the
## ILLUSTRATED DICTIONARY
of
## MICROCOMPUTERS

2ND EDITION

# the ILLUSTRATED DICTIONARY of MICROCOMPUTERS

2ND EDITION

### MICHAEL HORDESKI

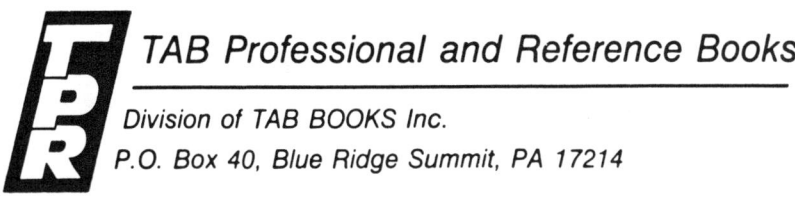

TAB Professional and Reference Books

Division of TAB BOOKS Inc.
P.O. Box 40, Blue Ridge Summit, PA 17214

SECOND EDITION
FIRST PRINTING

Copyright © 1986 by TAB BOOKS Inc.
Printed in the United States of America

Reproduction or publication of the content in any manner, without express permission of the publisher, is prohibited. No liability is assumed with respect to the use of the information herein.

Library of Congress Cataloging in Publication Data

Hordeski, Michael F.
  The illustrated dictionary of microcomputers.

  Rev. ed of: Illustrated dictionary of microcomputer terminology. 1st ed. ©1978.

  1. Microcomputers—Dictionaries I. Hordeski, Michael F. Illustrated dictionary of microcomputer terminology II. Title.
TK7885.A2H67    1986    004.16′03′21    85-27672

ISBN 0-8306-0488-X
ISBN 0-8306-2688-3 (pbk.)

# Contents

Preface .......................................................... vii

A .................................................................. 1

B ................................................................. 17

C ................................................................. 35

D ................................................................. 61

E ................................................................. 85

F ................................................................. 97

G ................................................................ 111

H ................................................................ 117

I ................................................................. 125

| | |
|---|---|
| J | 149 |
| K | 151 |
| L | 153 |
| M | 163 |
| N | 195 |
| O | 205 |
| P | 213 |
| Q | 245 |
| R | 249 |
| S | 269 |
| T | 305 |
| U | 323 |
| V | 329 |
| W | 335 |
| X | 341 |
| Y | 343 |
| Z | 345 |

# Preface

Since the time that this dictionary was first written, microcomputers have continued to be one of the most important developments in our lifetimes. We have always been driven towards the development of methods and machines that would produce the most output and require the least amount of equipment. This was the promise of the first microcomputers, which appeared in the early 1970s.

The changes that started with the introduction of the first microprocessors caused a whole new industry to evolve. This radical change in the method and nature of computing devices not only affected the computer and communications industries, but also continues to change our lives and lifestyles.

The development of microcomputers spawned a number of new techniques and industries with the vision and management required to use this new technology. Those who elected to participate and diligently pursue the new technology prospered.

A number of events have taken place since the first edition of this dictionary appeared in late the 1970s. Development and application range of more powerful microprocessors and the related circuits necessary for more complete microcomputer systems proceeded at a frantic pace. Many of these newer applications for microcomputers are included in this edition.

Order-of-magnitude improvements have been achieved in the power of these low-cost machines that are now within reach of almost everyone. The microcomputer user must now be aware of a greater range of concepts and terminology than in the recent past.

A major problem with any new revolutionary technology is the nomenclature. In a fast-moving explosive field such as microcomputers, terms and concepts develop with the technology, and the field soon has its own unique language. When there are rapid advances in a science, whole new branches of knowledge spring up, calling for a whole new vocabulary of terms. As new computer facts and concepts are created, the need for revised technical vocabularies is very great, and those involved will find what they need most conveniently in a specialized dictionary. Some of the terms included in this work represent new words, while others are words that have whole new meanings, which started in professional writing and communications and spread to a more common current use. Other terms may have had informal origins in the conduct of daily business and may be defined as the jargon or slang confined to special groups and situations.

This book was written to reflect the current usage of all terms related to the microcomputer industry. Both hardware and software terms are included, with particular emphasis on recent concepts. These concepts are the forces that will shape the products of tomorrow. Hardware and software concepts are discussed in those cases where the concepts are important in the understanding, selection, and use of microcomputer systems. This dictionary draws heavily upon the current use in literature including periodicals, product manuals, and industry conference presentations. Many specialized acronyms are included in this edition as an aid to those particularly troublesome terms that always seem to appear in the literature, without definition or apparent meaning.

All acronyms and terms in this dictionary appear in alphabetic sequence, ignoring hyphens, which are used sparingly and only to avoid ambiguity when the term is a single concept and common usage is dictated by the hyphenated form. Many concepts appear more than once due to the common use of acronyms in the electronics industry. The reader is directed to review related definitions and terms to obtain a fuller understanding of key concepts in microcomputer technology. These key concepts are treated in depth, while many other terms are related to microcomputers and computer development and are included to provide the broader understanding required for this complex and evolving field. Many examples are given to illustrate key concepts and to avoid confusion with similar or related terms. Cross references are included for similar terms as an aid to the reader.

The language that we use presents only rare examples of the out-and-out invention of new words. Sometimes a case occurs in which a new word is coined for an especially popular product; eventually the coined word comes to be used to refer to the general class or type of product.

You may also notice another process in which terminology, which is only in a certain sense new, furnishes an enrichment or clarification to the technical language. In more than one way this process appears to be more important than any other because it involves the composition of words, the putting together of independent elements to form a single designation. These words are logically abbreviated descriptive phases. The main ideas are put side by side, and the mind left to infer their relationship to one another form the known circumstances. These new words or acronyms are formed and used for the sake of brevity and convenience; this is one of the advantages of a language that has formative elements and form-words.

I wish to thank all of those who aided me in this project and especially my reviewer and editor, Dee, who read through the entire manuscript and provided many useful suggestions. My appreciation is extended to all of those in the electronic industry who have contributed to microcomputer literature and terminology, with a special thanks to Rockwell International and the Fairchild Camera and Instruments Corporation for permission to use illustrations from their product manuals and literature.

To become knowledgeable during this truly revolutionary period in the history of computer technology, one must be able to read the technical magazines and books, attend computer seminars and short courses, employ independent experts for consultation, and constantly keep up with the new developments. Without a firsthand grasp of the language and terminology of microcomputers, all of these efforts can be futile. This book is designed to contribute to your understanding of this required knowledge; it can be used as a reference at an almost infinite number of levels of understanding.

# A

**A** 1. Symbol for *accumulator*. 2. Symbol for *ampere*. 3. Symbol for *angstrom*.

**AAAS** Abbreviation for *American Association for the Advancement of Science*.

**AAC** Abbreviation for *Alaskan Air Command*.

**AADS** Abbreviation for *Army Air Defense System*.

**AAM** Abbreviation for *air-to-air missile*.

**A and not B gate** A binary logic coincidence (two input) circuit used to complete the logic operations of A and not B. The result is true only if statement A is true and statement B is false.

**A-axis** A is an angle defining rotary motion around the x axis. Positive a is in the direction to advance a right-handed screw in the + x direction. The standard coordinate system gives the coordinates of a moving tool with respect to a stationary workpiece. Used in CAD/CAM systems.

**ABAR** Abbreviation for *advanced battery acquisition radar*.

**abbreviated addressing** A process of shortening the address in the direct addressing mode by using only part of the full address. This process provides a faster means of processing data.

**ABC** Abbreviation for *advanced biomedical capsule*.

**ABD** Abbreviation for *advanced base depot* (Navy).

**ABEND unrecoverable** An error condition that results in abnormal termination of a program. Contrast with recoverable ABEND.

**ABL** Abbreviation for *atlas basic language*.

**ABLE** Abbreviation for *activity balance line evaluation*.

**ABMA** Abbreviation for *Army Ballistic Missile Agency*.

**ABRES** Abbreviation for *advanced ballistic reentry system*.

**ABSAP** Abbreviation for *airborne search and attack plotter*.

**absolute accuracy** Accuracy as measured from a reference that must be specified.

**absolute address** An identification of an exact location where information is stored in a computer system.

**absolute assembler** A type of assembly language program that produces binary (object) programs in which all addresses and address references are absolute addresses.

**absolute code** A code that specifies the memory location where an instruction operand is stored; thus, a code that uses absolute addressing and lists the exact location where the operand is to be found.

**absolute dimension** A dimension expressed with respect to the origin of a coordinate system. The origin of a coordinate system is arbitrary.

**absolute element** An executable computer program. An input program written in a source language, which is compiled and then the addresses are assigned for use during the execution of the program. The resulting element is termed *absolute* because the program can only be executed in a specific space in memory. This is to be distinguished from a *relocatable element*, which can be run in any memory space.

**absolute error** The amount or value of an off-tolerance state, expressed in the same unit of measure as the quantity being monitored or measured.

**absolute loader** A program loader used to load programs and associated data in absolute address format into memory for execution.

**absolute maximum ratings** The published limiting values for the operation and environmental conditions for electronic equipment. Absolute maximum ratings should not be exceeded in order to maintain the expected reliability of the equipment.

**absolute readout** A display of the true position as derived from the position commands to a control system.

**absolute system** A numerical control system in which all positional dimensions, both input and feedback, are measured from a fixed point of origin.

**absolute-value machine** A computer that processes all data using full values of all variables at all times. Absolute-value machines operate in a contrasting mode to incremental machines.

**absolute-value transducer** A device that produces an output proportional to the input, but always of the same polarity. The output does not change polarity and remains at the absolute value of the input proportion.

**absorption** The deposition of a thin layer of gas or vapor particles onto the surface of a solid. The process is also known as chemisorption when the deposited material is bound by a chemical bond.

**absorption current** The current flowing into a capacitor following its initial charge, due to a gradual penetration of electric stress into the dielectric. Also, the current that flows out of a capacitor following its initial discharge.

**AC** Abbreviation for *alternating current*.

**ACC and DEC** Abbreviation for *acceleration and deceleration*. An increase or decrease in velocity (tool feedrate); it provides smooth changes in velocity for machine tool slides. It may be provided for in hardware or software.

**acceleration time** The total elapsed time between the application of a read or write instruction, and the transfer of the acted-upon information to its storage medium.

**acceptance test** A test to show compliance of purchased equipment or services with the purchaser's stated requirements, specifications, or conditions of purchase.

**access** The process of obtaining data from or placing data into, a storage device or register.

**access time** The total time required to deliver data after the initiation of a command to retrieve it from its storage medium. Internal data storage usually provides the fastest access time, but tends to increase system costs. Processing with internal storage can be done in less than a microsecond, while external random access processing is typically expressed in terms of milliseconds. The ideal access time would of course be zero, and for many purposes the nanosecond speeds of some internal storage units appear to be virtually zero. When this is the case, it is called *immediate access* or *simultaneous access*.

**accounting machine** See *tabulator*.

**accumulator** A temporary storage register in a processing unit, where the results of arithmetic or logic operations are stored. The accumulator may operate on one word length, one word and one character, two words, or two words and two characters. Sometimes the accumulator is made up of two registers that function at a double word length.

**accumulator address** An address used when the operand is in an accumulator. For example, the 6800 uses two accumulators, a primary (A) and a secondary (B); the instruction

ASL A ; (shift A left)

shifts the contents of register A to the left by one bit length.

**accumulator extension register** The accumulator extension register in some microcomputers can be used for serial input and output. The extension register will function as a serial shift register using an instruction. The serial input and the serial output are controlled by an instruction, which shifts the contents of the register right by one bit.

**accuracy** 1. Conformity of an indicated value to a true value, an actual value, or an accepted standard value. 2. A measure of the difference between the actual position of a machine and the position demanded in control systems. The accuracy of a control system is expressed as the deviation or difference between the ultimately controlled variable and its ideal value, usually in the steady state or at sampled instants.

**accuracy rating** Refers to the limit, usually expressed as a percentage of full-scale value, not exceeded by errors when the equipment is used under reference conditions.

**ACDA** Abbreviation for *Aviation Combat Development Agency*.

**AC/DC** A term used to describe electronic equipment that is capable of operation from either alternating current (ac) or direct current (dc) sources.

**A C dump** The removal of alternating current from a unit either intentionally, accidentally, or conditionally. An ac dump results in the removal of all power from a unit unless special provisions are made for a backup system.

**ACE** Abbreviation for *aerospace checkout equipment*.

**achieved reliability** Refers to reliability that is determined on the basis of actual performance or on operations based on standards or benchmarks under equal or equivalent conditions and circumstances. Also known as operational reliability.

**ACIA** Abbreviation for *asynchronous communications interface adapter*, a unit that provides the data formating and control to interface asynchronous communications data to organized systems. The interface can include such functions as: select, enable, read/write, interrupt, and the logic for data transfer. The parallel data from the bus is transmitted in the serial mode using the ACIA. Error checking and variable word lengths are allowed with this adapter.

**ACIC** Abbreviation for *Aeronautical Chart and Information Center* (USAF).

**ACK** Abbreviation for *affirmative acknowledgement*. ACK, as used in block data transmission, signifies that a previously transmitted block has been accepted by the receiver and the receiver is now ready to accept the next block of data.

**ACM** Abbreviation for *Association for Computing Machinery*.

**acoustic coupler** An electronic device used in conjunction with a modem data set for transmitting data via a standard telephone handset. This is done by *coupling* via sound waves (acoustically) the handset and the modem.

**acquisition time** The time a sample/hold circuit takes to acquire the input signal to within the stated accuracy. It may include the settling time of the output amplifier. Since it is possible for the signal to be acquired and the circuit switched to hold before the output is settled, the user must be certain that the output amplifier is settled before he accepts the results as meaningful.

**ACR** Abbreviation for *advanced capabilities radar*.

**ACORN** Abbreviation for *automatic checkout and recording equipment*.

**ACRE** Abbreviation for *automatic checkout and readiness equipment*.

**active element** 1. An element in its excited or in use state. 2. A transistor or other device that is on or alive rather than off, dead, or in a ground state. 3. A file, record, or routine that is being used, contacted, or referred to. Computing components are active when they are directed or excited by the control unit.

**active filter** A filter, consisting of an amplifier and suitable tuning element, usually inserted into a feedback path. Active filters have a number of advantages over passive filters. They can eliminate inductors with associated saturation and temperature stability problems. The response of an active filter can be set by temperature stable capacitors and resistors. They overcome the problems of insertion loss and loading effects through the use of operational amplifiers. A typical active filter is manufactured with thick film hybrid technology. It uses the state variable active filter principle to implement a second order transfer function. Three operational amplifiers are used for the second order function while a fourth uncommitted op amp may be used as a gain stage, summing amplifier, or buffer amplifier, or to add another real pole. Two pole lowpass, bandpass, and highpass output functions are available simultaneously from three different outputs. Notch and allpass functions are available by combining these outputs in the uncommitted op amp. To realize higher order filters, several devices can be cascaded. Q range is 0.1 to 1,000 and resonant frequency range is 0.001 Hz to 200 kHz. Frequency stability is 0.1%/°C. Frequency tuning is done by two external resistors and Q tuning by a third external resistor.

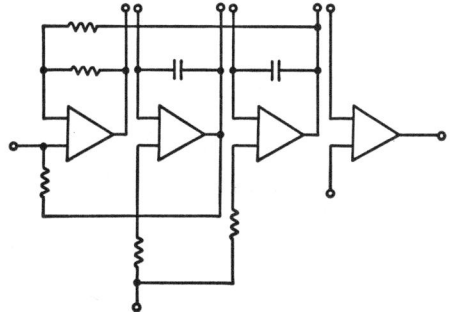

**Typical active filter IC**

**active storage** Data storage locations that hold the data actively being processed. See also buffer storage.

**active transducer** Any transducer in which the applied power controls or modulates locally supplied power.

**ACU** 1. Abbreviation for *address control unit*. 2. Abbreviation for *automatic calling unit*.

**ACWRON** Abbreviation for *Aircraft Control and Warning Squadron*.

**A/D** Abbreviation for *analog-to-digital*.

**ADA** Abbreviation for *automatic data acquisition*.

**adapt** Abbreviation for *air material command developed APT*, a computer aided numerical control programming language and processor. It is a subset of APT (automatically programmed tools) with limited capabilities compared to APT. It has been essentially limited to two axis contouring and has been implemented and supported on small and medium size computers.

**adapter** A device that allows operation between different components of a microcomputer system.

**adapter plug** A fitting designed to change the terminal arrangement or size of a jack, socket, or other receptacle, so that other than the original electrical connections are possible.

**ADC** Abbreviation for *analog-to-digital converter*.

**A/D converter** See *analog-to-digital converter*.

**A/D converter controller** When several analog inputs are connected to an analog-to-digital converter through an analog multiplexer, the controller selects an analog channel for conversion by the A/D converter. When conversion is complete, the end of conversion signal is issued. The converted signal's binary value is then read into the controller for processing. Errors are tested for and out of circuit checks are performed on the digital representation of the analog signal.

**add** 1. The mathematical operation of summing. 2. The command to perform a summing operation.

**addend** In a summing operation, the contents of a storage register addressed for addition to the augend. The resultant is the sum.

**addend register** The addend register serves as an addend store. When it stores both addends and answers, it is called the accumulator register.

**adder** A device that outputs the sum of two or more numbers presented as inputs. The adder is the main arithmetic element of the arithmetic and logic unit in some computers. The adder can perform addition, subtraction, multiplication, and division with the help of the accumulator and other storage registers.

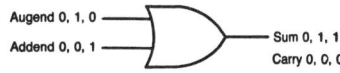

**Using the OR gate as an adder**

**adder-accumulator** In some systems the adder is a parallel binary adder with an internally connected carry for implementing precision arithmetic operations. The adder then operates with the accumulator to form the Arithmetic Logic Unit (ALU) section of the central processing unit (CPU). Functionally, the CPU has ten or more microinstructions dedicated to arithmetic and logical operations. All can be one cycle instructions and can enable direct arithmetic operation between the accumulator and the data in RAM or ROM storage. In addition to its arithmetic functions, the accumulator is the primary working register in the CPU and is the central data interchange point for most data transfer operations occurring in the system. During internal data transfer, the accumulator is the interfacing data register for both RAM and ROM. For external data exchanges (input/output) the accumulator is the source of the output data and the receiver register for the input data.

**adder, two input** A logic element that performs addition by accepting two digital input signals, a digit of a number and an addend or a carry, and that provides two output signals, a carry digit and a digit for the sum.

**addition** The summing of two or more numbers. Addition is always performed in a microcomputer by summing two numbers at a time, the augend and the addend. The augend is usually the contents of the accumulator, and the addend is the contents of a storage register that is addressed. A typical microprocessor contains a number of data registers. One of these registers functions as the accumulator with all arithmetic and logic operations being performed in it; the other registers hold temporary results and provide the operands of instructions to control the accumulator. When the operand is stored, for example, in register D, the instruction

ADD D ; (A = A + D)

adds the contents of the register D to the accumulator and stores the result in the accumulator.

Another type of microprocessor uses one register (A) as a primary accumulator and another (B) as a secondary accumulator; in this case the operand is likely to be stored in memory. To add the contents of the memory location to the accumulator, you can use extended addressing and write the following instruction.

ADD B $212 ; (add the contents of M (212) to B)

The symbol $ indicates that 212 is a hexadecimal number to the assembler.

**address** A label identifying a location where information is stored. An address can be represented by characters or bits that name, label, or number a location, a part of storage, a data source, or a destination. Also, an address can be that part of an instruction that identifies the location of the operand of that instruction.

A location in a city can be located if one knows the street address; similarly, if you know the computer storage medium's address for a desired piece of information, this information can be located in the storage unit. When the information is put into the storage unit, an address is assigned to each word; then when a particular word is desired, the address is used to find it.

Storage locations in a microcomputer can be thought of as being similar to a set of post office boxes, message boxes at hotel front desks, stock room bins, and the storage bins of hat-check services like this:

| 00 | 01 | 02 | 03 |
|----|----|----|----|
| 04 | 05 | 06 | 07 |
| 08 | 09 | 10 | 11 |
| 12 | 13 | 14 | 15 |

**Storage assignments**

All the storage locations are identified by a specific label and the locations are capable of holding various items. The contents of the locations change, but the locations and the location numbers remain the same. While post office boxes and storage bins can hold many different items at any one time, an address in a computer unit stores only one unit of data at a time.

If the storage unit had 2000 locations, then the addresses would be numbered from 0000 to 1999. Each of these numbers identifies a unique location; it says nothing about the contents of the location. Instructions deal only with address numbers; for example, let $144 be stored in address 1888. If it is desired to have the machine print this amount, the instructions will indicate that 1888 be printed. The microcomputer will interpret this to mean that the contents of 1888 be displayed, resulting in the printout of $144.

A simple payroll program might have the following English instructions:

(1) Start the machine.
(2) Read the employee's payroll data into storage for processing.
(3) Multiply hours worked by the hourly rate to find gross earnings.
(4) Multiply gross earnings by the withholding percentage to find the tax deduction.
(5) Add the hospitalization insurance deduction to (4) to compute the total deduction.
(6) Subtract the total deduction from the gross earnings to find the take-home pay.
(7) Print a check for the amount of the take-home pay with the employee's name and identification.
(8) Stop the machine at the end of processing for the last employee.

The storage locations for such a program can be assigned as shown in the accompanying pigeon-hole layout.

In this example the payroll data is stored in locations 00 to 04; location 05 is used for temporary storage, and the instructions are assigned to locations 06 to 17 (which become the program storage areas)! The first instruction sets the location of the payroll data 00 to 04. The location of this data is arbitrary.

| 00 STORE EMPLOYEE NAME | 01 STORE HOURS WORKED | 02 STORE HOURLY RATE | 03 STORE WITHHOLDING PERCENTAGE | 04 STORE HOSPITALIZATION DEDUCTION | 05 TEMPORARY STORAGE AREA |
|---|---|---|---|---|---|
| 06 READ DATA INTO 00, 01, 02, 03, 04 | 07 WRITE CONTENTS OF 01 INTO ARITHMETIC UNIT | 08 MULTIPLY CONTENTS OF ARITHMETIC UNIT BY CONTENTS OF 02 | 09 STORE RESULT OF 08 IN 05 | 10 MULTIPLY RESULT OF 08 BY CONTENTS OF 03 | 11 ADD RESULT OF 10 TO CONTENTS OF 04 |
| 12 SUBTRACT RESULT OF 11 FROM CONTENTS OF 05 | 13 STORE RESULT OF 12 IN 16 | 14 PRINT CHECK FOR CONTENTS OF 16 | 15 MAKE CHECK PAYABLE TO CONTENTS OF 00 | 16 IF 00 EMPTY STOP | 17 GO TO 06 |
| 18 STORE TAKE-HOME PAY | STORAGE ASSIGNMENTS | | | | |

**Storage assignments**

**address bus** An 8 bit microprocessor has a set of 16 pins to carry the binary numbers called addresses. These pins are called the address bus. The address bus carries information out from the microprocessor to ROMs, RAMs or I/O chips. Signals on the address bus are used to select a certain memory or I/O chip and to select a particular location inside that chip.

**address connections** This is how the ROM and RAM are wired to the address bus. Bits A11 and A1 are the chip selects. The RAM uses A7-A0 and the ROM A9-A0. The address bus is used to select a location within a component. To perform this function, two selections must be performed: 1. The device must be selected. 2. The location within the device must be selected.

**addressing capabilities** Much of the power of microcomputers is derived from wide ranges of addressing capabilities. Addressing modes include sequential forward or backward addressing, address indexing, indirect addressing, 16 or 32 bit word addressing, 8 bit (byte) addressing, and stack addressing. Variable length instruction formatting allows a minimum number of bytes to be used for each addressing mode. The result is efficient use of program storage space.

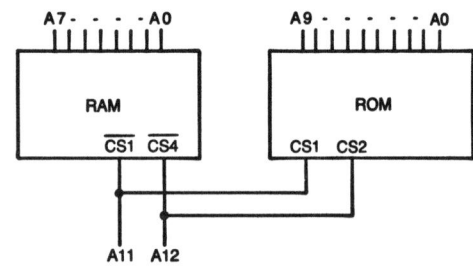

**RAM and ROM Address Connections**

**addressing, symbolic** Refers to a fundamental procedure or method of addressing using a symbolic address. The symbolic address is chosen for convenience in programming. A translation of the symbolic address into an absolute address is required before it can be used in the microcomputer.

**address field** The instruction segment that stipulates a specific memory location where an information element may be accessed.

**address modification** An alteration to the address portion of a program instruction that results in an internal transfer to a new memory location when the original address is called for after the first time in an iterative routine.

**add/subtract time** The time required for a circuit, system, or machine to perform addition or subtraction operations. The add/subtract time does not include the time required to obtain the numbers from storage, nor does it include the time involved in placing the answers into storage.

**add time** The time required to acquire from memory and execute one fixed point add instruction using all features such as overlapped memory banks, instruction lookahead and parallel execution. The add is either from one full word in memory to a register or from memory to memory, but not usually from register to register.

**ADF** Abbreviation for *automatic direction finder*.

**ADP** Abbreviation for *automatic data processing*.

**ADR** Abbreviation for *adder*.

**advanced BASIC** A form of BASIC with such features as extended color graphics commands, event trapping for communications adapters, joysticks, special function keys, and light pen and music support.

**ADX** Abbreviation for *automatic data exchange*.

**adventure** A game which is an exercise in logic, concentration and memory recall frequently using a fantasy background of caverns, dwarfs and giants.

**alarm systems, microprocessor** CPUs scan input/output points at preselected intervals. When the A conversion is completed, data are read, processed, and checked against alarm limits. Critical deviations from normal operating conditions are detected and alarms are sent to the control/acknowledgment terminal. The CPU at the terminal formats and routes the alarm data to an operator's display panel. The operator on duty observes the detected alarm and takes the necessary steps to correct the problem. Alarms corresponding to "crisis" situations can be detected directly by limit switches, by circuit continuity breaks, or by the manual depression of a button.

Crisis conditions require immediate attention and would therefore be assigned as priority vector interrupts in the CPU.

**algebra** Mathematical operations in which letters and other nonnumeral characters are used to represent variables and constants.

**ALGOL** Acronym for *algorithmic language*. With a few exceptions, this language is not being implemented on most microcomputers. It is an arithmetic language designed for scientific applications and involves computer processing of numerical procedures (algorithms). ALGOL is used more extensively in Europe than in the U.S.

**algorithm** A precisely defined set of rules or a structured procedure that provides the solution to a problem in a finite number of steps. An example of an algorithm follows:

Suppose that it is desired to compute the value of a polynomial of the form

$$f(x) = ax^n + bx^{n-1} + cx^{n-2} \ldots$$

For $n = 5$ you can write the following algorithm:

$$f(x) = (((((a) x + b) x + c) x + d) x + e) x + f$$

This algorithm indicates that the computation can be done by repeating a multiply-and-add step five times.

**algorithmic language program conversion** Refers to the steps involved in converting a program in a high-level language to a machine language program. Among these are decomposition of syntactic structure, allocation of storage, production of target program, editorial and optimizational function, and diagnostic provisions.

**algorithm, transfer** A specific algorithm design used in a demand fetching system to determine the order in which segments demanded by concurrent processes are transferred from a backing store to an internal memory.

**alignment** The process of adjusting components of a system for proper interrelationship. The term is applied especially to the synchronization of components in a system.

**alignment pin** Refers to any pin or device that will ensure the correct mating of two components designed to be connected.

**allocate** Refers to assignment of storage in a computer to main routines and subroutines, thus fixing the absolute values of symbolic addresses.

**alloy** Refers to a composition of two or more elements, of which at least one is a metal. It may be either a solid, solution, a heterogeneous mixture, or a combination of both.

**all points addressable mode** A graphics mode in which the programmer can control each dot on the screen.

**alphabet code** A set of letter-character abbreviations for computer instructions, which a computer can interpret as the instructions themselves.

**alphabetic coding** A system of abbreviation used in preparing information for input into a computer. Information can then be reported in the form of letters and words as well as in numbers.

**alphabetic-numeric** Alphanumeric.

**alphameric** A contraction sometimes used for *alphanumeric*.

**alphanumeric** Characters that include the letters of the alphabet, numerals, and other symbols used for punctuation and mathematical operations.

**alphanumeric instruction** An instruction containing both letters and numbers.

**alphanumeric mode** A graphics mode for text only.

**alphanumerics display, gas discharge** A gas discharge display that produces a light output that exceeds 300 microcandelas, which makes characters easy to read and viewable in high ambient light. These displays are suitable for point of sale and moving message applications, and are used in large audience information systems.

**alpha radiation errors** A potential problem in memories that occurs when positively charged alpha particles cause "soft errors" in dynamic RAMs. The phenomenon has also been observed in some static RAMs. As signal levels inside memory and logic devices continues to shrink, other noise sources (thermal noise, for example) may be isolated as error generators, but the assumption is that not all errors can be prevented, which has sparked new interest in error correction and detection. Simple parity checks can spot single bit errors, while more elaborate schemes such as the Hamming code can correct single bit errors and detect double bit errors. The Hamming code is gaining popularity in 16 bit microprocessors since the percent of overhead needed to perform the correction declines as word size increases. Five extra bits are required for an 8 bit word, while only six bits are needed to correct a 16 bit word. Error correction systems are a trend, and the logic necessary to perform this correcting is available in more and more integrated circuits.

**ALRP** Abbreviation for *APT Long Range Program*. An organization of private companies and government agencies who have pooled their funds for the purpose of developing a numerical-control computer-aided programming language, APT (automatically programmed tools). The management and development contractor hired by the organization has been the Illinois Institute of Technology Research Institute.

**ALRRI** Abbreviation for *airborne long range radar input*.

**alternating charge characteristic** Refers to the functions, under steady-state conditions, of the instantaneous values of the alternating component of transferred charge to the corresponding instantaneous values of a specified periodic voltage applied to a nonlinear capacitor.

**alternating current** Electric current whose flow alternates in direction; the time of flow in one direction is a half period, and the length of all half periods is the same. The normal waveform of ac is sinusoidal, which allows a simple vector algebraic treatment.

**alternation** Refers to one half of a cycle, either when an alternating current goes from positive to zero or from negative to zero. Two alternations make one cycle.

**alter switch** An alter switch, when toggled, causes the contents of the switch register to be copied into the register selected by the display switch or the memory location contained in the program counter if the display switch is so set.

**alt key** A key found on many microcomputers used to enter an ASCII character code directly from the keyboard. The key is held while the digits are typed on the numeric keypad.

**ALU** Abbreviation for *arithmetic and logic unit*.

**aluminum gate and silicon gate differences** An intrinsic determinant of the threshold voltage is the choice of gate electrode and substrate materials. This relates to the physics concept of work function, which represents the binding energy of an electron in a particular material. When polycrystalline doped silicon is used as a gate electrode instead of aluminum, the work function changes in such a way as to cause a lower threshold voltage. This is the basic difference between aluminum gate and silicon gate processes.

**ambient conditions** Ambient conditions are the conditions of the surrounding medium (pressure, noise, temperature, etc.)

**A/M** Abbreviation for *auto/manual*.

**AMD** Abbreviation for *Aerospace Medical Division* (USAF).

**AMD 2901** The Advanced Micro Devices (AMD) 2901 is a 4 bit slice unit that uses TTL technology. It is designed for use as a high speed element in controllers and other applications. The 2901 uses a 40 pin package and consumes 925 mw at 5 volts. Instruction word size is 9 bits and the chip uses a single phase clock with clock speeds of to 20 MHz. The basic structure for the 2901 is shown below. The 2901 uses a 16 word 4 bit RAM, a high speed ALU, and the Q register along with associated shift, decode, and multiplex circuitry. The microinstruction word is organized in three groups of three bits each, which are used to select the ALU source operands along with the function and destination registers.

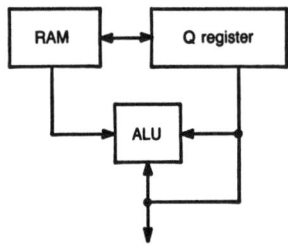

**2901 Structure**

**AMD 2901 system** The architecture of a 2901 bit slice system appears below. The complexity of the external control required to build such a system has been decreasing with the introduction of new control devices. The main use of bit slice devices has been in building large CPUs using components that reduce the parts count over other types of logic. Bit slices have become the major design tool for fast CPUs. A typical CPU implemented with the 2901 bit slice device can achieve speeds of 300 nanoseconds for 32 bits.

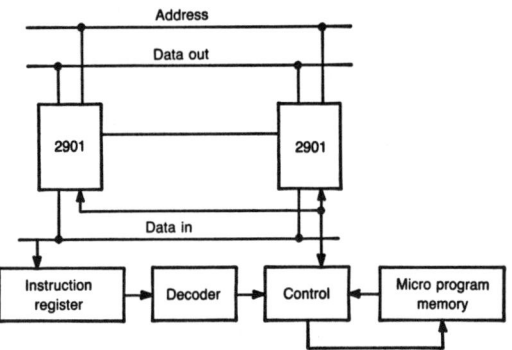

**Bit-slice system**

**American Federation of Information Processing Societies (AFIPS)** An organization of computer related societies. Its members include: the Association for Computer Machinery; the Institute of Electrical and Electronic Engineers Computer Group; Simulation Councils, Inc.; the American Society for Information Science. Its affiliates include: the American Institute of Certified Public Accountants; the American Statistical Association; the Association for Computational Linguistics; the Society for Industrial and Applied Mathematics; the Society for Information Display, and the Association of Data Processing Services Organizations.

**American Standard Code for Information Interchange (ASCII)** Usually pronounced "ASKEE," a standard data transmission code that was introduced to achieve compatibility between data services. It consists of 7 information bits and 1 parity bit for error checking purposes, thus allowing 128 code combinations. If the eighth bit is not used for parity, 256 code combinations are possible.

**ampere** Refers to a unit of electrical current or rate of flow of electrons. One volt across one ohm of resistance causes a current flow of one ampere. A flow of one coulomb per second equals one ampere. When an unvarying current is passed through a solution of silver nitrate of standard concentration at a fixed temperature, a current that deposits silver at the rate of .001118 grams per second is equal to 1 ampere, or $6.25 \times 10^{18}$ electrons per second passing a given point in a circuit.

**amplification, power** 1. The amplification of an input power to give a larger output power, as contrasted with voltage amplification. 2. The difference between output and input power levels of an amplifier, expressed in decibels.

**amplifier** A device for controlling power from a source so that more is delivered at the output than is supplied at the input. The source of the power can be of any type, including mechanical, hydraulic, pneumatic, and electric. Electric amplifiers may be classified into: (1) valve or tube, which operates on voltage, (2) repeater, especially used for telephone circuits, (3) transistor, which operates on current, (4) magnetic, which operates on very low frequency currents, and (5) solid state, which is operated by transistor action in a single semiconductor block.

**amplifier, transistor** A type of amplifier that uses transistors as the source of current amplification. Depending on impedance considerations, there are three types: base, emitter, or collector grounded.

**amplifier, tuned** A type of amplifier that contains tuned circuits, and therefore sharply responsive to particular frequencies.

**amplitude** The magnitude of a simple wave or simple part of a complex wave. Amplitude is quantified in terms of the largest or crest value measured from zero.

**amplitude distortion** A condition that occurs in an amplifier or other device when the output amplitude is not a linear function of the input amplitude. Amplitude distortion should be measured with the system operating under steady state conditions and with a sinusoidal input signal. When other frequencies are present, the term "amplitude" applies to the fundamental frequency only.

**amplitude modulation** Abbreviated AM. Refers to a process by which a constant frequency is varied in amplitude by a signal or information frequency. In this manner, the envelope of the constant frequency bears a direct relationship to the signal or information frequency.

**AMPS** Abbreviation for *automatic message processing system*.

**AMS** Abbreviation for *aeronautical material specifications*. Material and process specifications for aircraft components used to establish engineering and metallurgical practices in the aircraft industries.

**analog** A continuous direct current level of voltage or current, the magnitude of which is usually proportional to an unrelated parameter or function being monitored or measured.

**analog amplifier** In some analog/digital systems, the analog amplifier performs two functions. First, it supplies the dual-delayed sweep comparators with the proper direct current levels. Second, it accepts the direct current level from the vertical channel, processes this level, and provides two pieces of information for the processor through the input interface. The two pieces are polarity of the direct current level and whether the level is greater or lesser than some reference. If it is greater, the processor increases the reference until it is within 1 lower sideband of the unknown. Conversely, if it is lesser: the processor decreases the reference until it is within 1 lower sideband of the unknown. In both cases, it displays the reference level that is now equal to the unknown.

**analog channel** In an analog computer, a channel in which transmitted information can have any value between the defined limits of the channel.

**analog computer** A computer that uses variables represented by voltages, currents, or other parameters whose values are analogous to the quantitative magnitude of the variables.

**analog function circuits** Special purpose circuits that are used for a variety of signal conditioning operations on signals that are in analog form. When their accuracy is adequate, they can relieve the microprocessor of time consuming computations. Among the typical operations performed are multiplication, powers, roots, nonlinear functions such as those used for linearizing transducers, root mean square measurements, the computation of vector sums, integration and differentiation, and current to voltage or voltage to current conversion. Many of these operations can be purchased in available devices as multiplier/dividers, log/antilog amplifiers, and others.

**analog input/output** A capability required in many industrial systems. To provide analog input/output functions a digital-to-analog converter is used for digital to analog conversion and one or more analog-to-digital converters are used for analog to digital conversion.

**analog module testing** A binary-coded decimal digital-to-analog converter module that can be used to test any analog-to-digital module. Another way of testing an analog-to-digital module is by supplying 0 volts direct current through 10 volts direct current and observing the binary equivalents using light-emitting diodes; in this case a power supply is needed. Digital-to-analog converter modules can be tested using a scope.

**analog multiplexer** A device that allows the time sharing of analog-to-digital converters between a number of analog information channels. An analog multiplexer consists of a group of switches arranged with inputs connected to the individual analog channels and outputs connected in common, as shown in the figure. The switches can be addressed by a digital input code. MOS-FET switches are generally used and can be connected directly to an output load, if it has a high enough impedance, or to an output buffer amplifier that provides a high impedance to the switches.

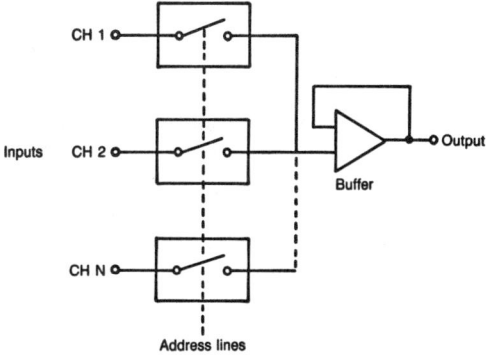

**Analog multiplexer**

**analog multiplier** An analog circuit or device that can be used to compute power by squaring voltage or current signals, or to multiply two or more inputs together, as shown in the figure.

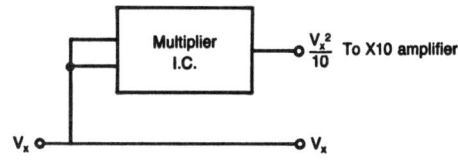

**Analog multiplication**

**analog output** As opposed to digital output, the output quantity is continuously proportionate to the stimulus, the proportionality being limited by the resolution of the device.

**analog recording** In the broadest sense, analog recording is a method of recording in which some characteristics of the record current, such as amplitude or frequency, is continuously varied in a manner analogous to the time variation.

**analog representation** A representation having discrete values but continuously variable.

**analog switches** A switching device that will only pass signals that are faithful analogs of transducer parameters. Many analog switches are available in electromechanical and solid state forms. Electromechanical switch types include relays, stepper switches, cross bar and mercury-wetted and dry-reed relay switches. The mechanical switches provide high direct current isolation resistance, low contact resistance, and the capacity to handle voltages up to one kilovolt. Multiplexers using mechanical switches are suited to low-speed applications as well as those having high resolution requirements. They interface well with the slower analog-to-digital converters, like the integrating dual slope types. Mechanical switches have a finite life, usually expressed in number of operations.

**analog-to-digital conversion** The process of representing precisely a varying voltage or current by a series of discrete pulses when the varying voltage or current itself is an analog of some other form of information. Analog-to-digital conversion techniques are required to convert any information that is in analog form into the digital form required by the microcomputer. Analog data is frequently encountered in data acquisition as voltage from a transducer, potentiometer, or other sensor of physical data.

Most methods of conversion involve division of the signal conversion device into two sections. The analog section contains all analog functions of the converter, and the digital section contains the digital functions of the converter. A major part of the digital portion can be done with microcomputer software, if software is available for this purpose. The software can control the analog section, determine the digital value of the input of the analog section, and perform calculations with the data. If a multiplexer is used in the data acquisition system, the software can perform the function of a controller for channel selection, end-of-conversion flags, and error checking.

Successive-approximation conversion is widely used and can provide both serial and parallel outputs. The conversion system uses a digital-to-analog converter in a feedback loop that generates a known analog signal. The unknown input is compared with this signal and then sensed by the digital section.

The successive-approximation register is implemented in the software of the microprocessor. Successive approximation provides medium conversion speeds when used in this arrangement.

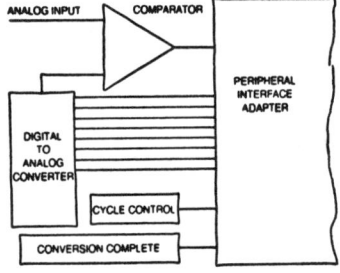

Successive-approximation converter

**analog transducers** Sensing devices that output either voltages in the 1-5, 2-10, 5-25, or ± 10 volt ranges for currents in the 1-5, 4-20, or 10-50 milliampere ranges.

**analytic relationship** The relationship that exists between concepts and their corresponding terms.

**analyzer** A routine to analyze a program. The routine usually consists of summarizing references to storage locations and tracing jump sequences.

**analyzer, electronic differential** A form of analog computer that uses interconnected electronic integrators to solve differential equations.

**ancillary equipment** A term, often interchangeable with peripheral equipment, that relates to all types of input/output, communication, and interface equipment.

**AND** A logic operator that has the property that if A and B are both statements, then A AND B is true if both statements are true, but it is false if either is false or both are false. Truth is usually expressed by the value 1, while 0 is used to indicate a false state. The AND operator is usually represented by a centered dot.

$$A \cdot B$$

or by no sign

$$AB$$

An inverted $u$ is sometimes used to denote the logical product

$$A \cap B$$

Finally, the standard multiplication sign may be used to express the AND function

$$A \times B$$

**AND circuit** A circuit that performs the AND function.

**AND element** One of the basic logic elements (gates or operators) that has at least two binary input signals and a single binary output signal. The answer or variable that represents the output signal is the conjunction, in set theory, of the variables represented by the input signals.

**AND gate** A gate that performs the AND function.

**AND operator** See AND.

**ANSI** Abbreviation for *American National Standards Institute*, a nonprofit, nongovernmental organization that acts as a clearing house for standards involving computers. ANSI establishes standards for character sets such as ASCII, high level languages such as FORTRAN and BASIC, and data communications protocols such as × .25.

**anticoincidence unit** A binary logic coincidence circuit for completing the logic operation of exclusive-OR. The result is true when A is true and B is false or when A is false and B is true and the result is false when A and B are both true or when A and B are both false. Also known as difference gate, nonequivalence gate, distance gate, diversity gate, add-without carry gate, exjunction gate, nonequality gate, symmetric difference gate, partial sum gate, and modulo-two sum gate.

**AOC** Abbreviation for *automatic output control*.

**APA mode** See all points addressable mode.

**APCHE** Abbreviation for *automatic programmed checkout equipment*.

**APL** Abbreviation for *a programming language*, a language in which an extensive set of operators and data structures are used. It is considered to be one of the most flexible, powerful, and concise of the algorithmic/procedural languages.

**APP** Abbreviation for *auxiliary power plant*.

**apparent power** The product of the root mean square value of the current and the root mean square value of the voltage.

**application** The system or problem to which a microcomputer can be devoted. Applications range from the computational type (in which arithmetic operations predominate) to the processing type (in which data-handling operations are the major function).

**application fit** Refers to the relative efficiency of an application program in solving a particular problem or improving a worker's output; for example, a word processing program would be appropriate for a typing task.

**application note** A published paper, usually from a product or device manufacturer, that offers suggestions, recommendations, or instructions for using the manufacturer's product or device in a specific manner or for a specific purpose.

**application package** A set of computer programs and/or subroutines used to solve problems and perform specific tasks in a particular application.

**application program** The ordered set of programmed instructions by which a computer performs an intended task or series of tasks, as opposed to a microprogram.

**application software** See application package.

**application study** The detailed process of determining the system and set of procedures for using the microcomputer in a particular application. This involves establishing the definite functions and operations of the machine along with specification development and machine and peripheral selection criteria.

**applications support** Applications support packages assist users in: (1) evaluating the operation of a microcomputer family of parts in an actual application, (2) reducing the engineering time and development costs required in developing and constructing prototype systems using a microcomputer family of parts, (3) comparing different system software and firmware programs, (4) reducing the time required to evaluate and debug system hardware, software, and firmware, (5) providing a working prototype of a microcomputer system.

**APT** Abbreviation for *automatically programmed tools*, a special computer language for programming the operation of numerically controlled machine tools.

**APU** Abbreviation for *automatic program unit*.

**AQ** Abbreviation for *any quantity*.

**AQL** Abbreviation for *acceptable quality level*.

**arbitrary function generator** A specific function generator (analog) that is not committed by its design function exclusively, so that the function which it generates can be changed by the operator or programmer.

**ARC** Abbreviation for *automatic ratio control*.

**arc clockwise** An arc in the clockwise direction with respect to the workpiece when viewed from the positive direction of the perpendicular axis. Used in automatic machining.

**arc counterclockwise** An arc in the counterclockwise direction with respect to the workpiece when viewed from the positive direction of the perpendicular axis. Used in automatic machining.

**arelem (arithmetic element)** A section of the APT (automatically programmed tools) processor that calculates cutter locations based on the motion commands that were input and the canonical forms of the geometry input.

**argument** An independent variable that identifies the location of a number in a mathematical operation. The argument can determine the value of a mathematical function when substituted; it can be the operand in operations on one or more variables.

**arithmetic and logic unit** That part of the microcomputer that performs arithmetic, logic, and related operations. It is the arithmetic and logic unit that performs the major part of the actual data processing. Calculations are performed and logic comparisons are made in this part of the chip set.

In a program involving a simple series of payroll calculations, we might have the following instructions:

| 07 WRITE CONTENTS OF 01 INTO ARITHMETIC UNIT | 08 MULTIPLY CONTENTS OF ARITHMETIC UNIT BY CONTENTS OF 02 | 09 STORE RESULT OF 08 IN 05 | 10 MULTIPLY RESULT OF 08 BY CONTENTS OF 03 | 11 ADD RESULT OF 10 TO CONTENTS OF 04 |
|---|---|---|---|---|

**Typical payroll calculation**

The first instruction requires that the contents of address 07 be written into the arithmetic and logic unit. The ALU must have the capability to store temporarily the data contained in address 01. Typically, registers would be used to store this data. The number of registers and the data flow pattern vary among microcomputers and this results in differences between arithmetic and logic units.

**arithmetic game** Refers to an educational program that is involved in some way with basic arithmetic skills. Examples include Rockets, Number Chase, Fact Track, and Discovery Machine.

**arithmetic logic register stack** A basic building block in some microcomputer chips. It often contains a four bit arithmetic and logic unit, an eight word by four bit RAM with output latches, an instruction decode network, control logic, and four bit output register. Eight arithmetic and logic functions can be implemented in the ALU by the input data, and a second four bit operand can be supplied internally from one of the eight RAM words.

**arithmetic mean** The arithmetic mean is found by summing the items of interest and then dividing by the number of items in the series.

**arithmetic operation** A mathematical manipulation of numbers or symbols performed for the purpose of solving a problem as stated by a prescribed formula.

**arithmetic progression** Any sequence of numbers in which the difference between two adjacent numbers is constant (as 5, 10, 15, 20 . . . ).

**arithmetic registers** Microprocessor arithmetic (or ALU) registers are those on which arithmetic and logic functions can be performed. The register can be a source or destination of operands for the operation. Registers that can supply but not receive operands for the ALU are not normally considered as arithmetic registers.

**arithmetic section** That portion of computer hardware in which arithmetic and logical operations are performed.

**arithmetic shift** Any shift that does not affect the sign position. An arithmetic shift results in the multiplication of a number by an integral power of the radix.

**arithmetic unit** The part of a computer system that performs arithmetic operations; an arithmetic and logic unit.

**armed interrupt** An interrupt that can accept and hold the interrupt signal. A *disarmed* interrupt ignores the signal.

**armed state** The state of an interrupt level in which it can accept and remember an interrupt input signal.

**ARQ** Abbreviation for *automatic request for repetition*.

**array** 1. A group of devices, components, or numbers arranged in a logical or meaningful pattern. 2. A matrix.

**artificial intelligence** 1. The study of computer techniques to supplement the intellectual capabilities of humans. Artificial intelligence is concerned with the more effective use of digital computers through improved programming methods. 2. The research and study in methods of developing a machine that can improve its own operations or can perform functions normally associated with human intelligence such as reasoning, adapting, or learning.

**artificial language** A language designed for a particular application area that has not evolved through long usage to a natural language.

**ARU** Abbreviation for *audio response unit*, a device that connects a computer system to a telephone to provide a verbal response to inquiries.

**ASCII** Abbreviation for *American Standard Code for Information Interchange*, an eight-level code (seven bits plus parity check) widely used for information interchange in data processing systems, communication systems, and associated equipment.

| CHARACTER OR SYMBOL | PARITY BIT | ASCII CODE | DECIMAL EQUIV |
|---|---|---|---|
| NUL | 0000 | 0000 | 0 |
| SOH | 1000 | 0001 | 1 |
| STX | 1000 | 0010 | 2 |
| ETX | 0000 | 0011 | 3 |
| EOT | 1000 | 0100 | 4 |
| ENQ | 0000 | 0101 | 5 |
| ACK | 0000 | 0110 | 6 |
| BEL | 1000 | 0111 | 7 |
| BS | 1000 | 1000 | 8 |
| HT | 0000 | 1001 | 9 |
| LF | 0000 | 1010 | 10 |
| VT | 1000 | 1011 | 11 |
| FF | 0000 | 1100 | 12 |
| CR | 1000 | 1101 | 13 |
| SO | 1000 | 1110 | 14 |
| SI | 0000 | 1111 | 15 |
| DLE | 1001 | 0000 | 16 |
| DC1 | 0001 | 0001 | 17 |
| DC2 | 0001 | 0010 | 18 |
| DC3 | 1001 | 0011 | 19 |
| DC4 | 0001 | 0100 | 20 |
| NAK | 1001 | 0101 | 21 |
| SYN | 1001 | 0110 | 22 |
| ETB | 0001 | 0111 | 23 |
| CAN | 0001 | 1000 | 24 |
| EM | 1001 | 1001 | 25 |
| SUB | 1001 | 1010 | 26 |
| ESC | 0001 | 1011 | 27 |
| FS | 1001 | 1100 | 28 |
| GS | 0001 | 1101 | 29 |
| RS | 0001 | 1110 | 30 |
| US | 1001 | 1111 | 31 |
| Sp | 1010 | 0000 | 32 |
| ! | 0010 | 0001 | 33 |
| " | 0010 | 0010 | 34 |
| # | 1010 | 0011 | 35 |
| $ | 0010 | 0100 | 36 |
| % | 1010 | 0101 | 37 |
| & | 1010 | 0110 | 38 |
| ' | 0010 | 0111 | 39 |
| ( | 0010 | 1000 | 40 |
| ) | 1010 | 1001 | 41 |
| * | 1010 | 1010 | 42 |
| + | 0010 | 1011 | 43 |
| , (COMMA) | 1010 | 1100 | 44 |
| - | 0010 | 1101 | 45 |
| . (PERIOD) | 0010 | 1110 | 46 |
| / | 1010 | 1111 | 47 |
| 0 | 0011 | 0000 | 48 |
| 1 | 1011 | 0001 | 49 |
| 2 | 1011 | 0010 | 50 |
| 3 | 0011 | 0011 | 51 |
| 4 | 1011 | 0100 | 52 |
| 5 | 0011 | 0101 | 53 |
| 6 | 0011 | 0110 | 54 |
| 7 | 1011 | 0111 | 55 |
| 8 | 1011 | 1000 | 56 |
| 9 | 0011 | 1001 | 57 |
| : | 0011 | 1010 | 58 |
| ; | 1011 | 1011 | 59 |
| < | 0011 | 1100 | 60 |
| = | 1011 | 1101 | 61 |
| > | 1011 | 1110 | 62 |
| ? | 0011 | 1111 | 63 |
| @ | 1100 | 0000 | 64 |
| A | 0100 | 0001 | 65 |
| B | 0100 | 0010 | 66 |
| C | 1100 | 0011 | 67 |
| D | 0100 | 0100 | 68 |
| E | 1100 | 0101 | 69 |
| F | 1100 | 0110 | 70 |
| G | 0100 | 0111 | 71 |
| H | 0100 | 1000 | 72 |
| I | 1100 | 1001 | 73 |
| J | 1100 | 1010 | 74 |
| K | 0100 | 1011 | 75 |
| L | 1100 | 1100 | 76 |
| M | 0100 | 1101 | 77 |
| N | 0100 | 1110 | 78 |
| O | 1100 | 1111 | 79 |
| P | 0101 | 0000 | 80 |
| Q | 1101 | 0001 | 81 |
| R | 1101 | 0010 | 82 |
| S | 0101 | 0011 | 83 |
| T | 1101 | 0100 | 84 |
| U | 0101 | 0101 | 85 |
| V | 0101 | 0110 | 86 |
| W | 1101 | 0111 | 87 |
| X | 1101 | 1000 | 88 |
| Y | 0101 | 1001 | 89 |
| Z | 0101 | 1010 | 90 |
| [ | 1101 | 1011 | 91 |
| \ | 0101 | 1100 | 92 |
| ] | 1101 | 1101 | 93 |
| ^ | 1101 | 1110 | 94 |
| _ | 0101 | 1111 | 95 |
| ` | 0110 | 0000 | 96 |
| a | 1110 | 0001 | 97 |
| b | 1110 | 0010 | 98 |
| c | 0110 | 0011 | 99 |
| d | 1110 | 0100 | 100 |
| e | 0110 | 0101 | 101 |
| f | 0110 | 0110 | 102 |
| g | 1110 | 0111 | 103 |
| h | 1110 | 1000 | 104 |
| i | 0110 | 1001 | 105 |
| j | 0110 | 1010 | 106 |
| k | 1110 | 1011 | 107 |
| l | 0110 | 1100 | 108 |
| m | 1110 | 1101 | 109 |
| n | 1110 | 1110 | 110 |
| o | 0110 | 1111 | 111 |
| p | 1111 | 0000 | 112 |
| q | 0111 | 0001 | 113 |
| r | 0111 | 0010 | 114 |
| s | 1111 | 0011 | 115 |
| t | 0111 | 0100 | 116 |
| u | 1111 | 0101 | 117 |
| v | 1111 | 0110 | 118 |
| w | 0111 | 0111 | 119 |
| x | 0111 | 1000 | 120 |
| y | 1111 | 1001 | 121 |
| z | 1111 | 1010 | 122 |
| { | 0111 | 1011 | 123 |
| | | 1111 | 1100 | 124 |
| } | 0111 | 1101 | 125 |
| ~ | 0111 | 1110 | 126 |
| DELete | 1111 | 1111 | 127 |

**ASCII code**

**ASCII keyboard** A typewriter terminal keyboard laid out in a specific format and containing the character symbol buttons and function switches required to generate signals representing the 127 different character variations of the American Standard Code for Information Interchange.

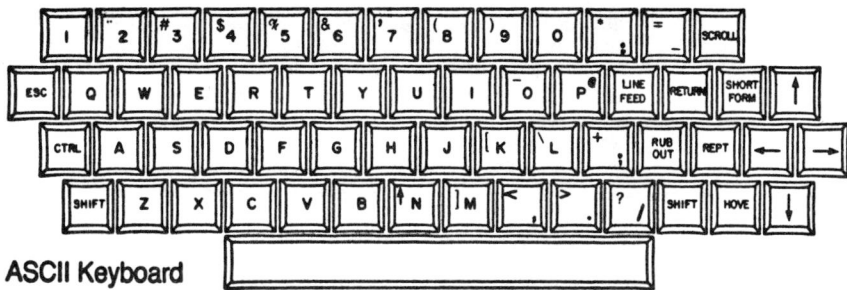

ASCII keyboard

**ASD** Abbreviation for *automatic synchronized discriminator*.

**ASM** The assembler used in the CP/M operating system.

**ASM-86** The assembler used in the 8086 version of the CP/M operating system.

**ASN** Abbreviation for *average sample number*.

**aspect card** A card containing the accession numbers of documents in an information retrieval system.

**aspirated thermocouple** A thermocouple with a means for achieving a gas velocity past the junction higher than that of free stream. This increases the heat transfer rate from the gas to the junction and lowers the response time.

**ASR** Abbreviation for *automatic send-and-receive*. A terminal that has the capability to send and receive messages without an operator.

**assemble** 1. To integrate subroutines into the main routine by adapting or changing relative or symbolic addresses to absolute addresses. 2. To prepare an object language program from a source language program by substituting machine operation codes for symbolic operation codes and absolute or relocatable addresses for symbolic addresses. See *assembler*.

**assembler** A computer program that is used to translate symbolic language into machine language. A typical program supplied by a microcomputer manufacturer is loaded and then executed using the same type of microcomputer to perform the assembly operation. The following is an example of an assembler program:

Source program (symbolic language) LD AC$,@. + 10
(load register AC$ through the address resulting from adding octal 10 to the current value of the program counter, shown on the list tape below)
10 000 9109 LD AC$,@. + 10
Where:
10 = line number on source tape in assembly language program.
000 = location of instruction.
9109 = hexadecimal equivalent of 16-bit machine language word.
LD AC$,@. + 10 = the statement in assembly language written by the programmer.
Object tape (machine language) 1001 0001 0000 1001

Assemblers also provide instructions that control the assembly of instructions into machine language. These assembler instructions can save programming time and reduce errors while allowing modifications to be processed more easily. Typical areas that assembler instructions can help in are:

*numbering* For example, B can be used to signify that literals in operand fields be interpreted as binary numbers, and 0 and D can be used to signify octal and decimal values.

*origins* To store the next instruction at location 112 decimal, the statement ORIGIN 112D can be used; consecutive locations follow 112 until a new origin statement appears.

*comments* To add comments in English in the source file, use symbols such as the solidus (/); comma (,), semicolon (;), or colon (:). The assembler can ignore symbols following this symbol on each line of the source text, at the same time reproducing the comments for the final list file.

*equals* For labeling registers, equal signs (=) can be used; thus either the original label or a more descriptive term can be used interchangeably as names for the register. Equal signs can also be used to set the contents of a register in either binary, decimal, or octal.

*tables and other sets of data* By using a statement such as TABLE D 23, 37, 41, three data words (in decimal) can be stored in successive locations in memory starting at a location labeled TABLE.

Another feature of assemblers is the ability to detect and flag errors. Syntactic errors—those errors that result from misuse of the language—are the only type that can be detected unless special routines are used; logic errors and errors of intent will be passed by. Statements containing errors are printed in the list file with flags (code letters signifying the error) or an entire error message. Errors that are easily detected include duplicate address labels, undefined address labels, undefined instruction mnemonics (misspelled operation codes), undefined operand field labels, incomplete numbers of operands, and invalid numbers or numbers from an incorrect number system. Here is an example of an error message from an assembler:

Program with errors:

```
                NUMBERS OCTAL
                ORIGIN 0
        ENTRY 1 LOAD R1, MEM 1
                LOAD R2, MEM 2
error           'LOAD' IS UNDEFINED
                OP-CODE*
        ENTRY 1 COMPARE R1, R2
error         * DUPLICATE  AD-
                DRESS LABEL*
                JCOND PLACE
error         * 'PLACE' IS UNDEFIN-
                ED    ADDRESS
                LABEL*
```

```
        error                      * OPERAND MISSING*
                                   JUMP FINISH
                                   STORE R1, MEM: IF R1
                                   GREATER THAN R2,
                                   EXCHANGE
        error                      * 'MEM' UNDEFINED*
                                   STORE R2, MEM 1
                            FINISH HLT
        errcr                      * 'HLT' IS UNDEFINED
                                   OPERATION*
                            MEM 1  = 1732
                            MEM 2  = 1840
        error                      * NUMBER IS INVALID
                                   OCTAL*
                                   END
Program with corrections:
NUMBERS OCTAL
ENTRY 1                            ORIGIN 0
                                   LOAD R1, MEM 1
                                   LOAD R2, MEM 2
                            ENTRY 2 COMPARE R1, R2
                                   JCOND GREATER,
                                   PLACE
                                   JUMP FINISH
                            PLACE  STORE R1, MEM 2; IF
                                       R1   GREATER
                                       THAN R2, EX-
                                       CHANGE
                            FINISH HALT
                            MEM 1  = 1732
                            MEM 2  = 2040
                                   END
```

Macro capability, a feature sometimes found in assemblers, can be very useful when similar but slightly different sections of coding are used over and over again. The differences in the coding do not allow the use of conventional subroutines for repeating.

The macro is defined in parameters such as data values, addresses, labels, or instructions. Once the macro is defined for the assembler, a single statement produces an expansion of the macro for all the parameters. The statement begins at the location the expansion is desired and contains a listing of the values of the parameters.

**assembler development system** A software development system. Some development systems permit the use of full macro capabilities, which means that a programmer can define special pseudo-instructions in the main program during the assembly process.

**assembly language** A hardware dependent, low-level source language employing crude mnemonics that are more easily remembered than their object language equivalents, which are "words" consisting solely of zeros and ones.

**assembly language processor** A language processor that accepts words, statements, and phrases to produce machine instructions. It is more than an assembly program since it has compiler powers. A macroassembler may permit segmentation of a large program so that sections can be tested separately. It also provides program analysis capabilities to aid in debugging.

**assembly list** A printed list that occurs as a by-product of the assembly procedure. The assembly list shows the instruction sequence with all details of the routine using coded and symbolic notations. The list is very useful during debugging operations.

**assembly system** A software system that includes a language and machine-code programs that perform such programming functions as checkout, updating, and others. An assembly system has two main elements, a symbolic language and an assembly program, that translate source programs written in the symbolic language into machine language.

**assembly testing** Refers to the testing of a group of functionally related programs to determine whether or not the group operates according to specifications. The programs may be related in that they have access to common data, occupy high speed storage simultaneously, operate under common program control, or perform an integrated task.

**assembly unit** 1. Any device that performs the function of assembly. 2. A portion of a program which is capable of being assembled into a larger program.

**assignable cause** A definitely identified factor that contributes to a variation in quality.

**Association for Computer Machinery (ACM)** A professional and technical society whose publications, conferences, and activities are designed to help advance the art, as regards machinery and system design, language and program development, and other related areas. It is a member of AFIPS, the American Federation of Information Processing Societies.

**associative storage registers** Various registers that are not identified by their name or position but are known and addressed by their contents.

**astable multivibrator** An oscillator, usually composed of one or two flip-flops, that produces a square-wave output as a result of self-triggering. See *bistable multivibrator*.

**astronomical unit** Mean distance of the earth from the sun, 92,907,000 miles.

**asynchronous** A system in which each event or operation starts as a result of a signal that the previous operation is complete and the microcomputer is now ready for the next operation. Synchronous machines have a master clock that sends pulses for timing to all critical circuits. Asynchronous machines do not use a master clock system for overall control; some timing circuits may be used for local control, but overall control is provided by the completion of a switching operation that serves to initiate the next operation.

**asynchronous communications** A data transmission that takes place using short, defined groups of bits.

**asynchronous communications adapter** Refers to the circuits or circuit board used to provide asynchronous serial communications between a microcomputer and other devices including modems and printers. The adapter is usually placed in one of the microcomputer's expansion slots.

**asynchronous computer** A computer that operates primarily in the asynchronous mode.

**asynchronous data transfer** Data communications can be either asynchronous or synchronous. Asynchronous data transfers usually occur in short bursts while synchronous data transfers are suited for long streams. Asynchronous messages are preceded by a start signal, which synchronizes the transmitting and receiving circuitry.

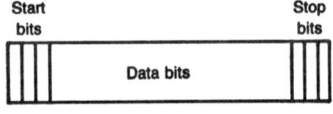

**Asynchronous data**

**asynchronous machine** Refers to any machine whose speed of operation is not proportionate to the frequency of the system to which the machine is connected.

**asynchronouos memory capability** A control function that allows a microprocessor to wait for memory or I/O. A small system, in which all components are access time compatible, may not require this asynchronous memory access, but as soon as users mix memory types and speeds, the need for asynchronous memory access becomes more obvious.

**asynchronous transmission** A transmission in which each group of code elements corresponding to a character signal is preceded by a start signal, which serves to prepare the receiving mechanism for the reception and registration of a character, and is followed by a stop signal, which serves to bring the receiving mechanism to rest in preparation for the reception of the next character.

**AT** Abbreviation for *automatic ticketing*.

**attendant phone** In a central dictation system, a phone that allows the word originator to communicate with an aide in the word processing center or other remote recorder location.

**attentuation** The decrease in amplitude of signal (current, voltage, or power) during its transmission from one point to the next. It may be expressed as a ratio or in decibels.

**attenuator** Circuits of resistors, capacitors, or other elements, which introduces a known attenuation into a measuring circuit or line.

**atto** A prefix for the numerical quantity of $10^{-18}$, e.g., attovolt.

**attribute** In the context of graphics, attribute refers to a graphical display feature or characteristic, such as shade or background.

**attribute code** A control byte used in some microcomputers to control a video feature such the intensity of a character or the darkness of the display background or foreground.

**auctioneering device** A specific device designed to automatically select either the highest or the lowest input signal from among two or more input signals. This is also known as a high or low signal selector.

**audio-cassette interface** An interface that allows tape cassette memory storage for data or software. The cassette operates by modulating audio frequencies in the record mode and modulating recorded data in the playback mode.

**audio response** A form of output that uses verbal replies to inquiries. A computer can be programmed to seek answers to inquiries made on an on-line system that utilizes a special audio response unit that elicits the appropriate prerecorded response to the inquiry. Inquiries must be of the nature for which the audio response output has been prepared.

**audio response calculator** A calculator that announces each entry and the results of every calculation using a synthesized voice stored in memory. The calculator's use is for vocational education of the blind and as an audio reinforcement of basic math concepts for sighted students.

**audio response unit (ARU)** A device that can connect a computer system to a telephone to provide voice response to inquiries made.

**audio system** Relates to the various types of special equipment that have the capabilities of storing and processing data obtained from voice sources, either recorded or transmitted.

**audit** A systematic examination of records, documents, and other evidence for determining the following:
1. The legality of transactions
2. If all transactions have been recorded
3. If transactions are reflected accurately
4. Assets and liabilities
5. Compliance with set procedures
6. The effectiveness of the accounting system

The audit can be an effective means of examining new procedures and systems in an organization.

**audit trail** A system for tracing items of data step by step. The audit trail begins with the recording of the transaction, follows through the processing steps and any intermediate records that may exist, and ends with the production of output reports and other generated records. A representative sample is chosen of previously processed source documents and an audit trail is traced through the system to test the adequacy of procedures and controls.

In manual systems, transactions are usually recorded in books of original entry; then they are connected to the final output by ledgers, summary books, and other documents. A visual and easily traceable path is left for the audit trail.

In automatic systems, steps in the processing function that were previously visible are now stored in reels of magnetic tape, disks, and other storage media. In many of these systems, an approach that circumvents the computer processing is used, the assumption being that if the input data is correct and the output is handled properly, then the processing *must* be correct.

An alternative method is based on the premise that if the input is correct and the internal processing is properly conducted, the output can then be assumed to be correct. The around-the-computer approach is usually suitable for many systems during the initial phases of construction or modification of a system. It is sometimes adequate for simple low-volume systems, but the through-the-computer approach is desirable for most larger systems. A combination of methods can allow cross checks in many applications.

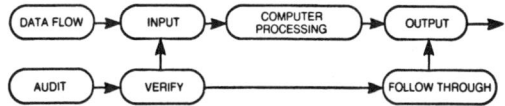

**Around-the-computer audit trail**

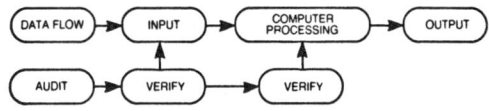

**Through-the-computer audit trail**

**augend** The numerical value to which an addend is added to obtain a sum.

**AUTOEXEC.BAT** An automatically-executing batch file.

**automatically-executing batch file** A disk file that allows a microcomputer to automatically run a program when turned on. VisiCalc uses this type of file, and when the VisiCalc disk is inserted into the disk drive, the VisiCalc program is automatically started without the entry of any commands. This type of capability is also referred to as *turnkey*.

**auto loader** A program that allows program loading to be initiated automatically, remotely, or from a front panel switch.

**automata theory** A theory that relates the study of principles of operations and applications of automatic devices to various behaviorist concepts and theories.

**automated factory** A factory that is capable of bringing together all materials required for processing and returning a final product.

**automated production management** Management using the assistance or under the control of data processing equipment that relates to production planning, scheduling, designing, or changing, and the reporting of output.

**automated typewriter** A general term covering all types of word processing keyboard equipment.

**automatic** Used to indicate that a process or device functions for a finite time period without human intervention. Automatic designates that the process or device has the ability to guide and control itself during the course of its operation. In the case of a computer, once the human operator has set up the machine to operate, it will function by itself within definite prescribed limits. The machine will digest the input data, perform the processing function, and produce the output data. The functional operation is predetermined during the setup of the system and preparation of the program. The program is stored, but not built into the machine.

**automatic calling unit** A unit that allows a business machine to dial calls automatically.

**automatic code** A code that allows a machine to translate symbolic language into machine language.

**automatic coding** Refers to a technique by which a computer is programmed to perform a significant portion of the coding of a problem.

**automatic dialing unit** A modem or device that is capable of automatically generating dialed digits.

**automatic dictionary** A translating device that provides word-for-word substitution from one language to another. An automatic dictionary is used in automatic searching systems for substituting codes for words and phrases during encoding.

**automatic feed punch** A card punch that incorporates an integral hopper, a track, and a stacker for the automatic movement of cards through the machine.

**automatic forward reset** In telephone dictation, a feature that enables the recorder to continue in playback mode to the end of recorded dictation, even though the person reviewing the dictation has disconnected. The next dictator can thus begin recording on an unused part of the medium.

**automatic interrupt** 1. An interruption caused by program instruction as contained in some executive routine. 2. An interruption not caused by the programmer but due to hardware devices. 3. An automatic program controlled interrupt system that causes a hardware jump to a predetermined location. There are at least five types of interrupts: (1) input/output, (2) programmer error, (3) machine error, (4) supervisor call, and (5) external, for example, timer turned to negative value, alert button on console, external lines from another processor. Unwanted interrupts such as an anticipated overflow, can be masked out on some computers.

**automatic loader** A program usually implemented in ROM (Read-Only Memory) that allows loading of at least the first record or sector of a mass storage device. The program is equivalent to a bootstrap loader plus a binary loader. When an automatic loader is installed, it is seldom necessary to key in a bootstrap program to load any other programs.

**automatic loader diagnostic** A program aid that reads out and verifies the contents of the automatic loader ROM (Read-Only Memory). It verifies the proper sequencing when the automatic loader switch is selected.

**automatic programming** A method of programming where the computer is used to translate the programming from a language that is easy for humans to write to a language that is efficient for a computer to operate with. Examples of automatic programming include assembling, compiling, and editing.

**automatic repeat key** A key, such as the underscore, that continues operating as long as the key is depressed.

**automatic reset** 1. A function that returns a control to its home position when a circuit fails to energize within a given time. 2. The function of an overload relay that restores the circuit as soon as the cause of the overload is corrected.

**automatic reverse** The ability of a recorder to rewind at the end of a tape for playback.

**automatic routine** A set of instructions that is executed independently of any manual operations. An automatic routine is usually triggered in response to certain conditions that are set within the program.

**automatic selector** In telephone dictation, a connection method that automatically links the handset to the first free recorder available.

**automatic stop** The automatic halting of processing as a result of error detection by built-in checking devices.

**automatic switchover** An operating system that has a standby machine that is capable of detecting when the on-line machine is faulty and once this determination is made, to switch to the alternate machine.

**automatic tape transmitter** A device that senses data on magnetic tape. It includes mechanisms for holding, feeding, controlling, and reeling up the tape, as well as sensing the data on the tape. It can be used as a computer input device to drive printers, plotters, or card punches, or to send information over a communications line.

**automatic typewriter** Refers to an automated typewriter that is used mainly for straight, repetitive output with little or no text editing.

**automatic voltage regulator** A device or circuit that maintains a constant voltage, regardless of variations of input voltage or load.

**automatic word recall** In dictation systems, an adjustable feature that enables the word originator or the transcriptionist to replay a measured portion of the previous dictation.

**automation** The technique and application of implementing a process such that human intervention is minimized. The microcomputer can be a useful tool in the automation of manufacturing and inspection of almost any product. The microcomputer can be programmed to operate milling and drilling machines, turret latches, and other machine tools with more speed and accuracy than is possible with human operators. A part or process can be inspected using suitable transducers; data from the transducers can be used by the microcomputer to control and adjust the machine tool or valve.

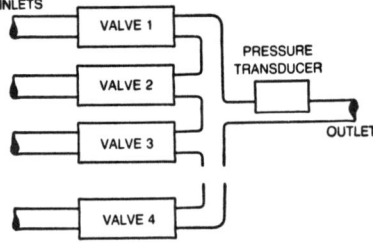

**Automation example**

An example of automation on a liquid pipeline illustrates the concepts of data collection, analysis, and control. Four valves are used for controlling the flow rate within the pipeline, and pressure transducers are used to monitor the liquid pressure on the pipeline walls. Data from the pressure transducers is used by the microcomputer to control the inlet valve openings. The desired pressure on the pipeline walls is 90 psi. The flow chart for the microcomputer program might be:

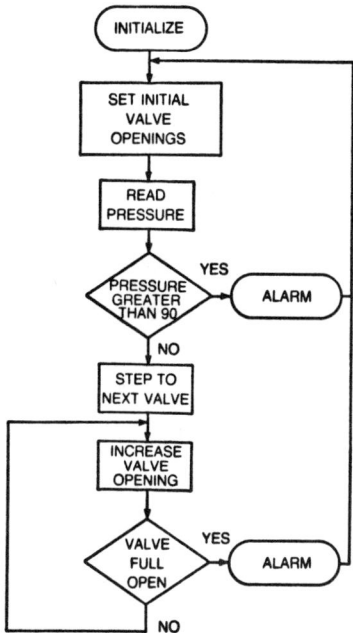

Microcomputer program flowchart

**automaton** A robot-like machine designed to simulate the operation of high-order living beings.

**automonitor** A microcomputer's record of its functions; also, a program or routine written for this purpose.

**automatic engine control** A microprocessor system installed in an automobile and used to monitor quantities such as fuel flow time and battery voltage. A block diagram that shows the operations of a typical automotive microprocessor system is shown below. The inputs to the microprocessor system are pressure, temperature, RPM (revolutions per minute) and EGR (exhaust gas recirculation) valve position. The inputs are provided by transducers or sensors located in the engine or EGR valve. One of the most difficult problems in the development of microprocessor systems for automotive applications has been in the design of low cost transducers. As reliable transducers are developed, they will provide the input signals that are converted to digital valves for use by the processor. These input signals may be temporarily stored in input latches until they are ready to be displayed or processed. The input latches are connected to the microprocessor through the system data bus. The outputs may be either to an actuator for performing engine control operations or to a display to enable the driver to monitor engine conditions and to alert him or her to critical conditions. The actuator performs spark advance and EGR value position adjustments. These adjustments will depend on the type of automobile and its operating environment and may be predetermined by the manufacturer and specified using parameters that are stored in a ROM. The microprocessor responds with the required engine adjustments on the basis of the stored information together with the current operating conditions sensed.

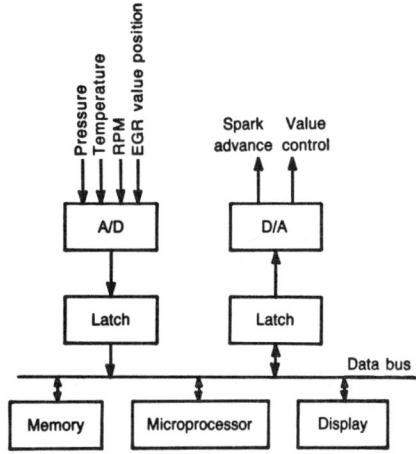

Automotive microprocessor system

**autonomous working** 1. A specific type of concurrent or simultaneous working; i.e., the carrying out of multiple instructions at the same time. 2. The initiation and execution of a part of a computer or automation system independent of a computer or other operations being performed on other parts of the system. The independent set of operations on various data are often monitored.

**auxiliary equipment** The peripheral equipment not in direct communication with the central processing unit. All auxiliary equipment must be interfaced with the CPU through a peripheral interface adapter.

**auxiliary function** In automatic machining, a function of a machine other than the control of the coordinates of a workpiece or cutter, usually on-off types of operations.

**auxiliary memory** Additional storage beyond the capacity of the main memory. Most computers accumulate and continue to accumulate large amounts of information. Not all the accumulated information is needed by the processor at the same time. It is more economical to use lower cost storage devices to store the information that is not currently in use. The memory that communicates directly with the central processing unit is called the main memory. The devices that are used to provide the backup storage are called auxiliary memory. Auxiliary memory devices may include magnetic disks and tapes.

**auxiliary processor** A specialized processor, such as an array processor, a fast fourier transform (FFT) processor, or an input/output processor (IOP), generally used to increase processing speed through concurrent operation.

**auxiliary PROM module** A PROM (programmable read-only memory) unit that is often treated as an input/output module. This means that data stored on these PROMs can be accessed only as data. These PROMs therefore cannot contain control programs to run the microcomputer.

**auxiliary routine** A routine designed to assist in the operation of the computer and in debugging other routines.

**auxiliary storage** A storage device that is used in addition to the main storage method. Auxiliary storage usually holds much more information than main storage, and the information is not as rapidly accessible as the information in the main storage.

**available machine time** The number of hours the computing machine is available for use. The available machine time is the time the machine is under power, when no maintenance is being performed and the machine is known or believed to be operating correctly.

**available power** The maximum power obtainable from a given source by suitable adjustment of the load.

**available time** Available machine time.

**avalanche** Refers to a rapid generation of a current flow with reverse-bias conditions as electrons sweep across a junction with enough energy to ionize other bonds and create electron-hole pairs, making the action regenerative.

**avalanche breakdown** In a semiconductor diode, a nondestructive breakdown caused by the cumulative multiplication of carriers through field-induced impact ionization.

**avalanche conduction** Refers to a form of conduction in a semiconductor in which the charged particle collisions create additional hole-electron pairs.

**avalanche diode** Also called a breakdown or zener diode, an avalanche diode switches the current through it rapidly whenever the applied voltage increases beyond a certain point (the zener voltage).

**avalanche noise** A phenomenon in a semiconductor junction in which carriers in a high voltage gradient develop sufficient energy to dislodge additional carriers through physical impact.

**average** 1. The typical value representative of any one of a group of values related to the same source; also called the median or median value. 2. The sum of a group of numbers divided by the quantity of numbers summed.

**average effectiveness level** A percentage computed by subtracting the total machine down time from the total performance hours and dividing this difference by the total performance period hours. Down time is usually measured from the time the defect has been reported to maintenance to the time the equipment is returned to the user in proper operating condition.

**average letter** A typed letter in the range of 92 to 115 words with from 18 to 23 lines of 12 pitch typing.

**average transfer rate** The transfer rate of blocks of data over a long enough time to include gaps between the blocks, words, or records. Regeneration time and other items not subject to program control are included. Programmed control items such as starting, stopping, and searching are not included.

**average transmission rate** Relates to the rate at which data is transmitted through a channel over an extended period of time to allow for gaps between words, blocks, records, files, or fields. Starting, stopping, rewinding, searching, or other operations subject to program control in the case of magnetic tapes, discs, drums, are excluded.

**axis** 1. A principal direction movement of the tool or workpiece in automatic machining. 2. One of the reference lines of a coordinate system.

**axis inhibit** A feature in automatic machining that prevents movement of selected slides with the power on.

**axis interchange** The capability of inputting information concerning one axis into the storage of another axis.

**axis inversion** The reversal of normal plus and minus values along an axis, which makes possible the machining of a left-handed part from right-handed programming and vice versa. Same as mirror image.

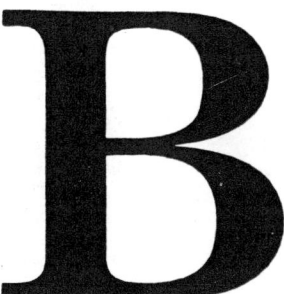

**BA** 1. Abbreviation for *binary add*. 2. Abbreviation for *bus available*.

**babble** The crosstalk from a large number of channels in a system. Also, the disturbing sounds in system operation resulting from such crosstalk.

**BAC** Abbreviation for *binary asymmetric channel*.

**back coupling** A form of coupling that permits the transfer of energy from an output circuit to an input circuit.

**background processing** Automatic execution of lower priority programs when higher priority programs are not using the machine. Batch processing, such as inventory control, payroll, and housekeeping, is often treated as background processing and can be interrupted on orders from terminals or inquiries from other units.

**background program** 1. In multiprogramming, the program with the lowest priority. Background programs execute from batched or stacked job input. 2. In time sharing, a program executed in a region of main storage that is not swapped. Contrast with foreground program.

**backlash** A property of many regenerative and oscillator circuits by which oscillation is maintained with a smaller positive feedback than is required for inception.

**backplane** Refers to the connecting slots available for the microcomputer circuit boards. A typical bus oriented backplane is used as the data highway between logic memory and process input/output modules. Some backplanes are configured so as to give each plugged-in module its own unique address. As a result of this *card address* design, users can interchange memory and input/output modules throughout the chassis. One typical backplane has in each chassis three control slots, one terminator slot, and 16 multipurpose addressable slots. Since only three of the 16 are used in many basic systems, 13 slots are available for users to plug in any additional memory or interfacing required.

**backplane testing** Refers to the testing of the backplane connections. Wiring error rates on backplanes may run between 0.1 percent and 5 percent depending on the type of wire-wrap equipment used. Manual wiring produces the highest error rates, between 2 percent and 5 percent. These errors are usually due to missed connections, misplaced wires, and loose solder. Semiautomatic connection errors run between 0.1 percent and 1 percent, with most errors resulting from machine malfunction, operator mistakes, and broken wires. Using completely automatic wrapping equipment, error rates seldom are above 0.2 percent. Newer solid-state-switched systems connect to the backplane via daisy-chained *fixture cards* to minimize the interface wiring.

**back-porch effect** The prolonging of the collector current in a transistor for a brief time after the input signal (particularly if it is large) has decreased to zero.

**back-to-back devices** Refers to two semiconductor devices connected in parallel but in opposite directions so that they can be used to control current without introducing rectification. Also referred to as an inverse-parallel connection.

**backspace code** A key-operated instruction that backspaces the carriage or carrier of a typewriter without backspacing the storage medium. It is used, for example, in underscoring.

**backup system** 1. A system that combines several error detection and correction techniques to spot and correct equipment and transmission errors. 2. A system that takes over when the primary system is down for various reasons.

**BADGE** Abbreviation for *base air defense ground environment*.

**BAGS** Abbreviation for *Bullpup all-weather guidance system*.

**balanced circuit** A circuit with two sides electrically alike and symmetrical to a common reference point, usually ground. These circuits may be terminated by a network whose impedance balances the impedance of the line so that the return losses are infinite.

**balanced instrumentation amplifier system** In balanced systems the output of the signal source appears on two lines, both having equal source resistances and output voltages in relation to ground or the common-mode level.

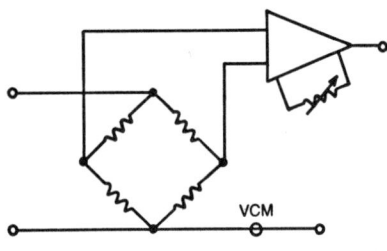

Balanced system

**balanced line** A transmission line consisting of two conductors; in the presence of ground, it is capable of being operated in such a way that the voltages of the two conductors at all transverse planes are equal in magnitude and opposite in polarity with respect to ground; the currents in the two conductors are equal in magnitude and opposite in direction.

**balanced line system** A system consisting of a source, balanced line, and a load adjusted so that the voltage of the two conductors at all transverse planes are equal in magnitude and opposite in polarity with respect to ground.

**balanced network** A network arranged for insertion into a balanced circuit and therefore symmetrical electrically about the midpoints of its input and output pairs of terminals.

**balanced oscillator** A type of oscillator in which the impedance centers of the tank circuits are always at ground potential and the operating voltages between either end and the centers are equal at all points and opposite in phase.

**balanced-to-ground** The state of impedance on a two wire line when the impedance to ground as measured from one side of the line is equal to the impedance to ground as measured from the other side of the line.

**balanced voltages** On the two conductors of a balanced line, balanced voltages are the voltages relative to ground, which are equal and opposite in polarity at every point along the line. Also referred to as push-pull voltages.

**balanced-wire circuit** A circuit with two sides that are the same electrically and symmetrical to ground and other conductors.

**balancing capacitor** A capacitor that impedes the flow of direct current in a circuit without affecting the flow of alternating current.

**BAM** Abbreviation for *basic telecommunications access method.*

**BAMBI** Abbreviation for *ballistic missile boost intercept.*

**band** 1. A range of frequencies or the frequency spectrum between two limits. 2. A continuous recording track on a storage device such as a magnetic drum or disk. The surface of the drum or disk is divided into more or less equally spaced rings, which are called bands, each with its own read/write head for reading in or writing out data (or both).

**band-edge energy** The band of energy between two defined limits in a semiconductor. The lower limit corresponds to the lowest amount of energy required by an electron to remain free, while the upper band is the maximum permissible energy of a free electron.

**band-elimination filter** A filter having a single attenuation band, with neither of the cutoff frequencies being zero or infinite, such as a filter to eliminate 60 cycle noise pickup from electrical power devices.

**bandpass filter** A filter that gives a "tuned" output consisting of frequency components of a signal within a specific range.

**band printer** A high speed printer in which the type moves on a band or chain. Not commonly used in microcomputer systems because of their expense.

**bank link** A software package used for electronic banking.

**bandwidth** A frequency range between minimum and maximum frequency points of stated attenuation. The attenuation limit is usually 3 dB (half power) at the bandwidth limits.

**BAR** Abbreviation for *buffer address register.*

**bar code** Optical binary code used on merchandise in retail stores.

**barrier layer** A double electrical layer formed at the surface of substances that have differing work functions; there is a diffusion of electrons up this work-function gradient.

**base** See *radix.*

**base address** The number in an address that serves as the reference for subsequent address numbers.

**base line** Refers to the horizontal or vertical line formed by the sweep of the electron gun as it moves across the cathode ray tube screen.

**base material** An insulating material used to support a conductive pattern. The material used most often is a copper clad laminate.

**base notation** A notation consisting of a decimal number, written as a subscript suffix to a number, its decimal value indicating the base or radix of the number. For example, $10_2$ indicates the number 10 has a binary base, and $11_8$ indicates the number 11 has a base of 8.

**base number** The radix of a counting system which indicates the quantity of characters available for use in each of the digital positions. With a binary number, only the characters 0 and 1 are used and the base number is two.

**base time** A precisely controlled function of time by which some particular process is controlled or measured.

**base voltage** The voltage between the base terminals of a transistor and the reference terminal.

**BASIC** An algebraic programming code developed at Dartmouth College. The name is an acronym formed from the initial letters of *beginners' all-purpose symbolic instruction code.* BASIC is a conversational type of programming language using English-like statements and mathematical notation. A BASIC program is made up of lines of statements that contain instructions for the interpreter or compiler.

The program is entered into the system, and it can be saved, listed, retrieved, or executed using the commands available in BASIC.

In the *immediate* mode it is not necessary to write a complete program in order to use BASIC. This mode is useful for debugging and desk calculation problems. Program loops are allowed, as shown in the following calculation of a table of square roots:

```
FOR L = 1 TO 9: PRINT L, SQR (L): NEXT L
```

| | |
|---|---|
| 1 | 1 |
| 2 | 1.41421 |
| 3 | 1.73205 |
| 4 | 2 |
| 5 | 2.23607 |
| 6 | 2.44949 |
| 7 | 2.64575 |
| 8 | 2.82843 |
| 9 | 3 |

**basic control system (BCS)** A system used in computer satellites that is interrupt-oriented, providing fast execution of dedicated programs, without any time scheduling capability.

**basic disk operating system** A part of the CP/M operating system.

**basic input/output system** A collection of subprograms that control the transfer of characters between the microprocessor and other devices in the microcomputer system such as the printer, video display, and keyboard.

**basic linkage** A program linkage that is used repeatedly in one routine, program, or system and that follows the same set of rules each time.

**basic telecommunications access method** An access method that permits read/write communications with remote devices. Abbreviated BTAM.

**basket** The typing mechanism of a standard typewriter in which each character, as a capital and lowercase pair, is conveyed on a separate typebar (the arm that contains the print that impacts the paper), the entire set of typebars is "basketed" in a curved array in front of the platen.

**batch** An assortment of data items that can be processed during a single computer program run.

**batch control** A way of apportioning predetermined quantities of work to users at regular intervals.

**batch mode** A computer mode in which the program is submitted on cards or some other medium and the results returned hours or days later.

**batch processing** A method of processing in which a number of items are grouped for processing during the same machine run. Batch processing systems usually do not require immediate updating of files, as data is gathered up to a specific cutoff time and then processed.

**batch total** The sum of certain quantities, related to batches of unit records, which is used to verify the accuracy for a particular batch. For example, in a payroll calculation, the batches could be employees and the batch totals would be the number of employee hours per each employee or the total pay per each employee.

**batten** See *cordonnier*.

**battery pack** A unit that provides backup power to support components, such as RAM.

**baud** A unit of signaling speed derived from the length of the shortest code element. The speed in baud is equal to the number of code elements per second transmitted. It is also the unit of modulation rate, with one baud equal to a rate of one unit interval per second, and the modulation rate equal to the reciprocal of the duration in seconds of the unit interval. The modulation rate for a unit interval of 20 milliseconds is 50 baud.

**Baudot code** A communications code that contains five binary symbols. The correct interpretation depends on knowing the previous history of the message; for example, whether a capital or lowercase character was last struck. If a sixth bit, called the case bit, is used, the Baudot code can be uniquely identified. Some examples of the code are shown below:

| CASE | 1 | 2 | 3 | 4 | 5 |
|---|---|---|---|---|---|
| A | 0 | 1 | 1 | 0 | 0 | 0 |
| B | 0 | 1 | 0 | 0 | 1 | 1 |
| S | 0 | 1 | 0 | 1 | 0 | 0 |
| Y | 0 | 1 | 0 | 1 | 0 | 0 |
| 4 | 1 | 0 | 1 | 0 | 1 | 0 |
| & | 1 | 0 | 1 | 0 | 1 | 1 |
| 8 | 1 | 0 | 1 | 1 | 0 | 0 |
| 0 | 1 | 0 | 1 | 1 | 0 | 1 |
| CASE | 1 | 2 | 3 | 4 | 5 |
| : | 1 | 0 | 1 | 1 | 1 | 0 |
| ; | 1 | 0 | 1 | 1 | 1 | 1 |

**baud rate** A measurement of data flow in which the number of signal elements per second is based on the duration of the shortest element. When each element carries one bit, the baud rate is numerically equal to bits per second (bps).

**B-box** A register that contains a quantity used to modify addresses; an index register.

**BC** Binary Code.

**BCD** Abbreviation for *binary-coded decimal*, a method of coding in which each decimal digit is coded into a separate 4-bit word. BCD is also known as the 8421 code due to the weight assigned to each 4-bit word.

| DECIMAL | BCD | | |
|---|---|---|---|
| | 8 4 2 1— | WEIGHT | |
| 0 | 0 0 0 0 | | |
| 1 | 0 0 0 1 | | |
| 2 | 0 0 1 0 | | |
| 3 | 0 0 1 1 | | |
| 4 | 0 1 0 0 | | |
| 5 | 0 1 0 1 | | |
| 6 | 0 1 1 0 | | |
| 7 | 0 1 1 1 | | |
| 8 | 1 0 0 0 | | |
| 9 | 1 0 0 1 | | |
| 10 | 0 0 0 1 | 0 0 0 0 | |
| 11 | 0 0 0 1 | 0 0 0 1 | |
| 12 | 0 0 0 1 | 0 0 1 0 | |

**BCFSK** Abbreviation for *binary code frequency shift keying*.

**BCO** Abbreviation for *binary coded octal*.

**BCS** Abbreviation for *basic control system*.

**BCW** Abbreviation for *buffer control word*.

**BDOS** Abbreviation for *basic disk operating system*.

**BDU** Abbreviation for *basic display unit*.

**beano** A computerized version of bingo, in which one adds, subtracts, multiplies, or divides a set of random numbers to get the numbers needed to complete the row on the bingo card.

**beating the shift** A typewriter action in which a very fast or erratic typist causes a character to misprint following or preceding a shift.

**BECO** Abbreviation for *booster engine cut off*.

**beginners's all-purpose instruction code** The BASIC language.

**bel** A nondimensional unit used for expressing the ratio of power units ($P_1$ and $P_2$).

$$N = \log_{10} (P_1/P_2) \text{ bels}.$$

A bel is ten times the size of the more frequently used decibel. In Europe *neper* is used instead of *bel*.

**BEMA** Abbreviation for *Business Equipment Manufacturers Association*.

**benchmark** A test criterion used for measuring the performance of a product. Microprocessors, for example, can be evaluated using a benchmark program to compare different types. A flowchart in assembly language can be used to test each type with respect to execution time, accuracy, and other critical parameters for a particular application.

**benchmark comparisons** These comparisons show the results of a benchmark test using a sample program. The results may reflect tests of available microprocessors as shown. In this task, microprocessor

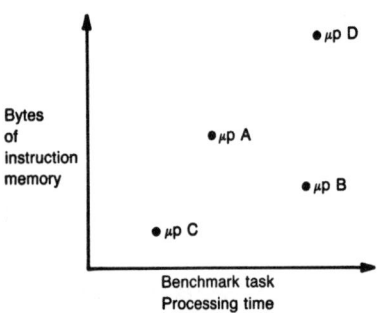

**Typical benchmark test results**

C requires the least amount of processing time and uses the smallest amount of memory for the benchmark program. Microprocessor D on the other hand uses more memory and requires the most processing time. Processing power favors an 8 bit design over a 4 bit one. If minimizing cost is the most important goal, 4 bit microprocessors should be considered. The domain of small to medium application problems, however, are dominated by 8 bit microprocessors.

Benchmark results using microprocessors may be based on a program that consists of the movement of a block of data using a sequence like the following:

```
SET UP   MOV;   move data to register A
         MOV;   move data to register B
         MOV;   move data to register C,
                (character move)
LOOP     MOV;   ; combine data in register A with B
LOOP 1          ; loop to register C
EXIT
```

Other criteria can consist of interrupt servicing, arithmetic operations, searching, or monitoring.

**benchmark problem** A routine used to evaluate the performance of computing machines and software. A typical problem might be to perform nine complete additions and one complete multiplication and measure the time to complete all operations, which include (1) operation acquisition from storage, (2) performance of the operation (3) storage of the result, (4) selection of the next instruction, and (5) instruction execution.

**benchmark program** A sample program or simple routine or operation mix that can be used to compare the performances of different processors. Since processors utilize different instruction sets, the benchmark programs are specified using flowcharts. As an example of a benchmark program, consider a simple program designed to test or poll a peripheral device. The figure below illustrates a flowchart for performing a polling function, labeling the data obtained, and storing it in memory. The blocks of the flow chart represent machine functions in this example. From the flowchart, a program for the particular microprocessor can be coded and run, and a timing memory size analysis can be computed based on execution times and instruction bytes. Thus the following key performance parameters could be obtained: (1) the number of memory bytes occupied by the program or task and (2) the speed of execution of the program or task. The relative importance of these parameters depends on the application, but a benchmark can establish a quantitative measurement for making a comparison. A complex program or actual operational application may contain numerous routines and conclusive information cannot always be drawn from simple benchmarks. It is not always easy to establish a single benchmark. One must then use judgment, or if time and resources are available, actual simulation. It has been found in practice that the majority of tasks to be performed by microprocessors can be performed by any standard 8 bit or 16 bit microprocessor, although there may be differences in speed and efficiency. When comparing microprocessors, an 8 bit by 8 bit multiplication may be faster on one, while an 8 bit by 16 bit multiplication may be faster on the other, due to design differences.

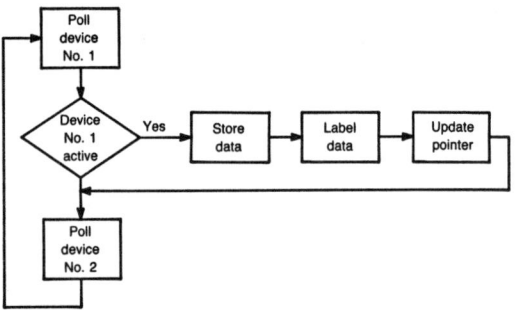

**Benchmark program flowchart**

**benchmark routine** A set of routines or problems that will help determine the performance of a given piece of equipment.

**benchmark task** Benchmark problem.

**BESS** Abbreviation for *binary electromagnetic signal signature*.

**BEV** Abbreviation for *billion electron volts*.

**BFO** Abbreviation for *beat frequency oscillator*.

**bias** 1. A term which denotes an electrical, mechanical, or magnetic force or voltage applied to a relay, transistor, vacuum tube, or other electrical device to establish an electrical or mechanical operational reference level. 2. The amount by which the average of a set of values departs from a reference value. 3. In teletypewriter applications, the uniform shifting of the beginning of all marking pulses from their proper positions in relation to the beginning of the start pulse.

**bibliographic retrieval service** A type of database service offered to microcomputer users that are properly equipped and subscribed.

**BIC** Abbreviation for *bus interface circuit*.

**bidirectional** Capable of operation in two directions; for example, toward the input and toward the output.

**bidirectional buffer** Since some chips cannot drive a heavily loaded data bus, it is sometimes necessary to buffer the data bus to this chip. This can be done as shown in the figure below.

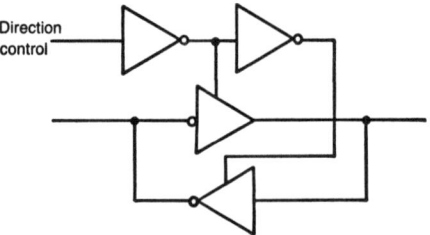

**Bidirectional buffer**

**bidirectional bus**  A bus that accepts both input and output signals on a single line.

**bidirectional bus driver**  A power driver that can operate with bidirectional signals.

**bidirectional data bus**  A bus that accepts both input and output data signals on a single line.

**bidirectional lines**  Bus lines with bidirectional and asynchronous communications. These lines permit devices to send, receive, and exchange data at their own rates. The bidirectional nature of a bus allows utilization of common bus interfaces for different devices and simplifies the interface design.

**bidirectional operation**  An operation in which reading, writing, and searching may be conducted in either direction, thus saving time and providing easy access to stored information.

**bidirectional printer**  A device capable of printing from right to left as well as from left to right, thus reducing wasted motion during operation. Also called *reverse printer*.

**bidirectional pulses**  Signal pulses that rise in one direction and repeat in the opposite direction.

**bidirectional signal**  A signal that appears to be symmetrical about an axis or bias.

**bidirectional transistor**  A type of transistor in which the emitter and collector can be used interchangeably. Either terminal can be used as the input or the output.

**bidirectional waveform**  A waveform that shows a reversal of polarity, such as the waveforms produced when a bidirectional pulse generator produces both positive and negative pulses.

**bifurcated contact**  A contact that is forked or pronged.

**bifurcation**  A condition under which two, and only two, outcomes can occur, such as on or off, and 0 or 1.

**BILE**  Abbreviation for *balanced inductor logic element*.

**bikini**  A lightweight battlefield reconnaissance drone, so named because of its simplicity, economy, and ability to cover strategic areas.

**billi**  A prefix that designates the quantity one billion power; synonymous with kilomega. Billibits mean one billion bits; billicycle, one billion cycles per second.

**binary**  Countable using two digits, zeros and ones. The basic requirement of a computer is its ability to represent numbers and to perform operations on the numbers represented; since any number can be represented by an ordered arrangement of ones and zeros, most computers use this system of counting. In the binary number system, the carry is used with the two digits. The numbers used to count to ten are as follows:

| DECIMAL | BINARY |
|---|---|
| 0 | 0 |
| 1 | 1 |
| 10 | 2 |
| 11 | 3 |
| 100 | 4 |
| 101 | 5 |
| 110 | 6 |
| 111 | 7 |
| 1000 | 8 |
| 1001 | 9 |
| 1010 | 10 |

A weighting table can be used to convert any binary number to its decimal equivalent. Each digit is multiplied by its position coefficient and the results added to obtain the decimal number:

| $2^3$ | $2^2$ | $2^1$ | $2^0$ | BINARY WEIGHT |
|---|---|---|---|---|
| 1 | 0 | 1 | 0 | BINARY NUMBER |
| 8 | 0 | 2 | 0 | DECIMAL EQUIVALENTS |

DECIMAL NUMBER = 8 + 0 + 2 + 0 = 10

The table can be extended to the left as far as desired. The 1 in the far left position is always called the most significant bit, abbreviated MSB. The digit in the far right position is called the least significant bit, LSB.

**binary arithmetic**  Mathematical operations performed using the binary digits of 1 and 0. In the binary number system, there are four addition rules:

$$0 + 0 = 0$$
$$1 + 0 = 1$$
$$0 + 1 = 1$$
$$1 + 1 = 0 \text{ and carry a } 1$$

These rules are demonstrated in the following example of adding the binary equivalents of 10 and 14.

```
carries ──→ 111
            1010 = 10
          + 1110 = 14
          ─────────────
           11000 = 24
```

The microcomputer could add these numbers by using three registers (A, B, and C). The program could have the following steps:

1. Load numbers to be added, 1010 and 1110, into registers A and B.
2. Clear C to remove any bits stored there.
3. Transfer the contents of A to C (they now hold the same value).
4. Add the contents of B to C, using the addition rules, and store in C.

The sum is now stored in C for transfer to another location or readout. Multiplication has a similar set of rules:

$$0 \times 0 = 0$$
$$0 \times 1 = 0$$
$$1 \times 0 = 0$$
$$1 \times 1 = 1$$

An example of a multiplications follows:

```
    1010 = 10
  ×  101 =  5
  ─────────────
    1010
   1010
  ─────────────
  110010 = 50
```

Multiplication can be done in a microcomputer by multiple additions, multiple shifts, or a combination of both. A shift to the left results in a multiplication by two. In the above example, 1010 is shifted left twice for a multiplication of four and then 1010 is added to the result to give a multiplication by five.

Subtraction is usually done by *complementing*, which involves changing all ones to zeros and all zeros to ones in a binary system. To perform binary subtraction:

(1) Complement the subtrahend.
(2) Add it to the minuend.
(3) Move the digit from the most significant position and add it to the value of the least significant position, performing the end-around carry.

For example, to subtract 1011 from 1100:

(1) Complement 1011 = 0100
(2) Add to the minuend:

$$\begin{array}{r} 1100 \\ + \ 0100 \\ \hline 10000 \end{array}$$

(3) Perform the end-around carry:

$$\begin{array}{r} 10000 \\ \hline 00001 \end{array}$$

Division is accomplished with binary numbers by repeated shifts and subtractions. For example:

$$\begin{array}{r} 101 \phantom{00} \\ 101 \overline{)11010} \\ \underline{101\phantom{00}} \\ 110 \\ \underline{101} \\ 1 \ \leftarrow \text{remainder} \end{array}$$

**binary cell** An elementary unit of storage that can be placed in either one of two possible stable states.

**binary chain** An entire series of separate binary circuits, each capable of existing in either one of two states. They are arranged so each circuit can affect or modify the condition of adjacent circuits.

**binary code** A code in which every element has only one of two possible values, which may be the presence or absence of a pulse, a one or a zero, or a high or a low condition for a voltage or current.

**binary coded decimal** See BCD.

**binary coded decimal number** The representation of a number using the binary coded decimal system. For example, the binary coded decimal number for 9 is 1001. For 8 it is 1000 and for 10 it is 0001 0000.

**binary counter** A counting circuit that produces an output for every two input pulses, producing a division by two.

**binary digit** A numeral in the binary system of notation. Usually known as a *bit*, the digit may be a one or a zero.

**binary dump** A portion of a program that allows for printing or displaying a binary copy of a portion of memory.

**binary loader** A device used to load a binary format, such as that required by a binary dump program, link editor, or assembler. In a binary tape loader, object tapes from the assembler can be loaded for debugging. The loader reads the tape using a teletypewriter reader and processes each record, which contains address, object, and checksum data, by placing the object data into the locations specified by the address data.

**binary number system** A number system having 2 as its base and expressing all quantities using the numerals 0 and 1. As in the decimal system, the value of binary digits is positionally weighted from right to left by ascending powers of the base:

$$2^6 \ 2^5 \ 2^4 \ 2^3 \ 2^2 \ 2^1 \ 2^0$$

Hence the binary number 011100 can be converted to decimal as follows:

$$\begin{array}{c} 0 \ 1 \ 1 \ 1 \ 0 \ 0 \\ 0 \times 2^0 = 0 \\ 0 \times 2^1 = 0 \\ 1 \times 1^2 = 4 \\ 1 \times 2^3 = 8 \\ 1 \times 2^4 = 16 \\ 0 \times 2^5 = 0 \\ \text{TOTAL } 28_{10} \end{array}$$

THEREFORE: $011100_2 = 28_{10}$

The two-state character of the binary number system makes it especially suitable for a digital computer that operates most conveniently on a bistable basis.

**binary object program** A program that can be directly executed by a digital machine. It substitutes the actual addresses in place of the symbolic ones and substitutes the actual binary encoding of the data along with the binary code of instructions in place of the mnemonics.

**binary point** 1. A point located half the distance between the integral powers of two in a binary number. 2. That point in a binary number that separates the integral from the fractional part. It is analogous to the decimal point for a decimal number.

**binary row** A method of representing binary numbers on a punched card using rows instead of columns. This system is convenient for computer systems using words less than 40 bits long; the card can then be used to store up to twelve words on each half.

**binary search** A method for locating an item in an ordered set of items by repeatedly dividing in half the set of items until only the desired item remains.

**binary signaling** A method of communications in which information is transferred by the presence or absence of the two state variations of the signal.

**binary synchronous** A mode of transmission in which the synchronizing of binary characters is controlled by signals generated at the receiving and sending stations. Also known as *bisynch*.

**binary tape assembler** A binary tape assembler converts source program tapes to the binary tape format that is loaded into memory and produces an assembly listing that shows the converted code alongside the original assembly language mnemonic source program text. Source tape input to the assembler can be via a high-speed reader. The binary tape may be punched on either a teletypewriter or a high-speed punch.

**binary-to-decimal conversion** The process of converting a binary number to its equivalent in decimal form.

**binary to Gray code conversion** A conversion between the two codes that takes place as follows: when the binary most significant bit (MSB) is zero, the Gray code MSB will be zero. Then going from the MSB to the LSB (least significant bit), each change produces a 1, each non-change a 0. A circuit in which binary to Gray code conversion may be achieved is shown below. See *Gray code*.

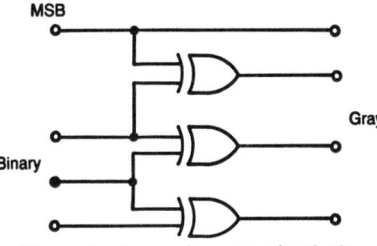

**Binary-to-gray code conversion logic**

**bionics** The application of biological techniques to the design of electronic hardware and systems. Bionics uses the knowledge gained from the study of living systems to create hardware that functions in a manner analogous to the biological systems being studied. The result sometimes creates hardware that strongly resembles the characteristics as well as the functions of living systems.

**BIOS** Abbreviations for *basic input output system*.

**biosensor** A sensor or mechanism for detecting and transmitting biological data from an organism in a way that permits processing, display, or storage of the results.

**bipolar** Having two polarity levels. Bipolar transistors are configured as npn or pnp "sandwiches," as opposed to the controlled channel construction of field-effect devices such as MOS (metal-oxide semiconductor) transistors and integrated circuits. Since bipolar devices have low capacitance, switching time (the time required to turn them on and off) can be very short, resulting in very fast computer operations.

Bipolar integrated circuit devices tend to have a higher surface area per unit volume compared to MOS, which tends to keep the cost of fabrication high for complex chips. Another disadvantage of bipolar IC construction is the requirement of isolation barriers between adjacent devices, which adds to fabrication costs. Bipolar devices also dissipate more power than MOS, since they operate on current rather than voltage.

Bipolar-device fabrication usually requires about 12 masking steps and four diffusion steps; MOS requires five masking steps and one diffusion. Bipolar processing can be complex because of the number of alternating diffusion steps required to produce the isolating barriers on the chip.

The first bipolar microprocessor chips to appear were 10 times faster than the MOS microprocessor available at the time. With a machine cycle time of 200 nanoseconds, the architecture of the bipolar chips was a two-bit slice approach and the instruction set was microprogrammable. The device was designed for products in which it would be tailored for a specific application.

Later bit-slice bipolar chips used sets of 4-bit chips, each chip consisting of a register file read by two address multipliers. Data in the registers passes through a set of latches. One of the chips contains the arithmetic logic unit and provides data routing control. An internal register is used for temporary storage of results and double-precision arithmetic storage. Bit-slice microprocessors are now being produced with Schottky-TTL logic, integrated injection logic ($I^2L$), and emitter-coupled logic (ECL), all of which are bipolar in form.

Schottky microcomputer chip sets have two major components—the microprogram control unit (MCU), and the central processing element (CPE). These can be combined with a bipolar memory to construct controller-processors using a minimum of auxiliary logic.

A programmable microcontroller can provide the best features of both program controllers and microprocessors. These systems can be used in high-speed instruments, control systems, and data processing acquisition systems. A unit can be put on a single circuit board and can perform 8-bit binary or 4-bit BCD arithmetic; it can test individual bits and perform data manipulation. A typical unit might have:

1. A 32-word × 8-bit register file.
2. A last-in, first-out (LIFO) stack of 16 levels for nesting subroutines.
3. High-speed multilevel interrupt capability.
4. Parallel and serial input/output.
5. Field-programmable ROM of 1000 words for program memory, expandable to 4000 words.

Available development aids include a control console for program development with a high-speed paper tape reader and time-sharing cross assembler. A typical central processing element can be used in an array of eight to construct a 16-bit controller-processor.

Bipolar read-only-memories are typically set up as 512 eight-bit words with an access time of 70 nanoseconds and are used as lookup tables, microprogram storage, code conversion, and function and character generation. For subroutine programming, the ROM can cover a particular area of the main memory with a window into the core at each ROM location containing a zero data word. Then a read or write operation allows an operand to be extracted from or entered into the core or main memory. The subroutines can then be programmed in ROM knowing that return addresses will be stored in and retrieved when the first location of the subroutine has a zero data word.

Bipolar random-access memories can be used as high-speed buffer memories or replacements for high-speed core memories. These can be organized as 256 words of one bit with eight-bit binary addressing. They usually have separate address and input/output lines. The eight address inputs select the proper bit location, and a write enable line is used to determine if a read or write mode is being used at any particular time. A series of chip enable inputs determine both the logic and impedance state of the output. Logical 1 or 0 is controlled by the chip enable along with an off or high impedance state. These states are used when connecting the output to a common bus.

Bipolar microprocessors offer a building-block approach from which complex processing systems can be constructed, using various hierarchies or levels of control memory. Both microinstruction and macroinstruction programming can be used in these systems.

Many bipolar chip sets that use the slice approach do not have fixed instruction sets. The user must develop these and store them in microprogram memory. Then the various peripherals including additional memory can be connected with the chip set to form a microcomputer, and additional programs are developed and stored as the design proceeds.

A typical chip set includes microprogram control units, central processing elements, and programmable read-only memories (PROM)s.

**bipolar CPU slice** A type of chip that provides many of the speed advantages of discrete logic and all of the processor oriented advantages of a microprocessor. It does require another level of system design: users must build their own instruction set (macroinstructions) using techniques like those used to create microprogrammed CPUs.

**bipolar current switching D/A conversion** A converter that uses offset binary or two's complement codes. An offset current equal and opposite to the most significant byte current is added to the converter output. This can be a resistor and a separate offset reference, but usually it is derived from the converter's basic reference voltage, to minimize drift with temperature. The gain of the output-inverting amplifier is doubled in order to double the output range, from 0 − 10V to + 10V. See the figure below.

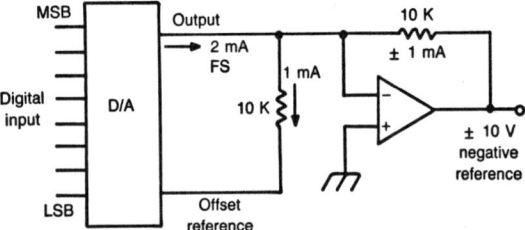

**Bipolar current switching D/A Converter connected for offset binary or 2's complement codes**

**bipolar decoders, Shottky** Systems that use input ports, output ports and memory components with active low chip select input can be expanded with these bipolar decoders. When the unit is enabled, one of its eight or more outputs goes low, selecting a single row of a memory system. One unit has three chip-enable inputs on the decoder, which allows easy system expansion. In large systems, decoders can be used in sets, with each decoder driving eight or more other decoders for memory.

**bipolar fabrication** Refers to the fabrication of bipolar devices. Bipolar fabrication typically requires 12 masking steps and four diffusion steps, versus 5 masking steps and one diffusion step for n-channel and p-channel MOS devices. Bipolar fabrication is complex because of the need for isolation rings around each device, and because a number of alternating diffusion steps are required to create the n-p-n-p layers.

**bipolar mask bus** A mask bus, unique to bipolar systems. The mask bus provides a mechanism for supplying constants to a central processor array and permits additional functions in the system.

**bipolar RAM** A bipolar random access memory. Bipolar RAMs are used in high-speed buffer memories and as replacements for high-speed core memories in older systems. The memories are generally organized with an 8 bit binary address field and separate data-in and data-output lines. Some memories have three active LOW chip select inputs and a three state output or open collector output. Inputs are generally buffered to present an input load of 0.5 TTL unit loads. Read/write operations may be controlled by an active LOW write enable input. When the write enable is LOW and the chip is selected, the data on the data input is written into the location specified by the address inputs. During this operation the output floats, allowing the data bus to be used by other memories or open collector logic elements that are tied to the inverting data output. Reading is accomplished by having the chip selected and the write enable input HIGH. Data stored in the locations specified by the address inputs is read out and appears on the data output inverter.

**bipolar random access memories** Bipolar random access memories use bipolar transistors arranged as flip flops in the basic cell configuration shown below. The memory, with its multiple emitter transistors, may be bit-organized or word-organized. If it is bit-organized, only one data bit is provided for each address. In a word-organized system, the flip flops are tied together in groups to obtain the desired word length. The address decoding circuits are usually included as a part of the chip.

**bipolar read-only memory** A read-only memory of bipolar transistors. Standard features permit the efficient use of ROM for subroutine pro-

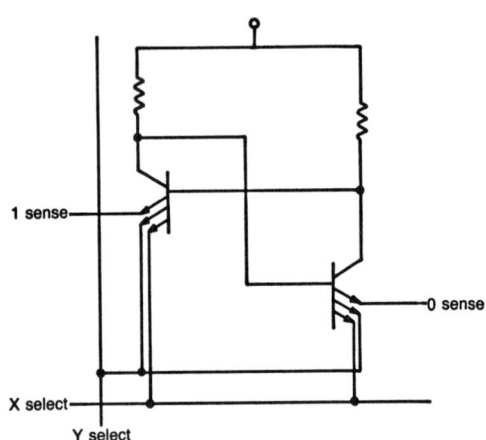

**Basic TTL memory cell**

gramming. An installed ROM in some systems covers a corresponding area of main memory and contains a window into the main memory at each ROM location containing a zero data word. A read or write operation into a zero ROM location will cause an operand to be read from or written into the corresponding main memory location. In particular, subroutines can be programmed into the ROM based on the fact that return addresses are automatically stored in and retrieved from main memory when the first location of a ROM subroutine contains a zero word.

**bipolar semiconductors** Refers to a semiconductor device fabricated with bipolar processes. The basic processes depend on the type of logic circuit built with the process, such as TTL (transistor transistor logic or ECL emitter coupled logic). All bipolar technologies are similar, being based on the formation of silicon layers with different electrical properties. The major difference is the number and sequences of diffusion operations required to manufacture the device.

**bipolar transistor** One of the two basic types of components that can be fabricated using integrated circuit technology. Bipolar devices have two types of charge carriers, while unipolar devices only have one type of charge carrier. Bipolar technologies used in microprocessors include transistor transistor logic (TTL), emitter coupled logic (ECL) and integrated injection logic ($I^2L$). A cross sectional view of a bipolar transistor is shown below.

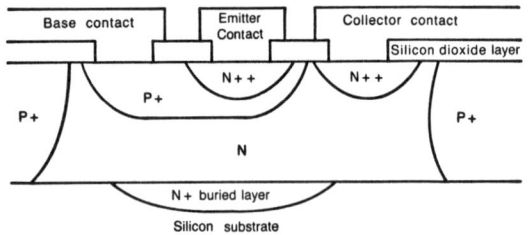

**Bipolar transistor**

The contacts are usually made of aluminum using an evaporation process. The buried layer is used to provide a more conductive path between the collector, base, and emitter regions. The figure shows only one transistor; a microprocessor or memory circuit would have thousands of these transistors connected together to form the logic elements required.

**biquinary** A method of coding that uses two parts of a binary code to represent a decimal number; one of the parts has the value of decimal zero or five, and the other part has the value of zero through four, as shown below:

| DECIMAL | BIQUINARY | DECIMAL INTER-PRETATION |
|---------|-----------|-------------------------|
| 0 | 0 000 | 0 + 0 |
| 1 | 0 001 | 0 + 1 |
| 2 | 0 010 | 0 + 2 |
| 3 | 0 011 | 0 + 3 |
| 4 | 0 100 | 0 + 4 |
| 5 | 1 000 | 5 + 0 |
| 6 | 1 001 | 5 + 1 |
| 7 | 1 010 | 5 + 2 |
| 8 | 1 011 | 5 + 3 |
| 9 | 1 100 | 5 + 4 |

This system is used in the hand-manipulated abacus and soroban. A modified biquinary system has been used in some early computers such as the IBM-650. The modified system uses seven bits with the following weights from left to right: 5, 0, 4, 3, 2, and 1 and 0. Since every decimal number is represented by two ones and five zeros, it is very easy to make a code check by counting the ones and zeros. Some arithmetic operations are difficult to mechanize with this system, which also requires a large amount of memory compared to other systems. More than 100 characters are required to represent just the first ten decimal numbers as shown:

| DECIMAL | BIQUINARY (7 bit) |
|---------|-------------------|
| 0 | 0100001 |
| 1 | 0100010 |
| 2 | 0100100 |
| 3 | 0101000 |
| 4 | 0110000 |
| 5 | 1000001 |
| 6 | 1000010 |
| 7 | 1000100 |
| 8 | 1001000 |
| 9 | 1010000 |

**bistable** Having the capability of assuming either of two stable states in a circuit or circuit element. A typical bistable circuit is a flip-flop or bistable multivibrator, which can store one bit of data. All computer operations are carried out by setting and resetting bistable elements. The action of bistable elements is such that if the circuit is in a stable state with a zero output, a change of the input produces a change of the output to a one state; and if it is in a stable state with a one output, a change of the input produces a change in the output to a zero state. The change in the input can be a pulse of limited duration, which allows a series of bistable elements to function as a counter or register.

**bistable circuit** A circuit capable of assuming either of two stable states (same as flip-flop).

**bistable components** Refers to a component that can exist in one of two states. Bistable states can be summarized as follows: If the bistable component is in stable state A, an energy pulse will drive it to state B; if the bistable component is in stable state B, an energy pulse will drive it to state A. Thus, a bistable component can represent the number 0 or 1:

Stable state A = 0
Stable state B = 1

A group of bistable components can be used to represent any number.

**bistable latch** A flip-flop circuit that can be enabled to store a logical one or a logical zero. One bistable latch device is required for the storage of each bit.

**bistable multivibrator** Flip-flop.

**bistable relay** A relay that requires two pulses to complete one cycle composed of two conditions of operation. Also referred to as locked, interlocked, and latching relay.

**bistable trigger circuit** A circuit that can be triggered to adopt one of two stable states.

**BISYNC** Abbreviation for *binary synchronous communications*.

**BIT** Abbreviation for *built-in test*.

**bit** A blend word formed from *binary digit*, a unit of information equal to one binary decision. It can be a single character in a binary number, a single pulse in a coded group of pulses, or a unit of information capacity.

When used as a unit of information capacity, the capacity in bits is equal to the logarithm to the base two of the number of possible states available. In a memory, for example, each element is capable of representing a zero or a one at any instant, and the total number of ones and zeros at any instant is the capacity of the memory.

**bit-bender** A computer hobbyist.

**bit check** A manual or machine-conducted examination of a word or bit group to verify presence of a parity bit in its prescribed position.

**bit density** The number of bits of digital data that can occupy a given volume or area of storage medium.

**bit location** 1. A storage position capable of storing one bit. 2. The position of a specific digit in a binary number.

**bit parallel** A method of simultaneously moving or transferring all bits in a contiguous set of bits over separate wires, one wire for each bit in the set.

**bit parity** The condition of an output group of bits when a check bit is used to parity-balance the total value for the purpose of error checking. A specific bit is used to indicate if the sum of ones in a series of bits is odd or even. The series of bits can be a word or a series of words, and the check bit must be separated from the counting operation. In a typical system, if a one parity bit indicates an odd number of ones in a series, then a zero parity bit indicates an even number of ones. If the total number of ones, including the parity bit, is always even, the system is called an even-parity system. If the total number of ones is odd, the system becomes an odd-parity system.

**bit position** A specific location in memory, space, or time at which a binary digit occurs or is located.

**bit rate** The number of individual data bits processed in a given period of time (usually in one second).

**bit serial** A method of sequentially moving or transferring a contiguous set of bits one at a time over a single wire, according to a fixed sequence.

**bit sign** The value of a binary digit used to indicate the polarity of data representing a number or quantity, such as an angle. The binary digit carrying this value is called the *sign bit*.

**bit slice** An approach in structuring microprocessors such that the resulting microcomputers are put together using a building block technique. A typical processor using bit-slice chips might use four 4-bit microprocessor chips. Some other bit-slice microprocessors (like the early 3000 series) are only two bits wide. The bit-slice approach lets the user configure the microprocessor and requires the development of a specialized instruction set during the initial design phase. A 16-bit processor can be built up with two dozen or less chips that will handle programs designed for popular minicomputers at similar speeds. The processor consumes only about 10W of power with an instruction time of about 1 ns and a cycle time of 300 ns.

**bit-slice devices** Large-scale-integration components that implement some of the functions of central, processing units but cannot be properly classified as microprocessors. The term microprocessor is often applied to bit slice devices, but they are not complete CPUs. Popular usage, however, labels them as microprocessors.

The bit-slice device is a section of an arithmetic logical unit along with its data paths. It may include registers, the ALU, multiplexers, and buses. It does not include the control section. This part of a bit-slice system is implemented with other devices and is generally microprogrammed as shown below. The complete microprocessor requires a significant number of devices that make bit-slice systems larger and more expensive than single-chip microprocessors.

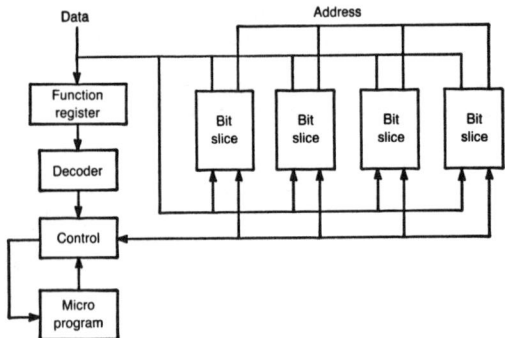

Bit-slice structure

The usual size for bit-slice devices is four bits. Bit slices are used for building the most powerful processors in use.

**bit stream** Refers to transmission methods in which character separation is accomplished by the terminal equipment, and the bits are transmitted in a consecutive line without regard to groupings by character. The term is often used in connection with synchronous transmission and the devices operating in this mode.

**bit string** A string of binary digits in which the position of each binary digit is considered as an independent unit.

**BIX** Abbreviation for *binary information exchange*.

**black box** A term for any functional electronic unit such as the central processing unit of microcomputer. It applies to any device that converts data from one format to another or changes the data or signal in any way.

**blank** 1. A location in a storage medium (character or space) that is used to provide a method of checking the accuracy of the operations. 2. A quartz plate.

**blank, switching** Dead band.

**blank transmission test** A feature that allows checking of the data field for all blank positions. Used as a control measure, a blank transmission can (1) prevent destruction of existing records in storage, (2) indicate when the last item on a card has been processed, and (3) instruct the computer to skip a calculation when a blank is encountered.

**block** 1. A group of words considered as a unit. On magnetic tape, a block is considered to be any group of words, recorded in the serial mode, that is separated by intervening blank spaces. Each block is considered to be made up of one or more records. The records can be reduced to blocks to decrease acceleration and deceleration times of the tape machine. Blocks are ten or more words in length and separated by enough blank spaces to allow the tape to start and stop accurately before read or write operations are attempted. 2. Geometric figures in block diagrams to show basic functional relationships, such as a part of a circuit or a part of a program.

**block delete** A feature that permits selected blocks of data to be ignored at the discretion of the user.

**block diagram** A graphic representation of any operational circuit or system when each functional element is presented as a box or block, and the relationship of each element to other elements is depicted by connected lines depicting hierarchy.

**block input** A group of words to be transferred from external storage to internal storage (input).

**block length** The number of characters, bits, or words comprising a defined unit word or character group.

**block output** A group of words to be transferred from internal storage to an external destination.

**block sort** A sort of one or more of the most significant characters of a key to serve as a means of making workable-sized groups from a large volume of records to be sorted.

**block transfer** The conveyance of a word or character grouping from one register or device to another.

**blockette** A subdivision of a block, that is treated as a unit, particularly during input and output transfer.

**blocking** The combining of two or more records into one block.

**blocking oscillator** A tuned oscillator that has more than sufficient positive feedback for oscillation, but in which a condition periodically causes a suspension of normal oscillation. As the cycle is continuously repeated, it produces sawtooth and pulse waveforms.

**blocks** Records are transferred to and from tapes in the form of *blocks* (also called physical records). A block or physical record may contain one or more logical records. Records can be reduced to blocks on tape to reduce the acceleration and deceleration times.

**blown fuse, polysilicon** Refers to semiconductor memory in which a formed fuse is blown with a pulse train of successively wider pulses, with a current of 20-30 mA typically needed to blow the fuse. During this operation, which determines the bit pattern in the read-only memory, temperatures close to 1400°C are reached in the notch of the polysilicon fuse. At these temperatures, the silicon oxidizes and forms an insulating material. The use of silicon eliminates conductive dendrites and the existence of conductive materials in the fused gap.

**blue-ribbon** Adjective used to describe a program that is handwritten and designed to run properly the first time. The blue-ribbon program is carefully written and debugged to remove all program errors before running (also known as a *star* program).

**blue sheet** A term sometimes used for a machine-language operator instruction sheet.

**BM** Abbreviation for *buffer module*.

**BMT** Abbreviation for *beginning of magnetic tape*.

**board** 1. A panel that can be changed by adding or deleting external wires. Also called a jumper board, plugboard, or panel. 2. A circuit board.

**bode diagram** A plot of log amplitude ratios and phase angle values on a log frequency base for a transfer function. This can be a control-element, output, or loop-transfer function.

**bode plot** A method of plotting control-element transfer functions that uses logarithms of gain or phase angles versus the logarithm of the frequency of the plotted function. For closed-loop system control, it is desirable to obtain the maximum gain while retaining control loop stability. The higher the gain of the system, the faster the system response and the better the control of the controlled variable.

Analysis of a closed-loop control system usually begins with an assessment of the frequency response of each component in the system. If this information is not known, frequency response tests are conducted. From the characteristics of the frequency response, the maximum gain for loop stability can be calculated using a bode plot.

In the bode plot, the gain and phase of the control component are plotted as a function of the log frequency as shown:

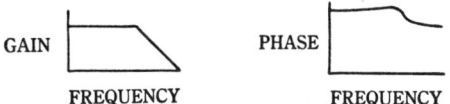

The frequency at which the phase is −180 degrees is called the critical frequency; the gain at this frequency must be less than one for loop stability.

Bode plots have the following advantages for control system analysis:

(1) Since logarithms are used, the expressions for gain are additive.
(2) For many electronic elements, the shape allows representation of the exact plot by straight line asymptotes.
(3) Since the bode plot is easy to construct, it provides a convenient starting point for more complex methods of control analysis.

**BOI** Abbreviation for *branch output interrupt.*

**bookkeeping** Maintenance of accounting ledgers, either manually or by machine. Bookkeeping represents an application area for microcomputers that involves variations of inventory control and general accounting. Generally the first stage in inventory control requires information collection, which is the recording in symbolic form of the level of inventory presently available, as indicated in various source documents. Following the collection stage, the information from the source documents is combined with information regarding the available balances of stock left in the processing stage. Next comes a comparison of the available balances with either of the reorder point figures or the maximum allowable stock amounts. The final stage involves some form of output such as a listing of the stock numbers and quantities on purchase order forms for the purchasing department.

For a general accounting operation, the typical primary end products are income statements and balance sheets with supporting documents.

**Boolean algebra** A deductive system or process of reasoning named after George Boole, an English mathematician who lived from 1815 to 1864. A system of theorems uses symbolic logic to denote classes of elements, true or false propositions, and on-off logic circuit elements. Symbols are used to represent operators such as AND, OR, NOT, EXCEPT, IF . . . THEN, etc. When Boole introduced his system in 1847, one purpose was to provide a shorthand notation for the system of logic originally set up by Aristotle. Aristotle's theorems dealt with statements that were either true or false, never partially true or partially false. Boolean algebra likewise consists of single-valued functions with only two possible output states.

For a long time Boole's system lay dormant, almost forgotten; however, it is now recognized as an effective method of handling single-valued functions with two possible output states. When Boolean algebra is applied to binary arithmetic, the two states become 0 and 1; when applied to switching theory, the two states become open and closed, as shown in the following analogy:

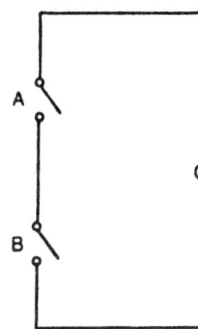

The convention normally used is 0 for an open or low state, and 1 for a closed or high state.

The AND function occurs if two or more gates are placed in series, and the resulting configuration is called an AND gate. This arrangement will transmit information if and only if all series gates are closed.

The equivalent equation in Boolean algebra is:

AB = C (A and B equals C)

Also, the following truth table can be written:

| A | B | C |
|---|---|---|
| 0 | 0 | 0 |
| 0 | 1 | 0 |
| 1 | 0 | 0 |
| 1 | 1 | 1 |

The OR function occurs if two or more gates are placed in parallel.

The result is called an OR gate, and transmission occurs when one or more gates are closed. This is shown in the following circuit:

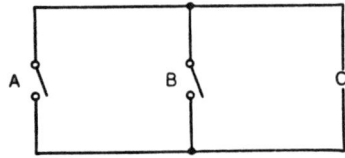

The equivalent equation in Boolean form is:

$$A + B = C \text{ (A or B equals C)}$$

and the truth table is:

| A | B | C |
|---|---|---|
| 0 | 0 | 0 |
| 0 | 1 | 1 |
| 1 | 0 | 1 |
| 1 | 1 | 1 |

The NOT gate occurs when two gates are connected such that a single signal will close one gate while opening the other. The NOT gate forms the complement of its input, thus a 1 on the input to the gate results in a 0 on the output, and a 0 on the input results in a 1 on the output. If the input is labeled A, the output is labeled $\bar{A}$ (A not, or not A). An entire function can be complemented. For example, if:

$$A = B(C + D)$$

Then:

$$\bar{A} = \overline{B(C + D)}$$

The commutative and associative laws apply in Boolean algebra:

$$AB = BA$$
$$A(BC) = (AB)C = ABC$$

Some other identities are:

$$1 + A = 1 \quad 0 + A = A$$
$$1A = A \quad 0A = 0$$
$$A(B + C) = AB + AC$$
$$A + A = A \quad A + \bar{A} = 1 \quad \bar{\bar{A}} = A$$
$$AA = A \quad A\bar{A} = 0$$

Also, De Morgan's laws, which only apply to Boolean algebra, can be verified as:

$$\overline{A + B + C + \ldots N} = \overline{ABC \ldots N}$$
$$\overline{ABC \ldots} = \bar{A} + \bar{B} + \bar{C} \ldots \bar{N}$$

**Boolean calculus** Boolean algebra modified to include the element of time.

**Boolean operator** An operator (gate) used in Boolean algebra as applied to logic units of computer architecture; the result of any operation is restricted to one of two values, generally represented as 1 or 0.

**Boolean variable** The use of two-valued Boolean algebra to assume either one of the only two values possible. Examples: true or false; on or off; open or closed. All digital computers use the two-state or two variable Boolean algebra in construction and operation.

**booster response** An automatic controller technique in which there exists a continuous linear response between rate of change of the controlled variable and the position of the final control element. Also called *rate action.*.

**bootstrap** A technique designed to cause a circuit, stage, or operation to bring itself into a desired state by means of its own action. The name is taken from the impossible situation of a person lifting himself off the ground by pulling on his bootstraps. Used as a machine routine, the bootstrap technique involves loading the first few instructions into storage; these instructions are then used to bring in the rest of the routine-usually by the entering of a few manual instructions or the use of a special key function.

A bootstrap is also that part of a program that is used to establish another version of the program. A bootstrap loader is used when there is no loader available in the main memory. The bootstrap is used to read into memory any series of bytes (usually without error checks) and is keyed into the console or implemented in ROM, where it is permanent. The bootstrap loader should contain as few instructions as possible in case it has to be keyed in via the console. The bootstrap is also sometimes used to load an absolute loader into the main memory.

In microprocessor systems, a bootstrap loader can allow the user to enter data and program into RAMs from a teletypewriter, keyboard, or paper tape and execute the program from the RAMs. The loader usually is a PROM that plugs into the prototype board.

In tape operations, a bootstrap is used as a subroutine that loads a binary loader when other loaders are not available (as in systems having no automatic loader). Bootstrap loaders are available for most input devices, and for paper tape systems they require only about eight words for manual keying.

**bootstrap loader (microcomputer)** A program that enables users to enter data or a program into RAM and execute the program. It may consist of a PROM that plugs into the system board.

**borrow** The negative carry that occurs in direct subtraction. In the direct subtraction of

$$\begin{array}{r} 10110 \\ -\phantom{00}101 \\ \hline 10001 \end{array}$$

the subtraction operation begins in the rightmost column, where a 1 is borrowed from the next-left column to convert the rightmost 0 to a 10. The process is repeated as the operations move leftward column by column.

**BOS** Abbreviation for *basic operating system.*

**BOT** Abbreviation for *beginning of tape.*

**boundary** A special register which selects the upper and lower addresses for each user's memory block in a multiprogrammed system.

**boundary register** In a multiprogrammed system, a special register used to designate the upper and lower addresses of each user's memory block.

**box** 1. Any block or enclosed area that is used to represent a function, circuit, stage, or element graphically. 2. The symbol used in flow charting to indicate a choice or branch in the path of the flow.

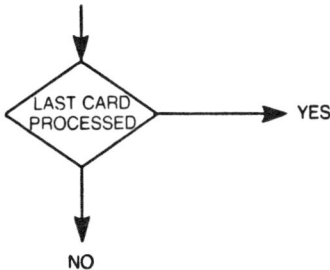

The diamond-shaped decision box always has one entrance line and two exit lines, or branches. The exit paths are determined by a yes or no, or other comparison test. In the example given, the condition to be determined is if the last card of a stack or deck has been processed. If the answer is yes, the program is allowed to branch away from the loop that it has been following. If the answer is no, then the processing of the cards continues until completion.

**bps** Abbreviation for *bits per second*. For serial transmission, bps is equal to the speed at which a device or channel transmits characters. See also *baud*.

**BR** Abbreviation for *break request*.

**branch** The selection of one or more paths in the flow of data or signals through a system or stage. Selection of a path is based upon some criterion that allow a decision to be reached. The instructions used to mechanize the selection are sometimes called *branch instructions*. Transfer of control and jump operations are also used in this context. In a microprocessor program, branching is done on the basis of computed results causing modification of the function or program sequence. The usual modification can be classed as (1) a change of the program direction, or (2) a departure from the normal sequence.

Very few programs do not take advantage of the microcomputer's ability to determine the direction that a program should take based upon intermediate results. For testing a condition and providing alternative paths for the program, microinstructions, which are sometimes called *conditional skip instructions*, are used.

A transfer of control can be handled in the 8080 as follows:

```
AAA:           ; (stack address)
    .JMP BBB ; (go to BBB,
               then return)
```

Control is transferred in this sequence to BBB, when that routine is completed, control goes back to AAA, the address at the top of the stack.

**branch circuit** In a wiring system the branch circuit is the portion that extends beyond the final overcurrent device that protects the circuit.

**branch impedance** In a passive branch, the impedance obtained by assuming a driving force across and a corresponding response in the branch, assuming that no other branch is electrically connected to the one under consideration.

**branch instructions** An instruction that when executed causes the arithmetic logic unit (ALU) to obtain the next instruction from some location other than the next sequential location. A branch may be one of two types: conditional or unconditional.

**branch-on** A term used to mark indicators or switches on a control console to indicate when branching is taking place. A branch-on indicator is used to show that conditions for a particular group of registers are such that branching will occur for the next block of data. Branch-on switches are used to control the use of certain memory locations or index registers. The setting of the switch determines if the program is to branch at that location.

**branch on indicator** Branching takes place when appropriate indicators (switches, keys, buttons) or conditions have been set. Thus, a branch may occur dependent upon whether the magnetic-tape unit is ready to receive a new block of data.

**branchpoint** The location in the program where one or more choices is selected, depending upon the character of the most recent data processed.

**breadboard** An initial or experimental model of a process, program, or device. Temporary arrangements of early electronic circuits used modifications of kitchen breadboards. These evolved to the many types of boards available for prototype work today, but the name held up and is still used today. Specialized breadboards are available for designing custom microcomputer interfaces. A typical board allows for data transfer over the data line using program control with or without interrupts. Board area is allowed for 14-, 16-, 24- 36-, and 40-pin integrated circuits along with discrete components. Power and ground buses are provided as well as edge connectors for input/output cables or card interconnections.

**breadboard construction** A temporary arrangement of electronic components fastened to a board for experimental work.

**break** 1. An open circuit. 2. An interruption that usually allows transmission from the user at the other end of the transmission system.

**breakdown impedance** Small signal impedance at a specified direct current in the breakdown region of a semiconductor diode. Often used interchangeably with the term *avalanche impedance*.

**breakdown voltage** The voltage at which a marked increase in the current through an insulator or semiconductor occurs.

**breakpoint** A point in a program that allows a conditional interruption to permit visual checking, printouts, or other analysis. Breakpoints permit debugging and are usually indicated by a breakpoint flag or controlled by a breakpoint switch on the console. With a breakpoint in the program, the user has an opportunity to check, correct, and modify the program before continuing its execution.

**breakpoint instruction** An instruction that causes the machine to either transfer control or stop and take some special action. The breakpoint instruction is usually triggered by some specific conditions placed into the program.

**breakpoint switch** A manually operated switch that controls conditional operation at breakpoints, used primarily in debugging.

**b-register** A register that can store words used to change an instruction before it is executed by the program. The b-register (also called index register or b-box) is sometimes used to extend the operation of the accumulator during multiply and divide operations.

Some machines use many index registers, their basic function being to add a number to part of an instruction after the instruction leaves storage on its way to the control unit and before it goes into the instruction register. The instruction entering the instruction register does not have to be identical with the one read from storage, since the contents of the index register may be added to it before it reaches the instruction register. B-registers allow changes to be made in the program just before program execution.

**bridge** 1. An inadvertent solder connection on a circuit board between two conductive paths. 2. A full-wave rectifier composed of four diode legs. 3. A circuit used in some data acquisition transducers to compensate for extreme temperatures and other error-inducing conditions. The system is derived from the Wheatstone bridge, a widely used method for the precision measurement of resistance. In strain gauge transducers used for pressure or stress measurement, a bridge circuit is required to display the small resistance change that occurs. The strain gauge is placed in one or more arms of the bridge as shown below:

**bridge circuit** A circuit of elements arranged so that, when an electromotive force is present in one branch, the response of a detecting device in another branch can be zeroed by adjustment of the electrical constants of other branches.

**bridge limiter** A unit intended to prevent a variable from exceeding specified limits. A diode bridge that is used as a limiter is called a *bridge limiter*.

**bridging connection** A parallel connection in which some of the signal energy in a circuit may be withdrawn with little effect on the normal operation of the circuit.

**bridging contacts** A set of electrical contacts in which the moving contact touches two or more stationary contacts simultaneously during operation.

**BRL** Abbreviation for *ballistic research laboratory*.

**broadband** In data communications, any bandwidth greater than the 4 kHz of voicegrade channels. Loosely, any relatively wide frequency bandwidth.

**broadband noise** A noise distribution that is relatively uniform over a wide spectrum of frequencies.

**BRS** Abbreviation for *break request signal*.

**brush** An electrical conductor for reading data from a punched card. The operation of punched-card readers depends upon the movement of the card past a sensing mechanism that has electrical contacts (brushes or photoelectric sensors). The cards are placed in the feed hopper of the reader in the order that they are to be read. They are taken one at a time from the bottom of the stack by the reader and passed to the reading station. The reading devices may be thin flexible springs or brushes that pass through the holes to be read; or light can be directed through any holes for sensing by rows of photoelectric cells. Sometimes the cards are passed through a second reader that is used as a check of the first reader.

**BS** Abbreviation for *binary subtract*.

**BSAM** Abbreviation for *basic sesquential access method*.

**BTAM** Abbreviation for *basic telecommunications access method*, a technique used in IBM equipment that utilizes macroinstructions for data communications between terminals.

**BTR** Abbreviation for *behind the tape reader* or *bypass tape reader*. A means of inputting data directly into a machine control unit from an external source other than a tape reader.

**bubble memory** A memory technology that makes use of magnetic bubbles generated from a single-crystal sheet. The bubbles are generated when two magnetic fields are applied perpendicular to the single-crystal sheet. A constant field is used to strengthen the field region, and a pulsed field is used to break up the field regions into small bubbles. The bubbles are free to move within the plane of the sheet. The presence and absence of bubbles can be used to represent digital information, and the bubbles can be manipulated by the external fields. Researchers have been somewhat successful with a single-mask technology that gives a simpler structure, but at the cost of higher access times and smaller bit densities than bubble units produced using other technologies. A typical device uses temporary changes in drive field rotation to read, write, and erase data.

A bubble generator is used to pass data through a generator lock to a major loop. Bubbles are also stored in minor loops using input switches. They are transferred back to the major loop with output switches. The unit can also selectively erase information in the data stream using an annihilator loop. The presence of a bubble is read as a one and the absence of a bubble is read as a zero. The bubbles are moved using a magnetic overlay system which forms a closed loop.

A bucket-brigade shift register, which is similar to that used by charge-coupled devices (CCDs); can be formed, the bubble devices have the advantage of being nonvolatile (retaining memory when power is interrupted). Besides shift registers, bubble technology may be used in the future for switching and logic functions.

In addition to nonvolatility, bubble memories require very small amounts of power; a 10 megabit unit uses about 10W and fits into a space of four square inches. Applications for bubble memories include an endless-loop recorder that would replace cassettes and floppy disks in data loggers, text editors, point-of-sale terminals, and other applications needing about one megabit of capacity. They will also find use in auxiliary memories that would fill the gap between 1 ns core types and 8 ns disks.

**bubble memory operation** Since the presence of a bubble is read as a one and its absence as a zero, data can be written by the selective formation of bubbles. This is accomplished by applying a weak external magnetic bias to the film, which in its normal state contains an equal mix of oppositely polarized magnetic regions. The external bias field groups regions of opposite polarity to the field into bubbles. By lining up and moving the bubbles via a magnetic overlay around a closed loop, a type of shift register is formed in a manner like that employed by charge coupled devices (CCDs). An essential difference between bubbles and CCDs is that bubbles, being magnetic rather than electronic, are nonvolatile, thus their bit pattern is retained if power fails.

**bubble shift registers** A shift register is the simplest bubble memory application, but it is not the only type of memory that can be made using bubbles, nor is bubble technology limited to memory applications. The properties of magnetic bubbles, related to their deformation or annihilation as a function of the bias field strength, allow switching and logic applications.

**bucket** An expression used to indicate a portion of storage reserved for accumulating data or totals of information. Buckets are labeled 1, 2, 3, etc., and are commonly used during initial system planning.

**bucket brigade** A continued shifting of data bits in a given direction.

**buffer** A device or unit that serves as an isolator or interface between two dissimilar elements. It is used to match impedances, speeds, or other characteristics while maintaining isolation between matched elements. As a register, a storage buffer would serve as an intermediary storage point between two registers or data handling systems with different access times or data formats.

In a typical communications interface, buffering provides asynchronous communications between Bell 103 or 202 data sets at speeds up to 9600 baud.

**buffer capacitor** A type of capacitor connected across the secondary of a transformer to suppress surging voltages that could cause damage to other circuit parts.

**buffer circuit** In a keyboard system, an electronic circuit that allows an operator to type ahead of the data output.

**buffered computer** A computer system that allows input and output data to be stored temporarily to match transfer speeds of the input and output devices with the speed of the computer. To accommodate a difference in speed changes, a buffer is used to accept the data at one speed, hold the data, and then release it at the required rate.

A card reader might be reading data from cards at about 1000 characters per second, and yet this data may be put into storage at a rate of about 50,000 characters per second. Part of the buffer operates at the lower speed and temporarily stores the data until it has enough data to transmit in a group at the higher speed. In the case of an output buffer, data is transmitted at the slower speed until a new group of input data can be accepted.

Some amount of buffering is required for all input and output equipment because of the translation needed in going from one language to another. Buffers are found in a variety of equipment functions, including controllers, synchronizers, electronic amplifiers, transmitters, selectors, adapters, and communicators. They may perform code changes, speed changes, mode changes, format changes, checking and time-sharing.

Format changing might include:

1. Rearranging data
2. Duplication of data
3. Code generation
4. Insertion and deletion of data

**buffering, simple** A technique for allowing simultaneous input/output operations and computation. This method involves associating a buffer with only one input or output file or data set for the entire duration of the activity on that file or data set.

**buffer storage** Buffer storage indicates:

1. A synchronizing element between different forms of storage, usually internal and external.
2. An input device for assembly of information from external or secondary storage for transfer to internal storage.
3. An output device that copies information from internal storage for entry to external storage.
4. Any device for temporary storage during data transfer.

**bug** 1. A usually elusive error in a program, circuit, or machine. 2. A dual-inline-package integrated circuit, so named because of the insect-like appearance of the device.

**bug patch** A temporary circumvention of a program element or automatic routine through manual control. The patches are worked out and inserted to fix the errors. After a number of patches are made, they are incorporated into the source program, which is reassembled to complete the documentation of the changes.

**building block** A self-contained element that can serve as a stage or subsystem by interconnection with other such elements. This concept of construction provides an approach to system and hardware design that allows expansion of a system using a modular technique.

**build-virtual-machine** A modeling process whereby a machine program duplicates an actual defined system configuration. A build-virtual-machine program allows the user to structure programs that will fit the limits of the memory of the actual system.

**built-in check** A system, usually implemented in hardware, for verifying the accuracy of information transmitted, manipulated, or stored in any part of the computer system. Also called an *automatic check*, *built-in automatic check*, or *hardware check*.

**bulk memory** A memory device for storing large amounts of data, such as a hard disk or magnetic tape unit.

**bulletin board** Refers to an electronic service that subscribers use, as they would use a traditional bulletin board, to post and circulate messages. These services operate through modems, which connect the subscriber's microcomputers to the information network.

**bundling** The lump sum pricing of computer equipment along with associated systems analysis and support services, in contrast to an "unbundled" arrangement in which each of these products or services is priced separately.

**buried layer** A heavily doped (N +) region directly under the N doped epitaxial collector region of transistors in a monolithic integrated circuit used to lower the series collector resistance.

**burn in** The operation of an item to stabilize its failure rate.

**burst** 1. A sequence of signals counted as one unit using a specified criterion. In burst transmission, messages are stored for a time period, then released at a much faster speed for transmission. The received signals are recorded and then slowed down for the user. 2. In color TV reception, the signal that serves as the reference for the 4.58 MHz oscillator; it occurs during video blanking.

**bus** A circuit used as a high-traffic path for data or power transmission. A bus often is used as a common connection between a number of locations or switching points and is sometimes called a *trunk* or *trunk line*. Buses are used in microprocessors to speed the data flow and transfer data, and for addressing and control. A single bus can be used in alternate time periods for data, addresses, and control signals. Multibus systems use a dedicated bus for data and another for addressing. Control may or may not be on a dedicated bus. The multibus system allows data and addresses on the same cycle without the serial delays found in a common-bus system.

Some of the features found in data and address buses used to minimize package count and improve performance are:

1. Multibus systems to eliminate multiplexing and latching.
2. Three-state output buffers to minimize the use of bus drivers.
3. Separate output-enable logic to allow bidirectional signal flow.

Most microprocessors are designed for 8-bit bus operation, and programs are more efficient if they use 8 bits or less per message to eliminate the need for multiple-word control.

Typical bus cycles found in microprocessors are:

1. Data word transfer in, followed by word transfer out.

2. Data word transfer in, followed by byte transfer out. Data transfer on the bus is sometimes interlocked so that communications can be independent of the length of the bus and response times. Asynchronous operation allows each device to run at maximum speed without the need for clock pulses.

Bus organization is an important part of a system's architecture. Many microcomputers use a single bus for address, data, and control information; others use a memory bus for data transfer between CPU and memory, and another bus for data transfer between the CPU and peripheral devices. A typical data bus may have 60 or more signal lines transmitting information.

The single-bus system acts as a universal interface connecting all parts of the system, while the dual bus treats the CPU as a focal point with separate interfaces to memory and peripheral units.

Buses are usually designed on some form of backplane with a bus motherboard to handle words up to 16 bits long. Bus construction requires control and power lines, variable- and fixed-frequency clocks, and connectors to peripheral devices.

Bus program counters are incorporated as counting registers on chips; one can be used for program location and another for stack counting. The counter contents are sent out on the address bus to allow the memory to fetch the correct instructions; the processor then increments the program counter after each use of the instructions.

Voltage levels and impedances at the bus interface allow rapid transmission and minimize effects due to noise. A number of units can share the bus without excessive loading. In some systems, a bus protocol allows a vectored interrupt. Device polling is not required for interrupts, which reduces processing time in cases where many devices are connected to a common bus. Usually, an interrupt vector is passed to the processor; the vector points to addresses for a new status word and the start of the interrupt service routine.

A priority structure is used to determine which device has control of the bus. Each device on the bus is assigned a priority number so that when two or more devices request use of the bus, the device with the higher priority receives control first.

**bus driver**  A power device designed to supply signals to all devices on a bus without signal degradation.

**bus extender module**  This module provides the capability to extend the bus for the purpose of signal tracing.

**bus interface**  A circuit or device designed to match a peripheral with a bus.

**bus interlocked communication**  Data transfer on the bus can be interlocked so that communication is independent of the physical bus length and the response time of the slave device. An asynchronous operation precludes the need for synchronizing with, and waiting for, clock impulses. Thus, each device is allowed to operate at the maximum possible speed. Full 16 bit words or 8 bit bytes of information can be transferred on many busses between a master and a slave. The information can be instructions, addresses, or data. This type of information transfer occurs when the processor, as master, is fetching instructions, operands, and data from memory, and storing the results into memory after execution of the instruction.

**bus master**  The device controlling the current bus transaction in a bus structure in which control of data transfers on the bus is shared between the central processor and associated peripheral devices.

**bus mother board**  A connecting board that handles bus resources such as control and power supply lines, frequency clocks, and plug-in connectors with provisions for auxiliary devices.

**bus organized structure**  A structure for the input/output of data and control information. Often in these bus systems, information can flow in both directions, and generally more than one talker and listener share a single interconnecting wire. The voltage levels and impedances at the bus interface are set to allow the transmission of information with minimum errors due to noise and to allow a number of units to share the line without excessively loading the bus line.

**bus priority structure**  Since many busses may be used by processors and I/O devices, there must be a priority structure to determine which device gets control of the bus. Every device on the bus that is capable of becoming the bus master is assigned a priority. When two such devices request use of the bus simultaneously, the device with the higher priority position will receive control.

**bus program counter**  Usually a sixteen bit counting register used for program location counting. The program counter contents are sent out on the address bus for use by memory modules in fetching the appropriate instructions; the processor increments the program counter by one after each use.

**bus slave**  The device currently receiving or transmitting data from or to the bus master in a bus structure in which control of data transfers on the bus is shared between the processor and peripheral devices.

**bus system**  The signals that are grouped together for various functions. A typical microprocessor bus system is shown below.

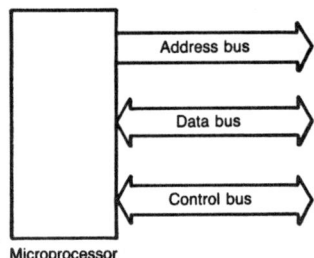

**Microprocessor bus system**

**Bust**  The bad performance of a programmer or machine operator.

**bus to peripheral interface**  Refers to the interface in some systems in which the interrupt control logic has separate interrupt sections. These provide interrupt requests to the CPU through unique vector addresses. Any specific vector addresses and bus request levels can be selected using wire wrap jumpers on the interface. An interrupt request can initiate a bus request sequence on a selected bus request line. A resulting bus grant signal then causes logic to issue a command to indicate that the interrupt sequence has begun and the interrupt request may be removed. Interrupt control logic executes the rest of the sequence, issuing control signals and causing the related vector select signal to gate the jumper selected address into specific data lines.

**bus transceiver**  Refers to a type of bidirectional buffer that is intended for bipolar or metal oxide semiconductor microprocessor applications. Such a device may consist of D type edge-triggered flip-flops with a built in two input multiplexer on each. The flip-flop outputs are connected to four open collector bus drivers. Each bus driver is internally connected to one input of a differential amplifier in the receiver. The four receiver differential amplifier outputs drive four D type latches that feature three state outputs.

**bypass**  A shunt or parallel path around a circuit, device, or unit. A bypass filter, for example, provides a low-attenuation path around the unit to be bypassed, as in the case of a carrier-frequency filter used to bypass a telephone repeater station.

**bypass capacitor** A type of capacitor used for providing a low impedance AC path around some other circuit, equipment, or device.

**bypass filter** A type of filter that provides a low attenuation path around some other circuit, equipment, or device.

**byte** A term developed to indicate a measurable number of consecutive binary digits that are usually operated upon as a unit. Bytes of eight bits representing either one character or two numerals are most often encountered. Words in some systems are divided into high and low bytes, and the byte addresses are either odd or even numbers. The high bytes are stored at the odd-numbered locations and the low bytes at the even-numbered ones.

**byte addresses** Some computer words are divided into a high byte and a low byte. In most systems the word addresses are even numbered. The byte addresses can be either even or odd numbered. Low bytes are stored at even numbered memory locations and high bytes are at odd numbered memory locations.

**byte manipulation** Refers to an ability to manipulate, as individual instructions, groups of bits such as characters. A byte is usually considered to be eight bits and forms either one character or two numerals.

**byte multiplexing** The processing of data in sequential chunks, by the assignment of time slots to individual input/output devices. Bytes, one after another, are then interlaced on the channel going to or from the main memory.

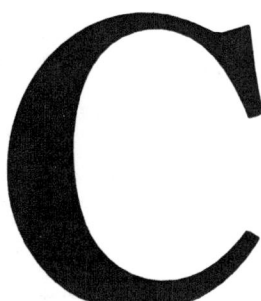

**C** A high level language developed in the early 1970s. It is a general purpose language that allows the programmer to create additional commands called functions.

**cable rack** Refers to the many types of racks designed for holding conductors with or without connectors or terminal strips. The cable rack is particularly useful in applications where the number of input and output lines is large.

**cable, twisted pair** A cable formed by twisting together two thin conductors which are each separately insulated. This arrangement reduces their intercapacitance.

**CAD** Acronym for *computer-aided design*. CAD techniques are used whenever conventional design methods prove excessively time-consuming. Considerable development has gone into computer methods and programs to solve complex network problems. Programs are also available for the design of integrated circuits. Some of these programs are ECAP, NET-1, CIRCUS, PREDICT, NASAP, and SCEPTRE, all of which handle lumped-parameter elements. Depending on the external construction of the device, sometimes frequency-response characteristics can be used to describe a device accurately. The response characteristics are obtained experimentally without regard to the internal structure of the device. This is known as the black-box method, and it offers the following advantages for integrated circuit design:

1. The model is able to accept experimental or analytical data.
2. The complete circuit is enclosed in a black box for repetitive analysis of a complete system.
3. Model parameters can be lumped or distributed.
4. Solution can be done in sections using small computers.

Some CAD programs are geared towards time-sharing using a larger machine. Here the computer serves many users at the same time at the output and input facilities, while the CPU actually services each user in sequence. The user dials the computer and operates the teletypewriter as if the machine were his alone, while other people are also being similarly served at many distant locations. The circuit designer is in contact with the machine and is able to make changes to save computing time and effort that are not possible with batch processing.

Time-sharing allows a turn-around time of a few minutes and provides the circuit designer with almost instant answers to calculations. This allows rapid interaction with the machine compared to batch processing.

**CADPO** Abbreviation for *communications and data processing operation*.

**cages, card frame** A unit that recesses the circuit card frame. It may be equipped with wings for 19-inch rack mounting. The system cage may also include a hinged front door panel for mounting controls and indicators. Some card cages are designed with extended depth to accommodata a middle component chassis allowing special components to be mounted within the standard chassis.

**CAI** Abbreviation for *computer aided instruction*.

**CAL** Abbreviation for *Cornell Aeronautical Laboratory*.

**calculator** 1. A data processor especially suitable for performing arithmetical operations that requires frequent intervention by a human operator. 2. A device for carrying out logic and arithmetic digital operations of any kind. Data and instructions are usually, but not always, inserted manually. A calculator can be used with a microcomputer and it can be a microcomputer that is used as a calculator. Early digital machines were used primarily for calculations and were assigned as special-purpose calculators.

Present-day calculators are small, highly specialized computers with a memory structure composed of a fixed and variable section.

35

The fixed section is in the form of a ROM and provides the control for changing instructions in a limited fashion.

The simple four-function calculator can be used to do advanced operations such as square roots, squaring, summing of products and quotients, trigonometric calculations and exponents. This is done by altering the order of computations and adding a few extra steps.

The scientific programmable calculator is typically used for complex scientific and engineering problems. These units can be used as portable scratch pads for problem solving and typically have a 10-digit display which operates in scientific notation. Results are computed in degrees or radians and some have 15 or more scientific functions, including trigonometric, inverse trigonometric, hyperbolic, exponential, and logrithmic. Units offer 64 or more steps or programming using eight or more registers. Decimal points systems include floating point and exponential with scientific notation to $10^{99}$.

Calculator systems that are operated as batch terminals typically use the following equipment:

1. A calculator with up to 4000 words of memory
2. A ROM for stringing variables
3. A thermal or matrix printer
4. A data communications interface and modem

Optional equipment for batch terminal use includes:

1. Tape cassette
2. Calculator card reader
3. Tape reader
4. Line printer or plotter
5. Memory subsystem

A typical display calculator organization uses:

1. 700 words of microprogramming
2. 75 words for storage in registers
3. 12 inputs and 12 outputs for external connections

The organization allows the user to emulate a ROM program before committing the microprogram to a custom ROM. Signal levels within the system are MOS compatible and all external lines are TTL compatible. The microprogram is written so that the keyboard is scanned in a desired sequence. The position of the keyboard switches provides the signals for the processor to carry out some operation or subroutine as a function of the microprogram stored in ROM.

Calculators are also used as editing systems in some batch terminals. Both cassettes and mass memory systems are used to add, delete, and insert card data into storage. Many of these systems are used to eliminate the bulkier punched cards or paper tapes as storage media.

Calculators typically operate in a sequential mode with one program step at a time. Following power-on initialization, the input data is strobed through a multiplexer as fast as the system clock will allow. Numbers representing one of the four functions are entered in a similar manner; then at the conclusion of the equation, a number representing the equals operation is entered. The output is then provided either to a display or as latched outputs to external equipment.

**calculator batch terminal** Refers to the operation of a calculator as a batch terminal. Such operation typically requires a calculator with up to 4K words of memory, string variables ROM, a thermal printer or equivalent, a data communications interface, binary synchronous ROM, and modem. Optional additions to the batch terminal environment may include one or more of the following groups of equipment: mass memory subsystem, external cassette, calculator card reader with extended I/O ROM, tape reader with extended I/O ROM, and line printer subsystem. A large calculator memory and a wide variety of other peripherals can also be included in a batch terminal environment.

**calculator chip** Refers to an integrated circuit dedicated to calculator use. A typical calculator chip might have the following characteristics:

1. Five functions (+, −, ×, ÷, %,) eight digit display.
2. Percent discount and percent add on.
3. Memory with automatic accumulation.
4. Algebraic keyboard with full chaining.
5. Automatic constant factor on five functions.
6. Floating decimal mode with decimal wraparound on overflow.
7. Automatic power on clear with leading zero suppression.
8. Square root, entry, percentage mark up, and percentage difference.
9. Register exchange, change sign, fixed decimal point with 5/4 rounding.
10. Conversion of liters/gallons, kilograms/pounds, and centimeters/inches.

**calculator circuit test unit** A unit designed to test calculator chips. It will reject devices on the basis of failures in substrate continuity, logic functions, input or output tests, power drain, and bounce delay. Data for test voltages, limits categorization, input stimuli, and output results are stored in a random-access memory. To minimize setup time, plug-in units containing the device adapter, pin assignment, level shifting, and special circuitry required for a particular device can be used. Test programs are generated and edited by means of a separate keyboard unit.

**calculator editing system** An editing system included with some calculator batch terminal programs. These systems allows users to add, delete, and insert data into an existing data base. This provides a fast, convenient medium for data storage before the information is transmitted over the data communications link.

**calculator I/O** Refers to a specific I/O circuit used in calculators that provides a general purpose time/impedance buffer between the metal-oxide semiconductor instruction/data bus and TTL logic signals.

**calculator, remote** Refers to the use of a desk calculator that can access on-line computing services. In a time sharing system, the terminal can be a remote calculator that provides direct, remote access to the computer. Remote connections can be made via standard telephone channels, through the common user dial networks. Answers are shown on the remote calculator display panel.

**calculator structure** A calculator can be defined as a small, highly specialized computer. The memory structure consists of both a fixed and a variable memory. The fixed portion, a read-only memory (ROM), provides a system control program called the firmware, with changeable instructions. This contrasts with general purpose computers programmed by software and random logic systems that use hard-wired circuitry.

**calculator terminal** A desktop calculator with microcomputer compatible inputs and outputs, and designed for interactive computations. Terminals designed around desktop calculators can handle such applications as inventory control, processing orders, payroll, and account maintenance with the help of the BASIC language. These applications also use alphanumeric stringing and matrix manipulation and require larger storage capacity than tape cassettes provide. Disk drive units are available for some desktop calculators; these will store up to 2 million 8-bit words at fast access speeds.

Other desktop calculators allow time-sharing for many users from their home or office. Remote connections are made through standard telephone channels, and the remote keyboard has all the functions and remote display, and many features of powerful minicomputers are symbols required for the application. Answers are flashed back to the available as options. Calculators are also used to communicate calculated data directly to large batch computers for additional processing and storage. The batch computer can then send a final message based on the data for display at the calculator. The batch terminals are usually used in an organization where centralized processing stations are required and large amounts of data are transferred between two or more points. Typical applications for batch terminals include:

1. Inventory Control
2. Payroll
3. Remote job entry
4. Numerical control tape preparation
5. Structural design engineering

Use of the calculator terminal brings all of these applications to the remote location. A typical calculator terminal may have the following characteristics:

1. 2000 bps transmission speed, with ranges from 1200 to 9600 available
2. Half-duplex mode with full duplex available
3. 80-column or 32-column output page width for display

**calendar age** Age measured in terms of time since the object was manufactured.

**calendar life** That period of time, expressed in days, months, or years, during which an item can remain installed in an operation environment and be expected to perform satisfactorily and reliably. The item should be removed at the expiration of the designated time and returned for repair, overhaul, or other maintenance action.

**calendar of conversion** A schedule prepared for the implementation of a new or different system.

**calibration accuracy** The limit of error in the finite degree to which a device can be calibrated. It is influenced by sensitivity, resolution, and repeatability of the device itself and of the calibrating equipment. Usually it is expressed in percent of full scale.

**calling sequence** The basic set of instructions used to begin, initialize, or transfer control to and return from a subroutine.

**CAM** Acronym for *content-addressable memory*. CAMs are special RAMs in which the addresses of data can be retrieved on command. Programming is usually done by writing into the unit using a separate addressing and control line. CAMs also allow a normal read/write across rows, which makes them useful for applications requiring quick data searches, correlation checking, and sorting. Fast CAMs find application in large virtual-memory systems or in applications like airline reservation systems, where searching for items like flight numbers, destinations, and departure times makes up a large part of the processing task.

The higher cost and low bit densities of CAMs have limited applications. Costs are higher compared to conventional RAMs because of the additional space needed for the equal-access system and the additional pins required for the dual control system.

**CAM** Abbreviation for *computer aided manufacturing*.

**CAMAL** Abbreviation for *continuous airborne missile launched and low level system*.

**CAN** The cancel character instruction, which is used to indicate data that is in error and should not be accepted.

**cancel** To stop or abort a process or selection in progress.

**CANCL** A status word used to indicate that the remote system has deleted information previously transmitted.

**CANEL** Abbreviation for *Connecticut Advanced Nuclear Engineering Laboratory*.

**canned cycle** A preset sequence of events (hardware or software) initiated by a single command.

**cannibalization** A maintenance modification or repair method in which the required parts are removed from a similar system or assembly for installation on another.

**capacitance** The property that permits the storage of electrically separated charges when potential differences exist between the conductors. The capacitance of a capacitor is the ratio between the electric charge that has been transferred from one electrode to the other and the resultant difference in potential between the electrodes. The value of this ratio is dependent on the magnitude of the charge.

$$C \text{ (farad)} = \frac{Q \text{ (coulomb)}}{V \text{ (volt)}}$$

**capacitive pressure transducers** A type of device that converts one quantity into another quantity, specifically when one of the quantities is electrical. A capacitive pressure transducer employs a metal diaphragm. A metal plate is positioned on one side of the diaphragm. Deflection of the diaphragm changes the capacitance between it and the fixed plate. An AC signal across the plates is used to sense the change in capacitance, or the capacitance change is used to alter the frequency of an oscillator circuit. The advantages of capacitive transducers are small size, high frequency response, and high temperature operation. It has the ability to measure both static and dynamic quantities. Shortcomings are a sensitivity to temperature variations, high impedance output, and complexity of associated circuitry. Capacitance transducers must be reactively as well as resistively matched. Long lead lengths and loose leads can cause a variation in capacitance. It is usually necessary to locate a preamplifier very close to the transducer.

**capacitor** 1. An electronic component consisting of two metal plates separated by a nonconductor that is also referred to as a condenser, but capacitor is the preferred term. A capacitor consists of two conductors, A and B, each having an extended surface exposed to that of the other, but separated by a layer of insulating material called the *dielectric*. The dielectric is designed so the electric charge on conductor A is equal in value but opposite in polarity to the charge on B. The two conductors are usually called the electrodes or plates.

**capacitor storage** A device that uses the electric field in an insulator held between conductive plates to store digital or analog data.

**CAPRI** Abbreviation for *coded address private radio intercom*.

**caps lock key** Refers to the key on a keyboard that locks all letters in uppercase.

**CAR** Abbreviation for *civil air regulations*.

**carbon set** A multi-ply form manufactured with carbon paper interleaved between the original and tissue copies.

**card** 1. An information storage medium of paper stock. Data is typically stored in the form of magnetic ink characters or punched slots in ordered positions on the card face. Such cards are typically 3 1/4 inches × 7 3/8 inches. 2. A plug-in circuit board containing printed-circuit connections and components. Circuit cards are designed to hold the integrated-circuit packages and other components that make up the electronics of a functioning microcomputer system.

**card address backplane** Refers to a microcomputer's card connec-

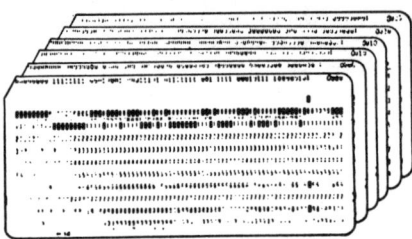

Card, 1

ting plane. This printed backplane, which serves as the bus, assigns an address to each card or module. Users can assemble nearly any combination of memory and interfacing modules and plug them into the standard backplane and still have a system that requires no hard wiring.

**card cage** The structure that holds the various printed-circuit cards required by the microcomputer. The card cage includes one or more output connectors and may be prewired to hold a minimum number of circuit cards such as the CPU, memory, and output controller. Expansion is allowed by connecting card cages together. The card and card cage system are modular in design, offering:

1. Simple assembly
2. Easy access for checkout and troubleshooting
3. Choice of output connections

**card chassis** A chassis that is designed to accommodate circuit cards or boards.

**card code** The combination of punched holes used in cards to indicate digital information.

**card column** The line of punched holes in a card that appears parallel to the short edge of the card.

**card deck** A pack of punched cards.

**card field** The columns on the card which are assigned to receive the same type of information for a group of cards.

**card frames** A card connector and guide assembly. Up to 40 cards may be mounted with some card frames. Frames can be supplied assembled with connectors, with bussed power terminations with connectors, and with bussed power terminations with connector options.

**card hopper** That part of a card processing machine that holds the card deck during processing. The card *hopper* holds the cards to be processed, and a card *stacker* typically holds the cards that have been processed.

**card image** A representation of the hole patterns punched in a card. In a card image, each card hole represents a one and each unpunched space represents a zero.

**card modules, microprocessor** The functional modules that are provided on printed wiring cards such as:

1. CPU modules: Typically, a card comprising the central processing unit, bus interface logic, and sockets for ROM and RAM.
2. Memory modules: These cards may contain memory timing and control logic as well as storage chips.
3. Interface modules: These cards contain the interfaces needed by the system; there may be one card devoted to each interface function.
4. Protyping cards: These are blank cards that are generally drilled to accept wirewrap pins and sockets. These cards are used for the development of special interfaces and other nonstandard circuits.

**card-programmed** A type of calculating system processing approach that uses punched cards for programming. Card-programmed calculating systems usually involve many different machines and multiple steps in the data flow.

**card punch** A device that records data onto cards by punching holes in them whose positions relate to alphabetic and numeric data in accordance with a specific code.

**card reader** A device that senses the hole patterns in punched cards and translates the data contained on the cards into the desired form. It is typically used with a controller that provides communications over a bus under direct memory access of CPU. The CPU issues commands to the controller through the bus, and the controller responds by issuing the correct timing and control signals to the reader. Data on the cards is then transferred to the system memory until the reader controller issues an interrupt signal to the CPU to signal the end of data transmission. Data can be transferred in one of two formats:

1. Standard, in which each column is stored right-justified within one word of memory.
2. Packed, in which eight bits from each column are stored in alternate half-words of memory.

**card row** The line of punched holes in a card that appears parallel to the long edge of the card.

**card sensing** The converting of information on punched cards into electrical impulses.

**card stacker** In a multiple-card processing system, a mechanical device that accepts each card after it has been processed and aligns it so that after the processing operation, all cards may be retrieved as a card deck.

**card to tape converter** A device that converts information directly from punched cards to punched or magnetic tape.

**card verifier** 1. A special card reader that senses card codes immediately following the punch operation check of their accuracy. The operator of the machine reads the source documents and presses the correct keys on the verifier keyboard. The machine checks each column to verify that the correct holes have been punched and notches the end of the card if all columns are correct. If the verifier cannot match all the holes in a column, a notch is made above that column. 2. An individual who checks card data as an accuracy verification step.

**carriage** The control mechanism for a typewriter or printer, which is usually automatically controlled for such operations as paper feed, spacing, skipping, and ejecting. The term *carriage* was assigned in the typewriter's early days, when the sheet being typed upon was physically carried back and forth in front of a stationary impact printer.

**carriage control tape** The tape that controls the line feed for a typewriter or printer.

**carriage return** The operation that causes the next character in a series to be printed at the first position on the next line.

**carriage return character** The character (abbreviated *CR*) that causes the print position to be moved to the first (usually flush left) space on a new line.

**carrier** A radio-frequency signal of a specific wavelength, usually modulated with frequency or amplitude variations that represent intelligence to be conveyed.

**carrier, exalted** Refers to the addition of a synchronized carrier before demodulation, to improve linearity and to reduce the effects of fading during transmission.

**carrier frequency** The frequency of the modulation signal.

**carrier noise** Noise that is produced by variations of a radio frequency

**carrier system** A means of obtaining a number of channels over a single circuit, or path, by modulating each channel with a different carrier frequency and demodulating at the receiving point to restore the signals to their original form.

**carrier transmission** A communications system in which a signal of one frequency (the carrier) may be modulated by signals of other frequencies to convey intelligence over many channels. The signals are demodulated at the receiving end to recover the original information signals.

**carrier wave** The basic frequency or pulse repetition rate of a signal with no intrinsic intelligence. It is modulated by another signal that does have intelligence. The carrier may be amplitude, phase, or frequency modulated.

**carry** The operation required when the sum of two digits equals or exceeds the base of the number being used as in adding:

$$\begin{array}{r} 1110 = 14 \\ + \; 1010 = 10 \\ \hline 11000 = 24 \end{array}$$

Four carry operations are required for this addition in binary notation. A carry within a computer results in a forwarding or transferring of the digits to a new digit place. When a carry into a digit place results in an additional carry and the normal adding circuit is bypassed, the carry is called a high-speed carry, or *standing-on nines* carry. If the normal adding circuit is used, a *cascaded* carry results, which produces a partial sum numeral and a carry numeral; these are added together until no new carries are produced. The *partial* carry results from forming the partial product during multiplication. If the partial carry is propagated to completion, a complete carry results. The *end-around* carry occurs in multiplication and other operations, such as the addition of two negative numbers in nines-complement notation. In subtraction operations, a carry results when the difference between the digits is less than zero. This type of negative carry is usually called a *borrow*.

**carry, cascaded** In parallel addition, a carry process in which the addition of two numerals results in a partial sum numeral and a carry numeral, which are in turn added together; this process is repeated until no new carries are generated.

**carry-complete** The signal used by parallel adders to indicate that all carries have been generated and propagated to completion for an addition operation.

**carry look-ahead generator** A unit that is used in some systems to provide a fast carry in arithmetic operations, considerably improving system throughput.

**carry time** The time required to perform the carry operation. The carry time consists of the time required to transfer a carry digit to a higher position and add it, or the time required to transfer all the carry digits to higher positions and add them to all the digits in the number.

**cartesian coordinates** A coordinate system in which the position of a point can be defined with reference to a set of axes at right angles to each other.

**cartridge** A container of magnetic tape, usually self-contained and generally larger than a tape cassette.

**cascade connection** Refers to two or more similar components or devices arranged in tandem; the output of one is connected to the input of the following device.

**cascade control** An automatic operations-controlling system in which control units are linked in such a way that each element regulates the input of the next succeeding unit.

**cassette** A magnetic-tape housing that contains a tape of a specific length. The cassette includes the supply reel, takeup reel, head pressure pad, and a slot for the capstan drive.

**cassette diagnostic** Refers to a test for the functions of a cassette controller.

**CAT** 1. Abbreviation for *clear air turbulence*. 2. Abbreviation for *computer of average transients*. 3. Abbreviation for *computer-aided-testing*.

**catalog** Refers to the list of files on the storage media. It also contains the information needed by the computer to keep track of the physical locations on the storage media of the various files. Also known as a *directory*.

**catastrophic failure** A change in the operation of an item resulting in a complete lack of useful performance of the item.

**cathode ray** The stream of negatively charged particles (electrons) normally emitted from the surface of the cathode in a rarefied gas.

**cathode-ray tube** A large vacuum tube with a viewing face, in which an electron beam is focused and controlled to form characters and other images. The beam and pattern are easily varied to produce almost any desired information format. The picture tube in a television is a special cathode-ray tube usually abbreviated *CTR*.

A typical application of the CRTs is in drawing display systems, whereby a designer uses a special stylus to draw on a piece of paper placed on a sensing tablet; as the designer draws, the information is sensed and displayed on the CRT screen. Quickly sketched lines are displayed straight, and rough corners appear precise on the display screen. Changes and modifications are easily made and lines are erased with simple stylus movements.

**c-axis** C is an angle defining rotary motion around the z axis. Positive c is in the direction to advance a right handed screw in the + direction. The standard coordinate system gives the coordinates of a moving tool with respect to a stationary workpiece.

**CAW** Abbreviation for *channel address word*.

**CC** Abbreviation for *carriage control*.

**CCD** Abbreviation for *charge-coupled device*, a memory medium that uses carrier movement between potential wells to store digital information. The carriers are stored in the potential wells under electrodes biased in the depletion mode. Pulsing of the electrodes moves the carriers from one electrode to the next. The electrodes are located very close to each other in order to allow the potential wells to couple and move the carriers between them. Two types of structures are used in CCDs:

1. The surface-channel type, which uses the surface of the substrate for storage and data transfer.
2. The buried-channel type, which uses both the surface and the bulk of the material for storing and transferring data.

The surface-channel type does not require as much doping, which results in a simpler fabrication. It does offer a higher total charge-carrying capability, but suffers from low transfer efficiency at higher charge transfer rates. (The transfer efficiency is the percentage of the data or charge packet which is actually transferred in a data shift and is typically greater than 99.9%.)

Charge-coupled devices offer high speed, high packing density, and low power requirements. Experimenters have operated CCD shift registers at frequencies greater than 100 MHz; however, their useful range for memories will probably be closer to 10 MHz, since the peripheral units will be in that range.

A CCD memory simulates the operation of a rotating drum

without any mechanical movement. A typical 16,384-bit chip is organized for both serial and random-access operation. Four-phase clock signals shift the data between the 64 shift registers of the device. Each shift register can be viewed as representing a single track in a conventional drum unit, with each track divided into 256 sectors, one for each CCD storage cell. The simulated rotation of the drum is controlled by the four-phase clock.

Applications include image sensing, signal processing, and semiconductor memory components. As memories, they may replace disks, drum, and other external storage devices.

**CCD internal memory array** A type of internal memory array that is comprised of surface channel charge-coupled structures. The CCD structure is formed by a series of metal-oxide semiconductor devices. These MOS devices do not have source/drain diffusions usually associated with other MOS structures. The clock phases are laid out perpendicular to the shift register channels. Electrical isolation between shift register channels is obtained by channel stop diffusions and thick film oxide methods. Data input/output connections to the registers are obtained from n+ diffusions at the ends of the registers.

**CCD line addressable random-access memory** Abbreviation, LARAM. A memory configuration that constitutes a combination of charge-coupled device (CCD) and metal-oxide semiconductor (MOS) concepts. By configuring an MOS selection matrix to several "lines" formed by CCD sequential shift registers, one can attain "pseudo random access" even though the CCDs are inherently serial. Selecting a given address in the MOS matrix causes the unit's driving waveforms to read, write, or refresh information in the chosen register. The access time of a LARAM depends on the number of elements in each of its lines. Because only one line is active at a time, power requirements are small. Each line can represent one or more words or one particular bit from several words. Because its data remains stationary most of the time, the LARAM is vulnerable to leakage current losses.

**CCD shift register** A series shift register of charge-coupled devices. If the unit's data remains stationary or moves slowly, the storage-element power requirement is low.

**CCD structure** The two common charge-coupled device structures are the surface channel and buried channel. The surface channel is characterized by the storing and transferring of charge (data) along the surface of the substrate. The buried channel type, because of additional substrate doping, stores and transfers the charge (data) further into the bulk of the substrate.

The primary differences in characteristics between the surface channel and buried channel is that the surface channel has a higher total charge carrying capability, a lower charge transfer efficiency at extremely high charge transfer rates, and a simpler fabrication process. Charge transfer efficiency is defined as the percentage of the total charge packet (data) which is actually shifted or transferred per shift. The efficiency is typically greater than 99.9 percent per shift.

**CCM** 1. Abbreviation for *constant current modulation*. 2. Abbreviation for *controlled carrier modulation*.

**CCR** Abbreviation for *central control room*.

**CDC** 1. Abbreviation for *combat development command*. 2. Abbreviation for *command and data handling console*. 3. Abbreviation for *code directing character*.

**CDCE** Abbreviation for *central data conversion equipment*.

**CDP** Abbreviation for *checkout data processor*.

**CEIP** Abbreviation for *communications electronics implementation plan*.

**celescope** A celestial telescope.

**cell** The storage memory element for one unit of information, usually one character or one word.

**center** 1. To position with a given measurement equidisant from the ends or margins. 2. A command that automatically center lines.

**central distributed system** A central system that usually has a control communication executive (CCE) that simultaneously handles and queues multiple satellite transactions.

**centralized processing** Data processing that is performed at a single central location from data obtained from several locations or managerial levels.

**central processing unit** The central processor of a microprocessor. Most microprocessors use a 4-, 8-, 12-, or 16-bit word with 1, 2, or 3 memory cycles required to complete execution of an instruction. The central processing unit (CPU) may contain the arithmetic unit, control registers, main storage, and scratch pad memories.

**central processor** That part of a computing machine that controls the interpretation and execution of instructions. The central processor is divided into three main sections:

1. Arithmetic and control, which performs the calculations, information routing, and control operations for the other sections.
2. Input and output, which handles all information going into and coming out of the central processor while controlling all peripheral equipment.
3. Memory, which provides the temporary storage for data and instructions.

The memory cycle time usually determines the overall speed of the central processor.

**ceramic capacitors** A capacitor with a dielectric of a ceramic material. Ceramic capacitors, both chip and packaged versions, have been a fast growing segment of the capacitor industry due to their use in microcomputers and related digital circuits. A significant step in ceramic capacitors was the successful transition from a precious metal system to a base metal system. Some units use a nickel alloy to make the internal electrodes and the terminations, permitting price reductions of up to 50 percent.

**ceramic package** Refers to an integrated circuit package made of ceramic material. A high reliability package is made of three layers of $Al_2O_3$ ceramic and nickel plated refractory metal. The cavity is sealed with a glazed ceramic lid, using a low temperature glass sealant. Package leads are of Kovar, nickel plated and solder dipped for insertion or soldering.

**cer-DIP** Acronym for *ceramic dual-in-line package*. Cer-DIP packages offer higher performance at costs closer to plastic packages than conventional ceramic devices. A military approved package with excellent reliability, this package is finding more and more applications now that some early stability and corrosion problems have been solved.

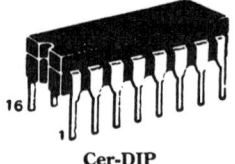

Cer-DIP

**cermet** Ceramic to metal seal.

**CERN reactor** The cyclotron at European Organization for Nuclear Research, Geneva, Switzerland.

**CF** Abbreviation for *central file*.

**CGB** Abbreviation for *convert gray to binary*.

**CGS system** A coherent system of units for expressing the magnitude of electrical and magnetic quantities. The fundamental units of these quantities are the centimeter, gram, and second.

**chad** The piece of material removed when a hole is punched in a card or paper tape.

**chadless** A type of paper tape in which a chad does not exist. Chadless tape is partially prepunched and each chad is left fastened by about 1/4 of the total circumference of the hole. It must be sensed by special readers that use mechanical fingers, as the loose chads interfere with conventional electrical or photoelectric sensors.

**chain** 1. The invoking or running of one program from another with the variable remaining intact. 2. A set of items that are serially linked together in specified segments that are processed in tandem, with only one allowed in the mainframe at any given moment. The items may be records or files that are dependent upon one another and each may have access to previously executed segments. Chained files allow open ended sequential data handling and consist of data blocks with forward and backward pointers.

**chain code** A cyclic sequence of words that are related by one bit position from the left or the right. A word must not be repeated before completion of the cycle. An example of a simple chain code is:

000   111
001   110
010   100
101   000
011

**chained files** Files that consist of a series of data blocks chained together with forward and backward pointers. They are used for open ended sequential data handling.

**chained list** A list of items in which each item has an identifier to locate the next item in the list.

**chaining search** A technique that uses an identifier to locate the next item in a search.

**chain printer** A printer mechanism that uses type carried on the links of a revolving chain.

**CHAMPION** Abbreviation for *compatible hardware and milestone program for integrating organizational needs*.

**change dump** A dump triggered by those storage locations whose contents have recently changed.

**channel** A data pathway for the transmission of signals and data. In a communications system, a channel connects the message *source* with the message *sink*. In a storage unit, a channel may be the track or band that is connected to the read or write circuits. Also called *circuit, line, facility, link* and *path*.

**channel, analog** A channel on which the information transmitted can take any value between the limits defined by the channel. A voice channel is an analog channel.

**channel capacity** The maximum number of bits or characters that can be handled in a particular channel at any one time. Also, the maximum transmission rate through a channel at a specified error rate. Channel capacity is usually measured in bits per second (for local media) or bauds (for data communications by wire or radio).

**channelizing** The subdividing of wideband channels into a number of channels with narrow bandwidths.

**channel pulse** A pulse used to represent intelligence on a channel by virtue of its time or modulation characteristic.

**channel synchronizer** A synchronizer, often housed in the peripheral control unit, that provides the proper interface between the central computer and the peripheral equipment. Other control functions of the channel synchronizer include primary interpreting of the function words, searching by comparing an identifier with data read from a peripheral unit, and providing the central computer with peripheral unit status information.

**character** A letter, numeral, or other symbol that is used to express information. A character is usually part of an ordered set and may be graphic, as in English and other spoken languages, and may be any form of letter, numeral, punctuation mark, or any other formatting symbols.

**character boundary** As used in character recognition, the largest rectangle having a side parallel to the reference edge of the document.

**character check** A verification that characters have been formed correctly.

**character code** An ordered pattern of bits that are assigned in a particular system to represent characters. Baudot and ASCII are character codes.

**character display** A device that allows the display of characters on a screen. A simple system for a television monitor is shown below. Typically the bit patterns for the characters are stored in a read-only memory. A television set in the United States operates with 525 lines, scanned at a rate of 30 frames per second. This corresponds to 64 microseconds for each picture line. For a display with 64 characters in each line, we must provide one character every microsecond. Shift registers or other recirculating memories are used to allow a character, which is written on the screen, to be continually rewritten or refreshed. The radio frequency section of the display consists of circuits for generating the correct RF signals to be supplied to the television monitor. The bit pattern is used to generate a modulating signal to modulate the RF output of an RF signal generator. The display pattern is a series of dots or scanning segments across a picture line. The arrangement shown is not limited to generating characters. Graphics and other images can be generated and displayed by the use of a programmed ROM. A game can be created by providing the means for moving images across the screen by opposing sides. As an example, each player side is provided with a miniaturized joystick. The movement of the joystick corresponds to a vertical and horizontal movement of the player's marker across the screen. In the control unit, the joystick movement is translated into delayed pulses from the horizontal and vertical sync signal generators, and the delayed pulses are applied to a coincidence gate, to modulate an RF signal that is applied to the television monitor.

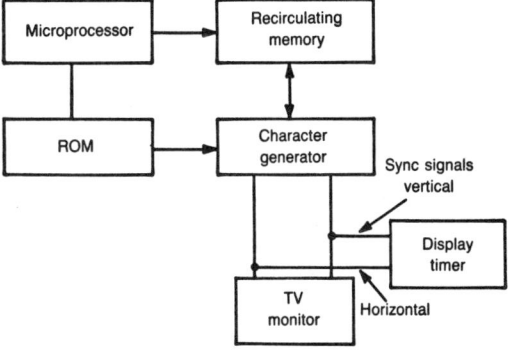

**Character display system**

**character element** 1. A basic information element as transmitted, printed, displayed, or used to control communications, when used as a code. 2. Groups of bits, pulses, etc. occurring in a time period normally representing that for a character or symbolic representation.

**character fill** The inserting of specific characters, usually all ones or all zeros, to delete unwanted data.

**character printer** A hard copy device that prints one letter at a time. Typewriters are character printers. These are slower than line printers that print a line of characters at one time.

**character reader** A device that senses and interprets printed or handwritten symbols and converts the information into machine-language code. Character readers are available for many type styles; they operate optically or magnetically for characters printed with magnetic inks.

**character recognition** The process of reading, identifying, and interpreting printed characters and converting them into a machine-language form for computers.

**character set** The complete group of representations used as characters. Examples include:
1. The letters of the alphabet
2. The binary digits 0 and 1
3. The complete set of signals used in Morse code

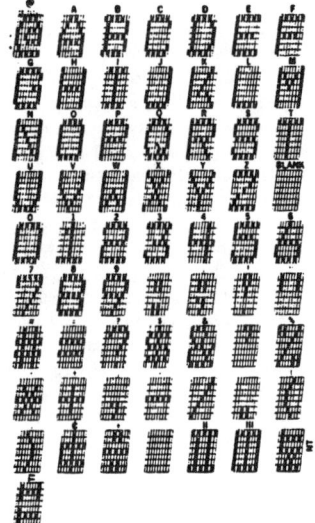

**Character set**

**character shift** 1. A code extension character used to terminate a sequence that has been introduced by the shift out character. 2. A code extension character that can be used by itself to cause a return to the character set prior to the departure caused by a shift out character.

**character string** A group of connected characters associated by coding, keying, or other programming techniques.

**character subset** Selected characters from a character set that have a specified common feature. For example, digits 0-9 are a subset of the ASCII character set.

**charactron** A cathode ray tube (crt) that is capable of displaying alphanumeric characters and other symbols.

**charge** A quantity of electricity associated with a body with an excess or deficiency of electrons.

**charge-coupled device** A storage medium that utilizes the transfer of stored charges to achieve high densities for memory applications. (See *CCD*.)

**chassis assembly** Refers to an assembly in many systems that provides mounting locations for the processor, power supply, and interface cards. The chassis assembly is often designed using a printed circuit backplane for all interconnecting wiring.

**chatter** The rapid closing and opening of contacts on a relay that reduces its life.

**check** Verification of equipment operation and the progress of desired operating conditions along with the correctness of resulting calculations.

**check, arithmetic** An operation performed by the computer to reveal any failure in an arithmetic operation. It may also be used to determine whether or not the capacity of a register has been exceeded after an operation.

**check, automatic** Refers to various provisions usually constructed in hardware for verifying the accuracy of information transmitted, manipulated, or stored by any unit or device in a computer. Synonymous with built-in check, built-in automatic check, and hardware check.

**check, balance** Refers to an analog computer control state in which all amplifier summing junctions are connected to the computer zero reference level (usually signal ground) to permit zero balance of the operational amplifier.

**check bit** A binary verification digit inserted with other digits as an automatic machine function. A parity check bit, for example, is inserted when the sum of a group of ones is odd, thus keeping the parity always even. When an output contains an odd number of ones, an error is indicated.

**check character** A character used to perform a checking operation.

**check digit** A digit used to perform a check. A check digit is carried as a part of a machine word to report on the other digits of the word. When an error occurs, the check is negative and an alarm is initiated. One or more check digits can be used with either batch processing or real-time computing operations. Data with the check digits can be periodically regenerated and compared with the source data.

**check indicator** A device that indicates that a checking operation has uncovered an error. A check indicator may use either visual or audible means to call the operator's attention to the error.

**checking routine** A diagnostic program that examines programs or data for the most obvious errors. A typical checking routine will discover errors in misspelling and keypunching, but usually does not execute the program to detect programming errors.

**checklists** These are lists that can be used with flowcharts. Here the programmer checks that each variable has been initialized, that each flowchart element has been coded, that the definitions are correct, and that all paths are connected properly. A good checklist can save time, but the hand checking of long or complicated programs should not be used since the programmer may be more likely to make additional mistakes when checking the program. Some loops and sections of programs can be hand checked to see that the flow of control is correct. In the case of loops, the programmer can always check to see if the loop performs the first and last iterations correctly. These are the sources of many loop errors. The program can also be hand checked for the trivial cases, such as tables with no elements. Program checking and debugging should always be done using a systematic method.

One can not assume that the first error found is the only one in the program.

**checkout** The use of diagnostic tests to verify the correctness of machine and program operation.

**checkpoint** A place in a program or routine where a check or a restart can be performed. The checkpoint allows the storage of sufficient information to allow restarting, or it records the information so that the step can be restarted at a later time.

**checkpoint and restart** A program verifying technique that allows processing to continue from the last checkpoint rather than from the beginning of the run following an error detection or other interrupt. The checkpoints are determined based upon a desired number of transactions out of the total number required.

**check problem** A test to detect errors in programming or machine operation. The check problem results in an error indication when it is not solved correctly.

**check register** A register used to store information for checking with the result of a succeeding transfer of data. The check register stores the information until a second transfer of the same information verifies that the information agrees.

**check reset** A key that is used to acknowledge an error and reset the program for restart.

**checkout routine** A routine to aid programmers during debugging operations. A checkout routine may consist of storage and printout subroutines.

**checksum** A summation of bits or digits used for checking purposes. Checksums are usually specified by an arbitrary set of rules fitted to the application. Summation checks provide a redundant checking method in which groups of digits are summed, usually without regard for overflow, and that sum checked against a previously computed sum to verify accuracy.

**check, summation** See *checksum*.

**check, unused command** A check, usually automatic, that tests for the occurrence of a nonpermissible code expression.

**chemical deposition** Refers to the process of depositing a substance on a surface by means of the chemical reduction of a solution.

**chemical etching** A process in which the dielectric and copper foil are sandwiched, and the circuit pattern is imaged on the copper with a material that is resistant to etching chemicals (the resist). The rest of the copper, which is not intended to be part of the circuit, is then removed by chemical etching.

**Chinese binary** The binary representation of data on cards that uses the card columns for storing information. Each column in a 12-row card would store 12 consecutive bits. (Also called *column binary*.)

**chip** A silicon slab selectively doped with impurities so that passive and active devices, circuit paths, and device interconnections are formed within the solid structure. Thus, a chip is the integrated circuit inside an IC housing.

Microprocessor chips typically utilize large-scale integration (LSI) techniques. Up to 10,000 transistors have been placed on chips of 6 mm square. The chips are usually mounted in dual-inline packages which may have up to 40 pins for mounting on circuit boards.

A microprocessor chip usually includes the arithmetic logic unit (ALU), general purpose registers, and bus controls. The microprocessor chip or chips are combined with memory and input/output chips to form a microcomputer system that will fit on a single circuit board.

**chip architecture** Refers to the functional structure of the microprocessor chip. The chip architecture generally includes the arithmetic logic unit (ALU), the general purpose registers, and the control bus structure. The architecture is to some degree dependent on the partitioning of the processor between one or more chips, the number of pins each chip has, the chip size, the off-chip memory, and the input/output bus structure.

**chip, circuit** Usually refers to an integrated circuit; a single device composed of transistors, diodes, and other interconnected components. It usually has been cut from a larger wafer, usually of silicon.

**chip materials** Refers to the kind of substrate to be used, its doping concentrations, the choice of silicon or aluminum for the gate electrode, and the parameters of the chip materials.

**chip selection** To select the proper ROM chip, the proper address lines must be wired to the ROM's chip select inputs. ROMs generally have four chip select inputs, which means that some external AND gates may be required. See the figure below.

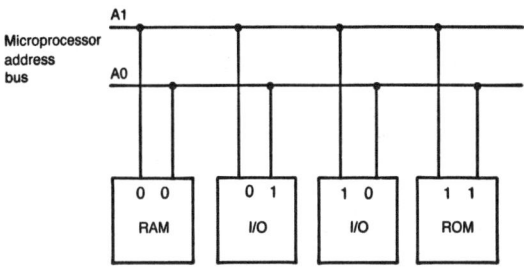

**Chip selection interface**

**chip system** Refers to a multiplicity of chips, together with addressing logic, interfacing circuits, and sometimes the power supply, in a convenient form for use in a microcomputer system.

**chip technology, LSI** Refers to the large scale integration (LSI) technology used to build microprocessor chips, which centers around metal-oxide semiconductor (MOS) devices. Chip densities on MOS devices range to over 100,000 transistors per chip. The chip's size typically ranges from 0.25 inch square to 0.45 inch square. The chips are mounted into packages that typically have 40 pins or more for mounting on a printed circuit card. The n channel MOS (NMOS) have been the predominant technology for most of the newer microprocessors. NMOS has become the preferred approach by many of the integrated circuit manufacturers.

**chroma** The characterization of a color quality without reference to its brilliance or hue (saturation only).

**CI** Abbreviation for *call indicator*.

**circuit** A closed communications path between two or more points. A circuit may have individual high paths and return paths, or the return path may be shared between many circuits. See *channel.2*. A group of electronic components interconnected to perform specific functions upon application of proper voltages and signals. 3. A closed path of current sources and sinks.

**circuit analyzer** Equipment that may consist of one or several test instruments and is controlled by a microprocessor that is used to measure one or more quantities or verify performance of a circuit. A typical circuit analyzer is capable of a variety of functional tests on TTL, DTL, MOS, CMOS, and HTL devices using either combinatorial or sequential logic. The equipment may consist of constant-voltage and constant-current supplies, pulse generators, comparators, and a connection matrix. Power supply levels, pulse levels, and comparator limits are all programmable, and the matrix is used to connect the forcing and measuring connections with any lead of the device under test.

**circuit, anticoincidence** Refers to a specific logic element that operates with binary digits and is designed to provide signals according to specific rules; for instance, one digit is obtained as output only if two different input signals are received.

**circuit, astable** Refers to a circuit that continuously alternates between its two unstable states. It can be synchronized by applying a repetitive input signal of slightly higher frequency.

**circuit, bistable trigger** A type of binary circuit that has two states, each requiring an appropriate trigger for excitation and transition from one state to the other. Also called binary pair, trigger pair, and flip-flop.

**circuit breaker** A resettable fuse device for opening a circuit path, usually when overcurrent conditions are exceeded. A circuit breaker may also be used to control and protect circuits from conditions of excessive heat, noise, vibration, voltage, radiation, and other parameters.

**circuit capacity** The information capacity and the number of total channels that can be operated in a given circuit at any one time, usually measured in baud or bits per second.

**circuit, closed** Refers to a complete circuit through which current can flow when voltage is applied.

**circuit components** Refers to the fundamental circuit parts that are connected by metallic conductors. Attached to the conductors may be coils, resistors, diodes, capacitors, transformers, integrated circuits, and other parts or devices.

**circuit hole** The component mounting hole that appears within or partially within the conductive lines of a printed circuit board; it may or may not be a through-the-board conductive path.

**circuit, integrated** Abbreviated IC. Refers to a circuit chip in which gates, or flip-flops are etched on single crystals of semiconductor materials. It is designed with the use of geometric etching and conductive ink or chemical deposition techniques.

**circuit, interlock** A circuit that originates a signal that is in the "on" condition only when all the following conditions are met: (1) Its internal circuits are arranged for signaling on a communication facility; (2) It is not in any abnormal or test condition that disables or impairs any normal function associated with the class of service being used.

**circuit limiter** A circuit of nonlinear elements that restricts the electrical excursion of service being used.

**circuit limiter** A circuit of nonlinear elements that restricts the electrical excursion of a variable in accordance with some specified criteria. Hard limiting is a limiting action with negligible variation in output in the range where the output is limited. Soft limiting is a limiting action with appreciable variation in output in the range where the output is limited.

**circuit, linear** A circuit whose output is an amplified version of its input or whose output is a straight line variation of its input.

**circuit load** The electrical load due to equipment current drain, usually expressed as a percentage of total circuit capability under specific operating conditions for a specific operating time.

**circuit noise** Erratic and random electrical impulses generated by electrical switching in a circuit; these impulses, when interpreted by circuits as legitimate signals, cause errors and improper data timing.

**circuit parameters** Refers to the values of the physical quantities associated with circuit elements. For example, the resistance (parameter) of a resistor (element) or the inductance per unit length (parameter) of a transmission line (element).

**circuit reliability** The percentage of time that a circuit meets specified operating conditions. The reliability figure is determined from the testing of enough parts to cause a desired number to fail based on the total population and the circuit application. The number of failures is then subtracted from the total number tested to obtain the circuit reliability.

**circuit single-shot** Refers to a circuit arranged to perform signal standardization to convert an imprecise input signal into one conforming to requirements.

**circuit tuned** Refers to a circuit with an inductance coil and a capacitor in series or in parallel that offers a low or high impedance, respectively, to alternating current at the resonant frequency.

**circuit, two-way** A bidirectional channel that operates in both directions.

**circuit video** A circuit capable of handling non-sinusoidal waveforms involving frequencies in the order of several megahertz.

**circular interpolation** A mode of contouring control that uses the information contained in a single block to produce an arc of a circle. Shorter lengths are possible when circular interpolation is used instead of linear interpolation.

**circulating register** A shift register operated as a closed loop with the data outputs circulated back to the input.

**circulating storage** A storage system that operates as a closed loop. Information is stored as a train or pattern of pulses; the pulse train at the output is usually sensed, amplified, and shaped before being inserted at the input.

**cldata (cutter location data)** The input to the postprocessor in some automatic machining systems. It consists of such items as x, y coordinates and postprocessor commands. The actual data is contained in a CLFILE or CLTAPE.

**clear** The placing of storage locations into a desired state, usually a zero or empty condition.

**clear area** As used in character recognition, the area that is to be kept free of any markings not related to reading the character.

**cleared condition** A destructive read operation that results in placing storage locations into cleared states. The cleared condition is usually permanent and is also called the zero condition.

**clfile (cutter location file)** The storage medium name for the CLDATA. It is common to use random access storage systems.

**clipper** Refers to a circuit that removes the portion of a waveform that would otherwise extend above or below a specified level. This is usually accomplished by diodes and capacitors.

**clipping** The removal of a portion of a waveform at a particular level; a condition in dictation where the first part of a word is not recorded because the mechanism does not engage fast enough.

**clock** The controlled timing signal of a precise frequency that is used to time events within a piece of equipment. The clock is the basic method of generating periodic signals for synchronization in electronic equipment, including computers. A clock may be a shift register that changes its contents at specified intervals to mark time, or it may be a data communications clock that controls and limits the number of bits in a data stream.

**clock counter** A memory location that records the progress of real time, usually by accumulating counts produced by a clock count pulse interrupt.

**clock generator** An oscillator, usually crystal controlled, that provides all timing signals within a computer system. A typical clock generator provides the multiphase signals using only one external crystal and internal dividers for signals that are MOS or TTL compatible. ROMs are used with counters for generating clock phases in systems requiring complex clocking.

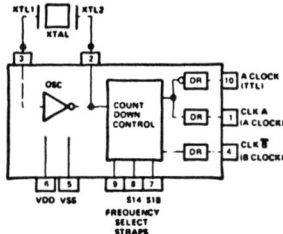

**Clock generator**

**clock pulse** A signal provided for synchronization of events.

**clock, input** That terminal on an integrated circuit whose condition or change of condition controls the admission of other inputs and thereby controls the output. The clock signal may perform two functions: (1) It permits data signals to enter the chip. (2) After entry, it directs the circuit to change state accordingly. Some circuits permit data entry when the clock goes to "1" and then causes the circuit to react to the data when the clock goes to "0," while others use the inverse of these signals.

**clock module, real time** A unit that provides programmable time bases. The time base reference is usually a crystal controlled oscillator. On completion of a time interval the microcomputer will receive an interrupt from the module if enabled.

**clock rate** 1. The number of pulses per unit time that are generated by a clock. The clock rate is typically measured in bits per second or hertz (cycles per second). 2. The rate at which bits or words can be transferred between elements within a system.

**clock signals** Those signals to an integrated circuit whose condition or change of condition controls the admission of other inputs and thereby controls the output. The clock signal may perform two functions: (1) It permits data signals to enter the chip. (2) After entry, it directs the circuit to change state accordingly. Some circuits permit data entry when the clock goes to "1" and then causes the circuit to react to the data when the clock goes to "0," while others use the inverse of these signals. Users must be concerned with the amplitude and frequency of the necessary clock signals, as well as requirements to gate or otherwise process the signals.

**clock track** The track upon which a pattern of signals has been cut or traced to provide a reference for the recording of time.

**closed loop** A circuit, system, or device in which the output is continuously sampled by the input for comparison and control purposes. Closed-loop or feedback control systems are used to control many industrial processes.

**closed-loop program** A program in which there is no exit other than by intervention from outside the program. The closed-loop program is used when a group of indefinitely repeated instructions is required.

**closed routine** A routine that is entered by basic linkage from the main routine, instead of existing as a block of instructions within the main program.

**closed shop** A computer facility that uses programming specialists for programming rather than using the originators of the problems, or one that uses full-time operators rather than user/programmers as operators.

**closed subroutine** A subroutine that can be stored in one place and connected to the main routine by one or more linkages. A closed subroutine is usually entered by a jump operation and is forced to return control to the main routine at the end of the operation. The instructions related to the jump and return are known as linkages.

**clprint** 1. An Automatically Programmed Tools statement that calls for the listing or printout of a CLFILE. 2. A CLFILE listing.

**cltape (cutter location tape)** The storage medium name of the CLDATA. It is common to store this on magnetic tape.

**CM** Abbreviation for *computer module*.

**C MOS** An acronym (pronounced "see-moss") for *complementary metal-oxide semiconductor*. Technology employing integrated field-effect transistors in a complementary symmetry arrangement, which simulates a "push/pull" operation because of the placement of opposing-polarity devices (p-channel and n-channel FETs).

As a logic family, CMOS offers the following advantages:

1. Low power requirements
2. Excellent noise immunity
3. High fanout to other CMOS circuits
4. High tolerance to power supply variations, allowing low-cost supplies
5. High temperature range

**CMOS characteristics** The characteristics and advantages of CMOS technology are in between those of NMOS and PMOS. CMOS is faster than PMOS, but slower than NMOS. Because it uses two transistors rather than one, CMOS offers less density than standard MOS. Its advantage is the very low power consumption (about 1.5 volts) and noise immunity. CMOS devices can operate between 2V and 12V. CMOS technology is suited for avionics, aerospace applications, and other systems that require portability and/or a very low power consumption. Several commercial microprocessors using this technology are available. A low cost, unregulated supply is sufficient to operate most CMOS devices. Since both n channel and p channel transistors are required, however, there is the disadvantage of having more processing steps involved in the manufacturing operation (two additional diffusions and photomasking steps). Also, more real estate is required for what are basically two separate MOS transistors.

**CMOS circuits** A circuit that includes CMOS components. In standard MOS circuit the upper transistor, which acts as a load, accounts for a significant amount of the power dissipation. In CMOS circuits with p and n channel devices as shown below, a complementary inverter is formed by applying an input to the gates of the two opposite polarity transistors. When a logical one is applied to this circuit, the upper channel transistor is off, while the lower n channel device is conducting. The output is shorted to ground, and current from the supply is only the leakage through the p channel device after the load capacitance is charged. When a logical zero is applied to the input, the upper transistor is on, while the lower device is off. The output is at +V, and the current will be a function of the load. If a similar high impedance MOS device is the load, the current will remain small.

**CMOS operation**

**CMOS IC contamination** CMOS ICs are subject to greater yield problems than other digital ICs. Contamination and mask registration problems are more critical, and moisture has an important influence. Water is the vehicle that makes ions form, makes them mobile, and then puts them where they can do damage. Water and ions can create contamination problems for the devices with the smallest geometries and most sensitive parameters.

**CMOS interface** When a CMOS is operated with a 5 V power supply, the interface to transistor-transistor logic (TTL) is straightforward. The input impedance of CMOS is very high, so that any form of TTL will drive CMOS without loss of fan-out in the LOW state. Most TTL, however, has an insufficient HIGH state voltage (typically 3.5 V) to drive CMOS reliably. A pull-up resistor (1K to 10K) from the output of the TTL device to the 5 V power supply will effectively pull the HIGH state level to 4.5 V or above.

**CMOS logic** A logic family that can reduce power supply costs and noise immunity. When operated with a 10 V supply, it has a worst case noise immunity of 3 V. Even when operated at 5V, ac and dc noise immunities are superior to those of other logic. The power dissipation is essentially zero at dc, climbing to that of lower power TTL at a few MHz. The low power regulation requirements allow power supply costs to be cut significantly.

**CMOS propagation delay** Compared to TTL, CMOS devices are slow and very sensitive to capacitive loading. Later devices use advanced processing (isoplanar) and improved circuit design (buffered gates) to achieve propagation delays and output rise times that are superior to junction-isolated CMOS designs. Silicon-on-sapphire, SOS, can achieve similar performance but at higher costs. Isoplanar processing achieves lower parasitic capacitances, which reduce the on-chip delay and increase the maximum toggle frequency of flip-flops, registers, and counters. Buffering all outputs, even on gates, results in lower output impedance and thus reduces the effect of capacitive loading. Propagation delay is affected by three parameters: capacitive loading, supply voltage, and temperature.

Propagation delay is a function of ambient temperature. The temperature dependence of CMOS is much simpler than with TTL, where three factors contribute: increase of beta with temperature, increase of resistor value with temperature, and decrease of junction forward voltage drop with increasing temperature. In CMOS, essentially only the carrier mobility changes, thus increasing the impedance and hence the delay with temperature. For some devices, this temperature dependence is less than 0.3 percent per degree Celsius practically linear over the full temperature range.

**CMOS structure** The CMOS structure requires a more complex fabrication process as shown below. The p channel device is formed directly from the n type substrate. A p doped tub must be created for the n channel device, which adds to the processing steps. Also, channel stops are required between the devices to prevent extraneous current flow between devices.

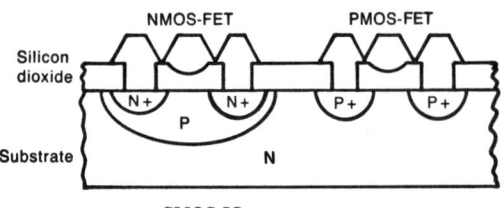

CMOS IC structure

**coalesce** The combining of two or more files into one.

**coaxial cable** Refers to a cable consisting of one conductor, usually a small copper tube or wire, within and insulated from another conductor of larger diameter, usually copper tubing or copper braid.

**coaxial line** A transmission line in which one conductor completely surrounds the other, the two separated by a continuous solid dielectric or by dielectric spacers. A coaxial line has no external field and is not susceptible to external fields from other sources. Also referred to as *coaxial cable, coaxial transmission line,* and *concentric line.*

**COBOL** Acronym for *common business-oriented language.* COBOL makes use of English-language statements and was designed by a committee to serve two purposes:

1. Provide a specific language for the business data processing industry.
2. Provide a language to help these users achieve program compatibility.

The committee was sanctioned by the U.S. Department of Defense and the language was released for publication in 1960.

There are two types of COBOL words—*reserved* and *supplied*. Reserved words such as SELECT, ASSIGN, and READ have a special meaning to the COBOL compiler and must be used according to COBOL rules. Supplied words are those supplied by the user and have meaning exclusive to the program without violating any of the language rules.

A COBOL source program has four basic divisions: identification, environment, data, and procedure. The identification division identifies the program, the program author, and the dates when the program was written and compiled. The environment division is used to describe the specific equipment being used. In the data division are two sections—a file section and a working storage section. The file section is used to describe all information that enters and leaves the CPU storage unit; the working storage section is used to specify the locations needed during processing to hold intermediate results, record descriptions, and items such as reserved words. The procedure division specifies the steps that the computer must use to process the program. The steps of this division make use of the names of records and items that were defined in the data division.

**CODASYL** Acronym for *Conference on Data Systems Language,* the assemblage that developed COBOL as a viable language.

**code** 1. A system of rules and ordered characters used to represent symbols and characters from a different character set. (See, for example, *Baudot code* and *Gray code.*) 2. As a verb, to write or form a routine, as in "code a program."

**code, biquinary** A mixed radix notation in which each decimal digit to be represented is considered as a sum of two digits of which the first is zero or one with significance five and the second is 0, 1, 2, 3 or 4 with significance one.

**code conversion** The process for changing the bit grouping for a character in one code to the corresponding grouping in another code. ROMs and other storage elements are useful for code conversion.

**coded character set** A set of characters with a code assigned to each character for computer purposes.

**code, cyclic binary** Also known as Gray code. A binary code in which sequential numbers are represented by expressions that are the same except in one place, and in that place differ by one unit as shown below

| | | Code | |
| Decimal | Binary | Gray |
| --- | --- | --- |
| 0 | 000 | 000 |

|         | Code   |      |
|---------|--------|------|
| Decimal | Binary | Gray |
| 1       | 001    | 001  |
| 2       | 010    | 011  |
| 3       | 011    | 010  |
| 4       | 100    | 110  |
| 5       | 101    | 111  |

**coded program** A program expressed in the form of a code: a program in its final form, ready for entry into the machine.

**code extension character** The control character that indicates that one or more of the succeeding code values is to be interpreted using a different code.

**code holes** The holes containing information in perforated tape as opposed to the sprocket holes (used for feeding the tape).

**coder** A person involved in writing program forms, but not in program design.

**code set** The complete set of representations defined in a code; for example, all of the three-letter international designations for airport identification.

**code, unit distance** A code format in which the characters of a character set are represented by some or all of the different words of n bits arranged in a sequence such that the signal distance between consecutive words is one.

**coding** The process of converting program flow charts into the desired language, or the use of codes to represent characters.

**coding line** A line on a coding form that is reserved for an instruction.

**coding scheme** The rationale behind a code, the understanding of which could prove helpful in determining character codes in the absence of explanatory data.

**coding, skeletal** Sets of instructions in which some addresses and other parts remain undetermined.

**coding tools** Hardware and software aids that are used in the various phases of microcomputer design, including techniques to simplify the designer's task. Some basic tools are: assemblers, editors, loaders, and compilers. In addition, there are hardware or software simulators for program testing and error locating.

**CODIT** Abbreviation for *computer directed to telegraph*.

**COGO** Acronym for *coordinate geometry*, a language used for solving coordinate geometry problems in civil engineering. COGO falls into the general group of production or process control language along with APT and STRESS.

**COHO** Abbreviation for *coherent oscillator*.

**coincidence** Refers to the property of a circuit or device in which an output is produced only when two or more inputs are received within a specified time period.

**coincidence AND signal** A circuit with two or more input wires in which the output wire gives a signal if and only if all input wires receive coincident signals.

**coincidence circuit** A circuit that produces a specified output pulse only when a specified number (two or more) or combination of input terminals receives pulses within a specified time interval.

**COL** Abbreviation for *computer oriented language*.

**COLIDAR** Abbreviation for *coherent light detection and ranging*.

**collate** To combine items from two or more similar sets to produce another similar set. The collated set may or may not be in the same order as the original set.

**collating sequence** The order that is assigned to a set of items, such that any two sets in the order can be collated.

**collation operation** A basic logic element (gate or operator) that has at least two binary input signals and a single binary output signal. The answer or variable that represents the output signal is the conjunction, from set theory, of the variables represented by the input signals. In set theory, the output is 1 only when all input signals represent 1.

**collator** A device used to collate or match sets of punched cards or other collatable data forms. Punched-card collators can combine two sets of cards into a single sequenced deck, or compare two decks of cards without combining them. The collator can also check trays of cards to determine the correct ascending or descending order.

**collector capacitance** Refers to the depletion-layer capacitance associated with the collector of a transistor.

**color display devices** Refers to the basic display devices that can be used with an adaptor such as a television, a high resolution monitor or an RBG (red, green, blue) color monitor.

**color/graphics monitor adaptor** An adaptor used to provide color or graphics to either a monitor or television set with an RF modulator.

**color monitor** A color CRT display unit.

**column** A vertical arrangement of characters, bits, or other data on cards, pages, or other matrixed lists.

**column binary** The representation of data on cards in which the significance of the punched positions are assigned along the card columns rather than the rows. Also called *Chinese binary*.

**column split** A method of sensing or punching card data that allows specified punch positions within single columns to be ignored or treated in a different manner than other punch positions in the same column.

**COM** Acronym for *computer output microfilm*. The COM printer transfers the output of the computer in use onto microfilm.

**combinatorial logic** Circuits or devices in which the outputs are completely determined by the present state of the inputs. Combinatorial logic includes AND, OR, NAND, NOR, and other circuits that do not rely on previous states to determine the present state.

**COMINT** Abbreviation for *communications intelligence*.

**command** As used in microprocessors and microcomputers, an "instruction" that signals the machine to start, stop, or continue a specific operation. A command is not an instruction in the usual sense, but it is a portion of an instruction word that specifies the operation to be performed. Some examples of commands used in the LSI-11 microcomputer are:

The solidus "/," which is used to open a memory location, a general register, or a processor status word.

The carriage return "CR," which is used to close an open location.

The "at cost" sign "@," which is used to keep a location open using the contents of the location as a pointer.

The GO or "G," which is used to start execution of a program at the location immediately before the "G".

**command, channel** An instruction that directs a channel, control unit, or device to perform an operation or set of operations.

**command.com** A section of the PC DOS operating system. It handles any interrupts that may occur, disk error problems, and end of program housekeeping, and loads and runs programs.

**command console processor** The CCP section of the CP/M operating system. It is the area where the programs are loaded.

**command control** Refers to a type of program that handles all user generated console commands sent into the system.

**command key** A key that is used to enter a particular command into a system.

**command language**  A source language that consists mainly of process operators. Each operator in a command language is capable of executing a particular function or command.

**command processor**  The command interpreter section of the PC DOS operating system.

**command readout**  A display of commanded dimension.

**command words**  A word that controls device operation. A command word may function to stop a motor or change a transmission rate.

**comment**  An expression used to identify or explain the steps in a routine. Comments have no effect on the execution of the routine or program and are often found to the right of instructions on printouts or program lists.

**common carrier**  A multiple-user communications system licensed and regulated by the Federal Communications Commission to provide services to all users at regulated rates.

**common field**  A field that can be accessed by independent routines.

**common hardware**  Refers to hardware items having multiple application in a number of functionally different systems.

**common memory**  A shared storage medium that many microcomputers can access.

**common mode range**  Refers to the common mode rejection signal that usually varies with the magnitude of the input signal swing, which is usually determined by the sum of the common mode and the differential voltages. Common mode range is the range of input voltage over which the specified common mode rejection is maintained. When the common mode signal is $\pm 5V$ and the differential signal is $\pm 5V$, the common mode range is $\pm 10V$.

**common mode rejection**  This is the ability to reject the effects of voltages applied to both input terminals simultaneously. It is usually expressed either as a ratio (CMRR = $10^5$) or as $20 \log_{10}$.

**common mode rejection ratio**  This is the ratio of the common mode voltage to the common mode error referred to the input and is generally expressed in dBs:

**common programs**  Programs that have common or multiple applications for more than one system. Programs in the following classes can be used for several routines if they are written in a language common to the computers:

1. Sorting routines
2. Report generation
3. Code conversion programs

**common software**  Common programs.

**communicating typewriter**  A typewriter that can send text to and receive text from another communicating typewriter or a computer, over phone lines or other telecommunications methods.

**communication channel**  A channel or circuit path reserved for transmitting and receiving. Microcomputers can handle full-duplex communication between a teletypewriter or RS-232 device and the CPU with the interface provided by a UART (universal asynchronous receiver/transmitter). To receive data, the UART converts the asynchronous serial characters from the teletypewriter or RS-232 device into a parallel format for transfer to the CPU bus. During transmission, the parallel characters from the CPU bus are converted into a serial mode for the printer or RS-232 unit. The data transfer is independent, allowing the system to achieve simultaneous two-way data communication.

**communication control character**  The character that is used to control the transmission of data over communication channels. A communication control character can be used to control printer operation by causing a back space or line skip.

**communication interface circuit**  A communication interface circuit (USART) is a peripheral device programmed by the CPU to operate using almost any serial data transmission technique currently in use. It can be used for synchronous operation or asynchronous operation. USART refers to universal synchronous/asynchronous receiver/transmitter.

$$\text{CMRR} = 20 \log \frac{V_{cm}}{e_{cm}}$$

where $V_{cm}$ is the common mode voltage and $e_{cm}$ is the common mode error referred to the input. CMRR is an important parameter of differential amplifiers. An ideal differential amplifier would respond to voltage differences between its input terminals without regard to the voltage level common to both inputs. In practice, there is a variation in the balance of the differential amplifier due to the common mode voltage which results in an output even when the differential input is zero.

**communication link**  The means of connecting one location to another for the purpose of transmitting and receiving information. A communications link may be a circuit, channel, or system of equipment that connects the two locations.

**communication modules, microcomputer**  These are modules that allow the use of devices such as printers and modems. Some modules permit serial communications over a current loop with optical isolation for distances up to several miles.

**communication, real time**  A real time system is a combined data processing and communications system that involves the direct communication of transaction data between remote locations and a central computer via communication lines and allows the data to be processed while the transaction is actually taking place. A real time system may be thought of as a communications oriented data processing system that is capable of performing batch processing functions while concurrently processing inquiries or messages and generating responses in a time interval directly related to the operational requirements of the system.

**communications control device**  Data devices that can be attached directly to the system channel via a control unit designed to perform character assembly and transmission control. The control unit may be either a data adapter unit or the transmission control.

**communications executive**  A program or routine that provides the handling and protocol management for the system of communication links and equipment.

**communications, microcomputer**  The use of microcomputers in a data communications system. Functions that efficiently utilize microcomputers include the storing and forwarding of data, switching to multipoints, providing backup circuits and systems, providing error detection and control, and correcting data before it is entered into a host computer. This includes the handling of both voice and data traffic and a capability to select from a variety of common carriers. One of the key results of this is that the host computer is relieved of extensive communications overhead processing.

**communications processor**  A microprocessor can be used as an interface or front end to the host processor, as shown in the figure on the next page. Some of the functions of the microprocessor are scheduling, data compression, polling, buffering, data link control, code conversion, and formatting.

**communications protocol**  A modem may use a particular type of

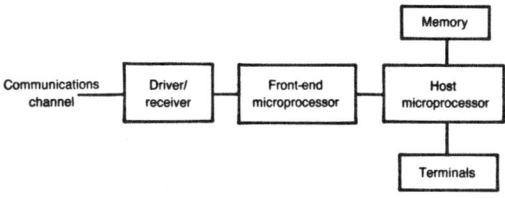

Typical communications processor applications

modulation as well as a particular communications protocol. The protocol sets the sequence in which the data is to be transmitted, the structure of the message, the method of synchronization for the transmitter and receiver, and the error checking procedure. Examples of protocols are IBM's binary synchronous communications (BISYNC), DEC's digital communications message protocol (DDCMP), and IBM's synchronous data line control (SDLC). The use of communications protocols has simplified many of the problems of data transfer between digital devices.

**communications satellite corporation** COMSAT. The United States representative in the international INTELSAT organization. COMSAT provides technical and operational services for INTELSAT under a management services contract and coordinates traffic from its operations center in Washington, D.C.

**communication statements** These are statements used to link a subprogram to a main program. The communication statements allow the subprograms to be called and returns to the main programs to be made. A few examples of communication statements are:
PROCEDURE CALL: Used to transfer control from a calling program to the called subprogram. Usually specific procedures are defined and used in this statement.
RETURN: Used to return control to the calling program from the subprogram.

**communications terminal** A point in a system or network at which data can be transmitted or received. A large amount of data communications is done over ordinary telephone lines using terminal devices and interfaces. Several leased lines are sometimes linked to improve the bandwidth and allow a heavier flow of traffic than is possible with single voice-grade lines.

**communications word** The partial set of characters used as a unit to store or transmit information in a communications system.

**community bulletin board** A message service that users with microcomputers can connect to using a telephone interface. These bulletin boards can handle notes of general interest as well as transfer programs among the participants.

**commutator pulse** A reference pulse that is used to mark, clock, or control a particular part of a word or a series of words.

**comp** A transient command of the PC DOS operating system that compares two disk files and reports where they differ. The files may be on the same or different diskettes.

**compaction** The methods used for reducing space, bandwidth, and costs in the transmission and storage of data. Compaction techniques tend to eliminate repetition and remove irrelevant operations and steps in coding data.

**comparator** A device or method used for checking two or more items for precise degree of similarity, equality, relative magnitude, or order.

**comparator check** A check made to compare original data and printed or punched data. The originals and the new data are run through a comparator check to uncover any errors made during processing operations. The checking of cards can be done on a match or nonmatch basis;

comparison of alphabetical and numerical data can be done either on selected columns and fields, or on entire cards.

**compare between limits** In some systems it is possible to do a comparison between upper and lower limits quickly and simply using only two compare memory and skip instructions.

**comparing unit** 1. A device used to compare two groups of time pulses and signals, on either an identity or a nonidentity basis. 2. A device used to check cards automatically on a match or nonmatch basis. Feeding, punching, and segregating are controlled by comparing cards from two separate files for a match or nonmatch condition. Comparison of both alphabetical and numerical data can be made on selected columns or fields or on entire cards.

**compatibility** The ability to interface without special adapters or other devices. The term relates to the ease of the transfer of data or programs between systems.

**compatibility, microprocessor** Refers to the electrical compatibility of microprocessors with other logic circuitry as required in most applications. Most microprocessors offer some degree of transistor-transistor logic (TTL) compatibility. The speed of metal-oxide semiconductor (MOS) circuitry frequently degrades as more loads are paralleled, requiring the addition of buffers even within portions of MOS only systems.

**compensator** A circuit used to alter the frequency response of an amplifier.

**compilation time** The time required to compile or translate a program, as opposed to the time when the program is actually being run.

**compile** To prepare a machine-language program from a program written in another language using the following techniques:
1. Using the overall logic structure of the program
2. Generating more than one machine instruction for each symbolic statement
3. Performing the function of assembly

**compiler** A coding or programming system that inputs source language data and outputs a program either in assembly or machine language. (Source languages used in compilers include FORTRAN, COBOL, APL, ALGOL, PL/1, Pascal, and others.)

The compiler provides a language that requires fewer statements for algorithm writing and eliminates the requirement for detailed coding to control loops, access data structures, and write complex formulas and functions. Below is a compiler statement with its equivalent in assembly language for the 8080 microprocessor. The compiler statements is in PL/M (a subset language for PL/1):

DECLARE (X, Y, Z) BYTE; IF X greater than Y
THEN Z = X − Y + 2; ELSE Z = Y − X + 2

The equivalent assembly language statement for the 8080 is:

```
              ORG 4000
BEGIN         LLI LOW X
              LHI HIGH X
              LAM;
              LLI LOW Y
              LHI HIGH Y
              LBM;
              SUB;

              ITS LOC2
LOC 1         ADI 2;
              LLI LOW Z
```

```
                LHI HIGH Z
                LMA
                JMP FINISH
LOC2            LCI 377
                XRC;
                ADI 1;
                JMP LOC1
FINISH          HLT
LOW X           EQU 70
HIGH X          EQU 10
LOW Y           EQU 71
HIGH X          EQU 10
LOW Z           EQU 72
HIGH Z          EQU 10
                ORG 4070
LOC X           DEF 0;
LOC Y           DEF 0;
LOC Z           DEF 0;
```

The compiler in this case provides instructions that are much easier to read, understand, and write. Programs tend to be easy to read and write, but sometimes at the cost of excessive storage space and slower execution times. A compiler that produces assembly language code allows the use of an assembly listing for checking and often helps to eliminate redundant data flow.

**compiler based system** A configuration that is organized on the structure of a language and operates by the direct execution or compilation of instruction sequences in that language. Compilation is done by translating instructions from a higher level language to instructions that are executed by the system. A system may arrange its configuration to conform with the program being compiled, to expedite the compilation and execution steps. Microprocessors can be used to implement the system based on a reconfigurable architecture. The system can be implemented by a multiprocessor array, along with supervisory and transfer functions controlled by other processors.

**compiler, consolidate** The final stage of compilation in which subroutines implicitly or explicitly called by a source program are inserted from a library file into the program being compiled.

**compiler level languages** High level languages that are normally supplied with computers by the computer manufacturer. APL, ALGOL, COBOL, BASIC, FORTRAN, are compiler level languages.

**compilers, high level** All higher level languages can use compilers or compiler programs to translate their commands and instructions into machine code before computers begin operations. See *interpreter*.

**compiling routine** A routine used to computer-construct a program.

**complement** In any radix system, the difference between any given digit and its base raised to the next higher power. For binary, the complement of 1 is 11. To check the accuracy of a complementing operation, add the number to be complemented with the complement to get the base or the next higher power of the base. Thus, to verify that 11 is the binary complement of 1, add 1 and 11:

```
        carry
          ↘ 1  1
            + 11
            ────
            100
```

In binary, $100 = 2^2$.

The complement $C$ can be obtained by subtracting the given number from the base raised to the power represented by the number of digits in the quantity, or

$$C = B^D - N$$

where $B$ = number base
$D$ = digits in number
$N$ = any number

**complement procedure** The method that relates the base and the system used to obtain the complement. See *complement*.

**complementary codes** Codes such as natural binary or binary coded decimal (BCD) in which bits are represented by their complements. In a 4 bit complementary binary converter, 0 may be represented by 1111, half scale (MSB) by 0111, and full scale (less 1 LSB) by 000. In a similar manner, for each quad of a BCD converter, a complementary BCD is obtained by representing all bits by their complements; thus, 0 is represented by 1111, and 9 is represented by 0110. The equivalents for 1 through 4 in the complementary binary and complementary BCD (with an overrange bit) are shown below:

| Decimal | Number | Natural Binary | Complementary Binary | BCD | Complementary BCD |
|---|---|---|---|---|---|
| 0 BIN. | DEC. | 0000 | 1111 | 00000 | 11111 |
| 1, 1/16, | 1/10 | 0001 | 1110 | 00001 | 11110 |
| 2, 2/16, | 2/10 | 0010 | 1101 | 00010 | 11101 |
| 3, 3/16 | 3/10 | 0011 | 1100 | 00011 | 11100 |
| 4, 4/16 | 4/10 | 0100 | 1011 | 00100 | 11011 |

**complementary metal-oxide semiconductor technology (CMOS)** A type of MOS transistor circuit used in microprocessors. This circuit uses complementary transistors (one p channel and one n channel device) for active pull up and pull down of the load. This complementary structure allows one transistor to be off when the other is on, resulting in a very low power dissipation. CMOS also offers designers high noise immunity, large fan out, and the use of inexpensive power sources.

**complementary MOS** CMOS. A process that combines both n-channel and p-channel MOS transistors (FETs) on the same chip in a complementary-symmetry configuration.

**complementary operator** A logic operator that produces the complement of any given logic operator (the NOT operator).

**complementary tracking** A system of interconnection of two regulated supplies in which one (the master) operates to control the other (the slave). The slave supply voltage is made equal (or proportional) to the master supply voltage and of opposite polarity with respect to a common point.

**complementation** An operation that results in the reverse significance in each digit position in a series of digits. If the word is:

$$0101100$$

then complementation gives 1010011.

**complementing** The use of complements to produce the negative equivalent of a number.

**complete carry** A technique used in parallel addition in which all carries are allowed to propagate to completion.

**complete operation** A computer operation that includes:

1. Obtaining all operands from storage
2. Performing the desired operation
3. Returning the results to storage
4. Obtaining the next instruction

**complex bipolar** This refers to a technique used to produce memories significantly faster than standard transistor-transistor logic (TTL) or emitter-coupled logic (ECL). It involves an extra diffusion that results in smaller resistors, low base and collector resistance in the transistors, and two layers of aluminum interconnections that reduce interconnection resistance. This technique produces fast memories, but at higher cost. Since speed is the prime requirement, the ECL circuit form is used. These ECL memory components can easily be made TTL compatible.

**complexity** A figure of merit or measure of the quantity of related parts or circuits. The total number of electronic parts is often used as the measure and complexity units are sometimes used as a preliminary and approximate measure.

**complex text** Refers to documents that require more flexibility and power for word processing operations. These operations can include searches, block movements, and automatic justification.

**compliance voltage** The output voltage range of a dc power supply operating in constant current mode. Compliance voltage is the voltage range required to sustain a given value of constant current throughout a range of load resistances.

**component** A functional part of a circuit, module, or system. A component can be a self-contained element or a combination of elements, parts, or assemblies.

**component density** The volume of a circuit assembly divided by the total number of discrete circuit components utilized.

**component error** Concerns the various errors related to a specific component such as the input and feedback impedances of an operational amplifier.

**component stress** The particular factors of usage or test, such as voltage, power, temperature, and frequency, which tend to affect the failure rate of electronic parts.

**composite cable** A cable in which conductors of different gauges or types are combined in one sheath.

**composite conductor** Refers to those conductors in which strands of different metals are used in parallel.

**composite filter** Relates to the combination of a number of filter sections or half sections all having the same cutoff frequencies and specified impedance levels.

**composite video** The signal for a cathode ray tube (CRT) consisting of picture signal, blanking, and sync pulses.

**compound logic** Logic that furnishes an output that is a function of many inputs.

**compound modulation** Modulation of signal that is already modulated, resulting in double modulation.

**compress** To reduce certain parameters of a signal while preserving the basic information content. Compressing usually reduces a parameter such as amplitude or duration of the signal to improve overall transmission efficiency.

**compute bound** The limiting of output rate due to delays caused by computing operations.

**compute limited** See *compute bound*.

**computer** A data processor that performs computations, including arithmetic and logic, usually without intervention by a human operator during the processing run.

**computer-aided design** The use of a computer for automated design purposes. See *CAD*.

**computer, analog** A computer that represents variables by physical analogies; any computer that solves problems by translating physical conditions such as flow, temperature, pressure, angular position, or voltage into related mechanical or electrical quantities and uses

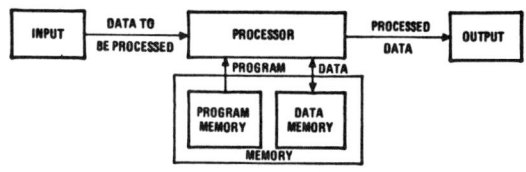

**Computer**

mechanical or electrical equivalent circuits as an analog for the physical phenomenon being investigated. It is a computer that uses an analog for each variable and produces analogs as output. An analog computer measures continuously, while a digital computer counts discretely.

**computer-assisted instruction** The use of a computer in a system that is used to assist in the instruction of students. These systems may involve a dialog between the student and the computer that informs the student of errors and offers guidance.

**computer, asynchronous** A computer in which the performance of each operation starts as a result of a signal either that the previous operation has been completed or that the parts of the computer required for the next operation are now available. Contrast with *computer, synchronous*.

**computer circuits** The circuits used in the construction of digital computers are the following: storage circuits, triggering circuits, gating circuits, inverting circuits and timing circuits. In addition, there may be other circuits used such as amplifiers for driving heavier loads, indicators, output devices, and amplifiers for receiving signals from external devices, as well as oscillators for obtaining the clock frequency.

**computer code** The machine language or code used within a computer system.

**computer configuration** A group of hardware units that are interconnected and arranged to operate as a system.

**computer dependent programs** Programs written using the specific language and/or features of a particular computer.

**computer instruction** A machine instruction used with a specific computer system.

**computer network** A system consisting of two or more interconnected computers. In addition to a host computer, a computer network usually contains the following facilities:

1. User communications interfaces
2. Communications networks
3. Network control hardware and software

**computer (computerized) numerical control (CNC)** A numerical control system wherein a dedicated, stored-program computer is used to perform some or all of the basic numerical control functions.

**computer output microfilm** A system (abbreviated *COM*) designed to replace a line printer as an output device; it is capable of producing high-quality text at 5000 lines or more per minute.

**computer part program** The definition of the workpiece geometry, motions, and commands, in a numeric/control (N/C) part programming language such as APT or Adapt. This is the input to the N/C language processor; the processor translates this input into CLDATA, and the postprocessor in turn translates this data.

**computer program** The series of instructions and statements prepared in order to solve a specific problem or achieve a certain result.

**computer run** The processing of a batch of transactions or the performance of one routine or several routines that are linked to form an operating unit. During a computer run, manual operations are usually not required from the human operator.

**computer, synchronous** A computer in which all operations and events are controlled by equally spaced pulses from a clock. Contrast with *computer, asynchronous*.

**computer system** An arrangement that uses several or many computing facilities in a cooperative manner. A computer system generally uses several small computers in dispersed locations for simpler tasks and a larger central computer for the more complex tasks. The central files are stored at the larger computer facility, and the smaller computers call on these files when required. This type of system reduces the load and cost of the central computer and results in overall cost savings.

**computer utility** A company that rents or leases computer facilities.

**computer word** The sequence of bits or characters that are treated as a unit and stored in one location. Same as *machine word*.

**COMSAT** Acronym for *Communications Satellite Corporation*, the privately owned United States communications carrier in charge of commercial communications satellite deployment.

**COM system** A *computer output microfilm* system serving the purpose of a line printer.

**concatenate** To link together in a series. A concatenated data set is one formed by combining the contents of several data sets in a specific sequence.

**concentrated data transmission** A form of data transmission that uses store and forward techniques for handling messages. These techniques include message switching and packet switching.

**concentrator** A processor, used in communication systems, that performs the following services:

1. Polling of local lines
2. Formatting of messages
3. Error correction and flags to operator

**concentricity** A measurement of the centering of a conductor within the insulation.

**concentric stranding** A technique used in stranding wire in which the final wire is built up in geometric layers so that the inner diameter of the succeeding layer is equal to the outer diameter of the underlying layer.

**concordance** A type of program that uses alphabetic lists of words and phrases with references. Concordance programs sometimes use a free-form assembler to produce the alphabetized listings, which are referenced by line numbers.

**concurrent** The occurrence of two or more events or activities within the same time period. Concurrent operating allows several programs to share a computer at the same time. Job processing is allowed to continue while the computer performs inquiry or utility operations using time-sharing or multiprogramming.

**concurrent operating control** Refers to operating systems that provide the ability for several programs to share the computer at the same time. Concurrent operations include task processing while performing inquiry or peripheral utility operations.

**concurrent processor** A machine capable of operating on more than one program at a time; a *multiprocessor*.

**condenser storage** A storage device that uses the capacitance of the medium to store information; capacitor storage.

**conditional breakpoint** A point in a program that causes the computer to stop because of a specified condition. The routine is continued from the breakpoint as coded, or another instruction is used to force a jump to another point.

**conditional code** Used to define a group of program instructions such as carry, borrow, and overflow. Conditional code instructions are important to program execution and are usually listed in a *condition code register*.

**conditional implication** A Boolean algebra operation defined by the following truth table:

| OPERAND | | RESULT |
|---|---|---|
| A | B | C |
| 0 | 0 | 1 |
| 1 | 0 | 0 |
| 0 | 1 | 1 |
| 1 | 1 | 1 |

**conditional jump** A jump that occurs only if specified criteria are satisfied. A conditional jump instruction may result in obtaining the correct addresses for the next instruction that produces a transfer of control. The next instruction can be dependent on the specified criteria as to whether or not a jump or skip to another instruction is called for.

**conditional stop** A program stop that is dependent upon specified conditions. Conditional stops can sometimes be controlled from the console by the operator.

**conditional transfer** A transfer of control that occurs only if specific conditions are met. If these conditions are not met, the program continues its normal sequence.

**condition code register** The condition code register in the 6800 is an 8 bit register used to indicate the results of an arithmetic and logic unit (ALU) operation such as negative (N), zero (Z), overflow (V), carry from bit 7 (C), and half carry from bit 3 (H). These bits are used to test conditions for conditional branch instructions. Bit 4 of the condition code register is used as the interrupt mask bit (I). Unused bits of this register are always ones. These bit positions are shown below.

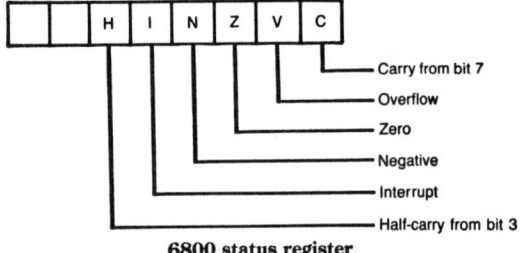

**6800 status register**

**condition codes** Codes that are used to contain information about the results of the last CPU operation, such as:

X = 1, if the result was zero
Y = 1, if the result was negative
Z = 1, if an overflow resulted

**conditioning** The processing of signals to make them more intelligible or more compatible in a given application. Signal conditioning may include pulse shaping, clipping, digitizing, and linearization.

**conditioning signal** A signal used to process the form or mode of data so as to make it intelligible to or compatible with a given device; includes such manipulation as pulse shaping, pulse clipping, digitizing, and linearizing.

**conductance** The physical property of an element, device, branch, network, or system that allows it to conduct electricity through a closed circuit.

**conductor** That part of a passive circuit path that carries electrical current.

**conduit** A tubular raceway for holding wires or cables.

**cone of error** The maximum error of dispersion of a missile at the point of reentry that can be corrected in time remaining until impact.

**confidence level** A measure of the degree of confidence of a device's or system's operation, usually expressed as a percentage of the probability of success.

**configurable array processor** A system in which the processors are arranged in an array for processing data that have some geometrical relationship to each other. A two dimensional array processor might operate on a two dimensional representation of the data to be processed, such as calculations with respect to a set of grid coordinates. If the two dimensional representation is changed to a different configuration of grid points, the system would reconfigure itself to another more suitable array configuration for the new task.

**configuration** A group or system of machines that are connected and programmed together.

**conjunction** The logic operation that uses the AND operator and results in the logical product. The AND function occurs when two or more gates are placed in series and follow the truth table below:

| GATE OR OPERAND A | GATE OR OPERAND B | AND OUTPUT C |
|---|---|---|
| 0 | 0 | 0 |
| 0 | 1 | 0 |
| 1 | 0 | 0 |
| 1 | 1 | 1 |

The conjunction of the two operands is written as AB or A • B or A × B.

**connection box** An electrical distribution panel similar in purpose to that of plug-board, which permits distribution or altering of the destinations of signals.

**connector** 1. A means of converging lines on a flow diagram. A flowchart connector can be used to represent a break in a flowline, or the divergence of a flowline into several lines. 2. A terminal designed for easy mating with a complementary terminal or adapter, as on a cable.

**connect time** The time period during which a remote terminal is connected to a time-shared system, usually marked by a *sign-on* and *sign-off*.

**consecutive** The occurrence of two sequential events without the interference of any other event.

**consecutive sequence computer** A computer in which all instructions are executed in a defined sequence unless specified to enter a jump operation.

**console** The part of a computer system that is used for communication between the computer operator and the central processing unit. The computer console may contain a start key, stop key, power control, sense switches, and register lights. Other console functions allow manual control, error correction, and status determination for counter and storage circuits. Some consoles allow the programmer to debug the program by slowly stepping the machine through each instruction and observing the status indicators; other consoles include a cathode ray tube terminal that may have pictorial capabilities as well as pointing aids such as light pens.

**console debugging** Refers to systems that permit the programmer to debug at the machine console or at a remote console by slowly stepping the machine through each instruction and observing the contents of appropriate registers and memory locations.

**console, visual display** Refers to a microcomputer development system that contains a visual display console to enhance operator system communications. The advantages of a visual display to the operator are great, and the possible display functions are large.

**constant** A fixed value or an item of data that does not vary. Constants are those quantities or messages that are available as data for the program and are not subject to change with time. A constant can be one character or a group of characters that represent a value and are used to identify, measure, or compare.

**constant area** That part of storage selected to store the invariable quantities required during processing.

**constant impedance multiplexer** A multiplexer in which the input resistor is terminated in a real or virtual ground; thus the input resistance is almost constant regardless of the channel selected.

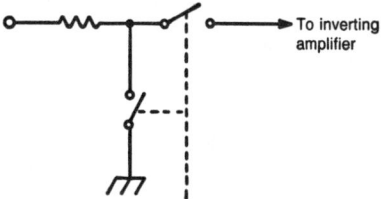

**Constant impedance multiplexer**

**constants, primary** Refers to those parameters of a transmission line such as capacitance, inductance, resistance, and leakage of a conductor to earth, per unit length of line.

**constructs** Detailed construction drawings produced using a patented process employing a computer and a plotter. Constructs allow human intervention when required and are commercially available through Control Data Corporation.

**contact** The part of a relay, switch, or connector that allows circuits to be closed by physically touching a similar part on a current carrying line. Circuits are opened by breaking the physical connection.

**contact alignment** Refers to electrical contacts and the sidewise movement or play in mating contact pins or other devices for plug or other contact insertions or surfaces.

**contact area** 1. The common area between two conductors through which an electric current flows. 2. The common surfaces between conductors or connectors of electricity.

**contact, bifurcated** Contacts used in printed circuits with slotted flat springs that increase flexibility of the spring and provide extra points of contact.

**contact float** Refers to the amount of give, movement, or side play that a contact has within the insert cavity to allow self-alignment of mated contacts and easy insertion of the plug or other contact surface.

**contact sensing** Refers to the techniques used to monitor and convert field switch contacts into digital information for input to a computer. Contact points are usually scanned at programmed intervals.

**contact separating force** Refers to the exertion or force necessary to separate or remove pins from sockets or connectors.

**content addressable memory** A type of random-access memory (RAM) in which the addresses of data can be retrieved upon command.

CAMs also provide a normal read/write technique, making them useful for:

1. Quick data searching
2. Correlation checking
3. Sorting items

Because of the dual accessing system and larger chips required, CAMs tend to cost more than conventional RAMs.

**contingency interrupt** An interrupt that occurs due to one of the following:

1. Operator requests use of the keyboard
2. Character typeout
3. Operator requests program stop
4. An overflow occurs
5. An invalid code

**continuous path operation** The controlling of the motion of a machine tool in space as a function of time such that the machine travels through the designated path at the specified rate. This generally requires the ability to simultaneously move more than one machine axis at coordinated rates.

**continuous simulation** A type of simulation represented by continuous variables scanned at regular intervals. Continuous simulation can be used for either linear or nonlinear differential equations.

**contouring** The ability provided by a continuous path system to produce a contour by moving the elements of a machine tool.

**control** The act or power of asserting authority in a specific plan of action. The control section of a computer will carry out the instructions in the proper sequence, interpret incoming instructions, and provide the proper output flags.

Instructions that determine jumps are called *control instructions*, and execution of instructions in the correct time sequence is called *flow of control*.

**control block** The circuitry that performs the control function of a central processing unit (CPU). In a typical microcomputer the control block will decode instructions and generate all control signals required for operation.

**control bus** A data pathway in a computer system that is used to regulate system operations. Control bus signals tend to operate like traffic signals or commands. They may originate in peripheral equipment and be under control of the bus register for access to the bus.

**control card** 1. A punched card that contains input data for initializing or modifying a program. 2. A punched card used in a sorting program for specifying the sorting parameters.

**control, cascade** Refers to a control system in which the various control units are linked in sequence, each control unit regulating the operation of the next control unit in line.

**control character** A character that initiates, modifies, or stops a control operation. A control character is generally not a graphic character, but it may have a graphic representation. A typical control character is used for nonprinting functions such as carriage return or line feed, or to control other operations such as recording, interpreting, transferring, and transmitting.

**control circuits** Circuits used to carry out program instructions in the correct sequence. Control circuits also interpret the program instructions and send the control signals through the system.

**control, common area** Refers to a memory control section used to reserve a main storage area that can be referred to by other modules.

**control console** A console that enables the operator to control and monitor all processing functions from a central location. The control console usually has a typewriter or other keyboard input to allow communication with the processor.

**control counter** A device used to record the location of the current instruction word. The control counter is sometimes used to select storage locations.

**control cycle** A cycle in the operation of a punch card machine in which feeding is stopped to allow a control change.

**control data** Any data item that is used to identify, select, modify, or execute an operation, routine, record, or file.

**control field** A location where control information is placed, usually constant and usually as a sequence of similar items.

**control function** Any action that affects the recording, processing, transmission, and interpretation of data such as starting and stopping, carriage return, font change, or rewinding.

**control instruction** An instruction that may (1) move data between the main memory and the control memory, (2) prepare main memory storage areas for processing, or (3) control the instruction sequence and interpretation.

**controller** A unit that operates automatically to regulate the performance of a controlled variable or system. Controllers use the data from the input and the output of a device to obtain the maximum and most efficient control of the device or process. Controllers are also used in computer systems for generation of signals to interface the CPU with memory and peripheral equipment. A typical controller chip performs all the control functions required for the flow of data at the interface.

**control logic** The control logic operates the sequence of operations within the microprocessor. It controls the various cycles and data transfers through the internal bus system. The control logic also provides external signals to let other modules know the status the microprocessor at any particular time. During a fetch cycle, the microprocessor generates a status signal to request an instruction from memory. During an execute cycle the microprocessor may be in a memory read, memory write, or input output status. The bidirectional bus buffers are controlled by the status request. When the microprocessor is requesting data from the external environment, the bidirectional bus is placed in an input mode. When it sends data to the external environment, the bus buffers are placed in the output mode and the information is placed on the data bus.

**control operation** Any action affecting the recording, processing, transmission, and interpretation of data; control function.

**control panel** The part of a computer console that contains the manual controls. The control panel may be implemented using switches, plugs, pins, or sockets to change instructions manually, or it may be implemented in software. Many microprocessors use a transparent control panel implemented in software with its own memory separate from the main memory. This frees the main memory and allows the control panel to be created as a unit and plugged in when needed without disturbing the main program.

**control program** A sequence of instructions that guides the central processing unit through the various operations or tasks programmed. Most often this program is permanently stored in read-only memory where it can be accessed but not erased by the CPU during operations.

**control ratio** The required change in control resistance to produce a one volt change in the output voltage of a power supply. The control ratio is expressed in ohms per volt.

**control read-only memory** CROM. A type of read-only memory that is designed and microprogrammed to decode control logic. A CROM

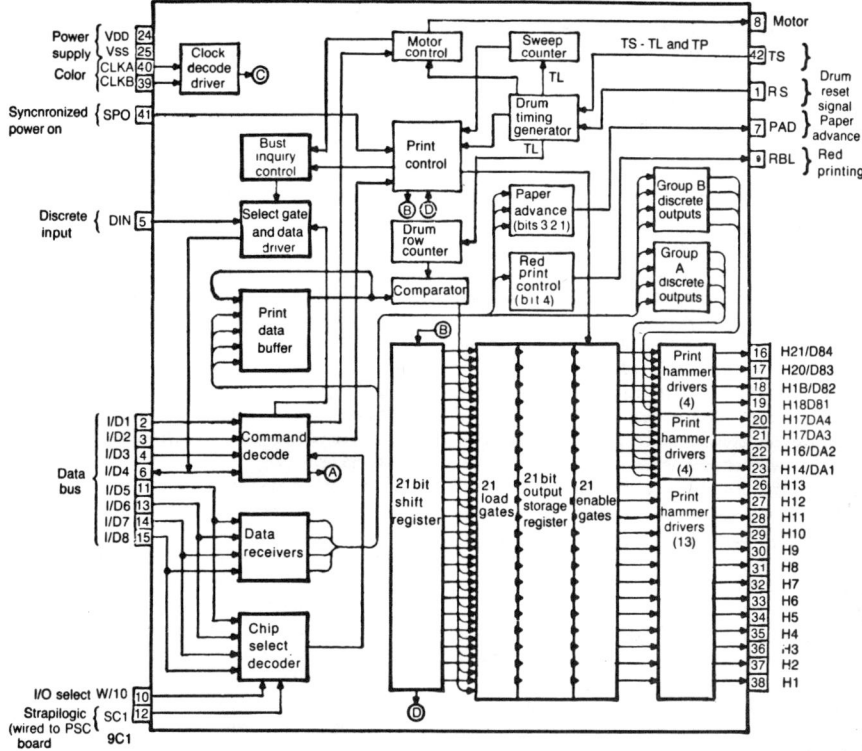

**Controller (For printer)**

is a major component of some microprocessors in which all actions of the CPU are controlled from the microprogram stored there. In general, the instructions are basic and have a short execution time, which makes it practical to use a large number of them in the program.

**control register** The register that stores the current instruction to control the CPU for the next cycle. Also called *instruction register*.

**control routine** Primary routines that control the loading and rerouting of other routines. Control routines are used in automatic coding and are sometimes considered as a part of the machine itself as opposed to another program. Sometimes called *monitor routine, supervisory routine,* or *supervisory program*.

**control section** The sequence of instructions within a program that can be replaced from outside the program segment that contains it. A typical control section is exchanged with control sections from other segments in many microcomputer systems.

**control sequence** The normal order for the selection of instructions for execution. The control sequence can be specified by an address in each instruction, or it may be consecutive except for jumps and transfers.

**control statements** These statements are instructions that direct the program flow and convey control information to the CPU. Control statements may cause transfers dependent upon specified conditions, but they do not cause the development of machine-language instructions.

**control store** An address register that allows the user to monitor the program point at which program operation is stopped. The control store register aids debugging and is usually monitored through the front panel of a ROM simulator.

**control system** A system that controls, analyzes, monitors, or measures a process or other equipment. Computers are integral parts of many modern control systems.

**control unit** The section of a computer that directs the sequence of operations, interrupts instructions, and sends control signals to other units in the computer system. Sometimes called the control section. A typical microcomputer has two control units: the CPU and the external logic control unit.

**conventions** Standard or accepted procedures in program and system analysis, which may include symbols, abbreviations, and special meanings.

**conversational** Descriptive of a program or system that can carry on dialog with the user. In the conversational mode, the system accepts input and then responds in real time. A conversational system can provide guidance to the user as to the form and content of the user response and is used in many teaching devices.

**conversational language** A language that uses a character set similar to English to aid communication between the user and the computer. BASIC is an example of a conversational language.

**conversion** The act of changing data or information from one form to another without changing the content of the data. Conversion equipment is used in many systems for transposing data from one form to another in order to make it acceptable to the input of another type of processing device.

**conversion device** Refers to various devices or pieces of peripheral equipment that convert data from one form into another form or medium, but without changing the data content or information.

**conversion equipment** Refers to the equipment that is capable of transposing or transcribing the information from one type of data processing medium to render it acceptable as input to another type of processing medium.

**conversion time** The time required to perform a conversion, such as a code conversion or a conversion from analog to digital data.

**convert** To change information from one base to another in order, for example, to transfer the data from the output of one unit to the input of another. Numerical data can be converted from binary to decimal, or from cards to tape.

**converter** 1. A device that changes the representation of data from one form to another and allows the form of data processing to change. For example, a converter may accept data on punched cards and store the information on magnetic tape with or without an editing function. 2. Any device that changes the level of a DC supply voltage to a higher value for powering hardware or peripherals.

**convex programming** A type of nonlinear programming used in operations research. The function is maximized or minimized to constraints that are convex or concave functions of the controlled variables.

**coordinate dimensioning** A system of dimensioning in which a point is defined as being a certain dimension and direction from a reference point as measured with respect to defined axes.

**coordinate dimension word** A word defining an absolute dimension.

**coordinate indexing** An indexing method in which all descriptors are correlated and combined to indicate interrelationships.

**coordinate storage** Storage in which all elements are arranged in a matrix so that any location can be identified using two or more coordinates. Examples of coordinate storage include cathode-ray storage, and core storage, which uses coincident-current techniques.

**copy** To reproduce data while leaving the source data unchanged. The physical form of the data may change as when a deck of cards is copied onto magnetic tape. A *hard* copy refers to any printed form of machine output, such as reports and listings.

**cordonnier system** An information retrieval system that uses cards with small holes drilled at the intersections of the column and row designations. Also called *peek-a-boo* and *batten* system.

**core** A toroidal memory array using small donut-shaped magnets, the fields of which may be used to represent digital ones and zeros. Magnetic core has been a major type of storage for many computers in the past.

**core allocation** The use of core memory as allocated in a system. Since memory is usually limited, core allocation is concerned with the division of memory for:

1. Programs to be permanently stored
2. Temporary storage of programs
3. Data to be permanently stored
4. Temporary storage of data
5. Working storage

**core memory** A memory that uses toroids in matrix arrays for storing binary digits. A core memory is a programmable random-access memory that uses ferromagnetic storage techniques.

**core storage** The storage of binary digits using magnetic cores, usually strung through wires in the form of a matrix array.

**correct** To fix errors or otherwise replace items in a program or document, usually by backspacing to remove unwanted items and rekeying to insert the desired material.

**correcting typewriter** A typewriter with the special capability of removing errors directly from the paper being typed, either by masking them over or directly lifting them off the sheet.

**correction program** A routine designed to be used after a failure, malfunction, or error. The routine is inserted at a point before the error, during a run or rerun of the program.

**corrective maintenance** Maintenance designed to eliminate existing faults. Corrective maintenance may occur as a part of emergency maintenance or deferred maintenance, and should not be confused with preventive maintenance, which is designed to prevent failures. Corrective maintenance time may be scheduled or unscheduled.

**correspondence center** 1. A word processing center. 2. A secretarial group performing typing activities.

**correspondence secretary** A secretary responsible for typing activities and assigned to a correspondence center; a word processor operator.

**correspondence study** A survey that identifies typing activities, including sources of input, and measures the volume of typing in an organization.

**COS** Abbreviation for *compatible operating system*.

**COSAR** Abbreviation for *compression scanning array radar*.

**cost/effectiveness** A constructed or designated measure of performance for the distinct evaluations of systems, products, or procedures. It is most often expressed as a ratio of some reference measure of cost and performance.

**coulomb** The quantity of electricity that passes any point in an electric circuit in one second when the current is maintained constant at one ampere.

**Coulomb's law** The law that states that the force of attraction or repulsion between two charges of electricity concentrated at two points in an isotopic medium is proportionate to the product of their magnitudes and is inversely proportionate to the square of the distance between them. The force between the unlike charges is an attraction, and between like charges a repulsion. Also called the law of electrical charge or law of electrostatic attraction.

**counter** A device used to measure and represent the number of occurrences of a specific event. Also known as an *accumulator*. Some types of counters can be set to an initial value and then increased or decreased (as an up-down counter). Others may be used as address counters or registers in which address data is loaded to specify the location where the next block of data is to be transferred.

A *counter* may be used as an index register that can be set to any number from storage, incremented by a certain number, and then tested against another number in storage. Index registers are used for address modifications and in programs involving repetitive steps.

Counters used as *cycle index counters* measure the number of times a cycle of instructions has been repeated. A cycle index register can be used to determine the number of repetitions required in a loop at any given time.

**counter comparator conversion** A type of analog-to-digital converter; the counter comparator A/D converter, as shown below, is analogous to the single ramp type, except it is independent of a time scale. The analog information is compared with the output of a D/A converter, and the digital input of the D/A is driven by a counter. At the start of a conversion, the counter begins the count, which continues until the D/A output exceeds the input value. Now, conversion stops and the converter is ready for the next conversion once the counter is reset to zero.

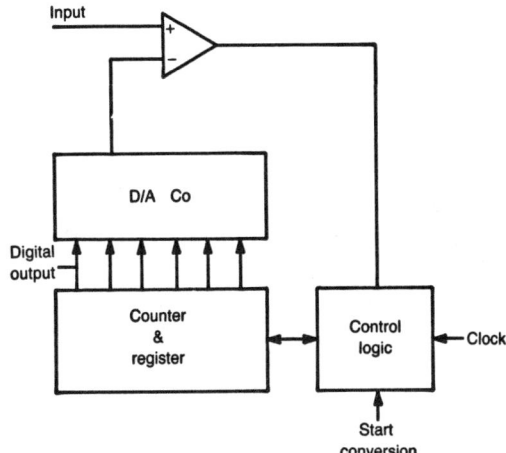

Counter-comparator A/D converter

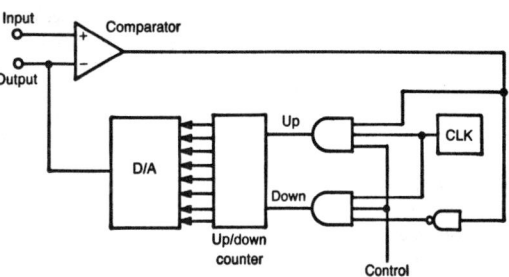

Counting sample hold

**counter, control** A device within a computer that records the storage location of the instruction word to be operated on following the instruction word in current use.

**counter, cycle** A counter constructed of hardware or software that is used to keep track of a particular set of events.

**counter, program** A register that holds the identification of the instruction word to be executed next in the time sequence, following the current operation. The register is often a counter that is incremented to the address of the next sequential storage location, unless a transfer or other special instruction is specified by the program.

**counting, sample hold** Sample hold counting uses a digital-to-analog converter, an up-down counter, a comparator clock, and logic gates. The initial acquisition time can be very long, since the clock period ($t_s$) depends on the least-significant bit settling time of the D/A converter, and the number of counts (n) depends on the resolution. For a full scale step, the acquisition time is approximately $(2^n - 1)\, t_s$. Smaller, slower changes are followed rapidly. The system can also be converted into a peak follower by disabling the up count function. The range of input signal levels and polarity will determine the choice of D/A converter. A binary coded decimal (BCD) counter and BCD DAC can be used with a display for a maximum peak digital voltmeter.

**couple, chip select decode** Refers to the use of chip selects of memories to achieve a partial decode of the high order addresses. For small systems this can be sufficient to discriminate among all memory locations.

**coupled circuit** A network that contains only resistors, inductors, and capacitors with more than one independent mesh.

**coupler** A device that transfers signals and has its input and output isolated electrically. Also known as an isolator, a coupler usually consists of a light-emitting diode (LED) and a light sensor. The input signal activates the LED, which in turn forces current through the output light sensor. When the two devices are separated by an air gap rather than glass or plastic, the coupler can be used to sense motion and encode cards, plates, and slotted disks.

**coverage** A percentage of the completeness with which a braid or shield covers the surface of the underlying insulated conductors.

**COZI** Abbreviation for *communications zone indicator*.

**CPE** Abbreviation for *central processing element*. An element of a bit-slice microprocessor that contains all of the major processing circuits necessary to build processors of longer word lengths. CPEs can be cascaded to form a processor of any desired word length. Multiple bus structures allow functions to be executed in a single microcycle instead of several cycles.

**CP/M** Control program for microprocessors, a popular disk operating system for microcomputers developed by Digital Research, Inc.

**CPS** Abbreviation for *character per seconds*, a standard unit of measurement for printer output.

**CPU** Abbreviation for *central processing unit*. A primary unit of the computer system that controls the interpretation and execution of instructions. A CPU may consist of registers, computational circuits such as the arithmetic and logic unit, control circuits, and input/output ports. The registers may include accumulators, index registers, and perhaps stack registers. All registers are treated as internal memory.

**CR** The carriage return character.

**CRC** The cyclic redundancy check character.

**crippled leapfrog** Refers to a variation of the leapfrog tests to discover computer malfunctions. The crippled leapfrog tests are done from a fixed set of locations rather than the changing locations used in the leapfrog tests.

**criterion** Refers to a value used for testing, comparing, judging, or determining whether a condition is plus or minus, true or false; also, a rule or test for making a decision.

**critical path** A scheduling system that uses milestones to check the progress of the task.

**CRO** Abbreviation for *cathode ray oscillograph*.

**CROM** Abbreviation for *Control Read-Only Memory*, a type of ROM that is designed and microprogrammed to decode control logic. The CROM is a major component of many two-chip microprocessors. One chip contains the CPU and the other a CROM that accesses the correct routine for each instruction, sequences through the routine, and provides the data control signals to the CPU.

**cross assembler** An assembler translates a symbolic representation of instructions and data into a form that can be loaded and executed by the microprocessor. A cross assembler is an assembler executing on a machine other than the microprocessor that generates object code for it. Initial development time can be significantly reduced by taking advantage of a larger scale computer's processing, editing and high speed peripheral capability. Some systems consist of a simulation program, which enables the computer to simulate the operation of a microcomputer, and an assembly program used to program the microcomputer.

**cross compiler** A program that prepares a machine-language program on one computer for another computer. A cross compiler can replace a cross assembler in many high-level language applications to allow extra convenience to the programmer.

**cross coupling** The usually unwanted inadvertent transfer of signals and signal components between circuits or channels.

**crossfoot** The punching of results of another field in punched cards due to the adding and subtracting of numbers from different fields in the same card.

**cross modulation** A form of signal distortion found in multiple-carrier systems; crosstalk. Cross modulation may be caused from the effects of the envelope of one carrier upon the other due to nonlinearity in the common transmitting medium.

**crosstalk** The undesirable energy transferred from one circuit to another. The source of the energy is called the disturbing circuit and the circuit receiving the energy is called the disturbed circuit. *Far-end* crosstalk propagates in the same direction as the signals, and *near-end* crosstalk propagates in the opposite direction.

**cross training** The switching of personnel among various work stations so that they may learn more than one job.

**cross validation** The verification of results by replicating an experiment under independent conditions.

**CRT** Abbreviation for *cathode-ray tube*. CRTs are used for both display and storage in computer systems. As a display, the CRT can be operated in the point mode to allow points to be established and displayed on the screen. CRT storage uses the electron beam to sense the presence or absence of spots on the CRT screen.

**cryogenics** The study and use of properties of materials at temperatures approaching absolute zero. Cryogenic elements offer high-speed storage from the superconductivity that occurs at near-zero temperatures. Since superconductors have no resistance, they also have the ability to store currents permanently.

**cryotron** A device operated at low temperatures to allow changes in small magnetic fields to control large currents; the cryogenic equivalent of an electron tube.

**CS** Abbreviation for *channel status*.

**cue** The action made by the calling party in a communications mode, which serves as the signal for a subsequent series of events to begin.

**cupping** Curvature of a tape in the lateral direction, which is usually measured in terms of the angle formed by the conjunction of lines drawn perpendicular to the tape surface at opposite edges.

**current** The rate of flow of electrical carriers past a given point, usually measured in amperes.

**current attenuation** The loss of current in a device or circuit or along a line, usually expressed as the ratio of output to input current in decibels.

**current balance** Refers to a form of balance in which the force required to prevent the movement of one current carrying coil in the magnetic field of a second coil carrying the same current is measured.

**current density** The amount of current passing through a given area of a conductor, usually expressed in amperes per square centimer ($A/cm^2$).

**current gain** In a transistor, the ratio of change in collector current at constant voltage, resulting from a change in emitter current.

**current instruction register** A register that contains the instruction presently being executed.

**current loop** The electrical interface to a magnetic bubble memory. At specific points within a bubble track, conductors are deposited under the permalloy element in the form of single loops. Passing a pulse of current temporarily alters the level of the bias field under the permalloy element.

**current multiplexer** In the current multiplexer the input resistor is removed to allow the multiplexing of current output transducers as shown below. When current output switching is used, the transfer accuracy is relatively unaffected by variations in line and connection resistance.

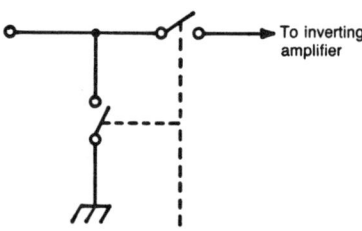

**Current multiplexer**

**current shunt instrumentation amplifier** Since instrumentation amplifiers can measure voltage differences at any level within their range, they are useful in current measurements. Typically, they measure and amplify the voltage appearing across a low resistance shunt, as shown below.

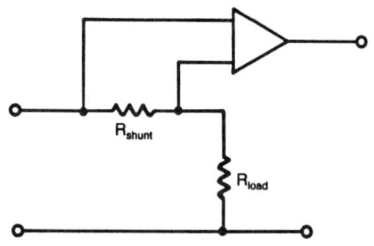

**Instrumentation amplifier**

**current source sample hold** A sample hold circuit that has an advantage in that the capacitor does not load the input source, which may either oscillate or lack the current to charge the capacitor fast enough. For faster charging at close to a linear slew rate, a diode bridge is used, as shown below. The current sources are switched on to charge the capacitor. If the bridge and current sources are balanced, current flow into the capacitor stops when the capacitor voltage is equal to the input voltage.

**current switching D/A converter** A digital-to-analog converter in which the switches and resistors are grouped as quads, with repeated

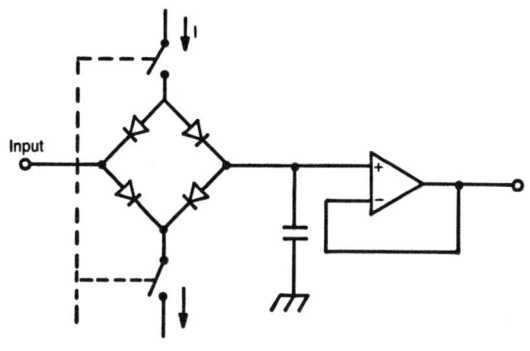

**Current source sample hold**

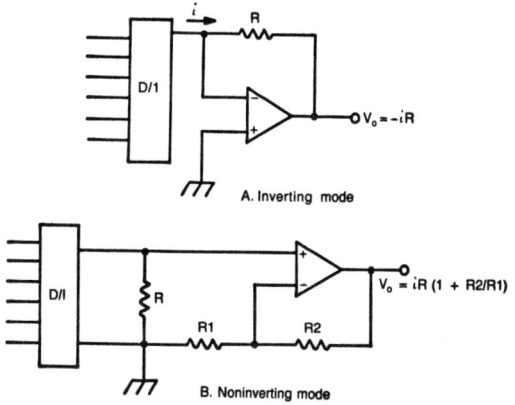

A. Inverting mode

B. Noninverting mode

**Current-to-voltage conversion**

2R, 4R, 8R, 16R resistance values and 8:1 maximum range for bit currents. The less significant bit currents are attenuated in the output line as shown. With the quad structure there are only four different current values, which eases current matching. The attenuation allows the tolerances on the resistor values and transistor tracking in the less significant quads to be relaxed. In the monolithic quads, the switching transistors have emitter areas with a power to two relationship to maintain a constant current density and equal tracking of $V_{BE}$ and beta. The reference transistor, on the same chip, is usually identical to one of the switching transistors.

**current to voltage converters** Converters that use current outputs or voltage outputs directly from resistive ladders can be considered as voltage generators with series resistance or current generators with parallel resistance. They can be used with operational amplifiers in either an inverting or the noninverting mode as shown below. Some types use internal feedback resistors for output voltage scaling. These track the ladder resistors to minimize temperature variations. The gain determining feedback resistances do not track the converter's internal resistors, only one another.

**current unidirectional** A current that, on the average, maintains the same direction in a circuit. It can fluctuate or go negative.

**cursor** A manually controllable pointer used as a position or location indicator in a display. A cursor is usually employed to indicate a character to be changed or corrected, or a position where data is to be entered via the display keyboard. The cursor may take the form of an underscore, an undertext caret, or an arrow.

**curtate** That part of a punched card consisting of adjacent punched rows.

**custom ROMs** Refers to a mask programmed read-only memory, in which the manufacturer places the binary information into the memory as specified by the user. Custom programming of ROMs is expensive when only small quantities are ordered. To reduce the high cost of small quantities of ROMs, one can use the field programmable ROM or PROM. The user can program information into the PROM by blowing selected on-chip fuses. The fuses are blown open by passing a specific amount of current through them.

**cutter diameter compensation** A method in automatic machining by which the programmed path may be altered to allow for the difference between actual and programmed cutter diameters.

**cutter path** The path described by the cutter in order to generate the desired part configuration in automatic machining.

**cutter radius offset** The distance from the part surface to the radial center of a cutter in automatic machining.

**cybernetics** The science of communication and control in living organisms and the corresponding simulation through the use of:

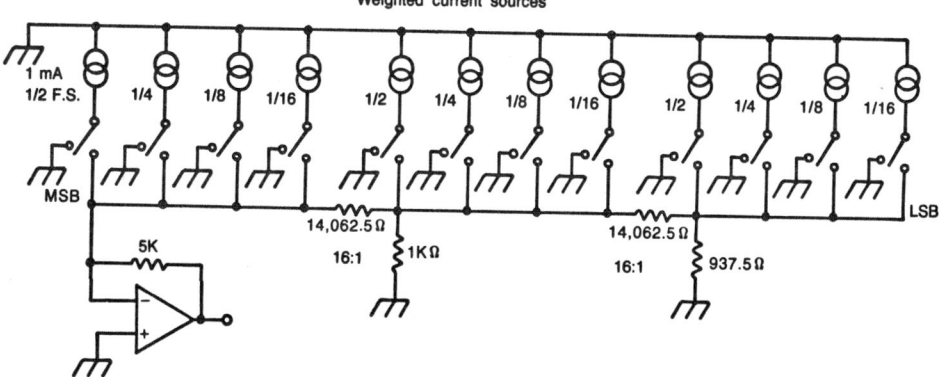

**12-Bit current switching D/A converter**

1. Integration of communication and control technology
2. Systems engineering development
3. Hardware and software application development

The field of cybernetics has aided technology forecasting and assessment, systems modeling, policy analysis, pattern recognition, and artificial intelligence development.

**cycle** One complete revolution in a repetitive sequence of revolutions; the operations are allowed to vary, but the sequence must retain a regular pattern. A computer cycle refers to a nonarithmetic shift in which digits are taken from one end of a word and moved to the other end, or to the repetition of a set of operations a required number of times. Cycling may include the supplying of address changes using a cycle counter to measure the number of times the cycle is to be repeated. An *action* cycle is the complete cycle operation performed on a block of data, including origination, manipulation, and storage.

**cycle availability** That specific time period during which stored information can be read.

**cycle counter** A mechanism or device that measures the number of times a specified cycle is repeated.

**cycle criterion** The total number of times the cycle is to be repeated; also the register that stores that number.

**cycled interrupt** A change of control to a specific operation, usually in a predetermined manner such as a specific sequence or operation cycle.

**cycle index** An index of the number of times a cycle has been executed or is to be executed. A cycle index register can be set to the number of cycles desired; then each cycle shifts the register down by one until it is empty and the cycle series is complete.

**cycle shift** The nonarithmetic shift in which digits are taken from one end of a word and shifted to the other end.

**cycle stealing** A method of delaying execution of a program to allow an operation that would normally require a complete cycle for completion. A cycle-stealing data channel will allow the storage of a data word without changing the processor logic. After the word is stored, the program can continue as though never stopped. A cycle steal is different from an interrupt in that it does not change the contents of the instruction register.

**cycle time** The interval between calling for and delivery of information from storage, or any regular sequential time interval such as required to complete specific operations or execute instructions.

**cyclic check** A cyclic method of error detection that is used to check the $x + n$ bit where $n = 1, 2, 3 \ldots$. The cyclic check is usually preferred over horizontal, vertical, or combinational checks.

**cyclic binary code** A binary code, also called *Gray code*, in which sequential numbers differ by only one place and in that one place differ by only one unit place. The cyclic binary code can be used to minimize the error at transition points in a code, since the error can be no greater than one unit space.

| DECIMAL | CYCLIC BINARY (GRAY) | BINARY |
|---|---|---|
| 0 | 0000 | 0000 |
| 1 | 0001 | 0001 |
| 2 | 0011 | 0010 |
| 3 | 0010 | 0011 |
| 4 | 0110 | 0100 |
| 5 | 0111 | 0101 |
| 6 | 0101 | 0110 |
| 7 | 0100 | 0111 |
| 8 | 1100 | 1000 |
| 9 | 1101 | 1001 |
| 10 | 1111 | 1010 |
| 11 | 1110 | 1011 |
| 12 | 1010 | 1100 |
| 13 | 1011 | 1101 |
| 14 | 1001 | 1110 |
| 15 | 1000 | 1111 |

**cyclic code** Any code that differs by only one bit between numbers. The cyclic binary code or Gray code is useful for positional measurement, since errors between positions will differ by only one significant bit. The cyclic decimal code uses 4-bit binary words to represent decimal numbers. In going from one decimal digit to the next sequential digit, only one binary digit changes its value.

**cyclic decimal code** Refers to a four-bit binary code word in which only one digit changes state between any two sequential code words, and which translates to decimal numbers. This code is one of a group of unit distance codes.

**cyclic memory** A memory that can be accessed only at multiples of the cycle time.

**cyclic polynomial** A detection method that uses division by a polynomial to check for errors. A cyclic polynomial check is a good test for single, double, and odd numbers of errors. If, after the division process, a remainder occurs, an error is present. The division can be done using a shift register, which also provides the checksum. A cyclic sum check results if the checksum data from the shift register is fed back through the register again.

**cyclic redundancy** An error detection method that uses redundant check bits. A cyclic redundancy generator is used to generate a stream of check bits that are divided by the same polynomial as the data bits; a nonzero remainder indicates that an error has been detected.

**cyclic redundancy check character** A character (abbreviated *CRC*) used as a redundant character for error detection in various modified cyclic codes.

**cyclic shift** A shift in which data is moved from one end of a word in a register to the other end. If the register holds:

00110011

then a cyclic shift of two bits gives:

11001100

This is also called a *circular shift, end-around shift, logical shift, ring shift,* and *nonarithmetic shift*.

**cyclic storage** A storage system which operates as a closed loop; sometimes called *circulating storage*.

**cyclic storage access** Descriptive of a storage unit that allows access only during specific, equally spaced intervals. Cyclic access is found in units such as magnetic drums.

**cycling** The periodic change allowed on a variable or function by a control system or controller.

**cycling control** A fundamental machine control that programs the machine using a dial or plugboard input.

**cylinder** A term used primarily with hard disks to refer to the number of tracks on a disk drive that can be accessed without repositioning the recording heads. Each side of a diskette or platter that holds information is considered a cylinder.

# D

**D/A** 1. Abbreviation for *digital-to-analog conversion*. 2. Abbreviation for *data acquisition*. 3. Abbreviation for *discrete address*.

**D/A converters** The basic D/A converter circuit consists of a reference, a set of binary weighted precision resistors, and switches as shown below. In this circuit, an operational amplifier holds one end of all the resistors at zero volts. The switches are operated by digital logic. Each switch that is closed adds a binary weighted increment of current $E_{REF}/R_j$ through the summing bus at the amplifier's negative input. The output voltage is proportional to the total current, which is a function of the value of the binary number. In an application that required 12 bit D/A conversion, the range of resistance values needed would be 4,096:1 or up to 40M for the least significant bit.

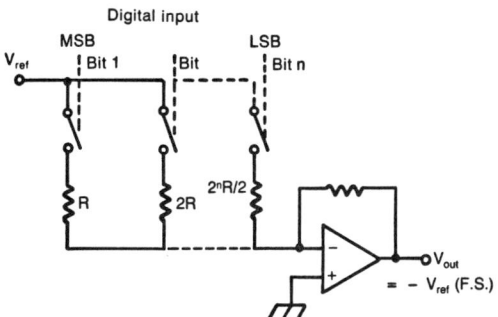

**Basic D/A converter**

**DAC** 1. Abbreviation for *digital-to-analog converter*. 2. Abbreviation for *data acquisition and control*.

**DAF** Abbreviation for *Department of the Air Force*.

**daisy chain** A bus system used in microprocessors in which units are interconnected and signals are transferred in serial fashion. The F8 microprocessor uses daisy-chain memory chips. Each unit is allowed to accept one interruption input, and the chips closest to the CPU have priority when requesting service. In a daisy-chain bus system, each unit can modify the signal before passing it on to the next device in the chain; when a device requires service, it blocks the signal. The first units in the chain thus have priority in the bus system.

**daisy chain bus** A bus that is similar to a party line, except that the connections are made in serial fashion. Each unit may modify the signal before passing it on to the next device. This approach is used mainly for signals related to interrupts or polling circuits. Whenever a device requires service, it blocks the signal. A priority is thus established, since the devices that are closest to the microprocessor usually have the first chance to request service.

**daisy chain polling** An I/O polling method that is software driven, with the help of additional hardware, and uses a linked chain to identify the device. This is shown below. After preserving the registers, the microprocessor generates an interrupt acknowledge, which is gated to device A. If device A generated the interrupt, it places an identification number on the data bus, where it is ready by the microprocessor. If it did not generate the interrupt, it will propagate the acknowledge signal to device B. Device B will then follow the same procedure.

**daisy chain structure** A bus structure in which the information passes through each system element until it arrives at the correct device. Each device acts as both a source and acceptor on the bus.

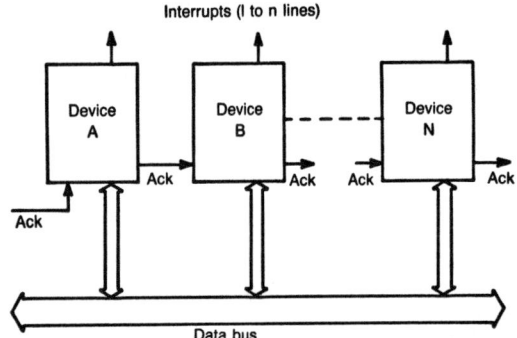

Daisy chain polling technique

**daisy wheel** A plastic or metal print wheel on certain types of impact printers, so called because of its symmetrical "petals."

**daisy wheel printer** A hard copy device that creates characters by use of a print wheel. Also known as a *correspondence printer*.

**DAM** Abbreviation for *data acquisition and monitoring*.

**DAMP** Abbreviation for *downrange antimissile measurement project*.

**damping** The reduction of oscillatory conditions in control devices and systems to improve stability. Damping may be done to electrical and mechanical components and generally falls within three classifications:

1. *Critically damped*—no overshoot or undershoot occurs (optimum response)
2. *Underdamped*—overshoot occurs (excessive oscillation)
3. *Overdamped*—no overshoot or undershoot (response too slow)

**DAMS** Abbreviation for *defense against missiles system*.

**DAR** Abbreviation for *data access register*.

**Darlington** A monolithic circuit consisting of two direct-coupled transistors connected to function as one. A Darlington circuit provides high current gains, which makes it useful as a driver circuit in computer applications.

**DART** Abbreviation for *data analysis recording tape*.

**DASA** Abbreviation for *Defense Atomic Support Agency*.

**DASD** Abbreviation for *Data Access Storage Device*.

**DASH** Abbreviation for *drone anti-sub helicopter*.

**DAST** Abbreviation for *Division for Advanced Systems Technology*.

**DAT** Abbreviation for *dynamic address translator*.

**data** A graphic or textual representation of facts, concepts, numbers, letters, symbols, or instructions suitable for communication, interpretation, or processing. Data may be source data or raw data, which is then refined to suit the user by processing. Data is the basic element of information that is used to describe objects, ideas, conditions, or situations.

**data access arrangement** An interfacing unit required between non-Bell and Bell equipment on a direct-dial network.

**data access register** A register used in some microcomputers for random-access memory stacking address arithmetic. A typical register system uses three registers: a program counter, a stack pointer, and the operand address. Sixteen instructions allow decrement/increment and register transfer within a single clock cycle.

**data acquisition** Data acquisition is typically concerned with the collection and processing of data for any or all of the following purposes:

1. Storage for later use
2. Transmission to another location
3. Processing to obtain additional information
4. Display for analysis or recording

Data can be stored in raw or processed form; it can be retained for short or long periods, transmitted over long or short distances, or displayed on a digital panel meter or a cathode-ray tube as shown in the figure.

**data acquisition and control** The system used to collect or gather data and prepare it for further processing. Data acquisition and control equipment may include transducers, transducer amplifiers, multiplexers, and data converters as well as logging units such as magnetic tape, disks, printers, plotters, and card and paper-tape units. A typical system samples analog voltages, scales them, and converts them to digital format for recording or printout.

**data acquisition module** A typical module for data acquisition may have 8 differential input channels and 16 single-ended input channels for 12 bit data acquisition in a 72 pin package. Acquisition and conversion time combined are 20 microseconds giving a throughput rate of 50 kHz. The twelve bit binary data can be transferred out in three four-bit bytes, by the three state data bus drivers. Output coding is straight binary in unipolar operation and offset binary in bipolar operation.

The circuit shown includes a multiplexer, programmable amplifier, sample hold circuit complete with hold capacitor, 10 volt buffered reference, and a twelve bit A/D converter with three state outputs along with digital logic.

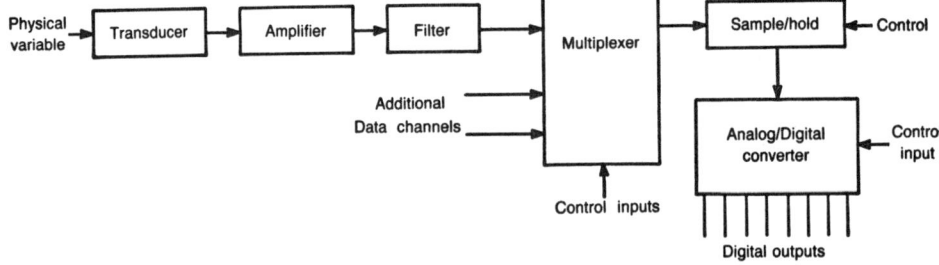

Typical data acquisition system

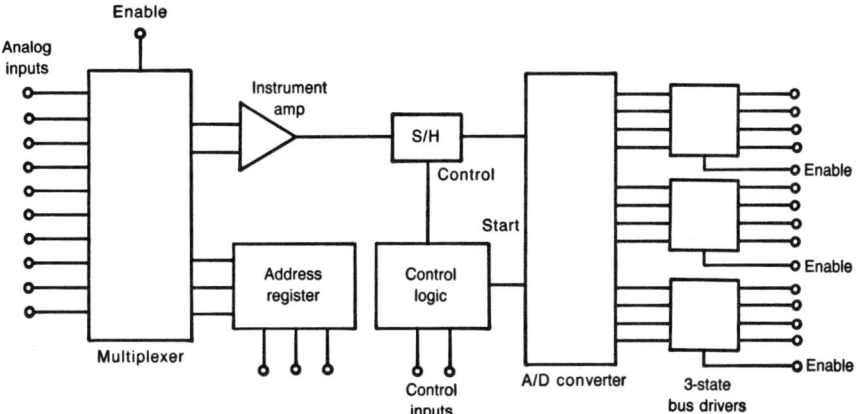

Data acquisition module

**data acquisition system board** A typical data acquisition system board might be capable of a 110 kHz throughput rate with 12 bit resolution. In this system a sample hold is used with a high-speed hybrid 12-bit A/D converter and a monolithic analog multiplexer. The basic configuration is shown below. The sample hold might have a 1 microsecond acquisition time while the A/D converter does a conversion every 8 microseconds.

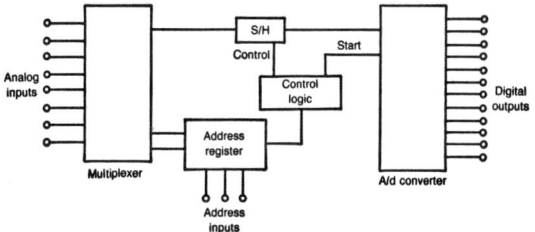

Data acquisition system board

**data, analog** A physical representation of information such that the representation bears an exact relationship to the original information.

**data bank** A collection or library of data. An invoice may form a *record* in an application, a set of records forms a *file*, and the collection of files becomes the data bank.

**data base** A collection of data, usually larger than a file, that is sufficient for a given purpose in a data processing application.

**data bus** A bus used in many microprocessor systems for transferring data to and from the CPU and the storage and peripheral devices. A typical microprocessor uses three buses: a data bus, a timing bus, and a control bus. The data bus is independent of the processor and handles all communications between any pair of devices connected to the bus.

**data bus system** In most microsystems all communication between modules in the microcomputer occurs over the system data bus. This bus is usually independent of the processor and handles communications between any two devices connected to the bus. In order to transfer information over the bus, a device first requests access through the bus priority network of bus control. If no higher priority request is present, control of the bus is granted, and the device then becomes bus master for one bus cycle. During this cycle, the master may address any other bus-connected device (which becomes the slave) and may command a transfer of data to or from the slave.

**data capture, direct** A technique employed for cash sales, using sales slips on which customer account numbers, the amount of the purchase, and other information are automatically recorded, read by an optical reading device, and sent to the computer to be processed. Its use permits the generation of more timely and accurate transaction data.

**data chain** A combination of two or more data elements in a sequence to provide meaningful information. A data chain called *Date* would consist of these data elements: year, month, and day.

The sequence would range from low to high or high to low for machine processing. Data chaining is used for the gathering of scattering of information within one record from or to more than one region of memory.

**data channel** A bidirectional data path or bus between input/output devices and the main memory, which usually allows concurrent operations.

**data code** A data code can be a set of numbers, letters, characters, or symbols used to represent a data item such as a record, a file, or a word.

**data collection, stations** Units on production floors used to collect employee payroll data and other information, for entry into computer systems.

**DATA com** Abbreviation for *data communications*.

**data communication** The transmission and reception of data generally using some form of electrical transmission. Data communication can be aided by using a data communications control unit, which scans the central terminal for messages and then transfers them to the processor. Another technique involves using a data station as a remote terminal for communication with a central computer. When not in use for transmission, the data station can be used for data preparation and editing tasks.

**data communication processing** Data communication processing functions that can be performed by microcomputers include:

1. Message switching by the processing and communication of messages over limited-channel capacity systems.

2. File management through the remote updating of a centralized file, or other file handling and processing functions from a remote location.
3. Inquiry/response systems, which are another form of a file-oriented system in which a remote station makes inquiries of a centralized file but does not change that file.
4. Data collection through the use of a remote station that provides updated or current information to a centralized file.

**data compaction** The methods used to reduce space, bandwidth, generating time, and other factors that add to the cost of data storage and transmission. Compaction methods tend to eliminate needless repetition and other irrelevancies.

**data compression** The methods that are used to increase unused storage space by eliminating gaps, redundancies, and unnecessary data, and shortening the length of records, fields, and blocks.

**data, continuous** 1. Continuous measures are those that may be found at any point along a continuous scale. Examples are thermometers, speedometers, and analog sensing devices. 2. Sometimes used in a broad sense to indicate all quantitative data, including that of a quantal nature.

**data conversion line** The channel used to transfer data elements between data banks.

**data converter** Devices that convert analog data to a digital format or vice versa. Converters are available in either hybrid or monolithic form.

**data descriptor** An identifier used to describe a data area by pointing to one or more data locations in storage.

**data element** The basic items of data appearing in a set of data. A data element can be used to denote a set of data items. For example, *Monday* is a data item denoted by the data element of *weekday*. Data elements can always be broken down into subcategories of data, usually data items.

**data element dictionary (DED)** An organized listing of data elements and their associated information in a given system.

**data entry** The transferral of information into a computer for processing. Typical data entry equipment includes terminal keyboards, card or tape readers, and teletypewriters. Data entry terminals contain a keyboard, a communications module, status panel, a display, and a power supply.

Many terminals use microprocessors to allow special functions to be programmed by the user. This technique produces cleaner data for the host computer and reduces reruns. Special collection methods can be designed for specific customers in payroll, accounts receivable, and other areas tailored for the application.

**data flowchart** A graphical representation of the path of data for a program or problem solution. The flowchart defines the major phases of the process. Also called *data flow diagram*.

**data format** The rules and procedures defining the system used to show the data used in records, files, or words. Data formats are usually defined by statements that can instruct the assembly program in the area of constants, spaces, and punctuation.

**data handling system** 1. A system of automatic and semiautomatic devices used in the collection, transmission, reception, and storage of information in digital form. 2. A system in which data is sorted, reduced, or stored in a particular form.

**data hierarchy** The structure of data consisting of sets and subsets of data in an ordered sequence. Each subset of data is of lower rank than each set of data.

**data input bus** A single-bus structure used in some microcomputers.

The processor, memory, and input/output devices all share this common bus. A switch register is used to transfer address codes and data between units.

**data item** An individual member of a set of data, usually classified under a data element. *Tuesday* is a data item of the data element *weekday*.

**data link** The communications circuits, lines, and other equipment used in the transmission of information between two or more stations.

**data link escape character** A communication control character used to form an escape sequence allowing supplementary communication control operations. Only graphic characters along with communication control characters are allowed to construct an escape sequence.

**data logging** The recording of data concerning events that occur in a time sequence. Data logging equipment ranges from simple visual readout devices to complex systems using microprocessors. Data logging applications include:

1. Process monitoring
2. Environmental monitoring and pollution measurements
3. Product research and development engineering
4. Structural testing for strength, stress, strain, and vibration

**data medium** The method used to transport or hold data or information. A data medium may be punched cards, punched tapes, magnetic tapes, or other physical methods that can be varied to represent data.

**data migration** The movement of data from online or offline as determined by the system or requested by the user.

**data movement, microprocessor** In microprocessor based systems, data movement is an important aspect of system operation. As new systems evolve, users must evaluate microcomputers with a critical eye toward input/output transfer. The number of instructions is less important than the nature of the instructions and usable addressing modes. There is a need to know how quickly the CPU can respond to a peripheral interrupt and how the interrupt is managed as well as what is available in the way of interface devices. The list of questions depends on the needs of the user.

**data name** An identifier for an item of data.

**data phone** A product trademark of AT&T used to identify the data sets manufactured and supplied by the Bell System for transmitting data over the telephone network.

**data processing** The execution of systematic operations performed on data using sets of defined rules and procedures. Data processing has evolved as a general term for using computers in business and other applications.

**data processor** A device used to perform data processing. A data processor may be a calculator, a microcomputer, a minicomputer, or a large-scale computer. Also called *processor*.

**data purification** The reduction of errors in data prior to using the data in the processing system.

**data record** A collection of data elements grouped together and considered as an entity.

**data reduction** The transformation of raw data into a more useful form using such methods as smoothing, scaling, or ordering.

**data reliability** A ratio used to measure a degree to which data is error free.

**data set** A set of data elements, or the electronic device used to provide the interface for data transmission to remote stations (as, for example, a modem). The data set is a potential combination, and all elements are not required to be present to complete the set. A *symbolic* data set is a data set used for coding a program; the *actual* data set is determined at a later time during a particular execution of the program.

**data sink** A device in a communications system used for accepting signals from a transmission device. A data sink may also check these signals and generate error control signals.

**data source** A circuit or device in a communications system used for originating signals for a transmission medium. A data source may also accept error control signals.

**dataspeak** Voice data communications that involve a teleprinter input and an audio output from a remote computer.

**data station** A device for supplying remote terminal capability. A data station allows a wide range of input/output devices, including paper tape, punched card, keyboards, page printers, and various readers.

**data stream** The serial data that is transmitted through a channel from a single read or write, or other specific operation.

**data system** The combination of personnel efforts, procedures, tools, media, and facilities that provide the means for recording, processing, and communicating data. The data system may be fully or partly automated. Also called *information system*.

**data terminal** The equipment that provides a complete data sink and/or source. A typical video data terminal combines data entry and display and has its own storage and character generator for selected displays of up to 480 characters on the screen.

**data transfer** As used in microcomputers, an instruction that provides the ability to break the normal sequence of control.

Three types of data transfers are used in microcomputers:

1. Programmed transfers—the easiest and most direct method
2. Interrupt transfers—peripheral devices initiate the transfer
3. Direct-memory-access transfers—the fastest method

A data transfer controller can be used to provide the signal sequences to allow data transfers through the bus system; a data transfer register can simplify the movement of data for transfers. The data transfer register is also called a memory data register (abbreviated *MDR*).

**data transmission** The sending of data to one or more stations or locations.

**data validation** The checking of data for compliance with requirements. Data validation can be determined with tests such as the *forbidden-code check* to verify reliability and validity.

**dB** Abbreviation for the *decibel*, a unit of measure representing a power ratio between two power sources or sinks, in which one decibel represents the ratio multiplied by 10 times its common logarithm. By extension, voltages and current can be similarly compared (in which case the multiplier must be doubled).

**DC** Abbreviation: 1. *Direct current.* 2. *Direct coupled.* 3. *Digital computer.* 4. *Direct cycle.* 5. *Display console.* 6. *Decimal classification.* 7. *Data conversion.* 8. *Design change.*

**DCA** Abbreviation: 1. *Defense Communications Agency* (DOD). 2. *Digital Computer Association.*

**DCAS** Abbreviation for *data collection and analysis system (NASA).*

**dc coupling** 1. Transmission with a modem using a steady stream of pulses. 2. Direct coupling using components other than capacitors so as to avoid loss of direct current.

**dc dump** The removal of any constant-sign voltage (and thus power) from a computer system.

**DCFEM** Abbreviation for *dynamic crossed field electron multiplication.*

**dc leakage current** The current that flows through a capacitor when the rated dc voltage is applied.

**DCS** Abbreviation for *distributed computer system.*

**DCSS** Abbreviation for *defense construction supply center.*

**DCTL** Abbreviation for *direct-coupled transistor logic,* a logic system that uses only transistors as active circuit elements.

**DD** Abbreviation: 1. *double density* diskette types. 2. *digital display.*

**DDA** Abbreviation for *digital differential analyzer,* an early type of computing machine.

**DDAS** Abbreviation for *digital data acquisition system.*

**DDP** Abbreviation for *digital data processor.*

**DDRR** Abbreviation for *directional discontinuity ring radiator.*

**DDT** Abbreviation for *dynamic debugging technique,* a sophisticated, online program debugger.

**DE** Abbreviation for *dictation equipment.*

**dead band** A range of values for which the incoming signal can be altered without also changing the output. Also called *dead space* and *dead zone.*

**dead front** Concerns the act of joining a connector that is designed in such a way that the contacts are recessed below the surface of the connector's body, in order to prevent accidental short circuits and to keep the contacts from touching other objects.

**dead key** A typewriter key that does not automatically advance the machine to the next character position when struck.

**DEADS** Abbreviation for *Detroit Air Defense Sector.*

**dead time** The interval between initiation of a stimulus change and the start of the resulting response.

**dead zone** A range of inputs for which no change in output occurs.

**debug** To detect and remove errors and malfunctions from a program, routine, or machine. Debugging usually involves the running and checkout of programs to detect the errors. One typical method of debugging includes running a similar problem with a known answer through the system for checkout. Debugging aids are available to allow quick development of microcomputer programs. These aids, normally used with a teletypewriter, allow the user to:

1. Print register contents
2. Modify memory and register contents
3. Use breakpoints for start and stop
4. Search memory

Debug commands are allowed in some systems for tracing errors, and a class of software known as debuggers features debugging programs that can be stopped and examined while slowly stepping the machine through the instructions. Debugging statements are often a part of these programs to permit the user to:

1. Start and stop the program
2. Insert and delete control statements
3. Print value changes as they occur
4. Transfer control
5. Cause printout of cross relationships

To facilitate a successful system debugging operation, the user should be able to start, stop, and single-step the system clock. If the system is microprogrammed, there must be a way to set the contents of the control store address register and lock this register so that it cannot be advanced by the system clock or jump instructions. These controls over the register will allow the user to select the starting point for coding and repeat a single instruction many times in order to completely debug that instruction. Monitoring the control store register is required to allow the user to know where the program is during debugging. This can be done in many microcomputer systems using the ROM simulator and the console control panel.

**debugger** A diagnostic aid that allows the user to analyze the program.

**debugging statements** The debugger allows the programmer to insert breakpoints and obtain register and memory dumps at desired points of the program excution. When the program detects an error, some debugger programs allow the user to make a modification and let the program continue to run.

**debugging statements** These statements are often part of the operating statements and provide a variety of methods for manipulating the program itself in an attempt to identify program errors or bugs. These statements may allow the user to: (1) insert or delete statements; (2) execute selectively; (3) print changes of values as the change occurs and transfer control as the transfer occurs; (4) obtain a static printout of all cross-reference relationships among names and labels, and dynamic exposure of partial or imperfect execution.

**decade** A group of assembly of ten units.

**decade switching** The use of a series of switches each with ten positions with the values 0 through 9, in which adjacent switches have a ratio of values 10:1.

**decay time** The time in which a voltage or current pulse will decrease to one tenth of its maximum value. Decay time is proportional to the time constant of the circuit.

**decentralized processing** Processing of data by individual subdivisions of an organization at different geographical locations.

**decibel** A unit (abbreviated *dB*) for expressing the relationship between two power levels, where the number of decibels is 10 times the logarithm of the ratio. Because of the relationship of voltage and current to power, their ratios may be similarly expressed in decibels using 20 log as a multiplier. A doubling or halving of power represents a 3 dB difference. An order-of-magnitude power difference is 10 dB.

**decibel meter** An instrument that is calibrated in decibels and used for measuring power levels above a usually arbitrary reference level. Where the reference is 1 mW across 600 Ω, the unit may be abbreviated *dBm*. In audio equipment, 1 dBm equals 1 volume unit (1 VU); 0VU or 0 dBm is the 1 mW reference.

**decimal** The number system that uses 10 as the radix or base.

**decimal code** A code in which each allowable position has one of ten possible states. The conventional decimal number system is a decimal code.

**decimal notation** A fixed radix notation that uses the characters 0-9 and the radix of 10. Using decimal notation, the number 601.2 is expressed as:

$(6 \times 10^2)$ plus $(0 \times 10^1)$ plus $(1 \times 10^0)$ plus $(2 \times 10^{-1})$

**decimal tabulation** A word processing function that provides for automatic vertical alignment of decimal points at predetermined locations.

**decimal-to-binary conversion** Refers to the process of converting a number written in base 10 into the same number written in base 2.

**decision** A determination of future action. A decision in computer systems usually involves a comparison to determine the existence or nonexistence of a specific condition before taking a specific succeeding action. The action may involve a conditional jump or transfer of control. The comparison may take place between words or numerical characters in registers or other temporary storage.

**decision box** A rectangle or other symbol used on a flow diagram to mark a choice or branch in a program.

**decision circuit** A circuit such as a decision gate that performs a logical operation on binary information.

**decision gate** A specific type of decision circuit that uses the states of two or more inputs to make a decision and provide the correct output indication.

**decision integrator** A digital integrator used in incremental computers. The decision integrator provides an increment that is maximum positive, maximum negative, or zero, depending upon the input values.

**decision instruction** An instruction that causes the selection of a branch of the program, as, for example, a conditional jump instruction.

**decision level** The signal amplitude that serves as a reference for determining the output of a comparison circuit. If the input signal is less than the decision level at the time of sampling, the output of the comparison circuit is negative or zero; if the input is greater than the decision level, the output is positive (with a binary 1 indication). Also called the *decision threshold* or *slicing level*.

**decision table** A table that contains all aspects of a problem along with the actions that could be taken. Decision tables can be used in place of flow diagrams and are usually arranged in a matrix or tabular format. The upper part of each column can list all conditions to be considered for the problem, and the lower part can list the action to be taken for each set of conditions.

**decision threshold** Decision level.

**deck** A collection of punched or magnetically imprinted cards.

**declarative operation** A coding sequence consisting of a symbolic label, a declarative operational code, and an operand. The declarative operation is used to write labels and codes for data and constants.

**decode** The act of applying a set of data rules to restore a previous representation or to reverse a previous encoding operation.

**decoder** A device that determines the meaning of a set of data and usually initiates some action based on the meaning. A decoder may be a matrix of switching elements used to select one or more channels according to the combination of input signals. Many decoder chips can be expanded so that each decoder drives eight or more other decoders for large system applications.

| E | A0 | A1 | 0 | 1 | 2 | 3 | |
|---|----|----|---|---|---|---|---|
| L | L | L | L | H | H | H | H = High voltage load |
| L | H | L | H | L | H | H | L = Low voltage load |
| L | L | H | H | H | L | H | X = Level does not affect output |
| L | H | H | H | H | H | L | |
| H | X | X | H | H | H | H | |

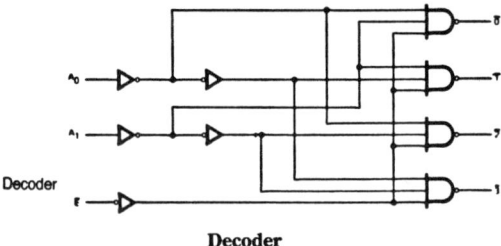

**Decoder**

**decoder chips** In decoded addressing the lines are connected to a decoder that linearly selects the components. An 8205 decoder appears on the next page. It accepts three inputs and selects one of eight possible outputs. The 8205 can be used to select an 8708 ROM or a pair of 8111 RAM's that provide 8 bit words.

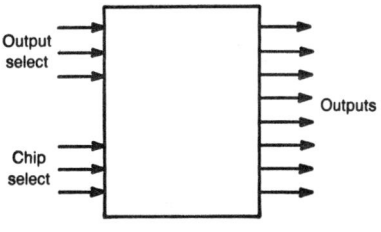

Decoder chip

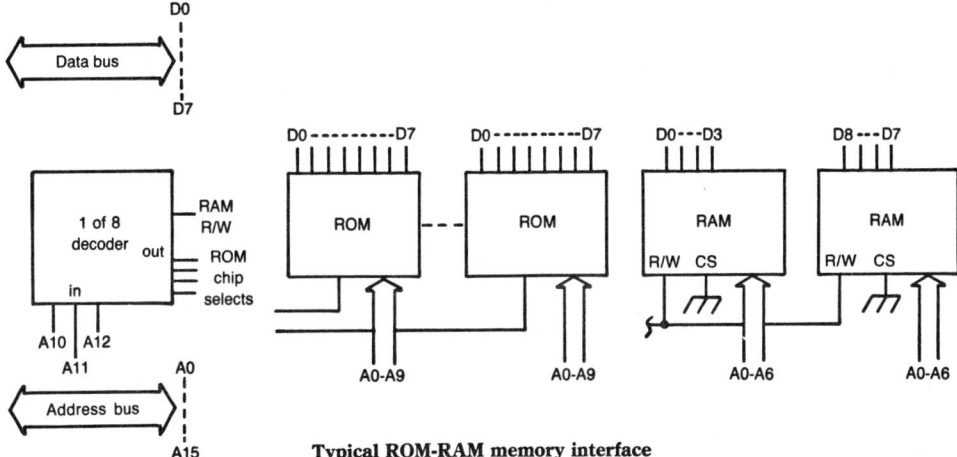

**Typical ROM-RAM memory interface**

of the processor waiting for external interruption, it is put to work analyzing the external situation, continuously scanning and testing for inputs. The processor has complete command of the operation knowing when to accept or ignore inputs. This simple but effective technique reduce the need for expensive and complex interrupt structures.

**deferred address** Indirect address.

**deferred entry/exit** An asynchronous event can cause a deferred entry by passing control of the central processing unit to a subroutine or to an entry point. This transfer causes a deferred exit from the program having control previously.

**deferred maintenance** Scheduled maintenance intended to correct an existing fault. Deferred maintenance can only be used for faults that do not affect the successful completion of a project or program.

**deflection yoke** The ring around the neck of a cathode ray tube that contains the deflection coils.

**defruiter** An interference suppression device for auxiliary radar equipment.

**degauser** A device that neutralizes magnetic charges; a device used to erase magnetic tape without removing it from the reel.

**degauss** A procedure that demagnetizes a magnetic tape. A coil is momentarily energized by an alternating current that disarranges the impulses on a magnetic tape when it is placed close to the coil.

**degeneracy** Refers to a condition in a resonant system when two or more nodes have the same frequency.

**degradation** 1. Refers to a gradual decline of quality or the loss of ability to perform within required limits. 2. A special condition under which a system operates at reduced levels of service.

**degradation factor** Refers to various measures of the loss in performance that results from the reconfiguration of a data processing system; for example, a slow down in run time due to a reduction in the number of central processing units.

**deionization** The process by which an ionized gas returns to its neutral state after all sources of ionization are removed.

**DEL** In ASCII, the delete character.

**delay** The amount of time an event is retarded. Delays can be generated

**decollate** To separate the parts of a multipart form or document.

**decrement** A device or instruction used to reduce, usually by one unit, the contents of a storage location and also the quantity by which the contents are decreased. Usually the decrement is a specific part of the instruction word.

**dedicated** Descriptive of machines, programs, or procedures that are designed, tailored, or reserved for specific uses. A dedicated communications line refers to a leased or private line that is used for a particular communications purpose. A dedicated microprocessor is one that is designed and programmed for a specific application, such as a instrumentation, traffic control, or arithmetic calculations.

**dedicated channel** A specific channel that has been reserved or committed or set aside for a very specific use or application.

**dedicated circuit** Refers to a communications circuit or channel that has been reserved or committed or allocated for a specific user or use.

**dedicated computer** A computer that is devoted to a singular processing type activity. For example, a microcomputer used in an NC system is dedicated to machine tool activity.

**dedicated line** A service offered by the common carriers in which a customer may lease, for exclusive use, a circuit between two or more geographic points.

**dedicated microprocessor techniques** Refers to tasks that are assigned to the microprocessor to maintain its productivity. Instead by special circuits, devices, elements, units, or lines. A *digit* delay device or circuit is one that retards digits and has the effect of a carry operation in arithmetic. Other elements and units have the ability to accept the data or signal, hold for a period of time *t*, and then emit the signal as a function of time minus *t*. Delays *lines* may be electrical, electromagnetic, or acoustical. Some registers use delay lines with feedback to achieve a circulating storage method.

**delay circuit** A specific circuit that can delay the passage of a pulse or signal from one part of a circuit to another.

**delay counter** A device that can temporarily delay a program long enough for the completion of an operation.

**delay device, digit** A logic device used to postpone digit signals and to achieve the effect of a carry from one digit location to another in arithmetic circuits.

**delayed access** Refers to an access that is delayed because of procedures relating to processing or to the speed of input/output or storage devices.

**delay element** Refers to circuitry or electronic devices that accept data temporarily and emit the same data after a specific interval.

**delay flop** Refers to a monostable multivibrator; a circuit that holds information for a fixed period of time. This period is determined by the nature and arrangement of the circuit components.

**delay line** 1. A device capable of retarding a pulse of energy between input and output, based on the properties of materials, circuit parameters, or mechanical devices. Delay lines may use material such as mercury, in which sonic patterns may be propagated in time, lumped constant electrical lines, coaxial cables, transmission lines, and recirculating magnetic drum loops. 2. A line or network designed to introduce a desired delay in the transmission of a signal, usually without appreciable distortion. 3. A sequential logic element with one input channel, in which an output channel state at any one instant, T, is the same as the input channel state at the instant T-N, where N is a constant interval of time for a given output channel. 4. An element in which the input sequence undergoes a delay of N time units.

**delay unit** Refers to a device in which the output signal is a delayed version of the input signal, if the input signal is f (t), the output signal is f (t − T) where T is the delay introduced.

**delete** A nonembedded command that permits removal of previously recorded material from the recording medium.

**delete character** A character used to obliterate erroneous or undesired data. In punched tape, the delete character will produce perforations at all undesired positions.

**delete code tape** A code used in punched tape to correct errors. Usually a punch in each of the first seven tracks of the tapes. The tape reader bypasses these rows of holes.

**delimiter** A flag or character that is used to separate and organize items of data. As a character, a delimiter is used to limit a string of characters, but it can never be a part of the string. A delimiter flag character can be used to mark the end of a series of bits or characters.

**delimiter, data** Refers to a flag character that ends or bounds a series or string of bits or characters; the delimiter is thus not a part or member of such a string unless it is the first or last member. Certain special patterns of data are also used as markers and end of message signals.

**delta** The Greek letter delta (Δ) represents any quantity that is much smaller than any other quantity of the same unit appearing in the same problem. 2. In a magnetic core, the difference between the partial select outputs of the same cell in a one state and in a zero state. 3. An increment.

**delta clock** A clock used for timing subroutine operations. A delta clock can be used to restart a computer using an interrupt after a fault forces the machine into a closed programming loop or causes a halt. The interrupt can be programmed to alert the operator that a fault has occurred.

**delta modulation** A type of digital speech encoding. Delta modulation uses a comparison of the input analog signal with a reference signal on a periodic basis. Depending on the result of comparison, a 1 or 0 is transmitted. The reference signal is typically obtained by a feedback loop from the previous input signals. The basic delta modulator has a limited dynamic range and a number of techniques are used to overcome this limitation. Most of these techniques increase the range by increasing the step size of the magnitude of the reference level each time a comparison results in an answer similar to the one previously obtained. If the first comparison reference signal is less than the input signal, the reference level is increased by a certain step. On the next comparison if the reference level is still less than the input signal, the step again is increased. This type of delta modulator is called a variable slope delta (VSD) modulator. The continuously variable slope delta (CVSD) modulator is a variation of the VSD type in which the comparison signal (which is an indication of the slope of the analog input signal) is sent through a low pass filter with a bandwidth of 25 to 35 hertz.

**demand** An input/output coding method in which read/write operations are initiated as the need for them occurs.

**demodulate** To recover the information carried by a modulated signal. Demodulation recovers the signal from the modulated wave so that it has the same essential information characteristic as the signal before modulation. Various demodulators are used to receive tone signals and convert them into digital bits for acceptance by computer circuits.

**demodulator-modulator** A *modem*, the common device that performs both modulation and demodulation for signals transmitted over communication lines.

**denial, alternative** Concerns a logical operation, applied to at least two operands, that will produce a result according to the bit patterns of the operand.

**density** The amount of space versus amount of information stored. Density refers to the compactness of the information stored on the available storage media or to the number of tracks per inch. Single density 5-1/4 inch mini floppy diskettes hold approximately 80-90 kilobytes (k), 8 inch diskettes hold 243 k. Double density floppies hold twice as much as single density diskettes; quad density diskettes hold four times as much as single density diskettes.

**departure frequency** The amount of variation of a carrier frequency or center frequency from its assigned value. This is also known as frequency deviation.

**derivative action** A type of response found in control systems, the output response of which is the derivative of the input.

**DES** Abbreviation for *digital expansion system*.

**DESC** Abbreviation for *defense electronics supply center*.

**descriptor** A word used to define characteristics of a program element such as a record, part of a program, or operation. Also known as *keyword*.

**design aids** Special software or hardware elements that are intended to assist in implementation of a data processing system. Design aids for microcomputers range from prototyping cards to software development systems. A prototyping card can reduce circuit design and fabrication time during the early development stage; the card usually contains the microprocessor, system clock, and input/output circuits.

(Additional cards may contain RAMs and ROMs along with peripheral controllers.)

**design cycle** The complete cycle of development for complex products, which includes breadboarding, prototyping, testing, and production planning. After each phase, the requirements are refined and the specifications modified to reflect everything that has been learned up to that time.

**design proof test** A test that verifies that the design specification has met the overall functional requirements of the finished product.

**desk check** Analysis of a program for errors in logic or syntax without using any equipment or electrical design aids.

**destructive read** A read operation that also erases the data from the source.

**destructive testing** Testing of any sort that drastically degrades the item tested.

**DETAB** Abbreviation for *decision table*.

**detector (primary element)** The first system element that performs the initial measurement operation and responds quantitatively to the measured variable.

**deterministic simulation** A type of simulation in which a given input always produces the same output.

**DEV** Abbreviation for *data exchange unit*.

**development processor module** Some development systems are constructed on a modular basis, with a number of boards for memory, I/O, and other functions. A block diagram of a typical development processor module is illustrated below. The various peripheral devices required can be connected to the I/O interface. This interface would not be used in the final system since it is only used to develop software for the system. The usual interface is to a keyboard and cathode-ray tube terminal, which allows the users to do the on line programming and editing. The modular development system is popular since the user may insert or delete modules from the system at will.

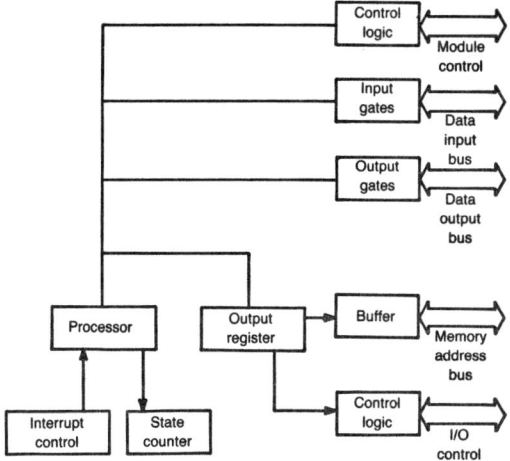

**Processor module structure**

**development system** A software design aid that enables the user to check and debug programs quickly. A typical development system allows the user to compose and edit programs, run them in real-time in the system environment, diagnose problems, program modifications, and document the required changes. The development system console may furnish program control signals such as STOP/STOP ACKNOWLEDGE, INTERRUPT/INTERRUPT ACKNOWLEDGE, and RESET IN/OUT. The user can then half, interrupt, and reset the resident CPU through the console interface. The console also allows the operator to manually write the data into memory, monitor bus contents during subcycles, and step the program to verify data flow.

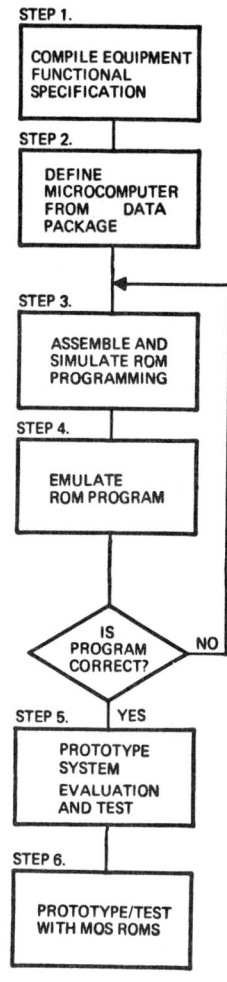

**Development system**

**development techniques** Refers to program development techniques, the most simple of which uses hand programming. Here, the program is developed directly in binary or hexadecimal; all that is required is a hexadecimal keyboard and LED displays for the output.

**development time** That part of operating time used for testing and debugging new routines and hardware.

**deviation ratio** Refers to a frequency modulation system in which the deviation ratio is the ratio of the maximum frequency deviation to the maximum modulating frequency of the system under specified conditions.

**device** A mechanical, electrical, or electro mechanical contrivance or appliance. Commonly used in conjunction with peripherals such as printers, CRTs, and disk drives.

**device control character** A control character used for switching various devices in and out of data processing and telecommunications systems.

**device independence** Refers to the ability to request I/O operations without regard to the characteristics of specific types of input/output devices.

**device selection check** A check to verify that the correct device was selected during a program instruction.

**device status word** A word used to indicate the status of devices such as registers in a computer system. (Abbreviated *DSW*.)

**DF** Abbreviation for *describing function*.

**DFG** Abbreviation for *diode function generator*.

**DFT** Abbreviation for *diagnostic function test*.

**DFT table** An area of main storage that serves as a logical connector between the user's problem program and a file. This table can also be used to provide control information for transfers of data other than for diagnostic purposes.

**DI** Abbreviation for *digital input*.

**DIA** Abbreviation for *Defense Intelligence Agency (DOD)*.

**Diablo** Trade name of a typing mechanism employing a high speed interchangeable printwheel.

**diagnosis, breakpoint conditions** A variety of breakpoint conditions can be specified to stop a program: memory read, memory write, I/O read, and I/O write. These conditions may be further qualified by prototype logic operations, combined with such functions as stack operations or instruction fetch. For example, one can monitor a device such as flip-flop A and specify a breakpoint halt when A is set and a specific stack address is being accessed. This enables one to make sure the flip-flop is set at the proper point in a control, data processing, or interrupt handling routine.

**diagnostic program** A program that facilitates testing through detection and isolation of malfunctions or mistakes.

**diagnostic routine** A routine designed to locate a malfunction in the computer or a mistake in coding, or both. Routines for diagnosing programming mistakes may be general routines, whereas routines for diagnosing mistakes in data are usually specific to a particular application.

**diagnostics** Techniques employed for detection and isolation of malfunctions and errors in programs, systems, and devices. Diagnostics in microcomputers usually involve the use of ROMs. Small systems can store their diagnostics in ROM control. If a compiler is used, diagnostics are available in the following forms:

1. Precautionary—PRINT WARNING AND CONTINUE
2. Correctable—CORRECT ERROR, PRINT MESSAGE, AND CONTINUE.
3. Uncorrectable—PRINT MESSAGE, REJECT STATEMENT AND CONTINUE
4. Catastrophic—TERMINATE COMPILATION

Diagnostic routines for programming mistakes are service-oriented; routines for detecting mistakes in data are much more specific. Many of the latter can be implemented from control store to test small portions of the system.

**diagnostic software** Software that may be provided on ROMs that are plugged into the system. This software or firmware can check the operation of the program and provide an error message when a failure is detected. A monitor program that can place TRAP instructions at specified addresses can be used for diagnostics.

**diagnostic test** The running of a program or routine to detect failures or potential failures. Diagnostic tests and routines will usually determine the location errors in programs.

**diagnostic trace** A program used to perform diagnostic checks on other programs. The output of the trace program can include the instructions of the program being checked along with the results of those instructions arranged in sequence.

**diagram, set up** A graphic representation showing how a computing system has been prepared and the arrangements that have been made for its operation.

**dialing, direct distance** An exchange service that enables a telephone user to specify subscribers outside the originator's local area.

**dial up lines** Refers to communications through normal dial or touch tone telephone lines.

**DIANE** Abbreviation for *digital integrated attack and navigation equipment*.

**DIB** Abbreviation for *data input bus*.

**dibit** A group of two bits. As used in some modulation systems, such as the Bell 201 data set, each *dibit* is encoded as one of four unique carrier phase shifts: 00, 01, 10, or 11.

**dicap storage** Storage using an array of diodes to control current directed to storage capacitors.

**diced elements** Subminiaturized component parts formed by deposition techniques in multiple on a substrate in checkerboard fashion and then separated by a slicing process.

**dichotomizing search** A search that divides an ordered set of items into two parts, one of which is rejected; the process is repeated on the saved part in an iterative routine that ultimately results in retrieval of the desired item.

**dictionary** A list of code names used in a system or routine along with their intended meaning in that system or routine.

**die** A single piece of silicon that has been cut from a slice by scribing and breaking. It can contain one or more circuits but is packaged as a unit.

**dielectric** 1. The insulating material separating the two plates of a capacitor. Dielectrics can be made of impregnated paper, plastic, mica, or ceramics. The dielectric provides a medium capable of recovering all or part of the energy required to establish an electric field. The field, or voltage stress, is accompanied by displacement or charging currents. 2. A nonconducting material through which induction of magnetic lines of force may pass. It is a medium in which an electrical field can be maintained.

**dielectric amplifier** A type of amplifier that operates through a capacitor, the capacitance of which varies with the voltage.

**dielectric current** The current that results when changing electric field is applied to a dielectric; it may consist of a displacement current, an absorption current, and a conduction current.

**dielectric diode** A capacitor sandwich whose negative plate can emit electrons, so that current flows in one direction. CdS crystals have this property.

**dielectric dispersion** Refers to the variation of dielectric constant with frequency.

**dielectric fatigue** The breakdown of a dielectric subjected to a repeated electric stress, which is insufficient to break down the dielectric if applied only a few times.

**dielectric guide** Refers to the possible transmission path of high frequency electromagnetic energy functionally realized in a dielectric channel, the dielectric constant of which differs from its surroundings.

**dielectric heating** Radio frequency heating in which energy is released in a nonconducting medium through dielectric hysteresis.

**dielectric isolation** An integrated circuit electrical isolation that is obtained by insulating each pocket with a dielectric layer. Normally, thermally grown silicon oxide is used as the dielectric material. It is used when the parasitic junction capacitances or leakage currents associated with the junction isolation methods may not be acceptable.

**dielectric polarization** A polarization due to the formation of doublets (dipoles) of a dielectric under electrical stress.

**dielectric relaxation** Refers to the time delay, arising from dipole moments in a dielectric when an applied electric field varies.

**dielectric strength** Refers to the electric stress required to puncture a dielectric.

**dielectric viscosity** Refers to the condition in which the polarization lags behind the changes in the applied field, depending on its rate of change.

**difference of potential** Refers to the voltage of electrical pressure existing between two points, which can result in a flow of electrons between the two points.

**differential analyzer** An analog computer that uses interconnected integrators for solving differential equations.

**differential delay** The difference between the maximum and minimum frequency delays occurring across a frequency band.

**differential instrumentation amplifier** An amplifier used to reject common mode signals, bias out the direct-current offsets, and scale the input as illustrated.

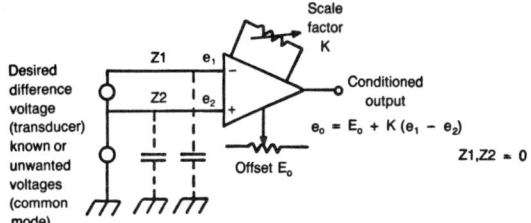

**Differential amplifier used as signal conditioner**

**differential multiplexer** A 2-wire differential multiplexer may be constructed with pairs of switches, as shown in the next column. The output amplifier is usually an instrument amplifier with a high common mode rejection. This rejection can only be achieved if the input lines are identical so twisted pairs for cabling and matching the parameters of the channels and switches are required. Integrated circuits and dual field-effect transistor switches can allow the matching required. Switch leakages and thermal electromotive forces may introduce errors in the low level inputs, and drift is a problem.

**differential transducer** A transducer that is used to measure two separate parameters and provide a single output that is proportional to the difference between them.

**differentiating amplifier** A type of amplifier whose output current

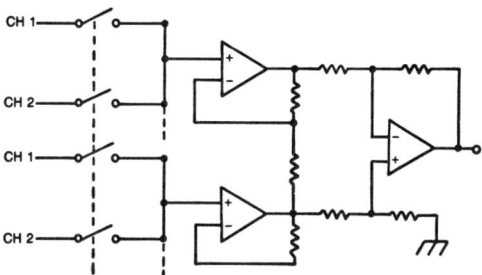

**Differential Multiplexer**

is proportional to the derivative with respect to time.

**differentiating circuit** Refers to a circuit whose output function is proportional to the derivative, or the rate of change, of its input function with respect to one or more variables.

**differentiator** A circuit or device with an output function that is proportional to the derivative of the input. A differentiator circuit accepts square waves and produces a spiked or peaked wave of the same rise time and frequency.

**diffused alloy transistor** A transistor constructed by combining diffusion and alloy techniques. First the semiconductor water is exposed to gaseous dissemination to produce the nonuniform base region. Alloy junctions comparable to a conventional alloy transistor are then formed.

**diffused semiconductor strain gages** Diffused semiconductor strain gages are based on the technology of integrated circuits. A sensing element is made by diffusing a four-arm strain-gauge bridge into the surface of a single crystal silicon diaphragm whose diameter and thickness is varied according to pressure range and application. The silicon has excellent mechanical properties, being elastic and free from hysteresis. These gauges have high gauge factors and give relatively high outputs at low strain levels. This basic sensor is built into an encapsulated transducer or transmitter using manufacturing techniques such as electrostatic or thermal compression bonding, and electron beam welding. Operational ratings such as those for shock, vibration, and overload are typical of high quality microcircuit devices. The combined linearity and hysteresis accuracy is typically less than 0.06%. The low mass silicon diaphragm gives fast response and minimum acceleration sensitivity.

**diffusion** The process used in the production of semiconductors to introduce impurities into the substrate material. The diffusion process allows the impurities to spread throughout the masked area.

**diffusion capacitance** The rate of change of injected charge with the applied voltage in a semiconductor diode.

**diffusion constant** The ratio of diffusion current density to the gradient of charge carrier concentration in a semiconductor.

**diffusion length** 1. The average distance traveled by current carriers in a semiconductor between generation and recombination. 2. A length significant in neutron diffusion theory. This length squared (termed the diffusion area) is one sixth of the mean square distance traveled by a thermalized neutron.

**diffusion theory** Refers to a current carrier migration theory based on Fick's law or the more detailed transport theory.

**DIGIRALT** Abbreviation for *digital radar altimeter*.

**digit** Any symbol that represents a positive integer smaller than the radix of a number system. In the decimal system, a digit is any one of the characters from 0 to 9; in binary, a digit is a 0 or a 1.

**digital** Employing discrete integers or voltage levels to represent data and information. A digital format can be used to represent any and all information required for problem solution.

**digital clock** A system clock that operates in a digital mode and produces precisely timed voltage pulses of fixed duration. The output signals have a digital representation and allocate time as set by the system priorities.

**digital computer** A computer that processes data using combinations of discrete or discontinuous data representations, and that can perform arithmetic and logic operations on data as well as on its own stored program.

**digital control** Descriptive of an automated system that uses a digital computer or other digital elements to perform processing and control tasks for production systems. Also called *direct digital control* (DDC).

**digital circuit** Refers to circuits that operate in the manner of a switch; that is, it is either on or off. May also be called *binary circuits*.

**digital data** Refers to quantities or variables expressed in digital form.

**digital differential analyzer** 1. An incremental computer that uses a digital integrator for computing. 2. A differential analyzer that uses digital representations for all analog quantities. (Abbreviated *DDA*.)

**digital filters** These are devices that produce a predetermined digital output in response to a digital input. They find applications in telephone, radar, and signal processing, and thus are an important area for the application of microprocessors. A digital filter may consist of elements for multiplication, addition, delays, and storage in order to obtain the desired transfer function.

**digital logic** Refers to the common types of logic families used for digital integrated circuits and systems, such as:

TLL—transistor-transistor logic
ECL—emitter-coupled logic
HTL—high-threshold logic
IIL—integrated injection logic

**digital multiplexing** For systems with small numbers of channels, medium scale integrated digital multiplexers are available in the transistor-transistor logic and metal-oxide semiconductor logic families. The 74151 is a typical example. Eight of these integrated circuits can be used to multiplex eight A/D converters of 8-bit resolution onto a common data bus.

This digital multiplexing example offers few advantages in wiring economy, but it is lowest in cost, and the high switching speed allows operation at sampling rates much faster than analog multiplexers. The A/D converters are required only to keep up with the channel sample rate and not with the commutating rate. When large numbers of A/D converters are multiplexed, the data bus technique shown below reduces system interconnections.

**digital pressure transducers** These transducers offer the accuracy and readability of digital readouts. Some use sensors such as bellows as the primary sensing device with analog-to-digital conversion circuitry. Others may use a bourdon coil pressure sensing element and an optical encoder. These are mounted on a common shaft that rotates 270 degrees in proportion to applied pressure providing a direct binary-coded-decimal or serialized output to a readout device that displays pressure in digital form. The outputs are compatible with microcomputers as well as with the monitoring and recording equipment in many chemical, paper, or similar industrial applications. By using selected transducers, engineers can produce high-performance instruments that can be used to calibrate other pressure transducers or gauges. Such instruments can be designed to produce digital displays in any pressure units.

**digital sample hold** A sample hold that uses an A/D converter and a D/A converter. When averaging is desired, the A/D converter used is an integrating type. The acquisition time is approximately equal to the sum of the A/D converter's conversion time and the D/A settling time. If the D/A output of a successive approximations A/D is used, a separate D/A converter is not required and the acquisition time is equal to the conversion rate.

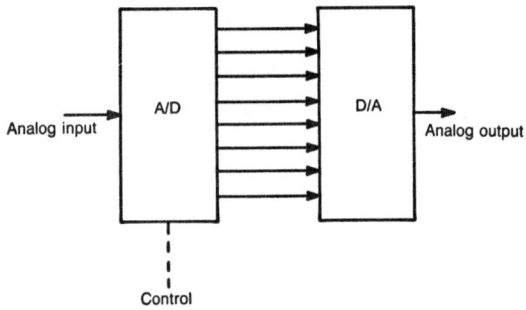

**Digital Sample Hold**

**digital subset** A collection of data in a specific format. The format is usually set by control information to which the system has access.

**digital-to-analog converter** A device for converting digital signals into continuous analog signals. Digital-to-analog converters usually buffer the input so that the output remains the same until the input changes. Units are available with up to 16 channels that can operate at 10,000 samples per second with a 100-microsecond conversion time. (Abbreviated *D/A* or *DAC*).

**digital transducers** These are sensing devices that fall into two basic groups: (1) those that incorporate a sensing unit as part of an oscillator circuit and determine the frequency of that circuit as a function of the

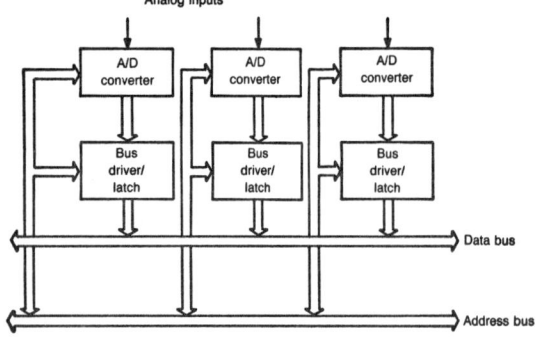

**Digital Multiplexing into the Microcomputer Bus System**

measured quantity and (2) those that detect the position of a primary sensor and convert that quantity into a coded digital word.

**digital transducer input interface** Digital transducers or encoders can simplify the system interface. For minimum software one can connect each of the parallel outputs of a digital transducer to a corresponding power amplifier line in a peripheral-interface adapter. Unclocked, the transducer outputs present a word, which the microprocessor can sample at almost any desired rate. Even for a relatively long sampling period, only the least significant bits will change during the measurement of most parameters. This configuration uses the software to define the connections as inputs, and the sampling rate is under main program control.

To achieve minimum hardware usage in an interface for a digital transducer one can use a software-oriented interface as illustrated in the figure. A digital transducer with a serial output requires only two connections.

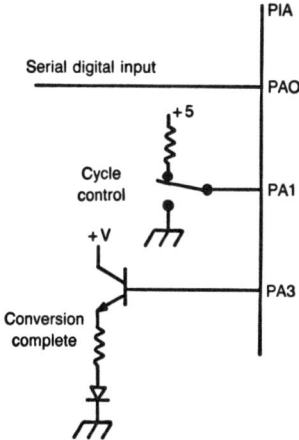

Digital transducer input interface

**digital transducer interface program** This interface with a peripheral-interface adapter is shown in the flow diagram below. The program simulates the serial to parallel register this interface requires. One defines the serial inputs and an output to control a conversion-finished light-emitting diode. One can eliminate this output by making the conversion a subroutine of a larger control program. A cycle loop causes the microprocessor to wait until the cycle control switches to high; then it clears a memory location to use as a pointer that tracks bit processing. The routine rotates the carry bit and resets the conversion-finished line. It uses a conditional branch to determine when all bits have been tested. Then the program sets the carry bit to signify that all bits have been checked. It uses another branch for bit testing and pointer control and prepares the bits for the microprocessor.

**digital up/down counter module** This module provides event counting capability for the microcomputer or external peripheral device. It detects counter overflow and sets a corresponding flag. All count parameters and reset are program selectable. The counter may be incremented or decremented at a 20 K Hz rate. It provides up to 50 VDC input for external event counting.

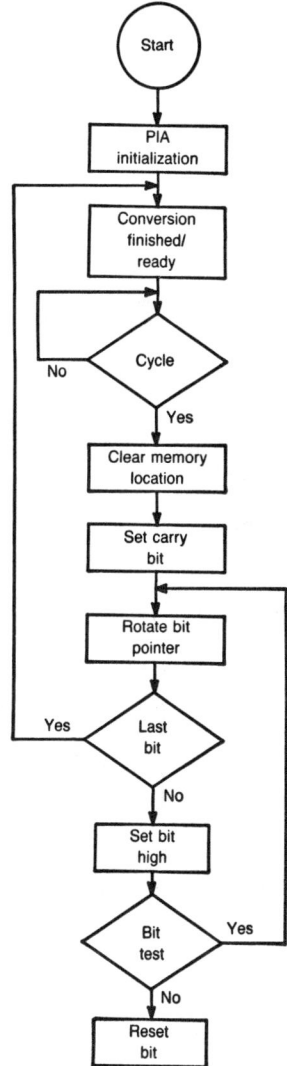

Digital transducer program flow

**digital voltmeter** 1. A type of indicator that provides a digital readout of a measured voltage as opposed to a pointer indicator. 2. An indicator that indicates a voltage by its nearest numerical magnitude.

**digit emitter** A character emitter limited to the 12 rows of a punched card.

**digitization** The conversion of analog signals to digital signals. Digitization creates steps at distinct levels of the analog signal.

**digitize** To convert an analog signal to a digital representation.

**digitizer** The device that converts an analog quantity to a digital format. Also called *quantizer*.

**digit place** As used in positional notation, the site where the digit is located in a word. Also called *digit rank* or *symbol rank.*

**digit punch**  A usually rectangular cutout in any of the rows representing 0 through 9 in a punched card or tape. A punch in the 0 row may also function as a zone punch.

**dimension**  A FORTRAN statement used to define arrays; used in assembler programming as the maximum number of values that can be assigned to the *set* symbol representing an array.

**diminished-radix complement**  A complement obtained by subtracting each digit from one less than the radix; for example, the nines' complement in decimal notation and the ones' complement in binary notation. Also called *radix-minus-one* complement.

**diode**  A usually solid-state electrical valve that permits current flow in one direction and inhibits flow in the other direction.

**diode amplifier**  A parametric amplifier that uses a special diode within a cavity to amplify signals at frequencies as high as 6,000 megahertz.

**diode arrays**  Multiple diodes, usually on a single chip and connected in some kind of matrix.

**diode function generator**  A device with the capability of generating an arbitrarily specified diode function or family.

**diode ROM**  A semiconductor ROM that uses diodes. They are characterized by small volume, low cost, and nonvolatility. Like a RAM, the ROM can be addressed in a fixed time interval, regardless of location. The figure below shows a simplified arrangement of ROM elements. The circuitry is much less complex than read/write memories and is ideally suited to metal-oxide-semiconductor (MOS) or bipolar manufacturing processes. Data storage is indicated by the presence

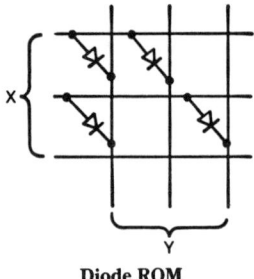

**Diode ROM**

or absence of a diode at the intersection point of the X and Y lines. Thus, any crosspoint can be identified as a "0" or "1" by making the X line positive and the Y line negative. A diode at the crosspoint will conduct, thus providing the readout. Both discrete or monolithic diode arrays can be used in ROMs. To program MOS arrays, the manufacturer uses a custom mask operation (with the mask being computer generated) to produce the required pattern of stored bits. ROM manufacturers provide forms on which users state the required contents. The data on these forms is translated into a computer program for automatic mask programming. There is also a variety of specialized ROMs for use in recurring applications. A block diagram of the organization of a typical ROM is shown.

**diode-transistor logic**  A logic family (abbreviated *DTL*) that uses diode inputs to transistors that are used as inverting amplifiers.

**DIP**  Acronym for *dual inline package,* a type of IC package that has double parallel rows of leads for connection to circuit boards. These packages are available in plastic for economy, or ceramic for high humidities and temperatures. Also known as *bugs.*

**dipole modulation**  The representation of binary digits in magnetic medium in which part of each cell is magnetically saturated in one of two opposing senses. The rest of the cell is magnetized as background and remains fixed.

**direct access**  A type of storage in which the access time is effectively independent of the location of the data. The items of data can be addressed or accessed in the same amount of time for each location, and program access is independent of any previous accessed location.

**direct acting**  Refers to a specific and defined operation of a final control element which is directly proportional to the control output.

**direct address**  An address that specifies the location of an operand. Direct addressing is a basic addressing method used in many microprocessors. It is designed to reach any point in main storage directly without using other registers. A direct addressed instruction for the 8080 is:

$$\text{LDA 2132H; load A with } 2132_{16}$$

This instruction loads the contents of location 2132 (hexadecimal) into the accumulator and is stored in memory as 3A2132.

**direct coding**  Refers to the writing of programs in binary or in hexadecimal form, which does not require much support in terms of hardware or software. This technique is used on simple systems that do not require much coding and where the coding must be very compact. The user communicates with the system through a hexadecimal keyboard and an LED display. The instructions and data are transferred into the system using the keys in a hexadecimal format.

The direct coding technique is cost efficient in terms of the hardware, but it is slow and tedious from the programmer's view point.

**direct-coupled transistor logic**  A type of logic (abbreviated *DCTL*) that uses only direct-coupled transistors as active elements.

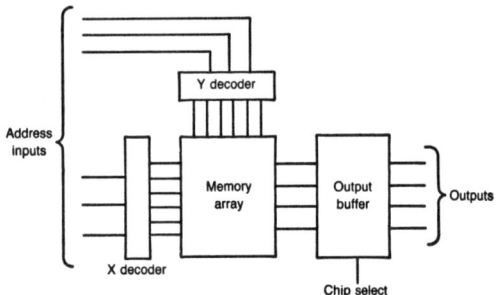

**ROM organization**

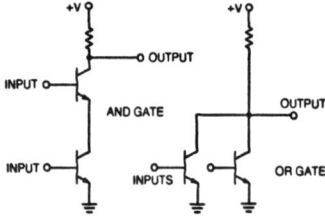

**Direct coupled transistor logic (DCTL)**

**direct coupling** The coupling of circuits by resistance or inductance so as to allow direct current to pass through the coupling.

**direct current** Current (abbreviated *DC*) that flows only in one direction at an essentially constant value.

**direct current balancer** Refers to the coupling and connecting of two or more similar direct current units or machines such that the conductors connected to the junction points of the machines are maintained at constant potentials.

**direct data transmission** The use of a single line or channel for the transmission of data. This system is the simplest type and is suitable for handling a predetermined volume of messages.

**direct digital control** Descriptive of the use of computers and other digital devices for the control of manufacturing processes. A typical direct digital controller might handle up to eight industrial control loops with more flexibility and options than possible with analog controllers.

**direct impression** A term applied to text production in which each character is struck onto the paper, as in conventional typing.

**direct insert subroutine** A subroutine that is inserted into a routine at each place that it is used. Also called an *open* subroutine.

**direct instruction** An instruction that contains the operand for the operation specified by the instruction. Also see *direct address*.

**direction of lay** Expressed as right or left hand lay, it is the lateral direction in which the strands of a cable run over the top of the cable as they recede from the observer.

**directive commands** As used in an assembler, a command that allows the user to generate data words and values for specific conditions in assembly time. Mnemonics are assigned to each instruction operation code in order to describe the hardware function of that instruction.

**directive statements** Statements that are used to define the program structure. Directive statements do not generate executable code. Examples of directive statements are ORIGIN STATEMENT, PROCEDURE STATEMENT, PROGRAM STATEMENT, and END STATEMENT.

**direct memory access** A technique (abbreviated *DMA*) to transfer data directly between memory and peripherals. Sometimes known as the *data-break technique*, DMA permits transfers to take place without CPU intervention on a cycle-stealing basis. The CPU is only used to set up the transfer, and the transfer rate is limited only by the bandwidth of the memory and peripherals. DMA is the preferred data transfer method for high-speed applications. Some DMA channels can transfer up to 500,000 words per second.

A DMA controller is used to handle several input/output channels. The controller generates the priority among the channels along with the interrupts required. The following tasks are required for DMA transfers:

1. Address selection
2. Interrupt control
3. Bus control
4. Word counting
5. Input/output data buffering

**direct memory access controller** (DMAC) This is a block transfer processor that implements automatically at hardware speed the transfer process, which would normally be executed by a program in the microprocessor. The principle application appears in the next column. Instead of sending an interrupt to the microprocessor, the I/O devices send the interrupt to the DMAC. The DMAC then suspends the microprocessor by putting it in a HOLD mode. It then takes over

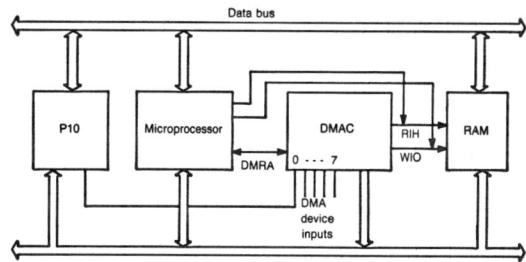

**DMA controller application**

the operation of the system and transfers the words between the memory and the I/O device.

**direct memory access (DMA), cycle stealing** A DMA technique used for high speed transfers. The DMAC transfers data on a cycle stealing basis directly between the memory and the external device, bypassing the central processor.

**direct memory access I/O** Some I/O devices must transfer large amounts of data too quickly to be controlled by a microprocessor. In this case, information can be transferred directly between the device and the memory of the microprocessor system using direct memory access (DMA). The transfer is controlled by a DMA controller, a dedicated circuit or chip that can operate independently of the microprocessor. In a DMA data transfer, the DMA controller takes over the control of the microprocessor memory in one of several ways. An external control line will stop the microprocessor after the current instruction is completed as shown below. The microprocessor memory control signals are disabled, and the DMA controller initiates the data transfer. After the DMA transfer is completed, the controller resets the halt line, and the microprocessor resumes execution of the next memory access instruction.

**direct numerical control** (DNC) Refers to the connecting of a set of numerically controlled machines to a common memory for part program or machine program storage, with provision for on demand distribution of data to the machines. Direct numerical control systems typically have additional provisions for collection, display, or editing of part programs, and operator instructions or data related to the numerical control process.

**directory** A list of files, their attributes, and their locations on the storage media. Sometimes known as a *catalog*.

**direct reference address** A type of virtual address that is not modified by indirect addressing. It can be modified by indexing.

**disable** A state of the CPU that does not allow certain types of interrupts to occur; also called a *masked* state. As used in communications, a state that does not allow a device to accept incoming calls.

**disarmed** A state used to define an interrupt level in a system that cannot accept an interrupt input signal.

**disaster dump** A dump that occurs as a result of a nonrecoverable error in the program.

**disc** Alternate spelling for disk.

**disc generator** A capacitive charge type of voltage generator.

**discrete** Individual and separate, as opposed to *integrated*. Discrete *circuits* are electronic circuits manufactured with individual diodes, resistors, capacitors, transistors, and other components. Discrete *data* pertains to variables that can assume one of several distinct states.

**discrete circuits** Refers to the various electronic circuits that can be

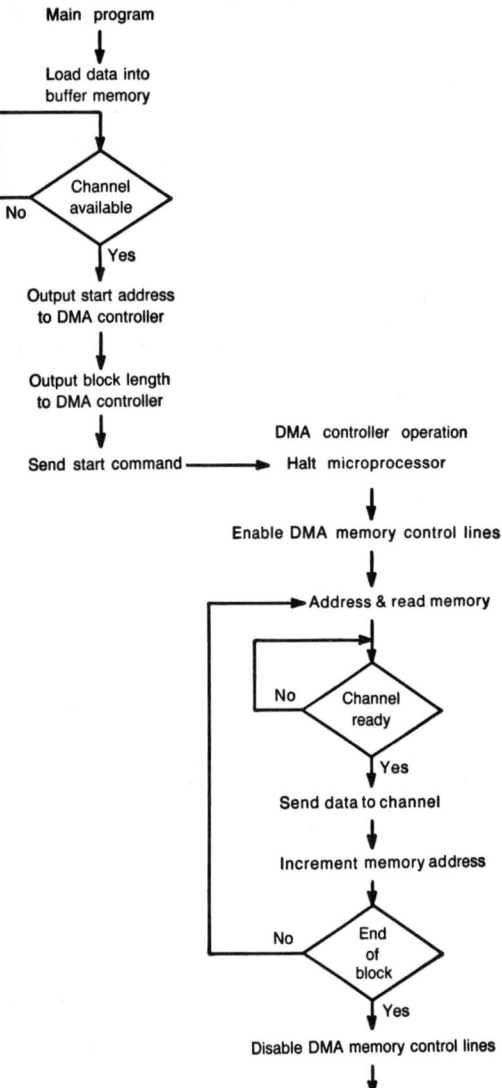

DMA control

built of separate, individually manufactured diodes, resistors, transistors, capacitors and other specific electronic components.

**discrete data** A representation for a variable that may assume any of several distinct states. They are usually coded.

**discrete media** A term applied to recording media that are individually distinct and can be filed, mailed, moved, and otherwise separately handled.

**discrete programming** A class of procedures used in operations research for locating the maximum and minimum values of a function. All variables must have integer values or similar constraints. If only integer values are used, the programming is called *integer programming.*

**discrete simulation** A type of simulation where all major components and events are identified individually and used at irregular intervals. Also called *event-oriented simulation.*

**discrimination** 1. The skipping of selected instructions as developed by the programmer. Usually in discrimination, if a conditional jump is not used, the next instructions are allowed to follow in a normal sequence. 2. The process of demodulating an FM signal.

**discriminator** In FM radio, a detector circuit used to recover the audio from an rf signal.

**disjunction** The logical operation that uses the OR operator and results in the logical sum. In Boolean form, the operation is written as:

$$A + B = C \quad (A \text{ or } B \text{ equals } C)$$

and follows this truth table:

| A | B | C |
|---|---|---|
| 0 | 0 | 0 |
| 0 | 1 | 1 |
| 1 | 0 | 1 |
| 1 | 1 | 1 |

**disk** A circular plate with magnetic material on both sides. This plate rotates for the storage and retrieval of data by one or more heads, which transfer the information to and from the computer. The computer readable information may be placed on a floppy or rigid (hard) disk, which may have information on one or both sides. Also known as *diskette* or *disc.*

**disk accessing** The process and methods used to transfer data in and out of a disk file. Access is usually accomplished by direct addressing, symbolic addressing, or keyed-record addressing.

**disk crash** When the disk drive unit's recording head makes destructive contact with the recording media. Also, a disk drive malfunction.

**disk drive** The piece of hardware that holds the motor, read/write heads, and electronics for use with a disk. The disk is inserted into the drive, which in turn is responsible for the communications between the disk surface and the computer.

**disk drive system** A complete unit that consists of a disk drive, power supply, cooling fan, buffer, and addressing electronics.

**diskette** See *floppy disk.*

**disk file** A disk unit consisting of drive, input/output, and disks, or an associated set of records of a similar format that can be grouped by a common label.

**disk operating system** A memory system (abbreviated *DOS*) using disks or diskettes that is designed to assemble, edit, and execute programs. A typical system includes an intelligent disk controller, a drive system, and a software system. Programs can sometimes be assembled, edited, and executed in seconds. Using the disk operating system requires the adding of additional memory to the executive.

DOSs allow the efficient use of ROMs for initial loading and storage of frequently used mathematical routines such as numerical integration, statistical test data, and math functions (powers, logs, sine, cosines).

**disk pack** Portable direct-access storage units that use magnetic disks. Disk packs are mounted on disk storage drives for read and write operations.

**disk storage** A memory system that stores data on magnetic disks. The disks are similar in size to a phonograph record and require a disk drive. A typical dual platter drive can provide 5 million bytes of storage with an average access time of 30 milliseconds and data transfer times of 2.5 million bits per second. Floppy disks are magnetic disks that are flexible and less expensive to produce and operate. More than 300,000 words can be stored on a floppy disk using a floppy-disk drive system.

**disk units** A disk unit is an electro mechanical assembly, containing a flat disk coated with magnetic material. Both sides of the disk may be used, and several disks can be stacked on a spindle. The disks rotate together at high speed. The bits are stored on the magnetized surface in spots along concentric circles called tracks. The tracks are divided into sectors. One sector is usually the minimum quantity of information that can be transferred. The division of disk into tracks and sectors is shown below. Some units use a single read/write head for each disk. In the unit below, address bits are used to move the head to the specified track position before a read or write. In other systems, separate read/write heads are used for each track on each disk. The address bits then select a particular track with a decoder circuit. This kind of unit is more expensive and is used in large systems.

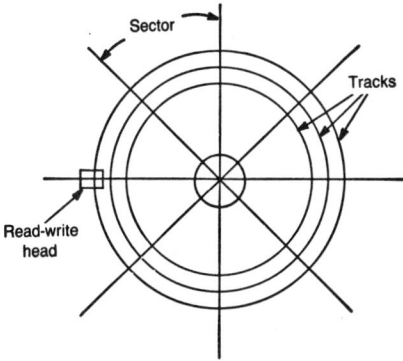

**Magnetic disk memory configuration**

Timing tracks are used to synchronize the bits and recognize the sectors. A disk is addressed by bits that specify the disk number, disk surface, sector number, and the track. As the read/write heads are positioned on the specified track, the system waits until the rotating disk places the specified sector under the head. Information transfers then starts once the beginning of a sector is reached. Some units have multiple heads for the simultaneous transfer of bits from several tracks. A track near the circumference is longer than a track near the center of the disk. If bits are recorded with equal density, some tracks will contain more bits than others. In order to make all the records in a sector of equal length, a variable recording density may be used with a higher density on tracks near the center than on tracks near the circumference.

**disorderly closedown** Stopping of a system due to an equipment error when it is not possible to shut down in a orderly manner. Special steps are usually taken to prevent the loss or duplication of data.

**dispersion** Refers to the variation of delay with frequency.

**displacement transducer** A device used to measure linear position or displacement and provide an analogous electrical output.

**display** A visual representation of data, which may take the form of numerals (as on a calculator), alphanumeric characters, or graphs. A display unit can provide viewing access into the operation of the microcomputer system.

A microcomputer *video-terminal display* unit might use a dot array of 1024 × 1024 dots for character generation. A bright dot can be produced anywhere on the screen, and a series of dots can be used to indicate lines on a graphical display. Data on the CRT display screen can be highlighted by blinking, underlining, use of a different color, increased intensity, or a combination of methods.

*Gas discharge displays* have a pleasing (orange or green) and large character size, but they are difficult to interface because of the high voltage required for ionization of the gas.

*Light-emitting diode displays* are compatible with TTL levels, but they have limited sizes and color selection.

*Liquid-crystal displays* (LCDs) require very little power and are compatible with MOS logic, but they produce no light themselves and are hard to see except under direct-lighting conditions.

*Incandescent* and *fluorescent displays* can produce high brightness with large character size, but because of costs and power requirements, they are used mostly in specialized applications.

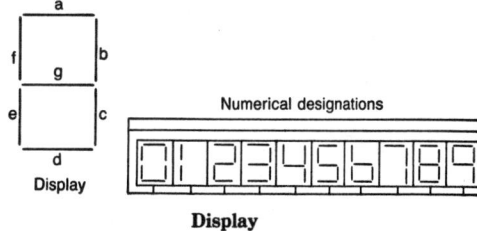

**Display**

**display adapter** An adapter unit that controls the transmission of data, control and status information, and the sequencing and synchronizing of the display units in the system. In general, the digital data received from computer storage is formatted for deflection commands for a CRT device.

**display highlighting** Refers to a feature that enables the user to distinguish or emphasize data on a CRT display by reversing the field, making it blink, underlining it, changing its color, changing its light intensity, or some combination of these.

**display modes** The various modes used in a display system to denote the points on the screen such as vector, increment, or character point.

**display register** A register with corresponding indicators on the display panel; used to display the contents of the register selected by the display switch.

**display station** A unit used to indicate alphanumeric information in a communications or computer system.

**display switch** Switches used to select the register that is to be shown on the display panel.

**display tube** An indicating type of vacuum tube (such as a CRT) that is used to display data in a form recognizable to humans.

**display types** These include cathode ray tubes, plasma and liquid crystal displays, light emitting diodes (LEDs), and incandescent and fluorescent displays.

**dissector** A mechanical or electrical transducer that detects in sequential order the light intensity of an illuminated space. The dissector is used in optical character recognition. Also known as an *image dissector*.

**dissipation, module** Refers to the power dissipation of a module calculated from the voltage current product, with an allowance for dissipation for load currents being supplied to other modules.

**distortion** Any variation in a reproduced waveform that was not present on the original waveform.

**distortion delay** The distortion that results when the phase angle of the transfer impedance is not linear with frequency within the desired range, thus making the time of transmission or delay vary with frequency in that range. Also called phase distortion.

**distortion, frequency** A type of distortion in which certain frequencies are lost or discriminated against.

**distributed control** Distributed control differs from distributed processing, in that it makes use of remote multiplexing. The processors communicate with field-located multiplexers, and each processor is usually dedicated to performing the same task in an online environment.

**distributed environment** See *distributed system*.

**distributed-intelligence microcomputer system** A multiprocessing method (abbreviated *DIMS*) in which the tasks assigned to the distributed system remain fixed. In a multiprocessing environment, the tasks are allocated by software algorithms. With the DIMS, each processor may be assigned a fixed combination of the following tasks:

1. Input/output controller activity
2. Data concentration
3. Information processing
4. Remote communication

Distributed intelligence is used in some modular instruments, POS terminals, networks of remote sensors, and scientific computers.

**distributed processing** Systems that use intelligent input/output controllers and direct-memory-access control to free the CPU of the details of block transfers. Distributed processing makes use of complex LSI chips similar to those used in microcomputers. These chips allow low-cost intelligent controllers for keyboards, displays, printers, card readers, modems, and floppy disks.

**distributed system** An arrangement of computers in an organization in which a number of computers at separate locations work in a cooperative manner. The system may use one large computer and several smaller machines, with the central files located with the larger machine and the smaller computers calling on the files when required.

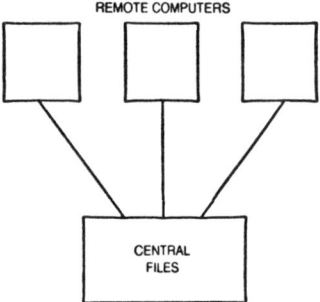

**Distributed system**

Distributed systems can provide fast response to local events, maximum availability for single failure modes, and simplified system programming with good user access.

**division circuits** A circuit that can be used to do division. A simultaneous type of circuit for numbers of larger than 8-10 bits involves a large number of gates and subtracters. These circuits are used where speed is essential. But since division, like multiplication, can make use of existing adder/subtracter circuits, most microcomputers do not use straight dividing circuits.

**DM** Abbreviation for *data management*.

**DMA** Abbreviation for *direct-memory access*, a method used to obtain direct access to the main memory without involving the CPU. The CPU is essentially disabled during DMA data-transfer operations. The approach usually taken bypasses the registers for direct access to the memory bus. DMA channels allow faster transfer speeds than otherwise possible, sometimes improving instruction times by as much as an order of magnitude.

DMA controllers are used to provide the interface between system buses and the user's peripheral. The controller provides the logic for the required tasks for DMA transfer: address selection, interrupt control, bus control, word counting, and input/output buffering.

**DME** Abbreviation for *distance measuring equipment*.

**DMED** Abbreviation for *digital message entry device*.

**DNC** Abbreviation for *direct numerical control*.

**DO** Abbreviation for *digital output*.

**document** 1. Any representation of data that can be interpreted by humans or machines, as well as the process of creating the same representation. 2. A paper voucher, form, report, or other record containing stored information; the information is usually recorded by the originator of the processing information and is usually more concerned with input information rather than output.

**documentation** 1. The presentation, organization, and communication of information. Documentation involves the creating, collecting, organizing, and disseminating of the information contained in documents. 2. A collection of documents or records on a particular subject.

**documentation techniques** The techniques most used for documentation are flowcharts, program listings with comments, memory maps, and parameter and definition lists. Structured programming and some of the other design techniques have developed their own documentation forms.

Flowcharts act as visual aids for program documentation. A general flowchart may serve as a pictorial description of a program, while a more detailed flowchart can be invaluable to the user who must use or maintain the program.

Comments are an important part of program documentation. A program with a clear structure and well-chosen names can be almost self-documenting.

**document reader** A device used to sense and interpret the codes contained in punched cards or printed materials. A typical card reader operates at speeds of up to 300 cards per minute.

**document reference edge** As used in character recognition, a specified edge of a document to which all alignment of characters is referenced.

**domain tip** A type of memory device that uses thin films to create magnetic domains for storing digital data. Thin aluminum layers are deposited on a glass substrate, and channels are etched into the aluminum and filled with a thin magnetic film which is used to form the domain regions. Costs are below core memory; applications include backup memories for microprocessors in areas like point-of-sale terminals, numerical control, and data logging.

**DON** Abbreviation for *Department of the Navy*.

**donor** Refers to those elements that enter or are introduced in small quantities as impurities to semiconducting materials and which have a negative valence greater than the valence of the pure semiconductor.

**donor ion** An atom that gives up an electron in a doped semiconductor crystal.

**dopant** An impurity added to a semiconductor to increase its ability to conduct electricity.

**dope additive** A specific impurity added to a pure semiconductor to give it the required electrical properties.

**doped junction** A semiconductor junction created by adding an impurity during crystal growth.

**doping** 1. Increasing the level of impurities of semiconductors in order to make N or P types. 2. The process of adding alien elements to a semiconductor crystal to supply it with the proper characteristics.

**DOS** Abbreviation for *disk operating system*.

**dot** Refers to pellet shaped components inserted into holes in a punchboard type of printed circuit board.

**dot leader** A word processing command that automatically places a series of periods between two items of copy.

**dot matrix printer** A hard copy device that creates characters using a series of wires that produce dots. Some high density dot matrix printers use up to 126 dots to form a character, which has a sharp, fully formed appearance. Although they are high speed printers, the characters from the lower density printers are usually not satisfactory for business correspondence.

**double bus system** A bus system that uses one bus for data and instructions and another for addresses. Control information may or may not have a special bus. In a double bus system, data and addresses can be transferred back and forth simultaneously in the same cycle without waiting for the sequential use of a common bus. A multiple bus requires a larger number of pins in the IC microprocessor package.

**double centrifuge** A centrifuge or rotating table on the boom of a second centrifuge.

**double doped transistor** A particular type of transistor created by growing a crystal and adding P and N type impurities while the crystal is being grown.

**double level polysilicon** The double level polysilicon process as shown below helps maximize RAM cell capacitance while cutting the bit sense line in half to reduce its capacitance. A sense amplifier is usually located in the center of the sense line and senses the differential voltage between the two halves of the line.

**double-precision** Descriptive of the use of two computer words to represent data. Sometimes called double-length processing. Double-precision arithmetic uses two words to represent numbers in order to obtain greater accuracy than is possible with a single word. If the normal word length is eight bits, then in double-precision arithmetic 16 bits are handled by breaking each number into two parts. Each part is handled separately, but in a manner that allows carries between them. Double-precision processing allows the system to operate as if its registers were twice as large, but operating at a slower speed.

**double-pulse recording** A type of recording in which each memory cell uses two regions magnetized in opposite polarities with neutral regions on each end. Zeros and ones are represented by the sequence of opposite polarities in the cell.

**double rail** A type of self-timed asynchronous logic circuitry that uses twin lines and three states: high, low, and undecided.

**double resistance—capacitance phase shift converter** A synchro to digital converter that eliminates at least two of those error sources that limited the performance of the single RC circuit. In this approach, $V_A$ and $V_B$ have equal but opposite phase shifts with respect to $V_{re}$. By measuring the time interval between the zero crossings of $V_A$ and $V_B$ and then using it to gate a clock pulse into a counter, the count can be scaled directly in degrees of $\theta$ at one half the clock frequency used in the single RC design.

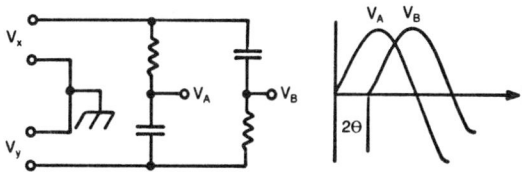

**Double RC phase shift configuration**

**downtime** The time interval when a system is malfunctioning or not operating correctly and is thus not being used. Downtime is opposed to available time, idle time, and standby time in which the system is functional.

**DP** Abbreviation for *data processing*.

**DPMA** Abbreviation for *Data Processing Management Association*.

**DPMA certificate** A certificate given by the Data Processing Management Association that indicates that a person has a certain level of competence in the field of data processing. The certificate is obtained by passing an examination that is offered yearly throughout the United States and Canada.

**DPS** Abbreviation for *data processing system*.

**DRA** Abbreviation for *dead reckoning analyzer*.

**draft** A rough and unedited outline of a document.

**drain** 1. The current taken from any voltage source. 2. The load device that absorbs the current or power in 1, above.

**DRI** Abbreviation for *data reduction interpreter*.

**DRIFT** Abbreviation for *diversity receiving instrumentation for telemetry*.

**drift** Refers to change in the output of a circuit, which takes place slowly. It may be caused by changes in environmental conditions.

**drift corrected amplifier** Refers to a high-gain amplifier that has been separately equipped with a means for reducing drift and thus preventing drift error.

**drift stabilization** Refers to the various methods used to minimize the drift of a dc amplifier.

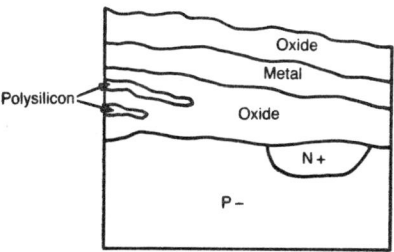

**Double-level polysilicon RAM structure**

**drift voltage equivalent** A voltage measurement or equivalent voltage that must be applied to the input of a high-gain amplifier to account for drift and to bring the output voltage to zero. This is a hypothetical voltage when applied to the input of the usual equivalent circuit of the amplifier.

**driver** 1. A small program used to execute other programs. 2. A circuit or device used to power or control other circuits or channels.

**driver modules** Modules that allow output signals to be power-amplified by bus drivers to allow them to drive a heavy circuit load.

**DRO** Abbreviation for *destructive read out.*

**droop** A drifting of an output at an approximately constant rate. It may be caused by the leakage of current out of a capacitor.

**drop-dead halt** A type of halt from which there is no recovery. A drop-dead halt may be programmed in deliberately, or it may be the result of an error in the program.

**drop-in** The reading or recording of a spurious signal with an amplitude greater than nominal by a specified percentage.

**dropout** A temporary loss of transmission or the failure to read a bit from a magnetic storage system. In transmission, a dropout is usually due to noise or a malfunction. Dropout in a magnetic storage system is mainly caused by an output too low to be detected.

**DRSC** Abbreviation for *direct radar scope camera.*

**drum storage** The storing of data in the form of magnetic spots on a cylinder coated with magnetizable material. Data is stored and retrieved by read/write heads positioned over the surface of the drum.

**dry contact** Refers to a part of a circuit containing only contact points and resistive components.

**dry reed contact** Refers to encapsulated units containing metal contacts that act as the contact points of a relay.

**dry run** A checking of the program flowchart, coding, and all program documentation before putting the program on a computer.

**DS** Abbreviation for *double-sided floppy diskettes,* where both sides of the flexible media are used to record data.

**DSA** Abbreviation for *Defense Supply Agency (DOD).*

**DSE** Abbreviation for *data storage equipment.*

**DSIF** Abbreviation for *deep space instrumentation facility.*

**DSL** Abbreviation for *deep scattering layer.*

**DSU** Abbreviation for *data storage unit.*

**DSW** Abbreviation for *device status word.*

**DTL** Abbreviation for *diode—transistor logic,* a logic family using diodes as inputs and transistors as inverting amplifiers.

**D-type flip-flop** A type of bistable multivibrator that is triggered on the leading or positive edge of the clock pulse. D-type flip-flops are typically used for buffer and shift registers, and ripple counters.

**dual diode** A combination tube consisting of two diode sections in a single envelope. Dual diode refers to monolithic dual diodes intended for use in applications requiring low leakage currents. Applications include coupling with reverse isolation, signal clipping and clamping, and protection of low leakage FET differential and operational amplifiers.

**dual-inline package** A popular type of IC package (abbreviated *DIP*) that uses twin rows of leads. This configuration allows standardization, low-cost manufacturing, and a degree of second-source replaceability.

**dual media** A term applied to equipment that is capable of utilizing two different types of media, such as tape and diskettes.

**dual operation** The negation of the result of the original operation. The dual operation is found by replacing all zeros with ones and all ones with zeros in the truth table of the original operation. The dual operation for a logical OR is the NOR operation.

**dual pitch printer** A unit capable of producing text at both 10 and 12 characters per inch.

**dual ramp A/D conversion** A type of analog-to-digital conversion. In the dual ramp or slope type of A/D converter the input signal is applied to an integrator, and a counter is started, counting the clock pulses. After a predetermined number of counts fixes the period of time, T, a reference voltage with an opposite polarity, is applied to the integrator. At this time, the charge on the integrating capacitor is proportional to the average value of the input over the period T. The integral of the reference is an opposite slope ramp with a slope $V_R/RC$. Now, the counter starts counting from zero. When the integrator output is zero, the counter is stopped and the analog circuit reset. Since the charge is proportional to $V_{IN}T$ and the charge lost is proportional to $V_R\Delta t$, the number of counts relative to the full period is proportional to $\Delta t/T$, or $V_{IN}/V_R$. The output of the binary counter is therefore a binary representation of the input voltage. When the input is attenuated and offset by half of the reference voltage, the output is an offset binary representation of a bipolar input.

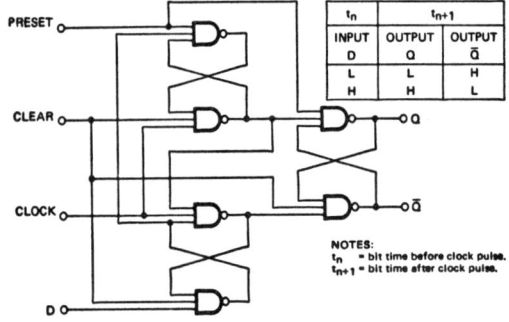

**D-Type flip-flop**

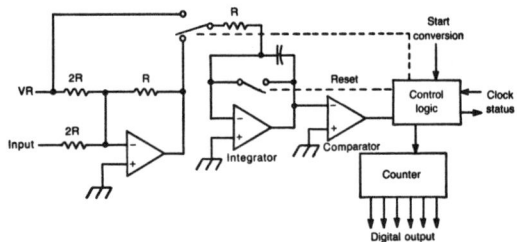

**Dual ramp A/D converter**

**dual ramp conversion interface** The dual ramp method uses an integrating technique to cancel out many of the drift problems that occur with successive approximation. The two ramps occur from a ramp time when the input voltage has been integrated for a fixed number of clock periods; then the input voltage to the integrator is switched to a reference voltage, and the ramp time required for the integrator to decrease to the level of the original input voltage is counted. Then the ramp times are compared to allow the calculation of the unknown transducer voltage. The interface and converter hardware for a dual ramp are shown below.

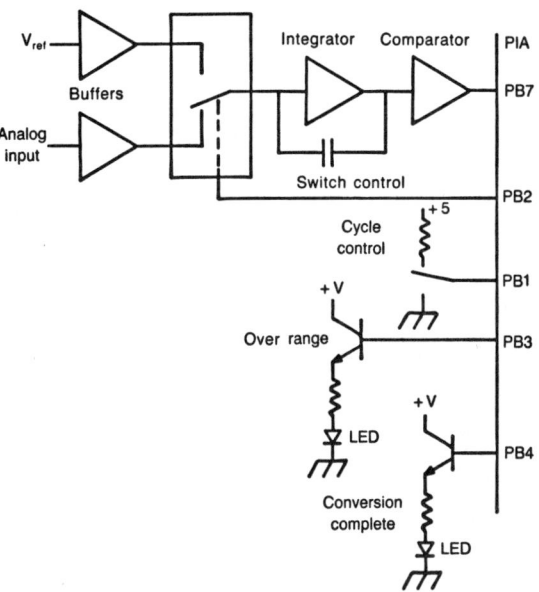

**Dual ramp conversion interface**

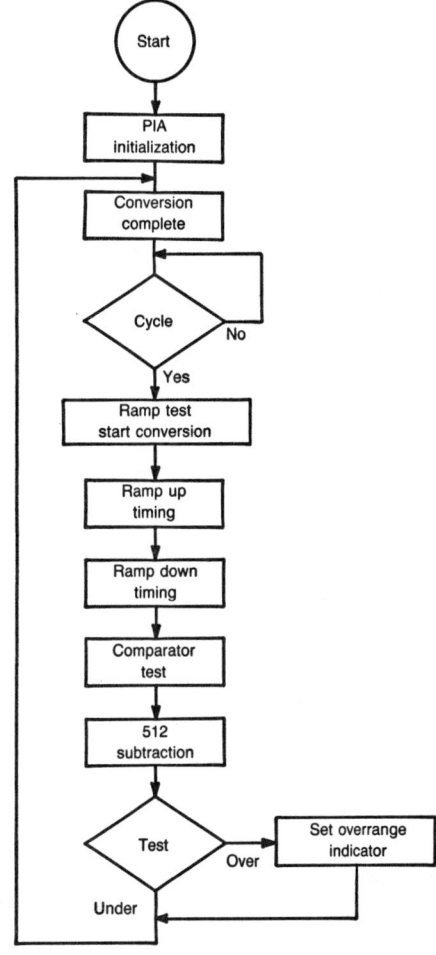

**Dual ramp conversion program flow**

**dual ramp conversion program** The program for the 6800 first requires instructions to initialize the input and output ports of the peripheral interface adapter (PIA). The ramp control is then set and the comparator tested. This insures that the comparator output is below the reference voltage level at the beginning of conversion. Then a conversion-finished flag is set, and the microprocessor enters a loop as shown in the flow diagram.

This loop uses the PB1 cycle input from the PIA, and it resets the conversion-finished flag when the ramp control goes low to start a new cycle.

The index register is loaded and then decremented to provide the ramp-up timing. As the ramp crosses the threshold level, the comparator output is switched, causing the microprocessor to enter the ramp-up cycle. The index register is decremented until empty. Then the ramp control switches to high and the index register is incremented. A dummy statement equalizes the count for the ramp periods. Then as the ramp down period ends, the contents of the index register are stored. The offset counts are obtained, and an overrange test then checks the contents of a location for a value.

**dual system** A system configuration in which two computers are used for processing and the results compared for accuracy. Identical inputs and routines are used. The dual system is employed for applications requiring a high degree of reliability.

**dummy** A nonfunctioning item used to satisfy some format or logic requirement or to fulfill prescribed conditions. A dummy may be an artificial character, statement, address, or instruction usually inserted to complete format conditions, such as fixed word length.

**dummy argument** A prototype field in a macro definition that is variable and is to be replaced with a parameter (quantity or symbol)

when the macro operation is used. It is also called a dummy definition.

**dummy instruction** Refers to an artificial instruction or address inserted in a list of instructions. It is used to fulfill certain conditions, such as a word or block length, without affecting the operation.

**dummy load** 1. The act of transfer to storage of a program without execution in order to determine if all specifications and requirements have been met. 2. A resistor that simulates electrically a sink for an electric current.

**dump** A transfer in operation or contents of a computer system. A power or *dc dump* results in the removal of power from the computer. Power dumps can result in the loss of operations and data unless specific measures are taken to prevent losses. *Binary* and *change* dumps cause a printout or output into binary form, or a printout or output only, for locations that have changed since the last dump. A dumping program usually has a restart provision to allow the program to start again at the last dump point if an interrupt such as that caused by a machine malfunction should occur.

Dump commands such as the following are used to transfer the contents of memory between two specific locations to a specified output format:

D x, y; (dump memory between locations x and y)

**dump and restart** Refers to software routines for taking program dumps at specified times and for restarting programs at one of these points in the event of program failure.

**dump, binary** Refers to a dump or printout of the contents of a memory unit in binary form onto some external medium such as tape or printout forms.

**dump, change** Refers to a printout or output recording of the contents of all storage locations in which a change has been made since the previous change dump.

**dump check** A check to verify data being transferred during dumping. One method adds all of the digits during dumping and checks the sum when retransferring.

**dump point** The point in a program where it is desirable to have a transfer operation. Dump points are usually designed to protect against machine failure.

**dumping resistor** A resistor that drains charge from a capacitor for safety purposes.

**dump, power** The removal of all power accidentally or intentionally.

**duodecimal** Relating to the number system with a radix of twelve.

**duplex** Containing two sets of operational elements that may or may not operate simultaneously. In communications, a duplex system is one in which data may be received and transmitted over the same lines simultaneously.

**duplex cable** A type of cable constructed of two insulating stranded-wire conductors twisted together. They may or may not share a common insulating covering.

**duplex channel** A channel providing simultaneous transmission in both directions.

**duplexed operation** A mode of operation in which a primary processor performs the control task. If a failure occurs, a backup processor takes over. The primary processor is then taken offline, repaired and returned to service without interrupting control of the process. Duplexed processors provide twice the computing capacity, since either processor may control the process. This excess power can often be used for other optional tasks.

To guarantee higher reliability, the entire system should be examined for the consequences of each possible failure. Also, software for the duplexed processors must be designed to achieve the higher potential reliability of the duplicated hardware.

Duplexed operation allows the selection of two processors to take advantage of special characteristics. One may be designed to perform fast floating point calculations; this would be its function during normal operation of the system.

In order for the backup processor to keep up-to-date, it must have access to the current process status information. With a shared file interconnection, the information is maintained in the shared file. With channel to channel connections, the primary processor periodically posts the process status information into the memory of the backup computer.

**duplexed system** A system with two distinct and separate sets of facilities, each of which is capable of assuming the system function while the other assumes a standby status. Usually both sets are identical.

**duplex operation** Refers to a simultaneous operation of transmitting and receiving apparatus at two separate locations.

**duplicate** 1. To copy such that the result is in the same form and indistinguishable in content from the original, such as, to make another punched card with the same pattern as the original. 2. A copy of an original document or program.

**duplication check** A check that requires that the results of two independent operations be identical. A duplication check may be performed at the same time on different equipment or at different times on the same equipment.

**durability index** A measure of the durability of a tape expressed as the number of passes that can be made before a significant degradation of output occurs divided by the corresponding number that can be made using a reference tape.

**duration, character** Refers to the time required for all of the pulses that are associated with a specific character to pass a given point on a communication channel.

**duty cycle** A specified operating time of an unit plus a specified time of nonoperation.

**Dvorak simplified keyboard** A rearranged typewriter keyboard; advocates of this keyboard claim that it permits 35 percent faster output than conventional keyboards. First patented in 1932 by Dr. August Dvorak of the University of Washington, Seattle.

**DVST** Abbreviation for *direct view storage tube*.

**DW** Abbreviation for *data word*.

**dwell** A programmed time delay of variable duration. A dwell is not sequential or cyclic, nor is it an interlock.

**dwell time reset** Refers to time spent in reset. In cycling the computer from reset to operate to hold and back to reset, this time must be long enough to permit the computer to recover from any overload and voltage changes.

**DXC** Abbreviation for *data exchange control*.

**dyad** An operator indicated by writing the symbols of two vectors with no symbol or other sign between them.

**dyadic operator** A Boolean operator with two operands. Dyadic operators include AND, OR, NAND, NOR, and exclusive-OR. A *dyad*.

**dynamic check** A test of any function or process that is conducted by subjecting the device, process, or function to the rigors of its anticipated operational environment.

**dynamic debugging** The debugging of routines at full system speed. The routines are first checked using the single-step mode; only when they are completely debugged at low speed should dynamic debugging be undertaken.

**dynamic dump** A dump that is performed during program execution.

**dynamic gain** The magnitude ratio of a steady state output to a sinusoidal input signal.

**dynamic memory** See *dynamic storage* and *dynamic RAM*.

**dynamic MOS RAMs** A kind of metal-oxide semiconductor random-access memory in which the memory cells must be electrically refreshed periodically to avoid loss of held data. A three transistor dynamic MOS cell uses a shared read or write select line and separate read and write data bit lines. The device capacitance shown in the figure in dashed lines is charged and discharged as a function of the write line. This type of MOS memory is relatively inexpensive to produce, but it requires additional circuitry for the refreshing operation.

MOS dynamic RAMs of 1024 bits were the first semiconductor memories to gain wide acceptance. Built from p channel MOS technology, these chips made large, solid state memory arrays possible. These dynamic memories used capacitive storage to hold each

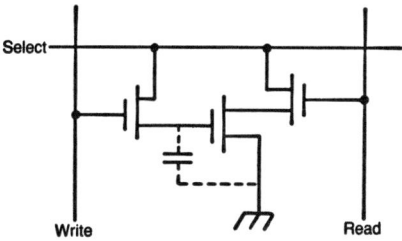

Basic dynamic MOS RAM cell

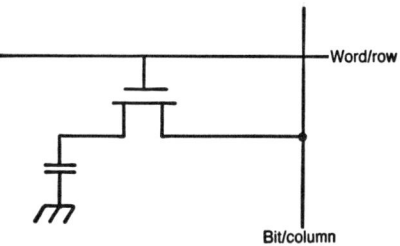

Single transistor MOS RAM cell

bit value and required periodic refreshing to retain data since the charge held in the capacitors leaked away. A three transistor cell was used for each bit stored, and the 1024 bits were housed in about 20,000 square mils of silicon. This density first promised to displace core memories and make large semiconductor systems simple to implement. But it was not until even higher density products were introduced that the takeover began occurring. The first of the higher density devices, the 4096 bit dynamic RAM, provided quadruple the density. To make those higher density and higher speed RAMs possible, p channel technology was abandoned and n channel processing was used. N channel allowed the low threshold voltages needed for TTL compatibility and its speed was greater. It also permitted device densities to grow larger. Along with n channel processing came a new cell design that permitted a bit to be stored with a single transistor and a capacitor, as shown in the figure.

**dynamic programming** Programming that allows a number of decisions for each stage of a multistage problem. Dynamic programming seeks to optimize the problem solution by the integration of the cumulative effects of each stage on the overall goal.

**dynamic RAM** A random-access memory in which data is stored capacitively and which must be refreshed, or it will be lost. Dynamic RAMs offer high bit densities, low cost, input/output compatibility with TTL levels, and speed compatibility with many microprocessors.

**dynamic relocation** A program that can be moved to a different location in a partially executed state without affecting its ability to complete the processing.

**dynamic response** The specific behavior of the output of a device as a function of the input, both with respect to time.

**dynamic storage** A type of memory, usually semiconductor, in which the stored data gradually leaks away and is lost, unless it is refreshed periodically by special circuitry.

**dynamic subroutine** A subroutine that has a skeletal form with regard to certain parameters that are selected later as the processing proceeds. These parameters may include the number of repetitions, decimal point position, or item size. The computer can be used to derive these parameters during program execution.

**dynamic worksheet** Refers to a program that allows "what-if" analysis for financial or planning analysis, such as the VisiCalc program. These programs allow act as hyper-editors that allow one to edit a balance sheet. They will automatically calculate any entries on the sheet that will change as a result of a directed change.

# E

**EA** Abbreviation for *effective address*.
**EAE** Abbreviation for *extended arithmetic element*.
**EAM** Abbreviation for *electrical accounting machine*.
**early failure period** An interval, immediately following the final assembly, during which the failure rate of certain items is relatively high. Synonym for infant mortality period.
**EAROM** Acronym for *electrically alterable ROM*, a specialized random-access read/write memory that may be programmed by writing into the array and used as a ROM. Read cycle time is 10-20 microseconds and writing takes about one millisecond. The contents can be erased in one operation. EAROM costs tend to be high due to low production yield and the long test times required to check the data patterns. EAROM testing may take up to 30 minutes per unit, while testing of conventional RAMs can be done in 30 seconds.
**earth stations** Refers to communications ground terminals that use antennas and associated electronic equipment to transmit, receive, and process communications via satellite. Future networks may be able to interconnect by domestic communications satellites, creating regional and national networks.
**earth, virtual** Refers to a live input terminal of a directly coupled amplifier that remains approximately at earth potential although not connected to earth.
**EAS** Abbreviation for *extended area service*.
**EASY** Abbreviation for *efficient assembly system*.
**EAX** Abbreviation for *electronic automatic exchange*.
**EBCDIC** Abbreviation for *extended binary-coded-decimal interchange code*, a code that uses a set of eight bit-coded characters. EBCDIC is used for representation and transmission in data processing systems, communications, and associated devices. Some examples of the EBCDIC code follow:

| EBCDIC SYMBOL | CODE |
|---|---|
| 1 | 1111 0001 |
| 2 | 1111 0010 |
| 3 | 1111 0011 |
| 4 | 1111 0100 |
| 5 | 1111 0101 |
| A | 1100 0001 |
| B | 1100 0010 |
| C | 1100 0011 |
| D | 1100 0100 |
| ! | 0101 1010 |
| $ | 0101 1011 |
| * | 0101 1100 |
| ) | 0101 1101 |

**EBICON** Abbreviation for *electron bombardment induced conductivity*.
**EBR** Abbreviation for *electron beam recording*.
**EBR-I** Abbreviation for *Experimental Breeder Reactor I*, the world's first reactor to produce usable amounts of electricity using plutonium in metal form as fuel.
**EC** Abbreviation for *error correcting*.
**ECAC** Abbreviation for *Electromagnetic Compatability Analysis Center;* Engineering College Administrative Council.
**ECAP** Abbreviation for *electronic circuit analysis program*, a language for modeling and analyzing electrical networks. ECAP allows the synthesizing of device models using function generators or tables of functions in conjunction with passive components.
**ECC** Abbreviation for *error checking and correcting*. Refers to self-diagnostic and self-correcting techniques used for RAM memory. ECC

memory prevents some improper computer operations due to soft errors.

**Eccles-Jordan trigger** A once-common tube-type bistable multivibrator in which the output of one section is directly coupled into the input of the other section. The circuit is capable of storing one bit of information.

**ECCM** Abbreviation for *electronic counter countermeasure*.

**ECG** Abbreviation for *electro cardiograph*.

**echo** The return of a sufficient portion of a transmitted signal to be recognized due to reflection. An echo is usually received as interference, but in an echo check, the received echo data is compared with the original for accuracy.

**echo check** Refers to error control techniques in which the receiving terminal or computer returns the original message to the sender to verify that the message was received correctly.

**ECL** Abbreviation for *emitter-coupled logic*, a logic family that uses signal coupling directly into the emitters of transistors. ECL is very fast, requires only a 1 volt of signal swing in 3-4 nanoseconds, and inherently generates little noise. Power requirements tend to be higher than other logic families. Microprocessors have been implemented with ECL using the bit-slice approach.

**ECL microprocessor** A typical ECL microprocessor set contains five chips: a 4-bit slice, a control register function, a timing function, a slice memory interface, and a slice look ahead. The various chips may be used as building blocks to construct a microprocessor with capabilities larger than four bits.

**ECM** Abbreviation for *electronic countermeasures*.

**ED** 1. The provided editor program for CP/M. 2. An abbreviation for *extended density*.

**EDC** Abbreviation for *external device code*.

**edit** To modify the form or format of data, such as inserting or deleting characters or decimal points.

**EDGE** Abbreviation for *electronic data gathering equipment*.

**edit commands** Refers to specific commands used with an editor. In some systems edit commands are implemented as single, double, or triple letter mnemonics followed by optional command parameters. Commands are usually terminated by typing a carriage return.

**editing** 1. The act of revising and correcting text or a program prior to its production as a final document or publication. 2. The act of operating the function and alphanumeric keys of an editor in a word processor or computer.

**editing terminal** Refers to a system for providing the following editing capabilities: replacement, insertion, deletion, and movement of characters, words, sentences, paragraphs, and blocks.

**editor** An interactive system or a program that allows users to prepare programs or text and to make changes using simple commands. Some time-sharing services offer such editor systems. Using the time-sharing programs, users can prepare assembly-language programs and correct them quickly. They can also add and store documentation as well as combine and retrieve programs. Editors allow the programs to be output into tape or printout with ease. Editing terminals allow the following functions:

1. Character replacement
2. Insertion and movement of characters, words, and blocks
3. Batch balancing
4. Check-digit verification

Text is punched using the teletypewriter or keypunch.

An editor allows the microcomputer designer to prepare the original assembly language programs and correct them using simple commands. Commands may be typed in at any time during the edit process in place of a source statement. Some types of editors are portable, with built-in displays and data entry keys.

**editor, linkage** 1. A utility program that edits the output of language translators and produces executable program phases. It relocates programs or program sections and links together separately assembled (or compiled) sections. 2. A program that produces a load module by transforming object modules into a format that is acceptable to fetch, combining separately produced object modules and previously processed load modules into a single load module, resolving symbolic cross references among them, replacing, deleting, and adding control sections automatically on request, and providing overlay facilities for modules requesting them.

**editor, microcomputer** Refers to an editor that allows designers to prepare assembly language programs and to change or correct them with simple commands. They can add documentation and store, combine, and retrieve programs.

**editor, portable** Refers to an editor unit with display and data entry keys to edit program programmable read-only memories (PROMs) in machine language. They are generally simple, which makes the portable units easy to use.

**edit statements** Refers to statements entered from the keyboard that can be placed into an internal edit buffer. Each statement entered can be preceded by a statement number that specifies the relative order of the statement in relation to all other statements.

**EDP** Abbreviation for *electronic data processing*.

**EEPROM** Electrically erasable programmable read-only memory, a PROM that can be electrically erased and electrically written into. This alterability allows in-circuit programming where the device can be erased, written, and read without being removed from the circuit. These devices are also known as EAROMs (Electrically Alterable ROMs).

There are two types of devices:

1. Metal-Nitride-Oxide-Semiconductors (MNOS)
2. Floating gate.

The floating gate EEPROMs are similar to ultraviolet EPROMs with the addition of a control gate. There is no quartz lid to allow erasing.

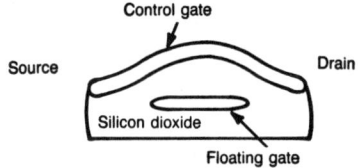

**EEPROM structure with control gate**

**EEROM programmer** A device that provides a means of programming a single EEROM or an EEROM module using an integral hex keyboard and display. EEROMS are electrically erasable and therefore need not be removed from the module or socket to be erased and reprogrammed.

**effective address** An address that is derived by indexing or indirect addressing techniques that is actually used to identify the current operand.

**effective instruction** A method used to modify a presumptive instruc-

**effector** A device used to bring about a desired response to a change in its input from another device where the end result is required.

**EFTS** Abbreviation for *electronic funds transfer system*, a computerized means of transferring financial information from one location to another.

**EGO** Abbreviation for *eccentric geophysical observatory*.

**ehf** Abbreviation for *extremely high frequency*, 30 to 300 gigahertz (FCC).

**EIA** Abbreviation for *Electronic Industries Association*, an organization of electronic manufacturers that maintains certain standards in various product areas. The EIA has interface standards that cover signal characteristics, voltages, currents, and time periods; connections to modem units; and the physical dimensions of hardware. The EIA also has standards for character codes and coding.

**EIA standard code** A code or coding system conforming to any one of the standards established by the Electronic Industries Association. The two EIA Standards for numerical control character coding are RS 244-A, the character code for Numerical Machine Control Perforated Tape; and RS-358, a subset of the USA Standard Code for Information Interchange for Numerical Machine Control Perforated Tape.

**EICM** Abbreviation for *employer's inventory of critical manpower*.

**eight-level code** Refers to a distinct code designed with eight impulses used to describe a single character, but with additional start and stop elements often used for asynchronous transmission.

**EIS** Abbreviation for *end interruption sequence*.

**electric** Refers to any phenomena that depend essentially on a peculiarity of electric charges.

**electrical contacts** Refers to paths, joints, or touchings of the two halves of a connector or contacts at points joined in electrical connections.

**electrical degrees** The angle, expressed in degrees of phase difference of vectors, representing currents or voltages arising in different parts of a circuit.

**electrical element** Any of the individual building blocks from which electronic circuits are constructed, such as conductors, resistors, capacitors, and inductors.

**electrical heating** Heating by an electrical means, such as current flow through a resistance, induction currents in a conductor, or displacement currents in a dielectric.

**electrical impulse** Any momentary transient voltage, whether inadvertent or intentionally produced.

**electrical interference** Interference due to the operation of electrical apparatus other than that arising from actual transmissions.

**electrically alterable ROM** A specialized random-access memory (abbreviated *EAROM*) that is programmed by writing into the array and used as a ROM. EAROM applications include machine controllers and replacements for semiconductor memories in minicomputers.

**electrically erasable ROM** A ROM that can be erased in one second or less. A typical EEROM is organized as 512 words of two bits each, and it can be erased and reprogrammed as many as one million times.

**electrical quantity** Usually denoted by Q, it is the amount of electric charge, the practical unit being the coulomb.

**electrical reset** Restoration of a device, such as a relay or circuit, usually by a reset signal.

**electrical schematic** A diagram that represents all circuit elements using symbols and interconnecting lines.

**electric axis** The direction in a crystal that gives the maximum conductivity to the passage of an electric current; the X-axis of a piezoelectric crystal.

**electric circuit** A continuous closed path consisting of wires and elements for the flow of current.

**electric delay line** A delay line that uses lumped or distributed capacitive and inductive elements.

**electric doublet** A system with a definite electric moment, mathematically equivalent to two equal charges of opposite sign at a very small distance apart.

**electric field** A region in which attracting or repelling forces are exerted on any electric charge present.

**electric flux** Refers to the electric field intensity normal to the surface. The electric flux is conceived as emanating from a positive charge and ending on a negative charge without loss.

**electricity** A fundamental quantity consisting of two oppositely charged particles, the electrons being negatively charged, and the protons positively charged. A substance with more electrons than protons is said to be negatively charged; conversely one with more protons than electrons is positively charged.

**electric motor** Any device for converting electrical energy into mechanical torque.

**electric oscillations** Electric currents that periodically reverse their direction of flow, at a frequency determined by the constants of circuit or source.

**electric polarization** The dipole moment per unit volume of a dielectric.

**electric potential** A measure of the energy of a unit positive charge at a point, expressed relative to that at infinite distance or at the surface of the earth (zero potential).

**electric susceptibility** A measure of the relative permittivity of a dielectric path, such as found in a transmission line.

**electric transducer** A device that converts nonelectric energy into electric energy, such as the microphone, solar cell, or strain gauge.

**electrochromeric display** A type of display that uses materials that change from transparent to opaque under the control of an electric field. A field can be used to turn the ECD on, and it will hold that state until a field of opposite polarity switches it back to its original state.

**electrode** The conducting element in an electronic tube, which does one or more of the following: emits or collects electrons or ions, or controls their movement by means of an electronic field on it. In semiconductors, the element does one or more of the following: emits or collects electrons or holes, or controls their movements by means of an electric field.

**electrode admittance** The admittance measured between an electrode and earth when all other potentials on electrodes are constant.

**electrode conductance** The in-phase or real component of an electrode admittance.

**electrode current** The net current entering or leaving an electrode.

**electrode impedance** The ratio of a sinusoidal voltage on an electrode to the corresponding sinusoidal current, all other electrodes being maintained at constant potential.

**electrodeposition** The deposition electrolytically of a substance on an electrode, as in electroplating or electroforming.

**electrodynamics** The science dealing with the interaction or forces between currents, or the forces on currents in independent magnetic fields.

**electroencephalograph** An instrument for studying voltage waves associated with the brain. It includes a sensitive detector (voltage or current), a dc amplifier of high stability, and an electronic recording system.

**electrofluor** A transparent material that has the property of storing electrical energy and releasing it as visible (fluorescent) light.

**electrokinetics** The science of electric charges in motion, without reference to the accompanying magnetic field.

**electrolysis** The chemical change, generally decomposition, effected by a flow of current through a solution of the chemical; the solution can be in its molten state. The process is based on ionization.

**electrolyte strength** A measure of the strength or extent towards complete ionization in a dilute solution. When concentrated, the ions join in groups, as indicated by lowered mobility.

**electrolytic dissociation** The splitting up (which is reversible) of substances into oppositely charged ions.

**electrolytic ion** A charged current carrier formed by dissociation of an ionic compound such as water.

**electrolytic polarization** A change in the potential of an electrode when a current is passed through it. As the current rises, polarization reduces the potential difference between the two electrodes of the system.

**electromagnet** Refers to a ferromagnetic core, surrounded by a current carrying coil, which exhibits appreciable magnetic effects only when current passes through it.

**electromagnetic delay line** A delay line whose operation is based on the time of propagation of an electromagnetic wave through the distributed or lumped capacitance and inductance.

**electromagnetic field** Refers to the field of influence produced around a conductor by the current flowing through it; it is a moving electric field and its associated magnetic field, the latter perpendicular to both the electric lines of force and their direction.

**electromagnetic flowmeters** These are flowmeters that follow Faraday's Law that relative motion, at right angles between a conductor and a magnetic field, induces a voltage in a conductor. This voltage is proportional to the relative velocity of the conductor and the magnetic field. The flowmeter is made with a nonmagnetic tube and uses a conductive liquid. On the tube are magnetic coils that, when energized, provide a magnetic field through the full width of the tube. As the liquid moves through the magnetic field, a voltage is generated proportional to the flow rate.

**electromagnetic induction** The transfer of electrical power from one circuit to another by varying the magnetic linkage.

**electromagnetic inertia** The energy required to stop or start a current in an inductive circuit. An electrical inductance behaves like a mass in a mechanical system.

**electromagnetic interference** The unwanted electrical energy or noise induced in the circuits of a device due to the presence of electromagnetic fields.

**electromagnetic wave** The radiant energy produced around a wire or other conductor when current passes through it.

**electrometallurgy** The branch of science concerned with the application of electro chemistry to the extraction or treatment of metals.

**electromotive force** Refers to the force that causes electricity to flow when there is a difference of potential between two points. The unit of measurement is the volt. Electromotive force is abbreviated emf.

**electron** One of the natural elementary constituents of matter, which carries a negative electric charge of one electric unit and has approximately 1/1840th the mass of a hydrogen atom or $9.107 \times 10^{-28}$ gram.

**electron affinity** The tendency of certain substances, notably oxidizing agents, to capture an electron.

**electron attachment** The formation of negative ions by the attachment of free electrons to neutral atoms or molecules.

**electron avalanche** A chain reaction that is started as one free electron collides with one or more orbiting electrons and frees them. The free electrons then free others in the same manner, as the reaction continues.

**electron beam** A narrow stream of electrons moving in the same direction under the influence of an electric or magnetic field.

**electron camera** A generic term for a device that converts an optical image into a corresponding electric current directly by electronic means, without the intervention of mechanical scanning.

**electron capture** Refers to the capture of a shell electron (K or L) by its own nucleus, decreasing the atomic number of the atom without changing the mass.

**electron conduction** Refers to the conduction that arises from the drift of free electrons in metallic conductors when an electric field is applied.

**electron device** A device that depends on the conduction of electrons through a vacuum, gas, or semiconductor.

**electron discharge** The current produced by the passage of electrons through air or vacuum.

**electron drift** The actual transfer of electrons in a conductor as distinct from energy transfer arising from encounters between neighboring electrons.

**electron emission** The liberation of electrons from a surface.

**electron gun** An electron source, with the necessary anodes, which accelerates electrons in a given direction while focusing or diffusing them, as required in a cathode ray tube.

**electronic** Descriptive of any circuit or network employing solid-state or vacuum-tube active devices.

**electronic beam recording** The use of an electron beam to store and read information on a target. Targets are usually silicon dioxide, and the data is sorted as electrostatic charges or magnetic bubbles on materials like vitrium iron garnet.

**electronic configuration** The arrangement of atoms or electrons in their various states or orbits in a molecule or crystal.

**electronic control** The general use of electronic devices for industrial and consumer control applications.

**electronic data processing** Data processing performed largely by electronic devices. EDP includes the functions of entering, classifying, computing, and recording information—and the devices such as internally stored program computers and automatic data processors. Disk units, but not disk packs, are considered as electronic data processing equipment.

**electronic digital computer** A machine that uses electronic circuitry to perform arithmetic and logic operations by means of an internally or externally stored program of machine instructions.

**electronic efficiency** The ratio of the power at a desired frequency, delivered by an electron stream to a circuit, to the average power supplied to the stream.

**electronic flash** Refers to a device that charges a capacitor, the latter discharging through a tube containing neon (stroboscope) or xenon (photography) and producing a burst of light when triggered.

**electronic funds transfer system** A type of national banking system that uses electronics for the transfer of funds, as well as for the clearing and settling of accounts.

**Electronic Industries Association** A trade association (abbreviated *EIA*) for electronics manufacturers which sets industry technical standards, disseminates market data, and maintains contact with government agencies affecting the electronics industry.

**electronic multiplier** An all-electronic device for forming the product of two variables.

**electronic oscillations** Refers to oscillations of high frequency, generated by moving electrons; the frequency is determined by the transit time.

**electronic packaging** Refers to the mechanical characteristics and features of an electronic assembly.

**electronic pen** A stylus that is used with a CRT display for input to the system computer. Also called a light pen, the stylus signals the computer with electronic pulses that the computer interprets.

**electronics** The branch of science and engineering that deals with the phenomena associated with the flow of electrons in devices and the utilization of these devices.

**electronic storage** Refers to memory units that utilize electronic charges or conduction, such as semiconductor RAM and ROM. The microcomputer's main or internal memory may be divided into read/write memory (RAM) and read only memory (ROM). RAM electronic storage is power vulnerable and is lost if there is any interruption of power to the microcomputer.

**electronic switch** A usually solid-state device that provides an automatic on/off switching action and functions primarily as an electronic circuit element.

**electronic tuning** The changing of the operating frequency of a system by changing the characteristics of a coupled electronic system.

**electronic voltmeter** A voltmeter that depends on the amplifying of the input signal.

**electron jet** A narrow stream of electrons, similar to a beam, but not necessarily focused.

**electron lens** A composite arrangement of magnetic coils and charged electrodes to focus or divert electron beams in the manner of an optical lens.

**electron microscope** A microscope that uses a tube in which electrons emitted from the cathode are focused, by suitable magnetic and electrostatic fields.

**electron octet** The up to eight valency electrons in an outer shell of an atom or molecule, which is characterized by great stability, in so far as the complete shell around an atom makes it chemically inert.

**electronogen** A photosensitive molecule that may emit an electron when illuminated.

**electron pair** Two valence electrons shared by adjacent nuclei, forming a nonpolar bond.

**electron scanning** The scanning or establishing of an image by an electron beam in a cathode ray tube, normally using a rectangular raster with horizontal lines.

**electron stream** A stream of electrons moving with the same velocity and direction in neighboring paths and usually emitted from a single source such as a cathode.

**electron trap** An acceptor impurity in a semiconductor.

**electroplating** Deposition of one metal on another by electrolytic action when a current is passed through a cell. Metal is taken from the anode and deposited on the cathode through a solution containing the metal as an ion.

**electropolar** Possessing magnetic poles or positive and negative charges.

**electrostatic adhesion** The adhesion between two substances or surfaces due to electrostatic attraction between opposite charges.

**electrostatic bonding** The valence linkage between atoms arising from the transfer of one or more electrons from the outer shell of one atom to the outer shell of another. The transfer leads towards near completion of the outer shells of both atoms.

**electrostatic printer** A printer that uses a special metalized paper and sends an electric charge through the paper thus creating the characters. These printers are principally used for draft work.

**electrostatic shield** A metal mesh used to screen one device from the electric field of another.

**electrostatic storage** A type of memory based on capacitor principles, in which a dielectric sandwiched between a pair of electrodes holds electrostatic charges representing information.

**electrostatic units** Refers to the units for electric and magnetic measurements in which the permittivity of a vacuum is taken as unity, with no dimensions in the centimeter-gram-second system.

**electrostatic wattmeter** A wattmeter that utilizes electrostatic forces to measure AC power at high voltages.

**electrostriction** The change in the dimensions of a dielectric accompanying the application of an electric field.

**electrovalence** The chemical bond in which an electron is transferred from one atom to another, the resulting ions being held together by electrostatic attraction.

**element** 1. One of the basic substances of matter that cannot be decomposed by simple chemical analysis. 2. A component of a circuit, such as a resistor or capacitor. 3. The typing component on an automated typewriter, such as the printwheel or the ball.

**element, delayed** A circuit or mechanism that accepts input, temporarily retains it, and emits it.

**ELGMT** Abbreviation for *erector-launches, guided missile, transportable*.

**ELINT** Abbreviation for *electromagnetic intelligence*, (USAF).

**elite** 1. The smaller of two common typewriter typeface sizes, the larger being pica. 2. A standard of typewriter spacing, 12 characters to the horizontal inch, also called 12 pitch.

**elliptic polarization** Refers to the polarization of an electromagnetic wave in which the electric and magnetic fields each contain two unequal components, at right angles in space and in phase quadrature.

**else** An operation such as disjunction, OR, or inclusive-OR that is programmed to take place when conditions are not explicit. The *else* conditions are handled as "don't care" or left blank. In a program, *else* conditions usually cause a halt that must be covered to allow recovery for continued processing.

**ELSEC** Abbreviation for *electronic security*.

**EM** The ASCII *end-of-medium* character.

**EMAR** Abbreviation for *experimental memory-address register*.

**embedded command** A word processing instruction generally affecting the format of text, but not its content.

**embedded hyphen** See required hyphen.

**embossment** As used in character recognition, the distance from the distorted surface of a document to a specified part of a printed character.

**EMI** Abbreviation for *electromagnetic interference*, a broad designation for any kind of interference occurring in the electromagnetic spectrum.

**emission** The release of electrons from atoms on absorption of energy in excess of the normal average. This can arise from (1) thermal (thermionic) agitation, as in X-Ray and cathode-ray tubes, (2) secondary emission of electrons, which are ejected by impact of higher energy primary electrons, (3) photoelectric release on absorption of quanta above a certain energy level, (4) field emission by the actual stripping from atoms by a high electric field.

**emissivity** The ratio of the amount of energy radiated by a body at some particular wave length to that emitted by a black body of the same temperature and at the same wave length.

**emittance** The power per unit area radiated by a source of energy.

**emitter bias** The bias voltage applied to the emitter of a transistor.

**emitter-coupled logic** A logic family (abbreviated *ECL*) that uses semiconductors that switch without being driven into full saturation. ECL circuits are faster than TTL, but more expensive because of the extra diffusion steps in device processing.

**emitter current** The current flowing in the emitter circuit of a transistor.

**emitter follower** Refers to a circuit that resembles a cathode follower but uses a transistor rather than a vacuum tube and an emitter rather than a cathode. The base also substitutes for the grid.

**EML** Abbreviation for *equipment modification list*.

**empirical** That which is based on actual measurement, observation, or experience versus that which is based on purely theoretical determinations.

**EMR** Abbreviation for *executive management responsibility*.

**EMT** Abbreviation for *electrical metallic tubing*.

**emulate** The process of using one system to imitate another such that the imitating system accepts the same programs and achieves the same end results as the imitated system. Emulation, which involves the software techniques used to imitate the other system, can minimize the impact of conversion from one system to another during program development.

Emulation of a number of devices can sometimes be done using a single general-purpose unit. The general-purpose device, adapted to several different configurations through microprogramming, becomes a host serving the more specialized devices. One in-circuit emulator system uses two processors—one to execute commands and control peripherals, and the other to interface directly with the user's prototype system. Emulation allows custom instructions through microprogramming, which permits software designed for larger machines to run on microprocessors. The user is also allowed to run programs and integrate hardware and software very early in the development cycle.

**emulsion** Refers to a light sensitive chemical coat on materials, commonly used on photographic film.

**emulsion laser storage** A storage system that uses a controlled laser beam to expose small sections of a photosensitive area.

**enable** To permit, either automatically or under manual control, the operation of a specific function.

**enclosure, microcomputer** Refers to an enclosure specifically designed to house a microcomputer system. The enclosure may be ventilated and often includes an air blower, air filter, power disconnect, card chassis, power supply, bus terminator, and termination panel with terminal strips.

**encode** To apply a code to represent data or information. Encoding may be done for convenience or to hide the meaning of information from others. Also called *encipher*.

**encoder** Any device or circuit that provides an enabling code to permit an otherwise unusable system or device to be used in an environment where the code is required. In a selective calling communications system, an encoder may be a simple tone oscillator of a specific frequency.

**end** In braiding operations, the number of fibers or wire per carrier.

**end-around carry** A carry from the most significant digit position to the least significant position.

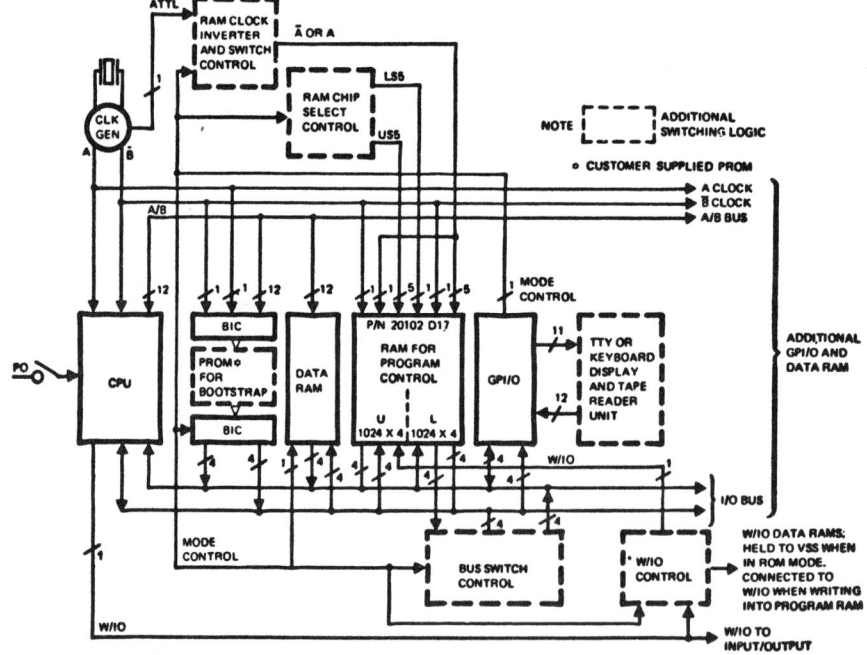

**Emulation of ROM with CPU-loaded RAM**

**end instrument** The final device in a communications loop. End instruments include all generating and loop-terminating units at receiving and transmitting stations.

**end item** A final combination of end products, component parts, and/or materials that is ready for its intended use.

**end-of-block character (EOB)** 1. A character indicating the end of a block of tape information. It is used to stop the tape reader after a block has been read. 2. The typewriter function of the carriage return when preparing machine control tapes.

**end-of-data marker** A character or code word that indicates that the end of all data held in a storage unit has been reached.

**end-of-file** The termination or completion of a quantity of data, usually indicated by end-of-file marks (abbreviated *EOF*).

**end-of-medium character** The ASCII EM character. A control character used to indicate the physical end of a data medium. The character usually gives ample warning to allow the user to make changes in the system operation. In the 7-digit ASCII, the EM is represented by a binary 25: 1001 1001 (the first character given is an even-parity indicator).

**end-of-message** A character or group of characters that indicates the termination of a message or record (abbreviated *EOM*).

**end of program** A miscellaneous function indicating completion of a workpiece in automatic machining. It stops the spindle, collant, and feed after completion of all commands in the block. It is used to reset control and/or the machine.

**end-of-run** A type of routine used for housekeeping just before a run is completed. An end-of-run routine may be used for rewinding tapes or printing out totals.

**end-of-tape arrangement** A programmed routine employed during the processing of the final tape in a multireel program. See also *end-of-run*.

**end-of-tape marker** A character or special device to alert an operator that the end of the recording area is approaching. The marker may be a photoreflecting strip, a transparent section of tape, a unique bit pattern, or any other flagging arrangement.

**end-of-text character** A control character used to denote the end of a text. In ASCII, this is the ETX character symbolized by a binary 3.

**end-of-transmission-block character** The ASCII ETB character, which indicates the end of a block of data being transmitted. The ASCII value of ETB is binary 23, or 0001 0111.

**end-of-transmission character** A control character used to indicate the conclusion of transmission. In ASCII, this is the EOT character symbolized by a binary 4.

**end point** An extremity of a span of measurement points.

**end use** The way a device is used by its ultimate consumer.

**energize** To apply the rated voltage to a circuit or device in order to activate it.

**energy band** In a solid, the energy levels of individual atoms interact to form bands of permitted levels with gaps between. Normally there is a valence band with a full complement of electrons and a conduction band, which is empty. When these overlap, metallic conduction is possible. In semiconductors there is a small gap and intrinsic conduction occurs only when some electrons acquire the energy necessary to surmount this gap and enter the conduction band. In insulators, the gap is large and cannot normally be surmounted.

**energy levels** Electron energies in atoms are limited to a fixed range of values termed *permitted-energy levels* and represented by horizontal lines drawn against a vertical energy scale.

**engineering data** Data contained in an original source document prepared under a design activity. Engineering data may include configuration description, performance specifications, reliability and maintainability goals, and operational practices and procedures.

**engineering improvement time** Machine time that is set aside for installing and testing modifications to the computer system. Engineering improvement time is a part of the total machine time necessary for servicing. Engineering time includes preventive servicing, repair time, and testing following repairs. Time spent to improve reliability without improving the facilities is called *supplementary maintenance time*.

**enlarger printer** A unit that projects an enlarged image from microfilm, and develops and fixes the image on a hard-copy medium.

**enquiry character** A control character used to request a response from a remote station. The ENQ character is usually for station identification or status data.

**entropy** 1. The measure of unavailable energy in a system. 2. The unavailable information is a set of documents. 3. An inactive or static condition (total entropy).

**entry block** A block of main memory storage assigned for receipt of each entry into the system and associated with that entry for the life of the system.

**entry conditions** The initial conditions required to be satisfied for the execution of a given routine.

**entry instruction** The first instruction to be executed in a subroutine. The entry instruction may have several entry points at different locations of the subroutine.

**entry point** A place where control can be transferred, other segments of the program can reference, and where the program can be activated by the operator or the system.

**envelope** The configuration of a modulation waveform in which the carrier may be seen as a different and more complex configuration.

**envelope delay** The propagation time between two fixed points of the envelope of a modulated wave. When the delay is variable over the frequency range of transmission, a distortion known as envelope delay distortion results.

**environmental conditions** External conditions of the surrounding environment such as heat, pressure, moisture, vibration and temperature.

**EOF** Abbreviation for *end-of-file*.

**EOM** Abbreviation for *end-of-message*.

**EOT** Abbreviation for *end-of-transmission*.

**EPBX** Abbreviation for *electronic private branch exchange*.

**epitaxial film** A type of film with a single layer semiconductor material that has been deposited onto a single crystal substrate.

**epitaxial growth** The process of manufacturing semiconductor material by depositing a vapor on a seed crystal. The deposited layer can then continue to "grow" a larger single-crystal structure.

**epitaxial planar transistor** A transistor in which a thin collector region is epitaxially deposited on a low resistance substrate, and the base and emitter regions are produced by gaseous diffusion with a protective oxide mask.

**epithermal** Having energy just above the thermal agitation level; comparable with chemical bond energy.

**EPROM** Acronym for *erasable programmable read-only memory*, a ROM in which the data pattern written in may be erased to allow a new pattern to be used. Some types use a transparent lid to expose the chip to ultraviolet light for erasure. The chip is supplied in the erased condition with all bits in the zero state. EPROMs allow fast turnaround times during the microcomputer development stage.

**EQ** Abbreviation for *Equalizer*.

**equalization** Circuit and techniques employed to compensate for the detrimental effects of methods used to reduce frequency and phase distortion in transmission lines. Equalization may involve the use of compensating networks to reduce delays due to frequency and phase shifts.

**equalizer delay** A corrective network that is designed to make the phase or envelope delay of a circuit or system substantially constant over a desired frequency range.

**equation solver** A technique used to solve systems of equations.

**equation statements** Statements that are used in high-level languages and appear as mathematical equations, but which might not have any mathematical validity.

An equation statement as used in FORTRAN, BASIC, or PL/1 is an instruction to replace the variable to the left of the equals sign with the value of the expression to the right.

Thus:

$$G = D/2 + G;$$ (replace G with D/2 plus G)

may not be valid algebraically, but it is a valid equation statement.

**equipment failure** Refers to a fault in the equipment that prevents the accomplishment of a scheduled task.

**equivalence** The logic operator that states: if P is a statement, Q is a statement, and R is a statement, then the equivalence of P, Q, and R is true if P, Q, and R are all true or all false.

**equivalence element** Any logic element that performs the following equivalence operation:

| INPUTS | | OUTPUT |
|---|---|---|
| A | B | C |
| 0 | 0 | 0 |
| 1 | 1 | 1 |
| 0 | 1 | 0 |
| 1 | 0 | 0 |

**equivalent binary digits** The number of digits required to express in binary notation a number expressed in another number system.

**equivalent network** A network identical to another network either in general or at some specified frequency. The same input applied to each would produce outputs identical in both magnitude and phase, generated across the same internal impedance.

**equivalent resistance** The value that the resistance of an equivalent circuit must have in order that the loss in it shall represent the total loss occurring in the actual circuit.

**equivalent sine wave** A sine wave that has the same frequency and the same root mean square value as a given wave.

**ERA** Abbreviation for *electronic reading automation*.

**erasable programmable ROM** A programmable ROM that allows fast turnaround time for prototype work. Some types use a package with a quartz lid to allow ultraviolet light to erase the bit pattern; then a new pattern is written into the device.

**erasable storage** 1. A storage device whose data can be altered during the course of a computation. 2. An area of storage used for temporary storage. 3. A storage medium that can be erased and reused repeatedly, such as magnetic tape or disk.

**erase** To clear or obliterate information in a storage medium. Erasing results in the replacement of all digits with zeros in magnetic storage, or the replacing of all digits in paper tape with holes, also called rubout or letter-out. Erasing in some EPROMs is done with a specified level of ultraviolet light.

**error** Any discrepancy between the observed or measured quantity, and the true or specified value. An error may be an incorrect step, process, or result in a data processing system; it may be attributable to a machine malfunction or a human mistake. Errors can tend to average out to produce a balanced error that may have no system effects.

Boundary errors can occur in a system when the processing arrives at a limit condition. This may occur in systems that have not been completely tested for overflow.

**error ambiguity** A gross error that occurs in the reading of certain digital codes as the parameters represented by the codes change. Error ambiguity is common in analog-to-digital conversion because of imprecise digit positions. It is usually transient in nature if the parameter continues to change. Antiambiguity circuits can be used to minimize this condition.

**error, balanced** 1. Refers to a set of error values with the maximum and minimum equal in magnitude but opposite in sign. 2. A range of error values that average a zero value.

**error, boundary** Refers to an error condition that occurs when processing arrives at a limit or division. This is a common type of error occurring in incompletely tested programs when untested overflow procedures are exercised for the first time, or when unanticipated concurrent conditions complicate an overflow or boundary handling procedure that had been tested only for a simple case.

**error budget** A tool for establishing tradeoffs for the performance requirements of a system. The error budget can be used for predicting the overall expected error. A worst case summation, a root sum of the squares summation, or a combination of the two may be used.

**error burst** A grouping of errors in a short period of time compared to error activity before and after the occurrence. In some transmission systems, a burst may be defined by a specific criterion such as three consecutive correct bits or words after any errors to terminate the error burst.

**error, component** Refers to an error related to the components of a unit or circuit such as the input impedance.

**error condition** The state that results from an attempt to execute programs or instructions that are invalid or that operate on invalid data.

**error control** The various methods that are used to detect and correct errors. Errors can be corrected by operating on the detected errors or by retransmission from the source. An error control character can be used to indicate if the data with it is to be disregarded or corrected. This character is also called an *accuracy control character*.

**error correcting codes** A code in which expressions must conform to specific rules of construction. The code may define equivalent expressions that are not acceptable so as to allow the correction of errors. Some codes may use retransmission for correction.

Error detecting codes may use similar methods for detecting without correcting errors. The code may be arranged so that single errors produce forbidden or impossible code combinations. Errors may be deleted or printed out for user correction.

Some compilers will continue through a program using error diagnostics; the errors are then listed along with the final printout.

**error detecting code** A code in which each acceptable term conforms to certain rules such that if transmission or processing errors occur, false results can be detected.

**error detection codes** These are codes that have been effectively used in many bus oriented systems. The information transfers are conducted with one or more added parity bits to provide error detectability through the use of parity checking circuits that are placed strategically in the microprocessor system. The parity circuits are used to count the number of ones or zeros in the data word.

**error dump** The dumping of a program into a medium so that the cause of an error interrupt can be analyzed.

**error message** An indication that an error has been detected.

**error ratio** The ratio of the number of units of data in error to the total number of data units.

**error signal** The feedback signal used in a closed-loop control system for correcting the output.

**ERX** Abbreviation for *electronic remote switching*.

**ESC** The escape character. A control character that signals a change in meaning for characters following it or forms an escape sequence for the development of additional operations. In ASCII, ESC is symbolized by the binary 27 (00011011).

**ESD** Abbreviation for *Electronics Systems Division*, USAF.

**ESI** Abbreviation for *externally specified indexing*.

**ESRO** Abbreviation for *European Space Research Organization*.

**ESS** Abbreviation for *electronic switching system*.

**ETB** The end-of-transmission-block character.

**ETCG** Abbreviation for *elapsed time code generator*.

**etched circuit** Refers to integrated circuits and the particular construction of a geometric design or pathing arrangement to form active elements by an etching process on a single piece of semiconducting material.

**etched printed circuit** Refers to a specific type of printed circuit, formed by chemically or electrolytically (or both) removing the unwanted portion of a layer of material bonded to the base.

**ETMWG** Abbreviation for *Electronic Trajectory Measurements Working Group*.

**ETV** Abbreviation for *Education television*.

**ETX** The end of text character.

**EURATOM** Abbreviation for *European Atomic Energy Community*.

**evaluation system** A group of parts from a specific microcomputer family that are mounted on a circuit board to allow the user to become familiar with the parts in a typical configuration. The user can run simple programs and connect the module to peripheral devices for operational tests. The evaluation module is usually interfaced with peripherals using a peripheral adapter for connection to keyboards, printers, displays, or other devices. A typical evaluation module may contain a CPU, RAMs, a clock generator, power-on initialization circuitry, and various input/output ports.

**evoke module** A module containing hard-wired circuits used for dedicated automatic control systems. Evoke modules are used where changes to the program are not expected. Up to 100 instructions are feasible and the system can be very fast, since fetching and decoding are not required. A low-cost system can be built using evoke module control, but if program changes are ever required, expensive rewiring must be done.

**EX** Exclusive OR.

**exalted carrier** A method used for receiving amplitude- or phase-modulated signals. The carrier is first separated from the sidebands, filtered, amplified, and then combined again with the sidebands for demodulation.

**except gate** A logic process designed for exception; if P and Q are two statements, then the statement P EXCEPT Q is valid only if P is true and Q is false.

**exception** A logic operation that states: if P and Q are statements, then the statement P EXCEPT Q is valid only if P is true and Q is false.

**exception reporting** A reporting of only the exceptions, such as values over limits, changes, or deletions.

**excess noise** Interference that results from the passage of current through a semiconductor material or any current-carrying substance other than a metallic conductor.

**excitation trigger** A circuit that has two stable states requires excitation triggers to cause a transition from one state to the other. The excitation may be caused by one and then the other of two inputs, by alternating two signals, or by causing the excitation of a single input.

**EXCH** Abbreviation for *exchange*.

**exclusion** A logic operator having the property: if P and Q are statements, then P EXCLUSION Q is true if P is true and Q is false; and P EXCLUSION Q is false if P is false or P and Q are both true. Exclusion can be represented by P AND NOT Q, or P NAND Q.

**exclusion gate** A binary logic coincidence (two input) circuit for com-

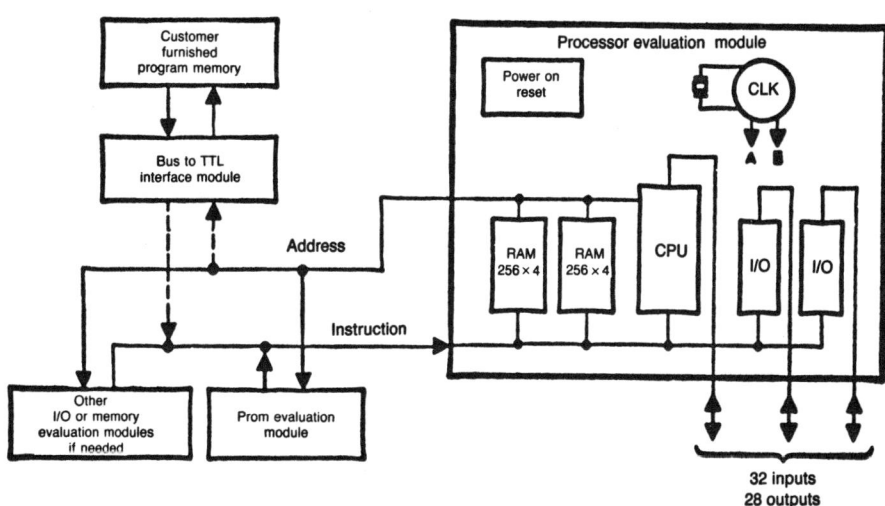

**Evaluation system**

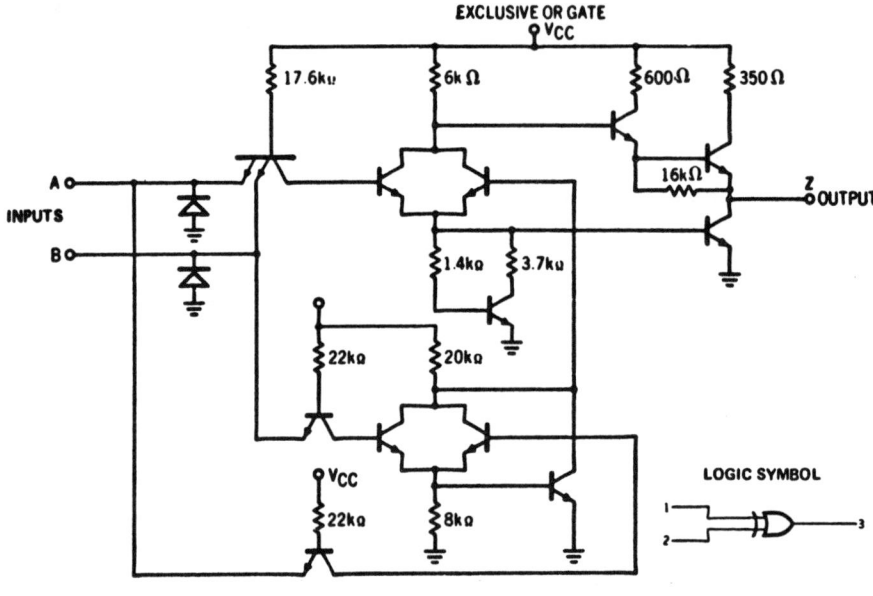

Exclusive-OR

pleting the logic operation of A AND NOT B; the result is true only if statement A is true and statement B is false.

**exclusive-NOR** A logic operation that has a true output if the input statements are the same, and a false output if they are different. The exclusive-NOR function is:

| INPUTS | | OUTPUT |
|---|---|---|
| A | B | C |
| 0 | 0 | 1 |
| 1 | 0 | 0 |
| 0 | 1 | 0 |
| 1 | 1 | 1 |

**exclusive-OR** A logic operation that has a true output only if the input statements are different or odd. The exclusive-OR operation can be shown as:

| INPUTS | | OUTPUT |
|---|---|---|
| A | B | C |
| 0 | 0 | 0 |
| 0 | 1 | 1 |
| 1 | 0 | 1 |
| 1 | 1 | 0 |

**EXEC** An abbreviation for *executive statement*, or *executive system*.

**execute phase** The part of the computer operation cycle when a command is performed.

**execute statement** A job control command that designates the load module to be executed along with the specific job steps.

**execution cycle** That part of the machine cycle when the execution of instructions is taking place. Divide and multiply operations may require a number of execution cycles to complete an operation. The execution cycle is usually the same as the clock period, which can vary from a few hundred nanoseconds to a few milliseconds.

**execution time** The time required to complete an instruction, procedure, or cycle. The execution time is the portion of an instruction cycle when the actual operation is taking place, such as decoding and executing an instruction. It is usually expressed in terms of clock cycles.

**executive** A program, routine, or system that has supervisory control over others. Executive instructions are designed and used to control the execution of other routines and programs. The executive command language should be open-ended to allow easy expansion for additional features and functions. Statements need not be restricted to card formats and may be of variable length.

An executive program usually consists of controlling loaders, an editor, an assembler, a FORTRAN compiler, a debug monitor, input/output devices, and a library of routines. After the executive program is loaded into memory, all operations are executed using teletypewriter commands to the executive, editor, and debug programs. The executive program coordinates and controls the running of all other programs and essentially converts a collection of software into an operating system.

Parts of the executive program are resident in the memory at all times. The main tasks of the program include job scheduling, storage allocation, and output control.

**executive cycle** Refers to a specific period of time during which a machine instruction is interpreted and the indicated operation is performed on the specified operand.

**executive diagnostics** A part of the executive system is an integrated system of diagnostic routines designed to provide the programmer with information of maximum utility and convenience in checking out programs. The programmer can select what is to be printed and may receive diagnostic listings with source code symbolics collated with the contents of both registers and memory. Both dynamic (snapshot) and postmortem (PMD) dumps of registers and memory may be provided.

**executive instruction** Similar to a supervisory instruction, this instruction is designed and used to control the operation or execution of other routines or programs.

**executive programs** These are programs that allow the computer to schedule, load, and execute each system software module. The executive which is also called the supervisor or monitor, is a program or set of programs that coordinates the controls and the running of other programs on the computer. As such, the executive is the key element that converts a collection of system software programs into an operating system. Portions of the executive are normally resident in computer memory at all times. The general duties of the executive are job scheduling, storage allocation, and monitoring the device control. The object programs rely on the executive and the library utilities for I/O and mathematical functions.

**executive routine** An automated computer procedure used to control the loading, relocation, scheduling, and execution of other routines. The routine usually maintains control of the computer at all times and returns control from all functional operations back to the executive routine upon completion.

**exit** A method used to interrupt or leave a repeated cycle of operations in a program.

**exjunction** A reasoning element applied to two operands that will create a result depending on the bit patterns of the operands.

**EXORciser development system** A system development tool for the 6800 microcomputer family of parts. It can be tailored to meet the user's need in the design and development of the system. It reduces the time required to develop a system and, at the same time, provides flexibility in configuring the system hardware for the application. The EXORciser's firmware, through its debug and program control features, minimizes the time required to develop the user's programs. EXORciser functions include displaying the contents of registers, stepping through user's programs, dynamically tracing through user's program, stopping the user's program on a selected memory address, triggering an oscilloscope on a selected memory address, aborting from the user's program at any time, and reinitializing the system at any time.

**EXP** Abbreviation for *exponential*.

**EXPERT** An expanded PERT.

**expert system** Refers to a computer system that utilizes artificial intelligence concepts and is patterned after an expert for the particular task or objective desired.

**explicit address** An address reference that is specified as two absolute values, one of which supplies the displacement value. The explicit address values are assembled from object code by a machine instruction.

**extended address** Addressing that allows the widest possible selection of locations. In the 6800 microprocessor system, extended addressing allows access to any of the 65,536 locations in the memory space. For extended addressing, the operand is specified by the memory location of the second and third bytes of the instruction. The location's address is always stored with the most significant byte first. In this extended address instruction for the 6800:

Add A $1256 (add the contents of M(1256) to A)

the $ indicates that 1256 is a hexadecimal number to the assembler.

**extended addressing** An addressing mode designed to reach almost anywhere in the memory system.

**extended arithmetic element** A central processor element (abbreviated *EAE*) that is implemented with hardware to multiply, divide, and normalize functions.

**extension** Refers to a three character suffix used with a file name to denote the file's usage.

**extension register** A register that provides expansion for the accumulator register or the quotient register.

**external clocking** A type of clocking used in synchronous communication in which the bit timing signal is supplied from a modem.

**external delays** Lost system time due to causes beyond the control of operators and service crews.

**external device code** An address code for an external device that specifies the operation to be performed. The code is used in systems with common bus lines for a number of external devices. The external device code addresses a particular device and only that device will respond to the instruction that is part of the code.

**external event module** A module used to detect power failures and control interrupts, and processor start-up and half functions. The module will implement the system priority scheme in the event of any power loss.

**external interrupt** An interrupt caused by an external event such as a device requiring attention.

**external label** A label defined in one program that is used in another. Usually the programs are assembled independently and executed together.

**external memory** An alternate term for auxiliary storage.

**external registers** Registers that are referenced by the program are located in control store as specific addresses. Also known as *location registers*.

**external storage** Storage that is separate from the computer unit. External storage includes magnetic tapes, punched cards, or paper tape. Also called *offline storage*.

**external symbol** A symbol that is used in several program modules, or in a program module dictionary.

**extracode** Machine instructions that are used to provide increased capability for machine software. For example, an extracode may provide floating-point arithmetic for a machine that does not already have floating-point capability. Extracodes are stored within the system, or in ROMs.

**extract** 1. To remove from a set of items all items that meet a particular criterion. 2. A procedure used to replace the contents of certain columns of data with the contents of other columns.

**extract instruction** An instruction that requests the formation of a new expression from selected parts of another expression. A typical extract instruction might remove the first, second, fifth, and sixth bits from an 8-bit word and combine them to form a new word.

**extrinsic properties** The properties of a semiconductor, modified by impurities or imperfection within the crystal.

**extrinsic semiconductor** A semiconductor whose electrical properties depend on its impurities.

**EWR** Abbreviation for *early warning radar*.

**E/Z** Abbreviation for *equal to zero*.

**F** Abbreviation for *feedback*.

**F-8 controller** Combining a Fairchild F-8 central processing unit and program storage unit results in a two chip system that may be used as a simple controller as shown below. The CPU recognizes inputs from the control panel keyboard and sensors located on the controlled item and produces output signals for motor control use. The PSU provides the control program storage along with the interface for the display unit. A hardwired logic system might require more than 250 components for a simple controller such as this. The system shown has about 50 components, which includes 28 devices for the display function and power.

**F-8 CPU** The Fairchild F-8 CPU chip contains 64 bytes of scratch pad memory, which may eliminate the need for random-access memory in simple control applications. The scratch pad can also serve as a workspace for simple calculations without transferring the data to external memory. The F-8 CPU contains a single accumulator, an ALU, an address register, an instruction register and two bus transfer gates.

**F-8 expansion** An expanded complex F-8 system is shown below. This system uses one CPU and two PSUs along with a memory interface unit for connecting a RAM to the system. The CPU accepts inputs from the system sensors and produces outputs for the system motors. One PSU interfaces with the printer and the keyboard input terminal. The rest of the PSU input/output ports are shared by a display unit and modem. This system approaches a small minicomputer in complexity and utility but it is more flexible with fewer parts and a lower cost.

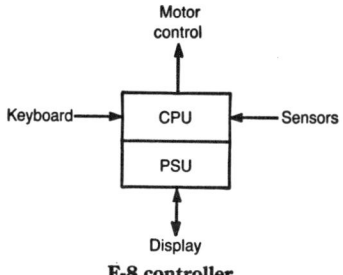

**F-8 controller**

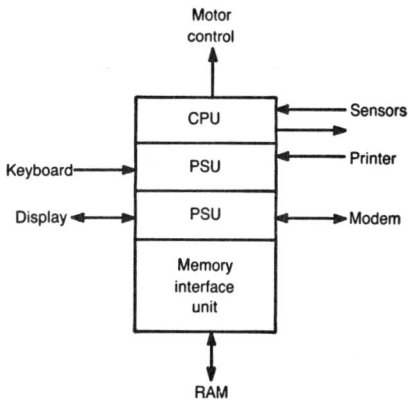

**F-8 expanded controller**

**F-8 multiprocessing** A multiprocessor system that can be used if additional functions are required. A typical system might use a common memory interface and RAM with CPUs to provide control signals to individual controllers for floppy disk, magnetic tape, and CRT display units. The use of the multiprocessor concept results in a system that may cost about half compared to conventional implementations with concurrent operations allowed for all devices connected to the controllers.

**F-8 system design** A potential problem can occur in systems with chips of both one and two data counters. This can happen in systems that contain both PSU chips (one data counter) and memory interface chips (two data counters). As the data counter is loaded, all DC0 counters are loaded, but when the data counter exchange instruction is used (XDC), the chips with only one counter ignore this, while in the other chips the data is exchanged between DC0 and DC1. Careful use of the exchange instruction in these systems is required to prevent erroneous memory addresses.

**FA** 1. Abbreviation for *frequency agility*. 2. Abbreviation for *final address*.

**FACE** Abbreviation for *field alterable control element*. A chip in the control logic unit of a field development system. Functionally similar to a CROM (Control ROM), the FACE chip uses external memory for the microprogram store. It is used in low volume applications. The system employs a writable control store, a control logic unit, and a display and debug unit.

**facsimile** A television-like system (abbreviated *FAX*) for the transmission of images of documents. The image is scanned and the information converted into signal waves for transmission to remote locations. The information is usually duplicated on hard copy for final use and documentation. Facsimile transmission involves scanning of the image with a revolving drum and use of photoelectric sensors to create the electrical signals.

**FACT** Abbreviation for *fully automatic compiler translator*.

**fade** Refers to a phenomenon represented by more or less periodic reductions in the received field strength of a station or device, usually as a result of interference between reflected and direct waves from the source.

**fading** The fluctuating in intensity of any or all components of a received signal due to changes in the characteristics of the propagation path.

**failsafe** Descriptive of a system, circuit, network, or component with built-in protective measures that preclude system failure. Failsafe systems usually allow some degradation of performance that does not prevent proper system operation.

**fail-soft** A method of system implementation that prevents the loss of data and facilities due to an outage in some part of the system. Degraded performance usually results from a failure, but the system may continue to run.

**failure logging** A procedure used in some systems to record the system state following the detection of an error. A section of the monitor using machine-check interrupts logs the data that is stored for diagnosing errors at a later time.

**failure, mean time to (MTTF)** The average time the system or a component of the system works without faulting.

**failure prediction** The methods and techniques used to determine when failures are most likely to occur in specific parts and equipment. Failure prediction attempts to allow a schedule for the replacement of parts and equipment before failure occurs. These methods are used to determine the *mean time to failure* (MTTF) and *mean time between failures*

(MTBF) for a part, based on test data that is used to calculate the average time that the part will operate under normal conditions before failure occurs.

**Fairchild F-8** The Fairchild F-8 is a multichip NMOS microprocessor system, which is designed around a bus architecture. The heart of the system is the CPU chip. When the CPU is combined with the program

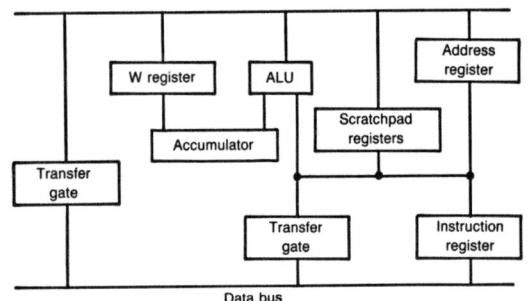

**F-8 architecture**

storage unit (PSU) that contains a masked ROM, along with timing and interrupt control, a minimal system configuration is obtained. A memory interface unit contains the memory address registers and address bus, which are not in the CPU unit. A DMA chip has the hold and wait circuitry required for direct memory access. The basic device family is shown below.

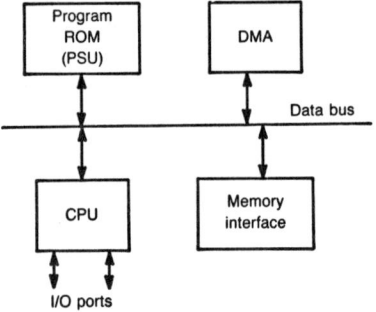

**F-8 family**

**Fairchild 3870** The 3870 is the single chip microcomputer version of the F8; it uses the F8 microprocessor along with a 2K ROM. It consumes less power using a 5 volt supply instead of a 12 volt supply. Besides the 2K of ROM, the device has 64 bytes of scratch pad RAM, a programmable timer and 32 bits of I/O.

The 3870 structure is shown on the next page. The instruction register receives the operation code of the instruction to be executed from the program ROM over the data bus.

**Fairchild 3870 instructions** The 3870 executes the instruction set for the F8 family of chips. The STORE instruction is not used in the same way, since the ROM addresses are within the range of the data counter. The STORE may be used to increment the data counter. For total software compatibility, the 3871 input/output circuit should be

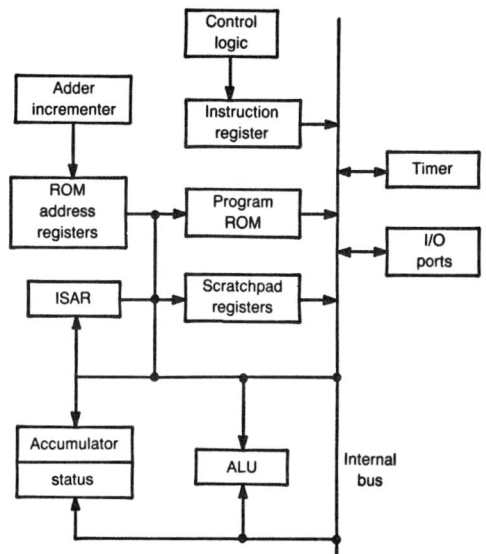

3870 architecture

used instead of the older 3861 PIO. The interrupt control bit of the status register is automatically reset when an interrupt is acknowledged, but when an external reset is recognized at the start of a machine cycle, the old contents of the stack register are lost since the program counter is then pushed into the stack. The new address in the stack may not be the address of the instruction to be executed next. If this is likely to occur, a hardware priority circuit can be used to inhibit external resets during critical times.

**Fairchild 3870 registers** The 3870 accumulator is the principal register for data manipulation. It provides one of the inputs to the ALU for all operations, and then the result of the operation is stored there. The status register holds the five flags shown below. An interrupt control bit is used to enable interrupts. If this bit is set, and an interrupt request is made to the CPU, the interrupt is acknowledged and processed when the first nonprivileged instruction is complete.

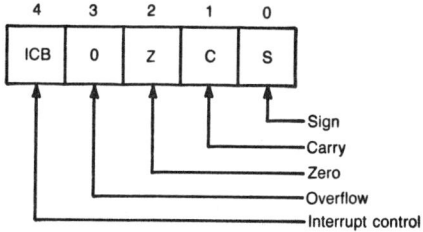

3870 status bits

**Fairchild 3870 timer** The timer is an eight big binary countdown unit, which is programmable in one of three modes: interval, pulse width,

or event. If there is both a timer interrupt request and an external interrupt request, the timer request is given priority.

**Fairchild 9440** The 9440 is a 16 bit microprocessor fabricated with the Isoplanar $I^2L$ process ($I^3L$). Housed in a 40 pin DIP, all of the 9440s software is compatible with the Nova minicomputer made by Data General Corporation.

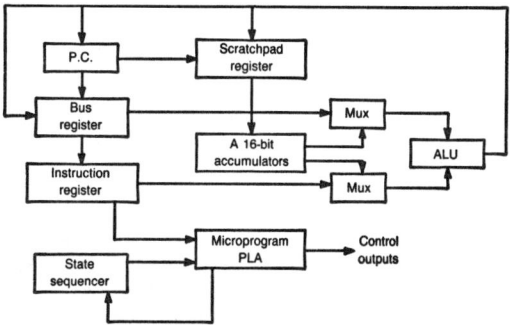

9440 architecture

**fallback** A condition in which substitute hardware is employed for malfunctioning systems. Fallback is used to increase capacity for malfunctioning systems or take over completely in the case of total system failure.

**fallback procedure** Refers to procedures used to circumvent equipment faults. The fallback may give degraded service and may include switching to an alternate computer or to different output devices.

**fallthrough** A software "step" that results in machine cycling to the operation represented by the next lower block on a flowchart.

**false add** To form a partial sum without carries.

**FAMOS** Acronym for *floating-gate avalanche-injection metal-oxide semiconductor*. A type of erasable PROM that uses ultraviolet light for erasing and an avalanche transport mode. The FAMOS device uses silicon-gate field-effect transistors with no connection to the silicon gate. Memory operation then depends on charge transport by avalanche injection from a source or drain.

**fan-in** The number of inputs connected to a specific logic device or function.

**fanout** The number of output circuits that are connected to a specific logic device or function. A device must be capable of driving the number of devices specified in the fanout specification.

**FAR** Abbreviation for *failure analysis report*.

**farad** The capacitance of a capacitor in which a charge of one coulomb produces a change of one volt in the potential difference between its terminals. The farad is the unit of capacitance in the meter-kilogram-second-ampere system.

**faraday** A unit equal to the number of coulombs (96,500) required for an electronic reaction involving one electrochemical equivalent.

**Faraday cage** An earthed wire screen in which a number of parallel wires are joined at one end, which is earthed. It completely surrounds a piece of equipment in order to shield it from external electric fields, so that there can be no electric field within. Also called a Faraday shield.

**Faraday's laws of electrolysis** 1. The amount of chemical change produced by a current is proportional to the quantity of electricity passed. 2. The amounts of different substances liberated or deposited by a given quantity of electricity are proportional to the chemical equivalent weights of those substances.

**Faraday's law of induction** The electromotive force induced in any circuit is proportional to the rate of change of the number of magnetic lines of force linked with the circuit, a principle used in every motor. Maxwell's field equations involve a more general mathematical statement of this law.

**FARET** Abbreviation for *fast reactor test facility*.

**fault** Any physical condition that causes an element of a system to fail or malfunction. A fault may be a broken wire, an intermittent device, or a failed element.

**fault-location** A type of program used for identification or information regarding equipment faults. The fault-location program is designed to identify the location and type of fault and is usually an important part of the diagnostic routine.

**fault tolerant systems** Systems that find their major application in high reliability systems, such as communications and telephone processing applications. These systems must perform the following fault processing operations: error detection, restriction of error propagation, and recovery from the fault or error. The system must reconfigure itself such that all data flows around the particular unit that is at fault once that unit has been localized as the source of an error.

**FAX** Abbreviation for *facsimile*, a system used to convert images to electrical signals for transmission to remote points.

**FBC** Abbreviation for *fully buffered channel*.

**FDC** Abbreviation for *floppy disk controller*, the integrated circuit that controls and communicates with the floppy disk drive.

**FDM** Abbreviation for *frequency-division multiplexing*, a type of multiplexing in which a communications channel is divided into a group of independent lower-frequency channels. Each channel is assigned a slot for its unique pair of transmission end frequencies, and channels are easily cascadable (allowing low costs in many applications). FDM is used on voice-grade lines where it provides asynchronous transmission speeds of up to 150 bits per second.

**FE** Abbreviation for *format effector*.

**feasibility study** A preliminary system analysis to allow decision-making. A feasibility study may be directed at the suitability, capability, or compatibility of a new system or modifications to present systems and equipment.

**FEB** Abbreviation for *functional electronic block*.

**feedback** Refers to the return of a part of the output to the input. As used in a closed-loop control system, feedback provides the information about the condition under control. Feedback is used in analog amplifiers using various feedback elements. Negative feedback is used in most amplifiers and control systems to stabilize the output and reduce distortion generated within the stage. Positive feedback in an amplifier increases gain, but causes instability and accentuates distortion. Positive feedback is not always undesirable, however, as an oscillator depends on positive feedback for its operation.

**feedback amplifier** Refers to an amplifier that uses the feedback principle to perform operations on signals, by using some function of the output signal as part of the input signal.

**feedback, analog** Feedback in amplifier circuits is usually obtained by means of a resistor from output to input. An important property of this type of amplifier is that if a suitable capacitor is used in the feedback path instead of a resistor, the output will be the derivative of the output. Thus, the operations of the calculus can be performed with the amplifier.

**feedback circuit** Refers to a circuit for producing current or voltage feedback from the output to the input of an amplifier.

**feedback control** A type of system control obtained when a portion of the output signal is operated upon and fed back to the input.

**feedback control loop** A closed transmission path that includes an active transducer and consists of a forward path, a feedback path, and one or more mixing points arranged to maintain a prescribed relationship between the loop input and output signals.

**feedback, degenerative** Refers to techniques designed to be used to return part of the output of a machine, system, or process and to input it in a way that causes a larger quantity to be deducted from the input.

**feedback device** An element of a control system that converts motion to an electrical signal for comparison to the input signal, such as a resolver, encoder, or inductosyn.

**feedback element** Refers to an element in a control system that changes the feedback signal as a response to the controlled variable.

**feedback impedance** Refers to the amplifier impedance between the input terminals and the output terminals that provides a feedback path. This impedance substantially defines the relationship of the input signals to the output signals.

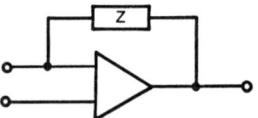

**Feedback impedance**

**feedback loop** A closed signal path in which outputs are compared with desired values to obtain the correct commands.

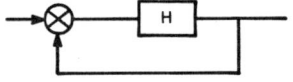

**Feedback loop**

**feedback resolution** The smallest increment of dimension that the feedback device can distinguish and reproduce as an electrical output.

**feedback sample-hold** A sample-hold circuit with a closed loop around the capacitor and a high loop gain for tracking accuracy. In this circuit the usual input follower amplifier is replaced by a high-gain dif-

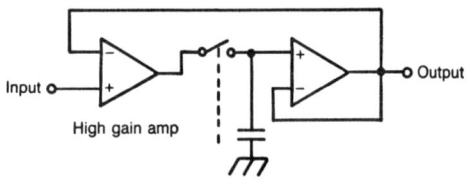

**Low-frequency sample hold with feedback**

ference amplifier. As the switch is closed, the output represented by the charge on the capacitor is forced to track the input, as a function of the gain and the current driving capability of the input amplifier. The common-mode and offset errors in the output follower are compensated by the charge on the capacitor. See the figure.

**feedback signal** The measurement signal indicating the value of a directly controlled variable, which is compared with a setpoint to generate a correction command.

**feedforward** A type of control action in which conditions that can disturb the control variable are minimized or converted into corrective actions.

**feedforward control** This is a technique in which the magnitude of the error is anticipated and the corrective action is taken prior to the occurrence of an error.

**feedforward/feedback control** The combining of both feedforward and feedback concepts resulting in an error anticipation and corrective action followed by readjustment. Feedforward/feedback control is illustrated below.

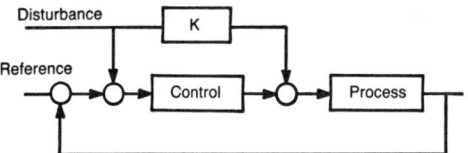

**Feedforward/feedback control technique**

**feed holes** The holes that are punched in a tape to allow it to be driven by a sprocket. The distance between the centers of the feed holes is called the feed *pitch*.

**feedrate bypass** A function directing the control system to ignore programmed feedrate and substitute selected operational rate.

**feedrate number** A coded number, read from a tape, that describes the feedrate function. Usually denoted as the "F" word.

**feedrate override** A variable manual control function used to reduce or increase the programmed feedrate.

**feed through** The fraction of the input signal that appears at the output of a sample hold in the hold or off mode, caused primarily by capacitance across the switch. It can be measured by applying a full scale sinusoidal input at a fixed frequency and observing the output.

**femto** Prefix for the numerical quantity of $10^{-15}$; for example, femtovolt.

**FEP** Abbreviation for *front end processor*.

**Fermi level** A point of a level of energy on a diagram that corresponds to the top of the Fermi distribution; the energy level in a semiconductor for which a Fermi-Dirac distribution function has a value of 50 percent or 1/2.

**ferric oxide ($Fe_2O_3$)** 1. A red, iron oxide coating for magnetic recording tapes. 2. The magnetic constituent of most present day tapes, in the form of a dispersion of fine particles within the coating.

**ferrite** A high-permeability iron compound used for the construction of magnetic cores. Ferrite compounds contain iron and other metallic oxides combined with ceramic materials to form toroidal cores with high magnetic flux properties. The cores are pulsed by electric currents in wires wound about them and assume one or the other states of magnetic flux to allow storage, switching, or gating. Ferrite-core memories are arranged in columns and rows to provide the function of state retention.

**ferrite core** 1. A core made from iron and other oxides usually shaped like a doughnut, used in circuits and magnetic memories; it can be magnetized and demagnetized very easily. 2. Concerns various types of magnetic materials, usually toroidal in shape, which are pulsed or polarized by electric currents carried in a wire or wires around them. These devices are capable of assuming and remaining at one of two conditions of magnetization, thus providing storage, gating, or switching functions.

**ferroelectric** Descriptive of a phenomenon in certain materials which exhibit spontaneous electric polarization along with dielectric hysteresis.

**ferromagnetic** Descriptive of the ability of certain materials to be highly magnetized and exhibit hysteresis. Ferromagnetic materials such as iron, nickel, and cobalt alloys have marked hysteresis properties and are used for storage in computers.

**ferromagnetic oxide parts** Refers to specific parts that contain primarily oxides and display ferromagnetic properties.

**ferrous oxide** One medium used to contain encoded information on magnetic tape.

**ferrule** A short tube used to make solderless connections to a coaxial cable or used to make stronger, wear-resistant shoulders or other protective devices on multiple contact connectors.

**FET** Acronym for *field-effect transistor*, a type of transistor that operates in a manner of field conduction and whose characteristics are similar to those of a vacuum tube. The field is set up in a channel of semiconductor material that is made more or less conductive, depending on the applied gate signal. Since FETs are controlled by voltages rather than currents, power requirements can be low and impedances quite high.

**FET advantages** Among the advantages of FET power devices are freedom from second voltage breakdown and thermal runaway, and reduced distortion in amplifiers. In some circuits the major advantage of FETs is that they are turned on and off by voltages rather than currents. And the voltages can be quite low, making FET switches compatible with digital ICs. Because FETs are majority carrier devices, they are essentially resistive when they are conducting.

Also they can be operated symmetrically, with the control voltage near ground potential, by using a second power supply.

**fetch** 1. To locate and load a program from storage, as in bringing a program phase into main storage for execution from the memory library. 2. That portion of a computer cycle from which the location of the next instruction is obtained. A fetch can also be used to retrieve phases of a program and load them into main storage, or transfer control to a system loader. A typical fetch routine includes:

1. Obtaining the requested phase of the program
2. Loading into main storage
3. Transferring control to the phase entry point

**fetching, demand** A memory multiplexing design in which segments are kept on a backing storage and only placed in internal storage when required.

**fetch instruction** The instruction or procedure used to locate and return instructions that have been entered in the instruction register.

**fetch phase** That part of the computer cycle in which the instruction is brought from memory into the program register. The fetch phase may be used to form the address, access the machine instruction from memory, and store it in the instruction register.

**FF** 1. The form-feed character. 2. Abbreviation for *flip-flop*.

**Fibonacci search** A dichotomizing search in which the set or remaining subset is divided, using successively smaller numbers in the

Fibonacci series. The Fibonacci series contains integers in which each integer is equal to the sum of the two preceding integers and is found from:

$$xi = xi - 1 + xi - 2$$

Where:
$$x0 = 0 \quad x_1 = 1$$

Thus:
$$xi = 0, 1, 1, 2, 3,$$
$$5, 8, 13, 21 \ldots \text{(Fibonacci numbers)}$$

If the number of items in a set is not equal to a Fibonacci number, then the number of items in the set is assumed to equal the next higher Fibonacci number.

**fibre optics** Refers to light-conducting materials that are used for high-speed digital communication cables. Since these operate with light pulses, they are insensitive to electrical noise.

**Fick's law** The rate of molecular diffusion is proportional to the negative of the concentration gradient. This law holds for mass and energy transfer and also for neutron diffusion.

**field** A group of data such as characters that can be treated as a single unit, or a specified area that is used for a particular category of data. A field might be a group of particular card columns or a set of bit locations assigned for specific items of information. Code fields can be assigned by source statements of the assembler or assembly program. Typical code fields include label, operand, comment, and operator. Fields are also used for data storage procedures: 8-bit words can be divided into two 4-bit fields, or eight 1-bit fields.

**field density** The number of lines of force passing normally through a unit area of an electric or magnetic field.

**field discharge** The passage of electricity through a gas as a result of ionization of the gas; it may take the form of a brush discharge, an arc, or a spark.

**field-effect transistor** A type of transistor (abbreviated *FET*) that uses conduction due to a field in a channel between depletion layers. The resistance of the channel can be altered by appropriately altering the applied gate voltage.

**field-enhanced** Refers to electron emission when a very strong field is effective at the emission surface.

**field-free** Refers to electron emission when there is no electric field at the emitting surface.

**field of force** Principle of action at a distance, such as mechanical forces experienced by an electric charge, a magnet, or a mass, at a distance from an independent electric charge, magnet, or mass, because of the fields established by these objects, which are described by uniform laws.

**field-protected** A display field in which the user is not allowed to enter, modify, or erase data from the keyboard.

**field strength** 1. Frequently referred to as field intensity. The value of the vector at a point in the region occupied by a vector field. Also the amount of magnetic flux produced at a particular point by an electromagnetic or permanent magnet. 2. A vector representing the quotient of a force and the charge (or pole) in an electric (or magnetic) field, with the direction of the force; also called *field intensity*. 3. An electromagnetic wave in volt/meter, which induces an electromotive force of one volt in an antenna of one meter effective height. Usually measured by a loop antenna.

**FIFO** Acronym for *first-in-first-out*, a priority basis used in many computer registers and storage elements. A FIFO system is useful for system applications where it is desirable to read out data in the same order that it was written. Excessive read time in a FIFO system may cause delays in communication rates. FIFO read and write operations should be completely independent of each other and system timing. In a FIFO system, the data to be written in memory is stored in the next available location, and the read operation advances the outputs to the next memory word. Once the read is advanced, the previous word cannot ordinarily be used again. The main advantage of a FIFO system is the absence of external addressing; since control is automatic, the system requires only data inputs, read outputs, and clock lines.

**FIFO queue** A first-in-first-out "waiting line" in which the most recent arrival is placed at the end of the line and the item waiting the longest receives service first. Also called a *pushup list*.

**FIFO stack register** A first-in-first-out stack register in which the register outputs are sequentially read in the same order that data is entered. A FIFO simplifies many information handling operations such as high speed compiling and code conversions.

**FIFO storage** A storage system that uses the FIFO technique. One method of FIFO implementation uses shift register circuits to insure the proper first-in-first-out order. When data is entered, it is shifted to the last register stage. The next data entry is shifted to the next-to-last register stage; this is repeated until the register is full. A status register is used to identify full locations so that data is shifted only to the last empty stage. FIFO is also used in stack registers and in stack storage systems where it is desirable to read data in written order.

**FIFO up/down counter** A minimum FIFO can be made using only the specified register files as storage elements and two binary counters for address control. Memory status indicators, however, are desirable to insure that memory capacity is not exceeded. The usual indicators are memory empty and full, although a half-full indication is sometimes used. Many FIFO designs employ an up/down counter to produce the required status indicators. This approach however, introduces serious timing problems with asynchronous data entry. Some systems overcome these problems by replacing the up/down counter with a binary subtractor. This circuit reads the difference between the numbers in the two address counters. When this difference is zero, the FIFO must be either empty or full.

**file** A collection of related records or data sets that are used as a unit. A line or an invoice may be an item, a complete invoice may form a record, and a complete set of records may form a file. A *permanent* data file is one maintained with new data, while a *working* file is a temporary collection of data sets that is destroyed once the data is utilized or transferred to another form.

**file, data** An aggregation of data sets for definite usage. The file may contain one or more different data sets. A permanent data file is one in which the data is perpetually subject to being updated; such as a name and address file. A working data file is a temporary accumulation of data sets that is destroyed after the data has been transferred to another form.

**file gap** The area of a data medium that is used to indicate the end of a file or the start of another. A file gap may also be used as a flag to indicate the beginning or end of a particular group of data.

**file maintenance** Any activity required to keep a file up to date by changing, adding, or deleting data.

**file manager** An online executive program that is used to create, delete, and retrieve programs by name from storage. A file manager can be used with disks, tapes, or cassettes in systems with as few as 4000 words.

**file protection** Any device or technique used to prevent accidental erasure of data from a file.

**file separator** An information separator used to identify the boundary between adjacent files.

**film resistor** A type of fixed resistor having a resistance element made of a thin layer of conductive material on an insulated form. Some type of mechanical protection is usually placed over this layer.

**film ribbon** Refers to a printer or typewriter ribbon made of mylar or polyethylene.

**FILO** Acronym for *first-in-last-out*, a pop-up register in which the most recent entry is retrieved first. Also called *stack*.

**filter** A device or program that "sifts" signals, data, or other materials according to specified criteria, with the purpose of separating usable portions from the unusable. An *electrical* filter may contain inductors, capacitors, and resistors that allow it to select desired frequencies in communication channels or to provide a path to ground for noise signals.

**filter, digital** A filtering process performed on a digitized signal by a general or special purpose computer. Although digital filtering is far more flexible than analog filtering, it may be slower and more expensive, which makes it largely limited to applications where relatively few frequencies are being filtered. When a power spectrum is desired across a larger frequency range, however, the fast Fourier transform (FFT) method offers advantages.

**filtering** When a microcomputer has access to a large number of samples over a period of time, the input can be filtered to eliminate spurious indications and to obtain a more precise result. This filtering can be done in software. If a digital multimeter samples 10,000 times every second, the simplest filtering is averaging 10,000 measurements, which are added together and then divided by 10,000. The result is the filtered or averaged voltage. Any unreasonable values would be averaged out, and the resulting measurement will have a higher precision in this programmable filter.

**final copy** A correct finished document.

**firmware** That part of software that cannot be easily changed once it is implemented. Firmware might consist of those microprograms that are contained in ROM, and may be an extension to the basic instruction package for creating microprograms for a user-oriented instruction set. If the extension is done in read-only memory instead of software, it is called firmware. The ROM is used to convert these extended instructions to basic instructions for the computer.

Firmware tends to have a hardware compatibility while offering software-type implementation techniques. Firmware is generally used only for the movement of data between hardware elements and tends to be defined by the hardware. Additional formats and data modes usually require additional hardware, if implemented with firmware.

**firmware building blocks** These are standard programs in programmable read-only memories that may include utilities such as macroassembly language interpreter, I/O control system, and disk file manager. For program development, the user can write, simulate, and debug programs using these building blocks.

**firmware limitations** Firmware generally is limited to moving data through the data paths and functional units already present; it is able to process effectively only the instruction formats, data types, and arithmetic modes that are defined for the hardware. Attempting to use firmware for new formats, types, and modes can be awkward and result in poor performances.

**first generation** 1. In the numeric control industry, the period of technology associated with vacuum tubes and stepping switches. 2. The period of technology in computer design utilizing vacuum tubes, electronics, offline storage on drum or disk, and programming in machine language.

**first-in-first-out** A priority basis (abbreviated *FIFO*) in which the item waiting the longest is serviced first. The FIFO system is used in many stack registers where the register outputs must be read in the same order that data was entered. It is also used for compiling and code conversions.

**first-in-last-out** See *FILO*.

**first-level address** See *direct address*.

**fixed area** That part of main storage occupied by the resident section of the control program.

**fixed block format** A format in which the number and sequence of words and characters appearing in successive blocks is constant.

**fixed capacitor** A type of capacitor with a specific capacitance that cannot be adjusted.

**fixed-cycle** Refers to a type of computer operation cycle in which a specific amount of time is used for each operation. Fixed-cycle operation involves clocking so that all events occur as a function of measured time.

**fixed data** Data that is not likely to change or affect the results, date, operator, designator, or dump format. Also known as *housekeeping data*.

**fixed heads** Refers to rigidly mounted reading and writing transducers for bulk memory devices.

**fixed length** Refers to records, words, or other elements that always contain the same number of characters, bits, or fields. A fixed length may be a restriction due to equipment or a requirement to simplify and speed processing operations.

**fixed-point** 1. A type of arithmetic in which the computer does not consider the location of the radix point. In a desk calculator using fixed-point arithmetic, the operator must keep track of the decimal point. In a computer, the location of the decimal point is the programmer's responsibility. 2. A type of arithmetic in which the operands and the results of all operations must be scaled to have a magnitude between certain fixed values. The LSI-11 allows fixed-point arithmetic with an extended arithmetic option. The following instructions are used for the manipulation of fixed-point numbers:

    MUL; (multiply)
    DIV; (divide)
    ASH; (shift arithmetically)
    ASCH; (arithmetic shift combined)

Operand formats are allowed for 16-bit single words or 32-bit double words.

**fixed-program** A type of computer that uses instructions that are wired in or stored permanently. In a fixed-program computer, the instructions are not changed except by rewiring or changing the storage locations.

**fixed resistor** A type of nonadjustable resistor designed to introduce a predetermined amount of resistance into an electrical circuit.

**fixed sequence format** A means of identifying a word by its location in a block of information. Words must be presented in a specific order, and all possible words preceding the last desired word must be present in the block.

**fixed storage** Storage in which contents are not changed by computer instructions, as in photographic disks or magnetic cores with a lockout feature. Also known as *read-only storage, permanent storage,* and *nonerasable storage.*

**fixed word length** Having the property that a word always contains the same number of characters or digits.

**F/L** Abbreviation for *fetch/load*.

**flag** An indicator used to signal the occurrence of a specific condition. A flag may be a specific bit that indicates a point of demarcation such as a carry, overflow, or interrupt. Also known as a *mark, sentinel*, or *tag*.

**flag bit** Refers to a specific information bit that indicates a type or form of demarcation that has been reached. This may be carry, overflow, or interrupt. Generally the flag bit refers to special conditions, such as various types of interrupts.

**flat fading** Fading in which all components of the signal change in the same way at the same time.

**flat pack** An integrated circuit package that has leads extending from the package in the same plane as the package so that leads can be spot welded to terminals on a substrate or soldered to a printed circuit board. The small size and low profile of the flat pack allows high density circuit packaging.

**FLBIN** Abbreviation for *floating point binary*.

**flex life** Resistance of a conductor to fatigue when repeatedly bent.

**FLF** Abbreviation for *flip-flop*.

**FLIP** Abbreviation for *floating instrument platform*.

**FLPL** Abbreviation for *FORTRAN list processing*.

**flip-flop** A circuit that is capable of assuming either one of two stable states; a *bistable multivibrator*. The flip-flop will assume a given state depending upon the previous history of the inputs. The circuit is capable of storing one bit of information. For a flip-flop with two inputs, the state of the outputs will correspond to the past and present conditions of the two inputs. Flip-flops can be coupled to other circuits with capacitors, or the circuits within the flip-flop can be coupled with capacitors, permitting operation only for alternating currents. Flip-flop circuits have a variety of configurations, including D, J–K, R–S, T and R–S–T.

*D flip-flops* perform a delay function since the output will be the input which appeared one pulse earlier. If a 1 appeared at the input, the output after the next clock pulse will also be a 1.

*J-K flip-flops* have a J input and a K input following the clock pulse; a 1 on the J input and a 0 on the K input will set the output to 1. A 0 on J and a 1 on K will reset the output to 0. Where a 1 appears on both inputs, a change of state results, regardless of any previous states; a 0 on both inputs inhibits any change of state.

*R-S flip-flops* operate like two NAND gates that have been cross-connected. The circuit has a reset (R) input and a set (S) input. A 1 on the S input and a 0 on the R input will clear or reset the output to 0. A 1 on the R input and a 0 on the S input will set the output to 1. If 1s are on both inputs, the output will remain the same; a 0 on both inputs is not considered.

*T flip-flops* have only one input. A pulse on the input causes the output to change states. T flip-flops are used for ripple counters.

*R–-T flip-flops* have three inputs labeled R, S, and T (reset, set, and trigger). The circuit operates like an R$–S flip-flop except that the T input is used to change the state of output.

Flip-flops can be strung together so that the state of one can be transferred to another. Then a number stored in one string can be transferred to another, allowing numbers to be transferred in computer systems. Flip-flops are used to form storage registers, counters, and controls as used for interrupt level signals. Level-enable flip-flops control the interrupt level from a waiting state to an active state.

**flip-flop, a-c coupled** Refers to a type of flip-flop circuit in which the active elements are coupled with capacitors.

**flip-flop, D type** A flip-flop whose output is a function of the input that appeared one pulse earlier; for example, if a "1" appeared at the input, the output after next clock pulse will be a "1". D stands for delay.

**flip-flop equipment** Refers to electronic or electromechanical devices that cause automatic alternation between two possible circuit paths. The term is often applied to any mechanical operation that is analogous to the principle of the flip-flop.

**flip-flop level enable** A specific flip-flop signal, the level enable signal, that partially controls the ability of an interrupt level to advance from the waiting state to the active state.

**flip-flop, sign** A specific flip-flop used to store the algebraic sign of numbers.

**flip-flop, storage** A bistable storage device that stores binary data as states of flip-flop elements.

**flip-flop string** A computer property in which the state of one flip-flop can be transferred to another by means of triggering circuits. A number stored in one string of flip-flops can be transferred to another string. In this way, numbers can be transferred from place to place in a computer. Many flip-flop circuits include a pair of triggering circuits for this purpose.

**flippy** Refers to a type of floppy diskette that can be used on single-sided disk drives. Two sets of write protect notches and index holes allow the diskette to be turned over and information recorded on both sides.

**floating address** An address that can be easily converted to a machine address by indexing, assembly, or some other means.

**floating-point arithmetic** A type of arithmetic in which the computer keeps track of the decimal point. Floating-point arithmetic uses the floating-point notation to eliminate carrying the great number of digits that may occur in many calculations. Seven or eight digits are retained along a two-digit characteristic:

| Number | Scientific Notation | Floating Point Notation |
|---|---|---|
| 0.024 | $0.24 \times 10^{-2}$ | .24E – 2 |

Some floating-point subroutines for conversion include:

1. Floating-point to ASCII
2. ASCII to floating-point
3. Floating-point to integer
4. Integer to floating-point

Floating-point instructions for the LSI-11 microcomputer are:

    FADD; (floating add)
    FSUB; (floating subtract)
    FMUL; (floating multiply)
    FDIV; (floating divide)

**floating point calculation** A specific number representation system in which each number, as represented by a pair of numerals, equals one of those numerals times a power of an implicit fixed positive integer base, where the power is equal to the implicit base raised to the exponent represented by the other numeral. Contrast with variable point representation.

| Common Notation | Scientific Notation | Floating Point Representation |
|---|---|---|
| 0.0001234 | $0.1234 \times 10^{-3}$ | .123E – 03 |

**floating point numbers** A noninteger number, real or imaginary, that uses the floating point representation.

**floating symbolic address** A label used to identify a word or other item in a routine independent of the location of the information within the routine.

**floppy disks** A magnetic storage medium that uses flexible disks that resemble phonograph records. Floppy disk systems provide random access storage for 300,000 or more bytes and are used to replace paper tapes or cassettes in many applications. Some systems use reusable diskette cartridges with up to four disk drives.

**floppy disk system** A magnetic storage system that provides random access program/data storage. A hard-sector formatted disk holds over 300,000 data bytes. Many floppy controllers offer features not practical in designs implemented with hardwired logic. The host computer driver need only issue a small sequence of commands to write or read data from the disk.

**flowchart** A graphical representation of the definition or solution of a problem, in which symbols are used to represent functions, operations, and flow. Also called a flow diagram. A flowchart might contain all of the logical steps in a routine or program in order to allow the designer to conceptualize and visualize each step. It defines the major phases of the processing, as well as the path to problem solution.

The flowchart can contain logical operations by using symbolic notation to describe the arithmetic operations in terms of inputs and outputs. Functional flowcharts define all operations sequentially, but do not contain enough detail to allow program coding. Detailed charts are derived from the functional flowchart and the command codes along with the way each command code acts in the system. The detailed charts include every operation that must be performed during coding in step-by-step form. The programmer is only required to know the microprocessor programming language.

**flowchart, logical** A detailed solution of a task or operation in terms of the logic or built in operations and characteristics, of the machine. Concise symbolic notation is used to represent the information and describe the input, output, arithmetic, and logical operations involved. The chart indicates types of operations through the use of a standard set of block symbols.

**flowchart symbols** A standard set of flowchart symbols is shown below.

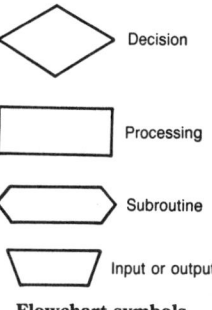

**Flowchart symbols**

**flow line** The line providing the connecting path between flowchart symbols. Flow lines are used to indicate the sequential processes of the operation they represent.

**flow process diagram** A graphic representation of work in process. The major steps of work in process are defined by illustrative symbols that represent documents, equipment, or operations.

**flow transducers** Flow sensing elements that respond directly to the flow rate of a fluid fall can be placed in three general categories:

1. A section of a pipe or duct that uses a restriction that produces a differential pressure proportional to flow rate. The differential pressure ($\Delta P$) is then measured with a pressure transducer.
2. A mechanical member that responds to moving fluid by rotating or deflecting, or by displacement in a tapered tube.
3. A sensing element that interacts with one of the fluid's physical characteristics.

**fluidics** A technique of control that uses a fluid as the controlling medium.

**flux** A type of material used to promote the joining of metals in soldering, such as rosin. Also refers to the flow of particles crossing a unit area per unit time, most commonly referred to in units of $cm^2$/sec. Integrated flux, after an exposure of time T, is equal to the total number of particles that have transversed a unit area during time T.

**flux guidance** Directing the electric or magnetic flux in high frequency heating by shaped electrodes or magnetic materials.

**fluxmeter** An electrical instrument for measuring the quantity of magnetic flux linked with a circuit; it consists of a search coil placed in the magnetic field under investigation and a detector.

**flying capacitor multiplexer** A low-level multiplexer that is used for combating common mode interference. The flying capacitor multiplexer is a two wire sample hold type as shown below. Switches X and X' are turned on with Y and Y' off to acquire the input signal.

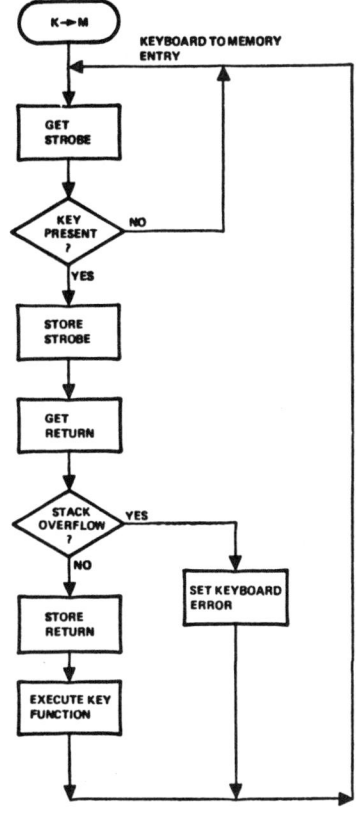

**Flowchart for a keyboard-to-memory routine**

When the capacitor is fully charged, all switches are momentarily turned off; then Y and Y' are turned on to transfer the signal to the output amplifier. No common mode voltage is transferred across the switches, and the output amplifier may be single ended and noninverting. This is effective in eliminating common mode voltages, but if normal mode interference is present as well, better rejection of both normal mode and common mode interference can be obtained with a straight multiplexer and a floating input integrating converter. An integrating converter used with the flying capacitor multiplexer will integrate the sample of the input rather than the input, and the sample will include variations from normal mode interference.

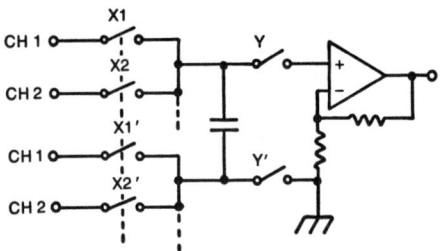

**Flying-capacitor multiplexer**

**flying-spot scanner** A device used in optical character recognition that uses a moving spot of light to scan each character's space. The difference in light levels as the light moves over dark lines and white spaces denotes the character printed.

**FM** Abbreviation for *frequency modulation*.

**FMI** Abbreviation for *failure mode indicator*.

**FO** Abbreviation for *fast operation*.

**FOIL** Abbreviation for *file-oriented interpretive language*.

**font** The family or group of characters of a given style. The characters in the text of this book are from one font; the characters in the captions are from another.

**forbidden combination** A combination of characters, bits, or other items that is not valid in a given operation, according to specified criteria.

**foreground** The computer program(s) in a multitasking or time sharing machine that have the highest priority.

**foreground processing** A type of programming in which top-priority programs are processed, usually through the use of interrupts, into other programs of lower priority. Foreground processing takes place in a multiprogramming environment or under time-sharing arrangements, in which programs are transferred in and out of main storage. This permits processing time to be divided among users. All command processor programs are executed in foreground processing, which saves memory in many applications and reduces or eliminates computer idle time. Foreground operations are initiated by interrupts into background programs.

**foreign attachments** Any nontelephone-company equipment connected directly to a commercial telephone wire pair.

**form** A predesigned document used for recording, transmitting, and summarizing data. Forms may be printed or reproduced in other manners; they usually contain spaces for the insertion of information.

**format** A predetermined arrangement of data, words, letters, characters, files, etc.

**format classification** A means by which parts, dimensional data, type of system, number of digits, and other functions for a particular ap-

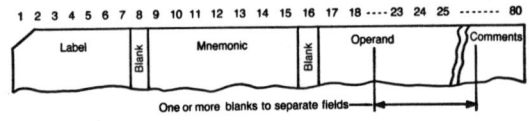

**Format for punched card**

plication can be denoted.

**format detail** Describes specifically which words of what length are used by a specific system in a format classification.

**format designator** The letters and symbols used in instruction words to specify and establish a given format.

**format effector** A control character (abbreviated *FE*) used for control of the layout and position of information in printing and display devices.

**form-feed** The format effector that controls the movement of the printing position to the next form or page. In ASCII this is the FF character represented by the binary 12 (0000 1100).

**FORTRAN** Acronym for *formula translator*, one of the most widely used languages for scientific and business problems. FORTRAN requires a compiler for each particular model of computer. It is well suited for problem solving with mathematical and English-language conventions. Statements, used as sentences in the language, do the following:

1. Define the arithmetic steps for the processor
2. Provide the control required during program execution
3. Define the required input and output operations
4. Define such additional areas as dimensions of variables

Arithmetic statements appear as equalities; the right side can involve parentheses, operation symbols, constants, variables, and functions. These are combined using a set of rules similar to ordinary algebra. The following operation symbols are used in arithmetic statements:

+; (addition)
−; (subtraction)
*; (multiplication)
/; (division)
**; (exponentiation)

An example of an arithmetic expression as it would appear on a FORTRAN coding sheet is:

A**B *C + D**E/F − G + H

Which is interpreted as:

$A^B C + D^{E}/F - G + H$

Besides the ability to indicate constants, variables, and operations, FORTRAN also allows you to use functions such as:

ABSF (X); (absolute value of $x$)
SQRTF (X); (square root of $x$)
SINF (X); (sin $x$)
COSF (X); (cos $x$)
ATANF (X); (arctan $x$)

Input/output statements such as the following bring data into the processor and output the results:

READ 1,A,B,C; (read the next card and the numbers stored in locations A,B and C)
PRINT 2, ROOT; (print the number identified as the variable ROOT in storage)
PUNCH 4, SUM A; (punch the value of SUM A on a card)

Control statements are used to state the flow of the program. Any statement that is referred to by another is given an identifying number, which allows branching from one part of the program to another. Some examples of control statements are:

GO TO 3; (the next statement to be executed is number 3)

GO TO (3, 18, 20) K; (the next statement to be executed depends on the previous value of $k$; if $k = 1$, the next statement is number 3)

IF (A*B) 3, 18, 20; (allows one of three alternate instructions if the value of $a$ times $b$ is less than, equal to, or greater than zero)

FORTRAN IV is an upgraded version that provides (1) more power for interfacing with more complex configurations, (2) greater flexibility, (3) improved accuracy, and (4) a more powerful instruction set. The FORTRAN IV compiler permits intermixing between assembly language and FORTRAN statements to produce an object listing for diagnostics. Programs are compiled in the *operating system* (OS) or as task modules under real-time executive control. Some extended features of FORTRAN IV are:

- $N$-dimensional arrays
- Mixed-mode expressions
- Unformatted inputs and outputs
- Alphanumeric stringing
- Conditional compiling
- Tracing and debug facility
- Inline assembly language capability

Many microprocessors use FORTRAN IV assembly and simulators which allow the use of large general-purpose computers for developing microcomputer programs.

**FORTRAN variables** Variables used in FORTRAN, which are restricted to integer values, consisting of one to six alphanumeric characters.

**forward bias** Refers to a voltage applied to a P-N junction such that the positive terminal of the voltage is applied to the P section and the negative to the N section.

**forward current** The current that flows through a semiconductor junction when a forward bias voltage is applied.

**forward direction** The direction in which the resistance to current flow through a semiconductor is lower.

**four-address** An instruction format that contains four address parts.

**Fourier analysis** A method used to determine the harmonic components of a waveform, based on the theory that any waveform can be constructed using the appropriate number of selected harmonics from a sinusoid of a given frequency.

**four-plus-one address** An instruction that contains four operand addresses and one control address.

**fourth generation** In the numeric control industry, the change in technology of control logic to include computer architecture.

**four-wire** A two-way communications circuit that uses two discrete paths for transmission. Data is transmitted in one direction only on one path and in the other direction on the other path. The circuit may or may not use four wires, but the *effect* of a 4-wire system is achieved in that no crosstalk or intercoupling exists between the two circuit paths.

**Fowler-Nordeim tunneling** A mechanism used to write and erase data. The device erases and writes by causing electrons to tunnel across a 200 Angstrom layer of silicon dioxide. The cells hold their charge in the same way as conventional EPROMs. Maintained at 125 °C, they retain data for years. Operation is fully static and refreshing is not required, regardless of read frequency. Byte erase/write or chip erase requires application of a 21 volt pulse for

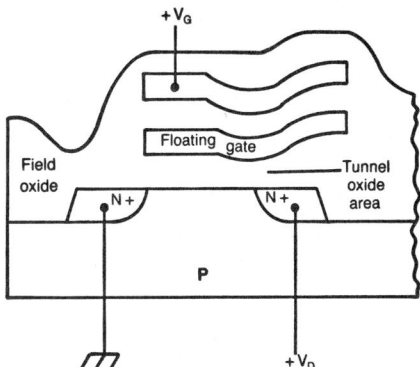

**Floating gate tunnel oxide EEPROM structure**

10 milliseconds. Any 2 kilobytes of the device can be erased and rewritten in 20 milliseconds. The tunnel structure is shown below.

**fox message** A standard message used to test communication systems, since it contains all of the alphamerics and many of the function characters. The standard fox message is:

THE QUICK BROWN FOX JUMPS OVER THE LAZY DOG 1234567890 (station name) SENDING

**FPLA** Abbreviation for *field-programmable logic array*, an array that uses fusible links for programming the logic configuration. High current is passed through the links to achieve the desired logic design. FPLAs offer 50-nanosecond speeds along with editing compatibility and good flexibility. In typical FPLAs, product terms can be added or deleted from any output function, input variables can be deleted from any output function or product term, and programmed active-high outputs can be reprogrammed to active-low. A typical device may provide eight output functions and 48 product terms; all outputs can be programmed active-high true or active-low true, which allows complements to be implemented using fewer product terms. FPLAs are used with a small auxiliary memory to repair core memory systems as an alternate to restringing methods.

**FPLA core patch** Refers to broken or marginal cores found in core planes that are not repaired by "restringing" methods. An alternate, dynamic repair technique is afforded by an FPLA in conjunction with a small auxiliary memory (RAM).

**FPLA fast multibit shifter** Computer performance can be increased by incorporating hardware capabilities for executing fast multibit shifts. Two FPLAs are sufficient to execute both arithmetic and logic shifts of an 8-bit byte any number of places, either left or right within 35 nanoseconds.

**FPLA priority resolver and latch** A tristate FPLA can be configured as a priority resolver and latch, which is useful in asynchronous multiport systems. It can be extended to implement a vectored interrupt system in a typical microprocessor application.

**FR** Abbreviation for *fast release*.

**fractional programming** This deals with optimizing the ratio of two linear functions subject to linear constraints.

**frame** An area that is one recording position long and extends across the width of magnetic or paper tape. A single frame may have several bits or punch positions through the use of different recording positions across the width of tape.

**frame connector** A portion of metal or plastic that surrounds a multiple contact connector that has a removable body or insert. The frame supports the insert and permits mounting the connector to a panel.

**frame grounding circuit** Refers to a conductor that will be electrically bonded to the machine frame and/or to any conducting parts that are normally exposed to operating personnel. This circuit may further be connected to external grounds as may be required by applicable codes.

**freeze mode** An operational mode whereby the computer is stopped with all values held as they were when the interrupt occured.

**frequency** The number of occurrences of a periodic phenomenon within a specified period of time, usually one second. The clock frequency refers to the master frequency of the periodic pulses used to schedule the operation of a computer.

**frequency, clock** Refers to a master frequency of periodic pulses that schedule the operation of the microcomputer.

**frequency divider** 1. A circuit that reduces the frequency of an oscillataor. 2. A counter that has a gating structure that provides an output pulse after receiving a specified number of input pulses.

**frequency modulation** A method of modulating a radio-frequency carrier of fixed amplitude, in which the instantaneous frequency deviates from the center frequency at a rate that corresponds with the signal. The amount of deviation is proportional to the *amplitude* of the modulating signal, but the frequency of the deviation is proportional to the *frequency* of the applied signal.

**frequency response analysis** A method of analyzing systems based on introducing cyclic inputs and measuring the resulting output at various frequencies.

**frequency response characteristic** The amplitude and phase relation between the inputs and the resulting sinusoidal outputs.

**frequency, unity gain** The open loop gain of an amplifier is equal to one at this frequency. The input signal must be restricted in amplitude such that the maximum rate of change of output (slew rate) is not exceeded.

**FRESH** Abbreviation for *foil research hydrofoil*.

**frictional error** Refers to frictional errors as applied to telemetering pick ups. It is the difference in values measured in percent of full scale before and after tapping, with the measurand constant. Friction causing this type of error is known as coulomb or dry friction.

**FRINGE** A language for information file processing that provides report generation.

**FROM** Abbreviation for *fusable read-only memory*.

**front-end processing** A processing system in which smaller processors such as microprocessors are used to interface the communication terminals to a larger host information processor.

**FSK** Abbreviation for *frequency-shift keying*, a form of signal transmission in which the 1 and the 0 are represented by two distinct frequencies (tones).

**FSM** Abbreviation for *frequency shift modulation*.

**FSR** Abbreviation for *feedback shift register*.

**full adder** A circuit or device that performs complete addition with carry operations. Many adders can be cascaded to increase word-length capability.

**TRUTH TABLE**

| $C_n$ | B | A | $\overline{C_{n+1}}$ | $\overline{\Sigma}$ | $\Sigma$ |
|---|---|---|---|---|---|
| L | L | L | H | H | L |
| L | L | H | H | L | H |
| L | H | L | H | L | H |
| L | H | H | L | H | L |
| H | L | L | H | L | H |
| H | L | H | L | H | L |
| H | H | L | L | H | L |
| H | H | H | L | L | H |

NOTES:
1. $A = \overline{A^* \cdot A_C}$, $B = \overline{B^* \cdot B_C}$ where $A^* = \overline{A_1 \cdot A_2}$. $B^* = \overline{B_1 \cdot B_2}$

**LOGIC DIAGRAM**

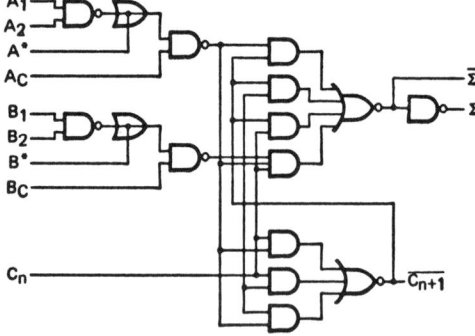

**Full adder**

**full-duplex** In communication systems and devices, refers to simultaneous two-way independent transmission in which transmission and reception occur mutually and on a noninterference basis.

**full proportional servo** A system with complete proportionality between output and input.

**full range floating zero** A characteristic of numerical machine tool control permitting the zero point on an axis to be shifted readily over a specified range. The control retains information on the location of the permanent zero.

**full-read pulse** As used in coincident current selection, the result of partial drive pulses that are applied at the same time.

**full shift** The capability of having more than just a single-place shift instruction. Full-shift includes single or multiple-place, left or right, or logical or circular shift instructions.

**full wave power supply** Refers to a power supply using two diodes that draw current during both the positive and negative half cycles of the input AC voltage.

**full-write pulse** The result of partial-write pulses that are applied at the same time in coincident-current selection.

**function** The purpose of an entity or its action, such as a machine action for carriage return or line feed.

**functional diagram** A diagram that represents the functional relationships of a circuit, device, or system in a logical sequence.

**functional interleaving** The technique of having input/output operations and computing operations proceed independently of one another, but sharing the memory.

**functional partitioning** A method of microprocessor partitioning directed towards user microprogramming. Microprogram storage is separate from the CPU and also from macroprogram storage. It is usually implemented in ROM, PROM, or RAM. Microinstruction address generation and internal register storage (along with all arithmetic processing) are also separated to allow a very flexible configuration.

**function digit** A coded instruction used for setting a branch order for linking subroutines into the main program.

**function element** The smallest building block in a computer system that can be represented by logical operators using symbolic logic. Typical function elements include AND, NAND, OR, and NOR gates.

**function generator** A circuit or device capable of generating sine, square, and triangular waveforms. Some analog function generators provide arbitrary output waveforms that can be changed at the discretion of the operator; others may follow a curve drawn on a surface to generate the waveform function automatically.

**function key** A specific button on a keyboard that initiates a desired functional operation. A function key might cause a carriage return, query the system, or have it perform a specific operation. Specialized function keys are used in airline consoles, badge readers, and stock quotation systems.

**function library** A set of subroutines used to perform common mathematical functions using floating-point arithmetic. A function library might include square roots, exponentiation, logarithms, and trigonometric functions.

**function multiplier** A device for changing the values of the product of two varying functions.

**function punch** A punched hole in a card that indicates (1) the nature of data or information coming, (2) which of various functions a peripheral unit is to perform, or (3) which instruction is to be followed. Also called *control punch, designation punch, function hole* or *hole*.

**function table** 1. The arrangement of two or more sets of data such

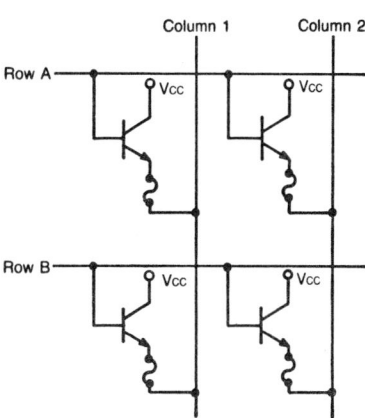

**Fusible link bipolar PROM**

that an entry in one set selects one or more entries in the remaining sets, providing a tabulation of the values of a function for a set of values of the variable. 2. A hardware device that decodes multiple inputs into a single output, or encodes a single input into multiple outputs.

**fuse** A protective device that melts and breaks a circuit when current exceeds rated capacity.

**fused connection** A circuit using components interconnected by a fusion or hot metal flow technique.

**fusible link** Refers to a type of programmable read-only memory integrated circuit in which bit patterns are formed by being fused open by a destructive current or being left intact.

**fusible link devices** Refers to ROMs that are programmed by fusible links. Fusible link devices are completely nonvolatile, and once they are programmed they cannot be erased. Continued improvements in fuse technology have resulted in the following types of fuse material: nichrome, platinum silicide, polycrystalline silicon, and titanium tungsten. The fuse material is deposited as a thin film link to the column lines of the PROM. The memory cell is constructed as a transistor switch. The fuses are blown during programming by saturating the transistor through the selection of the row and column by the decoding circuit. When the cell's transistor base is high and the column line near ground, a large current is switched through the transistor and through the transistor and through the fuse in the emitter leg. The emitter fuse link is open circuited by the current, resulting in the programming of the bit location.

A historical problem encountered in the use of metal link PROMs has been the regrowth of opened fused links over a period of time. In the regrowth process, cells go from a programmed state back to the unprogrammed (closed) state. Manufacturers, however, have refined the process of programming of metal link devices to achieve improved yields as well as reliability.

**fusible read-only memory** A ROM that is programmed by deliberately blowing fusible links. Fusing is done by the customer or at the factory; FROMs cannot be changed after fusing to allow errors to be corrected. FROMs require little tooling to generate a pattern, but their cost per bit is high compared to conventional ROMs; this tends to make them more suitable for low-volume low-capacity applications.

**GA** Abbreviation for *go ahead (cue)*.

**gain** The ratio of signal-level increase between the output and the input of a circuit or device.

**gamma ferric oxide** An oxide used to coat magnetic tapes for recording.

**galley proof** A preliminary printout for checking purposes.

**galvanometer** An instrument used to measure electric current, by measuring the mechanical motion produced by the electromagnetic or electrodynamic forces generated by the current.

**GAM** Abbreviation for *guided aircraft missile*.

**games** The first games implemented on television displays were created with standard logic. Low cost microprocessors allowed the use of a microprocessor system for the implementation of a variety of games on the monitor screen. Several manufacturers implemented these games and established a new market. Other manufacturers turned to companies for the direct implementation of those games with game chips. The new custom chips eliminated the prior designs using microcprocessor systems, as they accomplished the same function at a lower cost. The widespread use of these games resulted in more sophistication of the product. Manufacturers now compete not only in cost, but in the complexity and sophistication of the games. Newer, more complex games that can no longer be implemented on a single chip are now required. Many successful new games use a microprocessor system. Since it is possible to implement a complete microcomputer in one or two chips, and because of the low cost of such microcomputers in quantities, it is likely that games will be supplied as an option for color televisions in the future. This will allow a low cost computing facility with general purpose capability in the home. The availability of a microcomputer in the television means that it can be used for other tasks at no additional cost. It can be used for games, fine tuning, programmed selection, and data processing using the screen as a display. With the availability of cable TV networks, it may also be connected to a central computer.

**gang punch** The punching of identical information into a group of cards simultaneously.

**gap** A space or interval that appears between items of data. A magnetic gap refers to the air space in the magnetic circuit. A head gap refers to the separation between the pole pieces of a magnetic recording head. A data gap may appear as an interval of space or time to indicate the end of a word, record, or file on tape, or it may be the complete absence of information for a length of time or space on the recording medium.

**gap digit** A special character used to mark the beginning and end of gaps in some variable-word-length machines.

**gap length** The dimension of the gap of a reading and recording head measured from one pole face to the other. In longitudinal recording, the gap length is defined as the dimension of the gap in the direction of tape travel.

**gapless** Descriptive of a magnetic tape on which raw data is recorded in a continuous manner. The data is recorded onto the tape without word gaps, but it may still contain signs and marks in the gapless form.

**gapped** Refers to a magnetic tape on which blocked data is recorded. Gapped tape contains all of the flag bits required; the format can be read directly into a computer.

**GAR** Abbreviation for *guided aircraft rocket*.

**garbage** A term facetiously used for unwanted and meaningless information in a computer system.

**gas discharge** A type of display that uses the glow produced by ionized neon gas to illuminate segments of alphanumeric display characters. Gas-discharge displays can be viewed in bright sunlight and have lifetimes in excess of 200,000 hours. Their main disadvantage is the high voltage required to operate them and the interfacing circuitry required for computer applications.

**gate** A circuit or device having one output and one or more inputs with the output state completely determined by the previous and present states of the inputs. A gate can also be a trigger used to allow the passage of other signals through a circuit. Logical gates can take many forms, some of which are shown in the following table:

Gates can be implemented in software, individual hardware devices, or large gate arrays using integrated circuits.

| GATE TYPE | OPERATION |
|---|---|
| Conditional Implication | A OR NOT B: (output is false only if A is false and B is true) |
| EXCEPT | A EXCEPT B: (output is true only if A is true and B is false) |
| Exclusion | A AND NOT B: (output is true only if A is true and B is false) |
| IF-THEN | A OR NOT B |
| IF-THEN-NOT | A OR NOT B |
| Implication | A OR NOT B |
| Inclusion | A OR NOT B |
| Inclusive-OR | OR |
| Majority | Implements the majority logic operator |
| Negation | Reverses the signal or state into its alternate or opposite |
| NOT IF-THEN | A AND NOT B |
| AND | Output true if all inputs are true |
| OR | Output true if one or more inputs are true |
| OR-NOT | A OR NOT B |
| NAND | Negative AND |
| NOR | Negative OR |
| Coincidence | Any gate that depends on the input history |
| Sheffer stroke | NAND |

Logical Gates

**gate, AND** A signal circuit with two or more input wires in which the output wire gives a signal if and only if all input wires receive coincident signals. Synonymous with *AND circuit*.

**gate, B OR NOT A** A binary (two input) logic coincidence circuit for completing the logic operation of B OR NOT A, the reverse of A OR NOT B. The result is false only when A is true and B is false.

**gate circuit** An electronic circuit with one or more inputs and one output, with the property that a pulse appears on the output line, if and only if, some specified combination of pulses occurs on the input lines. Gate circuits provide much of the logical operations in a computer.

**gate, EXCEPT** 1. A logic process designed for exception; if P and Q are two statements, the statement P EXCEPT Q is valid only if P is true and Q is false. 2. A gate in which the specified combination of pulses producing an output pulse is the presence of a pulse on one or more input lines and the absence of a pulse on one or more other input lines.

**gate, exclusion** A binary logic coincidence (two input) circuit for completing the logic operation of A AND NOT B; the result is true only if statement A is true and statement B is false.

**gate, IF-THEN** Same as gate, A OR NOT B and gate, B OR NOT A.

**gate, IF-THEN-NOT** Same as gate, A OR NOT B and gate, B OR NOT A.

**gate, ignore** Same as gate, A IGNORE B and gate, B IGNORE A.

**gate, implication** Same as gate, A OR NOT B and gate, B OR NOT A.

**gate, inclusion** Same as gate, A OR NOT B and gate, B OR NOT A.

**gate, majority** A circuit designed to implement the majority logic operator.

**gate, NAND** A circuit that delivers a *zero* output signal only when two or more input signals are coincident ones; the opposite of an AND gate.

**gate, negation** A device with the capability of reversing a signal, condition, state, or event into its alternate or opposite.

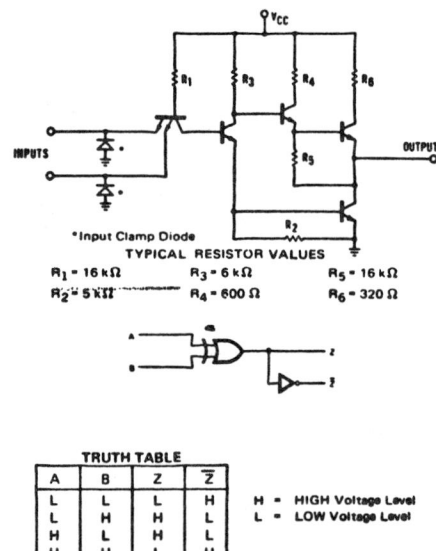

TTL NAND Exclusive OR Gate

**gate, negative AND** Same as gate, NAND.

**gate, OR** An electrical gate or mechanical device that implements the logical OR operator. An output signal occurs whenever there are one or more inputs on a multichannel input. An OR gate performs the function of the logical inclusive OR operator. Synonymous with OR circuit.

**gate, Sheffer stroke** Same as gate, NAND.

**gate, time** A circuit that gives an output only during certain time intervals.

**gating** The selection of a part of a waveform due to its time interval or amplitude, or the operation of a gating circuit when a signal is allowed to pass during a specific interval.

**gating circuit** Any circuit that operates in a selective manner, allowing conduction only under specified conditions.

**gating pulse** A pulse that permits the operation of a gating circuit.

**Gaussian** Refers to a distribution that is encountered when a large number of samples is collected. The Gaussian distribution is characterized by equal probabilities of values at equal positive and negative deviations from the mean. Also called *normal distribution*.

Gaussian noise occurs when unwanted signals are distributed in a Gaussian or normal manner. Some amplifiers are designed to furnish a response that can be differentiated with respect to time to match a Gaussian distribution curve.

**Gaussian noise** Noise in which the particular voltage distribution is specified in terms of probabilities related to a normal curve.

**Gaussian response** A response for a transient impulse, which, if differentiated, matches the Gaussian distribution or normal curve.

**Ga-YIG** Gallium substituted Yttrium Iron Garnet. A material useful in some specialized electronic applications. For example, small polished YIG and Ga-YIG spheres act as resonators at microwave frequencies.

**G-code** A command used in manufacturing process control that changes the mode of operation, as for example from positioning to contouring.

**GD** Abbreviation for *gate driver*.

**GE information services** Refers to a commercial network implemented to make available computing services. The network encompasses over 300 cities in North America, Japan, Australia, and Europe, making it international in scope. The communications network allows a user to make a local phone call that will then connect to the main computing facilities in Cleveland, Ohio, providing services ranging from light computation to remote batch processing. The network has the capability of connecting customer in-house computers to GE network service computers for the purpose of exchanging files. The GE network is a centralized hierachial network. Topologically, all communications paths lead to the central facility.

**GEM** 1. Abbreviation for *ground effect machine*. 2. Abbreviation for *guidance evaluation missile*.

**General Instruments 1600** The General Instruments 1600 is a 16 bit NOMS single-chip microprocessor that uses ion implantation. Ion implanting produces a device with a cycle time of 400 nanoseconds and the capability to add two 16 bit numbers in 3.2 microseconds.

The architecture of the 1600 is shown below. The chip is organized around a sixteen-bit bidirectional internal bus. Connected to the bus is the instruction register, the ALU, the input/output buffers and eight sixteen bit general purpose registers.

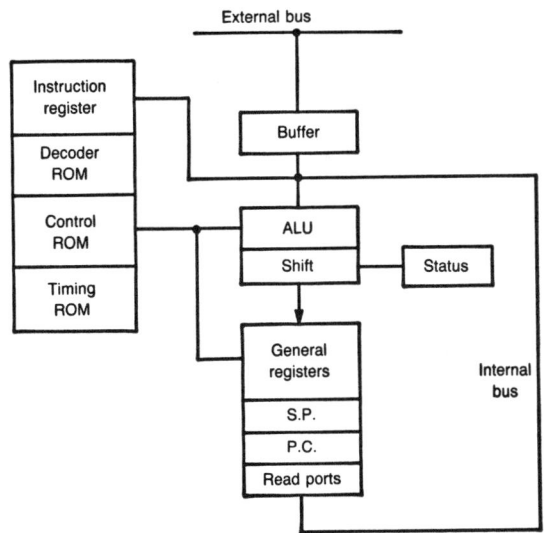

**1600 architecture**

**General Instruments 1600 assembler/simulator** Assembler/simulator routines for the 1600 are available on larger machines. These will accept assembly language statements to produce relocatable, linking object code. The microprocessor environment, which includes all input and output operations, can be simulated on the host machine to allow debugging and testing before the system is committed to hardware.

**generalized routine** A routine used to solve a general class of problem. The generalized routine is used to solve specific problems by inserting the appropriate values into the program.

**general numerical control language processor** A computer program developed to serve as a translating system for a parts programmer to develop a mathematical representation of a geometric form with the use of symbolic notation.

**general-purpose computer** A stored-program computer designed to solve a wide variety of problems and to be adapted to a large class of applications.

**general-purpose register file** A file (abbreviated *GPR*) usually made up of 2 to 16 registers for holding temporary memory data and addresses. GPRs are also used for calculating memory addresses and combining and moving memory data.

**general register** A register used for arithmetic operations and to compute and modify addresses. General registers perform such operations as addition, subtraction, multiplication, and division and are used in place of special registers such as accumulators in many microcomputer systems.

A typical central processor in a microcomputer might contain eight 16-bit general registers, can serve as accumulators, index registers, autoincrement registers, autodecrement registers, or stack pointers. Arithmetic operations are performed from one general register to another, one memory location to another, or between memory locations and registers. A general register unit may also serve as a scratchpad memory for the microprogram and provide a skeletal interrupt system to allow microprogram emulation.

**generate** To create or produce; especially, to formulate a program by selecting subsets from a set of skeletal coding under the control of specific parameters. Also, to produce assembly-language statements from model statements of macro definitions when called for by a macroinstruction.

**generated address** The number or symbol that is generated by instructions and becomes part of the address.

**generating routine** A compiling routine that performs a generating function.

**generator** A program or compiling routine that allows the computer to write other programs automatically.

**generator program** A program that permits a computer to write other programs automatically.

**generator, pulse** A circuit that generates pulses for the purpose of special timing or gating. Also known as a time-pulse generator.

**generator, signal** Refers to an oscillator designed to provide known voltages (usually from one volt to less than one micro volt) over a wide range of frequencies; used for testing equipment. It may be amplitude, frequency, or pulse modulated.

**generator, tone-burst** Refers to a circuit for producing pulses of short duration.

**generator, voltage** Refers to the concept of a total signal source, often with no internal impedance.

**germanium** A semiconductor material with properties similar to silicon. Germanium is used primarily for the manufacture of special-purpose

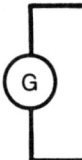

Voltage generator

diodes and transistors where sensitivity is a criterion, as in communications detectors and passive front ends.

**germanium diode** A type of rectifier or detector made from a germanium crystal.

**get** To locate, fetch, and transfer an item from storage, as the activity required to develop or make a record from an input file available, or to obtain or extract a coded value from a field. The GET command might be used to obtain a numerical value from a series of decimal digits.

**GFE** Abbreviation for *ground furnished equipment*.

**G-gradient** The radial difference in g-force from inner to outer radius points of a test article.

**gibberish** A term used for totals or accumulations of records or data. The totals have no meaning or particular sense on their own, but are useful for control purposes. An example would be the cumulative account number for a customer's accounts-receivable total.

**giga** A prefix denoting a quantity of $10^9$ and used for any unit in the International System of Units.

**gigacycle** One kilomegacycle, or one billion cycles.

**gigahertz** A term for $10^9$ cycles per second, used to replace the more cumbersome kilomegacycle.

**gigawatt** One thousand megawatts ($10^9$ watts). Abbreviates *gw*.

**GIGO** Acronym for *garbage-in, garbage-out*, a term used to describe the reason for meaningless computer output data: improper input.

**GIRLS** Abbreviation for *generalized information retrieval and listing system*.

**GLIPAR** Abbreviation for *guided line identification program for antimissile research*.

**glitch** A short-term voltage transient that usually occurs too fast for detection, but which causes improper machine operation because it is interpreted as a legitimate signal.

**global** That part of an assembler program that contains the body of any macro definition called from a source module and the open-code portion of the source module.

**global change** The ability of an editing system to change a word or other text element everywhere it appears in a document, with one instruction. Also called *global search* and *repetitive correction*.

**global variable** Any variable with a name that is accessible by the main program and all its subroutines.

**global variable symbol** A variable symbol used in assembler programming to communicate values between macro definitions and open-code sections.

**GLOCOM** Abbreviation for *global communications system*.

**GLOTRAC** Abbreviation for *global tracking network*.

**GM** Abbreviation for *mutual conductance*.

**GMR** Abbreviation for *ground mapping radar*.

**GND** Abbreviation for *ground*.

**GOE for OAO** Abbreviation for *ground operation equipment for the orbiting astronomical observatory*.

**gold** A metallic element of very high density used as a conductor in integrated circuits.

**gold doping** A process sometimes used in the manufacture of integrated circuits in which gold is diffused into the semiconductor material, resulting in higher operating speeds.

**gone west** A slang term used when a computer has entered an endless loop.

**goof sheet** A form in which personnel can write down suggestions to one another for improving service and avoiding problems.

**GOSS** Abbreviation for *ground operational support system*.

**go to** A multilanguage statement that directs the computer to leave the current sequence of instructions and begin operating at another point in the program. A typical FORTRAN go-to instruction might be:

GO TO 5; (the next statement to be executed is number 5)

In some languages such as BASIC, the space between the words is omitted, so the statement takes the form GOTO.

**GOR** Abbreviation for *general operational requirement*.

**GOX** 1. Abbreviation for *geostationary satellite*. 2. *global surveillance system*.

**GPC** Abbreviation for *general purpose computer*.

**grandfather cycle** A term used to indicate the time for magnetic records to be retained before they are rewritten, to allow records to be reconstructed in the event of losses or errors.

**graphic** 1. Any assembly of symbols or characters that is used to denote any concept, configuration, or idea nontextually. 2. Any symbol produced by printing, drawing, handwriting, etc.

**graphic character** A character represented using a graphic rather than a control character.

**graphic display** A nontextual display that reproduces data on a video screen, panel, or page.

**graphic panel** The master control panel used in automated control systems that displays all the relationships and functions of the control equipment using colored block diagrams.

**graphic plotter** A plotting machine used as a computer output device. Graphic plotters can provide high-quality graphics in several different colors for displaying complex patterns.

**graphic terminal** 1. A communications terminal that displays data on a screen or moving paper. 2. A video terminal.

**gravity, zero** The condition, as in an orbiting satellite, when centrifugal force exactly counterbalances gravitational attraction.

**gray body** A temperature radiator whose spectral emissivity is less than unity and constant at all wave lengths.

**Gray code** A cyclic binary code in which sequential numbers are represented by expressions that differ only in one place and in that place only by one unit. The Gray code is very useful in positional systems, since the maximum error between positions is never greater than the least significant bit. See code table under *cyclic binary code*.

**Gray cyclic code** See *Gray code*.

**Gray or cyclic binary code** The Gray code is a binary code in which the bit position does not signify a numerical weighting; each code corresponds to a unique portion of the analog range. A comparison of the Gray code with natural binary is shown below:

| Decimal Fraction | | | | | | | | |
|---|---|---|---|---|---|---|---|---|
| 0    | 0 | 0 | 0 | 0 | 0 | 0 | 0 | 0 |
| 1/16 | 0 | 0 | 0 | 1 | 0 | 0 | 0 | 1 |
| 2/16 | 0 | 0 | 1 | 1 | 0 | 0 | 1 | 0 |
| 3/16 | 0 | 0 | 1 | 0 | 0 | 0 | 1 | 1 |
| 4/16 | 0 | 1 | 1 | 0 | 0 | 1 | 0 | 0 |

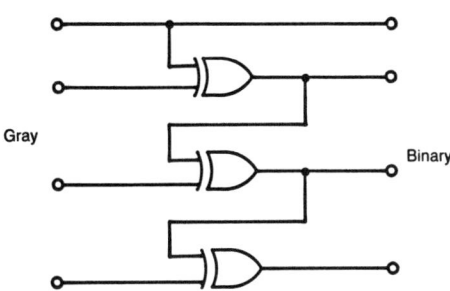

Gray-to-binary code conversion logic

In the Gray code, as the number value changes, the transitions from one code to the next require only one bit change at a time. The bits that change are underlined. Gray-to-binary code conversion can be done as shown.

**grid** As used in optical character recognition, and two mutually orthogonal sets of parallel lines used for specifying or measuring character images.

**grid base** The grid bias voltage required to produce anode current cutoff.

**grid bias** The DC negative voltage applied to control the grid.

**grid bypass** A capacitor that bypasses the signal from the grid.

**grid leak** A grid resistor through which DC grid current flows.

**grid spaced contacts** Refers to a type of electrical contact, usually spring types, pins arranged in parallel, or equally spaced rows and columns on a connector or the edges of printed circuit boards.

**gross error** In a measurement, an error may be expressed in units and a fraction (decimal) error; the gross error is that which is in the units but not in the fraction or decimal.

**ground** The point considered to be at zero potential voltage and to which all other potentials in the system are referred.

**ground absorption** The energy loss in radio frequency waves due to absorption.

**ground plane** The common ground electrical path for power and/or signals.

**grouped record** The combining of two or more records into single sections of information. Grouped records tend to decrease the time required for tape acceleration and deceleration and conserve tape space. Also known as *blocked record.*

**grouping** The combining of workstations to facilitate operations and improve support.

**group mark** A mark that identifies the beginning or end of a set of data, such as words or blocks.

**group separator** An information separator used to identify the boundary between groups of items (abbreviated *GS*).

**grown diffused transistor** A transistor made by combining diffusion and double doping techniques. Suitable N- and P-type impurities are added simultaneously while the crystal is being grown. The base region is formed by diffusion as the crystal grows.

**grown junction** The boundary between P- and N-type semiconductor materials, produced by varying the impurities during the growth of the crystal. These junctions have good rectifying properties.

**GRP** Abbreviation for *group*.

**guard band** 1. The frequency band left vacant between two communications channels to prevent overlapping and mutual interference. 2. The unused area that isolates components on a printed-circuit board.

**guard bit** A bit used to indicate the status of words or groups of words of memory. A guard bit can be used to indicate to hardware units or programs if the contents of a memory location can be changed by a program, or if a core or disk memory word is to be filed or protected.

**guard digit** The hexadecimal zero attached to each operand fraction in a single-word floating-point addition or subtraction operation.

**guard ring** An auxilliary electrode used to avoid distortion of the electric (or heat) field pattern in a working part of a system as a result of the edge effect, or to bypass leakage current to earth.

**guard ring capacitor** A capacitor consisting of circular parallel plates with a concentric ring maintained at the same potential as one of the plates to minimize the edge effect.

**guard signal** A signal that allows values to be read only when all values are not in a changing state. The guard signal is usually an extra output generated when all operations are completed.

**gulp** A term for a small group of bytes processed as a unit.

**gun** The group of electrodes constituting the electron beam emitter in a CRT.

**gun current** The total electronic current flowing to the anode, part of which forms the beam current.

**Gunn effect** The production of high field intensity domains in a semiconductor diode, usually by charges formed across a depletion layer, although other processes, such as charge accumulation, can produce similar effects. These domains are used in negative resistance microwave semiconductor oscillators.

**GVM** Abbreviation for *generating voltmeter;* a voltmeter that uses an induced field, rotating vane, and a stator device.

**GZ** Abbreviation for *ground zero* (atomic detonation).

**H** 1. Abbreviation for *halt.* 2. Abbreviation for *henry.*
**HAAW** Abbreviation for *Heavy Anti-tank Assault Weapon.*
**half-add** An instruction that performs bit-by-bit half-adder operations. Half-add can be done using an exclusive-OR operation without carries.
**half-adder** A circuit that has two input and two output channels that operate according to the following table.

| INPUTS | | OUTPUTS | |
|---|---|---|---|
| A | B | C | S |
| 0 | 0 | 0 | 0 |
| 0 | 1 | 0 | 1 |
| 1 | 0 | 0 | 1 |
| 1 | 1 | 1 | 0 |

Where S = sum without carry
C = carry

Two half-adders can be combined to perform binary addition.
**half-adjust** 1. A type of rounding in which the value of the least significant digit of a number determines whether or not a one shall be added to the next higher significant digit, or in which the two least significant digits determine whether or not a one is to be added to the next higher significant digit. If the least significant digits represent less than half, nothing is added to the next higher significant digit; if the least significant digits represent half or more than half, a one is added to the next higher significant digit. 2. To round by half of the maximum value of the number base of the counter.
**half cycle** The time interval for the operating frequency to complete half, or 180 degrees, of its cycle.
**half-duplex** A communications arrangement that permits alternate one-way transmission between two given points at any one time.
**half-duplex channel** A two-way channel used to transmit *or* receive at any one time.
**half-duplex circuit** A communications system, or portion of a system, with single loops to terminals for two-way nonsimultaneous operation.
**half-duplex operation** A communications mode in which transmission and reception take place, but not at the same time. Operating modes may be defined by the following:
S/O; (send only)
R/O; (receive only)
S/R; (send or receive)
**half-shift register** A term used for a type of flip-flop used in shift registers; it requires two half-shift registers to make one stage of a shift register.
**half sinusoid** The complete positive or negative portion of a single cycle of a sine wave.
**half splitting technique** A circuit tracing method in which tracing begins at a point where a fault is equally likely to exist ahead of or behind this point in the circuit path. The faulty half is found and then split in half again until the fault is isolated. The tracing from input to output can be time consuming and costly. Half splitting is faster and can be used for automatic board testers.
**halftime emitter** A device that produces pulses halfway between two other pulses. Halftime emitters are used in some punched-card equipment.
**half-word** A continuous sequence of bits or characters that make half a computer word and are capable of being addressed as a unit.
**Hall constant** The constant of proportionality R in the relationship:
$$E_h = R \times J \times H$$
where, $E_H$ is the transverse electric field (Hall field), J is the current density, and H is the magnetic field strength. The sign of the majority

carrier may be inferred from the sign of the Hall constant.

**Hall effect** The development of a voltage between the edges of a current carrying metal strip when it is placed in a magnetic field perpendicular to the faces of the strip.

**Hall mobility** The mobility, or mean drift velocity per unit field, of current carriers in a semiconductor as calculated from the product of the Hall coefficient and the conductivity.

**halt** A condition occurring after the sequence of operations in a program stops. A halt may be due to a halt instruction, an unexpected halt, or an interrupt. The program would normally continue after the halt unless a *drop-dead halt* occurs. In this case there is no recovery. A drop-dead halt may be programmed to shut down the system, or it may be due to an error in programming such as division by zero or transfer to a nonexistent instruction. A drop-dead halt is sometimes called a *dead halt*.

**halt, drop-dead** Refers to a machine halt from which there is no recovery. Such a halt is sometimes deliberately programmed. A drop-dead halt may occur through a logical error in programming. Examples of a drop-dead halt that could occur are division by zero and transfer to a nonexistent instruction word. Synonymous with *dead halt*.

**halt indicator** An indicator on the console or panel that shows true whenever the processor is in the halt mode.

**halt switch** A switch on the console or panel that causes the processor to stop executing instructions.

**Hamming code** A general term for a data code that is capable of being corrected automatically. The Hamming code contains four information bits and three check bits.

**Hamming distance** The number of digit positions in which two corresponding digits of two binary words having the same length are different. Also called the *signal distance*.

**handshaking** A term that implies an initial exchange between two units or items in a system connection. Handshaking usually requires a matching at an interface, as when signals are exchanged between data set devices when a connection is made. A typical handshaking procedure takes place when a connection between a modem and an asynchronous communications interface adapter (ACIA) channel is established:

1. Local modem is enabled from the ACIA *request to send* signal.
2. Remote modem answers the call and sends back its carrier frequency.
3. Local modem detects this carrier and enables its *clear to send* output, which is detected by the computer.

**handshaking protocol** A sequence in a program that greets and assists the programmer in the use of procedures or programs of the system. Handshaking in input/output control allows interfacing between peripherals with different response times. Control flags and jumps can be used to reduce decoding and software.

**hands-on** A descriptive term for actual operating experience of hardware and equipment as opposed to educational or tutorial knowledge of that equipment.

**hangup** A condition in which the central processor performs an illegal operation, keeps repeating the same routine, or stops execution. A hangup may be caused by the inability to escape from a loop, the improper coding of an instruction, or the use of an improper or nonexistent code.

**hangup prevention** The design of a program such that no sequence of instructions can cause a halt or a nonterminating condition. Hangup prevention may include nonterminating indirect addressing and an infinitely nested execution of instructions.

**hard copy** A printed record of a machine output, such as printed reports and program listings.

**hardcore section** A portion or kernal of the processor. This kernal is tested by an external processor or other hardware. The hardcore section is then used for the validation of another small portion of the system. The process is expanded until each successively larger level is validated.

In order to minimize the hardware in the hardcore portion, a portion of the diagnostic program is kept in ROM to avoid bootstrapping all the diagnostics from I/O devices. The hardcore section then includes only that hardware required to load the diagnostic.

**hard disk** A disk made of a rigid material with a magnetic coating. These disks spin at approximately 3600 rpm. and are contained in a sheltered environment to prevent damage from dust particles. Hard disk capacity is usually measured in the millions of bytes (megabytes). The heads fly over the disk surface at a distance less than the diameter of a human hair. They are often vertically stacked in groups called cylinders and allow hundreds of megabytes of storage. Hard disks come in two types. Removable disks or disk packs can be mounted and removed from the disk drive. Care must be exercised with removable disks as a fingerprint, hair, or dirt may cause the read/write head to skip and then fall into the disk surface. This is called *disk crash* and generally causes the loss of all data on the disk as well as damage to the heads. Winchester disks have their read/write heads sealed into the same shell with the platters, which reduces the chance of disk crash and improves reliability.

**hard drop** The malfunction of a RAM memory location. A hard drop causes an individual RAM bit location to freeze in either a one or zero mode; replacement of the defective RAM chip is required.

**hard limiting** A circuit that restricts the excursion of a variable with a very small variation of the limited output.

**hardware** The physical components of a computer system, including all electronic and electromechanical devices and connections.

**hardware assembler** An assembler that usually consists of PROMs that are mounted on simulation boards. A hardware assembler allows the prototype unit to assemble its own programs.

**hardware check** A check performed by built-in equipment. Also called a built-in check or an automatic check.

**hardware interrupt** Any interrupt that schedules input/output equipment. A hardware interrupt allows input/output operations to be performed simultaneously with processing.

**hardware priority interrupt** An interrupt that resolves priority when several events occur at the same time. Hardware priority interrupts can provide automatic vectoring and fast response to events. The routines are usually easy to write and take less memory space compared to polling methods.

**hardware selection, microcomputer** Hardware considerations begin with the microprocessor system functions of data, addressing, and timing and control. The bus system depends on the type of microprocessor chosen, the application and the need for flexibility and expandability. Smaller systems can take advantage of microprocessor family components, which use the bus for nothing more than the microprocessor's data, control, and address outputs. Larger systems can use the basic bus structure of the CPU chip, but to such systems users must add buffer elements or additional decoding logic to connect more functions to the system bus.

**hard-wired numerical control** A numerical control system in which the response to data input, the data handling, and the control functions are determined by the fixed and committed circuit interconnections of discrete decision elements and storage devices. Changes in the response, sequence, or functions are made by changing these interconnections.

**hard-wire logic** Any system of logic elements that uses formed or wired connections. Hard-wire logic includes hand-wired diode-matrix boards and any logic board that cannot be reprogrammed with little difficulty.

**harmonic** A sinusoidal wave whose frequency is an integral multiple of the fundamental waveform. The *second harmonic* is twice the frequency of the fundamental, although logically it is the first actual harmonic (multiple) of that signal.

**harmonic oscillator sampling S/D converter** This type of synchro-to-digital converter is illustrated below. The resolver format input signals are first sent to phase sensitive demodulators, with dc output levels:

$$V_x = K \sin \theta$$
$$V_y = K \cos \theta$$

where K is a constant and $\theta$ is the shaft angle to be digitized. It is the dc levels that are sampled at the proper time to set the initial conditions of the integrators in a harmonic oscillator converter.

The rest of the circuit has two major sections:

1. A two integrator and inverter chain in a positive feedback loop. This loop, under the command of the control logic, will oscillate at a frequency determined by the integrator time constants.
2. A clock pulse generator counter circuit that is on when the oscillator is on and off at the positive going zero crossing of the voltage at the second integrator.

Initially the loop is prevented from oscillating by the control logic, which also applies the sampled dc levels, $V_x$ and $V_y$, as initial conditions to the two integrators. As the integrators stabilize at the initial conditions, the oscillation begins, and simultaneously, clock pulses are sent to the counter. When the positive going zero crossing (point X) is reached, the counting stops.

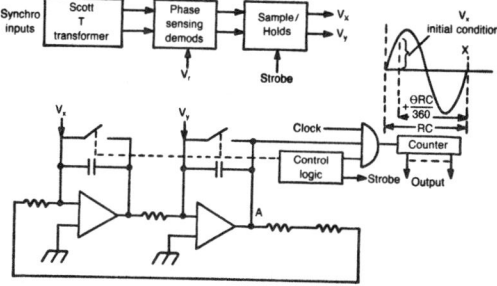

**Sampling harmonic oscillator S/D converter**

At this point, the total stored in the counter is the digitized value of $\theta$, the shaft angle, provided that the clock frequency has the correct relationship to the integrator time constants.

At point X, the positive zero crossing that stops the counting process, the following relationship will hold:

$$\sin \left( \frac{t}{RC} - \frac{2\pi}{360°} \right) = 0$$

or

$$\frac{t}{RC} = \frac{2\pi\theta}{360°}$$

If the clock rate is proportional to some convenient number of pulses like 3600, these are produced in $2\pi$ RC seconds and the count at point X will be:

$$\frac{3600}{360\theta}$$

Then the total stored in the counter represents the angle $\theta$ to a resolution of 0.1° (1 part in 3600). Any desired resolution can be obtained within the stability and accuracy limits of the system.

**HARP** Abbreviation for *high altitude relay point*.

**hartley** 1. A unit of information content equivalent to 3.32 bits. The hartley is defined as the equal of one decadal position, or the designation of one of ten possible and equally likely states or values. 2. (usually capitalized) A type of oscillator characterized by a feedback element consisting of a split inductance.

**hartley principle** The principle that the gross information content is the number of bits or hartleys required to transmit a message in a noiseless system with a specified accuracy, without regard to redundancy.

**HAS** Abbreviation for *high altitude sample*.

**hash** 1. Electrical interfering noise arising from vibrators or commutators. 2. Electrical noise that causes interference or unwanted and meaningless information to be carried in memory.

**hash total** A sum formed for error-checking purposes by adding fields or other items that normally are not related, such as the total of invoice serial numbers.

**HASO** Abbreviation for *houston automatic spooling operation*. Refers to a remote job entry system to fit IBM equipment.

**HASP** An extension to the System/360 operating system that provides supplementary job management, data management, and task management functions such as control of job flow, ordering of tasks, and spooling.

**HAWK** Abbreviation for *homing all the way killer*.

**HC** Abbreviation for *handling capacity*.

**HDX** Abbreviation for *half duplex*.

**head** A device used to read, write, or erase data in a storage medium. A head can be the small electromagnet for reading, writing, and erasing data on magnetic drums or tapes, or any of the marking devices used for punching, reading, and printing paper tape.

**header** The initial part of a message, which contains information such as routing, addressee, destination, and time of origin.

**header card** A card that contains supplemental information related to the data in cards to follow.

**header label** A block of data at the start of a magnetic tape that contains information to identify the file. A header label may include:

1. The date when recorded
2. File name and number
3. Reel number
4. Retention time

**head gap** The space between the pole pieces of a magnetic recording head.

**heading** 1. The sequence of characters preceded by the *start of heading* character, which is used as address and routing information. 2. Azimuth bearing of an aircraft or target.

**headliner** A photolettering machine that produces headlines and other large display copy.

**head meters** Some flow sensing elements are called head meters because the differential pressure across two points can be equated to the head or the height of the liquid column. The elements are characterized by a constant area of flow passage. The Venturi tube, flow nozzle, orifice plate, pitot tube, and other restricted sections are included in this group.

**head to tape contact** The degree to which the surface of the magnetic coating of a tape approaches the surface of the record or relay heads during normal operation of a recorder. Good head to tape contact minimizes separation loss and is essential in obtaining high resolution.

**heat of emission** The additional heat energy that must be supplied to an electron emitting surface to keep its temperature constant.

**heatsink** A device used to dissipate heat away from a component or chassis.

**HELP** Name of a program and system of files that provides assistance to the programmer in the use of software and hardware.

**henry** The unit of inductance in the International System of Units (SI) and equal to the inductance present when a current change of one ampere per second produces one volt of potential in a closed circuit.

**hermaphroditic connector** Refers to connectors whose mating parts are identical at their mating face; those which have no female or male members but still can maintain correct polarity sealing, and mechanical and electrical couplings.

**hertz** The SI unit of frequency equal to one cycle per second.

**hertzian wave** The electromagnetic radiation that carries a radio signal through space.

**heterodyne** To *beat* or combine two sinusoidal waves with a nonlinear device (such as a mixer) to produce sum and difference frequencies.

**heterodyne interference** Interference resulting from the simultaneous reception of two signals whose wavelengths are separated by a frequency difference in the audio range.

**HETS** Abbreviation for *hyper environmental test system* (USAF).

**heuristic** Refers to exploratory methods of problem solving in which solutions are found by evaluating the progress towards a final result.

**heuristic routine** A routine that uses a trial-and-error method using a learning technique rather than a direct algorithm approach.

**HEX** Abbreviation for *hexadecimal*.

**hexadecimal** Pertaining to the use of character sets with 16 possibilities, or number systems with a base or radix of 16.

**hexadecimal conversion chart** A conversion chart of the bit patterns and the hex letter/number codes as shown in the figure. Note that the first four-bit patterns begin with 00; the next with 01; the next four with 10, and the last four with 11. This is the sequence for a two bit binary number: 00, 01, 10, 11. Also notice that the groups of four (going down the table) start with 0, 4, 8, and C. Then the last two bits of each pattern go through the same sequence 00, 01, 10, 11— as you go through the set 4, 5, 6, 7. Next, look at the first two bits to get the starting point 0, 4, 8, or C. Then use the last two bits to sequence from there. So 1011 is in the group that starts with 8, and it is the last one in that group, so it is 11.

Starting with the letter/number code, first note the group; then write the first two bits; note where it is in the group; then write the last two bits. Note that you can easily convert from and address like 23FF to its binary equivalent, 0011 0011 1111 1110.

**hexadecimal notation** A notation system that uses 16 integers represented by the numerals 0-9 and the letters A-F, as shown in the following table:

| Binary | Octal | Decimal | Hexadecimal |
|--------|-------|---------|-------------|
| 0000 | 0 | 0 | 0 |
| 0001 | 1 | 1 | 1 |
| 0010 | 2 | 2 | 2 |
| 0011 | 3 | 3 | 3 |
| 0100 | 4 | 4 | 4 |
| 0101 | 5 | 5 | 5 |
| 0110 | 6 | 6 | 6 |
| 0111 | 7 | 7 | 7 |
| 1000 | 10 | 8 | 8 |
| 1001 | 11 | 9 | 9 |
| 1010 | 12 | 10 | A |
| 1011 | 13 | 11 | B |
| 1100 | 14 | 12 | C |
| 1101 | 15 | 13 | D |
| 1110 | 16 | 14 | E |
| 1111 | 17 | 15 | F |

**Hexadecimal and equivalent numbers**

**hex format** A technique that is used to put addresses in hexadecimal form with a base of 16. The 16 bits are broken up into four groups of four bits each; then a code of one letter or number is used to represent each group as shown below. An address that is 16 bits long can be given as four of these codes: for example FA34 or 05DC. These codes are easier to work with and remember. It is also easy to convert back and forth from the bit patterns.

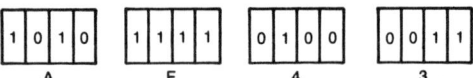

**Hexadecimal representation for a 16-bit address**

| 0 0 0 0 | 0 |
| 0 0 0 1 | 1 |
| 0 0 1 0 | 2 |
| 0 0 1 1 | 3 |
| 0 1 0 0 | 4 |
| 0 1 0 1 | 5 |
| 0 1 1 0 | 6 |
| 0 1 1 1 | 7 |
| 1 0 0 0 | 8 |
| 1 0 0 1 | 9 |
| 1 0 1 0 | A |
| 1 0 1 1 | B |
| 1 1 0 0 | C |
| 1 1 0 1 | D |
| 1 1 1 0 | E |
| 1 1 1 1 | F |

**Hexadecimal conversion chart**

**HF** Abbreviation for *high frequency*.

**HF/DF** Abbreviation for *high frequency direction finder*.

**Hg delay line** A sonic or acoustic delay line in which mercury is used as the medium of sound transmission, with transducers on each end to provide electrical signal. Related to acoustic delay line.

**HICAPCOM** Abbreviation for *high capacity communication system*.

**hierarchical networks** These networks use a multilevel master slave configuration. Various levels in the hierarchy have been assigned responsibilities for certain functions. The highest level in the hierarchy makes all major decisions, and the lower levels have the responsibilities for specific operations.

**hierarchical simulation** This simulation technique combines both gate level and functional simulation with several levels of detail. Gate level models can be used, for example, at functional interfaces or for critical internal faults. In some systems it is useful to simulate only critical sections that are known to cause most of the faults.

**hierarchical system** A system that uses a master processor and two or more slave processors in a hierarchical ordered relationship. The master processor controls or supervises the operation of the slave processors in either a tightly or a loosely coupled manner.

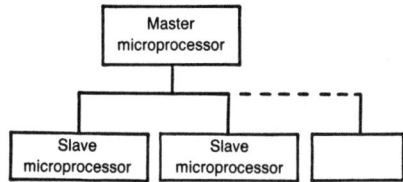

**Master-slave or hierarchical microprocessor system**

**hierarchy** A structure that consists of ranked sets and subsets. A hierarchical file system can eliminate the requirement for a separate data base definition language.

**high** Refers to the higher voltage or the most positive level in a two-level logic system. Usually, true states are represented by a *high* (relative to the alternate state) voltage, a binary 1, and a closed switch; false states are denoted by a logic *low*, a binary 0, and an open switch.

**higher order software technique** A software design technique developed on NASA projects as a means of defining reliable, large scale, multiprogrammed multiprocessor systems. This method is based on rules that define a hierarchy of software control; here the control is the specified effect of one software object on another:

1. A module controls the operation of functions at only its immediate, lower level.
2. A module is only responsible for elements of its own output space.
3. A module controls the access rights to a set of variables that define the output space for each immediate, lower level function.
4. A module can reject invalid elements of only its own input set.
5. A module controls the ordering of the tree for only the immediate, lower levels.

**high frequency** Any frequency falling between 3 MHz and 30 MHz.

**high frequency heating** Heating (induction or dielectric) in which the source of current is from rotary generators up to 3000 Hz and from electronic generators in the 1-100 MHz range.

**high frequency transformer** A transformer designed to operate at high frequencies. In these units the self-capacitance becomes important.

**high-gain amplifier** A voltage amplifier having little if any feedback.

**high-level compiler** A compiler for high-level languages.

**high-level language** A computer language that uses English-like statements for instructions. In high-level languages, each instruction or statement corresponds to several machine-code instructions. Tests using microprocessors show that such languages require 10 percent less time for programming and debugging than assembly languages.

**high-level modulation** A level of modulation produced in the output circuit of an AM transmitter system that permits 100% modulation.

**high-level multiplexers** High-level multiplexers are designed to operate with input signals greater than 1 V. The most common type uses a bank of switches connected to a common output bus as shown below. The bus output can be buffered by a noninverting amplifier as shown. The configuration is simple, and with an output amplifier, it offers a high input impedance. Depending on the switching device, this multiplexer can operate over a wide variation of input voltage. With solid state switches, the input voltage excursion is limited to about +20 V. Most multiplexers are designed for the standard analog range of 10 V; but some that use high threshold switches can be used for only ±5 range.

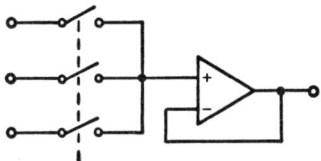

**High-level multiplexer**

**high-noise-immunity logic** A type of logic (abbreviated *HNIL* or *HiNIL*) that offers protection from noise generated in nearby sources. HiNIL offers a dc noise immunity almost ten times greater than TTL and will block transients large enough to cause TTL malfunctions.

**high-order digit** A digit that occupies a significant or highly valued position in a notational system.

**high-pass** Descriptive of a circuit or device (such as a filter) that permits the passage of all electrical signals above a certain critical frequency and shunts all other signals to ground.

**high-pass filter** A filter that freely passes signals of all frequencies above a reference value known as the *cutoff frequency*.

**high-speed bus** A set of wires that provides a path to transfer the electrical pulses that represent data and instructions to the various registers in the microcomputer.

**high-speed logic** A logic family such as ECL that offers relatively high switching speeds.

**high-speed printer** A typing machine that operates in excess of 300 lines per minute with 100 characters per line.

**high-speed read/punch diagnostic** A test for peripherals and controllers that uses a test tape for reading and punching operations.

**high speed storage loading** A I/O port option on some systems that adds a high-speed input/output path to ROM. This option permits high-speed transfer between the ROM and external devices such as cassettes. Through the I/O port, a microcomputer's storage, line printer, and keyboard are available to store assembled programs, obtain program listings, and examine and modify specific locations in ROM.

**HiNIL** Acronym for *high-noise-immunity logic*, a logic family designed especially for applications in which transients are likely to occur and create a noisy environment. HiNIL can be used directly with CMOS to protect the CMOS circuits from static electricity and transients during turn-on. HiNIL is also compatible with many analog circuits.

**HIPAR** Abbreviation for *high power acquisition radar*.

**HIPERNAS** Abbreviation for *high performance navigation system*.

**Hi-Pot** A contraction of *high potential*, which commonly refers to a device used for testing insulation breakdown or leakage with high voltage. High potting is the verb.

**historical data** Information concerning past production in a department; any data that have been accumulated from prior periods.

**hit** A momentary electrical disturbance in a circuit or system.

**HNIL** See *HiNIL*.

**hold** A condition that suspends operation of a system or circuit for a specified time (as, for example, to allow the user to study the parameters).

**hold, automatic** Refers to the attainment of a hold condition automatically through comparison of a variable or through an overload condition.

**hold button** A button used in analog computer consoles that allows the operation to be temporarily stopped for observation by the operator. All integrating capacitors are disconnected during a hold to maintain the correct charges.

**hold instruction** An instruction that causes data called from storage to be retained after it is called out.

**hole** 1. The blank left in a card after punching. 2. A mobile void in a transistor that is quickly filled by an electron and which gives the illusion of movement in a direction opposite that of electron flow.

**hole current** Current caused from the movement of electrons into holes, creating new holes in semiconductors.

**hole density** Refers to the density of the current carrying holes in a semiconductor.

**hole injection** The creation of mobile holes in a semiconductor by applying an electric charge using a metallic point or using other methods.

**hole mobility** The ability of a hole to travel easily through a semiconductor.

**hole pattern** The punched configuration in a card column that represents a single character or a character set.

**hole trap** An impurity in a semiconductor that can release electrons in the conduction or valence bands and so trap a hole.

**Hollerith code** A punched-card code that uses 12 rows per column and usually 80 columns per card. It is a 12-level code that represents the alphabet plus digits 0-9, using zone bits and data bits. The Hollerith code lends itself readily to error-detection methods.

**hologram** A type of imaging that uses lasers instead of lenses.

**home** On a video display, the position in the upper left hand corner where the first printable character is placed.

**homeostasis** A steady-state condition in a system where the input and output are precisely balanced.

**homogeneity** A state or condition of similarity of nature, kind, or degree.

**hopper** The portion of a card processing machine that holds the cards to be processed for the card feed mechanism.

**horizontal tabulation character** A format effector (the HT character) that causes the printing or display position to be moved to the next series of positions along the display or printing line. In ASCII, this character is represented by a binary 9 (0000 1001).

**host** The primary or controlling computer in a multiple computer installation. Host computers are also used to prepare programs for use by other computers and to compile, edit, link, and test programs used in other systems.

**host computer** 1. The primary or controlling computer in a multiple computer operation. 2. A computer used to prepare programs for use on another computer or on another data processing system; for example, a computer used to compile, link edit, or test programs to be used on another system.

**hot** A terminal or conductor that is connected, alive, or energized, but is not at ground potential.

**hot wire anemometers** A flow sensor that has a wire element, which is heated electrically, perpendicular to the flowing stream. Cooling by the flow changes the resistance of the wire as a function of the flow velocity. Other forms maintain the wire temperature constant and measure the current required to maintain the temperature; this current is then a function of the flow. Such instruments can measure mass flow as long as the product of the thermal conductivity, specific heat, and density remain constant. This is true for many gases at low pressures; thus this meter has the greatest application in the measurement of low flow rates of gases. They are also used for gas velocity determinations. They are sensitive to flow changes but tend to be expensive. Anemometers are widely used in air conditioning, in weather stations, and around cooling towers.

Some types of anemometers use the deflection of vanes measured with strain gage bridges in a limited number of designs. The vane in these flowmeters is usually installed perpendicular to the flow. A wedge-shaped vane anemometer with strain gages has been used for air turbulence measurements.

**hot zone** The area, adjustable in width, for controlling the right hand margin of text. When a line of typing is printed out under reset-margin conditions, the printer, having reached the hot zone, will decide either to start a new line or to pause so the operator can make a hyphenation decision.

**housekeeping** Any operation in a routine that does not contribute to the solution of the problem, but that is required for machine operation (such as setting up constants and variables).

**housekeeping instruction** An instruction pertaining to necessary but nonproductive instructions. Housekeeping instructions include bookkeeping instructions.

**housekeeping operation** Machine operations that must be performed before actual processing begins. Housekeeping operations include:

1. Establishing controlling marks
2. Reading the first record
3. Setting up auxiliary storage units
4. Initializing parameters

**housekeeping routine** Initial instructions that are executed only once, such as clearing storage locations or initializing instruction addresses.

**H/P** Abbreviation for *high position*.

**HPF** Abbreviation for *highest possible frequency*.

**HS** 1. Abbreviation for *half subtractor*. 2. Abbreviation for *handset*.

**HSBR** Abbreviation for *high speed bombing radar*.

**HSR** Abbreviation for *high speed reader*.

**HT** The ASCII horizontal tabulation (HT) character, designated by a binary 9 (0000 1001).

**HTL** Abbreviation for *high threshold logic*.

**hub** A receptacle into which an electrical lead may be connected in order to carry a signal.

**HUFF-DUFF** Abbreviation for *high frequency direction finder*.

**HUKFORLANT** Abbreviation for *hunter killer forces, atlantic* (USN).

**HUKS** Abbreviation for *hunter killer submarine* (USN).

**human engineering** The science and art of designing machines for use by human operators. Human engineering is concerned with the limits and habits of the human operator.

**human factors** Machine design considerations that are based on the inherent limitations and psychological or physiological needs of human operators.

**HUMRRO** Abbreviation for *human resources research office*.

**hunting** 1. A condition in which a system appears to seek a state of equilibrium continuously. 2. Repeated oscillation to limits above and below a desired value.

**hy** Occasional abbreviation for *henry*.

**hybrid circuit** A circuit fabricated by interconnecting circuits of different classes, such as tubes and transistors, transistor discretes and ICs, or thin-film and thick-film ICs.

**hybrid computer** A computer that uses both analog and digital representations. Hybrid computers are used in many simulation applications in which a close relationship with the physical world is required.

**hybrid integrated circuit** An integrated circuit that uses a combination of technologies or components that are interconnected on a common substrate or package.

**hybrid interface** An interface for connecting analog and digital devices together.

**hybrid system** A system in which digital and analog computing elements are used, or a system where a small computer is used for immediate quick-response processing and a larger remote location machine is used for off-site processing of large blocks of data.

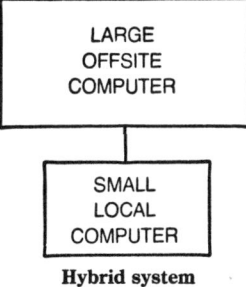

**Hybrid system**

**HYCOL** Abbreviation for *hybrid computer link*.

**HYCOTRAN** Abbreviation for *hybrid computer translator*.

**HYDAC** Abbreviation for *hybrid digital analog computer*.

**hyphen drop** A feature of word processing in which a hyphen that originally appeared at an end-of-line word break is automatically dropped if the word later appears in the middle of a line.

**hyperbridge** A computer game that uses the game of bridge as its main element.

**hypercards** Refers to a computer game that uses the characteristics of a deck of playing cards in its structure.

**hyperdice** A computer game that is based on the rolling of dice.

**hypereditor** An editor program, such as one used in a dynamic worksheet environment, that automatically recalculates results when changes are made.

**hypergame** A computer game that uses the characteristics of a familiar game such as dice or playing cards.

**hyperkaleidoscope** Refers to a computer game that automatically produces patterns or random events that allow the game to continue.

**hyperspace** Refers to higher-dimensional spaces such as the four dimensional universe of time and space.

**hypertape** A high-speed tape unit that uses cartridges to house the supply and takeup reels to permit automatic loading.

**hysteresis** 1. A lagging in the response of a signal or property, which may depend upon the past history of the signal or device being observed. 2. The difference between the turn-on threshold of a device or circuit, and the turn-off threshold of that same device after turn-on.

**hysteresis distortion** The distortion of waveforms in circuits that contain magnetic components. It is due to the hysteresis of the magnetic cores.

**hysteresis error** The difference in readings obtained in a system with and without hysteresis present.

**hysteresis loop** The loop or closed curve that results when parameters are plotted for devices exhibiting hysteresis.

**Hz** Abbreviation for *hertz (cycles per second)*.

**I** Symbol for current.

**IA** Abbreviation for *indirect addressing*.

**IAC** Abbreviation for *integration, assembly, and checkout*.

**IAEA** Abbreviation for *International Atomic Energy Agency*.

**IAF** Abbreviation for *International Astronautical Federation*.

**IAGC** Abbreviation for *instant automatic gain control*.

**IC** Abbreviation for *integrated circuit*, an electronic self-contained assembly fabricated on a single chip of semiconductor material.

An IC usually starts out as a schematic diagram; then a layout drawing that is 20-100 times larger than the final product. Mixtures of paste-like inks are used for conductors, and for each type of ink used a separate mask is produced by reducing the layout drawings. When the inking is completed, the chips are placed in a furnace, where the temperature is controlled and diffusion is used to achieve the proper resistivity of the semiconductor. Laser trimming can also be used for producing resistors with fine tolerances. Etching is used for trimming and removing unwanted paths on the chip.

**icand register** A register that contains the multiplicand during a multiplication operation (from the last two syllables of *multiplicand*).

**ICAS** Abbreviation for *International Council of Aerospace Sciences*.

**ICC** Abbreviation for *International Computer Center*.

**IC DIP package** An integrated circuit dual-inline package, a molded IC package generally available in 8-, 14- or 16-lead versions. It is somewhat larger (0.25 × 0.75 in) and easier to handle than the flat-pack. The inline bent structure makes it convenient for plugging into circuit sockets or for automatically assembling onto printed wiring boards. Its thermal resistance is comparable to that of a TO-5 transistor package.

**IC dopant impurities** Controlled amounts of dopant impurities are introduced into the preselected parts of the silicon surface through the diffusion windows in the oxide layer. Solid state diffusion of these dopants into silicon at high temperatures results in the formulation of a pn junction within the single crystal silicon. Since the diffusion of impurities proceeds sideways as well as downward from the diffusion windows at the surface, the resulting junction edge is not exposed to air on the surface, but is protected by the surface oxide layer.

**ICE** ICE is an in-circuit emulator that is plugged directly into the user's system in a real time environment. ICE is used to control, interrogate, revise, and completely debug a user's system in its own environment.

**ICES** Abbreviation for *Integrated Civil Engineering System*.

**IC electrical contact** Electrical contact to semiconductor regions can be formed by depositing thin metal films of high electrical conductivity, such as aluminum, over the windows cut in the oxide. These conductive films can then be etched into desired interconnection patterns on the surface of the silicon wafer thus completing the monolithic circuit structure.

**IC impurity diffusion** For digital integrated circuits, controlled amounts of interstitial impurities such as gold, copper, or nickel can be introduced into a silicon lattice to reduce the minority carrier lifetime.

**ICM** Abbreviation for *inverted coaxial magnetron*.

**icon** Refers to a descriptive picture or symbol on a CRT screen.

**IC photomasking** The wafer surface to be masked is initially coated with a photosensitive coating known as photoresist or resist. The resist coated wafer surface is then brought into contact with the masking plate and exposed under an ultraviolet light. The portions of the photosensitive resist not covered by opaque portions of the mask polymerize and harden as a result of this exposure. Then, the unexposed parts of the resist can be washed away, leaving a photoresist mask on the wafer surface. As a result of the masking step, the pattern to be etched through the oxide is transferred to the wafer surface in the form of a hardened photoresist pattern.

**ICT** Abbreviation for *insulating core transformer*, a type of high voltage generating device with high voltage/low current capabilities and compact design.

**IC tester** Abbreviation for *integrated circuit tester*, a type of automatic test instrument that interrogates the parametric and functional performance characteristics for a wide variety of integrated circuits. The instrument may display pass or fail information during the test cycle, detect out of specification supply current, and identify each input or output pin at which a parametric or functional failure is detected. The entire test sequence may be performed within milliseconds.

**ICU** Abbreviation for *instruction control unit*.

**IDA** Abbreviation for *Institute for Defense Analysis*.

**ideal filters** Ideal filters have flat response, infinite cutoff attenuation, and linear phase response. In practice one has the choice of a cutoff frequency, and an attenuation rate and phase response based on the number of poles and filter characteristic.

**idealized system** A conceptual system that is often used as a standard to measure the performance of other systems.

**idealized value** An expected or desired value of a parameter. The idealized value may be assumed to exist even though it may be impossible to determine.

**ideal noise diode** A type of diode that has an infinite internal impedance and in which complete shot noise fluctuations are suppressed.

**ideal sample hold** In an ideal sample hold, tracking is error free, acquisition occurs instantaneously with zero settling times, and hold time is infinite with zero leakage. Commercial units are specified in the ways in which they depart from the ideal.

**identification systems** Identification systems are an important industrial area for microcomputers. Such systems are used to monitor or control the location of moving objects, such as parts or vehicles, from a central location. The operator may issue commands to control the flow or direction to groups of parts or to a specific part or vehicle on the basis of the information that has been forwarded to the control station. A simplified block diagram of the system is shown below. This diagram shows the system for communicating with the central control station. A receiver and transmitter are shown, but a transponder could be utilized equally as well. Communications are conducted through a UART and the I/O interface to the data bus of the microcomputer system. The system includes a microprocessor, RAM and ROM, a keyboard for entry of information by the operator, and a display for indicating information.

**identifier** Any symbol that is used to tag, name, or indicate data.

**identifier word** A full-length word used in search or search-and-read operations. The identifier word may be stored in a special register and then compared with each word in the suspected sequence.

**identity element** A logical element that provides a true output when all inputs are the same. The term is usually used for circuits with only two inputs, while identity gates and units may have more than two inputs. Also called *equivalence element*.

**identity gate** A gate that produces an output when all of the inputs are the same.

| INPUTS | OUTPUT |
|--------|--------|
| 0 0 0  | 1      |
| 1 0 0  | 0      |
| 1 1 0  | 0      |
| 1 1 1  | 1      |
| 0 1 0  | 0      |
| 1 0 1  | 0      |
| 0 1 1  | 0      |

Also called an *identity unit*.

**identity unit** An N-input device or circuit that yields a specified output signal only when all N-input signals are alike.

**IDF** Abbreviation for *integrated data file*.

**IDI** Abbreviation for *improved data interchange*.

**idle time** That portion of available time when the hardware is not being utilized. Idle time may be the time when cards, tapes, and control panels are being prepared for the next run, or it may be the time between runs when no work is scheduled.

**IDP** Abbreviation for *integrated data processing*.

**IDS** Abbreviation for *integrated data storage*.

**IEC** Abbreviation for *International Electrotechnical Commission*.

**IEEE** Abbreviation for *Institute of Electrical and Electronic Engineers*.

**IEEE-488** A parallel bus standard also known as the general purpose interface bus (GPIB), the Hewlett-Packard interface bus (HP-IB), or ANSI bus (ANSI MC11978). The standard was originally developed by Hewlett-Packard for interfacing programmable electronic test equipment. The standard was later adopted by the IEEE and the American National Standards Institute.

There are many IEEE-488 bus-compatible devices, including computer peripherals. The IEEE-488 bus supports data transfer rates as high as one megabyte, and most microcomputer peripherals. Some personal computers use a 488 bus to interface with floppy disks.

The IEEE-488 bus uses a 24 pin wide cable for the sixteen signals: eight parallel data lines and eight control lines as shown below. Devices that interface to the bus always use a male plug. The bus cables have both male and female plugs at each end to allow multiple devices to be connected in a daisy chain. As many as 15 devices may share the bus. Devices may talk; transmit data, listen; receive data, and/or control the bus. Devices can be separated by 20 meters, but for maximum speeds, cable lengths should be limited to one meter for each device. Every device on the bus is assigned a control address. A listener can respond only to messages addressed to it. A control device can cause a talker to send data to a desired listener by issuing

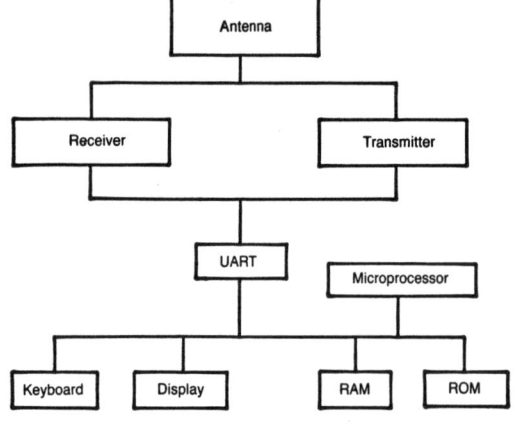

**Identification system**

the correct address. Thus, peripheral devices can transfer data among themselves without involving a host computer.

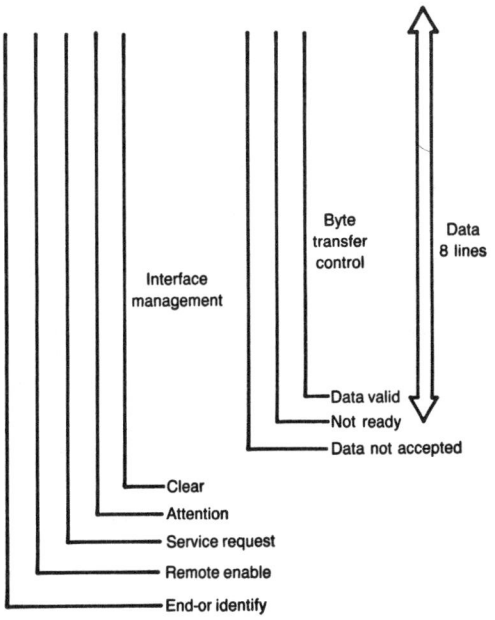

IEEE 488 bus

**ier register** A register that holds the multiplier during a multiplication operation (from the last two syllables of *multiplier*).

**IF** Abbreviation of *intermediate frequency*, the signal in a superheterodyne receiver that appears at the output of the first detector.

**IFIP** Abbreviation for *International Federation of Information Processing*.

**IF-THEN** A logical *inclusion* or *implication* operator that states: if P and Q are statements, IF P-THEN Q is false if P is true and Q is false; IF P-THEN Q is true if P is false and Q is true or P and Q are both true.

**IF-THEN gate** A gate that performs the IF-THEN operation. An IF-THEN gate may be implemented in hardware or software.

**IF-THEN, NOT** A logic operator possessing the property that if A is a statement and B is a statement, the NOT IF A THEN B operator is true if A is true and B is false, false if A is false and B is true, and false if both statements are true.

**IF-THEN operation** A logic operation with the property of IF-THEN; for example, A is a statement and B is another statement; A inclusion B is false if A is true and B is false.

**IF tube** An inclined field acceleration tube, a tube designed for use in particle (Van De Graaff) accelerators, invented by Dr. Robert Van de Graaff.

**ignistor** A device composed of a transistor and a matched zener diode, integrated into one package.

**ignore** 1. A typewriter character used to indicate that no action should be taken. 2. An instruction to inhibit execution.

**ignore gate** Same as gate, A IGNORE B and gate, B IGNORE A.

**ignore gate, negative** Same as gate, negative A IGNORE B and gate, negative B IGNORE A.

**IGY** Abbreviation for *International Geophysical Year*.

**illegal character** A character or character code that is not valid according to specified criteria. Illegal characters can be detected to indicate machine malfunctions.

**illegal code** A symbol that is not a true member of a defined code or language.

**illegal operating** An operation that cannot be performed or an operation that is performed with invalid results.

**Illiac** One of the world's earliest computers. Designed and built at the University of Illinois, it was the only one owned by a university in 1952. It was retired from service in December, 1962 after 10 years of operation at 24 hours a day.

**IM** Abbreviation for *integral modules*.

**image** A one-to-one representation of the hole patterns of a punched card. Also called a *card image*.

**image dissector** As used in optical character recognition, any transducer that detects the light intensity in different areas of a sample space. Also called an *image sensor*.

**image sensor** A type of light intensity transducer that can detect differences in light within a sample space. One type of image sensor uses silicon chips in a continuous array.

**IMC** Abbreviation for *image motion compensation*.

**IMI** Abbreviation for *intermediate manned interceptor*.

**imitation 2D** A technique of circuit fabrication using a thin film board containing a lattice of holes into which dot-type circuit elements are dropped.

**immediate access store** A store operation with an access time that is very small compared to other operating times.

**immediate address** An instruction in which the address contains the value of the operand. Sometimes called a *zero-level address*. In the 8080 microprocessor, the operand is provided by the second byte of the instruction as shown in the following example:

SBI 4 ;(A = A − 4)

which subtracts the constant 4 from the accumulator.

**immediate addressing** A form of addressing in which the operand contains the value to be operated on. Immediate addressing requires address reference, since the operands and instructions are in the same location. Almost all microprocessors use immediate addressing for jump and call instructions.

**immediate instruction** An instruction that contains the operand itself rather than an address. The use of immediate instructions allows only half as much memory to be required since instruction and operand are contained in the same word. Immediate instructions include addition, subtraction, load, and compare in some microprocessors.

**IMP** Abbreviation for *interplanetary monitoring probe* (program).

**IMP** Abbreviation for *inflatable micrometeoroid paraglide*.

**IMPACT** Abbreviation for *implementation planning and control technique*.

**impact printer** A device in which the typing element directly strikes the paper to produce a character or symbol.

**IMP computer** In the Advanced Research Projects Agency net, these are small computers that handle the store and forward communications of the packet network, and also have the capability of collecting message-handling statistics.

**impedance** The ratio of voltage to current in alternating-current circuits. Impedance contains a resistance term and a reactance term and is expressed in ohms.

**impedance bridge** A circuit used for the measurement of resistance, capacitance, and inductance.

**impedance compensator** A network used in a transmission path to

**impedance, output** Refers to an impedance measured at the output terminals of a transmission line, gate, or amplifier, under no load conditions.

**impedance, source** Refers to the impedance that is presented to the input of a device by the source.

**impedance, terminal** Refers to the impedance of a specific device such as a transmission line, gate, or amplifier, under no load conditions.

**impedance, transfer** In a network or transducer, the ratio of rms (root-mean-square, or effective) voltage applied at any pair of terminals to the rms current at some other pair.

**impedance, unilateral** Any electrical or electromechanical device in which power can be transmitted in one direction only.

**impedor** The physical realization of an impedance, as in an inductor, capacitor or resistor.

**imperative statement** A statement defining an action in a symbolic program that is converted into machine language. Imperative statements consist of verbs and operands, and usually express a complete unit of procedure.

**implementation** The phase following final approval of a system, during which the details of the system are developed and carried out.

**implication** A logical IF-THEN operation that states: if P and Q are statements, *P inclusion Q* is false if P is true and Q is false. *P inclusion Q* is true if P is false and Q is true, or P and Q are both true.

**implication gate** A device or circuit that performs the implication operation. Also called *IF-THEN* or *inclusion gate*.

**implicit address** An address reference used in assembler programming that is specified as one absolute expression. An implicit address is converted into explicit form before it can be assembled into object code.

**implicit differentiation** A procedure used in analog computers in which functions are derived implicitly. For example, if the output is the square of the input, then the input is the square root of the output; if the output is the integral of the input, then the input is the derivative of the output.

**implicit reference** A motor control technique that is suitable for implementation with a microcomputer. Usually an external reference source, such as a series of programmable counters, furnishes a clock train that the motor locks onto. With the implicit scheme, the processor calculates the desired rotation period and then forces the motor to conform. No phase angle is used.

**imprinter** A device for marking characters onto a form. Imprinters include typewriters, printers, presses, pressure plates, and stamping machine.

**imprinting** The act performed by an imprinter; the output function of an imprinter.

**impulse** 1. A pulse that begins and ends within so short a time that it may be regarded mathematically as infinitesimal. The change in the medium, however, is usually of a finite amount. 2. A change in the intensity or level of some medium, usually over a relatively short period of time. 3. A shift in electrical potential of a point for a short period of time compared to the time period.

**impulse excitation** 1. Excitation in which the current is allowed to flow for only a very short period during each cycle. 2. The maintenance of oscillatory current in a tuned circuit by pulses synchronous with free oscillations or at a submultiple frequency.

**impulse generator** A circuit providing a single pulse or a continuous series of pulses, generally by capacitor discharge; shaping is accomplished through the charging of capacitors in parallel and the discharging of them in series.

**impulse inertia** A property of an insulator in which the voltage required to cause disruptive discharge varies inversely with its time of application.

**impurity** A material added to semiconductor crystals to produce excess holes or electrons. Excess holes are produced by acceptor impurities, and excess electrons are produced by donor impurities.

**impurity level** The energy level in a material due to the addition of impurity atoms.

**IMS** Abbreviation for *Institute of Management Sciences*.

**IMU** Abbreviation for *inertial measurement unit*.

**IN** Abbreviation for *input*.

**Inaccuracies, systematic** Inaccuracies due to limitations in equipment design.

**INCH** Abbreviation for *integrated chopper*.

**incipient failure** A degradation failure that is just beginning to exist or appear.

**in-circuit emulator** A unit for emulating the user's prototype and production microcomputer in its actual operating environment. An in-circuit emulator allows early system control by using the emulator in place of the processor. The user is able to interrogate, revise, and debug the system in a real-time environment.

**in-circuit test** The testing of individual integrated circuits by checking their outputs. With an in-circuit test, logic inputs can be programmed while the outputs are measured to isolate pins stuck at zero or one, along with solder splashes and open connections.

**in-circuit tester** An automated test unit for performing in-circuit tests on mounted components. Some in-circuit testers can prescribe repairs and test simple components such as resistors in less than six milliseconds each.

**inclusion** See *IF-THEN*.

**inclusion gate** A circuit or device that performs the inclusion operation.

**inconnector** A connector used in flowcharting to indicate the continuation of a broken flow line.

**increment** To move ahead by one step at a time; it refers to a software operation used with stacks and stack pointers. The stack pointer is used to hold the addresses of information stored in the stack register. The pointer is incremented after each byte is removed from the stack and decremented (moved back one step) as each byte is added to the stack.

**incremental** An arrangement of outputs used in rotating sensors. The outputs are arranged such that the phase shift is 90 degrees apart, which allows the direction of rotation to be determined.

**incremental compaction** A data compaction method that uses only the initial value and changes in storage for transmission. Incremental compaction allows a saving in time and space because only changes at specific intervals are processed.

**incremental computer** A computer that mainly uses an incremental representation of data or a special-purpose computer designed to process changes in variables as well as the absolute values of the variables.

**incremental data** Data that represents the change from the value of the data that just preceded it; each data word or value is referenced to the prior position.

**incremental dimension** A dimension expressed with respect to the preceding point in a sequence of points.

**incremental feed** A manual or automatic input of preset motion command for a machine axis.

**incremental induction** Refers to one half of the algebraic difference between the maximum and minimum magnetic induction at a point in a material that has been subject simultaneously to a polarizing and a varying magnetizing force.

**incremental integrator** A digital integrator that has an output that is maximum positive, zero, or maximum negative when the input is maximum positive, zero, or maximum negative.

**incremental representation** A representation of a variable in which the changes in the variable are represented rather than the variable itself.

**incremental system** A system in which each coordinate or positional dimension is taken from the last position.

**IND** Abbreviation for *indicator*.

**indent** To bring a line or lines of typing in from the margin, as at the start of a paragraph.

**independent heterodyne** An oscillator, electrically separate from the detector, used for supplying local oscillations in heterodyne reception applications.

**independent program loader** A program that allows the *operation system* user to load nonsystem programs from *operating system* file devices.

**index** 1. A symbol or number used to identify a specific quantity in an array of similar items. 2. An ordered reference list of the contents of a file with keys for identification of the contents and the action required to prepare such a list. 3. In numerical control, the movement of a machine part to a predetermined location.

**indexed address** An address that is modified by the contents of an index register or similar technique. As used in the 6800 microprocessor system, the operand will be in a memory location with an address formed by adding the second byte of the instruction to the value contained in X, such as:

    ADD A 3, X ;(add X + 3 to accumulator A)

This instruction adds the contents of the memory location referenced by the contents of X + 3 to accumulator A. This instruction becomes the same as direct addressing if X contains zero. Sometimes called a *variable address*.

**indexed addressing** A form of addressing in which the address contained in the second byte of the instruction is added to the index register.

**indexed files** A file structure consisting of a series of pointers to data blocks throughout the disk. Indexed files are used for applications with a large amount of random-access data. They have the open-end characteristic of chained files with a much faster access time.

**indexing** A technique of addressing modification that usually requires an index register for implementation.

**index register** A register used to hold the addresses of information subject to modification prior to or during the execution of an instruction. The index register contents are available for loading into the stack when required. Modification may be either by addition or subtraction, yielding a new effective address.

**index value** A desired preset value of a controlled quantity used as a target value for an automatic control system.

**index word register** A register that stores a word used to modify addresses under the direction of the control section of the computer.

**indicator** A device that registers conditions resulting from computations.

**indicator chart** A chart or table used by the programmer to record items concerning the indicators in the program. The indicator chart can be a useful part of the program documentation, since indicators are often used to vary the sequence of operations within the program.

**indirect address** An address that specifies a location that contains either a direct address or another indirect address. Also called *multilevel address* or *deferred address*.

**indirect addressing** A system of addressing a location that contains the address of data instead of the data itself. Indirect addressing is any level of addressing other than the first level of direct addressing. It forms a system of computer cross referencing.

**induced** Produced by the influence of an electric or magnetic field.

**induced charge** An electrostatic charge produced by the electric field surrounding a nearby object, such as that produced on a conductor as a result of a charge on a nearby conductor.

**induced current** The current that flows in a conductor that is moved perpendicularly to a magnetic field or that is subjected to a magnetic field of varying intensity.

**induced environment** The environment of shocks, vibrations, temperatures, accelerations, and pressures that are imposed upon a system due to the operation or handling of the system.

**induced failure** A failure essentially caused by a physical condition or phenomenon external to the failed item.

**induced noise** Noise that arises because of sufficiently high frequencies in the area in space close to a conductor.

**induced voltage** Voltage that is produced in a conductor when the conductor is moved through the magnetic field of a second conductor, or when the field varies in intensity and cuts across the conductor space.

**inductance** The property of a metallic conductor or circuit element containing metal that opposes changes in the current flowing through the circuit.

**inductance bridge** An instrument, similar to a Wheatstone bridge, for measuring an unknown inductance by comparing it with a known inductance.

**induction coil** A device that uses induction for transforming a direct current into an alternating current.

**induction noise** The noise produced when two circuits or conductors are inductively coupled together.

**inductive** That property of an electric circuit or device that tends to prevent changes.

**inductive coupling** Coupling between circuits and conductors due to mutual inductance and a source of potential interference.

**inductive neutralization** A condition in which the feedback susceptance of the capacitance of the circuit elements is balanced by the equal and opposite susceptance of an inductor.

**inductive potentiometer** A type of toroidally wound autotransformer with one or more adjustable sliders.

**inductive pressure transducers** Inductive transducers use pressure to move a mechanical member that alters the self-inductance of a single coil. The inductance is changed by the relative motion of a core and inductive coil as shown below. Inductive single coil transducers have been used in L-C tank circuit oscillators, where they formed the frequency control. Their use has diminished because of difficulties in compensating for temperature effects, which required a matching of core and windings materials for temperature versus permeability characteristics.

**inductive resistor** A wirewound resistor having appreciable inductance at the frequencies in use.

**inductosyn scale** A precision data element for the accurate measurement and control of angles or linear distances, utilizing the inductive coupling between conductors separated by a small air gap.

**industrial control** The control of machines, processes, and systems involved in manufacturing operations.

**industrial control modules** Electronic control modules designed primarily for industrial control applications. Examples include analog

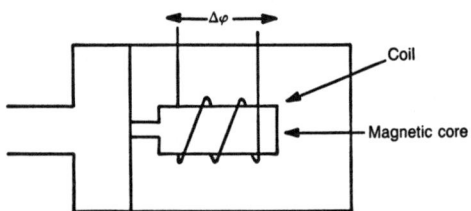

**Inductive pressure transducer**

multiplexers, transducer amplifiers, analog-to-digital converters, sample-and-hold devices, and digital-to-analog converters.

**industrial control communications** Communications equipment designed for industrial control applications.

**industrial data processing** Data processing used for industrial applications.

**industrial microcomputers** A microcomputer family designed specifically for industrial applications. Industrial microcomputers usually require a full range of memories and interface equipment for the specific applications. The microcomputer can monitor the process and transmit control signals when desired by the programmer. Typical applications include pollution control, utility control, machine tool control, and material control systems. Interface equipment should be rugged and simple (such as pushbutton controls with fixed displays), although more complex applications use keyboards, alphanumeric displays, printers, floppy disks, and tape cassettes.

**inequivalence** A Boolean *exclusive-OR* operator, which produces a true output if only one of the two input variables it connects is true.

| INPUTS | OUTPUT |
| A B | C |
|---|---|
| 0 0 | 0 |
| 1 0 | 1 |
| 0 1 | 1 |
| 1 1 | 0 |

**inequivalence gate** A device or circuit that performs the inequivalence operation.

**information** The aggregation of data that produces a whole idea, condition, or situation. Information may be a set of symbols that indicates alternatives for a situation. Information is usually derived from data.

**information bits** Any bits that are generated by the data source and not used for error control. Information theory provides that all information can be represented by some collection of bits, regardless of the complexity of the information.

**information content** The gross information content is the number of bits needed to transmit a message over a noiseless system with a specified accuracy, regardless of redundancy. *Net information content* is the minimum number required for essential information only.

**information feedback system** An information transmission system used in telecommunications that utilizes an echo check to verify the accuracy of the transmission.

**information heading** That portion of a message that contains control information such as the identification of originating station, the identification of a sending device or system, message priority, and message routing information.

**information processing** The execution of a systematic sequence of operations performed on data or information. In a typical microprocessor system, the processor accepts data, interprets it, and outputs the results. Information processing activities include routing, arithmetic, and diagnostic operations. In small systems, these operations will be performed by one processor or a single arithmetic processor and another processor for routing and diagnostics. Larger systems will use a separate processor for system diagnostics.

**information retrieval** The methods and procedures required for recovering specific information from stored data. Information retrieval may involve the cataloging of data so that all or part may be called out at any time.

**information separator** The IS character, used to identify the boundary of information in a message.

**information system** The network of all communication methods within an organization.

**information theory** A branch of science involved in the likelihood of accurate communications and transmission of information. Information theory uses mathematical analysis to determine the efficiency of communications techniques.

**inherited error** An error that is carried forward from a previous step in processing. An inherited error produces an initial error or offset for the next processing step.

**inhibit** A computer operation that prevents another operation from taking place. An inhibit might be used on a bus system to disable a channel to give another channel control of the bus.

**inhibit gate** A circuit used as a switch and usually placed in parallel with the circuit it is controlling.

**inhibiting input** A computer gate input that can prevent outputs that might otherwise occur.

**inhibiting signal** A signal that prevents an operation from taking place.

**inhibit pulse** A pulse used to prevent an operation from taking place.

**initial condition mode** A mode in analog computers in which all integrators are inoperative and the required initial conditions are applied to the system.

**initialize** To perform the preliminary steps for a routine that are not to be repeated, such as setting counters and addresses to zero.

**initializing** The preliminary, nonrepeating steps of arranging instructions and data in memory.

**initial program load** The procedure required to cause an operating system to begin execution. Also referred to as initial program loading, or initial program loader (abbreviated *IPL*). Load and loading usually refer to the procedure, while loader may refer to a routine that makes it possible to load and execute another program.

**injection logic, $C^3L$ (complementary constant-current logic)** A form of bipolar logic for the TTL (10 to 50 nanoseconds) application range. This logic form is complicated by five Schottky devices in each gate, but it allows compact processor circuits. $C^3L$ processor slices were first built at the end of 1975.

**injector grid** A grid that injects a modulating voltage into the electron stream of the first detector of a superheterodyne receiver.

**ink jet** A printing method in which characters are spray printed onto paper.

**ink jet printer** A nonimpact printer that sprays ink through an electrostatic field and onto paper to form the intended characters and symbols.

**inline** A method of processing in which all individual transactions are completely processed without the records being grouped or arranged.

**inline assembly** A mechanical assembly operation in which a line of assembly heads inserts electrical components into circuit boards.

**inline package**  See *dual-inline package*.

**inline procedures**  A set of statements used in COBOL for the controlling of program operations.

**inline processing**  A system that processes transactions in the sequence in which they arrive, without any sorting or arranging.

**inline subroutine**  A subroutine inserted directly into the operational sequence of processing. Inline subroutines are recopied at each point they are required in a routine.

**in-phase**  Two waves of the same frequency that pass through their maximum and minimum values of like polarity at the same instant are *in-phase*.

**input**  A device or set of devices used to bring data into another device. An input may be a channel for impressing or inserting a state or condition on another device, or a device or process involved in an input operation. Many times input is used as an all-encompassing term for input data, input signal, or input terminal when such usage is clear within a given context.

**input area**  Internal storage area into which data from external storage is transferred.

**input block**  A section of internal storage reserved for data from external storage (concerning processing and storage operations).

**input buffer register**  A register that receives data from input devices such as tapes and disks and then transfers it to internal storage.

**input channel**  A channel for impressing a state or condition on a device or circuit. Also called an *input*.

**input converter**  An analog-to-digital converter packaged for process control applications.

**input data**  Data entered into a computer system for processing.

**input device**  A device used for conveying data into another device, such as the units designed to bring information into a computer: card readers, transducers, and keyboards.

**input editing**  Operations done on input data to convert the format for more convenient processing and storage. Input editing may also check the data for proper format, completeness, and accuracy. Many times, the input data has been formatted for the convenience of humans and must be reformatted for efficient machine usage.

**input equipment**  Equipment used for transferring data and instructions into a data processing system. Input equipment includes all peripherals used to gather or collect data.

**input impedance**  An impedance that is measured at the input terminal of a device, usually under no-load or other specified conditions.

**input module**  A packaged functional device or unit used for conveying data into another device.

**input/output**  Pertaining to either input or output or both. Abbreviated *I/O*.

**input/output bus**  A bus that provides parallel lines for data, command, device address, status, and control information. It makes interfacing easier, faster, and less expensive.

**input/output channel**  A circuit path that allows independent communication between the processor and external devices. Input/output channels may transfer data between memory and external interfaces in blocks of any size without disturbing working registers in the processor. Multiple channels are allowed to operate concurrently with hardware priority control of each channel. Transfers are in full words, with automatic packing and unpacking allowed in some systems.

**input/output control program**  The control of input and output operations by the supervisory program.

**input/output control system**  A group of macroinstruction routines (abbreviated *IOCS*) for handling the transfer of data between main storage and external devices. The routines can be divided into two parts: physical and logical.

**input/output device controller**  A control unit with the necessary logic circuitry to interconnect one or more peripheral devices with the input/output interface. Many controllers can operate multiple devices as long as they are the same type.

**input/output devices**  Hardware capable of entering data into a machine and accepting data from the machine for processing into a form suitable for humans or other processing units. Also called *input/output equipment*.

**input/output equipment**  Refers to those units of the system that are designed to accept data and output the results of processing in a form readable either by humans or other processing units.

**input/output executive**  A modular programming technique for peripheral input/output device management and support. The executive program can free the user from time-dependent service routines and provide a well-defined protocol system.

**input/output interface**  A typical input/output interface might incorporate two input/output channels, a process input/output (PIO) channel, and a direct memory access (DMA) channel. The PIO channel interfaces with the process via the data input bus and provides simplex character-oriented data transfer capability. The DMA channel interfaces directly with the memory, via the data input bus, and provides high speed, record-oriented data transfer capability at rates of up to 500,000 or more words per second.

**input/output processor**  A secondary processor (abbreviated *IOP*) used to transfer operations to and from the main memory.

**input/output request words**  Control words that are used for input/output requests that are stored in the message reference block until the I/O operation is completed.

**input/output, simultaneous**  Generally refers to computers that can handle other operations concurrently with input and output operations, most often using buffers that hold input/output data and information as it arrives, on a temporary basis, while other operations are executed by the CPU. Thus the computer need not wait for data from the slower I/O units and may instead take it from the buffer in massive quantities.

**input/output switching**  Refers to the connection of input/output devices to more than one channel by using channel switching.

**input/output table**  A plotting machine that generates a function representing the input device plotted against the output.

**input/output unit**  A device such as a modem or terminal designed for manual, mechanical, electronic, video, or audio entry to and output from the computer.

**input program**  A routine to direct or control the reading of programs and data into the computer system. Input programs may be internally stored or wired and may use a bootstrap operation for housekeeping and control operations.

**input reference**  A value used to compare the deviation or error of a measured variable. The input reference is a selected value and is also known as the set point or desired value.

**input register**  A register that accepts data from outside the computer at one speed and supplies the information to the computer calculating unit at a different, usually much higher, speed.

**input resolution**  The smallest increment of dimension that can be an input to the system.

**input section**  That portion of machine hardware through which information passes into the computer.

**input signal**  The control loop signal when it enters a data block.

**input storage**  Containment of input data for processing. Successive

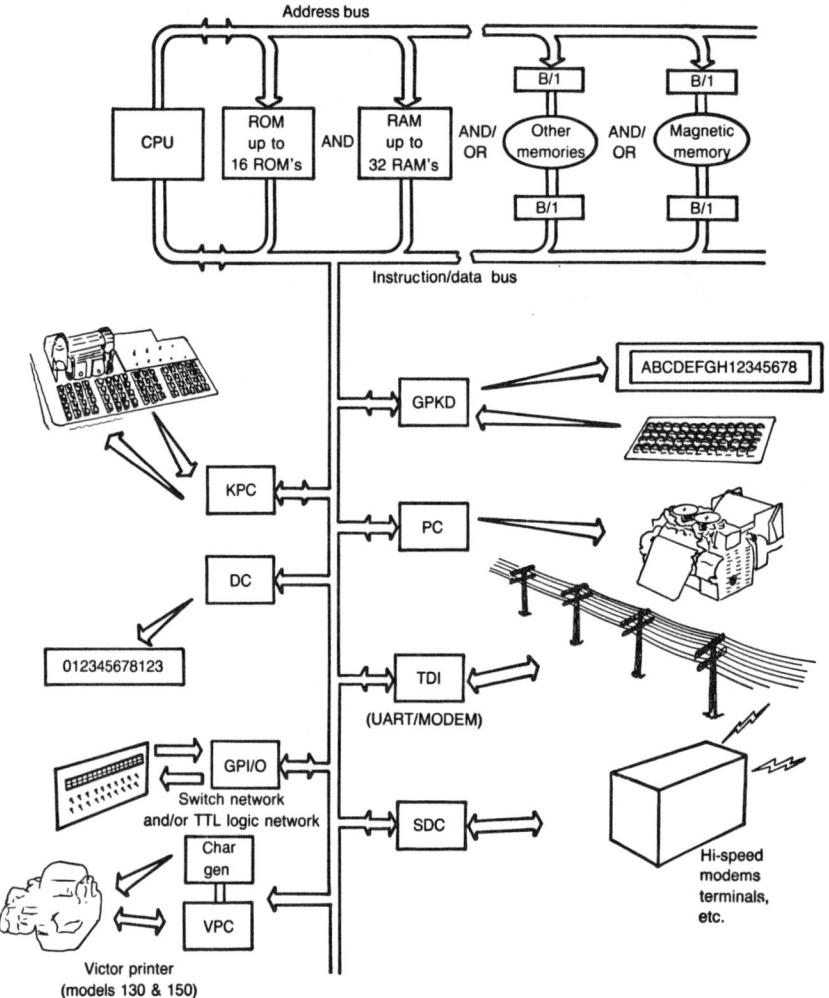

**Input-output devices**

groups of data can be compared for the correct format and are held until signaled for by the program.

**input stream** The sequence of job control statements submitted to an operating system on an input unit. Also called *input job stream* or *job input stream*.

**input transformer** A transformer for isolating a circuit from any other circuit.

**input translator** A section or a program that converts a programmer's instructions into operators and operands for the computer. A translator can also check the input for errors of syntax.

**input unit** Hardware used to supply the computer with coded information for processing.

**input word processing equipment** Dictation equipment.

**input work queue** A waiting line of job control statements from which jobs and job steps are selected for processing.

**inquiry** The interrogation of the contents of storage from a local or remote point by keyboard, keypad, or other device.

**inquiry processing** A type of processing in which inquiries and records from a number of terminals are used to interrogate and update one or more master files maintained by the central system. Also called inquiry and transaction processing.

**inquiry station** A remote terminal from which interrogation into computing or data processing equipment is made. Information is placed into the computer through an alphanumeric keyboard and is simultaneously displayed on a screen. A reply to the inquiry is then displayed on the screen until the operator desires to erase the display using an erase button on the console. Also called *inquiry terminal*.

**inquiry terminal** See *inquiry station*.

**INS** Abbreviation for *instrument*.

**insert** A word processing function that allows the introduction of new material within previously recorded text.

**inserted subroutine** A subroutine that must be relocated and injected into the main routine at each place it is used.

**instability** A measure of the fluctuations or irregularities in the performance of a variable, circuit, device, or system.

**installation time** Time required for installing, connecting, and testing either hardware or software (or both) until acceptance is complete.

**instantaneous power** In a circuit or component, the product of the instantaneous voltage and the instantaneous current. This may not be zero even for a nondissipative system because of stored energy, although its time integral must be zero.

**instruction** A statement containing information that can be coded and used as a unit in a digital computer to command it to perform one or more operations. An instruction usually contains one or more addresses and may specify arithmetic operations, such as addition or multiplication, or control operations for data manipulation. Instructions can be grouped as follows:

1. Data transfers between registers and memory
2. Branching operations
3. Input/output control
4. Loading and storing accumulators
5. Restoring registers and accumulators
6. Jumps and stack-pointer operations
7. Binary and decimal arithmetic
8. Set and reset interrupts
9. Increment and decrement registers and memory

**instruction address** The address that must be used to fetch an instruction.

**instruction address register** The register (abbreviated *IAR*) that holds the address of the instruction to be executed next in the program sequence without regard to branching or interrupts. Also called *program counter*.

**instruction area** That part of storage selected to store the group of instructions to be executed. The instruction area normally is used to hold the microcomputer program.

**instruction characters** Characters used as code elements to initiate, modify, and stop control operations. An example would be the CR (carriage return) character.

**instruction code** All of the symbols and definitions used to systemize the instructions for a given computer or executive routine.

**instruction control unit** Those parts of a computer (abbreviated *ICU*) that allow the retrieval of instructions in the proper sequence with the interpretation of each instruction and the application of the proper commands to the ALU and other parts in accordance with that interpretation. A typical ICU contains a read-only memory in which the microinstructions are stored along with the address control logic for microprogram branching.

**instruction counter** A counter used to indicate the location of the next instruction to be interpreted.

**instruction deck** A deck of punched cards that contain data defining the operations to be performed by the computer system.

**instruction diagnostic** A device using hardware and software that completely tests all CPU instructions, including interrupts, in all modes.

**instruction execution logic** The logic that allows each instruction to be retrieved or fetched from memory, decoded, and executed. The instruction execution logic may involve program counters, address registers, instruction registers, and the general-purpose register, along with many transfers between these units and memory.

**instruction formats** All instruction formats use an operational (OP) code that defines the basic operation. In general, all instructions must also address one or more elements to be operated on. The addressing is either implied by a unique Op code or it specifies the desired elements. The elements to be operated on may be internal registers or bits, or external memory or I/O. The number of elements that can be operated on by an instruction is related to the architecture of the processor and the instruction word size.

The two architectures that determine the instruction formats are register-oriented processors and memory-oriented processors. Register-oriented processors use the instruction formats to address internal registers; memory-oriented processors use the instruction format to select the modes for addressing memory. The 8-bit microprocessors, which have a limited instruction word size, have to choose between the two architectures. The 8080 favors a register architecture, and the 6800 favors a memory architecture. The 16-bit microprocessors have an instruction word size large enough for both architectures.

**instruction modification** An alteration in the operational code of a command or instruction such that if the routine is repeated, the computer will perform a different operation.

**instruction, n-plus-one address** Refers to a multiple address instruction in which one address specifies the location of the next instruction of the normal sequence to be executed.

**instruction operations** A typical microprocessor processes instructions that are used to provide the solutions to processing tasks. Instructions and programming techniques used in microprocessor systems fall into seven basic functional groups. They are:

1. Data transfer: the methods of moving data from one point to another or organizing it for processing.
2. Arithmetic operations: these may include binary or binary coded decimal, or decimal manipulations.
3. Logical operations: these include the methods for manipulating data as bits and the methods for obtaining logical functions of these bit combinations.
4. Data address modifications: the methods of modifying addresses in registers to facilitate data manipulation.
5. Control transfers: the techniques such as interrupts for modifying the normal sequence of the program for conditional and unconditional branching.
6. Register manipulation: the methods for storing data along with the manipulation of registers and individual segments of data within registers.
7. Input/output operations: the methods of using input/output instructions.

Subroutine usage including the techniques for calling routines, setting up data addresses, returning from subroutines, and nesting subroutines may be used in conjunction with the other operations.

**instruction register** A 4- to 16-bit register (abbreviated *IR*) used to hold the instruction currently being processed after it is brought to the control section from memory. The instruction register can be used to specify the initial step in a microprogram, and as an internal register, to store temporary data for microprogram control.

**instruction repertoire** The set of operations represented in a given operational code.

**instruction set** The total structured group of characters and definitions to be transferred to the computer as operations are executed. Usually the instructions are listed in alphabetical order and include binary and decimal arithmetic along with logic, shift, store, rotate, load, branch, interrupt, and stack operations. Instruction sets can be encoded in binary, octal, or hexadecimal, with the names of operations in mnemonic form using combinations of letters and numbers.

**instruction time** The portion of an instruction cycle during which the control unit is analyzing the instruction and setting up to perform the indicated operation.

**instruction word** The grouping of letters or digits into a single unit that defines operations to be performed by the computer. The instruction word may be a complete computer word, or part of the computer word that is executed as an instruction.

**instrumentation** Devices for measuring, recording, and controlling physical processes and quantitative phenomena.

**instrumentation amplifiers** A type of amplifier that may contain operational amplifiers, but are distinguished from op amps in that they are committed devices with a definite set of input/output relationships in a fixed configuration. They are designed for a high common-mode rejection ratio (CMRR) low noise and drift, moderate bandwidth, and a limited gain range, usually 1 to 1000, programmed by a fixed resistor.

**instrumentation calibration** A procedure to ascertain, usually by comparison with a standard, the locations at which scale graduations should be placed to correspond to the series of values of the quantity that the instrument is to measure, receive, or transmit.

**instrumentation correction** Refers to the calculated difference between the true value and the indication of the measured quantity; a positive correction denotes that the indication of the instrument is less than the true value.

**insulated** Separated from other conducting surfaces by a nonconductive material offering a high, permanent resistance to the passage of current.

**insulator material** A material on or through which essentially no current will flow, used to confine the flow of current within a conductor or to eliminate the shock hazard of a bare conductor.

**Int** Abbreviation for *interrupt*.

**integral action limiter** A program or device that limits the output value of a signal due to integral action at a predetermined value.

**integral boundary** A location in main storage at which a fixed-length field must be positioned. The integral boundary may be a half-word or double word; its address is a multiple of the length of the field.

**integral control action** A control action in which the rate of change of output is proportional to the input.

**integrated amplifier** 1. An analog-computer amplifier that has an output voltage proportional to the area under a time-curve plot of a variable between a reference time and any arbitrary point in time. 2. A high-fidelity stereo amplifier that includes an integral preamplifier with all necessary controls.

**integrated circuit** An interconnected array of components fabricated from a single crystal of semiconductor material by etching, doping, and diffusion; an IC is capable of performing at least one and sometimes many complete circuit functions.

**integrated circuit fabrication** In the actual fabrication of a single transistor, the silicon wafer is manufactured by cutting a single crystal of silicon in the proper direction (for example, direction 111 of the lattice). A layer of oxide is then deposited on the silicon.

The first mask is used to define the p-zones in the silicon. They are the source and drain areas of the transistor. A photosensitive emulsion is deposited on the silicon oxide, and a mask is used to print the areas that are to be doped. The oxide over the areas to be doped is then removed by chemical etching. Doping, using thermal diffusion, is then performed on the exposed areas, which allows p-type impurities into the silicon. Next, a layer of oxide is grown on top of the silicon as shown in the figure. Then, a mask is used to define the areas to be metallized. The oxide is then removed in these locations. Another oxidation for the gate is performed in order to grow a thin layer. A final oxide removal is performed to expose the source and the drain areas, which are then connected to the rest of the circuit during metallization.

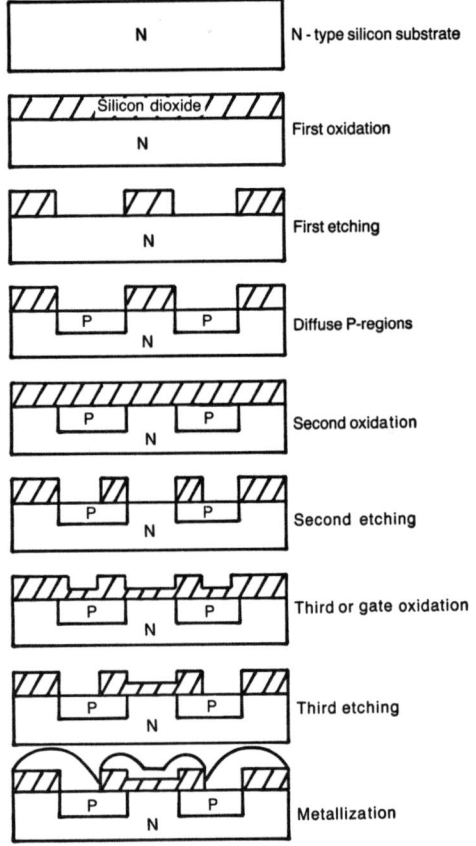

**Integrated circuit MOS transistor manufacture**

**integrated component** A single structure with a number of elements that cannot be separated without destroying the function or functions of the device.

**integrated data processing** A data processing approach (abbreviated *IDP*) in which all stages of processing are carried out using a coherent systems approach, such as a business system where data for orders and buying are combined to accomplish the functions of scheduling, invoicing, and accounting.

**integrated emulator** An emulator program whose execution is controlled by an operating system in a multiprogramming environment.

**integrated injection logic** An integrated circuit logic (abbreviated *IIL* or $I^2L$) that consists of interconnected bipolar transistors of both polarities. A cross section of an $I^2L$ chip consists of an npn transistor operated in a vertical mode, while a lateral pnp transistor is used as a current source and a load for the preceding stage. Isolation is automatically accomplished between the collectors, allowing high packing densities. Besides high packing density, it offers a good speed-power product along with versatility and low cost.

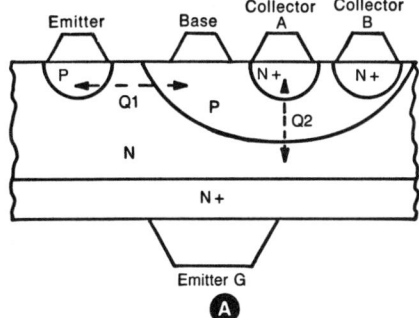

$I^2L$ Structure

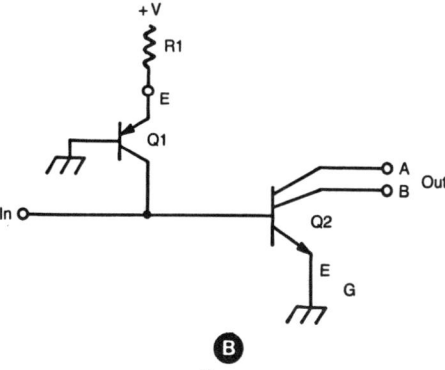

Basic $I^2L$ Circuit

**integrated monolithic circuit** A one-chip circuit that uses geometric etching and conductive ink deposition techniques to achieve circuit functions on a single semiconductor chip. Also called an *integrated circuit*.

**integrated system** 1. Programs that allow the introduction of new or allied data into an existing set without having to reenter the previous data. Thus a customer name need not be reentered for use with both accounts receivable and inventory control. 2. Hardware that works together without further need of additional circuits to allow communications between devices.

**integration A/D converters** These analog-to-digital converters perform an indirect conversion by first converting to a function of time and then converting the time function to a digital quantity by using a counter. The dual ramp converter is one example.

**integrator** A unit or device that performs the mathematical function of integration, usually with reference to time. Integrators include circuits that integrate signals over a period of time and any system with an output proportional to the input.

**integrator capacitors** Refers to devices that may be shunted by a resistor to permit the zero balance of an integrator.

**integrator, digital** An integrating device in which digital signals are used to show increments in input variables x and y and an output variable z.

**integrator, feedback sample hold** A sample-and-hold integrator in which a current amplifier is used with an integrator, permitting the switch to operate at ground potential and thus easing the leakage problem. See the figure.

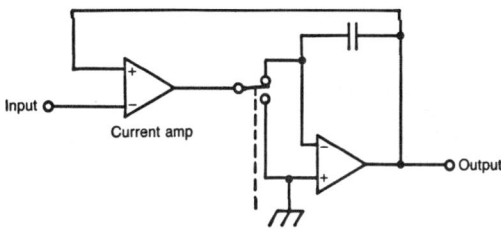

**Low-frequency sample hold with integrator feedback**

**integrator, hard-limited** Refers to a type of integrator in which the inputs cease to be integrated when the output tends to exceed specified limits. Unlike the output from soft-limited integrators output from hard-limited integrators does not exceed the limits.

**Intel 3002** The Intel 3002 is an early 2-bit slice microprocessor that used Schottky bipolar technology to achieve the first fast cycle times. The 3002 central processing unit was combined with the 3002 microprogram control unit to form a two chip microprocessor system based on user-generated microcode stored in the microprogram memory. The two components were combined with memory and peripherals for the first high-speed controllers and processors. Each 3002 represented only a 2 bit slice, and devices were connected in parallel to form processors of the desired word length. The basic architecture for the 3002 is shown below.

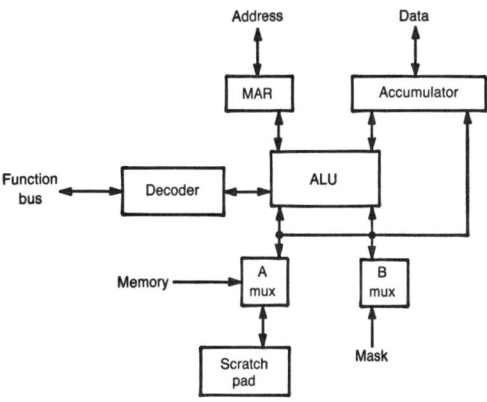

3002 architecture

In the 3002 the microfunctions were controlled by a function bus that instructed the decode unit to select the ALU functions to be performed, generate scratch pad register addresses, and control the A and B multiplexers. A microfunction action could be a data transfer, a shift, an increment or decrement, a test for a specified condition, an initialization for a specified condition, an addition or subtraction in two's complement, a bit mask, or a program counter operation.

**Intel 4004** The Intel 4004 was the first microprocessor. It was designed as the processing element of a desk calculator and introduced in 1971. The 4004 was never designed to be a general purpose computer. Its shortcomings in this area were soon recognized. It was, however, the first general purpose computing device in a chip to be on the market. Many other chips introduced at about the same time were called microprocessors, but were in fact, only calculator chips. Many of them used serial bit-by-bit arithmetic.

**Intel 4040** The Intel 4040, which was the first microprocessor, was rapidly replaced by an improved version, the 4040. In order to preserve the software investment of the 4004, the 4040 instruction set was made compatible with the 4004. The 4040 offers a number of improvements. It has an interrupt capability, and a larger number of internal registers. The register banks can allow a fast interrupt response. When an interrupt occurs (provided there are no more than two interrupt levels), one can switch from one bank of registers to the other. The program counter and the status word are not repeated within the register banks, which requires additional instructions to be executed for switching.

These registers can be used during interrupt processing for saving status variables, as already discussed, and during addressing to provide indexed capabilities.

The instruction register stores the next instruction to be executed by the processor. Instructions may be either 8 bits or 16 bits in length. The instruction register is 8 bits wide, so a one word instruction will be executed in one instruction cycle, while a two word instruction will take two instruction cycles.

The instruction decoder decodes the bit pattern of the instruction from the instruction register by translating it into a sequence of machine operations using the timing and control circuitry that in turn controls the internal operations of the 4040. A two-phase clock input is used in the 4040 to develop the synchronization signals that are transferred to the internal elements of the CPU.

A basic 4040 system is shown below. A 4289 memory interface is used with a 1 of 8 decoder for connecting a ROM. As a 4-bit microprocessor, the 4040 is intended for applications such as calculators, games, appliances, and simple control applications.

**Intel 8008** The 8008 is a first-generation 8-bit microprocessor that was introduced in early 1972. It was the second of the first-generation pro-

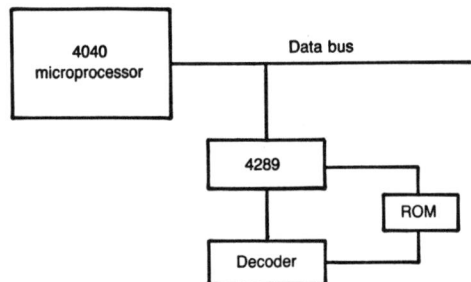

**Basic 4040 system**

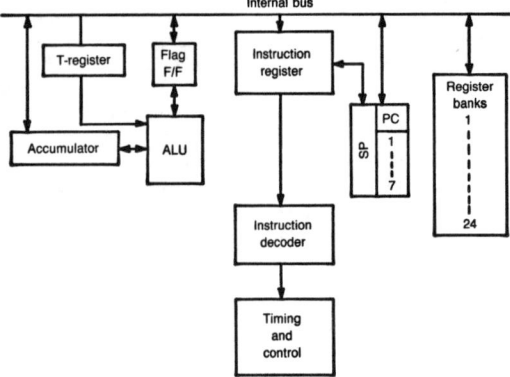

**4040 microprocessor architecture**

The basic architecture of the 4040 is shown above. The device is organized around a 4 bit internal data bus that interconnects the internal registers. Input and output functions are performed by a 4-bit bidirectional data bus that interfaces with the input/output pins. The accumulator is used as a latch for storing data that is ready to be processed by the ALU or for receiving data that has already been processed. A temporary register, T, which is not under user control, is used to temporarily store data that has been transferred from another register in the microprocessor.

The address registers operate as a last-in first-out push down stack. The address stack uses a program counter with seven levels. The address registers are 12 bits wide and are multiplexed to the 4-bit internal bus by a stack multiplexer. The register bank consists of 4-bit general purpose registers that can be used in pairs for 8-bit storage.

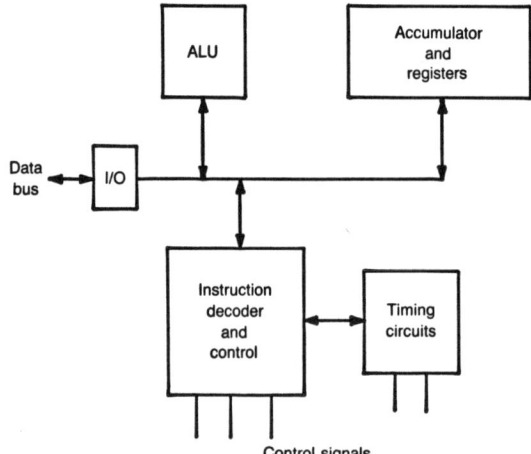

**8008 architecture**

cessors, following the 4004, which was introduced in late 1971. The 8008 is fabricated using the PMOS process. It is packaged in an 18 pin dual in-line package, and thus is compact for an 8-bit microprocessor.

Address information is multiplexed over the 8-bit bidirectional data bus as shown. At the beginning of each machine cycle requiring a read from or write to memory, the address information is put on the data bus. The address must be saved or latched by external circuitry.

**Intel 8021** The Intel 8021 is an 8-bit parallel microcomputer in a 28 pin package. The n-channel silicon gate chip contains a 1K × 8 program memory, a 64 × 8 data memory, an 8-bit timer/event counter, 21 input/output lines, and oscillator and clocking circuitry. The block diagram for the 8021 is shown below. The chip has a bit-handling capability and will perform either binary or BCD arithmetic. The 8021 program memory is mask programmable with no provisions for external expansion. All locations in the data memory are indirectly addressable with eight locations being directly addressable.

**Intel 8022** The 8022 is a member of the Intel group of single chip 8-bit microcomputers. It is designed for low cost, high volume applications that involve analog signals, capacitive keyboards, and/or large ROM space. The 8022 addresses these applications by integrating on the chip additional functions, such as analog-to-digital conversion, comparators, and zero cross detection.

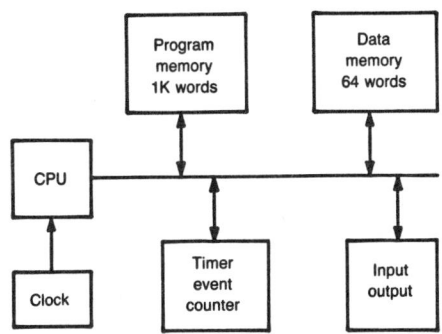

8021 microcomputer chip

The 8022 includes 2K bytes of ROM, 64 bytes of RAM, 28 I/O lines, an on-chip A/D converter with two input channels, an 8-bit port with comparator inputs for interfacing to low voltage capacitive touchpanels or other non-TTL interfaces, external and timer interrupts, and zero cross detection capability. In addition, it contains an 8-bit interval timer/event counter, oscillator, and clock.

The 8022 can be a controller as well as a basic arithmetic processor. It has bit-handling capability plus binary and BCD arithmetic. The instruction set consists mostly of single-byte instructions and has extensive conditional jump and table lookup capability. The 8022 contains an on-chip hardware implementation of an 8-bit analog-to-digital converter with two multiplexed analog inputs. The A/D converter uses the successive approximation technique and provides an updated conversion once every 40 microseconds using a minimum of software.

**Intel 8048 family** The 8048 is a self-sufficient 8-bit parallel computer fabricated on a single chip using the n-channel silicon gate MOS process. The 8048 has a 1K × 8 program memory, a 64 × 8 RAM data memory, 27 I/O lines, and an 8-bit timer/counter with oscillator and clock circuits. For systems that require extra capability, the 8048 can be expanded with standard memories. The 8035 is the equivalent of an 8048 without program memory.

Three interchangeable pin compatible versions of this microcomputer exist: the 8748 with user programmable and erasable EPROM for prototype and preproduction systems, the 8048 with factory programmed mask ROM program memory for low cost, high volume applications, and the 8035 without program memory for use with external memories.

The 8048 has bit-handling capability as well as facilities for both binary and BCD arithmetic. The instruction set consists mostly of single byte instructions with no instructions over 2 bytes in length.

The 8048 was designed for single chip applications and does not suffer from having to be compatible with more powerful predecessors.

The program memory of 1K × 8 can be expanded, but expanding the memory affects the hardware configuration drastically. Expanding the 8048 moves the device into the general purpose control market. In addition to expansion, the program memory can be completely external to the device. This requires a multichip system, but it allows more complete emulation during development.

The 8048 uses a register-oriented architecture with two banks of 8 bit registers in the 64 × 8 RAM. The selected bank operates with the accumulator, using a somewhat incomplete set of instructions. Incompleteness is due to a lack of compare and subtract operations. There is a full set of increments and decrements, and all of the registers, except the accumulator, may be decremented with a JUMP IF NOT ZERO instruction.

The data memory is a 64 × 8 RAM. Two register banks and the eight-level stack reside in the RAM, leaving half of the locations available as a scratch pad. RAM operations can be done with indirect register addressing using either of two registers in the selected register bank. The same operations that can be performed with the registers can also be performed with RAM locations (except the decrement operations).

**Intel 8051 family** The 8031, 8051, and 8751 are stand-alone single-chip computers fabricated with depletion load, n-channel, MOS technology.

The 8051 and 8751 contain a nonvolatile 4K × 8 read-only program memory; volatile 128 × 8 read/write data memory; 32 I/O lines; two 16 bit timer/counters; a five-source, two-level, nested interrupt structure; a serial I/O port for multiprocessor communications, a full duplex UART; and an on chip oscillator and clock circuits. The 8031 is identical, except it lacks the program memory. The 8051 can be expanded using standard TTL compatible memories.

The 8051 microcomputer, like its 8048 predecessor, was designed as a controller or a basic arithmetic processor. It has facilities for binary and BCD arithmetic as well as bit handling capabilities. The instruction set consists of 44 percent one-byte, 42 percent two-byte, and 15 percent three-byte instructions. With a 12 MHz crystal, 58 percent of the instructions execute in one microsecond and 40 percent in two microseconds; multiply and divide require four microseconds. Among the other instructions added to the 8048 instruction set are subtract and compare.

The 8031 is a control oriented CPU without the on-chip program memory. It can address 64K bytes of external program memory in addition to 64K bytes of external data memory.

For systems requiring extra capability, each device in the 8051 family may be expanded. The 8051 is an 8031 with the lower 4K bytes of program memory filled with on chip mask-programmable ROM, while the 8751 has 4K bytes of ultraviolet-erasable ROM.

**Intel 8080** The 8080 is an 8-bit N channel MOS device that is packaged in a 40 pin DIP. It is based on the older 8008 architecture, but it is capable of much more sophisticated applications. The architecture of the 8080, like the 8008 is organized around an 8-bit internal

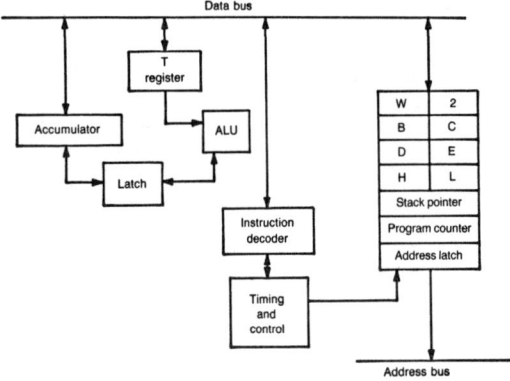

**8080 architecture**

data bus as shown below.

One of the limitations of the 8008 was its limited stack depth. The use of an external stack in the 8080 provides improved design flexibility, and the direct memory access feature allows peripheral devices to access the busses for direct memory data transfers without interfering with processor operation.

**Intel 8080 status decoder** The decoder shown below is necessary to synchronize the operation of the 8080 with the rest of the system.

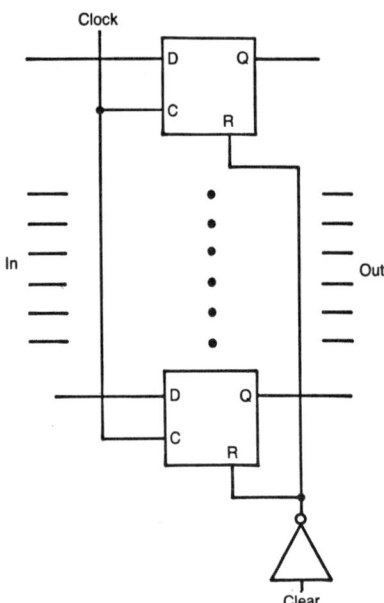

**Status decoding**

**Intel 8085** The 8085 is a faster version of the 8080. It has an on-chip clock along with a system controller to provide cycle status information. It is software compatible with the 8080, and it operates with a 1.3 microsecond instruction cycle for the A configuration.

The major value of the 8085 lies in the special chips that are available for a minimal 8085 system. These are memory and I/O combinations, that connect directly to the 8085 without the need for any additional components. They allow a complete 8085 system to be assembled with just three chips. Thus, we have a microprocessor with the same power as the 8080 requiring a minimal number of chips for a system. The limitation of the system is the amount of memory contained in these memory and I/O combinations, 2K words of ROM, and 256 words of RAM.

**Intel 8086** The 8086 is a 16-bit microprocessor based on the 8080. The 8086 uses silicon gate HMOS technology for faster performance and an expanded 8080 structure. Basically, it is an improved, 16-bit version of the 8080. The 8080 multiplexed bus has been expanded into a 16-bit external bus. Like the 8080, the instructions are byte oriented.

The basic structure of the 8086 is shown below. The 8086 consists of two separate processing units, an execution unit, or EU, and a bus interface unit, or EIU, connected by a 16 bit ALU data bus and an 8-bit Q bus. The EU obtains instructions from the instruction queue, maintained by the BIU, and executes instructions using the 16-bit ALU. Execution of instructions involves maintenance of the status and control logic, manipulation of the general registers and instruction operands, and manipulation of segment offset addresses. The EU accesses memory and peripheral devices through requests to the BIU, which performs all bus operations for the EU. This involves generating the physical addresses from the segment register and offset values, reading operands, and writing results.

The execution unit and the bus interface unit operate in-

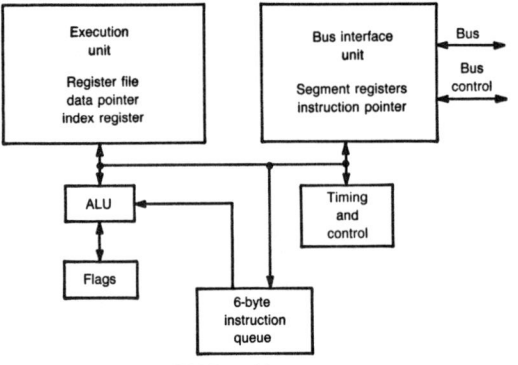

**8086 architecture**

dependently of each other, enabling the 8086 to overlap instruction fetch and execution. While the 8086 is decoding the current instruction, the bus interface unit (BIU) fetches the contents of the next sequential memory addresses and loads them into the queue. If the current instruction is not a branch instruction, the next instruction is available to the processor's execution unit (EU) upon completion of the current instruction without the need for a memory access. If the current instruction is a branch instruction, the next instruction is fetched from memory. The queue decreases address bus/data bus idle times by prefetching data, thus increasing processor speed.

The 8086 register structure is similar to the 8080's. The 8086 execution unit contains four 16-bit point and index registers and four 16-bit data registers addressable on a byte basis. These eight registers are used to provide compact coding at the cost of flexibility. The BIU contains one 16-bit instruction pointer, which holds the offset of the next instruction to be fetched. This pointer is updated by the BIU but is not directly accessed by the program. The BIU also contains four 16-bit segment registers for segment base addressing, which allows access of up to four 64K segments at a time. The EU also contains 1-bit status flags and three 1-bit control flags.

**Intel 8257** A controller for the 8080 system. It requires an external latch in order to preserve the eight-address bits. A typical configuration of the 8257 appears below. It shows four DMA levels for controlling four different disk units, each connected to its own DMA level.

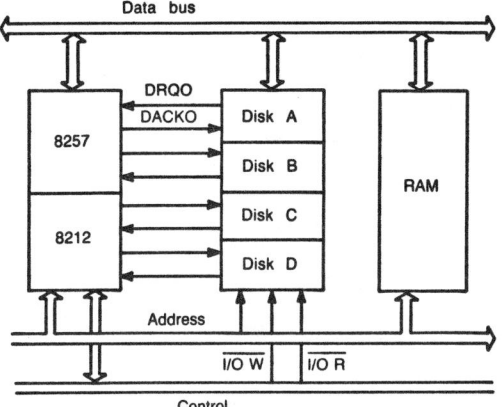

**8257 DMA**

**Intel 8259 interrupt controller** A priority interrupt controller chip. The structure of the Intel 8259 appears below. It provides interrupt management including priorities, interrupt mask, and automatic vectoring. It is implemented in an NMOS 28 pin package. The chip can be cascaded with up to eight other PICs to manage 64 separate interrupt levels.

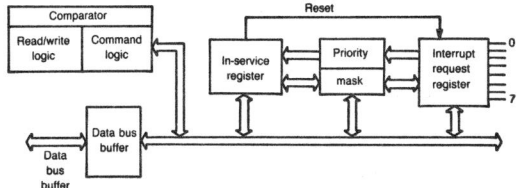

**8259 interrupt controller**

**intelligent bus interface** A technique that reduces some of the costs required during the development of special purpose interfaces. The intelligent interface as shown below consists of a microprocessor system specially designed with a limited instruction set to emphasize I/O control and interface operations instead of the usual general-purpose instructions. The microprocessor system has a bus that is compatible with the host microprocessor system and extensive I/O facilities along with on-chip data and program memories. The system can be programmed to perform the interface functions required by the particular I/O device.

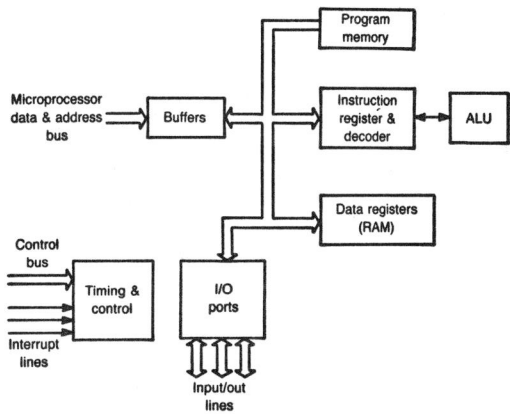

**Intelligent interface**

**intelligent cable** An interfacing system that allows input and output operations along with word and byte transfers to occur in any mix on all channels concurrently. An intelligent cable provides a low-cost parallel interface while freeing the designer from costly development time involved in interfacing the peripherals. Some features of intelligent cables include:

1. TTL compatibility with low-power Schottky circuits
2. Handshaking and strobing capability
3. Multiple device control
4. Microprogrammed interface control
5. Standard ribbon cabling

**intelligent disk storage** A disk system that does its own data-base management; only commands from the host computer and data field information need to be passed to the system controller. All indexing, searching, and deblocking are done on the disk system controller.

**intelligent keyboard system** A keyboard system that performs all alphanumeric and numeric operations for keying, editing, calculating, storing, compressing, and printing.

**intelligent terminals** A terminal capable of data processing using storage and a stored program, which is available to the user. Typical configurations include 4096 bytes of user memory with a minidisk system or magnetic tape cassettes. Expansion allows up to 16,384 bytes with additional cassette stations and panel displays. Intelligent terminals allow more of the communications function to be done outside of the host computer, thus increasing the potential for terminal applications.

**INTELSAT** The International Telecommunications Satellite Consortium, known as INTELSAT, was established under a pair of international agreements originally signed by 14 nations in August 1964. With the ratification of definitive agreements by the required 54 partner member countries, the International Telecommunications Satellite Organization came into being on February 12, 1973. An Office of the Secretary General was established and a Secretary General appointed, assuming office in late 1973. INTELSAT is the international joint venture created to establish the global communications satellite system.

**intensity level** The level of power as expressed in decibels above an arbitrary zero power level.

**interacting simulator** A simulator that precisely duplicates the timing of the microcomputer to allow the user total interactive control to execute and alter the program.

**interaction factor** A factor allowing for insertion loss due to the connection between source and load. This vanishes when the impedance of a network equals that of the load or source.

**interactive** Refers to the point at which two systems, two devices, or a person and a device come into contact with each other.

**interactive multiprocessor systems** Multiuser systems that are used for the simultaneous processing of a large number of jobs with dif-

**interface** 1. A common or shared boundary between instruments, devices, or systems, which is functionally compatible with connected units. An interface enables devices to exchange information among devices and implies a connection to complete the interchange. 2. The specification required for the interconnection between two systems. For example, the EIA interface is a standard set of signal characteristics including voltages, currents, and time durations for communication terminals.

**interface bus** A bus that provides the interface connections and timing to interconnect different types of instruments, and either programmable calculators or computers to form complete instrumentation systems.

**interface cards** Circuit boards or cards that permit the connection of various instruments and peripherals to the CPU.

**interface channel, peripheral** The interface form that is designed or agreed upon so that two or more devices, systems, or programs may be easily joined or shared.

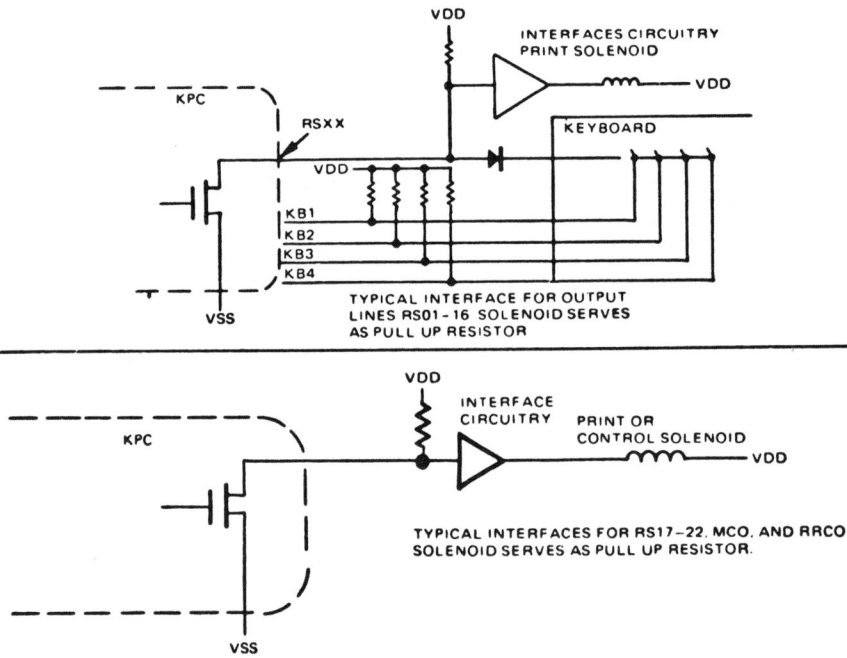

**Interfaces**

ferent characteristics. The system may reconfigure itself by partitioning the system into independently operating units, on a space or time-division multiplex basis.

**interbase current** The current flowing between the two base connectors in a junction type tetrode transistor.

**interblock gap** The area on a data medium used to indicate the end of a block or record. Also called *block gap*.

**interconnection line** A transmission line connecting two systems or networks that allows energy to be transferred in either direction. Also called *tie line*. A large interconnection is called *giant tie* or regional interconnection.

**interface debugging** Some microcomputer interfaces can be checked out in part by writing short programs that test portions of the interface. Suppose you wished to check out the interface to a tape unit. A short loop can be written that advances the tape and checks for data. This loop can be executed in a single step mode. The final routine for driving the tape unit will be more complex because it will have to time out the interval between characters. The short routine determines that the circuits are working. In this way the problem of determining whether the bugs are in the program or in the circuitry can be solved.

**interface module** A hardware unit that provides the interface between a bus and the user's peripheral or instrumentation. Integrated circuits mounted on the module provide logic for address selection, interrupt control, and byte input/output transfers. Interface modules for industrial microcomputer systems may include modules for digital communication, power switches, analog-to-digital and digital-to-analog conversion, time-keeping clocks, and pulsers.

**interface standard** A format that allows matching the characteristics of two or more units, systems, or programs so that they can be easily joined together.

**interfacing, analog** In many systems, it is necessary to provide an interface for analog devices such as transducers for pressure, temperature, or other variables. The output of the transducer can be a voltage or current that may or may not require amplification for interfacing. The transducer output is converted into a digital word to be used by the microprocessor.

**interference** Electrical or magnetic disturbances that cause unwanted responses or effects (usually voltage spikes or *transients*).

**interference fading** The fading of signals because of interference among the components of the signals that have taken slightly different paths to the receiver.

**interference trap** A means of reducing interference, such as a tuned-rejector circuit for a single steady transmission or a band-pass filter that will reduce the accepted band of frequencies to a minimum.

**interferometer** An instrument that uses light interference techniques for the determination of wavelength, spectral lines, indices of refraction, and small linear displacements.

**interior label** A label magnetically written on a magnetic tape to identify the remainder of the contents of the tape.

**interlace** 1. To assign successive storage location numbers to physically separated storage locations on a magnetic drum to reduce access time. 2. To superimpose two TV raster scans so that the lines formed by one scan appear as alternating lines of the other.

**interleave** To arrange parts of one sequence or group with parts from another such that each sequence or group retains its identity.

**interleaved status checking** In a program, the status check may be repeated continuously until I/O device is ready. This loop effectively stalls the program execution, which can use too much processing time. To avoid this, one can interleave the status check with other microprocessor operations as shown below.

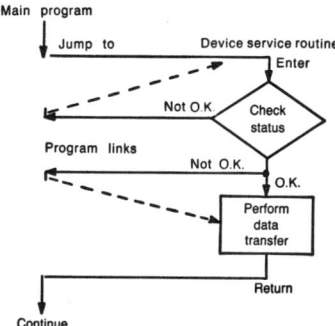

**Interleaved status checking**

**interleaving** 1. The inserting of segments of one program into another program to allow the two to be executed essentially in a simultaneous mode. 2. A process of splitting memory into two sections with two paths to the central processor to speed processing. Interleaving allows a second word to be read during the half-cycle when the previously read word is being written back into the memory.

**interlock** To arrange the control of machines or devices so that their operation is interdependent in order to assure their proper coordination.

**interlock bypass** A command, device, or circuit, used to temporarily circumvent a normally provided interlock.

**intermediate cycle** An unconditional branch instruction that may address itself.

**intermediate frequency oscillator** An oscillator used in heterodyne reception that is coupled with the output of the intermediate amplifier for demodulation in the second or final detector.

**intermittent control** A control system in which the control variable is monitored periodically with an intermittent correcting signal supplied to the controller.

**intermittent error** A sporadic error that may not be detected when diagnostic programs or routines are run.

**intermodulation distortion** Amplitude distortion in which the intermodulation products are of greater importance than the harmonic products, as in audio amplifiers for high quality reproduction.

**internal arithmetic** Computations performed by the arithmetic and logic unit.

**internal interrupt** A control signal that diverts the attention of the computer to consider an extraordinary event or circumstance. An internal interrupt causes the control of the program to be transferred to a subordinate, which then corresponds to the stimulus. Internal interrupts are used primarily to synchronize the program with the termination of input/output transfers, and to signal the occurrence of errors.

**internally stored program** The set of instructions stored in internal memory as contrasted with those stored on cards, disks, or tape.

**internal memory** Addressable storage directly controlled by the CPU of the microcomputer. Internal memory is the total memory or storage accessible to the CPU and forms an integral part of the microcomputer. Also called *internal storage*.

**internal storage** See *internal memory*.

**international electrical units** (ohm, watt, amp, volt). Values of the practical units adopted internationally until 1947, when MKSA (meter-kilogram-second-ampere) units were employed. The international watt differs by 16 parts in $10^5$ from the absolute watt (1 J/sec).

**interpolation** The process of finding a value between two known values, and the procedure for determining values of a function between known and observed values.

**interpolator** A device that is part of a numerical control system and performs interpolation.

**interpret** To translate or decode, as in converting nonmachine language into machine language, or to print the graphic characters represented by the holes in a punched card.

**interpret program** A program that translates and executes each source language statement before operating on the next statement.

**interpreter** 1. A machine that will accept a punched card with no printing on it, read the information from the punched holes, and print a translation using characters in specified rows and columns. 2. A routine that translates a stored program expressed in a code into machine code and performs the indicated operations, using subroutines as they are translated.

The interpreter is used like a closed subroutine that operates successively on the sequence of instructions and operands. It is usually entered as a closed subroutine and left with an exit instruction. Since the interpreter operates on the instructions one by one, and executes each statement before starting on the next, it tends to be slower than other methods of translation.

**interpreter operation** Refers to a routine that, as the computation progresses, translates a stored program expressed in some code into machine code and performs the indicated operations, by means of subroutines, as they are translated.

**interpretive code** Interpretive routine.

**interpretive routine** A routine that decodes and immediately executes instructions written as pseudo codes. The essential characteristics of an interpretive routine is that a particular pseudo-code operation must be decoded each time that it is executed. This is contrasted with a compiler, which decodes the pseudo codes into a machine language routine for execution at a later time.

**interpretive translation program** A program designed to translate each instruction of a source language into computer instructions and allow each one to be executed before translating the next instruction. If the program allows programs written for one type of computer to be run on a different type, it is often called a *simulator program*.

**interrecord gap** An interval of space or time left between recording portions of data or records. Interrecord gaps are used to prevent overwrite errors and permit tape start-stop operations.

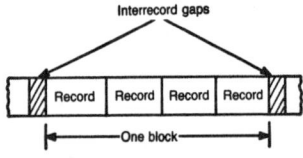

**Interrecord gaps**

**interrupt** To temporarily disrupt the normal operation of a routine by a special signal from the computer. Usually the normal operation can be resumed from that point at a later time. As the peripheral units interface with the CPU, interrupts occur on a frequent basis. Multiple interrupt requests will require the processor to delay, to prevent further interrupts, or to break into a procedure to modify operations.

With the use of interrupts, throughput increases because the processor is allowed to perform calculations concurrent with input/output operations. The major characteristics of interrupts include:

1. *Latency*, the time to recognize the interrupt and branch to the service routine.
2. *Response*, the time to identify the interrupted device and begin execution of the device service code.
3. *Software overhead*, the time required to get to the service routine and return to the main program.

An example of interrupt usefulness occurs in printer buffering. Serial printers tend to be slow and to print a line of characters without interrupts; a microprocessor transfers a character to the printer and then waits until that character is printed until it transfers the next character. Character transfer takes only a few microseconds, while character printing may take up to 100 milliseconds per character; the microprocessor spends most of the time waiting for printing completion. A program interrupt can eliminate this waiting time, so that when the printer is busy, the microprocessor can be involved in other tasks and return only when required to transfer a character.

**interrupt, active** Refers to the state of an interrupt level that is the result of the CPU starting to process an interrupt condition.

**interrupt control** An example of interrupt control is a real time application such as an online data acquisition system that uses a microprocessor-controlled multichannel analog-to-digital converter. The flow is shown below.

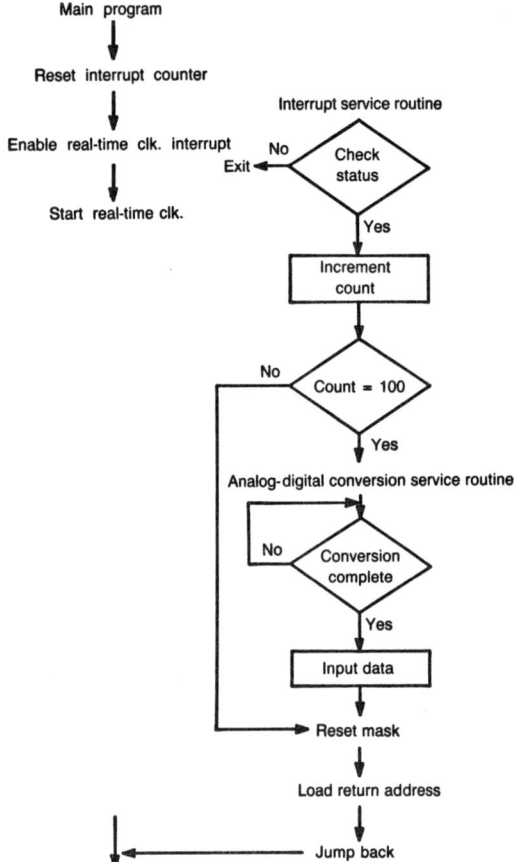

**Interrupt-controlled data acquisition system**

**interrupt controlled I/O** When the polling technique for I/O does not provide a fast enough response, or uses too much microprocessor time, interrupts can be used. In the interrupt driven scheme, the devices have the initiative for requesting service. An extra line is used as an interrupt line, which is connected to the MPU. Each of the devices is connected to this line. Every one of devices wishing to get service has the option of using this line to request service. A device that requests service generates an interrupt pulse or level on this line. The microprocessor then detects the presence of interrupts on the line and manages them as illustrated in the diagram.

**interrupt count pulse** An interrupt level that is triggered from pulses provided by the clock. Each pulse causes an instruction in the count-pulse location to be executed.

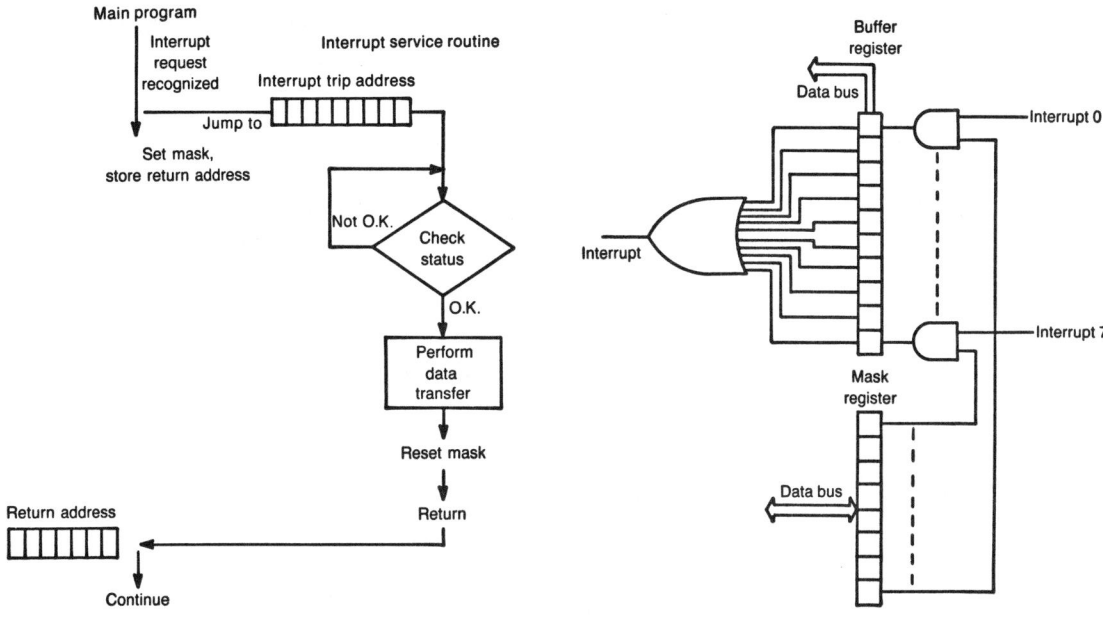

**Interrupt-controlled input/output**

**Interrupt priority logic**

**interrupt device** The external device requesting an interrupt, such as a communications unit or timing signal.

**interrupt enable and disable** Instructions used to set and reset an interrupt control flip-flop.

**interrupt freeze mode** A condition in analog computers under which all computing action is stopped and all values are held as they were when the interrupt occurred.

**interrupt identification** Identification of the device and channel causing the interrupt are often stored as a program status word (PSW). In addition, the status of the device and channel is stored in a fixed location in memory.

**interrupt input lines** Signal channels that are used for inputs that set the interrupt flags of the control registers.

**interrupt mask bit** A specific bit used to prevent the CPU from responding to further interrupt requests until cleared by execution of programmed instructions. It can also be manipulated by specific mask bit instructions.

**interrupt mask word** A word used to enable or disable interrupts in a system. Each bit of the word is interrogated to enable or inhibit a specific device interrupt.

**interrupt module** A device that acts as a monitor for a group of field contacts and notifies the computer when an external priority request is generated.

**interrupt priority logic** Refers to the priority scheme used in managing interrupts. Most hardware interrupt handlers use a masking register. This is shown in the basic interrupt management logic shown below, which does not include priority-encoding or a vectoring facility.

This circuit, which is on the right of the diagram, manages eight interrupts. The mask register appears at the bottom. When the contents of a bit of the mask are 0, this will block the propagation of the corresponding interrupt signal towards the left of the circuit. The interrupt level is then masked. The presence of a 1 in the mask register allows the interrupt to propagate towards the left. When all interrupt lines are used, or allowed, the mask register contains all 1s. If interrupt line 2 is not allowed, then bit 2 of the mask register is set to 0. The interrupt levels that are not masked out will set a bit in the interrupt register. The contents of this register can be read out of the circuit via the data bus.

This register allows the implementation of the software priority decoding. An exclusive OR of the lines of this register provides the final interrupt signal shown on the left of the circuit. This interrupt request line is connected to the microprocessor interrupt line.

In normal operation, the mask register is loaded by the programmer with the correct bit pattern to enable the selected interrupt lines. If all interrupt lines are used, the mask register will contain all 1s. When one or more interrupts are requested, they propagate to the left of the circuit when an interrupt request results. The microprocessor then reads the contents of the interrupt register and finds 1s in every bit where a device has requested service.

**interrupt, processor** In many systems, processor interrupts are automatic procedures designed to alert the system to conditions arising that may affect the sequence of instruction being executed.

**interrupt response time** The elapsed time between an interrupt and the start of the interrupt-handling subroutine. The difference between the total time elapsed and the actual execution time is the overhead time.

**interrupt signal feedback** A signal indicating that the interrupt signal has advanced to the waiting or active state. The signal is not present once the interrupt level is reset to the disarmed or armed state.

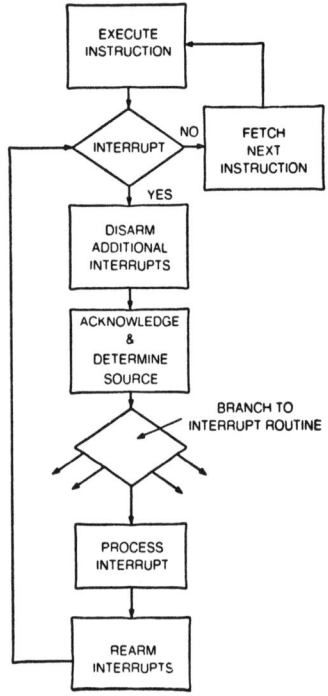

**Interrupt flow**

**interrupt vector** 1. An interrupt channel reserved for the highest priority external function; in many cases this is a real-time interrupt from the 60 Hz line source. 2. A polling scheme in which the highest priority device or devices are hard-wired to achieve fixed-priority encoding. The encoded value is then used as a system address to transfer control to the interrupt response routine.

**interstage punching** A form of card punching in which either the odd or even columns are not used.

**interval polling timer** A control program that keeps track of the time of day in order to interrupt the system periodically as required.

**interword gap** The time or space allowed between words on a tape, disk, or drum. The interword gap allows the medium to be switched and is used for the control of individual words.

**intrinsic conduction** Conduction in a semiconductor when electrons are raised from a filled band into the conduction band by thermal energy, thus producing hole electron pairs. Intrinsic conduction increases rapidly with rising temperature.

**intrinsic mobility** The mobility of electrons in an intrinsic semiconductor.

**inversion** 1. Any procedure that is used to reverse the order of items of data. 2. The process of reversing the polarity of any dc voltage or signal.

**invert** 1. To place in contrary order, as to exchange the numerator with the denominator in a fraction. 2. To reverse the polarity of any voltage or signal, whether dc or pulsed.

**inverter** 1. A circuit or device that takes in a positive signal and outputs a negative one, or takes in a negative signal and outputs a positive signal. 2. A device that changes direct current to alternating current, with or without a voltage level change.

**inverted rectifier** A rectifier arranged to convert direct current to alternating current. See also inverter.

**inverted R-2R ladder** A network used in data conversion to give an unattenuated noninverting output by connecting the output to a high impedance load, such as the input of the follower amplifier shown below. The MSB (most significant bit) output is 1/2 V (2R - 2R divider). Since the entire network may be considered as an equivalent generator having an output voltage NV (where N is the fractional digital input) and an internal resistance R, the output may be scaled accurately by connecting precision resistors to ground.

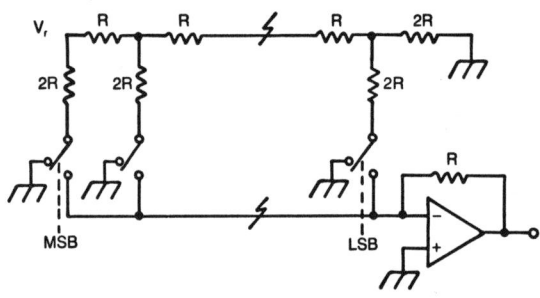

**Inverted R-2R ladder for current switching**

**inverting amplifier** An amplifier with an output voltage that is equal in magnitude to the input, but opposite in sign.

**inverting current switch multiplexer** For switching as much as several hundred volts with solid state speed, the inverting current switch multiplexer (MUX) can be used as shown in the illustration. Since switching takes place at the summing junction, with the protective diodes to ground, the switches are not subjected to the high voltages. This MUX has a high immunity to transient voltages and a constant but low input resistance while conducting; it assumes a safe state when power is removed. Each channel can be adjusted for gain. This multiplexer is rugged and suited to industrial system control.

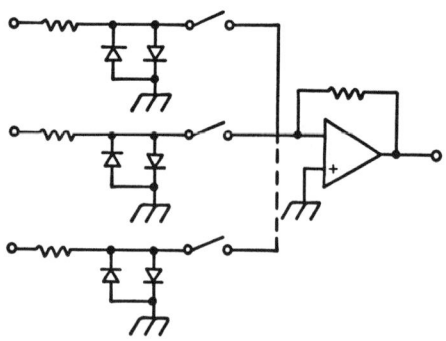

**Inverting current switch multiplexer**

**involuntary interrupt** An interrupt that is not caused by the object program, but affects the running of the object program. An example is the termination of a peripheral transfer that causes the operating system to stop the object program while the interrupt is serviced.

**I/O** Abbreviation for *input/output*.

**I/O architecture, microcomputer** A microcomputer's I/O architecture generally breaks down into these areas: transfer techniques, instruction formats, busses, bus structures, interrupt schemes, and memory-access techniques. Most microprocessors allow for three types of I/O transfer techniques: programmed transfer, interrupt program control, and hardware control. In the first two cases, found in most simple applications, the microprocessor controls the transfer. In the third case, system hardware controls transfer.

**I/O cable** A bus connecting various input/output devices to the microcomputer.

**I/O controllers** I/O controllers are usually required for devices having complex time-dependent mechanical operation. The controller may incorporate a processor that receives instructions and also executes them. The controller will implement the control sequence required by the I/O device. It might advance a mechanical linkage, perhaps using a stepping motor in a specified number of steps. These device controllers can range from simple circuits to complex boards. Device controllers are available in LSI chips for the most common I/O devices. *IOCS* Abbreviation for *input/output control system*.

**I/O device polling** In the process of I/O device polling, the interrupt causes a jump to the service program by using the interrupt trap address. The interrupt service program checks the status word of each I/O device to determine which one caused the interrupt. The figure below shows the flow of a interrupt service program for two I/O devices. The interrupt status bit indicates whether or not a device has generated an interrupt request, and it is checked for each device. The device status word is read into the status register of the microprocessor. If the bit is set, a jump is then made to the device service program.

**I/O M** Abbreviation for *input/output multiplexer*.

**I/O mapped system** Here the processor uses control signals to indicate that the present cycle is for input or output and not for memory. Fewer address lines are used to select the input/output ports, since normally the system needs fewer input/output ports than memory locations. One advantage to I/O mapped input/output is that because separate I/O instructions are used, they can be distinguished from a memory reference instruction for ease in programming. Also, with the shorter addressing, less hardware is required for decoding, and instructions are shorter and usually faster. The disadvantages are the loss of processing power and the necessity of using two control pins for I/O read and I/O write. This technique is not used with most microprocessors. The 8080 is an exception to this rule.

**I/O memory addresses** It is almost always possible to use memory addresses for I/O devices. I/O ports are considered as if they were RAM locations; an input is performed by reading memory and an output by writing into it. The program may seem somewhat more obscure, because I/O operations become more difficult to find if the program isn't properly documented. This technique allows a greater number of I/O devices, limited only by the size of the memory that can be addressed by the microprocessor.

**I/O ports** As shown below, a simple I/O port requires the following: an input latch to hold external information until the system can read it, an output latch to hold data from the system until required, and bus buffers to receive and drive the data bus. There should also be an internal status register to indicate if there is data to be read, or if the data is to be output.

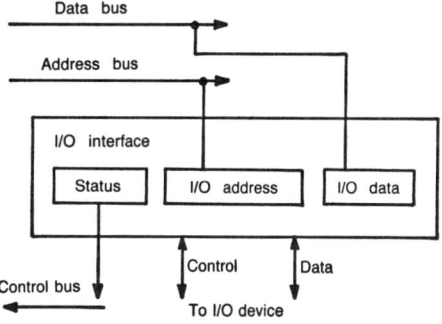

**I/O port requirements**

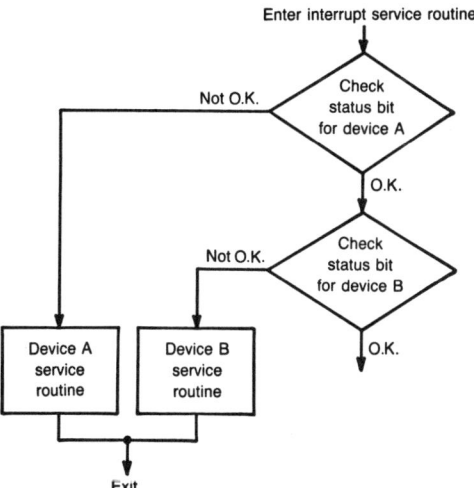

**Device polling with separate status bits**

**ion** Any atom or molecule that has an electric charge due to loss or gain of valence electrons.

**ion, accept** An atom in a doped semiconductor crystal that accepts an electron or gives up a hole.

**ion beam** Refers to a directed stream of ions moving in the same direction with similar speeds, usually produced by some form of accelerating machine.

**ion cluster** A group of molecules loosely bound by electrostatic forces to an ion in a gas.

**ion counter** A tubular chamber for measuring the ionization of air.

**ionic** Pertaining to or associated with gaseous or electrolytic ions. *Ion* is frequently used interchangeably with *ionic* as an adjective, as in *ion(ic) conduction*.

**ionic radius** The approximate limiting radius of ion crystals, ranging, for common metals (including carbon), from a fraction to several angstroms.

**ion implantation** A method of introducing impurities into semiconductors that uses high energy ion impingement on the silicon surface. Ion implantation allows shallow emitter junctions with a high degree of control. Ion implantation is used in CMOS circuits, shift registers, semiconductor memories, solar cells, and even resistors.

**ionization heat** The increase in heat necessary for complete ionization of a gram molecule of a substance.

**IOP** Abbreviation for *input/output processor*. A typical input/output processing unit performs bidirectional data transfer between main memory and the peripheral devices. Up to 32 devices can be attached to the IOP, but the high data transfer rates may allow only one device to operate at a given time in some microcomputers.

**IOPS** Abbreviation for *input/output programming system*.

**IOR** Abbreviation for *input/output register*.

**I/O test program** Refers to a special PROM containing a program which plugs into and checks input/output circuit boards.

**IOU** Abbreviation for *immediate operational use*.

**IP** Abbreviation for *initial point*.

**IPC** 1. Abbreviation for *industrial process control*. 2. Abbreviation for *information processing center*.

**IPE** Abbreviation for *interpret parity error*.

**I phase** A carrier phase separated by 57 degrees from the color subcarrier. Also referred to as the in-phase carrier.

**IPL** Abbreviation for *initial program loader*, a program that reads the supervisor into main storage and then transfers program control to the supervisor.

**ipot** Acronym for *inductive potentiometer*, a variable resistor that uses a metallic resistive element such as nickel-chromium wire rather than deposited carbon.

**IPS** 1. Abbreviation for *interceptor pilot simulator*. 2. Abbreviation for *interpretive programming system*. 3. Abbreviation for *inches per second*.

**IQSY** Abbreviation for *International Quiet Solar Year*.

**IRAN** Abbreviation for *inspect and repair as necessary*.

**iraser** A laser having an infrared output frequency.

**IRIG** Abbreviation for *Interrange Instrumentation Group*.

**iron (Fe)** A metallic element, atomic number 26, atomic weight 55.847, specific gravity 7.88, melting point 1535°C, boiling point 2450°C. It has magnetic properties and high strength.

**IRP** Abbreviation for *initial receiving point*.

**irreversible process** A device or mechanism that does not return to its original state after a disturbance is removed.

**IS** 1. Abbreviation for *internal signal*. 2. Abbreviation for *information separator*.

**ISAL** Abbreviation for *information system access line*.

**ISM equipment** The Federal Communications Commission designation for industrial, scientific, and medical equipment capable of causing interference.

**ISO** 1. Abbreviation for *International Organization for Standardization*. 2. Abbreviation for *individual system operation*.

**isolated digital output module** A unit that provides an output interface along with electrical isolation between the microcomputer and a process control or peripheral device. Isolation is typically 1500V, and outputs of up to 50V can be provided.

**isolating diode** A diode that passes signals in one direction through a circuit but blocks signals and voltages in the opposite direction.

**isolation amplifiers** Isolation amplifiers are used in those application conditions that require an actual galvanic isolation of the amplifier's input circuit from the output and the power supply. Typical applications include:

1. High common-mode voltages between input and output.
2. Medical electronics equipment.
3. Two wire inputs with no ground return for bias currents.
4. High CMRR (common-mode rejection ratio) required with a large source unbalance.

**isoplanar oxide isolation** An isolation technique applicable to all bipolar processes. The oxide isolation technique primarily results in high packing densities and slightly higher speeds and is accomplished by using silicon oxide to isolate the various components. A common form of oxide isolation is called isoplanar. Other bipolar processes achieve electrical isolation of the circuit elements with reversed biased P-N junctions, but these junctions occupy more space and have higher capacitance.

**isotron** A device in which pulses from a source of ions are synchronized with a deflecting field. This separates isotopes, since their acceleration varies with mass.

**isotropic** Used to describe a medium with physical properties that do not vary with direction.

**isotropic dielectric** A dielectric insulator material with electrical properties that are independent of the direction of the applied field.

**ISR** Abbreviation for *information storage and retrieval*.

**item** A unit of information relating to a single object, as a set of one or more fields, or a collection of data characters that are treated as a unit. For example, a record may contain a number of items such as fields, and a file may contain a number of items such as records.

**item advance** A technique used for the grouping of records by operating successively on different records in storage.

**item design** A specification that contains the fields that make up an item, the order in which the fields are to be recorded, and the number of characters to be allocated to each field.

**item size** The magnitude of an item expressed in words, characters, or blocks.

**iterate** To repeat a loop or a series of steps in a program or routine.

**iterative** Descriptive of a procedure or process that repeatedly executes an operation or series of operations until some condition is satisfied.

**iterative impedance** The impedance of a four-terminal network when a large number of identical networks are cascaded.

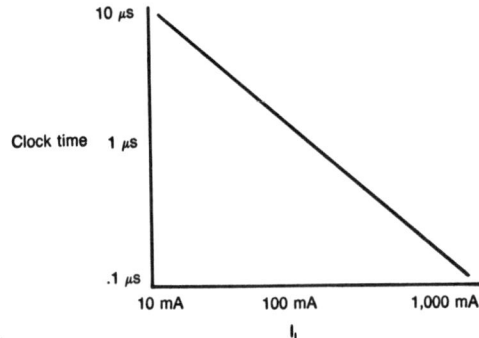

$I^2L$ speed-power characteristics

**iterative process** A process for calculating a desired result by repeating a cycle of operations, which comes progressively closer to the result. For example, the square root of a number may be approximated by an iterative process using addition, subtraction, and division.

**I$^2$L** Abbreviation for *integrated injection logic*, a logic family that uses only npn and pnp transistors. I$^2$L offers high performance and low costs along with ease of interfacing with other circuits.

**I$^2$L microprocessor** The user of an I$^2$L microprocessor is able to adjust the injection current, allowing a trade off between speed and power consumption. When injection current is low, power consumption is low, but the speed of operation is reduced. Higher injection currents permit higher speed operation with an increase in power consumption. Typical speeds as a function of injection current for an I$^2$L microprocessor at room temperature are shown below. I$^2$L circuitry may be powered with a supply voltage as low as 0.8V. Since the performance characteristics are controlled by the injection current, the voltage/resistance combination can be used to an advantage, and the low power consumption make this an ideal technology for the consumer market. I$^2$L has not yet achieved the speed characteristics of TTL devices. One advantage is the high-integration level that may be achieved. I$^2$L is an important technology for portable microprocessor applications.

# J

**JA** Abbreviation for *jump address*.

**jack** A connecting device into which the wires of a circuit or device are attached.

**jack panel** An assembly of a number of jacks mounted on a board or panel.

**jack part** Refers to an electrical connector at the end of a wire designed to fit into a hub or other connecting device.

**Jackson method** In the Jackson software design method, the program is viewed as the means by which the input data is transformed into output data as shown below; thus paralleling the structure of the input data and the output report insures a well-designed system. Some other assumptions of this method are that the resulting data structure will be compatible with a rational program structure, that only serial files will be used, and that the user of the method knows how to structure the data.

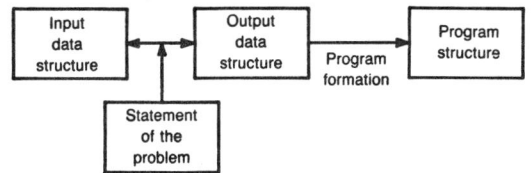

**The Jackson methodology of software design**

**jam** A pileup of cards in a card processing machine.

**Janus** The first nuclear reactor designed entirely for biological research. It is employed in studies of the effects of radiations on living organisms.

**JCL** Abbreviation for *job control language*, a programming language specifically used to code job control statements.

**J-FETS pair** Refers to matched FET (Field Effect Transistor) pairs for differential amplifiers. These general purpose FETs are utilized for low- and medium-frequency differential amplifiers requiring low-offset voltage, drift, noise, and capacitance.

**JIC** Abbreviation for *joint industry conference*.

**jitter** A distortion caused by shifts in the time or phase position of pulses which can cause difficulty in synchronization and detection.

**J-K flip-flop** A flip-flop with two inputs, J and K, with the following features:

1. A clock pulse will not cause a transition if either input is enabled.
2. If both inputs are enabled, the output will change states.
3. No indeterminate conditions are allowed.

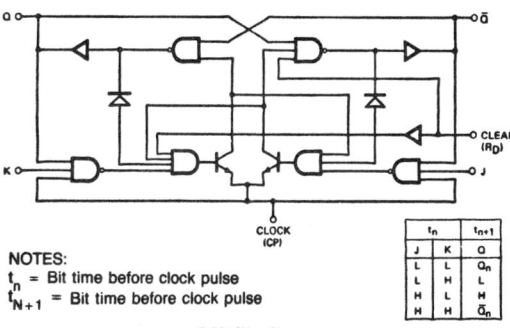

NOTES:
$t_n$ = Bit time before clock pulse
$t_{N+1}$ = Bit time before clock pulse

**J-K flip-flop**

**job** A group of tasks prescribed as a unit of work for the computer. A job consists of one or more steps and may include programs, linkages, files, and instructions for the operating system.

**job control language** A language (abbreviated *JCL*) used to code job control statements.

**job control program** A program that is called into storage to prepare each job or step to be run. It may assign input/output devices and set switches for program use.

**job control statement** A statement used in identifying a job or describing its requirements to the operating system.

**job input stream** The input, usually consisting of tape or punched cards, that is first sent to the operating system. The job input stream may contain the beginning of job indicators, directions, and programs.

**job-oriented terminal** A type of terminal designed to receive source data associated with the job to be performed and capable of transmission with the operating system of which it is a part.

**job processing control** That portion of a program that starts job operations, assigns input/output operations, and controls the transfer from one job to another.

**job scheduling executive** Refers to executive programs that sequence the loading and execution of programs as directed by the user via system commands to the executive. Users can enter instructions, or commands may be supplied with the user program (as on cards placed at the beginning of a job deck). The control program function controls input job streams and system output, obtains input/output resources for jobs and job steps, attaches tasks corresponding to job steps, and otherwise regulates the use of the system by jobs or tasks.

**job step** The execution of that portion of a program identified by a job control statement. Most jobs will have several job steps.

**job stream** The set of computer jobs in an input queue waiting for initiation and processing.

**JOG** A function that provides for the momentary operation of a drive for the purpose of accomplishing a small movement of the driven machine.

**Johnson noise** The electrical noise across the terminals of a resistor when it has no current flowing through it. It is caused by the thermal motion of charge and is greater for larger resistances, higher temperatures, and wider bandwidths.

**join** To form the logical sum or union.

**joint denial** A logical operation that has a true output only if all inputs are false.

**joint denial gate** A circuit or device that provides a true output only if all inputs are false.

**Josephson junction** A thin-film junction that uses a tunneling mechanism for current flow.

**Josephson junction memory** A type of memory cell that contains two Josephson junctions and a sensing junction. Experiments show that very fast and very low-power memories may be provided using this technique.

**Josephson memory cell** A memory cell that contains two data junctions and a sensing junction. A write current temporarily changes the magnitude of the current flowing and allows the sensing device to determine the current's original magnitude and direction: clockwise signifies a one and counterclockwise a zero.

**Josephson ratio** A frequency-voltage ratio symbolized by $2e/h$ and equal to $4.835\ 939 \times 10^{14}$ Hz per volt.

**joule** The unit of energy (symbol, J) that describes the work performed when the point of application of one newton is displaced a distance of one meter in the direction of force.

**joule effect** The production of heat due to current flow in a conductor.

**joule magnetostriction** The effect that causes the length of an iron core to increase when subjected to a longitudinal magnetic field.

**JOVIAL** A computer language used for command and control applications that is a version of the *international algebraic language*, an early version of ALGOL. JOVIAL contains facilities for numerical computations along with some data processing.

**JPL** Abbreviation for *Jet Propulsion Laboratory*.

**JPW** Abbreviation for *job processing word*.

**jump** A departure from the normal sequence of executing instructions. Jumps usually differ from branches in that they do not use the relative addressing mode. Also called *transfer*.

**jump instruction** An instruction designed to control the transfer of operations from one point to another in a program.

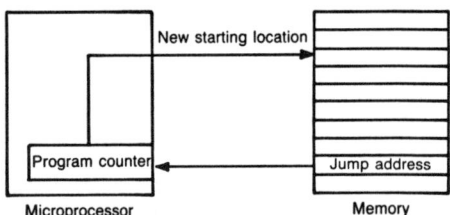

**Jump instructions change the program counter**

**jump routine** A routine designed to have the computer depart from the regular sequence of instructions and shift to another routine or program. For example, the following sequence in the 8080 microprocessor calls the *ZZZ* routine:

    YYY

    .

    CALL ZZZ    ; (call routine for ZZZ)
    RET    ; (return to caller of YYY)

A better way of performing the same task uses a jump routine.

    YYY

    .

    JMP ZZZ    ; (go to ZZZ then return)

**junction** A connection between two or more conductors, flow paths, metals, or semiconductors.

**junction box** An enclosure used for connecting different runs of cable in a raceway or conduit.

**junction circuit** A circuit connecting two exchanges that are closer than those found in trunk lines or circuits.

**junction diode** A two-terminal device with a single-crystal structure that permits current flow in only one direction. Also called a *junction rectifier*.

**junction rectifier** Junction diode.

**junction summing** A technique used in computing amplifiers and control systems in which various signals are connected to a common point at the input of the amplifier or control unit.

**junction transistor** 1. Bipolar transistor. 2. Field-effect transistor without an insulated gate.

**junk** A term used for unintelligible signals, especially those received from a communications channel. Also called *garbage* and *hash*.

**justify** 1. To adjust the printing positions of characters on a page such that the rightmost edge of each line is flush with all other lines. 2. To shift the contents of a register such that the least significant bit is at a desired position.

# K

**K** 1. Symbol for *kelvin*. 2. Symbol (on drawings) to indicate presence of an electromechanical relay. 3. Symbol for *cathode*. 4. Nonstandard but often used symbol for *kilohm*. 5. In lowercase form, the SI prefix for *kilo-*, the prefix meaning thousand. 6. In lowercase form, symbol for *constant*. 7. In lowercase form, symbol for *coupling coefficient*. 8. In microcomputer usage, symbol for 1024 (which is the first power of 2 above 1000).

**Karnaugh map** A chart or table that shows the combination of logical functions and tends to eliminate duplicate logical expressions by listing all of the similar functions. The Karnaugh map is drawn as a rectangular diagram of variables with overlapping subrectangles such that the intersection of the subrectangles represents a unique combination of variables, and such an intersection is shown for all logical combinations.

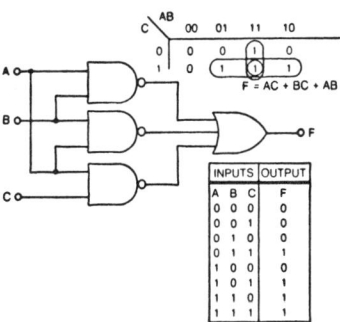

**Karnaugh map with logic and truth table**

**kayser** The obsolete unit for wave number, which is the reciprocal for wavelength. The SI unit for wave number is *reciprocal meter*.

**KB** Abbreviation for *kilobytes*.

**Kelvin ampere-balance** A laboratory instrument for measuring current. The force between two coils carrying the current to be measured is balanced by the force of gravity on a weight sliding along a beam.

**Kelvin effect** A property of high-frequency currents in which most of the current flow concentrates near the surface. Also called *skin effect*.

**Kelvin temperature** Temperature expressed on the Kelvin thermodynamic scale, in which measurements are made from absolute zero.

**key** A group of characters used to identify an item or record. 2. A marked lever or switch used for entering a character or command into the system.

**keybar** A term applied to typewriters having conventional typebar or basket typing mechanisms.

**keyboard** A unit containing keys for entering data or information into a system. Keyboards may be *alphanumeric* (as used for word processing, text processing, and data processing) or *numeric* as used for Touch-Tone telephones, accounting machines, and calculators.

**keyboard control keys** Switches used in terminals to control and move the cursor on CRT displays, to change the terminal application, or to change the communications mode.

**keyboard display** Some keyboards offer possible interpretive operations. A particular job is assigned by the computer program, and the keys for that job are identified by removable overlays.

**keyboard encoder** A circuit or device that identifies each key function and produces a word corresponding to that function. Some encoders allow the use of custom encoding with the use of PROMs, and error detection for stimultaneous key depressions.

151

**keyboard function key** A key that sends out a unique string of characters that represents a code (to the computer), a set of data, or a command to activate a peripheral.

**keypunch** 1. A device used to record information in cards or tape by punching holes that represent letters, digits, and characters. 2. To operate a device for punching holes in cards or tapes.

**key-verify** To make certain that the information desired in a punched card has actually been punched properly.

**key-verify unit** A machine designed to check keypunched information. When the depressed key and punched card do not agree, a signal alerts the operator. Also called *verifier* and *key verifier*.

**keyword** A significant word in the title, abstract, or text that can be used alone or with other significant words to describe a document. A keyword or set or keywords may describe a document's contents, label the document, or assist in identifying or retrieving the document.

**keyword-in-context** An index of programs (abbreviated *KWIC*) that lists the programs in alphabetical order with entries for each keyword in the title. The index is prepared by highlighting each keyword of the title in the context of the words on either side of it, and aligning the keywords of all titles alphabetically.

**kHz** Abbreviation for *kilohertZ* (1,000 cycles per second).

**kill** 1. The achievement of the desired destructive effect against a target. 2. The command to erase a disk file in certain operating systems.

**kill radius** The distance from the center of a detonation to the point on a spherical surface where there is a 50 percent probability of destroying specific targets.

**kilo** Prefix indicating multiplication by a factor of $10^3$; thousand.

**kilobauds** 1,000 bauds, used to define the capacity of data channels.

**kilobyte** 1,024 bytes or characters, which is 2 to the 10th power. This roughly corresponds to one-half of a typewritten page.

**kilocycle** Abbreviated *kc;* One thousand cycles per second.

**kilomega** A prefix meaning one billion; a *kilomegacycle* is one billion cycles (same as *billicycle* and *gigacycle*), and a *kilomegabit* means one billion bits (same as *billibit*).

**kilomegacycle** Also called *gigacycle;* one billion cycles per second.

**kilovolt-ampere** A unit of apparent electrical power equal to 1000 volt amperes.

**kilowatt** A unit of electrical power equal to 1000 watts.

**kilowatt hour** The equivalent energy supplied by a power of 1,000 watts for one hour.

**Kipp relay** An alternative term for an electromechanical one-shot or monostable multivibrator, a circuit that has a stable and an unstable state, and goes through a complete cycle in response to a single triggering action.

**Kirchoff's laws** 1. The current flowing to a given point in a circuit is equal to the current flowing away from that point. 2. The algebraic sum of the voltage drops in any closed path in a circuit is equal to the algebraic sum of the electromotive forces in that path. 3. At a given temperature, the emissive power of a body is the same as its radiation-absorbing power for all surfaces.

**kit** A set of parts and software assembled by the user for a specific application or specification. Microcomputer kits allow the user a cost-effective system without special hardware design. Kits are available as complete standalone systems for writing, debugging, and executing programs on the microprocessor. They include not only the processor and memory, but also a low-cost set of peripherals. A typical system has an alphanumeric display, an ASCII keyboard, and cassette tape units. Software may include a monitor, editor, and assembler package. A universal system bus may be included to allow the connection of memory and peripherals with several microprocessors.

**kit, breadboard** A circuit kit that usually comes with an assortment of sockets for custom circuitry. A number of circuit kits that allow the user to add special functions to the modular microcomputer system are available. Designed for insertion into a breadboard, they include a collection of parts and sockets, and full instructions.

**kit, extender card** A kit that allows all cards on the bus to be extended out of the card rack for easy maintenance.

**kludge** A humorous term for a quick-fix circuit or device. Also refers to a hastily formed interface between devices.

**KPC** Abbreviation for *keyboard/printer controller.*

**KSR** Abbreviation for *keyboard send/receive,* a teletypewriter transmitter and receiver unit that has transmission capability from the keyboard only.

**kurtosis** A statistical quantity that expresses the peakedness of a distribution.

**KWIC** Abbreviation for *keyword-in-context,* a title index based upon the use of keywords for programs. The keywords are listed in alphabetical order for identification.

# L

**L** Abbreviation for *label*.

**LAADS** Abbreviation for *Los Angeles air defense sector*.

**label** 1. A set of symbols that identify or describe an item, record, message, or file. 2. A code name that classifies a name, term, phrase, or document.

**LAC** Abbreviation for *load accumulator*.

**LACE** Abbreviation for *liquid air cycle engine*. (Air Force).

**laced card** A card with extra multiple punching in a column to signify the end of a card run. The term is derived from the lacework appearance of the card.

**lacing** The extra punching used in a card to indicate the end of a run.

**LADAR** Abbreviation for *Laser Detection and Ranging*.

**lag** The relative difference between two events, states, or mechanisms.

**LAGS** Abbreviation for *Laser Activated Geodetic Satellite*.

**language** A system for representing and communicating information or data between people or different types of machines. A language consists of a carefully defined set of characters and rules for combining the characters into larger units such as words or expressions. There are also rules for word arrangement and usage to achieve specific meanings. Most computer languages have the following features:
  1. Data objects or structures with descriptions that correspond to nouns and adjectives in natural languages.
  2. Operations and commands that act upon the data objects, corresponding to verbs and adverbs in a natural language.
  3. Control structures to specify the sequence of operations, which correspond to phrasing and forming paragraphs in natural languages.

**language, ALGOL** This language allows problem description in an internationally defined language. It includes all the major elements with a number of features such as unrestricted nesting of conditional statements and the intermixing of real and integer identifiers.

**language assembler** A development-oriented system that is used to assemble source code and convert it into binary output, which is then loaded and executed on the CPU. Input to the assembler is usually prepared with the aid of an assembler program.

**language interpreter** A processor, assembler, or other routine that accepts statements in one language and produces equivalent statements in another language.

**language, list processing** Refers to a language developed by symbol manipulation and used in the construction of compilers and in simulations.

**language translator** A program or routine that converts statements in one language to equivalent statements in another language. The languages may be computer or machine languages, or natural languages such as English.

**Laplace's law** The differential form of Ampere's law for the magnetic field produced by a current carrying conductor. In vector notation:

$$dH = \frac{I\,(dl \times r)}{r^3}$$

where dl is an element of the conductor, I the current, and r the vector drawn from the element to the point at which the field component dH is required.

**lapping** The final abrasive polishing of a quartz crystal to adjust its operating frequency; also the smoothing of the surface of crystalline semiconductors.

**LARAM** Abbreviation for *line addressable random-access memory*.

**large-scale integration** Fabrication of integrated circuits with more than 1000 equivalent transistors on a single semiconductor chip. Abbreviated *LSI*.

**Larmor frequency** The angular frequency of precession for the spin vector of an electron acted on by an external magnetic field.

**Larmor precession** The motion experienced in a small uniform magnetic field by a charged particle (or system of charged particles) when subjected to a central force that is directed towards a common point.

**Larmor radius** Radius of the circular or helical path followed by a charged particle in a uniform magnetic field.

**lase** To undergo laser operation.

**laser** Once an acronym for *light amplification by stimulated emission of radiation*, the term has become legitimized as a word describing an amplifier and generator of a narrow and coherent beam of energy in the visible light spectrum.

**laser emulsion storage** Refers to various types of digital data storage media that uses a controlled laser beam to expose very small areas on a photosensitive surface, producing the desired information patterns.

**LASL** Abbreviation for *Los Alamos Scientific Laboratory*.

**lasons** The ultrahigh energy produced by lasers.

**latch** An arrangement or circuit used to hold data in a ready position until required, usually controlled by another condition or circuit. Also called *lock*.

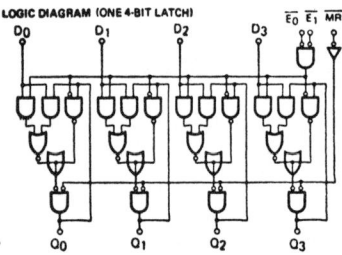

Latch

**latching** A technique in which data is held in a circuit until other circuits are ready to change this circuit.

**latency** Refers to the time required by a computer to deliver information from its memory. In a serial storage system, the latency time becomes the access time minus the word time. In a rotational system, it becomes the time required for the desired location to appear at the heads.

**latency time** The time lag between a command for data and the delivery from memory.

**lattice dynamics** Refers to the mechanical properties of the thermal vibrations of crystal lattices.

**lattice filter** A wave filter composed of four branches connected together to form a mesh that functions as a section of the filter. The filter may have a single section, or it may be composed of several sections.

**lattice network** A circuit with four branches connected together to form a mesh, with the two nonadjacent junctions serving as inputs and the other two serving as outputs. Also called *bridge network*.

**lattice spacing** Refers to the length of an edge in a unit cell of a crystal.

**lattice vibration** The vibration of atoms or molecules in a crystal due to thermal energy.

**LAW** Abbreviation for *light anti tank weapon*.

**lay** The length of a turn of the helix of any helical element.

**layout** The overall plan, structure, or design of a circuit, system, or device. The layout may include the arrangement of data, sequence, size, schematic diagrams, flow diagrams, and outlines of operation or procedure.

**LB** Abbreviation for *line buffer*.

**LCD** Abbreviation for *liquid-crystal display*, a display technique that uses segments of a liquid crystal solution in a sandwich of glass plates. The light-reflecting properties of the solution are controlled by an electric field.

**LCL** Abbreviation for *local*.

**LD** Abbreviation for *load*.

**LDS** Abbreviation for *local distribution system*.

**leader** 1. A record that precedes a group of detailed records, giving information about the group that is not in the detailed records. 2. An unused or blank length of tape or film at the beginning of a reel.

**leading** The amount of space between lines of type, usually referred to in terms of point size. The notation *10/12* or *10 on 12* means 10 point type in a 12 point space, or expressed in another way, 10 point type with 2 points of leading between lines.

**leading zeros** Zeros preceding the first nonzero integer of a number. Leading zeros may be employed in the numeric fields of some input blocks to indicate the position of the decimal point within the field.

**leakage** Refers to undesired losses due to stray conductive paths in components and circuit boards.

**leakage current** Current flow due to undesirable conductive paths across or through insulating surfaces or barriers.

**leakage radiation** Spurious radiation in a transmitting system; radiation from other than the system itself.

**leakage reactance** The reactance represented by the difference in value between two mutually coupled inductances when their fields are aiding and then opposing.

**LEAP** Abbreviation for *lift off elevation and azimuth programmer*.

**leapfrog test** A checking routine that copies itself using storage. A typical leapfrog routine might:

1. Perform a series of operations on one group of storage locations.
2. Transfer to another group of storage locations.
3. Check the correctness of the transfer.
4. Repeat the series of operations for the new locations.
5. Continue transferring and repeating until all storage locations are occupied.

**left-justify** 1. To adjust the printing positions of characters on a page such that the left margin is aligned flush. 2. To shift the contents of a register so that the most significant bit is at a specified position.

**LEM** Abbreviation for *lunar excursion module*.

**Lenz's law** A current resulting from an induced electromotive force is in such a direction as to oppose any change in the current that generates the emf.

**LEP**  Abbreviation for *lowest effective power.*

**LEPT**  Abbreviation for *long endurance patrolling torpedo.*

**letter quality printer**  A printer that uses a full-formed character like a typewriter or the text on this page. Also known as correspondence-quality printers because they are preferred for most business communications.

**level**  1. The absolute magnitude of a quantity. 2. The degree of subordination in a hierarchy, as in the different levels of recorded information on paper tape.

**level-enable signal**  Refers to a signal generated by the CPU for the purpose of changing the state of the level-enable flip-flop from 0 to 1.

**leveling, zone**  An analogous process to zone refining carried out during the processing of semiconductors in order to distribute impurities evenly.

**LF**  Abbreviation for *low frequency,* 30Hz to 300Hz.

**LG**  Abbreviation for *line generator.*

**liar's dice**  A computer game based on the statistics of dice.

**library software**  A collection of routines and subroutines available for many a microcomputers. A typical microcomputer library includes:

1. A loading and debugging program
2. A text editor
3. A resident assembler
4. A cross assembler
5. A floating point arithmetic program
6. A PROM programming software
7. A multiply/divide package

**library, user**  A basic library of general purpose software is furnished by manufacturers to perform most common jobs; to this the user can add developed programs and routines.

**LIC**  Abbreviation for *line integrated circuit.*

**life characteristic**  Operating life as a function of failure rate. The life characteristic is usually plotted showing three phases: (1) an infant mortality or debugging phase; (2) a normal operating phase; and (3) a wearout phase.

**LIFMOP**  Abbreviation for *linearly frequency modulated pulse.*

**LIFO**  Acronym for *last-in-first-out,* a queue technique in which the last item in is the first to be operated on. LIFO is used to pushdown stack operations. Also called *FILO.*

**light-emitting diode**  A diode with a light-producing characteristic used as a low-cost, low-power indicator on panels and in displays. Light-emitting diodes are available in several colors and operate at current levels of 5-10 mA.

**light pen**  A photosensitive device that detects the CRT beam when pointed towards the screen and generates a narrow electrical pulse that can be fed to the computer as an interrupt signal. Also see *light pen functions.*

**light pen attention**  An interruption generated by a light pen when it senses light on the screen of a CRT display device.

**light pen functions**  1. When the penlike device is pointed at information displayed on the screen, it detects light from the cathode ray tube (CRT) when a beam passes within its field of view. The pen's response is transmitted to the computer which in turn relates the computer action to the section of the image being displayed. In this way, light pens can be used to delete or add text, maintain control over the program, or choose from alternative courses of action. 2. The light pen is a highspeed, photosensitive device that the operator can use to cause the computer to change or modify the display on the cathode ray tube. As the pertinent display information is selected by the operator, the pen signals the computer by generating a pulse. Acting upon this signal, the computer can instruct other points to be plotted across the tube face in accordance with the pen movement.

**light sensitive**  Refers to surfaces in which the electrical resistance, emission of electrons, or generation of a current depends on the incidence of light.

**limited integrator**  An integrator that ceases to integrate when the output exceeds a specified limit.

**limiter**  1. A transducer in which the output does not vary above a critical threshold value. 2. A circuit that restricts amplitude to a specified level. 3. In an FM receiver, a circuit that eliminates variations in amplitude to prevent AM components from being processed.

**limiter tube**  An amplifier so biased that the output resulting from a large input voltage is substantially the same as that from a small one.

**linac**  Abbreviation for *linear accelerator.*

**lindemann electrometer**  A form of electrometer that uses a metal-coated quartz fiber located between an arrangement of electrodes to which the potentials are applied. The fiber is mounted on and perpendicular to a quartz torsion fiber that provides the controlling couple.

**linear**  A function that varies in direct proportion to the input.

**linear amplifier**  A class A or AB amplifier that develops an output in direct proportion to the input signal.

**linear control**  A rheostat or potentiometer having a uniform distribution of graduated resistance along the entire length of its resistance element.

**linear displacement transducer**  A transducer that produces an output that is a direct function of position along a single axis.

**linear distortion**  1. Amplitude distortion in which the output and input signal envelopes are not proportionate, but no alien frequencies are involved. 2. Distortion that results in the nonlinear response of a system, such as an amplifier, to the envelope of a varying signal, such as speech, without distorting (within acoustic perception) the detailed waveform.

**linear energy transfer**  The linear rate of energy dissipation by particulate or electromagnetic radiation while penetrating absorbing media.

**linear integer programming**  The use of linear programming models where only integer solutions are admissible. A special case of integer programming is selective programming. In this case the variables in the solution can take only one of the preselected values.

**linear interpolation**  A mode of machine-tool control that uses the data contained in a block to produce constant velocities for two or more axes simultaneously.

**linearity**  A relationship between two quantities when a change in one is directly proportional to a change in the other.

**linear magnetostriction**  Refers to the relative change of length of a ferromagnetic object in the direction of magnetization when the magnetization of the object is increased from zero to a specified value.

**linear modulation**  A modulation in which the amplitude of the modulation envelope is directly proportioniate to the amplitude of the modulating wave at all audio frequencies.

**linear network**  A circuit with electrical elements that remain constant in magnitude with varying currents.

**linear optimization**  The set of procedures used to find maximum and minimum values of a linear function subject to specific constraints or conditions.

**linear potentiometer**  Refers to a potentiometer in which the voltage at a movable contact is a linear function of the displacement of the contact.

**linear power amplifier** A power amplifier in which the output voltage is directly proportionate to the input voltage.

**linear program** An algorithmic program used to select one solution from a set of possible solutions to a given problem based on desired maximum or minimum requirements.

**linear rectifier** Refers to a rectifier with the same output current or voltage waveshape as that of the impressed signal.

**linear resistor** A resistor that obeys Ohm's law; under certain conditions the current is always proportional to the voltage. Also called ohmic resistor.

**linear selection** An addressing technique that uses a line of the address bus to select a component. If a system requires a 4K memory, this implies that 12 bits of the address be reserved for this function. ($2^{12}$ = 4K). The other four bits can be used as chip selects. One bit can be allocated to selecting ROM or RAM memory. In most cases the RAM requirements are smaller than the ROM requirements. The 12 bits allocated for word selection will also provide the addressing for the RAM, when it is selected. This leaves a maximum of three bits available. Excluding one of the codes, such as 000, for memory selection, 7 combinations of these 3 bits can be used to address the I/O devices. Any of the 12 address bits are reused to select locations within the devices.

**linear variable differential transformer** The linear variable differential transformer (LVDT) uses a movable core in a transformer configuration. Depending on the particular sensing element and linkage, transducers of this type can be sensitive to vibration and mechanical wear.

**line** A row of typing often used as a unit in work measurement. There is no universal standard, but a common definition sets a line at 6 inches of elite type or 72 keystrokes.

**line circuit** A physical circuit path, as a transmission or communication line.

**line code** A single instruction contained on one line in a program. A line code may contain one or more addresses, or one or more operations. Also called *program line*. A line code for addition in the 6800 system is:

ADD A 1, Y ; (add Y + 1 to accumulator)

**line control block** An area of main storage (abbreviated *LCB*) used to hold control data for operations on communication lines.

**line discipline** The procedures and rules used to adjust the operating values of transmission systems for the desired control. Line discipline includes considerations in polling and queuing priority.

**line driver** An amplifier used to transmit analog or digital signals over a transmission line or circuit.

**line feed character** The LF character, a format effector that causes the print to display position to be moved to the next line. In ASCII, the LF character generates a binary 10 (0000 1010), which is decoded to cause line feed at the receiving terminal printer.

**line impedance** Refers to the impedance of a transmission line. It is a function of the resistance, inductance, conductance, and capacitance of the line, and the frequency of the signal. Also called the characteristic impedance.

**line integral** A mathematical concept associated with vector fields. It is given by the summation along any path of the product of an element of the path and the component of the field vector parallel to it.

**line number access** A means of addressing points within a recorded text through codes that generally correspond to lines of the document, numbered sequentially.

**line of flux or force** Refers to a line drawn in a magnetic (or electric) field so that its direction at every point gives the direction of magnetic (or electric) flux (or force) at that point.

**line printer** A machine that prints an entire line of characters at one time. The characters are typically contained on a series of continuously rotating disks. The machine stops the disks at the right characters and stamps a single line in a fraction of a second. Highspeed line printers may operate at a rate of 1000 lines per minute or more.

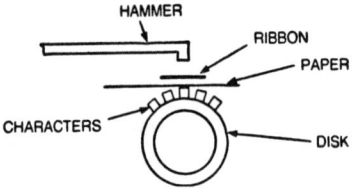

**Line driver**

**line spectrum** An area in which the radiation is in narrow energy bands, called lines, which are characteristic of the atomic state.

**lingering period** The time interval during which an electron remains in its orbit of highest excitation before jumping to the energy level of a lower orbit. The difference in energy will be in the form of radiation.

**link** 1. A transmit and receive system for connecting two terminal loca-

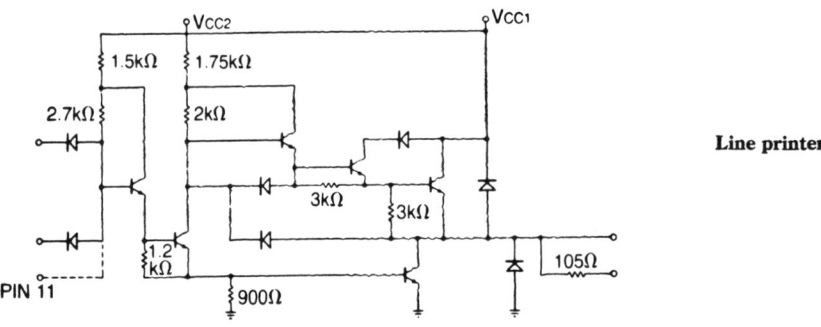

**Line printer**

tions. 2. A connecting path between two units of switching apparatus, or that part of a subprogram that connects it with the main program. 3. A 1-bit register used as an extension of the accumulator in some systems. As a link register, the link is used in arithmetic operations and can be cleared, set, and complemented as part of the accumulator.

**linkage** A technique for providing connections for entry and exit of a closed subroutine from the main routine.

**link bit** Refers to the single bit contained in the link register. The link bit can be used as an indicator for overflow from the accumulator or other diagnostic operations. (See also *link,* 3).

**link editor** A software system used to load and connect the object program output from a BASIC or FORTRAN compiler, or an assembler into a main program.

**link indicator** An indicator used to display the contents of the link register.

**linking loader** A relocatable loader that completes memory address calculations that were partially processed by the relocatable assembler, allowing users to load and execute a program anywhere in memory.

**liquid crystal** A type of display technology that uses segments of a liquid crystal solution between glass plates. An electric field at the plates causes the solution to change its light-reflecting properties selectively. Energizing the proper segments produces the desired display output.

**liquid drop model** A model of the atomic nucleus using the analogy of a liquid drop in which such concepts as surface tension and heat of evaporation are employed.

**liquid photoresists** These are photosensitive materials used for etching patterns through masks on semiconductor surfaces and thin films. Both negative and positive resists are available. In a negative resist application, ultraviolet light is shone through a photomask onto a resist covered surface. The resist film beneath the clear areas of the photomask undergoes a physical and chemical change that renders it insoluble in the developing solution. In a positive resist system, the identical action produces areas that are soluble in a developing solution. Most resist applications use the negative type.

**LISP** Acronym for *list processing,* an interpretive language designed for the handling of symbolic lists and recursive data. LISP can also be used for manipulation of mathematical and logical operations.

**list** An ordered set of items. A pushdown list is a set of items in which the last item entered is the first item of the list, and the position of the other items is pushed back by one. A pushup list has items entered at the end of the list, and the other items maintain the same relative position in the list.

**listing** A printed list that is a by-product of a program or operation. For example, an assembly listing would contain in logical instruction sequence the details of a routine with the coded and symbolic notation along with the actual notation established by the assembly routine.

**listing, assembly** Refers to a printed list that is the by-product of an assembly procedure. It lists in logical instruction sequence all details of a routine showing the coded and symbolic notation next to the actual notation established by the assembly procedure. This listing is often useful in the debugging of a routine.

**list processing** A method of processing data in the form of lists. Chained lists are used to allow the order of items to be changed without altering their physical contents.

**list-processing language** A language such as LISP designed for symbol manipulation. List-processing languages are used mainly as research tools and have proved valuable in the design of compilers and problem-solving simulation. Other uses of list processing languages include:

1. Mathematical proofs
2. Information retrieval
3. Pattern recognition
4. Algebraic programming
5. Artificial Intelligence

**list-processing structure** A technique in which list structures or sets of data items are used to organize the memory in computers. The memory is organized into several lists having symbolic names, headers, or starting records, and a number of entries. The header contains the first data entry address; each data entry contains one or more data items and the address of the next entry in the list.

**list structure** A set of data items with each element containing the address of the successor item or element. It is relatively easy to insert or delete data items in a list structure, and such lists tend to reach the capacity of fixed storage systems.

**literal** A symbol that represents the value expressed rather than a reference to data. A literal in a source program is data and not a reference to data. The literal 8 represents the value eight.

**literal operand** An operand that specifies precisely the value of a constant rather than an address where the constant is stored. Literal operands allow coding to be more concise than operands using data name references.

**lithium (Li)** An element, atomic number 3, atomic weight 6.939, melts at 186 °C, boils at 1360 °C, specific gravity 0.534. It is the lightest known solid, chemically resembling sodium but less active. It is used in alloys and in the production of tritium.

**LLL** Abbreviation for *low level logic.*

**LLR** Abbreviation for *load limiting resistor.*

**LLS** Abbreviation for *lunar logistics system.*

**LLSV** Abbreviation for *lunar logistics system vehicle.*

**LLV** Abbreviation for *lunar logistics vehicle.*

**LMO** Abbreviation for *lense modulated oscillator.*

**load** The process of filling a storage unit in a computer. Loading includes the reading of the beginning of a program into virtual storage and the modifications necessary to the program for transfer of control for execution. Loading also includes the transfer of storage between memory units. A typical load operation transfers the contents of a memory byte and stores it in the accumulator. The memory is read bit by bit, and as each bit is read, the next sequential accumulator bit will be set or reset to reproduce the status of the memory bit just read.

**load-and-go** A machine operation and compiling technique that uses pseudo language for conversion directly into machine language. The program is then run without the need of an output machine language.

**load capacitor** A capacitor that tunes and maximizes the power to a load in induction or dielectric heating.

**load coil** The coil in an induction heater used to carry the alternating current, which induces the heating current in the object being heated.

**load curve** Refers to a curve of power versus time showing the value of a specified load for each unit in the period covered.

**loaded impedance** The impedance at the input of a transducer when the output load is connected.

**loader** A program that operates as an input device to transfer data from offline memory to online memory. A loader usually performs the following functions:

1. Load a string of bytes into memory.
2. Check each byte for correct transmission.

3. Check each word to insure that is is a valid instruction.
4. Check the number of bytes read.
5. Convert relocatable addresses to absolute addresses.
6. Satisfy all external references and labels.

**loader routine** A routine generated to perform program-loading operations. A loader routine usually includes printout of memory content upon request. Also called loading routine, since once it is in storage, it is able to bring other information into storage.

**loading routine** *Loader routine.*

**load line** On a set of characteristic curves for an active device, a line representing the load. It is straight if entirely resistive, elliptical if reactive.

**load matching** 1. As pertaining to induction and dielectric heaters, adjustment of the load circuit impedance so that the desired energy will be transferred from the power source to the load. 2. Adjusting circuit conditions to meet requirements for maximum energy transfer to load.

**load regulation** Refers to the maximum change in the output of a power supply as the result of a specified change in output load current, usually from no load to full load.

**LOBAR** Abbreviation for *long baseline radar.*

**location** A storage position that can store one word and that is usually identified by an address.

**location counter** 1. The control section of a computer that contains a register with the address of the instruction currently being executed. 2. The control section register that contains the address of the instruction currently being executed. 3. A register in which the address of the current instruction is recorded. Synonymous with instruction counter and program address counter.

**lock-in amplifier** A synchronous amplifier that is sensitive to variations in signal at its own frequency.

**locking** 1. The use of code extension characters to change the interpretation of a specified number of following characters. 2. Control of an oscillating circuit using a correction signal. 3. Latching.

**log** The process of recording, or collecting messages pertinent to a machine run. These include:

1. Run identification
2. Input/output identification
3. Identification of stops and action taken
4. A history of manual switch settings or key-ins

**logarithmic amplifier** An amplifier with an output that is a logarithmic function of the input signal, such as in decibel meters and some types of recorders. Also called *log amp.*

**logarithmic decrement** Relates to a logarithm to the base of the ratio of the amplitude of successive oscillations that are diminishing through energy dissipation.

**logarithmic range compression** A logarithmic amplifier for data compression can be used as shown below. The logarithmic amplifier allows the encoding of signals, which would ordinarily require a 20-bit data conversion to cover the dynamic range, with a 12-bit converter.

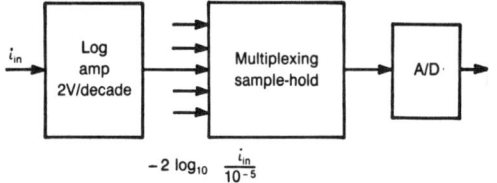

$-2 \log_{10} \dfrac{i_{in}}{10^{-5}}$

**Logarithmic range compression**

**logger** A device that records physical processes and events, usually chronologically. Loggers or data loggers are used in control systems to scan and record pressure, temperature, humidity, and other parameters.

**logic** 1. The systematic scheme that defines the interaction of signals in data processing systems. Logic includes the application of truth tables and the relationships between switching circuits involving arithmetic computation. 2. The science dealing with the formal principles of reasoning and thought.

**logic analysis** The determination of the specific steps required to produce the desired output or intelligence from given input data.

**logic analyzer** A device used to test and troubleshoot equipment containing digital logic. Logic analyzers can be used to trace logic states and timing; to examine the activity on each line of a data bus by displaying that line on a CRT screen or using a string of light-emitting diodes; and to design microprocessor-based products for examining the flow of command and data words on multiline buses. Logic analyzers perform the first steps in locating the problem; from there conventional instruments such as signal generators and oscilloscopes can be used.

**logic card** A circuit board that contains components and wiring that perform one or more logic operations or functions.

**logic circuit** A set of elements connected or programmed to perform logic operations or represent logic functions such as AND, OR, and NAND.

**logic coincidence element** An operation defined by the equivalence operator. A logic coincidence element produces a true output when the two input signals are the same and a false output when they are different.

**logic comparator** A testing device that compares an in-circuit integrated circuit with a tested device. Any differences in the outputs are detected and displayed, usually by light-emitting diodes. A fault can be traced to a specific IC using a logic comparator.

**logic design** The specification of the operation of a system in terms of symbolic logic without primary regard to the hardware required to implement the system.

**logic diagram** A graphic representation of the logical elements and their interconnections without regard to construction details.

**logic, diode transistor (DTL)** The earliest form of integrated circuits combining a diode and a transistor in a monolithic structure.

**logic element** The smallest part of a computer system that represents a function or operation of symbolic logic. Typical logic elements are flip-flops and gates.

**logic file** A data set that is composed of one or more logical open records. A logic file may operate through the use of a file-definition macroinstruction.

**logic flow chart** A detailed solution of the work order or arrangement in terms of the logic for a specific machine or process. Symbolic notation is used to represent the information and describe the inputs and the outputs, arithmetic and logical operations. Types of operations can be shown using block symbols.

**logic gates** A circuit or single component capable of performing a logic operation. A gate may have several inputs but only one output.

**logic high** The voltage state furthest from zero in a two-state logic system, usually signifying a true, yes, on, or closed state. Also called *high level.*

**logic instruction** An instruction that executes an operation defined in symbolic logic.

**logic level** The voltage levels that represent binary conditions in a logic circuit.

**logic low** The voltage state nearest zero in a two-state logic system, usually signifying a false, no, off, or open state. Also called *low level*.

**logic operation** An operation in which logical quantities expressed in ones and zeros are used to make comparisons, decisions, and extractions.

**logic operator** Any of the Boolean operators such as AND, OR, NOR, and NAND.

**logic probe** A logic testing tool that provides a direct readout of logic levels by connecting to or placing over in-circuit ICs. The logic probe uses one or more lamps to indicate if a logic signal path is at logic one or logic zero or toggling between these levels. Some units use the relative brightness to indicate duty cycle, some rely upon blinking effects for frequency indication, and others are designed to be used in conjunction with a high-quality oscilloscope.

**logic product** The result obtained from the logical multiply operation or the AND operation.

**logic, programmable** Programmable logic devices can be defined as relatively simple entitites that of themselves, do not comprise an entire computing system. Included in this category are random logic, FPLAs, PLAs, ROMs, EAROMs, RAMs, CAMs, and microprocessors.

**logic pulser** A testing tool that drives a logic path to a desired state for a short time to check for faults and short circuits.

**logic shift** A shift in which all bits are treated the same with no special consideration given to the sign bit as in an arithmetic shift. A logic shift affects all positions.

**logic swing** The voltage difference between the two logic levels representing a zero and a one in a gate or circuit.

**logic symbol** A graphic character used to represent a logic operator.

**logic, transistor-transistor (TTL)** An integrated circuit logic in which transistors are combined in one monolithic structure.

**logical add** A Boolean operation performed on two bits at a time such that the result is one if either or both are one, and the result is zero if both bits are zero. Logical add is the same as the OR operator.

LOGICAL ADD

| INPUTS | | OUTPUT |
|---|---|---|
| A | B | C |
| 0 | 0 | 0 |
| 1 | 0 | 1 |
| 0 | 1 | 1 |
| 1 | 1 | 1 |

**logical connectives** Operators or words such as AND, OR, OR ELSE, IF-THEN, and EXCEPT, which make new statements from given statements.

**logical construction of programs method** The logical construction of programs (LCP) software design as shown in the figure assumes that the data structure is the key to software design. This method is procedure oriented and has the following steps:

1. Identify and organize the input data in a hierarchical manner.
2. Define and note the number of times each element of the input file occurs and use variable names to note the ratio of occurrences such as: N records.
3. Repeat steps 1 and 2 for the desired output.
4. Obtain the program details by identifying the types of instructions required for the design using a specific order: (1) read instructions (2) branches (3) calculations (4) outputs and (5) subroutine calls.
5. Using flowchart techniques, graph the logical sequence of instructions using Begin Process, End Process, Branching, and Nesting labels.

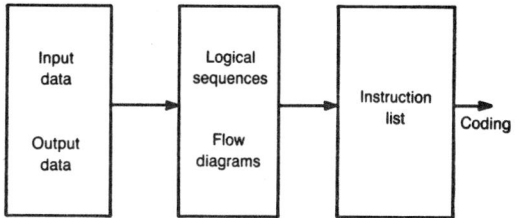

The LCP method for software design

**logical decision** The choice between two alternatives based upon certain criteria pertinent to the application.

**logical difference** A relation in set theory that includes all members of one set that are not members of another. For example, if set A includes 1, 3, 5, 7, 9, 11, and set B includes 2, 3, 5, 6, 7, 8, then the logical difference is 1, 2, 6, 8, 9, and 11.

**logical multiply** The AND operator.

LOGICAL MULTIPLY

| INPUTS | | OUTPUT |
|---|---|---|
| A | B | C |
| 0 | 0 | 0 |
| 1 | 0 | 0 |
| 0 | 1 | 0 |
| 1 | 1 | 1 |

**logical relation** A term used in assembler programming in which two expressions are separated by a relational operator such as EQ, GE, LE, LT or NE.

**logical shift** A shift in which the sign is treated as another data position.

**log sheet** A document used to list such items as incoming and outgoing work.

**logical sum** Logical add.

**longevity** The period of time during which the failure rate of a group of components is basically constant.

**long instruction format** An instruction that occupies more than one standard position or length, such as a two-word instruction. The second word may be used for address modification or as an operand.

**longitudinal current** A current that flows in the same direction in both wires of a parallel pair, the earth being its return path.

**longitudinal delay line** Delay lines are often named according to a propagating medium, such as mercury delay line, quartz delay line, or according to vibrational modes such as longitudinal.

**longitudinal magnetization** A magnetization used in magnetic recording that is in a direction parallel to the line of travel.

**longitudinal redundancy checking** A checking method that adds an additional block to the message. Each bit in this check block is obtained by performing an Exclusive OR on corresponding bits in the other blocks in the message. The receiving device calculates the contents of the check block from the data received. If the check block received is the same as the one calculated, the message has been received correctly.

**look-ahead** 1. A logic characteristic resulting in machine-sensing that all carries required for addition are generated. 2. The ability of a CPU to mask an interrupt until the following instruction is completed.

**look-ahead carry**  See *look-ahead*. 1.

**look-ahead-carry generator**  An adding circuit that anticipates carries to provide high-speed operations.

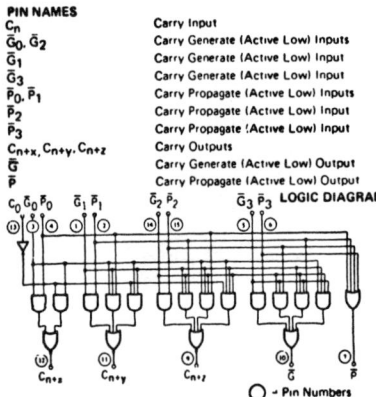

Look-ahead-carry generator

**lookup**  A procedure for obtaining the value of a function from a table of function values. If the values of the function are equally spaced, the locations of associated functions can be generated by a linear relationship. If the arguments are not equally spaced, the addresses can be separated using constants and a comparison operation.

**lookup, binary**  Relates to techniques designed for finding a particular item in an ordered set of items by repeatedly dividing in half the portion of the ordered set containing the sought-for item until only the sought-for item remains. Binary searching is more efficient than sequential searching, even when the number of items is small.

**lookup table**  A collection of data in a form suitable for ready reference, frequently stored in sequenced machine locations or in the form of rows and columns. The intersection of rows and columns can serve to locate specific items of data or information.

**loop**  1. A communications circuit between two private subscribers or a subscriber and the local switching center. 2. A direction-finding antenna. 3. A closed-circuit path within an electronic circuit or collection of circuits (such as a ground loop). 4. A self-contained series of instructions in which the final instruction can modify itself, causing the process to be repeated until a terminal condition is reached. Productive instructions in the loop are used to manipulate operands while housekeeping or bookkeeping instructions modify the productive instructions and keep track of the number of operations and repetitions. A loop may be terminated under any number of conditions. Loops are also used as return paths in control systems and other functions or operations requiring a feedback path.

**loop approach**  A technique of distributed control that uses satellite microcomputers to perform a fixed number of functions. A single microcomputer could perform a single function in a number of different loops. Normally, a microcomputer is dedicated to a single loop, so a single failure will cause the loss of only one loop.

**loopback test**  A test or check in which signals are looped from a test center through a loopback switch or data set, and then back to the test center for measurement.

**loop checking**  A method for checking the accuracy of transmission of data in which the received data is returned to the sending unit for comparison with the original data.

**loop code**  Coding that uses a program loop for repetition of a sequence of instructions. Loop coding generally results in storage savings, but it also requires more execution time compared to straight line coding.

**loop configuration**  The loop configuration as shown in the diagram is used in remote multiplexing. If a single link breaks, the nodes can still communicate. This is also called a ring configuration. The loop may begin and end at a loop controller, which is a computer that controls the communications. Messages between computers in the loop are handled as a string of words containing information on the originator and addressee. When a computer recognizes a message addressed to it, it accepts the message. Loops can be difficult to control, and the way that messages are sent past the computers requires higher data rates.

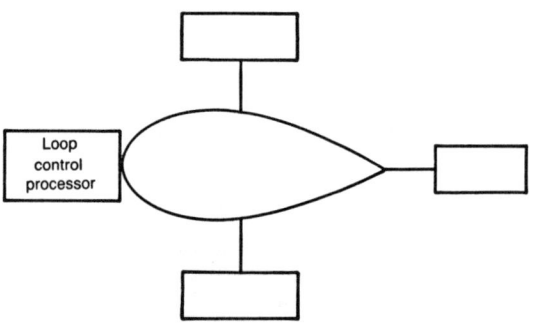

Loop network configuration

**loop counter**  A counter used in assembly programming to prevent excessive looping during conditional processing.

**loop error**  The error due to departure of the loop output signal from its desired value.

**loop feedback**  The signal that is fed back to the input to produce the loop actuating signal in a feedback control system.

**loop gain**  The ratio of output to input amplitude in a control loop.

**looping**  A repeating or recursive property of many programs and instructions used in microcomputers. Looping is often performed at delayed speeds, and many looped instructions are stored in ROM and then jumped to when required. Looping can also occur when the CPU is in a wait condition or as a result of errors and malfunctions.

**loop initialization**  The instructions prior to a loop that set addresses and data to their initial values.

**loop input**  Refers to an external signal applied to a feedback control loop in control systems.

**loop jump**  A jump instruction that causes a jump to itself.

**loop output signal**  Refers to the output signal at a point in a feedback loop produced by an input signal applied at the same point.

**loop program**  A series of instructions that are repeated until a terminal condition is reached.

**loop tape**  A short piece of tape containing a complete program task or operation, with the ends joined.

**loop test**  A series of instructions used to determine when a loop function has been completed.

**loop transfer function** The mathematical function representing the relationship between the output of a feedback loop control system and its input.

**loop update** Refers to the process of supplying the current parameters associated with a particular loop for use by the loop's control algorithm in calculating a new control output.

**LOR** Abbreviation for *lunar orbit rendezvous*.

**LORAC** Abbreviation for *long range accuracy*.

**LORAD** Abbreviation for *long range active detection*.

**LOS** Abbreviation for *loss of signal*.

**loss** The decrease in power of a signal as it is transmitted from one point to another, usually expressed in decibels.

**loss angle** A measure of the loss due to hysteresis in an imperfect dielectric, being the angular difference between its lead angle and 90°.

**Lossev radiation** The radiation due to the recombination of charge carriers injected into a p-i-n or p-n junction biased in the forward direction.

**loss factor** 1. The characteristic that determines the rate at which heat is generated in an insulating material, equal to the dielectric constant of a material. 2. The ratio of the average power loss to the power loss under peak loading.

**lossy** Pertaining to a material or apparatus that dissipates energy, such as a dielectric material or a transmission line with a high attenuation. The attenuation loss will be expressed in decibels (dB), while the rate of loss in the dielectric is proportional to its loss factor, which is the product of the power factor and dielectric constant.

**low-cost microcomputers** One of the major applications of the microprocessor is in low-cost general-purpose computers. For under $1,000, one may purchase a microcomputer that is able to perform various tasks. Such a low-cost computer is appealing for educational or home use. There are a number of ways in which this microcomputer may be sold: as components to be assembled, as an already-assembled unit, and or as a unit programmed for specific applications. The lowest cost microcomputers are those preprogrammed and packaged for a dedicated operation, such as educational toys. A simple system may sell for less than $100 using a minimum number of parts.

One example of such a system is shown below. This configuration is among the simplest that could be assembled. Many microcomputer chips could be used as a CPU.

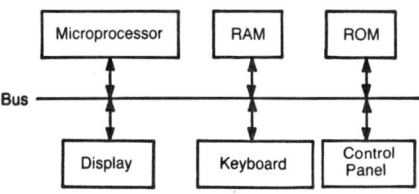

Low cost microcomputer

**lower-case** Refers to the small letters of type, rather than the capitals or uppercase.

**lower sideband** In an AM signal, that band of frequencies adjacent to and immediately below the carrier and spaced from the carrier by an amount equal to the frequency of the modulating wave. Since the sidebands (upper and lower) contain the intelligence, the carrier and one of the two sidebands may be discarded before transmission, so that only one of the two sidebands (upper or lower) is sent.

**low frequency** Electromagnetic radiation between 30 and 300 kHz.

**low level** 1. The most negative voltage in binary logic systems. If the true level is most positive, as it is in positive logic or positive true logic, then the low level is the false or zero level. 2. Characterized by a comparatively small value, as in *low-level signals*. 3. Relatively crude or primitive when compared with other members of the same genre or class.

**low-level language** A "primitive" language that resembles a machine code or has a one-to-one relationship with a machine code, by contrast to a *high-level language*, which uses English-like statements.

**low level modulation** Refers to modulation at a point in a system when the power level is low compared to the power level at the output of the system.

**low-level multiplexers** The multiplexing of voltages in the millivolt range, up to 1V, requires low-level multiplexers. Low-level interference and thermal effects can be great, so lines are run in pairs, and differential techniques are commonly used to remove interference that is present as a common mode signal. When high common-mode voltages are present, guarding techniques are used along with three-wire multiplexing of shielded input pairs.

**low loss** A component or system with little power dissipation, such as a low-loss line.

**low-order** Refers to the weight or significance assigned to the digits of a number. For example, in the number 2,345,768, the low-order digit is 8.

**low or high selector** Refers to devices designed to automatically select either the highest or the lowest input signal from among two or more input signals. This is also called a high or low signal selector.

**low-pass filter** A device or circuit that permits the passage of relatively low-frequency signals and attenuates high-frequency signals.

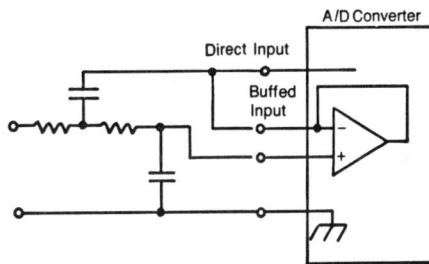

A/D input amplifier connected as low-pass filter

**low-performance equipment** Equipment that has insufficient performance characteristics to allow its use in trunk or link circuits. This equipment may be used in subscriber line circuits whenever it meets line circuit requirements.

**low-power Schottky** A variation of the Schottky TTL logic family. Low-power Schottky circuits allow smaller, less costly power supplies, improved packing density, and less noise generation, along with simplified MOS-to-TTL interfaces.

**low-speed storage** Descriptive of storage devices that have long access times compared with the time required for arithmetic operations of the CPU, and low access times compared to other peripheral units.

**low tension** A term applied to the currents and voltages associated with low voltage-circuits.

**LP** Abbreviation for *linear programming*.

**LPH** Abbreviation for *lines per hour*.

**LPL** Abbreviation for *list programminig language*.

**LPM** Abbreviation for *line per minute*. Used in measuring printer output speed.

**LRS** Abbreviation for *long range search*.

**LSB** Abbreviation for *least significant bit*.

**LSI** Abbreviation for *large-scale integration*, a name applied to integrated circuits with 1000 or more functional units or gates on a single chip.

**LSI board tester** An automated tester designed for troubleshooting and repair stations. A typical system provides stored program capability, which permits the testing of boards, devices, and the entire module with the exact patterns timing necessary to do a functional test. With the stored program capability, testing of LSI boards and devices is possible.

**LSTTL** Abbreviation for *low power Schottky TTL*.

**lug** A device provided on the end of a conductor for inserting screws at terminal strips.

**Lukaseiwicz notation** A notation used in forming mathematical expressions in which the operator precedes its operands. For example, the term *A plus B multiplied by C* is written as +*ABC*. Also called prefix notation, parentheses-free notation, and Polish notation.

**lumped** Circuit elements that are concentrated in discrete units rather than distributed over a transmission line or circuit path.

**lumped loading** Refers to the process of inserting uniformly spaced inductance coils along a line.

**lumped parameter** A circuit parameter that may be considered to be localized for the purpose of analysis.

**lumped voltage** A voltage formed by adding the sum of the products of a number of intermediate electrode voltages and the respective amplification factors associated with those electrodes. The total space current is a function of this quality.

**LWD** Abbreviation for *larger word*.

**M** Symbol for the avalanche multiplication factor in transistors.

**m** Symbol for the empirical determined avalanche constant in transistors.

**MA** Abbreviation for *memory address*.

**machine** 1. A general term for a device such as a microprocessor or microcomputer that can store and process numeric and alphabetic information. Machine is used to refer to both analog and digital computers along with related data processing equipment. 2. An automatic radio receiving and transmitting station.

**machine address** Absolute address.

**machine-check indicator** A device that is switched on when programmed conditions are detected by the machine-checking circuits. The system is then programmed to run a diagnostic routine to find the cause of the interruption.

**machine code** An operation code that a machine is designed to recognize directly and without translation.

**machine-code instruction** The symbols that state a basic computer operation that is to be performed. The machine-code instruction is the combination of bits specifying the machine-language operator, which becomes a part of the instruction that designates the operation of logic.

**machine cycle** The shortest complete action or process that is repeated in order; also, the time required for this action or process. Also called *microcycle*.

**machine equation** The equation that an analog computer is programmed to solve.

**machine hardware** Refers to the circuits contained in the five parts of the computer: input, output, control, storage, and arithmetic and logic sections.

**machine instruction** Any instruction that a machine can recognize and execute; machine-code instruction.

**machine language** A language that can be used directly by a microprocessor; a binary language. All other languages must be translated or compiled into binary code before entering the processor. Users generally write the program in coded instructions that are more meaningful to them. Then assembly programs are used to translate the symbolic instructions into binary machine code. Also called *object code*.

**machine learning** The ability of a device to improve its performance based on its own prior experience.

**machine length** Refers to the working word length used by a device.

**machine logic design** Refers to the methods of computer design problem approach and function execution; the way a system is designed to do its operations; what those operations are, and the type and form of data it will use internally.

**machine-oriented language** A language designed for interpretation and use by a specific machine or class of machine. The language may include instructions that define and direct machine operations along with any information to be acted upon by the machine during specific operations.

**machine-readable** The capability of being sensed or read by a specific device. Cards, drums, disks, and tapes are all machine-readable media.

**machine unit** The voltage used in an analog computer to represent one unit of the simulated variable.

**machine variable** Refers to the signal in an analog computer used to reproduce the variations of the simulated function.

**machine word** A word with the standard number of bits that a computer normally handles in a register or during a transfer. Typical machine words in microcomputer systems are 4, 8, and 16 bits long.

**machining center** A machine tool, usually numerically controlled, capable of automatically drilling, reaming, tapping, milling, and boring multiple faces of a part and often equipped with a system for automatically changing cutting tools.

**macro** 1. A large mainframe computer facility able to handle very large volumes of data. 2. A single instruction as written in source code, which may require a number of successive operational machine steps to execute, each step involving a machine instruction in *microcode;* a macroinstruction. 3. A group of often-used instructions treated as a unit entity.

**macroassembler** A language processor that accepts words, statements, and phrases to produce machine instructions. A macroassembler allows segments of a large program to be created and tested separately. The full macro capability of a resident macroassembler eliminates the need to rewrite similar sections of code repeatedly and simplifies program documentation.

**macroassembler, resident** An assembler that enables users to translate assembly language program into the appropriate machine language instructions. The macro capability eliminates the need to rewrite similar sections of code repeatedly, and simplifies the user's program documentation. The conditional assembly feature of the macroassembler, which may vary from system to system, permits users to include or delete optional code segments.

**macroassembler, two-pass** A two-pass assembler used on some computers that is available with subprogram, literal, and macro facilities. Some can be directly processed by debugging programs. These can provide symbol tables for program checkout in terms of the source language symbols.

**macro call** A call for a subroutine jump to a macro command.

**macro code** 1. That coding system that permits a macroinstruction to call upon specified groups of instructions for execution as if it were a discrete machine operation. 2. Any instruction that results in a call for a jump to a routine that is not machine-peculiar, and which usually consists of a body of inseparable instructions. 3. Collectively, the procedures used to provide code segments that are used frequently throughout a program.

**macro command** A command or statement used to bring a string or strings of frequently used instructions into operation.

**macro cross assembler** An assembler that runs as a conversational program on a machine other than the target system. Many variations are available, including macro cross assemblers that allow the use of a few simple pseudo operations, that allow you to specify the radix of the assembler listing as octal, decimal or hexadecimal, that number every statement, and that provide clear and extensive error messages.

**macro definition** The specification of a macro operation, including the name of the operations and the definitions of fixed and variable fields.

**macro facility** That feature of an assembler that allows it to produce a sequence of statements from a macro definition.

**macro flowchart** Refers to tables and charts utilized in designing the logic of a specific routine in which the various segments and subroutines of a program are represented by blocks.

**macro generating program** A program designed to construct a group of instructions in object code from a macroinstruction in the basic source language.

**macro generator** Macro generating program.

**macroinstruction** An instruction in a source language that is equivalent to a specified sequence of machine instructions and requires several microcycles to execute. A macroinstruction is a powerful command that results from combining several operations into a single instruction. A macroinstruction may also generate a debugging routine to be used with a particular program.

A macroinstruction set may be register- or stack-oriented, and may be original or a copy from another machine. Lower cost and higher performance usually result when an original macroinstruction set is developed. If more than eight bits of operation code are used in a macroinstruction, the interpretation becomes complex and additional logic may have to be added to the hardware design.

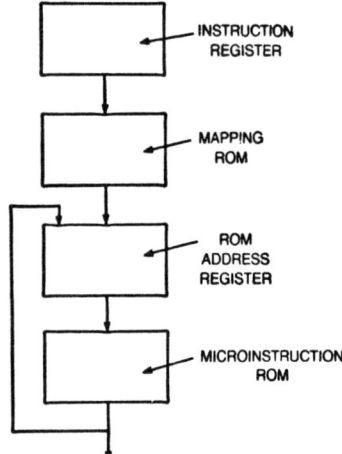

**Macroinstruction decoding system**

**macroinstruction, inner** A macroinstruction that is nested inside a macrodefinition. It is the opposite of *outer macroinstruction.*

**macroprogramming** The procedure and methods used for writing machine statements in terms of macroinstructions.

**macroscopic state** A state described in terms of the overall second-statistical behavior of the discrete elements from which it is formed.

**macros, debug** Refers to aids built into a program by the applications programmer, in addition to those supplied by the supervisory program.

**MAD** 1. Abbreviation for *magnetic airborne detection.* 2. Abbreviation for *Michigan algorithm decoder.* 3. Abbreviation for *magnetic anomaly detection.*

**MADT** Abbreviation for *micro alloy diffused-base transistor.*

**MAG** Abbreviation for *marine aircraft group.*

**magnadur** A ceramic material made from sintered oxides of iron and barium, used for permanent magnets and as an electrical insulator.

**magnesium (Mg)** A metallic element, Atomic number 12, atomic weight 24.312, specific gravity 1.74, melts at 651 °C, boils at 1120 °C. A light metallic element, often alloyed with aluminum and used in constructing electronic components.

**magnet** A body that has the property of attracting iron and when freely supported in isolation from other bodies will tend to set in the north-south direction. Occurs naturally in stones containing magnetite. Once known as a lodestone. Now permanent magnets are made artificially from hardened steel that has been magnetized by a strong magnetic flux.

**magnetic** Descriptive of phenomena and devices depending essentially on magnetism.

**magnetic analysis** The separation of a stream of electrified particles by a magnetic field, in accordance with their mass, charge, or speed.

**magnetic bias** A steady magnetic field added to the signal field in magnetic recording. A magnetic bias can improve the linearity of response during recording.

**magnetic bubble memory** A technology that uses a single-crystal sheet with perpendicular magnetic fields to produce magnetic "bubbles." A pulsed field is used to break up and control the bubbles as groups of data bits. Densities of 10 million bits per square inch have been realized, and densities to one billion bits per square inch have been projected for this technology.

**magnetic character reader** A device that reads magnetically inscribed data from cards and paper documents into a computer. The reader may be used for both online and offline operations.

**magnetic circuit** A closed path for magnetic flux.

**magnetic coating** The magnetic layer consisting of oxide particles held in a binder applied to magnetic recording materials such as tapes, disks, and drums.

**magnetic code** The specific manner in which data bits are represented on magnetic recording materials. A phase-encoding format records a one as a flux transition at the midpoint of the data cell towards the level representing erased tape. A zero is recorded as a flux reversal in the opposite direction.

**magnetic core** A memory device in which information is represented by the magnetic polarity of a wire-sensed permeable ring. Small rings called cores are used to represent bits 0 and 1. The cores are made of ferrites; variations of the ring form include tapes, rods, and thin-film configurations. The cores are usually arranged in the form of a matrix.

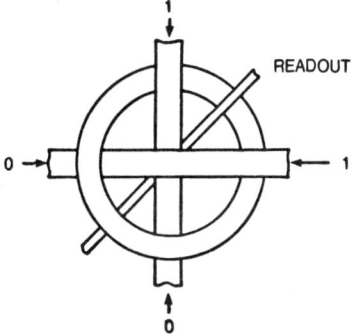

**Magnetic core**

**magnetic core storage** A storage system that uses a core of magnetic material coupled by wires or other conductors. The cores are magnetized to represent binary ones or zeros.

**magnetic cycle** The sequence of changes in magnetization of an object corresponding to one cycle of alternating current.

**magnetic damping** The damping of motion of a conductor by induced eddy currents in it when moving across a magnetic field. It is particularly applicable to moving parts of instruments and integrating meters.

**magnetic delay line** A delay medium that uses magnetic material to slow the propagation of magnetic or sound waves.

**magnetic disk** A storage device or medium that uses a coated disk for storing information. The data is stored in the form of magnetic spots representing binary data and is arranged in circular tracks around the disks. The tracks are accessed by movable read and write heads that are positioned to the desired disk, and then to the desired track. The information is obtained sequentially as the disk rotates.

**magnetic disk storage** A storage device or system consisting of magnetically coated disks.

**magnetic drum** A storage device that uses a rotating cylindrical drum surfaced with a magnetic coating. The data is stored as magnetized spots on closed tracks that circle the drum. A read-write head is used for each track, and the proper head is selected by switching. Data is read or written sequentially as the drum turns.

**magnetic energy** The product of flux density and field strength for points on the demagnetization curve of a permanent magnetic material; this product enables researchers to measure the energy established in the magnetic circuit. It is normally required to be the maximum possible for the amount of magnetic material used.

**magnetic ferrite** A ceramic-type material that possesses strong magnetic properties along with good insulating qualities.

**magnetic field** A modification of space near a magnetic body or a current carrying body. The forces due to the magnetic body or current can be detected in this area of space. It is associated with electric currents and the motions of electrons in atoms.

**magnetic field intensity** The magnitude of the field strength vector in a medium; the magnetic strain produced by neighboring magnetic elements or current carrying conductors. The MKSA (meter-kilogram-second-ampere) unit is the ampere-turn/meter, and the CGS (centimeter-gram-second) unit is the oersted. Also called *magnetic field strength, magnetic intensity, magnetizing force.*

**magnetic field interference** Refers to interference induced in the circuits of a device due to the presence of a magnetic field. It often appears as common-mode or normal-mode interference in the measuring circuits.

**magnetic flip-flop** A bistable amplifier that uses magnetic amplifiers. The two stable states are determined by changes in the control voltage or current.

**magnetic hysteresis loop** A closed curve that shows the relation between the force and the induction in a magnetic substance when the field or force is determined for a complete cycle.

**magnetic induction** Refers to the vector associated with the mechanical force exerted on a current carrying conductor that is located in a magnetic field.

**magnetic ink** An ink containing magnetic particles that can be detected by magnetic sensors.

**magnetic ink character recognition** Machine recognition of characters printed using magnetic inks. Abbreviated *MICR.*

**magnetic instability** The property of magnetic material on tape that causes variations to occur from temperature, aging, and mechanical strain. Magnetic instability is a function of particle size and magnetization.

**magnetic keyboard** A device that records keystrokes and editing changes on a magnetic medium.

**magnetic leakage** That part of the magnetic flux in a system that is lost for most practical purposes; it may be a nuisance that affects nearby apparatus.

**magnetic media** Any of a wide variety of cards, disks, or tapes coated or impregnated with magnetic material, for use with the appropriate equipment and on which data or information are recorded and stored.

**magnetic memory** The use of magnetic materials for registering and recovering information in the form of bits.

**magnetic mirror** A device based on the principle that ions moving in a magnetic field tend to be reflected away from high magnetic fields.

**magnetic moment** 1. A vector such that its product with the magnetic induction gives the torque on a magnet in a monogenious magnetic field. 2. The dipole moment of an atom or nucleus associated with electron orbitals and/or electron and nuclear spin.

**magnetic oxides** The oxides that are ferromagnetic and are used to fabricate permanent magnets and coat tapes and other media.

**magnetic path** Refers to the track or route followed by magnetic flux lines; a closed line that involves all media through which the lines of flux pass, such as the interior of a ferrite toroidal core.

**magnetic potential** A continuous mathematical function the value of which at any point is equal to the potential energy, relative to infinity, of a theoretical unit north-seeking magnetic pole placed at that point.

**magnetic potentiometer** A flexible solenoid used with a ballistic galvanometer to explore the distribution of magnetic potential in a field.

**magnetic pumping** The use of radio frequency currents in coils to modulate the axial field and provide heat to a plasma. This process is most efficient when there is resonance between the rf signals and vibrations of the molecules of plasma. The process is then called resonance heating.

**magnetic quantum numbers** These numbers determine the components of orbital and spin angular momentum in the direction of the applied field.

**magnetic recording** The registering of data on a magnetic medium such as a tape, disk, or drum. Magnetic recording parameters include tape speed, transfer rate, and packing density. Tape speed refers to the speed or velocity at which the tape moves past the recording head and is usually expressed in inches or centimeters per second. Transfer rate is a measure of how fast data can be handled by the recording system and is expressed in bits or bytes per second, or in baud. Packing density refers to the number of bits per unit length stored on the tape.

**magnetic resonance line width** The width of the absorption lines depends upon the interaction of the spins with each other and with the crystal lattice. It is measured by the random fluctuating magnetic field (H) that is exerted on a spin by its neighbors; $\Delta H = \mu/d^3$, where $\mu$ is the magnetic moment of each spin and d is the interatomic spacing.

**magnetic rigidity** A measure of the momentum of a particle. It is given by the product of the magnetic intensity perpendicular to the path of the particle and the resultant radius of curvature of this path.

**magnetic saturation** The limiting value of magnetic induction in a medium when magnetization is complete.

**magnetic shield** Any surface of magnetic material that reduces the effect on one side of a magnetic field on the other side. A shield is used to protect some instruments from errors arising from external alternating magnetic fields.

**magnetic shift register** A shift register in which the pattern of a row of magnetic cores is moved one step along the row by each new pulse.

**magnetic spectrometer** An instrument in which the distribution of energies among a beam of charged particles is investigated by means of magnetic focusing techniques.

**magnetic storage** A storage system that uses the magnetic properties of materials such as magnetic cores, tapes, and disks to store data.

**magnetic strip** A line of magnetic ink on the back of a ledger card which contains coded information. The magnetic strip may or may not be printed on the face of the card.

**magnetic susceptibility** The amount by which the relative permeability of a medium differs from unity, positive for a paramagnetic medium and negative for a diamagnetic one.

**magnetic tape** A flexible oxide-coated tape on which data can be stored by selective polarization of portions of the surface. One side is usually coated with a uniform layer of dispersed magnetic material. The tape can be used for audio, video, or binary data recording.

**magnetic tape diagnostic** A routine used to check tape controller and tape transport operations.

**magnetic tape reader** A unit that transforms the pattern of magnetic spots on a tape into pulse signals for a computer.

**magnetic thin film** A layer of magnetic material used for logic and storage elements. Thin films are usually less than one micrometer (micron) in thickness.

**magnetic units** Ampere-turn, gauss, gilbert, line of force, maxwell, oersted, and unit magnetic poles are some examples of magnetic units that are used in measuring magnetic quantities.

**magnetic wire** A wire composed of or coated with a magnetic material and used for recording.

**magnetism** 1. The science covering magnetic fields and other magnetic phenomena. 2. A property of devices or bodies due to the unbalanced spin of electrons in atoms.

**magnetoelectric** The property of certain materials, such as chromium oxide, of becoming magnetized when placed in an electric field. Conversely, they are electrically polarized when placed in a magnetic field. Such materials can be used for measuring pulsed electric or magnetic fields.

**magnetohydrodynamics** The study of the motion of electrical conducting fluids in the presence of a magnetic field.

**magneto ionic** Refers to the components of an EM wave passing through an ionized region and divided into ordinary and extraordinary waves due to the magnetic field of the earth.

**magnetoresistance** The resistivity of a magnetic material in a magnetic field, when carrying an electric current, depends on the direction of the current with respect to the field. If they are parallel to one another, the resistivity increases, but if they are mutually perpendicular it decreases.

**magnetostriction** A phenomenon in which certain materials increase in length in the direction of a magnetic field and return to their original length when the field is removed.

**magnetostriction transducer** A device that uses the property of magnetostriction to convert electrical energy to mechanical energy, or vice versa.

**magnetostrictive delay line** A delay device that uses the magnetostrictive effect to convert electrical signals to sonic waves or sonic waves to electrical signals. Also called *magnetostrictive acoustic delay line.*

**magnetron** A uhf diode oscillator containing its own cavity resonator in which electrons assume a circular path due to the magnetic field.

**mailbox** A set of locations in a common RAM storage area that is reserved for data addressed to specific peripherals and other microprocessors located in the immediate area. The mailbox arrangement helps the coordinator microprocessor and the supplementary microprocessors transfer data among themselves with minimal hardware.

**mainframe** 1. The heart of a computer system, which includes the CPU and ALU. 2. A large computer, as opposed to a mini or a micro.

**mainframe computer** Larger than minicomputers are mainframe computers, often used in large offices such as insurance companies. These computers deal with large files of data such as millions of insurance policies. With mainframes many magnetic disks and tapes are connected to the computer in order to store data so the input/output scheduling can become a major task. Mainframe computers may be used to handle "scientific" computations such as those needed to produce the daily weather forecast for a section of the nation. Here, speed and efficiency in using arithmetic computations far beyond what is found in most microcomputers are needed.

**main memory** The main memory in a computer system occupies a central position through which information passes to and from peripheral units and CPU. A large computer system may have several CPUs and several I/O processors communicating with the memory through a bus system.

**main storage** The general-purpose storage area of a computer. Main storage is usually accessed directly by the operating registers and may be the fastest storage device in the computer, since it is used to execute all instructions.

**maintenance** Activity used to eliminate faults and keep hardware and programs in satisfactory working condition. Maintenance may include tests, measurements, replacements, adjustments, and repairs.

**maintenance control panel** A panel of indicators and switches used to display a sequence of routines for repair checks.

**maintenance processor** A processor used to remotely check a microprocessor through the checking of memory or register contents. The maintenance processor can also be used to single step the clock of the microprocessor in order to search out faulty register contents. Other circuitry could be checked in a similar manner.

**maintenance time** Time used for hardware repair, including corrective and preventive operations.

**major control data** The various high-priority items of data used to select, execute, or modify another data value, routine, record, file, or operation.

**major cycle** The time interval between successive appearances of a given storage element. Usually it is the time of one rotation of a recirculating storage element, and it is composed of a number of minor cycles.

**major item** An obsolete military term, replaced by the term "end item".

**majority** The logic operator having the property of unanimity: if P, Q, R are statements, then the majority of P, Q, R is true if more than half the statements are true, and false if more than half the statements are false.

**majority carrier** Refers to the predominant type of current carrier in a semiconductor region. For npn transistors, the majority carrier is the *electron;* for pnp is the *hole.*

**majority decision gate** A device or circuit used to implement the majority logic operator.

**majority element** Related to a threshold element or a decision element: if the weights are equal to 1 and the threshold is equal to (n + 1)/2, the element is called a majority element.

**majority gate** Majority decision gate.

**major state** A basic control state in a computer, such as fetch, defer, or execute. Major control states are used to determine and execute instructions. During any one instruction, a state lasts for one cycle.

**major state logic generator** The logic circuits of the CPU that are used to establish the major state for each computer cycle. The major state logic generator determines the machine state as a function of the current instruction, the current state, and the conditions of the peripheral units.

**makeup time** 1. The part of available time that is used for reruns due to malfunctions and mistakes from a previous operating time. 2. The unproductive time required to prepare a system to perform a specific task.

**malfunction** A failure in the operation of a computer system.

**malfunction routine** A routine used to locate a malfunction in a computer or as an aid in locating mistakes in the program. Also called *diagnostic routine.*

**management information system** An organized assemblage of management activities performed with the aid of automatic data processing. One example is a data processing system that provides management with the information required to manage or supervise a particular organization or function. Another example is a communications data processing system in which data is recorded and processed for operational purposes. The problems are isolated for different levels of decision-making, and information is fed back to upper management to reflect the progress made in achieving objectives.

**manganese (Mn)** A grey pink, hard, brittle metallic element: atomic number 25, atomic weight 54.9380, specific gravity 7.20, melts at 1260 °C. Alloyed with other nonferromagnetic elements of copper and aluminum, it forms a ferromagnetic material. The element is used in some primary batteries.

**manganin** A copper base alloy, containing 12 percent manganese and 4 percent nickel, used for making resistor wire, because of its low temperature coefficient and low contact potential.

**manipulated variable** The quantity or condition that is altered by the computer to initiate a change in a regulated process.

**MANOP** Abbreviation for *manual of operations.*

**manual data input (MDI)** A means of inserting data manually into the control system.

**manual feedrate override** A device enabling the operator to reduce or increase the feedrate.

**manual input** The entry of data by hand.

**manual input generator** A device that accepts manual input data and holds the contents for sensing by the computer or controller.

**manual part programming** The manual preparation of data in machine control language and format to define a sequence of commands for use on a numerical control machine.

**manual storage** A type of storage in the form of manually set switches, usually arranged in an array or matrix.

**manuscript** A form used by a part programmer for listing detailed manual or computer part programming instructions.

**map** A graphic portrayal of the correspondence between the elements of one set and the elements of another set, such as a listing that relates data names to addresses.

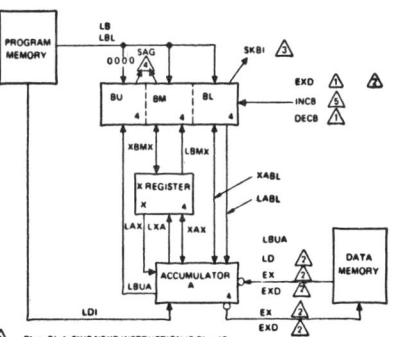

**Map**

**MAR** Abbreviation for *memory address register*.

**marginal check** A preventive maintenance technique that uses the variation of operating conditions such as voltages and frequency to detect and locate incipient defective components.

**marginal test** A built-in check system that uses resistor networks and variable voltages. All working registers are usually displayed on the console panel.

**marginal voltage check** Refers to a means of testing a unit by reducing the power supply voltage. The theory is that if there is a marginal circuit, it will fail at the reduced voltage.

**mark** 1. A sign or symbol used to signify or indicate an event in time or space. Examples include end of message marks, file marks, drum marks, and end-of-tape marks. Also called a *marker* or *flag*. 2. The radioteletype signal that causes a character to print.

**marker** 1. An intentionally displayed pip on a scope to show a specific frequency 2. Mark, 1.

**Markov chain** A probabilistic model in which the probability of an event is dependent only on the event that preceded it.

**mark reader** A device used to detect pencil marks on documents.

**mark sensing** The electrical detection of manually recorded conductive traces on a nonconductive surface such as paper.

**mark-to-space ratio** In radioteletype, the ratio of the duration of positive and negative cycles of a square waveform; the positive cycle is a mark or a one, and the negative cycle is a space or a zero.

**M-ary** A term used to refer to devices and operations with more than two states or conditions.

**mase** To undergo maser operation.

**MASER** Abbreviation for *microwave amplification by simulated emission of radiation*.

**mask** 1. A machine word that specifies by selective inhibition the parts of another machine word that is to be operated on. 2. A thin sheet with open and closed portions used in device photoprocessing.

**mask bit** A specific bit used with a pattern of bits to extract selected bits from a string.

**masking** The process of extracting certain bits or sensing certain binary conditions while ignoring others by inhibition. One technique of masking uses zeros in bit positions of no interest and ones in positions to be sensed.

**mask programmable read-only memory** A type of PROM that is programmed during the final steps of manufacture. The surface of the wafer is coated with a layer of aluminum that is selectively etched to give the desired interconnecting pattern. The devices are fabricated up to this step of manufacture and then held in storage until a customer's data pattern is defined. Then the chips are mask-programmed and delivered to the user.

**Massey formula** A formula giving the probability of secondary electron emission when an excited atom approaches the surface of a metal.

**mass spectrometer** An instrument in which charged particles of different atoms are separated by their mass-to-charge ratios. Separation takes place in a high vacuum to eliminate collision with other molecules. A sample is admitted and ionized under reduced pressure by an electron beam. The charge particles pass through a magnetic field to determine the mass-to-charge ratios. Space collectors pass the charges to an electrometer where they are amplified into voltages proportional to the compositions. A closed loop control system compensates for any changes in sensitivity. The use of a microcomputer makes the system self-calibrating and able to operate without human attention.

A central computer can be used with a microprocessor that scans all the analyzer units and converts and stores the signals for use as required. A block diagram of the system is shown.

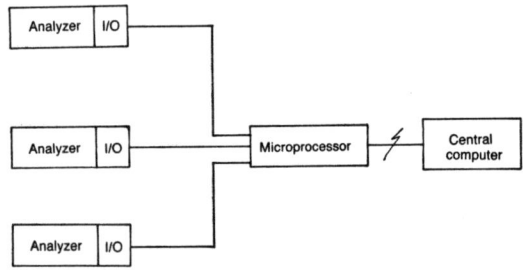

**Microprocessor controlled gas chromatograph system**

**mass storage** A mechanical, nonvolatile memory device. Mass storage units include magnetic tape and disks, punched cards, paper tape, bubble memories, and video tape and disks.

**mass-storage device** A device with a large storage capacity such as a magnetic disk or drum.

**mass-storage dump** A program used to transfer a specified area of memory to a mass-storage device. If an autoloading format is used, the accuracy of the dumped program is automatically verified.

**mass store** Random-access memory.

**master clock** The primary source of all timing signals in a digital computer. Most master clocks use a crystal to provide a stable source. The clock pulses are then used for precision time-triggering of events.

**master control interrupt** A signal that transfers control of the computer to the master control program. It may be generated by input/output devices, operator error, or processor request.

**master control program** A program designed to direct all phases of the operation of the system. The master control program usually is designed for minimum human intervention and may provide the following functions:

1. Schedule programs to be processed
2. Control input/output operations
3. Allocate memory
4. Direct compiling operations
5. Provide error-detection and correction
6. Provide printed instructions
7. Adjust operation according to system environment

**master control routine** 1. A part of a program used to control linking of other routines and subroutines, or calling selected program segments into memory. 2. A routine used to control the operation of hardware.

**master instruction tape** Master tape.

**master scheduler** A control program that allows the operator to initiate special actions designed to override the normal functions of the system.

**master—slave** A term for a configuration in which one device or function, the master, always has control over another device or function, the slave. In a computer system, the master computer schedules and transmits tasks to the slave, which performs the computations as directed. Bus control can also be under a master-slave relationship. The processor is the master when fetching an instruction from memory, which is the slave.

**master/slave network** In the simplest master/slave network, a host processor is connected by one line to a satellite processor. The communication line between the processors is referred to as a link. A link may be any communications channel, such as a coaxial cable or telephone line. Each device in a network is sometimes referred to as a node.

**master slice** Refers to silicon wafers containing 30 or more clusters of components. These elements can be interconnected with paths of aluminum to form desired circuits. The wafer is then diced to form single devices.

**master synchronizer** The primary source of timing signals in some systems. A typical configuration uses a ring counter synchronized by a crystal-controlled oscillator.

**master tape** A tape that contains the program or master data file with most of the routines. Other data units such as cards may serve the same purpose in some systems.

**master unit** Refers to various units that handle a variety of jobs being executed simultaneously and have the capability of regrouping several units together to control a complete processing system or job independently.

**match** A check to determine identity, similarity, or agreement between items of data. A match is similar to a merge except that instead of producing a sequence of items from the input, sequences are matched against each other on the basis of a key.

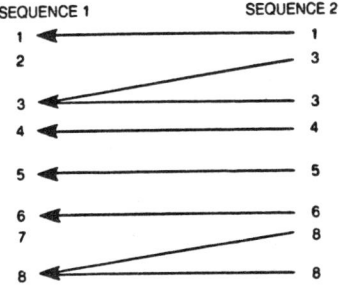

**Match schematic for two items**

**matching** A technique used to verify coding. Individual codes can be compared by machine against master codes to detect any that are invalid.

**matching impedance** The impedance value that must be connected to the terminals of a signal voltage source of matching.

**material control** Material control is concerned with the counting, sorting, and identification of raw materials and manufactured parts.

**material implication** A Boolean operation defined by the following truth table:

| OPERANDS | | RESULT |
|---|---|---|
| A | B | C |
| 0 | 0 | 1 |
| 1 | 0 | 0 |
| 0 | 1 | 1 |
| 1 | 1 | 1 |

**mathematical check** A check that uses mathematical relationships. Also called *arithmetic check*.

**mathematical control mode** The control mode or control action used in a control system, such as proportional, integral, or derivative.

**mathematical model** The mathematical representation of a process, device, or system.

**mathematical programming** A procedure used in operations research for locating the maximum or minimum values of a function subject to specified conditions.

**matrix** An array of quantities or elements in a prescribed form. A matrix is usually capable of being subject to a mathematical operation using an operator or another matrix. A matrix of circuit elements can be capable of performing functions such as code conversion. The matrix elements may be diodes, transistors, magnetic cores, or other binary devices.

**matrix printer** A device that uses an array of dots to form characters. Dot-matrix character formation is also used in some display devices. Sometimes called *dot matrix printer*.

**matrix storage** A storage system with elements arranged such that access to any location requires the use of two or more coordinates. Examples are magnetic-core storage and CRT storage.

**matrix switch** An array of circuit elements used to perform a specific function as interconnected. Functions include word translation, encoding, and number-system transformation. Elements include switches, transistors, diodes, and relays.

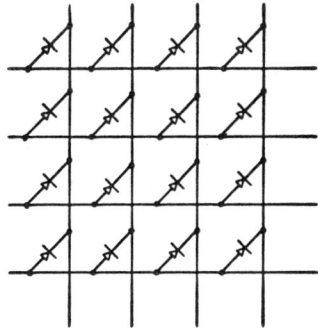

**Matrix of diodes**

**matrix table** A set of quantities arranged in a rectangular array according to specific mathematical rules and conventions.

**MATS** Abbreviation for *Military Air Transport Service*.

**maximum frequency operation** The maximum repetition or clock rate at which the electronic circuits will perform reliably under continuous worst-case conditions.

**maxwell** In the centimeter-gram-second system, the unit of magnetic flux. One maxwell is equal to $10^{-8}$ webers.

**Maxwell's circulating current** Refers to a cyclic current inserted in closed loops in a complex network for analytical purposes.

**Maxwell's law** A movable portion of a circuit will always travel in the direction that gives maximum flux linkages through the circuit.

**MB or M** Abbreviation for *one million bytes* (1,048,576).

**MBR** Abbreviation for *memory buffer register*.

**MCD** Abbreviation for *master clerical data*.

**MCP** Abbreviation for *master control program*.

**m-derived filter** An electric filter element derived from the constant-$k$ element by transformation.

**mean repair time** The average repair time per failure. The mean repair time, if taken over a given performance period, can be used to assess reliability of the equipment.

**mean-time-between failure** The average time between failures (abbreviated *MTBF*) taken as a function of the operating time. The MTBF represents the expected failure-free operating time for the equipment. Also called *mean-time-to-failure (MTTF)*.

**mean-time-to-failure (MTTF)** The average or mean life of an irreparable device, circuit, or part.

**measurand** A measured physical variable such as pressure, temperature, flow, or distance.

**measure** A line standard usually expressed in terms of character units.

**measured signal** Usually refers to the analog of the measured variable produced by a transducer; a measured signal concerns various electrical, pneumatic, mechanical, or other variables that are applied to the input of the device.

**measured variable** A specific physical quantity, condition, or property that is to be measured, often referred to as the measurand. Common measured variables include pressure, temperature, rate of flow, thickness, and speed.

**measurement error** Anticipated deviations in a measurement due to:

1. Sampling variability
2. Sample preparation variations
3. Stability variations or lack of precision

**measurement reproducibility** The degree of agreement between repeated measurements under the same operating conditions over a given period of time.

**mechanical dictionary** A language translating machine used to provide a word-for-word substitution from one language to another. The mechanical dictionary is used in automatic searching systems for encoding.

**mechanical differential** A device used in analog computers to provide a mechanical rotation equal to the difference of two input rotations.

**mechanical interface** Refers to the mechanical mounting and interconnections between system elements.

**MEDLARS** Abbreviation for *Medical Literature Analysis and Retrieval System*.

**media** The material on which data is stored; media includes punched cards, floppy and hard disks, and magnetic and video tape. The magnetic devices use a metal oxide coating which can store thousands to millions of bits per inch of surface. Magnetic media is sensitive to stray magnetic fields, and care must be exercised when handling the media in the proximity of such sources.

**median** The average of a series of values, or that value for which there are an equal number of items with lesser magnitudes and greater magnitudes.

**medium** 1. The physical substance upon which data is recorded, such as magnetic tape, disk, or card. 2. Any carrier of any commodity, especially data.

**medium frequency** Radio frequencies from 300 kHz to 3 MHz, sometimes called *hectometric waves*.

**medium-scale integration** Integrated circuits with more than 100 but less than 1000 circuits or gates on a single chip. Abbreviated *MSI*.

**meet** A Boolean operator that gives a true output only when both variables connected by the operator are true.

**MEG** Abbreviation for *megohm*.

**mega** Prefix denoting one million, abbreviated *M*.

**megabit** A unit equal to one million bits.

**megabyte** One million bytes, actually 2 to the 20th power (1,048,576).

**megacycle** A million ($10^6$) cycles per second.

**megahertz** A unit of frequency equal to one million cycles per second.

**Meissner circuit** Refers to an oscillating circuit in which the resonant circuit is inductively coupled to two coils included in the anode and grid circuits.

**Meissner effect** The apparent expulsion of lines of magnetic induction from a superconductor when cooled below superconducting transition temperature in magnetic field.

**memories** Memories are used to hold programs and any data that must be manipulated by the instructions. Programs are stored in the memory as a series of binary words, each word having from 4 to 16 bits, depending on the microprocessor used. Each word or series of words represents an instruction or data that the microprocessor will decode or act upon when that information is presented at the processor input.

**memory** A basic component of a computer that stores information for future use. Memory and storage are interchangeable terms.

A memory is used to accept and hold binary numbers until required. To be effective, a computer must be able to store the data that will be operated on as well as the program that directs what operations are to be performed. Memory units are designed to store large amounts of information and must allow rapid access to any desired part of that information in time of need. These two requirements tend to increase the cost of the memory. Various types of memory in use include core, disk, drum, tape, and semiconductor. Typical access times are:

| | |
|---|---|
| TTL RAM | 60 ns |
| MOS RAM | 300 ns |
| FIXED HEAD DISK OR DRUM | 8 ns |
| MOVING HEAD DISK | 50 ns |
| FLOPPY DISK | 100 ns |
| CASSETTE AND REEL TAPES | 10 s |

**memory address counter** A register used to point to the next location in memory for an instruction-fetch operation. The memory address counter may be a regular working register or a specially designed unit.

**memory address driver** A device or circuit used to supply signal requirements over transfer lines in memory systems.

**memory address register** A register (abbreviated *MAR*) used to hold the address of a data word to be read from or written into memory. The memory address register can also be used as an internal register for microprogram control during data transfers to and from the memory and peripherals.

**memory and device control unit** A unit that provides the external signals to communicate with peripheral devices, switch registers, and other memories.

**memory, backing** Considered to be the same as auxiliary storage; those units whose capacity is relatively larger when compared to working (scratch pad or internal) storage, but which have longer access times; their transfer capability is usually in blocks between storage units.

**Memory organization—hexadecimal addresses**

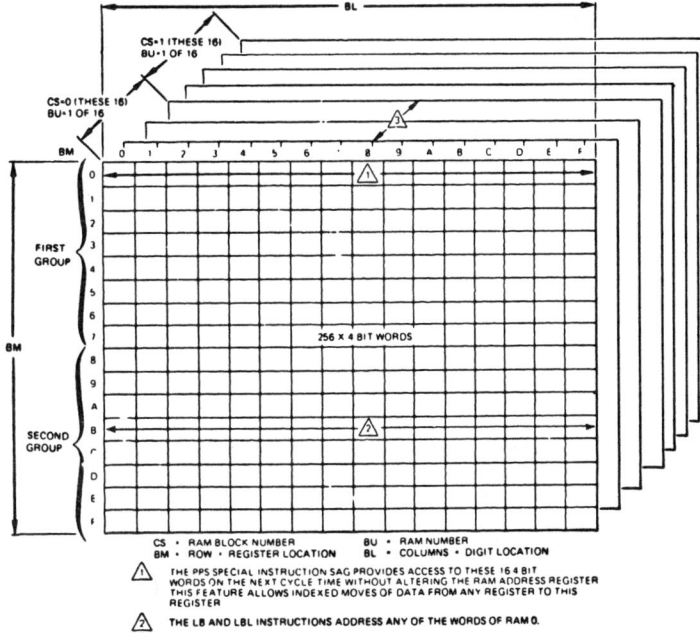

**memory buffer register** A register used to store words as they come from memory (read operation) or prior to entering memory (write operation).

**memory bus** The circuit path for communication between the CPU and memory. A memory bus may actually consist of three buses that are time-shared over a single bus:

1. Memory address bus
2. Memory-to-CPU data bus
3. CPU-to-memory data bus

**memory cache** A memory system that uses a limited but very fast semiconductor memory along with a slower but larger capacity memory. The overall effect of a larger and faster memory is achieved at reduced cost. Look-ahead procedures are used to locate and deposit the right information into the fast memory when it is needed.

**memory, CAM-cache** In some systems, when the CPU requests a word from memory, it checks a *content-addressable-memory* (CAM) for the location of the data. If the word is already in cache, it is sent to the CPU. If not, it is retrieved from main memory and sent through the cache to the CPU. Simultaneously, the cache is loaded with the addressed word plus the words from the adjacent memory locations. Because programs tend to be sequential in nature, the next location requested is likely now to be in cache. If requested, that word will then be transmitted to the CPU. In some systems, each memory board contains its own local cache and so the ratio of cache to memory remains constant no matter how many memory boards are used. This allows easy memory expansion.

**memory chip density** Refers to a fundamental form of raw semiconductor memory that typically ranges from 1024 to 16384 bits in a package that is 1/4 or 1/2 square inch.

**memory cycle** The operation and the time required for reading from and writing into memory.

**memory data register** A register (abbreviated *MDR*) that holds the last data word read from or written into the memory location addressed by the contents of the memory address register.

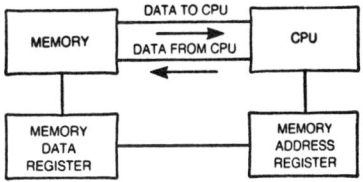

**Memory data and address registers**

**memory diagnostic** A routine used to check all memory locations for proper operation with a set of worst-case pattern tests.

**memory dump** An operation that causes a microcomputer to produce a listing of the contents of a storage device. A *dynamic* memory dump is concerned with only certain sections of memory under program control as a main routine is executed. A *differential* memory dump is concerned with only those words and bits that have been changed during execution of a routine.

**memory extender** A unit designed to provide powered channels for additional memory modules. A power fail recovery system is also available that will support a memory system for a minimum of hours in the event of a total power failure.

**memory, FIFO** Refers to a first-in-first-out memory scheme. These memories operate with a minimum of addressing logic; their separate write and read address inputs eliminate critical timing problems.

**memory fill** The placing of patterns of bits in memory registers not in use in order to stop the computer if the program seeks instructions from these registers.

**memory, interlaced** A memory with sequentially addressed locations occupying in physically separated positions in the storage media.

**memory latency time** The time required for the memory control hardware to move the memory medium to a position where it can be read.

**memory, magnetic** In magnetic memory technology, bits are represented by the presence or absence of magnetism at a certain spot or region on a magnetic medium that can be mechanically scanned. Mechanical scanning puts some limitations on the speed and convenience of such memory, but the low cost per bit and the high capacity of such memories has produced a high market demand that continues to grow.

**memory, main** Refers to the fastest storage device of a computer and the one from which instructions are executed. Contrast with *auxiliary storage*.

**memory management** Refers to the control and addressing scheme used for the total memory system. In some microcomputers, the memory management system controls the operation of user programs in a multiprogram environment.

**memory-mapped I/O** Refers to the use of memory type instructions to access the I/O devices. A memory-mapped system allows the processor to use the same instructions for memory transfers as it does for input/output transfers. An I/O port is treated as a memory location. The advantage is that the same instructions that are used for reading and writing memory may be used to input and output data. The traditional computer usually had many more memory instructions than I/O instructions. In a memory-mapped I/O computer, arithmetic can be performed directly on an input or output circuit or register without having to transfer the contents in and out of temporary intermediate registers. One disadvantage is that for each I/O port used this way, there is one fewer location available for memory. If all memory locations are needed as memory, memory-mapped I/O cannot be used. Also, instructions that operate on the memory may require three bytes to address the location of the port, but some I/O instructions may need only one byte to specify a port. Memory-mapped I/O instructions can also take longer to execute than I/O instructions because of the extra bytes. This problem can be solved by using short addressing modes.

**memory maps** These list the memory assignments made for the program. These maps prevent different routines from interfering with each other and help in determining the amount of memory needed as well as in finding the locations of subroutines and tables.

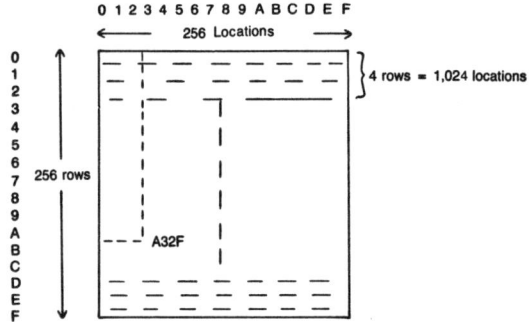

**Memory map**

**memory, metal oxide semiconductor (MOS)** A memory using a MOS semiconductor circuit.

**memory module** Refers to a semiconductor memory unit. One typical module contains 4096 words of 16 bits each. Modules may be stacked to obtain up to 65,536 words.

**memory parity** Refers to a procedure that generates and checks parity on each memory transfer and provides an interrupt if an error is detected.

**memory protect** A CPU option that protects the system from accidental modifications. The memory is set up into two segments, separating the operating system from user programs. If the user program attempts to modify the system, an interrupt occurs and the system takes control.

**memory protection option** Memory protect.

**memory, read only (ROM)** Refers to memory that cannot be altered in normal use of the computer. It usually contains often-used instructions in the form of firmware.

**memory register** A register used in all data and instruction registers between memory, the arithmetic unit, and the control register. The memory register may be involved in all transfers of data and instructions in either direction between memory and the ALU. The contents may be added to or subtracted from and are usually available until cleared. Also called *distributor, high-speed bus, arithmetic register, auxiliary register*, and *exchange register*.

**memory scan** An option that provides a rapid search of any part of memory for any word. With a memory-scan option, any block of locations may be searched using a single instruction.

**memory scratch pad** Refers to the central, high priority, small, immediate-access memory area of the CPU, with a significantly faster access time than the larger main store. This is normally used by the hardware and/or operating system for storing frequently used operands or instructions.

**memory, semiconductor (LSI)** 1. Refers to semiconductor flip-flop circuits in the form of large-scale storage units. They were originally used primarily for microcomputer storage registers and computational logic units (such as the arithmetic logic unit). 2. A memory whose

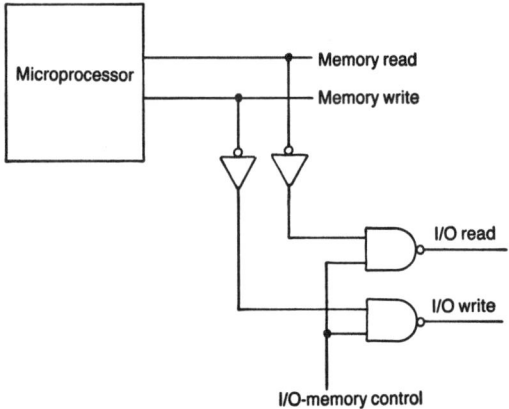

**Memory-mapped I/O configuration**

storage medium is semiconductor circuits, now the primary storage devices for most computers due to the use of large-scale integration (LSI) semiconductor chips.

**memory, static** Refers to a memory device that contains no mechanical moving parts or one that contains fixed information. Also refers to memory chips that do not need to be refreshed or clocked.

**memory timing generator** Circuits used in multiple-memory systems to determine where addresses should be written, which words should be sent to the CPU, and in what order they should be sent.

**memory typewriter** A kind of electronic typewriter with limited powers and capacities.

**memory unit** A memory unit is specified by the number of words (m) it contains and the number of bits in each word (n) as shown. The address selection lines select a particular word out of all the m words. Each word is assigned an identification address, starting from 0 and continuing up to m-1.

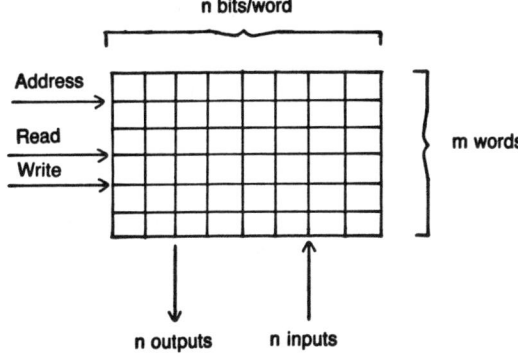

A typical memory unit

The selection of a specific word inside the memory is done by placing its address value on the selection lines or address bus. A decoder in the memory accepts this address and connects the paths required to select the word specified. Thus, k address bits will select one of $2^K$ = m words. Microprocessor memories may range from 1024 words, requiring an address of 10 bits, up to 1,048,576 = $2^{20}$ words or more, requiring an address of 20 bits. We usually refer to the number of words in a memory with the unit K, where K refers to 1024 = $2^{10}$ words; thus 1K = 1024 words, 4K = 4096 words, and 64K = 65,536 words.

**mercury (Hg)** A metallic element: atomic number 80, atomic weight 200.59, melts at 39°C, boils at 357°C; used in arc rectifiers and switches.

**mercury delay line** A delay circuit or system in which mercury is used as the medium of sound transmission.

**mercury storage** A storage system that uses the acoustic properties of mercury to store data.

**mercury tank** A container of mercury holding one of more delay lines.

**mercury vapor tube** 1. Any device in which an electric discharge takes place through mercury vapor. 2. A triode with mercury vapor, which is ionized by the passage of electrons and reduces the space charge and the anode potential necessary to maintain a given current.

**merge** To combine items into one sequenced file from two or more similarly sequenced files without changing the order of the items.

**mesa** A type of transistor in which one electrode is made smaller than the other to control bulk resistance. The base and emitter are raised above the collector.

**mesh** A set of branches forming a closed path in a network.

**mesh network** One formed from a number of impedances in series.

**mesic atom** A short-lived atom in which a negative muon has displaced a normal electron.

**meson field** That which is considered regarding the interchange of a proton and a neutron in a nucleus, with the mesons transferring energy.

**message** A transported item of information or a group of words that is transported as a unit.

**message blocking** The linking of several messages into a single transmission or record. Message blocking results in lower transmission overhead by reducing the delays due to changing the transmission direction of the communications link.

**message control program** The top-priority program that controls the sending and receiving of messages to and from remote terminals.

**message exchange** A device placed between a communication line and a computer to free the computer for other functions.

**message routing** The function of selecting the path or the alternate path by which the message will proceed to the next point in reaching its destination.

**message switching** The operation in which a message is received at a central location and stored on a direct-access device until the proper outgoing circuit is available for transmission to its destination.

**meta stepwise refinement** A software design method that uses the philosophy that the more times one does something, the better the final result is. The designer assumes a simple solution to the problem and then gradually builds in detail until a final solution is derived. Several refinements at the same level of detail are used by the designer each time the additional detail is required as shown in the figure. The best of these refinements is used for building more detailed versions.

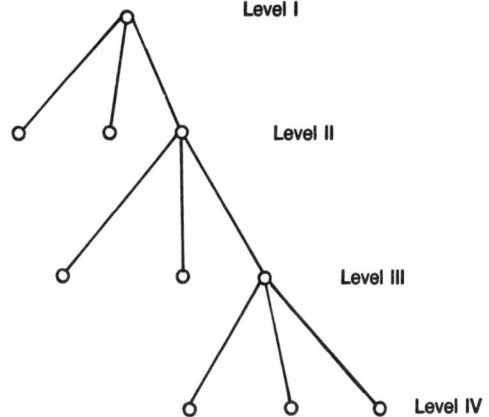

The MSR method for software design

**metal, base** Refers to the metal substrate on which one or more coatings of other materials or metals are deposited such as in printed circuits or connections.

**metal ceramic** An alloy of a ceramic and a metal that retains its useful properties at very high temperatures.

**metallic bond** A bond in which the valence electrons of the constituent atoms are free to move in the periodic lattice.

**metallic film resistor** A resistor formed by coating a high temperature insulator, such as mica, ceramic, glass, or quartz, with a metallic film.

**metal-oxide semiconductor** A semiconductor (abbreviated *MOS*) device in which a conducting channel is induced in the region between two electrodes by applying a field created by a voltage. MOS devices are self-isolating and can be fabricated in a smaller area than bipolar devices. They are less expensive to make in LSI configurations, but switching speeds are slower than bipolar units. MOS devices employ field-effect transistors in one of three functional configurations: NMOS, PMOS, and CMOS (for negative, positive, and complementary).

**metal-oxide-semiconductor memory** A memory using MOS technology.

**MEW** Abbreviation for *microwave early warning.*

**mf** Abbreviation for *medium frequency,* 300 kHz to 3 MHz.

**MFB** Abbreviation for *mixed functional block.*

**MFC** Abbreviation for *magnetic-tape field scan.*

**MFM** Abbreviation for *mixed functional module.*

**MFS** Abbreviation for *magnetic-tape field scan.*

**MHz** Abbreviation for *million hertz or cycles per second.* A computer that operates at 4 MHz has a clock cycle time of 25 billionths of a second.

**MIC** Abbreviation for *microwave integrated circuit.*

**mica** A naturally occurring mineral that may be sheared into very thin sheets. In the very clear form it is an extremely good insulator even at very high temperatures and is used in capacitors. It is also employed as an insulator for high temperature connections.

**MICR** Abbreviation for *magnetic-ink character recognition.*

**MICR code** A magnetic-ink character-recognition code developed for the American Bankers Association. It uses a set of 10 numeric symbols along with 4 special symbols; the characters are visually readable through the use of magnetic sensing heads in various types of sensing equipment.

**micro** 1. Prefix for one-millionth ($10^{-6}$). 2. A microcomputer, a microprocessor, or the system built using either.

**microampere** ($\mu a$) Equal to $10^{-6}$ ampere.

**microcircuit** A circuit fabricated from integrated elements in such a way as to make the elements inseparable and the circuit miniaturized.

**microcircuit isolation** The electrical insulation of circuit elements from the electrically conducting silicon wafer. The two main techniques are oxide isolation and diode isolation.

**microcode** The microprocessor operational instructions that cause the device to respond to user-programmed instructions. A single user-programmed instruction may involve many microcode instructions, and each microcode instruction occurs during a microcycle. Some microcodes are user-programmable, and this allows tailoring a microprocessor to fit a particular language, making it competitive with larger machines that do not allow modifications of their basic structure.

**microcommand** A command issued in microcode used to specify elementary machine operations or microcycles that are to be performed within a basic machine cycle.

**microcomputer** A complete small computing system consisting of hardware and software. The hardware includes the microprocessing unit, memory, auxiliary circuits, power supply, and control panel. The main processing blocks are typically fabricated with LSI circuit packages.

Dramatic decreases in the costs of microcomputer hardware, achieved through a high level of circuit integration, have opened up new applications for computers. These include consumer and control applications in which low-cost programmable logic is required.

Microcomputers have been applied to games, controllers, terminals, and instruments with considerable success. A number of features of microcomputers have led to this success.

1. Product costs are greatly reduced
2. Products get to market faster
3. Product capability is greater, allowing a higher product price
4. Development time and costs are lower
5. Reliability is increased, reducing service costs

A typical microcomputer has the CPU on a single chip or circuit board; the system also contains ROM, and storage for programs and data along with clock circuits, input and output units, selector registers, and control circuits. The console control panel typically has an alphanumeric keyboard and a display screen. The keyboard is an input port available for microcomputers. Software includes assemblers, loaders, source editors, debugging and diagnostic routines, and cross assemblers. All microcomputers can use assemblers and most are supported by cross assemblers on commercial time-sharing networks, which allow the user to develop and debug the software using a high-level operating system.

Software can also be developed on the microcomputer; this approach tends to be slower, but it does have other advantages:

1. Low cost for the software development tools
2. Online program execution
3. Debugging of the actual hardware

Despite their many advantages, microcomputers do have some disadvantages. They are not as efficient for high-speed applications such as data acquisition and communications as minicomputers and larger machines. Because of the high level of integration, testing is difficult and sometimes places a burden on the user in trying to develop effective diagnostics during product development.

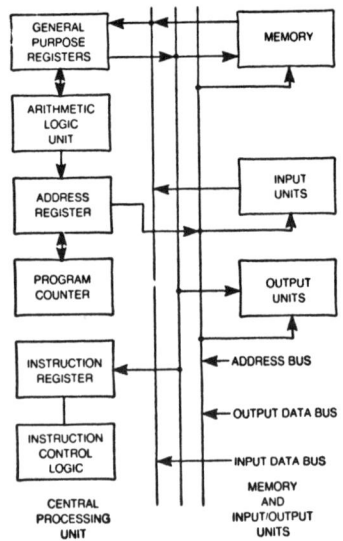

**Microcomputer structure**

**microcomputer applications** The typical microcomputer application is a task that is small, relatively fixed, not too demanding of input/output paths, and requiring fast, efficient arithmetic.

The typical "applied" microcomputer itself is a small box with a convenient mounting arrangement. It has its own self-contained power supply, along with terminals to which wires or cables are connected that lead to sensors and output devices such as keyboards, as well as temperature and pressure sensors, level detectors, and flowmeters. Output devices include automatic typewriters, printers, video screens, electric motors, valves, solenoids, lighted displays, and actuators of various types.

The microcomputer may also "talk" to larger computers, floppy disks, magnetic tapes, remote terminals, and other peripherals.

**microcomputer control system** In a typical input/output system four chips are required, as shown below. The 4040 microprocessor and a clock chip, the 4201 are used. The 4002 RAM provides the read/write I/O capabilities. A 4308 I/O chip provides the program storage and I/O capabilities.

In most designs it is desirable to reduce the number of components, so chips that incorporate both memory and I/O facilities are used when available. In a larger system, where expansion capability would be essential, the memory and I/O chips would be separate. The 4002 and the 4308 chips allow both memory and I/O facilities. Each has 16 lines of I/O. The use of these lines will be discussed shortly. The basic I/O controller provides input facilities through the keyboard and display facilities through a four digit display. It also communicates with an external microcomputer using a 16 bit bus. The program is contained in the 4308 ROM. A scratch pad area for storing temporary data and for intermediate computations is contained in the 4002.

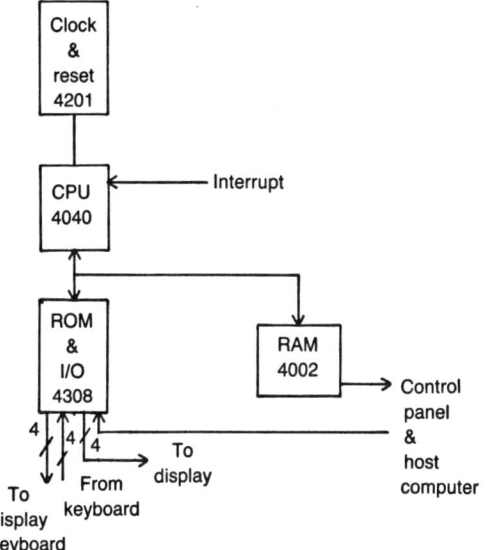

**Basic microcomputer control system**

In the input/output functions provided by the 4308, four pins were used to connect the columns of a 16 key keyboard. The scanning technique was used. Four pins collect the data from the four keyboard rows. Four other pins connect the LED display. Three lines would be used for seven segment LEDs. The remaining four bits are used for a control panel or for communicating with the host computer. Communications to this computer used 16 lines from the 4002.

**microcomputer CPU** Generally, the CPU consists of the following: program counter (PC), instruction register (IR), instruction execution logic, a memory address register (MAR), general purpose register file, and an arithmetic logic unit (ALU).

**microcomputer development system** A prototyping system of hardware and software that allows the user to design, debug, and modify programs. These systems can compose programs; emulate the CPU, memory, and input/output units; and automate all debugging operations. Errors in the programs can be detected before masks are made, and implementation of high-level languages is allowed. Many systems operate in parallel with the standard instruction set. A typical development system includes:

1. Console or panel for control and monitoring functions
2. Processor card or board
3. Random-access-memory card
4. Programmable read-only-memory card
5. Input/output ports
6. Teletypewriter interface
7. PROM programmer
8. Self-contained enclosure with power supplies

Software includes a debug program, editor, assembler, and PROM programmer. Standard documentation consists of instruction books and programming manuals.

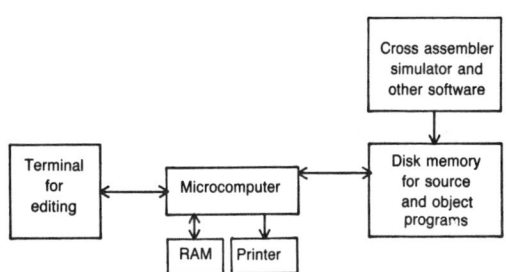

**Microcomputer development system**

**microcomputer disk development system (MDOS)** A hardware development aid that generally features self-diagnostic capability and a comprehensive repertoire of software for error free data. Software development on this system has several advantages. During the assembly process, the entire program listing need not be printed to find assembly errors. Instead, the system prints out only those statements that contain assembly errors.

**microcomputer execution cycle** The microcycles required for a microcomputer to execute an instruction. A typical execution cycle is:

1. Fetch instruction from memory
2. Store in instruction register
3. Decode instruction
4. Execute operation defined by instruction

**microcomputer hydraulic system** When the microcomputer control concept is extended to hydraulic motors, it works as follows: an electric machine is used to create hydraulic pressure that will drive the hydraulic motor. A control valve, arranged between the hydraulic pressure generator and the hydraulic motor, is opened or closed depending upon the motor's status. The microcomputer can be used to activate the valve.

**microcomputer instrument** A scientific instrument that used microcomputers to control the collection, conversion, and recording of data. Examples include spectrometers and interferometers.

**microcomputer interfacing kit** A set of hardware designed to permit customer interfacing of peripherals. A typical kit has a prewired card frame that will accommodate from 6 to 18 modules. The user selects the proper modules and wires in the mating system connector.

**microcomputer kit** A set of hardware or software or both that allows the user to configure a microcomputer system to a particular product application. A kit can be a collection of logic modules that are assembled by the user to a prewired system unit. Kits that allow the processor to communicate with a variety of peripherals are available. Provisions that are included allow interrupts at a hard-wired priority level and conversion of analog monitoring voltages.

Many kits are complete enough so that they can be wired for the user's configuration and used immediately. They include all the components needed as well as full documentation. Many have enough input/output and memory capacity to implement an instrument controller, a point-of-sale terminal, a communications interface, an industrial robot, or a sophisticated game. Kits contain the microprocessor, RAM, EROM, input/output ports, and support circuitry including a master clock, interrupts, DMA control, control panel circuits, and display. Some kits have interfaces for a teletypewriter and cassette tape unit.

Software usually includes a monitor, an editor, and an assembler program. The programs can be run directly on the CPU and loaded on cassette tape in less than 60 seconds. System capabilities include:

1. Program load and dump on cassette tape
2. Debug commands
3. Display and store memory
4. Display, set, and clear breakpoints
5. Display and set contents of all registers
6. Manual interrupt for program start and restart
7. Execute programs from memory
8. Memory protect

**microcomputer kit assembler** A software package used to generate object programs from a source program written in symbolic assembly language. Some assemblers process the source program in two passes. In the first pass, the assembler reads the source tape and generates a symbol table for storage in the memory. During the second pass, the symbolic instructions from the symbol table are converted into binary data. This system allows a number of options during the second pass, such as:

1. Generate a listing on the CRT display
2. Generate a listing for the printer
3. List only lines with errors
4. Generate an object tape

**micrcomputer machine control** Microcomputers can be used as machine controllers. Besides economical considerations, other important features to be considered are the space it takes compared to relays, the reliability of the integrated circuits, and the noise immunity level. Programmable controllers take very little space; the components are extensively tested, and excellent noise immunity is accomplished through the use of high threshold logic.

**microcomputer POS** A *point-of-sale* system in which the cash register is a special-purpose computer terminal. The POS system can monitor and record transactions directly in the store's data files, perform credit checks, and handle other marketing functions.

**microcomputer prototyping system** A hardware and software kit that allows the user to develop a prototype system to his own specifications. The system includes a chassis, control panel, power supplies, and one or more RAMs in addition to the processor cards. Using a teletypewriter unit, the system provides everything needed for evaluation of the processor cards.

**micrcomputer support devices** Equipment used to complement such peripherals as paper-tape readers and punch machines, card readers, printers, floppy disk drives, cassette drives, PROM programmers, and terminals.

**microcomputer terminal** A terminal that uses a microcomputer for intelligence. Microcomputer terminals usually have formatting and error-correction capability and can act as stand-alone data collection centers.

**microcomputer timing modules** Circuits used to clock the microcomputer. The real-time clock module, the resettable clock module, the pulse accumulator, and the time-of-day module are considered as *special* timing modules.

**microcomputer word processing** Microcomputer applications include the office equipment application of word processing. Before the appearance of microcomputers, this application clearly required a minicomputer. To support a small office, the minicomputer was relatively costly; the microcomputer helped bring the cost down to a reasonable level. This application also benefited from the development of the floppy disk as a relatively inexpensive text storage medium. Microcomputers are also used in small business accounting and recordkeeping systems. A microcomputer can handle these functions in a relatively standardized format if the information traffic is not too heavy.

**microcontroller** A device or instrument that controls a process with a high degree of resolution; it typically consists of a microprocessor, memory, and appropriate interfaces. A microcontroller is distinguished from a data-processing microcomputer by its shorter word length and inability to accommodate some types of arithmetic operations.

**microcontroller design system** A microcontroller design system provides resources to aid in design implementation. Emphasis is placed on the designer's application knowledge rather than a knowledge of component design. Software support is usually provided to facilitate programming and minimize errors during the design. In addition, resources are available to the designer to operate and diagnose a system in real time at the hardware level.

**microcontroller interface** A microcontroller can become a tool for the designer to use to implement a programmable logic design. The capability exists in the system to store and execute control sequences. A typical interface uses a uniform method of input/output connection that accepts variable field length sizes; additional, expensive, custom circuitry for I/O is often not required. The programmed microcontroller becomes the controlling subsystem in the overall specified system.

**microcycle** One of the operational steps required for a microprocessor to execute an instruction. Typically, one microcycle might be used to fetch the instruction, one or two more might be used for data access, and several more may be required for execution.

**microdiagnostic** A test routine used to exercise the microprocessor and detect faults. Microdiagnostics are usually controlled by the microprocessor control store, which may be a RAM to allow writing capability. On most systems, microdiagnostics can detect a problem in a few seconds.

**microelectronics** The technology of fabricating functional circuits using subassemblies comprised of integrated-circuit packages.

**microfiche** A sheet of film, usually 4 by 6 inches, used to store printed or graphic material that has been reduced 12 to 38 times by photographic methods.

**microfilm** A film in the form of a strip that is used to hold a photographic record of printed or graphic material that may be enlarged for viewing or reproduction.

**microfunction decoder** An MSI arithmetic logic function especially useful in microcomputer systems. Microfunction decoders perform look-ahead operations for carry and shift functions, usually in a single microcycle.

**microinstruction** The microcode required for a microcyle. Microinstructions are stored within a microprogram; they specify the sequential operations of individual computing elements.

**microinstruction decoder** The logic used to interpret the microinstructions and provide signals to control data transfers, arithmetic operations, and sequences.

**microinstruction display** Refers to a display that can be implemented in binary, octal, or hexadecimal. During a single step execution, it is useful to display the current microinstruction being executed; with the help of the display, errors can be more quickly identified and corrected.

**micronstruction sequence** The series of microinstructions that the microprogram control unit selects from the microprogram to execute a single macroinstruction or command.

**microkit** A microcomputer system kit that usually consists of a CPU, keyboard, CRT display, and cassette tape units.

**micrologic cards** Circuit boards that provide a logic family for use in wired or programmable logic systems. Typical micrologic cards include flip-flops, arithmetic functions, counters, converters, timing circuits, analog and digital converters, line and lamp drivers, motor controls, signal shapers, and input/output isolation circuits.

**microm** A read-only memory integrated circuit containing microcode.

**microminiaturization** The production and use of circuits and components with very small dimensions, especially with regard to the scaling down of already-miniature circuits. An example of microminiaturization is the development of LSI chips that perform the functions once performed by circuit cards containing several MSI chips.

**micromodule** A small electronic device capable of performing one or more circuit functions, and possessing the feature of replaceability as a (usually) plug-in element.

**micron** A unit of length equal to one millionth of a meter. The term has recently been supplanted in the International System of Units (SI) by *micrometer.*

**microprocessing unit** The main part of the hardware (abbreviated *MPU*) for a microcomputer. The MPU consists of the microprocessor, the main memory, input/output ports, and the clock circuit. It does not contain power supplies, enclosure, or control panel, and it is usually on a single circuit board. The level of complexity of the microcomputer is a direct function of the MPU.

**microprocessor** The LSI equivalent of a computer's central processing unit, designed to work as a sequential computational or control unit by executing a defined set of instructions contained in memory. In a microcomputer with a fixed instruction set, the microprocessor may consist of an arithmetic logic unit and a control logic unit. For a microcomputer with a microprogrammed logic set, it may contain an additional control memory unit. The microprocessor determines what devices should have access to data and makes these decisions based upon timing requirements. It also correlates the activities of the memory and input/output units.

All microprocessors use large-scale integrated circuit technology; some feature a single-chip construction while others use several chips. The division or partitioning of functions is based on considerations of word length, flexibility, and performance.

Programmability can be obtained on one or two levels. The microinstruction level provides a very detailed level of control. The microinstructions can be combined to obtain a macroinstruction set which is then used to write control programs.

Control programs can sometimes be written in microcode to provide increased execution speed and more detailed control at the expense of more difficult programming. Microprocessors that are not microprogrammable use fixed, general-purpose instruction sets which are usually adequate for most applications.

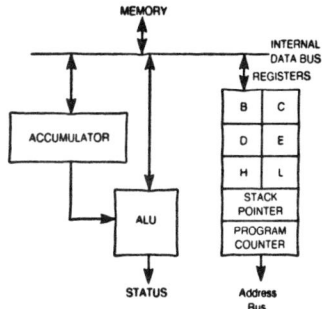

**Typical Microprocessor Structure**

Key features of individual microprocessors include word length, architecture, speed, and programming flexibility. Word length depends upon the requirements for resolution, accuracy, and the width of parallel inputs and outputs.

Microprocessors are structured for fixed word lengths, or for modular expansion using the bit-slice approach. In some microprocessors, the word lengths used for addresses are greater than those used for instructions. Longer word lengths for either instructions or addresses provide higher system throughput and more powerful memory addressing; shorter word lengths can require less hardware and smaller memories.

Architecture can include general-purpose registers, stacking, interrupts, interface structure, and some integral memory. General-purpose registers may be used for addressing, indexing, and status. They can simplify programming and reduce memory by eliminating memory buffering. Stacking permits subroutine nesting and temporary storage of data when programs are placed in ROM. Stacks consist of RAM memory locations maintained by software or stack register hardware.

The interface structure should be simple to use and not too costly for the application. Separate buses for addressing, data and memory are usually the best solution.

Memories can be a major portion of hardware cost. PROMs are used for program storage in many systems, while RAMs are used for variable data storage and program storage during development. The modular concept tends to reduce overall costs while allowing the most efficient system to be determined during development.

Cycle and instruction times along with other functional operational times do not give as good an indication of useful speed as a benchmark program for a specific task.

Programming flexibility can be determined from the nature of the instruction set. Multiple addressing modes conserve memory, simplify programming, and increase processing speed. Indexing and pointer addressing can be used to access tables stored in ROM or PROM. Custom instructions using microprogramming can improve overall performance by optimizing the microprocessor structure. Other features that aid programming include bit and byte manipulation, microprogram emulation, multiply and divide instructions, and double-precision arithmetic capability.

A typical microprocessor has an ALU and a number of registers to provide temporary storage. The accumulator is usually the one essential general-purpose register. It can serve as both a source and a destination register for operations involving another register, the ALU, or memory. Other general-purpose registers are used to store intermediate data and operands.

The program counter is a dedicated register used to count and track the program instructions by maintaining the address of the next instruction in memory. Each time that the microprocessor fetches an instruction, it increments the program counter so that it always indicates the following instruction. The fetched instruction, in the form of an operation code, is sent to the instruction register to be decoded.

**microprocessor alarm systems** A system, based on light, sound, and temperature, that uses various transducers and sensing devices to measure the required variables and provide inputs to a multiplexer. The microprocessor scans these input points at operator-selected time intervals by supplying a point address to the multiplexer. The data is read, processed, and checked against alarm limits.

Critical deviations from normal operating conditions are detected and alarms are sent to the control/acknowledgment terminal. The terminal formats and routes the alarm data to an operators display panel. The operator on duty observes the detected alarm and takes the necessary steps to correct the problem. Some alarms can be detected directly by limit switches or continuity breakage, or by manually pressing a button. Examples include spills, fire, burglary, or accident alarms. These crisis conditions require immediate attention and would therefore be implanted as prioritized vector interrupts in the monitor. Fast response and quick operator notification may require the sounding of an audible alarm.

**microprocessor analyzer** An instrument used for designing, troubleshooting and testing both hardware and software in systems that use microprocessors. The analyzer is used with an oscilloscope and can display data related to a selected instruction cycle. Some types interface to the system using a connector that clips directly onto the microprocessor.

**microprocessor architecture** The architectural features of a microprocessor include the number and type of general purpose registers, stacks, interrupts, interface structure and memories. General purpose registers are used for addressing, indexing and status and as multiple accumulators. They simplify programming and conserve main memory by eliminating the memory buffering of data. Multiple accumulators are especially useful for programs that require much arithmetic or data movement.

**microprocessor assembler simulator** A program that accepts microprocessor assembly language, edits the text, and then allows the user to debug the software on a simulation of the microprocessor. A microprocessor assembler simulator provides about 60% to 80% assurance that the final software product will work.

**microprocessor automation** This remains as one of the most resourceful areas yet for the valuable design tools available using microprocessors. By using the new techniques one can turn vague requirements into firm specifications and near flawless programs quickly.

**microprocessor cache memory** A storage area that is used in addition to the main memory. A typical cache memory contains a cluster of bipolar devices in four blocks of four words each. When addressing memory, the CPU checks the cache and the main memory. If the cache is full, data is transferred to the main memory. A cache system can save CPU time when checking for errors.

**microprocessor card** A circuit board that contains a microprocessor or microprocessing elements. A 144-pin edge connector is used for interfacing to other units.

**microprocessor chip** The single piece of doped silicon upon which the microprocessor CPU is fabricated.

**microprocessor chip set** A group of LSI semiconductors that can be connected to form a microcomputer.

**microprocessor code assembler** Assembler programs for microcodes. The code assembler can also test the microprogram and is generally written in FORTRAN IV for running on a large computer system.

**microprocessor compiler** A program that translates the source program into machine language. Compiler programs can be run on medium to large computers, and are available from time-sharing service firms.

**microprocessor components** The hardware parts of a particular microprocessor configuration such as ALU, control logic, and register array.

**microprocessor configurations** At the core of the microcomputer system is a microprocessor with its arithmetic processing circuits and control memory for its instruction set. Even a simple microcomputer system and its microprocessor require a list of instructions in order to perform a task along with control of input/output operations and communications. A typical microprocessor configuration is shown in the figure.

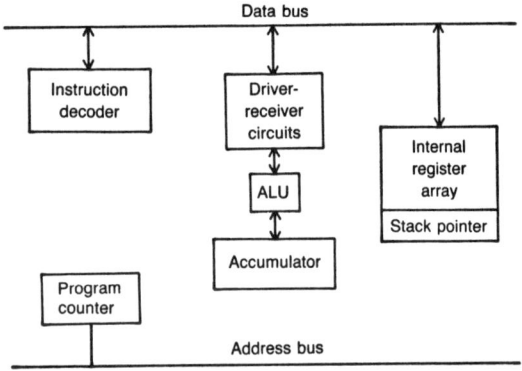

**A typical microprocessor configuration**

**microprocessor controller** A usually dedicated controller built around a microprocessor; a microcontroller.

**microprocessor, CRT display** Refers to a display built around a microprocessor controller. The microprocessor controls both information readout by the operator and the setting methods.

**microprocessor data logging** Data logging systems that are fundamentally instruments are now available with integral microprocessors. With a wide variety of available peripherals, the microprocessor can analyze the data, perform computations, limit tests, and averages. It can also record the entire data set or only portions or summaries. Most systems provide internal processing of the data by the microprocessor, replacing the online analyzing previously performed by a minicomputer. In addition, the micro can perform functions such as the linearization of thermocouple curves.

**microprocessor debugging program** A program that resides in microprocessor memory and is used during system development to assist in debugging operations. A typical debugging program has the following capabilities:

1. Load contents of external storage
2. Write contents of memory
3. Inspect memory
4. Move and set program breakpoints
5. Start program printout
6. Modify memory

**microprocessor economic feasibility** The crossover point between fixed and programmable logic depends on the application, but economics tends to favor the microprocessor when the number of integrated circuit packages required to implement the control of a dedicated logic system approaches thirty or forty. The improving cost/performance ratio, however, makes the programmable approach attractive for many less complex circuits, especially when product line continuity is important.

**microprocessor educator system** A microprocessor-based communications terminal used for program development. A typical system contains:

1. 53-key input keyboard
2. A 64-character, 31-line CRT display
3. 110 bps teletypewriter
4. Composite video output for remote display

**microprocessor-equipped traffic control** This system uses a standard microprocessor plus the required interface. All system functions are accomplished by the program. A typical system is illustrated in the next column. A microprocessor-based board provides the memory, I/O, and CPU facilities. Two modules are shown on the top of the illustration: they are the real time clock, for precise timing of external events, and the power fail restart unit for restarting the system after a power failure and for preserving data when a power failure is detected. Sensing and control are based on the information provided by the vehicle detectors. A rectangle is cut in the pavement and two or more loops of wire are deposited inside the groove. The loop is connected to an RC oscillating circuit. The frequency of oscillation will depend on the impedance of the loop. The presence of a large magnetic mass, such as a car, over part or all of the loop causes a change in inductance and oscillating frequency.

**microprocessor, industrial control** Microcomputers are cheaper

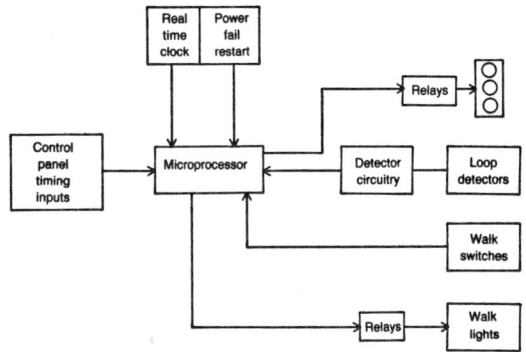

Traffic control system

than minicomputers; they are smaller, and some are even more flexible, and they are being rapidly applied in warehouse equipment, numerical and process controllers, and manufacturing machines. The use of microprocessors in industrial equipment can require special design techniques. Industrial environments present several design problems that include noise, physical distance between sources of variables, power consumption and dissipation, I/O interfacing, and future expansion plans. Ambient electrical noise and line transients that typically occur in plant environments often require special circuitry and components to ensure reliable system operation.

**microprocessor instruction set** The group of instructions that are a part of the basic software for a given microprocessor. A typical instruction set may have 50 to 100 different instructions, including binary and decimal arithmetic, shift, rotate, load, store, interrupt, and stack.

**microprocessor instrument** A scientific instrument that contains a microprocessor for calculations and error corrections due to drift and other variations.

**microprocessor intelligence** The control program used to guide the microprocessor through the various operations it must perform.

**microprocessor language assembler** A software package used to assemble source code on a minicomputer and convert it into binary output for loading into the microprocessor.

**microprocessor language editor** A software set provided in the form of a binary tape that is then loaded into memory using a special program. Language editors are used primarily for creating and modifying source program tapes. Once in memory, the program text can be changed, deleted, and reformatted.

**microprocessor maintenance console** A diagnostic tool that interfaces with some types of microprocessors. The maintenance console can display and simulate the contents of any memory location and register in the microprocessor system. It can also display outputs and simulate inputs.

**microprocessor master/slave systems** Processor organization or configuration depends to some extent on factors such as the number of I/O ports and their location, the type of I/O ports and activity rate, the type of processing required, and the microcomputer cost performance characteristics. Two basic organizations used are master/master and master/slave. Either organization (or any other) can perform the four basic system functions. The master/slave arrangement imposes a rigid hierarchy on subsystem components. All slave processors communicate to a single master, which acts as either a concentrator or information switch assigned to control the subsystems communication activity.

**microprocessor, military** For military designs it is necessary to consider microprocessors that have the required environmental characteristics. Many microprocessors are available in an M version for the extended temperature range as well as some of the other military specifications. Few microprocessors, however, are qualified to the specifications of the 38510 JAN program.

**microprocessor modem** A modulator-demodulator device under dedicated microprocessor control.

**microprocessor monitor** A system monitor gives users complete control over the operation of the system. All necessary functions for program loading and execution are provided, while additional commands implement extensive debugging facilities. These facilities include the capability to examine and modify memory or CPU register contents, set program breakpoints, and initiate program execution at any given address. Users can dynamically reassign system peripherals via monitor commands through calls to the system monitor's I/O subroutines.

**microprocessor registers** A typical set of registers in a microprocessor is shown. Registers have different purposes; some microprocessors allow the programmer to assign different functions to registers. Most registers, however, are permanently assigned.

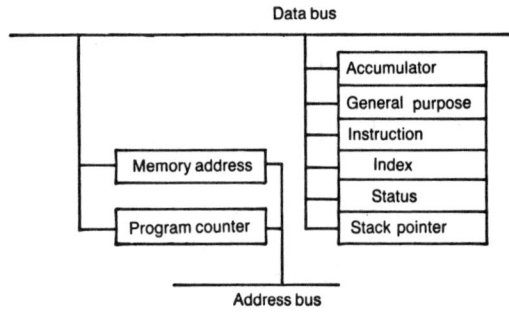

**Microprocessor registers**

**microprocessor ROM programmer** A program that is used to load, verify, and modify programs in a PROM device. Data is usually entered by means of paper tapes produced from a teletypewriter keyboard.

**microprocessor, 6800** A typical microprocessor like the 6800 has eight pins to which wires are attached for the movement of data into and out of the device. These eight wires constitute the data bus, and information can flow in both directions along the bus (during different times). This technique is called multiplexing. In addition to the data bus, the 6800 microprocessor has a group of 16 pins to which wires that are used to move binary words called addresses can be attached; together they are called the *address bus*. The address bus carries information outward only from the microprocessor to memory and input/output chips. The signals on the address bus are used to select a certain part of memory or I/O section.

There is also a group of assorted control signals that enter and leave the microprocessor. Some of these may carry control signals back and forth between the microprocessor and the memory and I/O chips. They are usually grouped together and called the *control bus*. Other wires may go back and forth between the microprocessor and support chips. No connection is made directly to the registers, the ALU, or other internal components. Microprocessors have many of the features common to all computers. The characteristic that makes the microprocessor unique is that the CPU is contained in just a few integrated circuit packages.

**microprocessor slice** Refers to the building-block approach of a 2- or 4-bit microprocessor that can be ganged to build 8-, 16-, 24-, or 32-bit systems. A longer word length provides higher throughput and easier programming, while shorter word lengths require less hardware and smaller memories.

**microprocessor system analyzer** An instrument used to design, troubleshoot, and test both programs and hardware in microprocessor systems. A system analyzer can test programs and hardware either together or individually and can be connected or disconnected in a short time using clip-type connectors.

**microprocessor terminal** A terminal that uses microprocessor circuits for intelligence capabilities; a smart terminal.

**microprocessor timing** The timing cycle for a microprocessor can be generated from a pair of signals that are obtained from a clock generator circuit that uses a quartz crystal as a frequency source. Two timing signals to generate the phases are shown below. By outlining the two instruction periods of influence, you can see that the instructions are overlapped in order to make better use of the bus system.

A new instruction is obtained every clock cycle and a single cycle instruction is completed every clock cycle. The actual time to complete an instruction is dependent upon the specific instruction being executed. Even though there may be variations in the actual instruction times, these variations are transparent to the programmer and the system user.

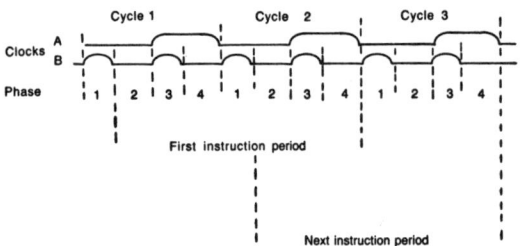

**Typical microprocessor timing**

**microprocessor training aid** A hardware unit designed to help the user master the software of 4- and 8-bit microprocessors. The training aid contains memory circuits for program and data storage, with a front panel for display and control of addressing and CPU status. It gives the student training in the use of the instruction set and provides software solutions to hardware problems.

**microprogram** A program of instructions that do not reference the main memory. The microprogram is constructed from the basic subcommands, and it is sometimes a sequence of pseudo commands that are translated into machine commands by hardware. A microprogram tends to obtain maximum utilization of the subcommands by directly controlling the operation of each functional element in the microprocessor by using microcode. The microprogram can be used to implement a higher-language program by storing the microinstructions in ROM.

**microprogram, bipolar** The microprogrammed approach is useful for bipolar microcomputers because complex macroinstruction sets can be realized as sequences of relatively primitive microinstructions. The logic of the final macromachine remains relatively simple, with most of the complexity being represented by the contents of the control memory. When used with a Central Processing Element (CPE) slice, the basic microinstruction functions are established, although additional logical elements drawn from standard TTL families may be added, which may alter or enhance the microinstruction set.

**microprogram control section** Refers to the area of a microprogrammed computer that determines control action for the microprograms. The control section is similar to a processor within a processor; actions are usually determined by a microprogram stored in ROM, the control store. Instructions usually are very basic, and control is at a detailed level with a very short execution time.

**microprogram control unit** A functional unit (abbreviated *MCU*) used in bipolar microprocessors to maintain and generate microprogram addresses. It is also used to control carry and shift operations, and with an interrupt control unit, to set the interrupt structure. The MCU uses the next address field rather than a program counter. The microprogram addresses are arranged in a two-dimensional array or matrix. Each microinstruction is selected by its row and column address.

**microprogram display** A special board used on some systems for display and debug operations. It can be used to trap, latch, and display the control signals from the microprogram for an interface into the machine operations.

**microprogram emulation process** Microprogrammed devices are sequential logic circuits using ROM, which within some time constraints can be used to simulate the performance of any sequential logic network. The simulation process is referred to as *emulation*. The ability of the device to emulate effectively is determined to a great degree by the address selection or sequencing portion of the unit. In microprogrammed devices with short microinstruction words, the design usually involves combining a program counter technique with a global branch instruction format. In larger systems truncated addressing schemes are more frequent.

**microprogram indexing** A technique used to locate data within a memory and count the number of times an operation is performed in a microprogram. Indexing can be used to point to a data item in a list of words, or count the number of times an inner loop in an instruction is used.

**microprogrammable instruction** An instruction that does not reference main memory and may have several shift, skip, or transfer commands to be performed.

**microprogrammable processor** A processor in which the instruction set is not firmly fixed. The instruction set is defined in memory, which is fetched to control the data paths of the machine. Since the contents and interpretation are defined in memory, the meaning and effect of the instruction can be changed by changing the contents of the memory.

**microprogrammed processor** A processor or computer whose instruction set is not fixed, but can be tailored to specific needs by the programming of ROMs or other memory units; a microprogrammable processor.

**microprogrammed sequencer** A device that generates, increments, and stores addresses. It can branch anywhere in memory, perform a subroutine, and then return.

**microprogrammed subroutines** Subroutines are programs designed to be used by other routines to accomplish a particular purpose. These routines can be called from numerous points within the main body of the program. In microprogramming, subroutines are also used. This is because many microprograms contain similar or identical sections of code. For example, many memory reference instructions in a computer system all use the same logical sequence in generating the address for an instruction, and therefore, this sequence could be a subroutine called from within a body of code that executes the addressing algorithm.

**microprogramming** The techniques of modifying an instruction set by building higher-level instructions from basic elemental operations. The higher-level instructions can then be directly programmed. For example, if a machine has basic instructions for addition, subtraction, and multiplication, an instruction for division could be defined by microprogramming. Microprogramming adds flexibility to the microcomputer. Compared to conventional programming, the distinctive feature is the storage associated with the control unit. In microprogramming, a user instruction determines an address in control memory that provides the starting point for executing the microprogrammed steps.

The development of inexpensive semiconductor memory has resulted in a wider use of microprogramming techniques. Microprogramming, enhances flexibility by allowing the machine to optimize its control memory for specific applications. This ability to adjust can greatly simplify programming. Microprogramming is generally slow, since each user instruction requires that a sequence of programmed steps be executed. Control storage ROM must be fast enough to allow the use of a separate clock that is five to ten times faster than that used for main memory.

In *monophase* microprogramming, each microinstruction requires a clock pulse period for execution, while in *polyphase* microprogramming, the microinstruction requires more than a single clock period. Monophase operation involves shorter instructions and a shorter instruction set. Polyphase operation needs fewer instructions and is faster, but more complex to implement.

Microprogramming can aid system testing. Checking all data paths is difficult at the machine-language level, but microdiagnostics can check each path to isolate faults by checking functions rather than combinations of functions, as with conventional diagnostics.

Microprogramming is not, however, without its disadvantages:

1. Expensive compared to writing programs
2. Tends to be application- and machine-peculiar
3. Relatively slow
4. High debugging costs

Microprogramming techniques have been implemented in terminals, calculators, peripheral controllers, processors, and instruments with success.

**microprogramming parameterization** A technique of microprogramming that uses stored parameters to characterize the state of the program. These parameters can be stored as program status words that are then tested to determine what actions should be initiated.

**microsecond** A time period equal to $10^{-6}$ second (one millionth of one second).

**microwave** Electromagnetic wavelengths shorter than 300 cm (frequencies above 1 GHz).

**migration** Refers to the movement of atoms within a metal or among metals in contact, such as the problem of the movement of atoms during plating of one metal over another. Migration can occur during the production of printed circuit boards and often prevents one metal from performing its function as a protective coating.

**MIIS** Abbreviation for *metal-insulation-insulation-semiconductor*, a semiconductor "sandwich" which uses stored charges between two layers of insulation for nonvolatile memory. MIIS is used with the silicon-on-sapphire process to produce a memory that is independent of the external power supply.

**mil** A unit of length equal to $10^{-3}$ inches used in measurements of small thicknesses, such as thin sheets.

**Miller-Pierce oscillator** A crystal stabilized oscillator in which a quartz crystal is connected between the grid and cathode of a triode, a parallel resonant circuit being formed in series with the anode.

**million bit CCD** A memory of charge-coupled devices that has a storage density of 1 million bits per board. One board contains 64 memory devices plus the logic and drive circuits to operate it as a complete memory system or as a plug-in subsystem of a larger memory. At maximum operating speed the million bits of data on the card can be read out in 64 milliseconds, which represents a system data rate of 32 million bits per second.

**millisecond** A thousandth of a second. (1 section of 1,000 milliseconds.) Abbreviated *ms* or *msec*.

**miniaturization** The reduction in size of components and circuits to increase packing density and reduce power dissipation and signal propagation delays.

**minicartridge** A magnetic tape holder that is smaller than a cassette. A typical minicartridge holds 140 feet of tape, 54% less than a cassette. The drive unit records on a single track at 800 bpi with storage for 115 kilobytes. The minicartridge is expected to outlast the life of a cassette by a factor of six or seven.

**minicomputer** A small general-purpose computer with a central processor, memory, and interface components that has more computing power than a micro, but less than a full-scale mainframe computer. Minicomputers are characterized by word lengths of 12, 16, or more bits; high-level language programming; extensive data processing capability; and a capacity that permits time-sharing.

**minicomputer communication processor** 1. A processor unit containing a minicomputer that is connected between a central computing facility and a communications network to perform communications control functions for a full-scale mainframe central computer. 2. A communication processing unit that interfaces with a minicomputer system.

**minicomputer interfaces** Microprocessors like the Z80 are used to implement front end processors in minicomputers. The microprocessor replaced the hard-wired logic that was used to interface the minicomputer to remote communications hardware. Typical microprocessor tasks include bit detection, signal qualification, character assembly, character detection, modem status, buffering, error handling, protocol management, message acknowledgment and handling, file management, and transaction handling. A basic Z80 system for asynchronous communications operation is shown *below*. The Z80 and the UART

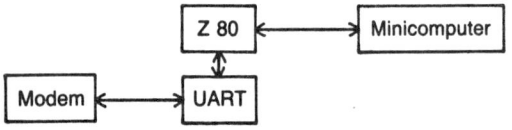

Z80 minicomputer interface for asynchronous operation

provide the complete interface between the minicomputer and modem.

Expanding this concept into a distributed microprocessor system for synchronous communication operation results in the configuration shown *below*. The Z80 and random access memory now provide the interface between the minicomputer and a system bus. Connected to the bus are additional microprocessors with specialized tasks for a number of modems and communications lines.

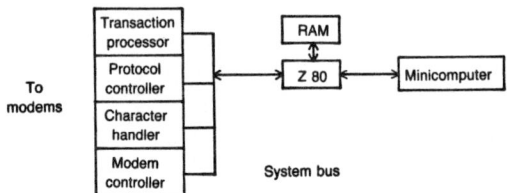

Z80 minicomputer interface for synchronous operation

**minicomputer terminal** 1. A terminal that contains a minicomputer for computation and processing, as well as interface control; a smart terminal. 2. A user-interactive input/output device that interfaces with a minicomputer system.

**minimal latency coding** A method of programming in which the access time for a word depends upon its location; the location is chosen to reduce or minimize the access time. Also called *minimum delay coding* or *optimum coding*.

**minimum access code** A coding system in which the effects of delays for the transfer of data or instructions between storage and other sections is minimized.

**minimum access programming** Programming aimed at minimizing the waiting time required to obtain information from storage; minimum latency programming.

**minimum access routine** A routine coded such that the *actual* access time is less than the *expected* random access time.

**minimum latency code** Minimum access code.

**minimum latency programming** Minimum access programming.

**minimum latency routine** Minimum access routine.

**minor cycle** The time interval between the appearance of corresponding parts of successive operations used to provide serial access in a storage device. A major cycle usually contains several minor cycles.

**minority carriers** Nondominant charge carriers in a semiconductor device.

**minuend** The quantity from which another quantity is subtracted or is to be subtracted.

**minus zone** The bit positions in a code or coding that represent the algebraic minus sign.

**MIR** Abbreviation for *memory information register*.

**MIS** Abbreviation for *Management Information System*.

**miscellaneous function** An off-on function of a machine such as fan or a coolant device.

**mistake** A human action that produces an unintended result such as faulty arithmetic, an incorrect formula, or incorrect instructions. Mistakes are sometimes called gross errors to distinguish them from rounding and truncation errors. In the strict sense of the word, humans make mistakes and do not malfunction, while computers malfunction and do not make mistakes.

**MITRE** Abbreviation for *Massachusetts Institute of Technology Research and Engineering*.

**mixed-base notation** A positional representation in which the ratios of significances for all pairs of adjacent digits are not the same. For example, let three digits represent hours, tens of hours, and minutes. The significances, taking one minute as a unit, are:

60, 10, 1

The radixes of the second and third digits are 6 and 10. The ratio of the significances must be an integer.

**mixed-radix notation** Mixed-base notation.

**MK** Abbreviation for *master clock*.

**MKS system** The MKS (meter-kilogram-second) system is used in preference to the CGS (centimeter-gram-second) version of the metric system. The metric system uses a series of multipliers, all powers of ten, that together with Greek and Latin terminology, indicate the actual size of its units. A kilogram, for example, is 1000 grams.

**ML** Abbreviation for *machine language*.

**MMRBM** Abbreviation for *mobile, mid-range ballastic missile (Air Force)*.

**mnemonic** 1. A word-like symbol used in assembly languages to code a computer to execute an instruction whose description resembles the word symbol. For example, the term MOV A, B is a mnemonic for "move the contents of register B into arithmetic register A." 2. Descriptive of any technique involving memorization of simple words and elements to recall complex words, rules, names, etc.

**mnemonic address code** An address code that uses an easy-to-remember abbreviation related to the destination, such as LAX for Los Angeles International Airport.

**mnemonic operation code** Refers to an operation code in which the names of operations are abbreviated and expressed in mnemonic terms to aid programmers. Examples include:

| | |
|---|---|
| ADD | for addition |
| CLR | for clear |
| SQR | for square root |
| MPY | for multiply |

Source statements are usually written using mnemonic code for translation by an assembler into machine code, which consists of only ones and zeros.

**MNOS memories** Memories that utilize NMOS transistors with thresholds that are altered by applying a large gate voltage. Erase time is between 10-100 milliseconds and write time between 1-10 milliseconds. Devices may use word, row, or chip erasable configurations. Serial addressing and output is also available.

MNOS memories have not been widely used. Although a variety of devices has been available, problems in data retention and high cost due to the complex manufacturing process has limited their application.

**MO** Abbreviation for *master oscillator*.

**mobile systems** Computer, radio, and other complex systems that are to be installed on ships, planes, or motor vehicles.

**mobility** Refers to the characteristics of the movement of charge carriers in vacuum or in materials.

**mode** Any of the various methods of operation in a system, or the most frequent value in a series of values. Examples of modes in a system include:

1. access mode
2. interpretive mode
3. binary mode
4. alphameric mode
5. byte mode
6. conversation mode

**mode, burst** The movement of a continuous bit stream between devices until an interruption or completion of the stream occurs.

**mode, byte** Refers to the movement of one byte at a time between devices, separated by an interrupt and the release of channel control. Used in multiplexing, the byte mode permits the handling of data from several low-speed devices simultaneously.

**mode, conversation** Refers to a real time communication activity between one or more remote terminals and a time sharing computer, in which each entry from a terminal requests an immediate response from the computer. The remote terminal thus can control, interrogate, or modify a task within the computer.

**model** A characterization, usually involving mathematical terms, of a process, device, concept, or system. A model may be a schematic representation of a system or process. It usually allows some manipulation of variables to enable a study of the system or process under various conditions or modifications.

**modem** An electronic device that performs the modulation and demodulation functions required for communications. A modem (formed from a blending of *modulator* and *demodulator*) can be used to connect computers and terminals over telephone circuits. On the transmission end, the modulator converts the signals to the correct codes for transmission over the communications line. At the receiving end, the demodulator reconverts the signals for communication to the computer using the computer interface unit. Also called *data set*.

**modem chip** An LSI chip that can be used to build a stand-alone modem unit. A modem chip can be used to develop full-duplex, half-duplex, simplex, automatic answer, automatic disconnect, answer only, or answer/originate configurations. All that is required for a complete unit that can perform all supervisory functions, including handshaking routines, is an input filter, output buffer, and threshold amplifier.

**modem, digital** Digital modems provide the necessary modulation, demodulation, and supervisory control functions to implement a serial data communications link over a voice grade channel utilizing frequency shift keying (FSK) techniques.

**modem multiplexer diagnostic** Refers to a device that tests all data and control functions of an asynchronous modem multiplexer.

**modem, simplex/duplex** Modems may be designed to operate in three modes: (1) Simplex: data are transmitted in only one direction, (2) Half-duplex: data can be transmitted in only one direction at a time, but that direction can be reversed, and (3) Full duplex: data can be transmitted in both directions simultaneously.

**moderating ratio** Refers to the ratio of the slowing down power of a moderator to the macroscopic absorption cross section.

**modification loop** A group of instructions that form a closed path to alter or change instruction addresses or data.

**modifier** A quantity used to alter the normal interpretation and execution of an instruction, such as an index tag or indirect address tag.

**modify** To alter a portion of an instruction or subroutine such that its interpretation and execution will be different from its usual interpretation and execution. The modification may permanently change the instruction or affect only the current execution. A typical modification is the changing of effective address through the use of index registers.

**modulator** Possessing a building-block capability, whereby standard replaceable components can be grouped to form a variety of configura-

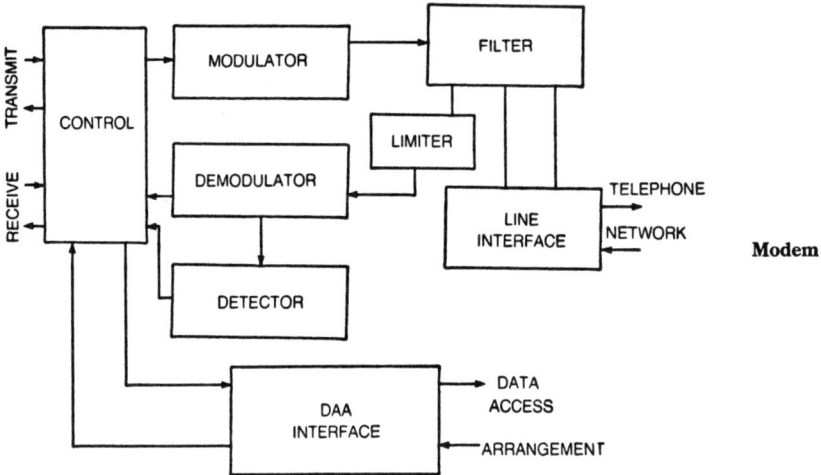

Modem

tions of subassemblies, assemblies, or systems.

**modular connector** Refers to an electrical connector with sections that are used like building blocks or modules.

**modular converter** A data conversion unit that can be interconnected to form data acquisition systems and subsystems. These modular converters are available in epoxy-encapsulated form for analog-to-digital and digital-to-analog conversion along with sample-and-hold circuits and multiplexers.

**modular design** When the bigger problem is broken down into smaller problems, one has the basis of modular design. In a modular hardware design, the modules tend to isolate and separate the functions making the designing, troubleshooting, and debugging tasks easier.

There are several advantages in using program modules. The modules can be run and tested separately before they are linked into the main program. The modules can be designed for open end locations to allow changes without affecting the other parts of the program.

Modular programming is based on techniques in which the programs modules are written, tested, and debugged in small units that are then combined. Top-down design may use modular programming, but modular programming is more common and older, and it is often used independently of any other techniques.

The modules are often divided along functional lines. In microprocessor systems, this division is most useful, since the modules can be used to form a library of programs for use in other designs.

By partitioning the program into small modules and interconnecting these modules into larger programs it is possible to create larger complex programs rather easily.

The modular programming technique limits the size of programs that need to be debugged and tested at any one time. It also provides basic programs that may be reused and allows a division of functional tasks.

The disadvantages include the additional program interfacing that is required and the extra memory needed to transfer control to and from the modules. The need for separate testing of modules can also be more time consuming without duplicate facilities. Modular programming can be difficult to apply if the structure of the data is critical and cannot be modified.

Modular programming can be used for developing microprocessor software in conjunction with any other design techniques that may be used. Some examples of typical modules might be: 1. A program that signals an A/D converter to begin conversion, waits for the conversion to be completed, and then places the results in memory. 2. A program to read a keyboard for key closures. 3. A program that divides two signed decimal numbers.

The modular program design technique coupled with the proper documentation discipline tools is a simple but effective microprocessor design technique.

**modular programming** A technique in which programs are divided into smaller programs or modules that are then designed, coded, and debugged separately and linked together later.

**modular systems** A system that allows the user to plug in additional boards and to build up progressively to a bigger system. This technique, along with the use of other computers, may be used for developing microprocessor software. One may purchase assembler and simulator programs to use on an in-house computer.

This technique is less expensive than using time sharing services over the long term, but it requires the purchase of hardware and software and perhaps some modifications to meet the requirements of the in-house computer. Any computer may be used to execute these cross programs.

**modulate** To vary the amplitude, frequency, or phase of a carrier wave (such as light or a radio signal) proportionally with intelligence (such as speech), for transmission and ultimate demodulation.

**modulated carrier** A wave whose magnitude, frequency, phase, or other characteristic has been varied according to the intelligence to be conveyed.

**modulating electrode** An electrode in which a voltage is applied to control the size of electron beam current.

**modulating signal** The signal that causes a corresponding variation in the characteristics of the carrier wave.

**modulation** The variation of any wave or parameter in direct correspondence with an intelligence-bearing signal.

**modulation code** The code used to cause variations in a signal in accordance with a predetermined scheme.

**modulation, dipole** Refers to the representation of binary digits on a magnetic surface medium, such as disks and tapes, in which a specified part of each cell is magnetically saturated in one of two opposing senses, depending upon the value of the digit represented. The remainder of the cell is magnetized in a predetermined sense and remains fixed.

**modulation, four phase** Refers to a digital type of modulation designed for the carrier to shift between four distinct phases; the four possible phases serve to encode the bits.

**modulation index** Refers to a measure in a frequency modulated wave; the ratio of the frequency deviation to the maximum modulation frequency.

**modulation meter** A meter placed in shunt with a communication channel, giving an indication of the changing power level due to varying the modulation current.

**modulation rate** A measure of the reciprocal of the unit interval measured in seconds. This rate is expressed in bauds.

**modulator-demodulator** A device that converts data signals to a form suitable for transmission and decodes transmitted signals to a form suitable for processing; a *modem*. Also called *data set*.

**module** A software or hardware device that is of standardized design for easy replaceability or system expandability.

**module boards** Interchangeable circuit boards that may contain a complete or partial functional circuit for building up a microcomputer system.

**module extender boards** The connecting boards that, when inserted between a modular circuit board and its receptacle, permit access to the circuit without breaking the existing electrical connections. Module extender boards are used during system testing and maintenance operations.

**modulo check** A checking operation that anticipates a remainder when the processed number is divided by a number carried through with data during the process.

**modulo $n$** A ring of integers derived from the set of all integers:

Let $n$ be an integer greater than one, and $A$ and $B$ two other integers; if $n$ is a factor of $A - B$, then $A$ is congruent to $B$ modulo $n$.

**modulo $n$ check** A check that makes use of a check number that is equal to the remainder of the desired number when divided by $n$. For example, if $n = 4$, the check number will be 0, 1, 2, or 3 and the remainder of $A$ must equal the check number $B$ when divided by 4.

**MOL** Abbreviation for *machine oriented language*.

**molar conductance** The electrical conductance between electrodes 1 cm apart in an electrolyte having one mole of solute in one liter of solution.

**mol(e)** The amount of any defined chemical substance that weighs its molecular weight in grams. Also gram molecule. Symbol *mol*.

**molecular beam** A directed stream of ionized molecules issuing from a source and depending only on their thermal energy.

**molecular bond** The bond in which the linkage pair of electrons are provided by one of the bonding atoms; the atomic bond.

**molecular volume** The volume occupied by one mole of a substance in gaseous form at standard temperature and pressure.

**molecule** The smallest part of an element or compound that exhibits all the properties of that specific compound or element.

**mole electronics** The technique of growing solid-state crystals to form transistors, diodes, and resistors in one mass for microminiaturization. Also called *molecular electronics*.

**MON** Abbreviation for *monitor*.

**monadic Boolean operator** A Boolean operator with only one operand, such as the NOT operator.

**monadic operation** An operation on one operand, such as negation. Sometimes called *unary operation*.

**monitor** 1. To supervise and verify the correct operation of a program during its execution. 2. Software, hardware, or a human that observes, supervises, controls, or verifies the operation of a system or process. 3. A unit in a computer that prepares machine instructions from a source code. It may use built-in compilers for one or more program languages. The machine instructions are sequenced into the processing unit once compiling is complete.

**monitor program** A computer software routine used to check for error conditions that may occur when the program is being executed. These error conditions may consist of numerical overflow, infinite loops, or attempts to access protected areas of memory. The monitor will attempt to provide error recovery along with diagnostics.

**monitor system** The hardware and software used to control computer system functions. The monitor system can simulate the processor, maintain continuity between jobs, observe and report on the status of input/output devices, and provide automatic accounting of jobs.

A time-sharing monitor system usually remains permanently in memory to provide overall coordination and control of the total operating system. It allows several user programs to be loaded simultaneously into memory and prevents one user's program from interfering with another's during execution and control of all input/output devices.

**monochromator** A device for converting a heterogeneous beam of radiation (electromagnetic or particulate) to a homogeneous beam by the absorption or refraction of unwanted components.

**monolithic** Fabricated on a single silicon chip.

**monolithic integrated circuit** An integrated circuit in which both active and passive elements are simultaneously formed in a single small wafer of silicon by diffusion techniques. Metallic stripes are then evaporated on to the oxidized surface of the silicon to interconnect the elements.

**monolithic microcircuit** A semiconductor microcircuit in which circuit elements are not readily identified as individual components. Also called molecular electronics or monolithic circuit.

**monolithic storage** A computer memory made up of monolithic integrated circuits.

**MONOS** Abbreviation for *monitor out of service*.

**monostable circuit** 1. A circuit that has one stable state. A monostable circuit repeats one complete cycle of operation for each trigger pulse. 2. A one-shot multivibrator.

**monostable multivibrator** A one-shot device that provides a single output pulse for each input trigger pulse.

**Monte Carlo generator** A random-number generator or program for obtaining a random number.

**Monte Carlo method** 1. A trial-and-error method of obtaining a solution to a problem by repeated calculations. 2. Any technique for generating a number that is truly random.

**MOPAR** Abbreviation for *master oscillator*.

**Morse code** A system used in signaling and telegraphy, which uses combinations of dots and dashes to represent characters.

**mosaic** A photoelectric pattern composed of a large number of photoemissive granules on an insulating support.

**mosaic detector** A detector containing a number of active elements arranged in an array. It is generally used as an imaging device.

**MOS** Abbreviation for *metal-oxide semiconductor*, a basic technology for fabricating integrated active devices employing field-effect transistors in any of a variety of different configurations. MOS devices tend to have a high capacitance, which makes them slower than their bipolar counterparts; but MOS devices achieve a higher functional density with fewer process steps, so fabrication costs are lower.

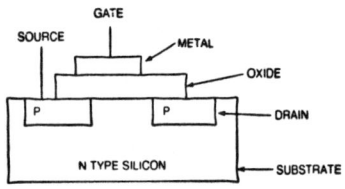

**MOS structure**

**MOS character generator** An LSI device that uses MOS circuitry to generate the voltage patterns required to form numbers, letters, and symbols for visual displays.

**MOS DMOS** A double-diffused MOS device. The second diffusion process results in a product capable of handling higher voltages and currents with very little parasitic capacitance and low noise.

**MOS (DMOS) transistors** Refers to double diffused MOS transistors. These have been used in a noninvasive, nonradiating imaging system for observing the body's internal organs. Operating prototypes of this ultrasonic imaging system have been used by cardiologists to observe human heart action in real time. A two dimensional 10 by 10 array of piezoelectric transducers are sequentially excited by bursts of energy at about 3 megahertz. Each element transmits an ultrasound pulse into the region of interest in the body. Echoes from tissue interfaces are focused back to the array, are time gated out, and undergo the appropriate signal processing. When the array is scanned in time periods much shorter than the cardiac cycle, real time images of the heart movement can be displayed.

**MOSFET** Acronym for *metal-oxide-semiconductor field-effect transistor*, a field-effect transistor made from a sandwich of metal and oxide layers.

**MOSFET multiplexer** The MOSET multiplexer has reversed biased diodes that protect the input channels from being damaged by overvoltage signals. The input channels are protected for up to 20 V beyond the supplies and can be increased by adding series resistors (Ri) to each channel. This input resistor limits the current flowing through the protection diodes to 10 mA. See the diagram below.

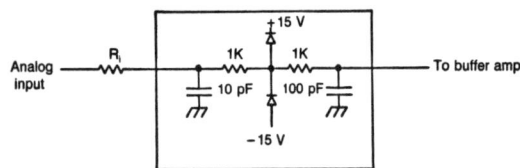

**MOS-FET multiplexer equivalent circuit**

**MOS memory** A computer storage medium that uses MOS LSI devices rather than devices such as drums or disks.

**MOS ROM** Acronym for *metal-oxide-semiconductor read-only memory*, a storage medium that uses MOS transistor cells to store binary ones and zeros.

**MOST** Abbreviation for *metal oxide semiconductor transistor*.

**MOS technology 6500** The MOS technology 6500 microprocessor series are 8-bit devices produced using n-channel MOS with silicon gate processing. Ten CPU devices are available, with various options including addressable memory (4K - 65K), interrupts, and on-chip oscillators and drivers. These ten CPU devices are software compatible among themselves and bus compatible with the 6800 series. Six of the family use on-chip clock oscillators in which a single input from a crystal or RC oscillator circuit provides the time base. The other four devices are designed for multiprocessor applications where some flexibility in clock timing is desired. A pipelined architecture is used for improved speed. The architecture can be divided into two sections as shown below, a register section that contains the ALU and registers and a control section containing the decode logic and timing.

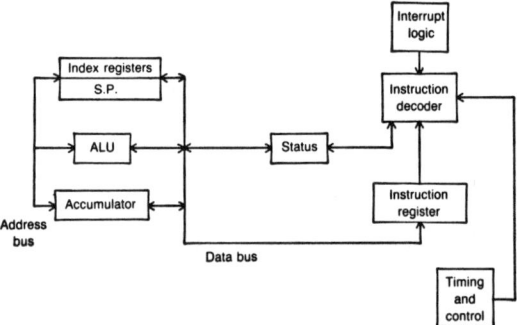

**6500 architecture**

**MOS technology 6500 system** There are several types of peripheral devices for the 6500. A peripheral interface adapter (PIA) provides two 8-bit bidirectional ports and four control or interrupt lines. Another type is called a versatile interface adapter (VIA) and in addition to the PIA it also contains two interval timers along with a shift register and latch for serial-to-parallel and parallel-to-serial conversion. These devices include handshaking capability for data transfers in multiprocessor systems.

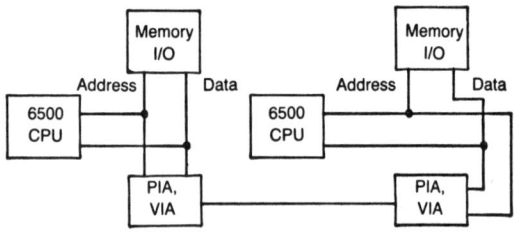

**6500 multiprocessor configuration**

**MOS transistor** Abbreviation for *metal-oxide-semiconductor* transistor, a field-effect transistor that uses a sandwich of metal and oxide layers. Also called *MOSFET*.

**most significant bit** The leftmost bit (abbreviated *MSB*) in a word. The MSB contributes the most weight to the numerical value of the word in most codes.

**motor control system applications** Microprocessors find many uses in stepping motor controls. The microprocessor can be used with hardwired logic to advance the motor by a step when an output appears from a state generator.

The logic sequence can also be stored in memory and one bit sent out at a time. A step counter can be used to ensure that the motor goes through the correct number of steps. Two modes of operation may be used: constant speed operation and automatic acceleration and deceleration. In the constant speed mode, the motor covers the steps at a constant rate. The acceleration-deceleration mode uses progressively decreasing time delays between steps to increase the stepping rate.

**Motorola DMA controller** The operational structure of the 6800 DMAC is shown. This is a cycle stealing DMA controller.

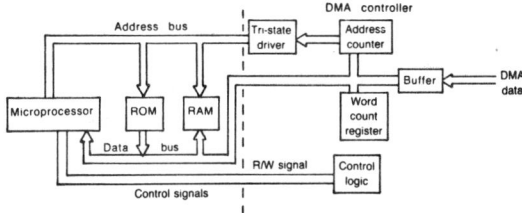

**6800 DMA controller operation**

**Motorola 6800** The Motorola 6800 is an 8-bit NMOS single-chip microprocessor. The architecture of the 6800 microprocessor has three 16 bit registers and three 8 bit registers that are available to the programmer. Another register, the instruction register is used for temporary storage of instructions for the instruction decoder.

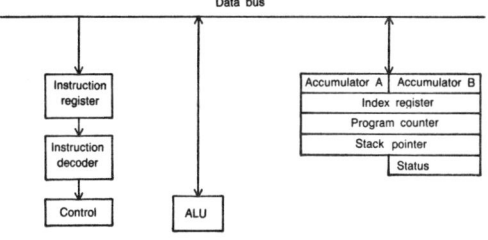

**6800 architecture**

Two 8-bit accumulators are used to hold operands and results from the arithmetic and logic unit (ALU). The A accumulator serves as the primary accumulator, while the B unit functions as a secondary accumulator. The 6800 performs all arithmetic computations using one of these registers. The index register is a two-byte unit for storing data or 16-bit memory addresses for use in the indexed mode of addressing. The program counter is a 16-bit, two-byte register that points to the current program address.

The stack pointer register serves the same function for subroutine linkage as the stack pointer in the 8080. It contains the address of the next available location in a last in first out pushdown stack. The stack itself, is normally a RAM.

**Motorola 6800 interfacing** The 6800 uses the 6820 PIA to interface with I/O equipment. The control bus channels the data flow in the PIA's data bus, and the address bus lets the 6800 read or write into the PIA's registers, which are divided into two independent sections, each with a control data and address register.

**Motorola 6800 signal interface** The 6800 uses an 8-bit bidirectional data bus for transferring data to and from memory and peripheral devices. The address bus is 16 bits wide, and when the bus is turned off, it acts as an open circuit for direct memory access (DMA) operations as shown in the diagram.

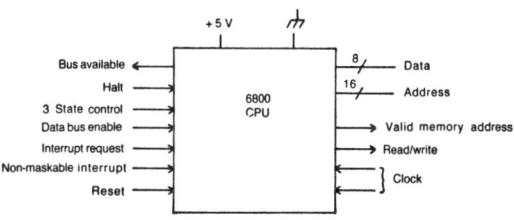

**6800 signal interface**

**Motorola 6800 UART** In the 6800, the UART chip is called an *Asynchronous Communications Interface Adapter*, or *ACIA*. The ACIA operates by placing the eight-bit byte into a shift register. Then the bits are shifted one bit at a time each time the register is shifted. The shifting is done in synchronism with a clock pulse, which may come from the device or may be generated locally.

The ACIA also has a data register to accept the eight-bit byte from the microprocessor data bus and store it until the shift register is ready for it. This tends to smooth out the transmission rate of the bits. While the shift register is shifting, the data register can accept the next eight bits. When the shift register finishes, the movement of data from the data register to the shift register is done by the chip to keep the bits flowing in an uninterrupted manner.

The ACIA has other registers that use the data bus to and from the microprocessor. To save pins, the commands are given to the chip by transmitting control bits into a register in the ACIA.

Since the ACIA receives and transmits on separate wires, it has two shift registers. Each of these has its own data register. One is used for receiving and the other one for sending as shown.

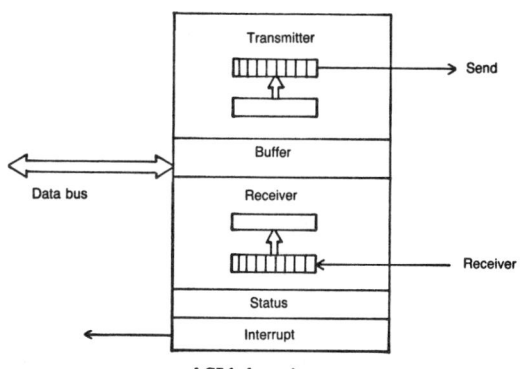

**ACIA functions**

**Motorola 6801** The Motorola 6801 is a microcomputer chip that contains 2048 bytes of mask-programmable ROM, 128 bytes of RAM, a 16-bit counter/timer, a UART, 31 parallel I/O lines, and an expanded instruction set of the 6800. The 6801 is object code compatible with the 6800. It has improved execution times for some instruction, plus new 16- and 8-bit instructions. It is expandable to 64k words.

The basic architecture of the 6801 microcomputer is shown below. In addition to the 6800 CPU, the program memory, scratch pad memory, counter, clock oscillator, UART, and I/O ports are on the microcomputer chip.

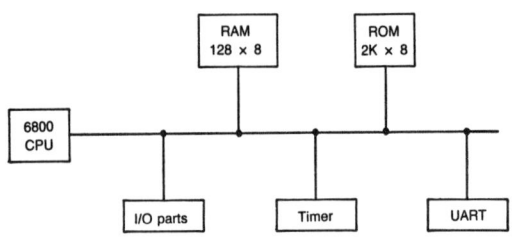

**6801 microcomputer**

Besides being code compatible with the 6800 processor, the 6801 has 10 new instructions. Added are instructions for performing 8-bit multiplication, double-precision addition, double-precision load operations, and double-precision subtraction. There are also some new shift, rotate, and index register operations.

**Motorola 6802** A second version of the 6800 is the 6802. This chip includes all of the features of the 6800 along with an on-chip clock oscillator and 128 bytes of RAM. The RAM locations are at hex addresses 0000 to 007F with the first 32 bytes at addresses 0000 to 001F having a low-power mode for memory retention during power outages. The 6802 can be used with a 6846 timer for a complete system for simple control applications in just two packages.

**Motorola 6803** The 6803 chip is similar to the 6801 except that it doesn't have on-chip ROM storage and some of the port lines are used as a multiplexed data and address bus. The 6803 has a 16-bit counter/timer, 13 parallel I/O lines, UART, clock, and a 128-byte RAM.

**Motorola 6809** The 6809 is a 16-bit internal version of the 6800. It uses an extended 6800 instruction set with instructions like 8-by-8 bit multiply; it has 16-bit modes with the same mnemonics as the 6800. The operational codes differ so that object code cannot be directly transferred from 6800 to 6809, but the programs can be reassembled with a 6809 assembler to provide a more efficient program resulting from the improved internal structure of the 6809. A stack pointer defined by the user, another index register, and a page register have been added. The 6809 also has a number of long branch instructions, which were absent in the 6800.

An additional addressing mode in the 6809 is auto increment addressing. This capability improves the software in sequential indexing applications since index updating commands are not required. A new SYNC instruction stops the processor until an interrupt occurs to resume processing. This instruction can be used to synchronize the processor to real time events in a system.

The instruction set has fewer instructions than the older 6800; however, the 6809 has more powerful commands that replace multiple instructions of the older processor. The 59 instructions include 16-bit arithmetic, extended range branches, enhanced pointer register manipulation, and auto-increment/decrement operations with any of four pointer registers.

**Motorola 6820 control register** The control register format is shown. Bit 7 indicates a transition of the CA1 input, and it is used as an interrupt flag. Bit 6 monitors the CA2 input. Bits 5, 4 and 3 establish the eight different modes of the device and the function of the CA2 pin. Bit 2 indicates if the direction register or data register is to be selected. Bits 1 and 0 are the interrupt enable/disable control bits.

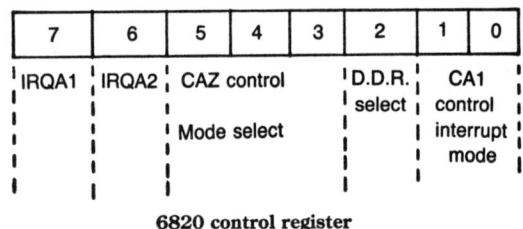

**6820 control register**

**Motorola 6820 PIA** This is a double I/O chip with two sets of eight lines as shown. Each PIA has two data registers, or peripheral registers, as they are called. One is used for each set of input/output lines. There are also two other registers used with each peripheral register, which results in a total of six for each PIA.

The PIA has a data direction register to control the directions of the input/output lines. One data direction register has eight bits, one for each input/output line.

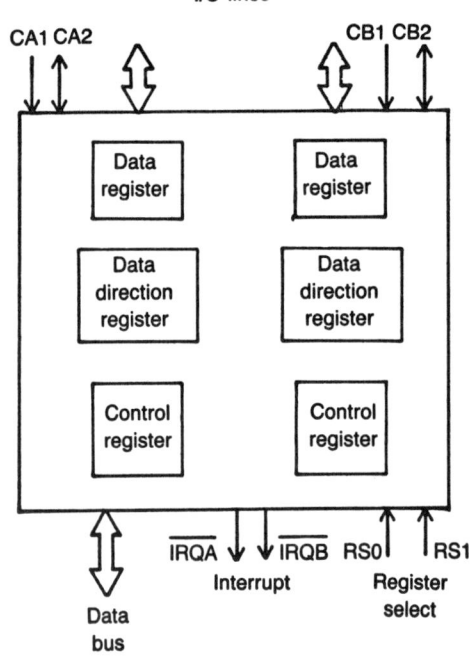

**6820 PIA**

**Motorola 10800** The Motorola 10800 4-bit slice uses emitter-coupled logic (ECL) to achieve high speed performance. A 48-pin quad inline package is used and both lateral and vertical expansion are allowed. Lateral expansion can be used to increase the bit length in increments of 4-bits and vertical expansion can be used to increase throughput by pipelining.

The 10800 arithmetic logic unit is combined with a microprogram control unit, a timer unit, and a memory interface unit for the microprogrammed system. The memory and register file complete the configuration.

The ALU components include a 4-bit adder, which uses a shift network and accumulator for arithmetic operations. A latch and multiplex system are used to control data flow within the ALU, and bus control logic is used to control the flow of data over the input and output busses.

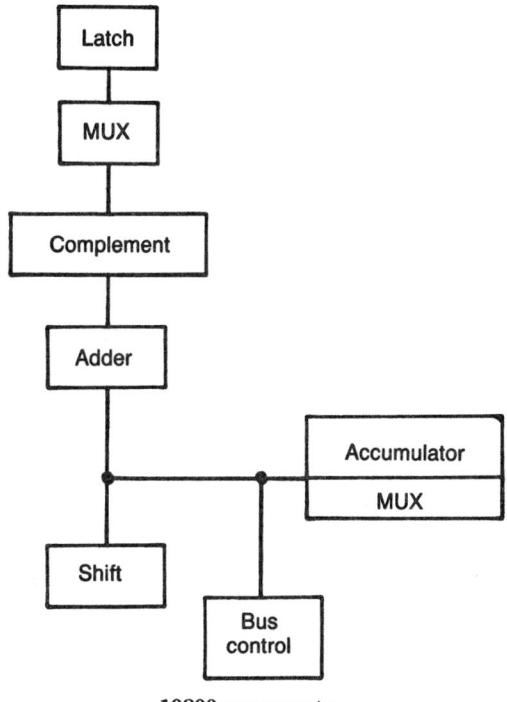

**10800 components**

**Motorola 10801** The 10801 is a microprogram control unit that was designed as a component for the 10800 microprocessor system, but it may also be used as an independent device for controller applications. The 10801 contains bit-control registers that are expandable to any number of bits. It also contains a control memory address register and a 4-bit, 4 deep LIFO stack register for subroutine nesting. Sixteen address control functions are used for jumps, which may be conditional or unconditional, and for subroutine control. This chip also has an internal instruction register, a repeat register, and a 4-bit status register.

A single 10801 allows addressing of 256 words using row and column jumps. Two chips allow addressing for 65,536 words. A two-chip system also allows eight way branching for three separate branch inputs. Multiple chip operation uses the extender bus.

**Motorola 10802** The 10802 is a timer unit that contains a 4 phase counter with a start synchronizer for ECL circuit chips. The phases as well as the phase time are programmable. One control function allows the microprocessor to be stepped through a routine for diagnostic testing.

**Motorola 10803** The 10803 is an ECL memory interface unit that is used as an interface between memory and processor for generating memory addresses and routing data. It contains an ALU for generating memory addresses, which also may be used as the prime ALU in a simple system. It contains the memory address register, the memory data register, and a set of four 4-bit register files for minimum systems. The 10803 can perform 17 transfer or store operations for data manipulation and 12 register/bus/ALU functions.

**Motorola 68000** The Motorola 68000 is a 16-bit microprocessor with an external 16-bit bus that is multiplexed from the 32-bits inside. A 32-bit ALU is used. The 16 32-bit registers of the 68000 are partitioned into eight data registers and seven address registers. An eight address register exists as a stack pointer.

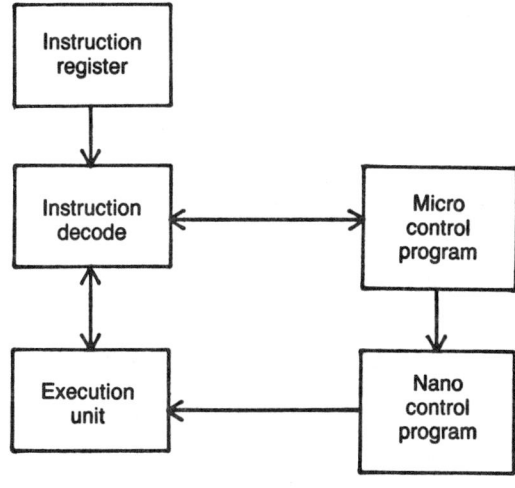

**68000 structure**

The 68000 structure has the CPU centered around the microprogram controlled execution unit. Control store area size is minimized by the use of a two level control structure. First, machine instructions are produced by sequences of microinstructions in the microcontrol program. These microinstructions are actually addresses to nano-instructions in the nano-control program. This memory contains a set of machine state words to control the executing unit. Information that is timing independent bypasses the control programs and is transmitted directly to the execution unit. About 22.5K bits of control memory is used, 50 percent less than required for a one level implementation.

Since the two-level structure increases access time, an effort has been made to reduce this effect by a pipelined architecture, in which the instruction fetch, decode, and execute cycles are overlapped.

The 68000 uses eight 32-bit data registers, seven 32-bit address registers, and two implied 32-bit stack pointers. The data registers can be addressed as byte, word, or double word registers. The address registers are used for 32-bit base addressing, 32-bit software stack operations, and word or long word address operations. The stack pointers are used for the 32-bit base addressing and word or long word address operations. The 68000 uses a 32-bit program counter and a 16-bit status register.

**Mott scattering formula** This gives the differential cross section for the scattering of identical particles arising from a coulomb interaction.

**mounting, table top** Some microcomputers may be mounted in a table top cabinet. There are several types of table top mountings available; a single row for single rack mounting and a double row for double rack mounting. Rear cable panels are available for internal/external connections.

**moving-domain memories (MOD)** A type of memory that can be batch-fabricated using conventional microcircuit techniques. Moving domain memories are nonvolatile, like core memories, but much smaller; they operate reasonably fast; they need no external magnetic bias to form and hold the domains, as do bubble memories. Some MOD units have densities of 128k per substrate.

**MPE** Abbreviation for *maximum permissible exposure* (of radiation).

**MPS** Abbreviation for *microprocessor system*.

**MP tandem** A 20 million volt particle accelerator used for neutron research.

**MPU** Abbreviation for *microprocessor unit*.

**MQ** Abbreviation for *multiplier quotient*.

**MRBM** Abbreviation for *medium range ballistic missile*.

**MRSV** Abbreviation for *maneuverable recoverable space vehicle*.

**MS, Ms** Abbreviation for *manuscript*.

**MSI** Abbreviation for *medium-scale integration*, that level of active-device integration that yields more than 100 but less than 1000 active devices on a single substrate.

MSI interconnections

**MSB** Abbreviation for *most significant bit*.

**MSSS** Abbreviation for *manned space station simulator*.

**MSTS** Abbreviation for *Military Sea Transportation Service*.

**MT** Abbreviation for *magnetic tape*.

**MTBF** Abbreviation for *mean time between failures*, the predictable average time between anticipated malfunctions of an equipment item or system.

**MTL** Abbreviation for *merged transistor logic*, a type of logic that uses multicollector transistors. Also called *integrated-injection logic ($I^2L$)*.

**MTTF** Abbreviation for *mean time to failure*.

**MTTR** Abbreviation for *mean-time-to-repair*.

**MU** Abbreviation for *machine unit*.

**mu-circuit** The part of a feedback amplifier in which the vector sum of the input signal and that of the feedback portion of the output is amplified.

**mu-factor** The voltage amplification factor of grid to anode (or another grid), the current and all other voltages being constant.

**multiaccess** Descriptive of a system that permits several users to interact with a single central computer using a number of online terminals. Access points are connected to the central processor by data transmission lines from remote terminals which may use teletypewriters, CRT displays, or satellite processors. Most multiaccess systems operate in a conversational mode with a fast response time.

**multiaddress** An instruction format that contains more than one address part.

**multiaspect** Descriptive of searches or systems that allow more than one facet of information to be used to identify and select operations.

**multibus** The bus structure for interfacing Intel's 8080/8586 products. It supports a one megabyte address space. The 8289 bus arbiter controls accesses by multiple processors. The control lines use a master/slave concept: a master processor takes control of the bus; then the slave device, I/O or memory, acts upon the command provided by the master. An asynchronous handshaking protocol allows units of different speeds to use the bus.

**multichannel** A system that divides the frequency spectrum of a signal into a number of bands that are separately transmitted and then recombined.

**multichip IC** An integrated circuit that uses two or more semiconductor chips in a single package.

**multidrop configuration** A multidrop configuration as shown is also called a *data bus*, *data highway*, or *multipoint* configuration. The host controls the flow of data between any two nodes. Any satellite can communicate with the host or any other satellite at any one time.

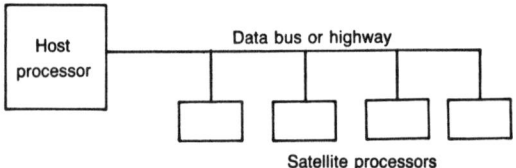

**Multidrop network configuration**

**multilayer board** A printed circuit board that has two or more layers of circuit tracks (abbreviated *MLB*). Multilayer boards increase logic speed and packing density, and cut electrical crosstalk.

**multilevel address** Indirect address.

**multiphase program** Refers to a program in absolute form that requires more than one fetch or load operation to complete the execution.

**multiple address code** An instruction code in which an instruction word may specify more than one address to be used during the operation. Examples include the *two-address* code and the *four-address* code. In a typical instruction of a *four-address* code, the addresses specify:

1. The location of the two operands

2. The location where results are stored
3. The location of the next instruction

**multiple-aperture core** A magnetic core with two or more holes for wires. Multiple-aperture cores can be used for nondestructive reading.

**multiple bus structure** Refers to a bus structure in which any memory module may send or receive information from several processors operating concurrently.

**multiple channel systems** In multichannel data systems, parts of the data acquisition chain are usually shared by two or more input sources. The sharing may occur in a number of ways, depending on the desired specifications of the system. Large systems might combine several different types of multiplexing and perhaps even use cascaded tiers of the same type.

**multiple device** Two or more semiconductor chips in a single package, connected together to function as a single unit.

**multiple interrupts** In systems with several sources of interrupt, one or more interrupt requests may occur during the servicing of an earlier request. In simple systems, the interrupt mask bit is set when the first request is recognized. Subsequent requests are placed in a queue, waiting until the service of the first interrupt is complete before they are recognized and serviced. The order in which the queued interrupts are recognized determines the time delay before service. This order, or priority, is dictated either by software or by hardware with software priority. After recognizing an interrupt request, the service program can poll the devices in an order that determines the interrupt priority of each device. The devices polled first are serviced first.

**multiple modulation** A modulation technique that uses a succession of modulation processes in which the wave from one stage becomes the modulating wave for the next stage. For example, PPM-AM is a system where pulse-position modulation is used to amplitude-modulate a carrier.

**multiple-precision** The use of two or more words to represent a quantity or numeral, resulting in increased accuracy for computation.

**multiple programming** Programming that allows two or more logic or arithmetic operations to be executed simultaneously.

**multiple system** A computer system that contains two or more central processing units with input/output devices and other hardware units that are related and interconnected for simultaneous operation.

**multiplex** The concurrent transmission of two or more messages or information streams over the same channel.

**multiplex data terminal** A device that transfers data from units operating at low transfer rates to units operating at high transfer rates in such a way that the high-speed devices are not required to wait for the low-speed units.

**multiplexed operation** Refers to simultaneous operations that share the use of a common unit in such a way that they are considered independent operations.

**multiplexed sampling S/D converter** A circuit in which a pair of sample holds are switched from input to input, where each is sampled and its value held during conversion, which takes less than one carrier cycle. The sampling is done at the peak of the carrier cycle.

**multiplexer** A device that samples a number of channels and produces data that is the composite of all sampled channels, for transmission over a single channel. On reception, demultiplexing recreates all original channels.

**multiplexer channel** A channel designed to operate with a number of devices simultaneously. A multiplexer channel allows several devices to transfer records at the same time by interleaving items of data. The

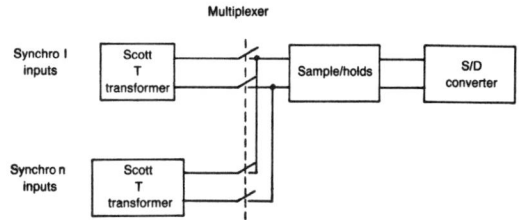

**Multiplexed sampling S/D converter system**

multiplexer channel acts as a communications coordinator in many complex system configurations.

**multiplexer polling** A method of polling or voting that allows each remote multiplexer to query the terminals connected to it. Multiplexer polling is usually more efficient than polling from a central computer, since it involves fewer control messages.

**multiplexers** When more than one channel of data requires analog to digital conversion, it is necessary to use time division or multiplex the analog inputs to a single converter, or to provide a converter for each input and then combine the converter outputs by digital multiplexing.

**multiplexer settling time** The time required for the analog signal to settle to within its error budget, as measured at the input to the converter. In a 12-bit system, with a ±10V range, the multiplexer units typically settle within 1 microsecond, and a typical conversion time might be 20 microseconds.

**multiplexing** The process of transmitting more than one signal at a time over a single channel, usually by sequentially sampling all signals and

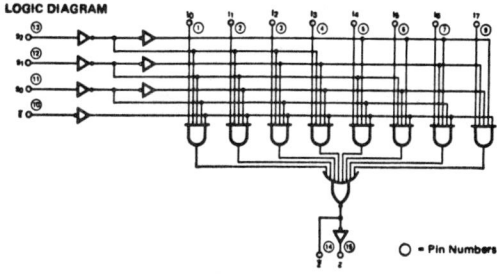

**Multiplexer**

coding them into a single data stream. Frequency-division multiplexing (abbreviated *FDM*) allows a number of devices to share a link by dividing its frequency spectrum into a number of subchannels. Time-division multiplexing (abbreviated *TDM*) assigns a time slot into which each device may place information.

**multiplexing, byte** Refers to a process in which time slots on a channel are delegated to individual input/output devices so that bytes from one and then another can be interlaced on the channel.

**multiplication** 1. The secondary emission of electrons due to impact of primary electrons on a surface. It varies from zero for graphite to 1.3 for nickel and up to 12.3 for nickel-beryllium alloys. 2. The ratio of neutron flux in a subcritical reactor to that supplied by the neutron source alone. It is equal to 1(1 − k), where k is the multiplication constant.

**multiplication shift** A shift that results in multiplication of the number by a positive or negative integral power of the radix.

**multiplication time** The time required to perform a multiply operation. In most binary operations, it is equal to the total of all addition times and shift times.

**multiplier** A device that generates a product from two numbers. A digital multiplier generates the product from two digital numbers by additions of the multiplicand in accordance with the value of the digits in the multiplier. It then shifts the multiplicand and adds it to the product if the multiplier digit is a one, or shifts without adding if the digit is a zero. This is done for each successive digit of the multiplier.

**multiplier, digital** Refers to a circuit or device that generates a digital product from the representation of two digital numbers, usually by additions of the multiplicand in accordance with the value of the digits in the multiplier. It is necessary only to shift the multiplicand and add it to the product if the multiplier digit is a one, and shift the multiplicand without adding, if the multiplier digit is a zero, for each successive digit of the multiplier.

**multiplier-quotient register** A register in which the multiplier for multiplication is placed, and the quotient for division is developed.

**multiply** The logic operation that makes use of the logical product and is given by:

| MULTIPLIER | MULTIPLICAND | LOGICAL PRODUCT |
|---|---|---|
| 0 | 0 | 0 |
| 1 | 0 | 0 |
| 0 | 1 | 0 |
| 1 | 1 | 1 |

Same as the AND operation.

**multiply-divide instruction** An instruction or set of instructions that allow multiply and divide operations directly. Multiply and divide instructions are standard or optional on some microcomputers.

**multiply-divide package** A collection of subroutines that perform single- and double-precision multiplication and division for signed and unsigned binary numbers. The multiply-divide package is usually supplied in the form of a source program tape with an assembly listing for the specific microcomputer.

**multiplying D/A converters** A special class of digital-to-analog converters with the capability of handling variable reference sources. Their output value is the product of the number represented by the digital input code and the analog reference voltage, which may vary from full scale to zero, and in some cases, to negative values.

**multipoint network** A type of network with multiple slaves. In this network, a single processor has control and determines which slave computer shall operate on a task. Communications between slave computers is under control of the master. After it is assigned a task, the slave proceeds asynchronously with respect to the master until completion of the task, or until it requires services from the master.

**multipole moments** Refers to magnetic and electric measures of charge. These static multipole moments determine the interaction of the system with weak external fields. There are also transition multipole moments that determine radiative transitions between two states.

**multiport register** A register that is capable of reading two locations and writing one location simultaneously. A typical 8-bit multiport register uses two sets of eight latches for address selection.

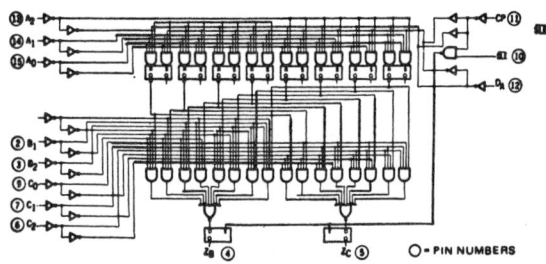

**Multiport register**

**multiprocessing** The use of more than one independent processor and the processing of several programs or program segments concurrently. Each processor is active on only one program at any one time, while operations such as input/output transfers are performed in parallel on the programs. The processor can address adjacent storage modules in an odd or even fashion to reduce storage access conflicts in a multiprocessing system. Modules 0, 2, 4, and 6 would be referenced for even addresses, while modules 1, 3, 5, and 7 are referenced for odd addresses.

Multiprocessing microcomputer systems can be used to provide increased computing power, but hardware and software costs can outweigh the advantages compared to larger computers.

**multiprocessing, interleaving** Relates to various techniques or processes of addressing adjacent storage modules in an even/odd fashion. It significantly reduces storage-access conflicts in a multiprocessor system and thereby increases overall system performance. With interleaving, the modules are divided into even and odd locations (although the addressing structure within the modules themselves remains unchanged.) Thus, in a fully expanded eight-module system, modules 0, 2, 4, 6 are referenced for even addresses, while modules 1, 3, 5, 7 are referenced for odd.

**multiprocessor operating modes** Multiprocessor systems may use a number of operating modes. The processors may cooperate in solving a problem that requires more computing speed than a single processor provides. Each processor can control a portion of the process. The necessary coordination may be effected through the interconnection.

**multiprocessor systems** Systems that use more than one central processing unit in the system configuration.

**multiprogramming** Refers to the concurrent execution of two or more programs. Multiprogramming generally uses overlapping or interleaving techniques to allow more than one program to time-share machine components.

**multiprogramming executive** A software block that provides the operating system for concurrent execution of more than one program. A typical multiprogramming executive includes a priority scheduler along with memory allocation and deallocation.

**multiprogramming, master-slave** Refers to a system designed to guarantee that one program cannot damage or access another program sharing memory.

**multistage** 1. A control system that uses several levels of gain or amplification. 2. A tube in which the electrons are progressively accelerated by anode rings held at increasing potentials.

**multistate noise** Refers to noise that is found occasionally in transistors and more often in diodes. It consists of erratic switching that is generated within the device at various sharply defined levels of applied current.

**multitasking** The procedures in which several separate but interrelated tasks operate within a single program identity. Multitasking differs from multiprogramming in that common routines and disk files may be used. Multitasking may or may not involve multiprocessing.

**multitasking operating system** An operating system that is desirable in applications that have a significant number of random, asynchronous inputs. An application of this nature is illustrated. Most of these applications have sections that are functionally similar and an overall organization that is structurally similar.

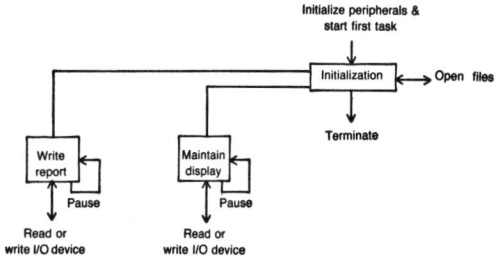

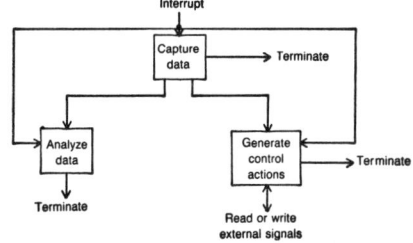

**Multitasking operating systems**

**multithread** A section of a program that can have more than one logical path through it executed simultaneously.

**multiuser** The ability to have more than one person using the resources of the computer at one time.

**multivibrator** An electronic switching circuit with two distinct states. When the device alternates rapidly between the two states, with no external crystal for frequency control, it is said to be *free-running*. When it is crystal-controlled, it is usually called an *oscillator*. When one of the two states is stable, it is called a *one-shot*. When both states are stable, it is called a *flip-flop*. In the free-running or crystal-controlled state, the multivibrator is said to be *astable*. As a one-shot, it is said to be *monostable*. As a flip-flop, it is considered *bistable*.

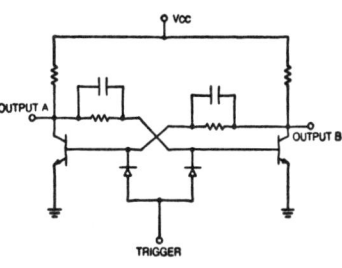

**Multivibrator**

**multivibrator, astable** Refers to an oscillator that generates desired shapes of signals, normally of the relaxation type. Operation is dependent on two interacting devices, such as two transistors connected in such a manner that one governs the operation of the other. One device causes the charging of a capacitor, resulting in a rise in voltage, which triggers the other to discharge the capacitor, causing an output voltage pulse.

**multivibrator, bistable** Refers to an electronic circuit having two stable states, two input lines, and two corresponding output lines such that a signal exists on either one of the output lines if and only if the last pulse received by the flip-flop can store one binary digit (bit) of information.

**multivibrator, monostable** Refers to a type of multivibrator that has one stable state and one unstable state and goes through a complete change cycle. The circuit provides a single signal of proper form and time from a varying shaped, randomly timed signal. Upon receiving a trigger signal, it assumes another state for a specified length of time, at the end of which it returns, of its own accord, to its original state.

**multivariable control** A control technique that uses built-in intelligence to simultaneously monitor many variables and to choose, based on the situation, the optimum of several programmed control strategies.

**multiwire pc board process** A wiring process that involves a customized pattern of insulated wires laid down on an adhesive coated substrate. Multiwire competes with multilayer boards *(MLB)* in two areas: packaging density, and as an interconnection method for high speed bipolar logic. Some multiwire boards with an etched ground and powerplane and signal layers on each side are the equal of a six-layer MLB. Equivalents of a 12-layer MLB are also available.

**multiwire process** A customized pattern of insulated wires laid on an adhesive-coated surface to form a circuit board.

**muting** Refers to the suppression of an electronic signal to improve the signal/noise ratio.

**mutual conductance** The differential change in the space or anode current divided by the differential change of grid potential that causes it. Also called the slope or slope conductance, it is used as a figure of merit for an amplifier.

**mutual inductance** The generation of an electromotive force in one conductor by a variation of current in another conductor that is linked to the first conductor by magnetic flux.

**MUX** Abbreviation for *multiplex, multiplexing,* or *multiplexer.*

**MXR** Abbreviation for *mask index register.*

**Mylar** Tradename for a type of polyester film widely used as a base for magnetic tape and for the dielectric of capacitors.

# N

**n** A notation describing depletion layer behavior in transistors.

**NA** Abbreviation for *not assigned*.

**NACA** Abbreviation for *National Advisory Committee for Aeronautics*. Later became NASA.

**NAK** The negative acknowledge character. A signal sent by the receiver as a negative response to the sender to indicate that the previous block was unacceptable and the receiver is now ready to accept a transmission.

**NAND** The use of an AND gate followed by an interverter is called a NOT AND or NAND gate. If all the inputs have a value of 1, the output is 0, and if any of the inputs have a value of 0, the output will be 1. This is the opposite of an AND gate. (Also called *interval AND* and *negated AND*.)

**NAND flip-flop** A flip-flop, such as the R-S type that can be constructed from NAND gates.

**NAND gate** A device or circuit that performs the NAND operation.

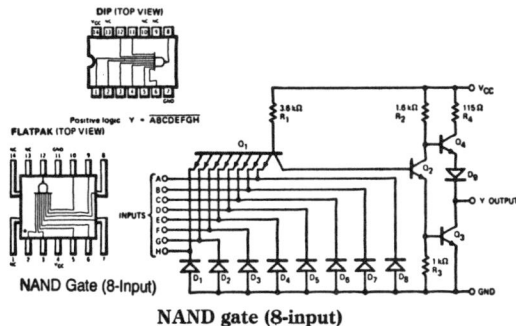

**NAND gate (8-input)**

**n- and p-channel MOS capacitance** When a voltage is applied to the metal gate of a MOS device, a finite amount of time is required to charge the capacitance due to the oxide insulation between the gate and channel. The time taken to charge this capacitance represents the gate settling time. Just as the oxide layer between gate and channel presents a capacitance, the metal oxide substrate formations also present a capacitance, referred to as parasitic capacitance.

**nano** Prefix for $10^{-9}$ (a billionth) times a specified unit.

**nanocircuit** An integrated microelectronic circuit in which each component is fabricated on a separate chip or substrate for maximum high-speed performance.

**nanoprocessor** A processor that operates with a cycle time in the nanosecond range.

**nanosecond** An amount of time equal to $10^{-9}$ second. Abbreviated *ns*.

**nanosecond circuit** A circuit that processes pulses or waveforms with rise and fall times measured in billionths of a second or less.

**NAREC** Abbreviation for *naval research electronic computer*.

**narrowband** Descriptive of a communications channel whose bandwidth is restricted to some specified value less than originally allocated for such channels.

**National Semiconductor IMP 5750** The National IMP 5750 register and arithmetic logic unit (RALU) was a microprocessor element utilizing p-channel enhancement-mode, silicon gate technology. It provided a 4-bit slice of the register and arithmetic portion of a general purpose controller/processor. RALU's could be stacked in parallel for longer word lengths. Each RALU provided 96 bits of storage in the form of four bits in each of seven general registers, a status register, and a 16 word last-in, first-out (LIFO) stack. The arithmetic and logic unit performed ADD, AND, OR and exclusive OR operations.

**National Semiconductor INS8900** The NMOS INS8900 is architec-

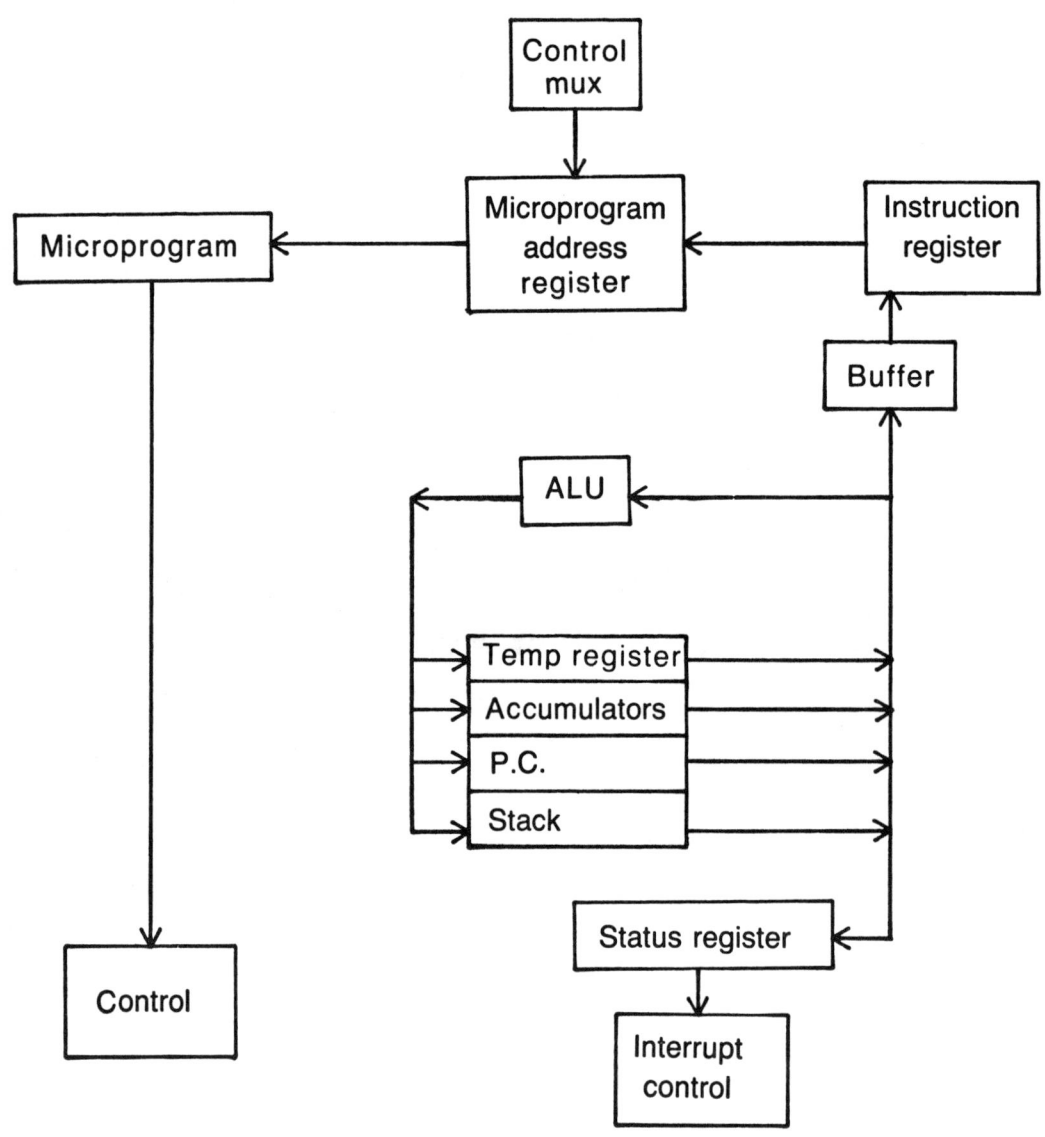

**8900 architecture**

turally similar to the PACE PMOS microprocessor. This NMOS processor is recommended for all applications instead of the PACE. The microprocessor uses an on-chip 10 word stack, indirect addressing, 8 or 16-bit data operation, memory-mapped I/O, four accumulators, and vectored interrupts.

The architecture shown for the INS8900 and PACE provides the 10-word stack as well as four general-purpose registers and a 16-bit status and control flag register. A minimal system consists of the CPU, the clock and memory.

**National Semiconductor NS16000 Family** In the NS16000 microprocessor chip family, the 16008 and 16016 chips are 8080 code compatible. The 16008 is designed for eight-bit systems while the 16016 has a 16-bit data bus. The 16032 has an internal 32-bit ALU bus and a direct address range of 16M bytes using 24 bit address pointers. Unlike the 16032, and 16016, the 16008 cannot be used with an MMU to increase the address space beyond 64K.

The 16000 family offers symmetric addressing, including top of stack, memory relative, external, and scaled. This provides modular software capabilities, permitting a user to develop software packages independent of other packages and without regard to individual addressing. This can provide flexibility in system design and lower programming costs.

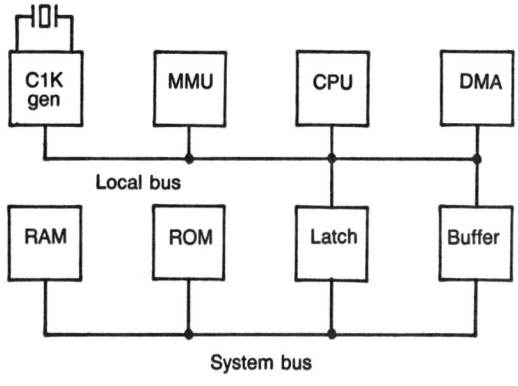

16000 system structure

**National Semiconductor SC/MP** The National Semiconductor SC/MP (simple, cost-effective microprocessor) is an 8-bit PMOS processing unit. The SC/MP uses a 16-bit memory bus for addressing up to 64K bytes of memory with four address pointer registers.

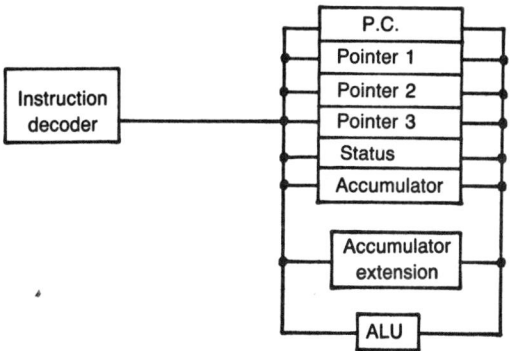

SC/MP architecture

A preprogrammed, programmable logic array (PLA) is used for instruction decoding.

The SC/MP ALU has 8-bit binary ADD, AND, OR and EXCLUSIVE OR operations and can perform two digit BCD additions. The pointer registers are 16 bits long; one register serves as the stack pointer and the others can be used by the programmer. The chip operates on a single power supply of +10 to +14 volts and uses a 40 pin package. The single supply voltage can allow direct interfacing with CMOS components.

The instruction set for the SC/MP is smaller than that for most 8-bit microprocessors. There are 40 basic instructions. Addressing modes in SC/MP include indexed addressing, auto indexed addressing, immediate addressing, and extension register addressing.

**natural binary** The most common digital code, in a natural binary code of bits, the most-significant bit has a weight of 1/2: ($2^{-1}$), the second bit has a weight of 1/4: ($2^{-2}$) and so on to the least-significant bit, which has a weight of $2^{-n}$. The value of the binary number represented is obtained by adding up the weights of the nonzero bits. A 4-bit representation is shown with the binary weights and the equivalent numbers shown as both decimal and binary fractions.

| | | Digital code | | | |
|---|---|---|---|---|---|
| Decimal Fraction | Binary | MSB | Bit 2 | Bit 3 | Bit 4 |
| | Fraction | (x1/2) | (x1/4) | (x1/8) | (x1/16) |
| 0 | 0.0000 | 0 | 0 | 0 | 0 |
| 1/16 = $2^{-4}$ (LSB) | 0.0001 | 0 | 0 | 0 | 1 |
| 2/16 = 1/8 | 0.0010 | 0 | 0 | 1 | 0 |
| 3/16 = 1/8 + 1/16 | 0.0011 | 0 | 0 | 1 | 1 |
| 4/16 = 1/4 | 0.0100 | 0 | 1 | 0 | 0 |
| 5/16 = 1/4 + 1/16 | 0.0101 | 0 | 1 | 0 | 1 |

Natural binary code

**natural frequency** The frequency of free oscillation; thus, the frequency of resonance of any device or circuit.

**natural function generator** An analog hardware unit or a software program used to solve differential equations using methods based upon physical laws.

**NC** 1. Abbreviation for *numerical control*, a system that uses prerecorded intelligence prepared from numerical data to control a process or machine. 2. Abbreviation for *normally closed*, and used to describe relay or switch contacts, or the electronic equivalent of such contacts. 3. Abbreviation for *no connection*, usually written adjacent to a depicted contact or conductor on a schematic to show that the absence of another conductor is not an inadvertent omission.

**n-channel** A semiconductor material using n-type dopants and used for the conduction channel in MOS field-effect devices. N-channel MOS devices have several advantages over p-channel types. The majority carriers are electrons rather than holes, as in p-channel devices; thus, the mobility is increased, thereby allowing a theoretical improvement in speed. Threshold voltages are lower than with p-channel devices, which allows circuits to operate at lower supply voltages. The lower voltages result in fewer parasitic effects and permit tighter packing densities.

Compared to bipolar devices, n-channel MOS offers lower power consumption for the same speed, but bipolar offers higher speed if power is not a consideration.

**n-channel enhancement mode** Refers to a MOS FET device that features low switching voltages, fast switching times, low drain source resistance, and low reverse transfer capacitance. Manufactured using the silicon nitride process.

**n-channel JFET** A junction-type discrete field-effect transistor that uses an n-doped conduction channel. N-channel JFETs are characterized by high gain and low noise.

**n-channel modem** A modem that uses n-channel MOS circuits. N-channel modems operate from a single power supply and are fully TTL-compatible.

**n-channel MOS** MOS devices that use an n-channel region for field-effect conduction. Such devices tend to be faster and use less semiconductor real estate than p-channel units. Also called *NMOS*.

**NCP** Abbreviation for *network control program*, a communication system involving the VTAM virtual telecommunications access method.

**NCR paper** NCR company's brand name for carbonless copying paper; 3M company's Action Paper is another brand.

**ND** Abbreviation for *no detect*.

**NDRO** Abbreviation for *nondestructive readout*.

**negate** To perform the logical operation of reversing a signal, condition, or state to its alternate or opposite state.

**negation element** A device, circuit, or gate with the capability of reversing a two-state signal, condition, or event into its alternate or opposite state.

**negation gate** Negation element.

**negative** 1. Less than zero, the opposite of positive. 2. Having a surplus of electrons (negative charges). 3. The minus terminal of a battery or power supply. 4. The *NOT* function. A negative OR gate is the same as a NOT OR or NOR gate; a negative AND is a NOT AND or NAND.

**negative-acknowledge character** A communication control character (abbreviated *NAK*) transmitted by a receiver as a negative response to a sender. The negative acknowledge is sometimes used as an accuracy control character.

**negative bias** A potential, negative with respect to ground, applied as a constant voltage to an electronic circuit element for the purpose of keeping the circuit element in a ready-to-operate state. A negative bias on an amplifier input electrode, for example, establishes the operating point of that stage.

**negative conductance** Refers to the use of hot electrons in some form of a two-terminal negative conductance, forming the basis of both avalanche transit time devices and those devices relating to the Gunn effect. In the former, the negative conductance arises from a phase shift (greater than 90° and preferably near to 180°) between current and voltage. In the Gunn devices it arises within the Ga As crystal in a strong electric field, the local current density decreasing whenever the local electric field exceeds a certain threshold. Other materials showing the Gunn effect are In P, In As, Cd Te and Zn Se.

**negative conductor** Refers to a conductor or cable that is connected to the negative terminal of a voltage source.

**negative crystal** Refers to a solid state crystal structure in which the velocity of the extraordinary ray is greater than that of the ordinary ray.

**negative electricity** Refers to the phenomenon in a body due to effects associated with excess of electrons.

**negative electrode** The anode of a primary cell; the electrode by which conventional current returns to the cell; the cathode of a tube or voltmeter connected to the negative side of the power supply.

**negative feedback** A circuit or system in which a part of the output signal is fed back out of phase and summed with the input for control purposes. Negative feedback decreases amplification and distortion because of polarity-difference signal cancellation. Also called *degeneration*, *inverse feedback*, and *stabilized feedback*.

**negative ignore gate** Same as *gate, negative (A ignore b)* and *gate, negative (B ignore A)*.

**negative impedance** A condition occurring in electronic devices in which an increasing voltage at some point begins to produce a proportionate decrease in current.

**negative impedance converter** An active network for which a positive impedance connected across one pair of terminals produces a negative impedance across the other pair.

**negative ion** Refers to an atom with more electrons than normal. Thus, it has a negative charge.

**negative resistance** See *negative impedance*.

**negative transconductance** A property of tubes in which an increase in positive potential on one electrode accompanies a decrease in current flowing to another electrode.

**negatron** A four-electrode thermionic tube for obtaining negative resistance, comprising an anode and grid on one side of a cathode, and an anode on the other.

**NERVA** Abbreviation for *nuclear engine for rocket vehicle application*.

**nesistor** A type of transistor that operates as a result of a bipolar field effect.

**nest** 1. To store subroutines or other data within subroutines or data of a different hierarchy such that the different levels can be accessed or executed recursively. 2. To store subroutine addresses or general register data in such a fashion that the most recent stored data must be accessed first, and all subsequent data accessed in that same order (the reverse order of storage).

**nesting** 1. Stacking of index addresses and other register data so that they can be accessed sequentially, in reverse order of storage. 2. A program technique of enclosing subroutines within program subroutines; the blocks of data or subroutines in the inner "ring" or loop are not necessarily part of the outer ring or loop.

**nesting level** Refers to the relative hierarchical level at which a term or subexpression appears in an expression in assembler programming, or the level at which a macro definition containing an inner macro instruction is processed by an assembler.

**nesting loop** Refers to a loop of instructions that can also include inner loops, nesting subroutines, outer loops, and rules and procedures relating to the in and out procedures for each type.

**net lines** Refers to finished lines of typing of final documents. Also called net output.

**net loss** The sum of gains and losses between two terminals of a device, circuit, or system.

**network** 1. An interconnected combination of elements used to provide a communications path between two or more points. 2. An assemblage of components usually containing many similar elements and devoted to a common function. 3. Any system of multiple interrelated circuits or elements.

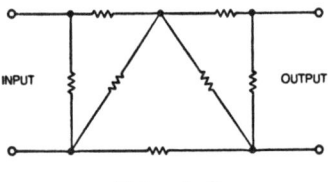

Network, 2

**network, analog** Refers to a circuit or circuits that represent physical variables in such a manner as to permit the expression and solution of continuous mathematical relationships between the variables or permit the solution directly using electric or electronic means.

**network analysis** The process of calculating the transfer characteristic and other properties of a usually passive circuit from its configuration, elements, voltages, etc.

**network analyzer** 1. A group of circuit elements that can be interconnected to form a model of a network or system. Electrical measurements can then be used to determine desired quantities in the simulated system. Also called a *network calculator*. 2. An electronic

**network buffer** test-equipment item designed to make qualitative tests on specific circuit networks.

**network buffer** A storage device used to compensate for a difference in the rate of flow of data received and transmitted in a computer communications system. The buffer has memory and control circuits for storing incoming messages and holding outgoing messages that must be delayed because of busy lines.

**network calculator** A combination of electrical elements used to simulate the operation of a system such as a power generating plant.

**network constant** Any one of the resistance, inductance, mutual inductance, or capacitance values in a circuit or network. When these values are constant, the network is said to be linear.

**network relay** A relay used for the protection and control of alternating current networks.

**network service** A multiuser computer service. Typical network services include highly systematized programs and data bases.

**network stabilization** Relates to techniques used to shape the transfer characteristics in order to eliminate or minimize oscillations when feedback is provided.

**network synthesis** The process of formulating a network with specific requirements.

**network topology** Network topologies can be centralized or distributed. *Centralized* networks are those in which all nodes connect to a single node. The alternative topology is the *distributed* network, in which (in the pure sense of the term) each node is connected to every other node; however, the terminology is commonly applied to topologies approaching this full connectivity.

**network transfer function** The ratio of output to input in a network, usually expressed in incremental units over a specific time period.

**Neumann principle** The physical properties of a crystal are never of lower symmetry than the symmetry of the external form of the crystal. The tensor properties of a cubic crystal, such as elasticity or conductivity, must have cubic symmetry, and the behavior of the crystal is isotropic.

**neuron network simulation** Refers to the study and duplication of neuron cells and networks in order to build multiple purpose systems using analogous electronic components.

**neuron simulation** Refers to the study of neuron cells and networks using electronic devices and systems.

**neutral** A conductor, device, or contact with no net charge or voltage with respect to another similar element in the same system, or with respect to ground.

**neutral conductor** The conductor nearest in potential to a neutral point in a polyphase power system.

**neutralization** The nullifying of inadvertent feedback within a device, circuit, or system for the purpose of preventing generation of spurious signals and unwanted radiation.

**neutralizing capacitor** A capacitor, usually variable, employed in a receiving or transmitting circuit to provide a feedback path for a portion of the signal voltage.

**neutral state** A condition of a ferromagnetic material when completely demagnetized. Also called *virgin state*.

**neutral temperature** The temperature for a thermocouple at which the e.m.f. curve has a turning value, for Cu-Fe it is 270 °C.

**neutral zone** 1. An area in space or time in which no control action takes place. 2. A period between words used for switching or other operations. Also called *dead band*.

**neutron** An uncharged subatomic particle with a mass approximately equal to that of a proton. It is a part of the structure of atomic nuclei and interacts with matter primarily by collisions.

**new input queue** Refers to a group of new messages in a system awaiting processing. The main scheduling routine will scan them along with the other queues for processing at the right time.

**new line character** A format effector that causes the printing or display position to be moved to the first position of the next printing or display line. Abbreviated *NL*.

**newton** The unit of force in the MKS system, being the force required to impact, to a mass of one kilogram, an acceleration of one meter per second per second.

**next-higher assembly** A term used to designate an assembly of the next-higher order in the breakdown of a system.

**NFB** Abbreviation for *negative feedback*.

**nibble** A set of 4 or 5 binary digits or bits. Usually this term refers to 4 bits.

**NIC** Abbreviation for *not in contact*.

**nichrome** A nickel chromium alloy used for heating resistance elements because of its high specific resistance and its ability to withstand high temperatures.

**nickel (Ni)** A silver white metallic element: atomic number 28, atomic weight 58.71, melts at 1450 °C, boils 3000 °C, electrical resistivity at 20 °C, 10.9 microhm/cm. It is magnetostrictive, showing a decrease in length in an applied magnetic field; in the form of wire, it has been used in computers, in which data is circulated and extracted when required.

**nickel delay line** A delay line utilizing the magnetic and/or magnetostrictive properties of nickel.

**nickel iron secondary cell** An alkaii cell that uses potassium hydroxide electrolyte. It is lighter and more durable than lead cells and has an e.m.f. of 1.2 V. Also known as an Edison cell.

**nines' complement** The radix-minus-one complement in decimal notation.

**ninety-column card** A punched card with 90 vertical columns representing 90 characters.

**Nixie tube** Tradename for a gas discharge tube used as a visual alphanumeric display unit.

**NLC** Abbreviation for *new line character*.

**n-level logic** A collection of gates connected in such a way that no more than gates appear in series.

**NLS** Abbreviation for *no lead speed*.

**NMOS** Abbreviation for *n-channel metal-oxide semiconductor*, a semiconductor technology that uses MOS devices with n-channel regions for conduction.

**NMOS driver** A circuit used to interface NMOS memories with emitter-coupled logic. A typical NMOS driver has a propagation time of 10 ns and a transition time of 20 ns with a 400 pF load.

**NMOS EAROM** A completely nonvolatile bit ROM with moderate access speed. Memory contents can be electrically erased and altered externally from the device leads with no restrictions. The output can be either TTL or MOS compatible. Using the EAROM, a single hardware design can be applied to multiple product lines. The required programming for individual applications can be done on site. Conventional ROMs require the development of different chip masks for each application. The EAROM eliminates such duplication, providing significant savings, especially in applications using only a few devices.

**NMOS 40-pin package** A 40 pin package permits separate data and address buses, thereby eliminating most external control circuitry and reducing the required interface circuitry.

**NMOS RAM** A random-access memory that uses NMOS technology for high speed and lower power. NMOS RAMs compete with bipolar units for many high-speed cache applications. A typical NMOS RAM has the following features:

1. Access time of less than 100 ns
2. Maximum power dissipation of less than 600 mW
3. Fully static operation
4. Single 5V supply
5. Standard 16-pin package

**NMOS technology** NMOS technology is the most widely used technology for microprocessors today. The first NMOS microprocessor was the 8080. The original 8080 was designed for a maximum clock frequency of 2 MHz. Advances in n-channel technology now permit NMOS microprocessors to use clock rates higher than 12 MHz. An important feature of MOS microprocessors is that the load resistors are MOS transistors that are used as resistors. MOS transistors can also be classed as depletion mode or enhancement mode devices. *Depletion mode* transistors are normally on and require a gate voltage in order to be turned off. *Enhancement mode* devices are normally off and require a gate voltage in order to be turned on. The early NMOS microprocessors (such as the 8080) used enhancement-mode transistors for load resistors. This required a separate power supply to provide the gate voltage for the loads. Newer MOS microprocessors such as the 6800 use depletion mode loads, which eliminated the need for the extra power supply voltage. These processors operate from a single 5 volt supply using circuits as shown below.

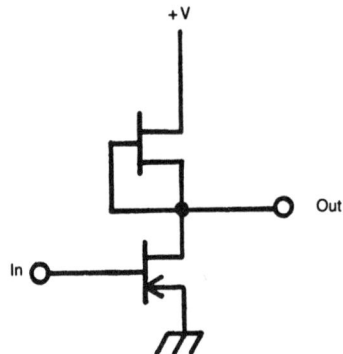

**NMOS-FET amplifier with depletion Mode load**

Since NMOS is faster than PMOS, and newer versions such as H—MOS and V—MOS give excellent density, NMOS is the most popular technology used to implement microprocessors today.

**n-n junction** A junction in a semiconductor device produced between two n-type regions having different electrical properties.

**NO** Abbreviation for *normally open*.

**no-address instruction** An instruction specifying an operation that the computer can perform without referring to its storage or memory unit.

**node** A terminal common to two or more branches in a network or system. Also called *junction point, branch point, nodal point,* and *vertex*.

**noise** Any unwanted disturbance in a system, such as random variations in voltage or current, or bits or words that are extra and must be removed before the data is used. *Steady-state* noise may consist of Gaussian noise, thermal noise, white noise, and random noise. *Impulse* noise

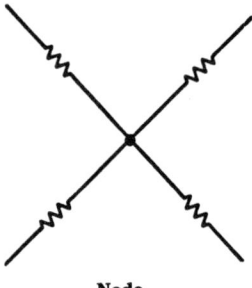

**Node**

is characterized by peaks of large amplitude and pulses of short duration. This type of noise can block out data signals and cause errors, especially in high-speed systems where more bits are affected in a given time period.

**noise, ambient** Refers to acoustical or electrical noise existing in a room or other location.

**noise, background** 1. Refers to extra bits or words that must be ignored or removed from data at the time the data is used. 2. Errors introduced into data in a system. 3. A disturbance tending to interfere with the normal operation of a device or system.

**noise, delta** Refers to the difference between the 1-state and the 0-state; a half-selected noise condition.

**noise diode** 1. A standard electrical-noise source consisting of a diode operated at saturation. The noise is due to the random emission of electrons. 2. A diode operated as a noise generator, under temperature-limited conditions.

**noise equivalent bandwidth** The useful bandwidth of a thermistor bolometer for different frequencies in the input radiation. Normally equal to 1/4t, where t is the time constant of the bolometer.

**noise, gaussian** Refers to noise in which the voltage distribution is specified in terms of statistical probabilities.

**noise immunity** Refers to the insensitivity of a circuit or device to spurious signals or noise. CMOS logic offers a noise margin of 1.5V compared to a noise margin of 0.4V for TTL circuits.

**noise, impulse** A type of noise characterized by high amplitude and short duration, sometimes occurring as a group of impulses or burst. Impulse noise is a common source of error, originating from switching equipment or electrical storms.

**noise level** Refers to the strength of extraneous signals in a circuit or system.

**noise margin** The difference in potential between a signal and either the noise existing when the signal is removed or the threshold level of the device being rated.

**noise, natural** Refers to noise caused by natural phenomena such as thermal emission or electrical storm static.

**noise ratio** The ratio of the noise level to the signal level, usually expressed in decibels.

**noise, systematic** Noise may be classified as random, periodic, or systematic. Systematic noise is a form of noise found in imperfect equipment. For example, if the signal for the character "u" were always replaced by the signal for character "s" in a message because of some failure, this would be a systematic error.

**noisy digit** A digit (usually zero) that is produced during the normalizing of a floating-point number and inserted during a left shift operation into the fixed-point part.

**noisy mode** The mode during the normalization of a floating-point number in which digits are inserted with a left shift operation into low-order positions.

**NOMA** Abbreviation for *National Office Management Association*.

**nominal bandwidth** The band of frequencies, including guard bands, assigned to a channel.

**nominal impedance** The impedance of a circuit or device under normal conditions, usually specified for a specific frequency. For example, a loudspeaker with a nominal impedance of 8 Ω is considered to have an 8 Ω impedance when the speaker's input signal is a 1000 Hz sine wave.

**nonarithmetic shift** A shift in which the digits dropped off at one end are returned at the other in an end-around carry operation. If a register holds 23456789, a nonarithmetic shift of two bits produces 45678923. Also called *end-around, ring shift,* or *cyclic shift*.

**nonconductor** An insulator through which no current can flow.

**nondestructive read** A read operation that does not result in erasure of the data in the source (abbreviated *NDR*).

**nondestructive readout** 1. A reading process that does not result in destruction of the data in the source. 2. A storage medium that cannot be erased and reused.

**nondissipative network** A network in which the inductances and capacitances are assumed to be free of power dissipation, since they are constructed as components with minimum losses.

**nonembedded command** A program instruction that effects an immediate change in the data to be processed, such as a command to delete a given line.

**nonequivalence element** A two-input logic element that furnishes a *true* output only when its two input signals are different.

**nonequivalence operation** A logical operation applied to two operands which produces a 1 for those bits that are different and a 0 for those bits that are the same.

```
OPERANDS         RESULT
110110           101100
011010
```

**nonimpact printer** A mechanism that produces text output on plain or special paper without contact between the printing mechanism and the paper, in contrast to an impact printer.

**noninductive capacitor** A capacitor designed to have its inherent inductance reduced to a minimum.

**noninductive circuit** A circuit in which effects arising from associated inductances are negligible.

**nonlinear capacitor** A capacitor that has a nonlinear mean charge characteristic or peak charge characteristic.

**nonlinear distortion** Distortion that is caused by a deviation from a linear relationship between the input and output of a system or device.

**nonlinearity** A relationship between the output and input that cannot be represented by direct proportioning.

**nonlinearity monotonicity** 1. The ability to include all digital code numbers in a conversion operation. 2. The amount by which the plot of output versus input deviates from a straight line.

**nonlinear network** A network of circuit elements that cannot be specified with linear variables such as differential equations or functions.

**nonlinear programming** A procedure used in operations research for locating the maximum and minimum of a function subject to nonlinear constraints.

**nonlinear resistance** A resistance with a nonproportionality between the potential difference and the electrical current.

**nonlinear system** Refers to a control system model that cannot be represented by linear equations.

**nonloading lines** Refers to cable pairs or transmission lines with no added inductive loading.

**nonnumerical data processing** Specific languages have been developed using symbol manipulation; they have been used primarily as research tools rather than for actual data processing. These have proved valuable in the construction of compilers and in the simulation of human problem solving. Other uses include the generalization and verification of mathematical proofs, pattern recognition, information retrieval, algebraic manipulation, heuristic programming, and the exploration of new programming languages.

**nonoperable instruction** An instruction whose only effect is to increment the instruction index counter. Usually written as CONTINUE.

**nonpolarized return-to-zero recording** A recording method in which the reference condition is the absence of magnetization. Ones are represented by a specified condition of magnetization, and zeros are represented by the absence of magnetization.

**nonrecursive filter** This type of filter uses only the input to the filter to determine the output signal. The figure shows how a microprocessor is applied to a recursive digital filter. The microprocessor and ROM replace the coefficient generator, multipliers, and address of a hardwired digital filter. The three microprocessors in this example are synchronized and connected by the I/O interface along with a common data bus. The recursive data is applied to the three microprocessors as shown in the right hand part of the diagram where particular parts of the circuit assume functional values f (n), f (n−1), and f (n−2).

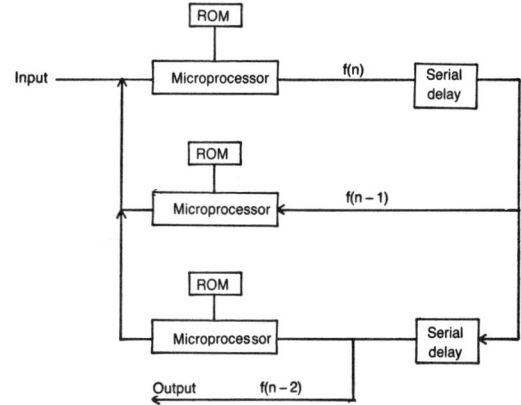

**Digital filter implementation**

**nonreturn-to-change recording** A recording method in which ones are represented by a specified condition of magnetization and zeros are represented by another condition.

**nonreturn-to-reference recording** A recording method in which ones are represented by a change in the condition of magnetization, and zeros are represented by the absence of change. Also called *nonreturn-to-zero recording*.

**nonreturn-to-zero** A method of writing information on a magnetic surface in which the current through the write head does not return to zero after the write pulse. Abbreviated *NRZ*.

**nonreturn-to-zero recording** Nonreturn-to-reference recording.

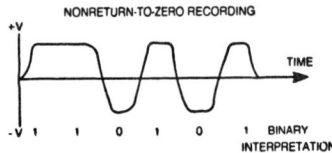

Nonreturn-to-zero recording

**nonswitched line** A service or connection between a remote terminal and a computer that does not have to be established by dialing.

**nonsynchronous** Not related in speed, frequency, or phase to other quantities in a device or circuit.

**nonvolatile** Descriptive of a memory or storage medium that retains data in the absence of power so that the data is available upon restoration of power. A magnetic memory is nonvolatile; most semiconductor read/write memories are volatile. PROMs and EAROMs remain intact after they are programmed if power is removed and then reapplied.

**nonvolatile memory** A memory, such as magnetic tape or disk, that retains information if power is removed.

**nonvolatile storage** Storage media that retain information in the absence of power and which allow the information to be available when power is restored.

**NO OP** A no-operation instruction, which causes the computer to do nothing except proceed to the next instruction in sequence. Also, *NOP*.

**no-operation** The computer instruction which causes the computer to do nothing except proceed to the next instruction. Abbreviated *NO OP*, *NOP*.

**NOP** The no-operation instruction, *NO OP*.

**NOR** A logical operation that has a true output only if all inputs are zero. The negative-OR operation.

**NORAD** Abbreviation for *North American Air Defense Command*.

**NOR circuit** A circuit or gate that has a true output only if all inputs are false.

**NOR element** A gate circuit having multiple inputs and one output that is energized only if all inputs are zero.

**NOR gate** A circuit that performs the NOR operation.

**normal contact** A contact that in its normal position closes a circuit and permits current to flow.

**normal direction flow** A flow in a direction from left to right or top to bottom in a flow chart.

**normal failure period** That period of time during which an essentially constant failure rate exists.

**normalization** The multiplication of a variable by a numerical coefficient to make it assume a desired value. Also called *scaling*.

**normalization routine** A floating-point arithmetic operation related to the normalization of numerals in which digits other than zero are developed in the lower order or less-significant positions during a left shift.

**normalization signal** Refers to the generation or restoration of signals that comply with specified requirements in amplitude, shape, and timing. Such signals are often generated from another signal, and the requirements are often conventions or rules of specific computer systems.

**normalized form** A form used in a floating-point number that is ad-

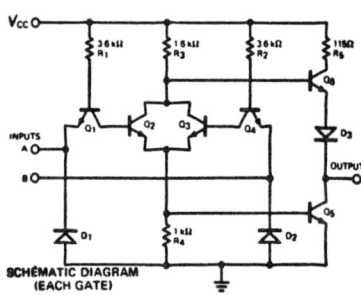

NOR gate (Quad 2-input)

justed so that its mantissa lies in a specified range. Also called *standard form*.

**normally closed** The designation applied to the contacts of a switch, relay, or solid-state switching device such that the circuit is completed when no input power is applied. Abbreviated *NC*.

**normally open** The designation applied to the contacts of a switch, relay, or solid-state switching device such that the circuit is not completed until power is applied. Abbreviated *NO*.

**normal magnetization** The locus of the tips of the magnetic hysteresis loops obtained by varying the limits of the range of alternating magnetization.

**normal stage punching** A card punching system in which only the even-numbered rows are punched.

**normal state** Refers to the condition of operation in a computer in which instructions are concerned with conventional aspects of computation such as adding, subtracting, and data transfer.

**Norton's theorem** A theorem that states that any linear network of impedances and sources, if viewed from any two points in the network, can be replaced by an equivalent impedance in shunt with an equivalent current source.

**NOT** A logic operator having the property: if P is a statement, then the NOT of P is true if P is false; and it is false if P is true. The NOT operator is represented by an overline.

**NOT AND** The NAND operation.

**NOT AND gate** An AND gating circuit combined with an inverter; a NAND gate.

**notation** The act, process, or method used to represent technical facts or quantities. In computer practice, the term typically describes the number radix, as follows:

| NOTATION | RADIX |
|---|---|
| BINARY | 2 |
| TERNARY | 3 |
| QUATERNARY | 4 |
| QUINARY | 5 |
| DECIMAL | 10 |

| NOTATION | RADIX |
|---|---|
| DUODECIMAL | 12 |
| HEXADECIMAL | 16 |
| DUOTRICENARY | 32 |
| BIQUINARY | 2,5 |

**notational system** Any of the various number systems used to indicate radix values, such as binary, decimal, or hexadecimal. See *notation*.

**notation, infix** A method of forming one dimensional expressions, arithmetic or logical, by alternating single operands and operators. Any operator performs its indicated function upon its adjacent terms, which are defined subject to the rules of operator precedence and grouping brackets that eliminate any ambiguity.

**NOT circuit** A circuit or gate in which the output is opposite in polarity to the input.

**NOT gate** A circuit that has a true output when the input is false, and a false output when the input is true.

**NOT if-then gate** A gate that performs the *A AND NOT B* and *B AND NOT A* operations.

**NOT operation** A Boolean operation that specifies that the output will always be the inverse of the input. A circuit or device that performs the NOT operation is called an *inverter*.

**NOT OR** The *negated OR* operation; *NOR*.

**NOTS** Abbreviation for *naval ordnance test station*.

**NP** Abbreviation for *new program*.

**npin transistor** A transistor that has an intrinsic (undoped) layer between the base and collector to extend the high-frequency range.

**npip transistor** A transistor that has an intrinsic layer between two p regions.

**np junction** The region in a semiconductor where the n-doped and p-doped areas meet. It is characterized by a high resistance in one direction and a low resistance in the other.

**n-plus-one address instruction** A multiple address instruction in which one address serves to specify the location of the next instruction in the normal sequence of execution.

**npn** A transistor with a p-region base and an n-region emitter and collector. Such transistors are characterized by electrons as majority carriers (rather than holes).

**npn transistor** 1. A junction transistor with a thin slice of p-type material forming the base between two pieces of n-type semiconductor, which form the collector and emitter. 2. A junction transistor with a p-type base, n-type emitter, and an n-type collector.

**NPO** Abbreviation for *Navy Purchasing Office*.

**NRL** Abbreviation for *Naval Research Laboratory*.

**NRZ** Abbreviation for *nonreturn to zero*, a recording technique in which write-pulse voltages do not return to zero following application.

**NRZO** Abbreviation for *nonreturn to zero one*.

**NSEC** Abbreviation for *nanosecond*.

**NSF** Abbreviation for *National Science Foundation*.

**NSIA** Abbreviation for *National Security Industrial Association*.

**NSV** Abbreviation for *nonautomatic self-verification*.

**n-type** A semiconductor region that is doped to provide excess electrons.

**n-type conductivity** The conductivity associated with conduction electrons in a semiconductor.

**nuclear energy** In principle this refers to the binding energy of a system of particles in an atomic nucleus. More usually this refers to the energy released during nuclear reactions involving the regrouping of such particles due to fission or fusion processes.

**nucleonic flowmeters** These flow instruments utilize radioisotopes and the detection of nuclear radiation. One type uses a source mounted to the outside of the pipe some distance upstream from the detector. The source neutrons collide with the moving fluid and cause particle and electromagnetic radiation to be emitted. Most of the emitted radiation occurs at the source location, but some is emitted as the fluid passes the detector. The number of counts produced by the detector are an indication of the flow rate of the fluid. Another type obtains an output by adding minute amounts of a radioactive trace element to the fluid. Nucleonic flowmeters offer no obstruction to the fluid and are useful for the measurement of difficult fluids such as multiphase variable composition fluids, slurries, and suspensions.

**null** A balanced condition that results in zero output from a circuit, device, or system.

**null character** A control character that serves to accomplish media fill or time fill functions. For example, in ASCII the null character is a string of zeros. Null characters can be inserted or removed without affecting the meaning of a sequence, but control of equipment or the format may be affected. Abbreviated *NUL*.

**null cycle** The time required to cycle through a program without introducing data. The null cycle represents the lower boundary for program processing time.

**null indicator** A device that indicates when a parameter is zero.

**null matrix** A matrix of values in which every element is zero. Also called *zero matrix*.

**null set** A set that contains no numbers. Also called the *empty set*.

**null suppression** The bypassing of all null characters in a data string to reduce the number of characters transmitted. Also called *data compaction*.

**number** A mathematical entity that indicates quantity or amount of units; a numeral.

**number, check** Refers to a designated number composed of one or more digits and used to detect equipment malfunctions in data transfer operations. If a check number consists of only one digit, it is synonymous with check digit.

**number system** Notation system.

**numeral** A discrete representation of a number using a single-digit symbol. For example, the number 12 is composed of two numerals.

**numeral, double length** Refers to a specific numeral that contains twice as many digits as ordinary numerals in particular kinds of computers and that usually requires two registers or storage locations. Such numerals are often used for double precision computing.

**numeral system** A system for representing numbers by agreed sets of symbols according to agreed rules.

**numeration** The representation of numbers by agreed sets of symbols according to agreed rules.

**numeration system** Numeral system.

**numeric** 1. Pertaining to numerals or representation by means of numerals. 2. A set of numerals with an established meaning within a given context. For example, 10-4 is a communications numeric for "okay."

**numerical** Pertaining to numerals or representations using numerals.

**numerical analysis** The study of methods for obtaining useful quantitative solutions to problems that have been expressed mathematically. Numerical analysis also includes the study of errors and the bounds of errors in obtaining these solutions.

**numerical control** The automatic control of a machine or a process using numerical data that is introduced using punched tapes or other input methods. Most numerical-control devices have limited logical capability, and they rely on the input medium for detailed guidance.

A computer is generally used to prepare the control media. Direct numerical control uses a system of numerically controlled machines that are connected to a common memory. Direct numerical control systems may have provisions for collection and display of data along with limited editing and operator instruction capabilities.

Other types of numerical control systems may use methods with interchangeable connections for modifying the control sequence.

**numerical control, hand-wired** A numerical control system wherein the response to data input, data handling sequence, and control functions is determined by the fixed and committed circuit interconnections of discrete decision elements and storage devices. Changes in the response, sequence, or functions are made by changing the interconnections.

**numerical control system** A system for controlling industrial machine operations automatically by insertion of numerical data at some point.

**numerical control tape** A punched-paper or magnetic tape that is used to feed instructions to a numerical control machine.

**numeric code** A code that consists only of number symbols and associated special characters.

**numerical data** Data in which information is expressed by a set of numbers that can assume only discrete values or configurations.

**numerically controlled machine** A machine that is under the control of numerical data. See *numerical control*.

**numeric coding** A system of abbreviation in which all information is reduced to numerical quantities, in contrast to alphabetic coding.

**numeric constant** A term that is treated as an octal or decimal number, depending upon the conversion mode in effect at the time.

**numeric word** A word composed of characters from a numeric code. For example, in the Dewey decimal classification system, 621.39 is a numeric word used to identify a specific class of literature.

**Nusselt number** The significant nondimensional parameter in convective heat loss problems, defined by $Qd/k/O$, where Q is the rate of heat loss from a solid body, /O is the temperature difference between the body and its surroundings, k is the thermal conductivity of the surrounding fluid, and d is the significant linear dimension of the solid.

**nylong** A generic term for any long chain synthetic polymeric amide that has recurring amide groups in an integral part of the main polymer chain and that is capable of being formed into a filament in which the structural elements are oriented in the direction of the axis.

**Nyquist rate** Refers to the maximum rate at which code elements can be resolved in a communication channel of limited bandwidth.

# O

**OAR** Abbreviation for *Office of Aerospace Research*.

**object code** The output from a compiler or assembler that is itself executable machine code or is suitable for processing to produce executable machine code. A line of object code might be a 16-bit string of ones and zeros whose combination is the machine-language equivalent of an instruction.

**object deck** A stack of punched cards forming a computer program in machine language. The object deck is usually prepared from an equivalent source deck by a compiler.

**object language** The language that is the output of an automatic coding routine. Object language and machine language may be the same; however, if the coding routine is done in a series of steps, the object language of one step may serve as the source language for the next step.

**object program** A source program that has been translated into machine language, or the final or target program which is the end result of processing. Typically, translator modules are used to translate the user-generated code into executable machine code; other operating modules add the utility routines to generate the executable object program.

**OCAL** Abbreviation for *Online cryptanalytic aid language*.

**OConUS** Abbreviation for *outside continental U.S.*

**OCP** 1. Abbreviation for *optional character printing*. 2. Abbreviation for *output control pulse*.

**OCR** Abbreviation for *optical character recognition*, the recognition by machines of printed or written characters using optical sensing devices.

**octal** A number system whose radix is 8, composed of the digits 0 through 7.

**octal debug technique** A debugging and loading program used in octal systems. It is usually supplied on two preprogrammed PROMs with a supplementary tape and includes the following features:

1. Memory list/modify
2. Register list/modify
3. Tape load/punch
4. Memory dump

**octal digits** The symbols 0 through 7 when the radix is 8.

**odd-even check** Parity check.

**odd-even interleaving** The splitting of memory into several sections and independent paths with the odd and even addresses in alternate sections. Odd-even interleaving allows additional segmenting over normal memory interleaving.

**odd-parity** A parity checking scheme in which the parity bit is set so that the total number of ones in the block is always odd.

**odd-parity check** A check in which the sum of all binary digits in a word is odd. An additional character position permits insertion of a 1 when the total is even, and insertion of a 0 when the total is odd.

**OEM** Abbreviation for *original equipment manufacturer*.

**oersted** A unit of field strength in the eeu system, such that 2 oersted is the field produced at the center of a circular conductor, 1 cm in radius, carrying 1 abampere (10 amperes). In the MKSA system

$$1 \text{ oersted} = \frac{1000}{4} \text{ ampere-turns/meter.}$$

**off emergency** A console or control panel switch that can be used to disconnect all power in the event of an emergency situation.

**offline** 1. Equipment that is not under direct control of the CPU. 2. Terminal equipment not connected to a transmission line.

**offline operation** An operation that is independent of the system's operating time base. Offline operation usually refers to the operation of peripheral units independent of the CPU.

**off-punch** A punched hole in a card or tape that did not compare favorably with the proper position for that hole.

**offset** For a zero input, the extent to which the output deviates from zero, usually a function of time and temperature.

**offset amplifier, current** Current offset (or bias current) multiplied by the feedback resistor produces an output error. This effect can be minimized by using the differential offset (the difference in offset currents for the two inputs) when the resistance seen from both inputs to ground are equal.

**offset binary code** A code that for three bits plus sign is the same as natural binary for four bits, except for the following: zero is at negative full scale; the LSB is 1/16 of the total bipolar range; and the MSB is on at zero. An offset binary 3 bits plus sign converter can be made from a 4 bit D/A converter with a 0 to 10V full scale range. The scale factor is doubled to 20V, and the zero is offset by half of the full range to $-10V$. For an A/D converter, reduce the input by half, and increment a bias of half the range. Offset binary is more compatible with microcomputer inputs and outputs since it is easily changed to the more common two's complement (by complementing the MSB). It also has a single unambiguous code for zero.

**OFHC** Oxygen Free High Conductivity, a grade of electrolytic copper wire.

**off-the-shelf** Refers to production items that are available from current stock, or software that can be used as purchased.

**OG** Abbreviation for *OR gate*.

**ohm** The unit of electrical resistance.

**ohm-cm** The CGS unit of resistivity.

**ohmic contact** A contact in which the potential drop is proportional to the current across the contact.

**ohmic drop** The voltage drop over a part of a circuit because of current passing through resistance.

**ohmic loss** The power dissipation in a circuit due to pure resistance losses.

**ohmic resistor** A resistor can be described to be ohmic or nonohmic, according to whether or not its resistance is described by Ohm's law.

**ohmmeter** A portable battery-operated instrument for measuring electrical resistance and determining electrical continuity.

**Ohm's law** 1. A law formulated by B. S. Ohm in 1827 that states that in metallic conductors at a constant temperature and zero magnetic field, the resistance is independent of the current. 2. The voltage across an element of a circuit is equal to the current in amperes through the element, multiplied by the resistance of the element in ohms. Expressed mathematically as $E = I \times R$ or $I = E/R$ and $R = E/I$.

**O/L** Abbreviation for *operations/logistics*.

**one or 1** In binary code, the representation of an "off", "no", or "false" state. The compliment to zero (0).

**one-address** A system of instructions such that each complete instruction explicitly describes one operation and one storage location.

**one-address instruction** An instruction that consists of an operation and exactly one address. The instruction code of a single-address computer may include both zero and multiaddress instructions as special cases.

**one-cell switching** Refers to an array of magnetic cells and the selective switching of one cell in the array by the application of selected drive pulses.

**one-digit adder** A binary adding circuit that adds one digit at a time.

**one-for-one** A term used with assembly routines where one source-language instruction is converted into one machine-language instruction.

**one-level storage** A concept that treats all online storage as having one level of appearance to the user. One-level storage makes all online storage appear as main storage.

**one-plus-one address** An instruction that contains one operand address and one control address.

**ones' complement** The radix-minus-one complement in binary notation.

**one-shot** 1. A monostable multivibrator. 2. Any circuit or device having only one stable state.

**one-shot multivibrator** A multivibrator that has one stable state.

**one-step operation** A method of operating a computer manually in which a single instruction or part of an instruction is performed in response to a single manual control operation. One-step operation is generally used for debugging procedures.

**one-to-zero ratio** The ratio of a one output level to a zero output level.

**online** 1. Equipment, devices, and systems in direct interactive communication with the CPU. 2. Descriptive of terminal equipment connected to a transmission line.

**online data processing** Data processing in which all changes to records and accounts are made at the time that each transaction or event occurs. Online processing generally requires random-access storage.

**online debugging** The debugging of a program while sharing its execution with an online process program. Online debugging must be accomplished in such a way that any attempt by the program being debugged to interfere with the process program will be detected and inhibited.

**online diagnostics** The running of diagnostics while the system is online, but off peak to save time and to take corrective action without shutdown of the system.

**online equipment** Equipment under the direct control of the CUP.

**online mode** A mode of operation in which all devices are responsive to the CPU.

**online storage** Storage devices that are under direct control of the computing system.

**online system** 1. A system in which the input data enters the computer directly from the point of origin and the output data is transmitted directly to where it is used. 2. A system that has no need for human intervention between the source of data and the processing by the CPU.

**online test facilities** Refers to test facilities including line loop tests, error recovery procedures, checkpoint, restarts, and the collection of traffic and error statistics while directly connected to the CPUs.

**on-state drain current** The current into the drain terminal of a MOS device with a specified forward-gate source voltage applied to bias the device to the on state.

**oops** An off line operation simulator that does high speed printing operations as peripheral support.

**OP** Abbreviation for *Operation*.

**OPAL** Abbreviation for *optical platform alignment linkage*.

**op codes** Operation codes that are decoded to serve as instructions in microcomputer systems. The op code usually contains source statements that are used to generate machine instructions after assembly.

**open circuit** Refers to the nondelivery of current from a source that is not loaded.

**open circuit impedance** The input or driving impedance of a line or network when the output is open circuited and not grounded or loaded.

**open code** In reference to assembler programming, the portion of a source module that lies outside of any source macro definitions that may be specified.

**open-loop** A control system in which there is no self-correcting action and no feedback path; also a family of control units, which may include computers which are linked together manually by operator action.

**open-loop control** A type of control in which no feedback is employed.

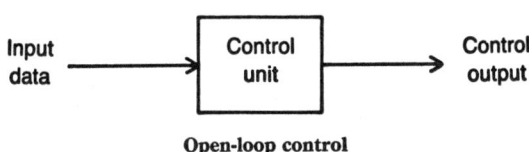

Open-loop control

**open-loop control system** A control system without feedback in which the output is directly controlled by the system input.

**open loop follower sample hold** An open loop follower circuit is shown. As the switch is closed, the capacitor charges exponentially to the input voltage, and the amplifier's output follows the capacitor voltage. As the switch is opened, the charge and voltage level remain on the capacitor. The capacitor's acquisition time depends on the series resistance and the current available. Once the charge is complete to the desired accuracy, the switch can be opened, even though the amplifier may not have settled, without affecting the final output value or the settling time greatly, because the amplifier's input stage should not draw any appreciable current (the switch is typically a FET and the amplifier has a FET input).

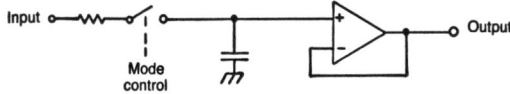

Basic open-loop follower sample-hold

**open loop gain** Refers to the ratio of the change in the return signal to the change in the corresponding error signal at a specified frequency.

**open loop response** The response of a closed loop system with the feedback path interrupted for test purposes.

**open loop system** A control system that does not compare the output with the input for control purposes.

**open routine** A routine that can be directly inserted into a larger routine with a linkage or calling sequence.

**open running** Refers to a teletypewriter that is connected to an open line. The teletypewriter appears to be running, as the type hammer continually hits the type box, but does not move across the page.

**open shop** The operation of a computer facility in which most of the problem programming is performed by the problem originator rather than by a group of programming specialists.

**open subroutine** A subroutine that is directly inserted into the linear operational sequence where it is used. It does not require a jump and must be recopied at each point where it is needed in the routine.

**operand** 1. The fundamental quantity on which a mathematical operation is performed. A statement usually consists of an operator and an operand; in an add instruction, the operator will indicate "add," and the operand will indicate what is to be added. A result, parameter, or the address portion of an instruction.

**operand call syllable** A specific syllable that calls for an operand to be brought from the stack either directly from the program reference table or indirectly using a descriptor.

**operating code** A specific code containing source statements that generate machine code after assembly. Also called *op code*.

**operating conditions** Refers to the various conditions, such as ambient temperature, ambient pressure, and vibration, to which a device is subjected to. Operating conditions do not include the variable measured by the device.

**operating console** A unit that contains all controls and indicators necessary for the operation of the processor. A typical microcomputer operating console may include the following functions:

1. Run indicator and switch
2. Halt indicator and switch
3. Reset switch
4. Link indicator
5. Interrupt indicator
6. Accumulator, program counter, and memory display

**operating system** A basic group of programs under the control of a data processing program or an integrated collection of service routines for supervising the sequencing and processing operations.

Operating systems may provide scheduling, debugging, input/output control, accounting, compilation, storage assignment, data management, and other services. A typical disk operating system features extended file management, program chaining, page loading, and mixing programs of different languages. Up to 100 million bytes of storage can be accessed with some systems.

Floppy disk operating systems have replaced paper tape and cards during microcomputer development. The source programs are written and edited at the system keyboard and stored on the floppy disk for assembly.

Supervisor and executive operating systems include a supervisory program, system programs, and system routines. The executive brings together the system software components to make an operating system.

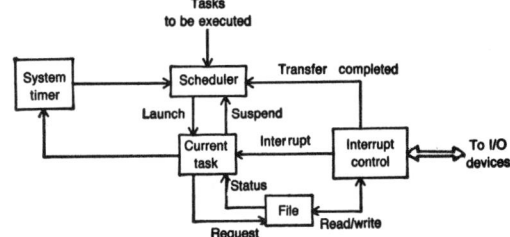

Basic tasks of an operating system

**operating system, disk** Refers to a software management package for a magnetic disk memory system. Typical units provide system features such as extended file management, program chaining, current page loading, and mixing programs of different languages. They may include data communication facilities to allow the time-critical allocation of machine response time and data protection features. Hundreds of megabytes of random storage can be directly accessed with some systems.

**operating system, floppy disk** Refers to software developed to control the floppy disk systems used in microcomputer systems. Programs written and edited at the system keyboard and stored on the floppy may be managed and controlled by the operating system.

**operating system, supervisor** Refers to an operating system that consists of a supervisory control program, system programs, and system subroutines. It may include a symbolic assembler and macroprocessor, a compiler, and debugging aids. A library of general utility programs may also be provided.

**operation** A defined action, usually specified by a single instruction or pseudo instruction. An operation may be arithmetic, logical, or transferral; it may be executed under the direction of a subroutine.

**operational amplifier** A usually integrated amplifier with high gain and wide bandwidth that can be used to perform mathematical operations. Also called *op amp*.

**operational character** A character used as a code element to initiate, modify, or stop a control operation. A typical operational character is the *carriage return*.

**operational relay** A relay that is controlled by an operational amplifier or a relay amplifier.

**operation code** A code that represents specific actions. Also called *instruction code*.

**operation cycle** The portion of a machine cycle during which the actual execution of the instruction takes place. Operations such as multiply or divide may require a large number of these cycles for completion. Also called an *execution cycle*.

**operation decoder** A device that selects one or more channels of operation according to the operation part of the machine instruction.

**operation, dyadic Boolean** A specific Boolean operator that is applied to pairs of operands, in particular the operators: AND, equivalence, exclusive OR, inclusion, NAND, NOR, and OR.

**operations analysis** The use of analytic methods to provide criteria for decisions in systems involving repeatable operations. The usual objective is to provide management with a logical basis for making predictions and decisions. The following techniques may be used:

1. Linear programming
2. Probability theory
3. Information theory
4. Game theory
5. Monte Carlo methods
6. Queuing theory

**operations manual** A manual that contains instructions and specifications for a given application. Typically it includes the components of operator's manual and programmer reference manual; it may also include a log section.

**operations research** Operations analysis (abbreviated *OR*).

**operator** 1. The mathematical symbol that represents the process to be performed on an associated operand. 2. The portion of an instruction that indicates the action to be performed on the operands.

**operator console** A hardware unit that allows the operator to communicate with the computer. The operator console is used to enter data or information, to request and display stored data, and to actuate the various command routines.

**operator indicator** Any display light used to show conditions on the operator console. The operator indicators can usually be set, cleared, and tested under program control.

**operator interrupt** In some systems an operator interrupt trap is armed, and the fixed interrupt location is patched each time the monitor program receives control. When an operator interrupt occurs, control is given to a routine in the monitor.

**operator intervention section** That portion of the control equipment in which operators can intervene in normal programming operations.

**op register** A register used to hold the operation code of computer instructions.

**OPTEVFOR** Abbreviation for *operational test and evaluation force*.

**optical character recognition** The machine identification of graphic characters using photosensitive devices. Optical character recognition (abbreviated *OCR*) includes characters of all fonts or types.

**optical coupled isolation amplifier** A common approach for obtaining electrical isolation is optical coupling. Optical coupling is effective for isolation, since it uses a portion of the electromagnetic spectrum that completely eliminates voltage, current and magnetic flux for energy transmission.

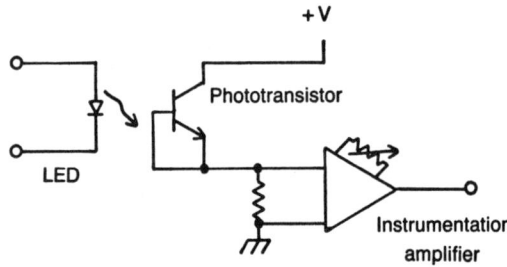

**Optical coupled isolation amplifier**

**optical coupler** A photon-coupled amplifier used to isolate electrical outputs from inputs. Optical couplers can operate at speeds of up to 10 MHz with isolation voltages as high as 5kV. Also called *optocoupler* and *optoisolator*.

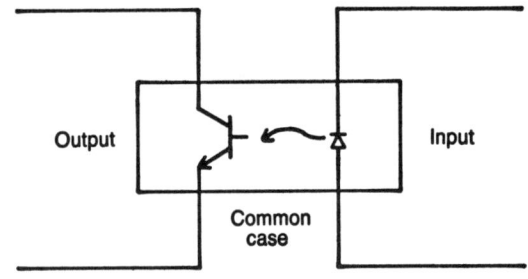

**Optical coupler**

**optical image chip** An integrated circuit that converts optical images into electrical signals. Optical image chips are used in some TV monitors and in small inexpensive TV cameras.

**optical isolator** Optical coupler.

**optical mark reader** A device that can read forms with pencil marks, punches, and printed marks.

**optical scanner** A device that scans patterns of incident light and generates signals that are functions of the data represented. The data may be printed or written using a bar code or other representation.

**optical sensor** A device or transducer capable of detecting light and producing an electrical output.

**optimize** To rearrange instructions or data in storage such that a minimum number of jumps or transfers are required in the running of the program.

**optimizing control action** Refers to a type of control action that automatically seeks and maintains the most advantageous value of a specified variable, instead of maintaining it at a set value.

**optimum code** A computer code that is particularly efficient in regard to a specific aspect, such as:

1. Minimum time of execution
2. Most efficient use of storage space
3. Minimum coding time

**optimum programming** Programming in order to maximize efficiency with respect to some criterion.

**optional stop** A miscellaneous command similar to a program stop except that the control ignores the command unless the operator has previously actuated a manual selector to validate the command.

**option board** A circuit board family that allows customers to implement certain basic system options. Typical option boards include real-time clocks, serial interfaces, and input/output circuits.

**optocoupler** Optical coupler.

**optoisolator** Any device using a light-sensing element and light source to avoid direct contact in a circuit.

**OR** A logic operator having the following property for logical quantities P and Q:

| P | Q | P OR Q |
|---|---|--------|
| 0 | 0 | 0 |
| 0 | 1 | 1 |
| 1 | 0 | 1 |
| 1 | 1 | 1 |

The OR operator is represented in electrical and FORTRAN terminology by a "plus" symbol.

**OR circuit** A circuit or device that implements the logical OR operator. An output occurs whenever there are one or more inputs present.

**order** 1. The weight or significance assigned to a digit position in a number. 2. To sequence or arrange in a series according to specified conditions.

**orderly closedown** The stopping of a system in such a way that allows an orderly restart with no destruction of data. An orderly closedown or shutdown provides that all records are updated that should be updated, and no records are erroneously updated when the restart begins.

**ordinary symbol** A symbol used in assembler programming to represent an assembly time value when used in the name or operand field of an instruction in assembly language. Ordinary symbols are also used to represent operation codes for assembly language instructions.

**OR ELSE** A logical operator that states that if P and Q are statements, then P OR ELSE Q is either true or false. Also called *EITHER/OR*.

**OR ELSE logic** A logical operator that has the property that if P and Q are two statements, then the statement (P or else Q) is true or false.

The OR-ELSE operator is often represented by an inverted vee. This operator is the same as either/or.

**ORG** Abbreviation for *ORiGin*, a pseudo command in assembly language to specify the starting memory address of a program. Most CP/M systems use an address of $100 ($ indicates hexadecimal notation) for the start or origin of their programs. Some computers use $4200 for their CP/M program's origin as these use read-only memories, which occupy the lower memory spaces.

**OR gate** OR circuit.

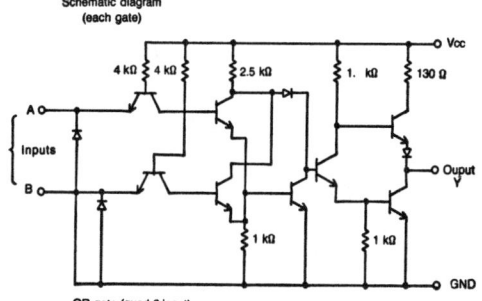

OR gate (quad 2-input)

**origin** The absolute storage address in relative coding to which addresses in a region are referenced.

**origination** Refers to the creating of a record in machine sensible form, directly or as a byproduct of a human readable document.

**OR NOT gate** Same as gate, A OR NOT B and gate B OR NOT A.

**OR operation** The logical operation defined for two integers as follows: if A OR B = 1, then the result is 1; otherwise the result is 0. The OR operation is represented by a plus sign, A OR B = A + B.

**OR operator** The logical operator that produces an OR function.

**Orthocode** An arrangement of black and white bars resembling a piano keyboard that can be read by a photoelectric device.

**orthoscanner** An optical scanning device that reads coded information (Orthocode) at the rate of 1,850 characters per second. Coupons, on which the code is printed, are read at the rate of 1,500 per minute.

**orthotrack** A complete row of orthocodes.

**OR unit** OR gate.

**OS** Abbreviation for *operating system*, the basic software used for scheduling, debugging, and other operations in a computer system.

**OS bulk storage diagnostic** Refers to tests and verifies the long term reliability of operating system (OS) bulk storage devices by continuously copying test files between devices.

**oscillation** The cyclic alternation of conditions (as voltages, currents, etc.) in a circuit or system.

**oscillation constant** The square root of the product of inductance (henry) and capacitance (farad) of a resonant circuit.

**oscillation frequency** This frequency is determined by the balance between the inertia reactance and the elastic reactance of a system that includes an open or short circuited transmission line, a cavity, a resonant circuit, or a quartz crystal.

if  $C$ = capacitance
   $L$ = self inductance or circuit

then frequency $f = 1/(2 \pi LC)$.
In a mechanical oscillating system,
$$f = 2 \pi M/S$$
where $M$ = Mass
   $S$ = restoring force/unit displacement

**oscillations, free** Refers to oscillating currents and voltages that continue to flow in a circuit after the voltage has been removed. This is due to the interchange of electromagnetic and electrostatic energy and is a function of the time constant of the circuit.

**oscillator** A low-current source of an alternating voltage at any frequency. Oscillators may be electrical, electronic, or mechanical. Most microcomputer systems use an oscillator with a piezoelectric crystal to provide a stable reference frequency for clocking.

**oscillator, Armstrong** Refers to an oscillator in which the feedback is achieved through coupled plate and grid circuit coils.

**oscillator, blocking** Refers to a form of dynamic circuitry that makes use of block oscillators that either oscillate in step with the clock or do not oscillate at all. A single input pulse is sufficient to start the oscillations; then the output is fed back to the input through the appropriate delay to maintain the oscillations. The presence of oscillation can represent a "1," while the absence of oscillation can represent the "0" state.

**oscillator, Colpitts** Refers to an oscillator in which two resonant circuit capacitors with a tap between them are used.

**oscillator crystal** A piezoelectric crystal used in an oscillator to control the frequency of oscillation.

**oscillator, Hartley** Refers to an oscillator circuit in which the coil of the resonant circuit is tapped.

**oscillator, local** Refers to the front-end oscillator in a superheterodyne circuit.

**oscillatory discharge** The discharge of a capacitor through an inductor when the resistance of circuit is sufficiently low; the current persists after the capacitor has discharged, so that it charges again in the reverse direction. This process is repeated until all initial energy is dissipated in the resistance.

**oscilloscope** A test instrument that uses a cathode-ray tube to display graphic representations of pulses and waveforms. Digital testing requires oscilloscopes with wide bandwidths and short rise times. Several manufacturers have combined oscilloscopes with microprocessors and display units to produce a high-performance troubleshooting unit. The microprocessor is used to calculate time intervals, computer voltage levels, convert time intervals to frequency, and calculate percentages.

**oscilloscope tube** Refers to a cathode ray tube (CRT) used to display waveshapes.

**outer macroinstruction** A macroinstruction in assembler programming that is specified in open code.

**output** The produced signals used to drive peripheral terminals.

**output area** A segment of internal storage reserved for output data. Also called the *output block* or *output working storage*.

**output block** Output area.

**output bus driver** An amplifier used to drive the impedance loads used for the output lines in a system.

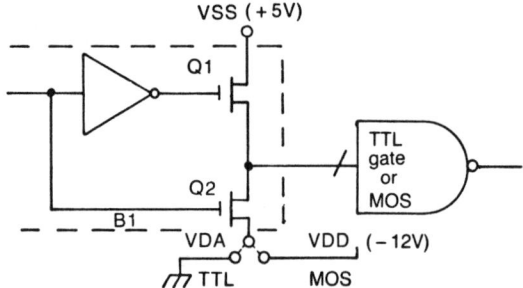

Output bus driver

**output capacitance** Refers to the capacitive component of the output impedance of a device or circuit.

**output channel** A path for conveying data from a device or logic element.

**output data** Data delivered from a device or program, generally after processing.

**output device** A unit used for conveying data out of another area, block, or unit.

**output formatter** A special program used to produce punched card or tape versions of assembled microprocessor programs in formats compatible with available storage media. Output formatters are available for the following media:

1. Mask-programmable ROM
2. Laser-encodable ROMs
3. Assemblers
4. ROM emulators

**output impedance** The idealized load impedance of a device producing signals for use in another system or another part of the same system.

**output meter** A meter that measures the output voltage of a circuit or line. It may be calibrated in volts or power level. In dB the zero power level is usually set at one milliwatt when the circuit is properly terminated.

**output module** Refers to a machine or part of a machine that translates electrical impulses representing data into permanent results such as printed forms, punched cards, or magnetic recordings.

**output module valve** A section of the computer that converts output data into analog control signals.

**output ratings, amplifier** The output voltage and current ratings of an amplifier imply a minimum value for the load resistor. In an inverting amplifier, the feedback resistor is a load for the output, and the current through this resistor must be subtracted from the amount of current still available at the output. Most operational amplifiers can be shorted to ground without damage, but shorting to a voltage can destroy some of the circuitry.

**output record** The current record stored in the output area prior to being output, or a specific record written to an output device.

**output register** The register used to hold data until it can be output to an external device.

**output regulation** Refers to the variation of voltage with load current in a power supply.

**output steering** Refers to the sharing of one UART serial output among two separate serial output devices under program control.

**output stream** The messages and other output data issued by a system or program on the output device or devices activated by the operator. Also called *job output stream* or *output job stream*.

**output table** A device that plots curves, graphs, charts, and other graphic output.

**output word processing equipment** Refers to automated typing systems.

**outside loop** A program loop that executes the control parameters being held constant while the current loop is being carried through possible values. Outside loops are considered nested loops when loops within it are entirely contained.

**oven** Refers to a component processing enclosure and associated sensors and heaters for maintaining components at a controlled and usually constant temperature.

**overall loss** Refers to a term adopted to represent the composite attenuation, the transducer loss, and the insertion loss of a circuit.

**overcoupling** A condition of two electrical circuits or mechanical systems tuned to the same frequency when there is sufficient interaction between them for the frequency response curve of the system to show two maxima, displaced to opposite sides of the maximum for either circuit alone.

**overdamping** Damping in excess of critical damping in a control system. Overdamping produces a slow nonoscillatory return to equilibrium following a disturbance.

**overflow** 1. The condition that occurs when the result of an arithmetic operation exceeds the capacity of the storage space alloted for it. 2. The digit or digits that occur from overflow conditions. Overflow develops when attempts are made to write longer fields into a location of specific length; for example, a 10-digit product will overflow an 8-digit accumulator.

**overflow, arithmetic** 1. In reference to an arithmetic operation, the generation of a quantity beyond the capacity of the register or location that is to receive the result; over capacity; the information contained in an item of information that is in excess of a given amount. 2. The portion of data that exceeds the capacity of the allocated unit of storage. Overflow develops when attempts are made to write longer fields into a field location of a specific length; a 12 bit product will overflow a 10 bit accumulator.

**overflow check indicator** A device that indicates an overflow condition.

**overflow indicator** A device that changes state when an overflow occurs in the register it is monitoring. The overflow indicator can be interrogated and restored to its original state.

**overflow operation** An operation that exceeds the capacity of the storage device, leading to the generation of an overflow condition.

**overflow position** The extra position in a register used to hold an overflow digit.

**overhead** The distribution of operating time of the executive routine for checking, monitoring, and scheduling all jobs or tasks related to the total cost of the complete system, usually expressed in percentages or ratios.

**overlapping data channel** Refers to a data channel that allows asynchronous operation of its input/output devices and processing by the central processing unit.

**overlay** A technique for bringing routines into high-speed storage from some other form of storage during processing, such that several routines will occupy the same storage locations at different times. Overlay is used when the total storage requirements for instructions exceed the available main storage. New information that is required is laid over information no longer needed. Usually the sets of information are not related, except that they are needed in the same program at different times. The use of the same data for successive cases is not an overlay.

**overlay module** A software load module that has been divided into overlay segments and provided with the information to implement the desired loading of the segments when requested.

**overlay path** Refers to the segments in an overlay tree between a particular segment and the root segment of a program.

**overlay program** A program in which certain control sections can use the same storage locations at different times during execution.

**overlay region** An area of main storage where segments can be loaded independently of paths in other regions. Only one path within a region can be in main storage at any one time.

**overlay segments** Refers to overlaying or replacing one program segment with another.

**overlays, memory** In many systems, the monitor remains resident in lower memory at all times. Object programs are loaded into memory, starting at the end of the monitor. The program loader resides in upper memory. Object programs cannot be loaded into the loader area. This area can be overlayed by common storage. Part of the loader can also be overlayed by library subroutines. In addition, programmers can specify that sections of their own program may overlay each other when needed.

**overlay supervisor** A routine that controls the proper sequencing and positioning of segments in limited storage during execution.

**overlay tree** A graphic representation showing the segments of an overlay program and their relationships.

**overload** A condition in a computing element that results in a substantial error in computation because of the saturation of one or more parts of the computing element.

**overload capacity** The excess capacity of a circuit or system over that of its rating.

**overload module test** A hardware test designed to detect substandard units by using operating conditions or parameters outside the normal.

**overload recovery time** The time required for the output to return to its proper value after an overload condition is removed.

**overmodulation** Amplitude modulation which exceeds 100 percent. Overmodulation can produce the loss of signal transmission for a fraction of the modulation cycle, along with considerable distortion.

**overpunch** To add holes in a card column that already contains one or more holes.

**overrun** A condition that occurs when data is transferred to or from a nonbuffered control unit operating with a synchronous medium, and the total activity initiated by the program exceeds the capability of the channel.

**overshoot** 1. The extent to which a control device or system carries the controlled variable or output past a final or desired value. 2. The amount by which an output pulse exceeds its stabilized value momentarily.

**overwrite** The act of placing information in a location and destroying all previous information contained there.

**Ovshinsky effect** The switching action found in some types of glass semiconductor materials. The impedance of the device changes with an applied electric field and is independent of the polarity.

**oxide** A chemical coating used in semiconductor devices, magnetic tapes, and other electronic products.

**oxide buildup** The accumulation of magnetic tape residue on the surface of magnetic heads from repeated use. Oxide buildup causes a loss in output and accelerates tape and head wear.

**oxide isolation** The separation of elements on semiconductor chips using oxidized regions. Oxide isolation results in high packing density along with higher speeds. Without oxide isolation, the electrical isolation is achieved with reversed-biased junctions that occupy more space and have higher capacitance.

**oxide isolation, isoplanar** A fabrication variation applicable to bipolar processes. This technique results in higher packing densities and slightly higher speeds and is accomplished by using silicon oxide to isolate the various components. A common form of oxide isolation is isoplanar. Other bipolar processes achieve electrical isolation of the circuit elements with reversed biased pn junctions, but these junctions occupy more space and have higher capacitance than oxide isolation circuits. The technique can be applied to the complex bipolar products to achieve cost reduction.

**oxygen** An odorless gaseous element: atomic number 8, atomic weight 15.994, melts at $-218.8\,°C$, boils at $-182.970\,°C$. It is chemically very active and forms one fifth of the atmosphere.

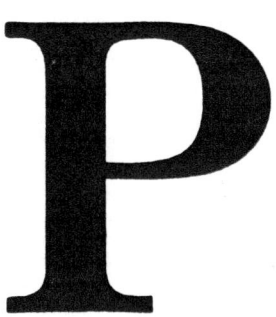

**P** 1. Symbol for *power*. 2. Symbol for *poise*. 3. Symbol for *permeance* (webers per ampere). 4. Symbol for prefix *peta* ($10^{15}$). 5. Abbreviation for *positive*. 6. In lowercase, symbol for *pico* ($10^{-12}$).

**PABX** Abbreviation for *private automatic branch exchange*, equipment that switches calls between the public telephone network and inside extensions.

**pack** To compress data by taking advantage of known characteristics of the data in such a way that the original data can be recovered. Packing involves the use of bit or byte locations that would otherwise go unused and may be used to combine several fields of information into one machine word.

**package** The container used to house an active semiconductor device. Packages are available in plastic and ceramic housings with up to 40 pins. In general, microprocessors with fewer pins are easier to physically install, while those with larger numbers of pins are easier to interface with the rest of the equipment required for the microcomputer system.

**package, ceramic** Refers to a standard high reliability package, made of three layers $Al_2O_3$, ceramic, and nickel plated refactory metal. In some types the cavity is sealed with a glazed ceramic lid, using a controlled devitrified low temperature glass sealant. Package leads are of Kovar, which is nickel plated and solder dipped for socket insertion or soldering.

**packaged** Descriptive of equipment that is complete and ready for use, such as modules which are sealed or encapsulated; thus, *off-the-shelf*.

**package, plastic** Usually refers to a plastic dual-inline package (DIP), which is a widely accepted industry standard refined by manufacturers for MOS/LSI applications. Many packages use a silicon body that is transfer molded directly onto the assembled lead frame and die. The lead frame is often Kovar or Alloy 42, with external pins tin plated. Internally, some use 50 microinch gold spot on each die attach pad and on the bonding fingertips. Gold bonding wire is attached with the thermocompression gold ball bonding technique.

Materials of the lead frame, the package body, and the die attach are all closely matched in thermal expansion coefficients, to provide optimum response to various thermal conditions. During manufacture every step of the process must be rigorously monitored to assure maximum quality of the plastic package. Generally they are available in 14, 16, 18, 22, 24, 40 and 48 pin configurations.

**package, SLAM** Single layer metalization. A dual-inline package that offers a low cost alternative to three layer ceramic packages. The package uses the same basic materials as a ceramic unit, but it is constructed in a simpler manner. It uses a 96 percent alumina base, one basic refractory metallization layer, an alumina passivation layer, and brazed-on Kovar leads. The leads are suitable for either socket insertion or soldering. Either a glazed ceramic or a Kovar lid is used to hermetically seal the package. The glazed ceramic lid is attached with a low temperature controlled devitrified glass frit sealant; a gold silicon eutectic solder is used for Kovar lids. It is available in various 14 to 40 pin configurations.

**package, TO** Refers to a standard metal can package for small lead count chips. The package generally consists of a Kovar body, a pure nickel lid, and Kovar leads, brazed in with a glass seal. The lid is sealed onto the body by cold welding to assure hermeticity of the package.

**packaging** The process of containing, connecting, protecting, and sealing components and their associated circuitry into standardized enclosures (such as dual-inline devices and transistor housings).

**packaging density** The relative number of units of information or devices in a dimensional unit area or volume of a system. Also called *packing density*.

**packaging, microprocessors** Package size is important in many system designs, particularly those with cramped layouts. In general, package sizes with small numbers of pins are easier to physically install into a system, while microprocessors in packages with large numbers of pins are easier for interfacing.

**packet broadcasting** A technique that uses the simultaneous transmission of a packet to several remote stations. Each remote station is equipped with decoding circuitry to decode each incoming packet to determine if it is addressed to that station. Packet broadcasting is basically a radio broadcasting communication system. A packet broadcasting system can also be implemented by means of a satellite transmission network.

**packet communications** This is based on the transmission of message packets. There are two forms of packet communications, packet switching and packet broadcasting.

**packet data link interface** In the functional diagram below the communication processor links the transmission lines with the buffer store that is connected to the host processor. The user interfaces with the host processor through a CRT terminal.

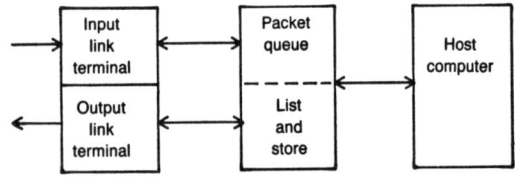

Packet data link interface

**packet data link processor** Here a microprocessor is connected to the control, address, and data busses that lead to the memory and interface units. The microprocessor data link interface performs the following operations: serial/parallel conversion; error checking, such as the arithmetic check sums and cyclic redundancy checks; header and frame information encoding on outgoing data; and header and frame information decoding from incoming data, assembling data into packets; and link and synchronization control.

The processor performs the packet handling functions based on a protocol flowchart. From the information in the flowchart, the system designer will code the program that performs the desired operation. The program may then be stored in a ROM to be called by system control or user command.

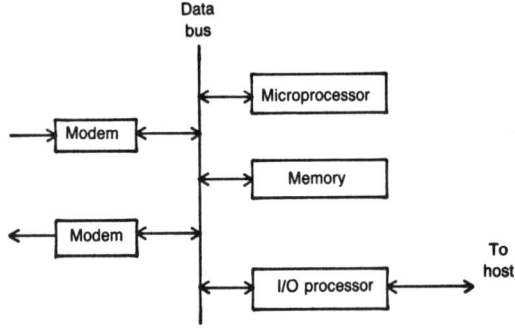

Packet data link processor

**packet switching** The formation of messages into a packet or group with a predetermined length.

**packet transmission** The segmentation of messages and the subsequent transmission and reassembly at the destination. The separate routing of packets can be completely invisible to the host computers and terminals. The packets are typically stored in memory, and flow control procedures insure that the storage does not become overloaded while still maintaining loadings close to maximum. Packets can be checked for errors during transmission and retransmitted until they are correctly received. All messages can also be acknowledged from destination to source to insure against their loss.

**pack field strength** Refers to a limit of magnetizing forces associated with a magnetic field.

**packing density** The relative number of useful storage units or components per unit of dimension, such as the number of bits per inch on a magnetic tape, or the number of equivalent FETs on an LSI chip.

**packing factor** The number of words, bits, or characters that can be written or stored in a given length or volume or a device or medium.

**pad** 1. A device used to match or control impedances in a transmission line or between an rf generator and receiver terminals. 2. To add capacitance in parallel with existing capacitors to alter the frequency of a tuned circuit. 3. To add dummy characters for the purpose of maintaining bit or timing integrity.

**PADAR** Abbreviation for *passive airborne detection and ranging*.

**pad character** A character inserted to fill a blank time slot in synchronous transmission, or to fulfill the character count requirement for transmission of fixed block lengths.

**padding** 1. A technique used to fill out a block of information with dummy records, words, or characters. 2. See *pad*, 2.

**page** 1. A segment of a computer program that has a virtual address and can be located in main storage or in auxiliary storage. A page can be moved into main memory by the operating system whenever the instructions of that subdivision need to be performed. A program can be divided into pages in order to minimize the total amount of main memory allocated to the program at any one time. Pages are normally stored on a fast-access store. Pages are typically a set of 4096 consecutive bytes, with the first byte located at a storage address that is a multiple of 4096.

**page addressing** A procedure of addressing in which memory is divided into segments to make full use of addressing capability. See *page*.

**page protection** Refers to the memory protection and control of page-mapped memories. The programmer may have control of read and/or write protection for each of the pages in memory. If the system and the user have independent memory maps, the programmer can specify a page of memory be unprotected for the operating system, but write-protected for the user. The result is a page of memory that can be altered by the operating system, but only read by the user.

**pager** A tiny pocketable receiver designed to receive personalized messages from a central dispatcher in a communication network.

**pages, multiple base** In multiuser systems, each user can have a complete base page while the system also maintains a base page. The large space for base page links or direct addressing for both user and system allows users to write large programs without linking or common area limitations.

**paging** 1. The procedure used to locate and transmit pages between main storage and auxiliary storage, or to exchange them with pages of the same program or other programs. Paging can be used to assist in the allocation of a limited amount of main storage among several concurrent programs. 2. The process of calling a nontransmitter-equipped member of a communications network.

**pair, binary** An electronic circuit having two stable states, two input lines, and two corresponding output lines such that a signal exists on either one of the output lines if and only if the last pulse received by the flip-flop is on the corresponding input line. A binary pair can store one binary digit (bit) of information since it is a bistable device.

**paired cable** A cable with two insulated conductors or with several sets of two conductors each.

**PAM** Abbreviation for *pulse-amplitude modulation*, a form of pulse modulation in which the amplitude of the pulses is varied.

**pancake** A small sealed package for a transistor.

**panel** The part of a computer console that provides an operator interface. A panel may be an interconnection unit with removable wires, or plugs, which allow specific functions to be changed by the operator. Other panels may pictorially show the relationship of system equipment using graphic indicators. Many panels contain all the switches and indicators required for the operation of the CPU and allow bit-by-bit manual entry into registers for program setup and debugging operations.

**panel, control** A component of some data processing units that permits the user to change the operational characteristics of the computer using switches or the insertion of pins, plugs, or wires into sockets and thus making electrical interconnections that may be sensed by the data processing machine.

**panel, maintenance and control** Refers to a panel of indicator lights and switches on which are displayed a particular sequence of routines, and from which repairs can be determined.

**panel, operator control** Generally, a control panel that contains all the switches and indicators for the operation of the central processor. Bit-by-bit register display and manual entry into the registers may be provided. The control panel is used primarily for initial set up prior to a program run or for debugging purposes, rather than to exercise control over a running program.

**panel, removable** Refers to a removable front panel that allows replacement or installation of a module from the front.

**paper checking exercise** A technique used to check out a design on paper. It can be used to test the logical design of the program.

In a paper checking exercise, one executes the program by hand and fills out entries in a table corresponding to the values of critical registers or outputs. This requires no development hardware but it can be long and tedious.

Paper checking is more often done at the flowchart level to verify the overall design. It may not result in a reasonable evaluation of actual performance.

In order to evaluate performance, development tools normally must be used. In many cases, paper checking is used to evaluate different microprocessors or different control schemes using a common benchmark or set of benchmarks.

**paper tape** The long, narrow paper strips used to record and store information in the form of punched holes, partially punched holes, chemical impregnation, or magnetic-ink imprinting.

**paper tape automatic development system** A software system consisting of loaders and utility programs for paper tape users. The system includes an executive that causes the utilities to be loaded at the highest memory address to leave maximum room for the user's program. A typical system includes programs for debug, binary load, binary dump, verify, and object loader.

**paper tape controller** A tape controller that will read seven or eight bits of ASCII coded data from the tape and punch data with the

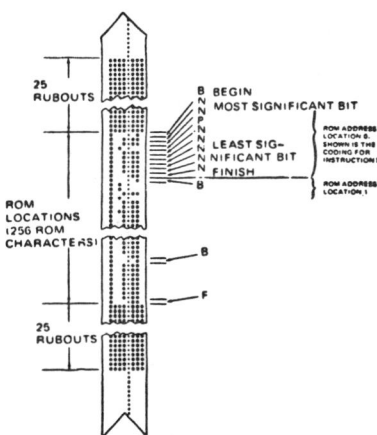

**Paper tape**

punching mechanism. It also has a front test panel that uses eight lines for communication. Four lines are used to give commands to the mechanism, and four sense lines are used for the switch and status indications. The required functions are obtained by adding two more chips to the basic system. A block diagram of the system is shown below. A 4308 ROM can be used for the program storage required for this application. For the 16 lines of I/O, a 4211 GPI/O chip is used. This is a general purpose interface chip with 16 lines that are individually programmable for direction.

The 4308 ROM uses eight lines to interface with the mechanism and eight lines that go to the operator's panel. The data transfer uses an 8-bit directional bus, which is in the ASCII format. Communication with the host computer can be accomplished by using a second 4308 ROM. The control logic required to interface to the reader-punch mechanism is accomplished with six chips.

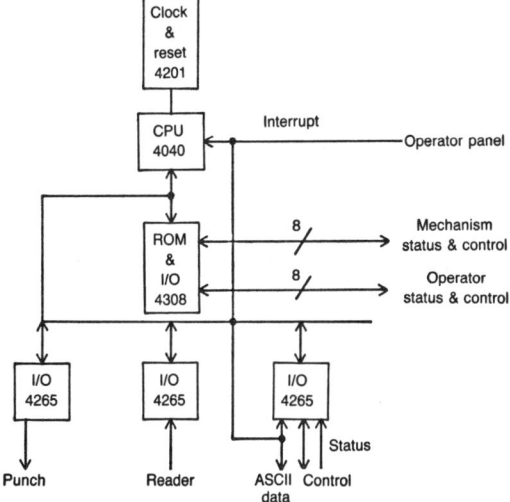

**Paper tape controller**

**paper tape reader** A device that senses the positions of holes in perforated tape and translates them into electrical signals. High-speed paper tape readers operate at 200 characters per second and are compatible standard software and hardware interfaces.

**PAR** Abbreviation for *precision approach radar*.

**parabola** A plane curve generated by a point moving so that its distance from a fixed second point is equal to its distance from a fixed line.

**parabolic interpolation** A procedure used in the numerical control of a machine tool to control the centerline of a cutter path. The method uses parabolic segments defined by three programmed points.

**parallel** Arranged in blocks for simultaneous transmission, storage, or logical operation of items (as opposed to *serial*).

**parallel adder** An adding circuit that processes all of the corresponding pairs of two numbers simultaneously.

**parallel addition** An addition method in which all the corresponding pairs of digits of two numbers being added are simultaneously processed.

**parallel bidirectional bus driver/receiver** Refers to a type of data bus buffer driver. The bidirectional bus driver has a high output drive capability for driving the system data bus. Use of this family member reduces the number of components required to construct microcomputer systems.

**parallel by character** The handling of all characters of a machine word simultaneously in separate lines, channels, or storage units.

**parallel circuit** A circuit in which all elements are connected to two common points with the same applied voltage across all elements.

**parallel connection** The connection of two or more parts of a circuit to the same pair of terminals. Also called *shunt connection*.

**parallel conversion** A parallel 3-bit converter with Gray code output is shown. It has $2^n - 1$ comparators, biased 1 LSB apart and starting with $+1/2$ LSB. For zero input, all comparators are off. When the input increases, the number of comparators in the on state increases. For any given bit position for the code, those comparator outputs that should give a logic 1 for a given input level are connected to the first NOR gate, and those that should be zero are connected to the next NOR gate, thus generating the correct code. Natural binary can be implemented in the same way. In this approach conversion occurs in parallel, with the speed limited only by the switching times of the comparators and logic gates. When the input changes, the output changes as a function of the switching times. This is the fastest approach to conversion, but the number of elements increases geometrically with the resolution. A 4-bit converter uses 15 comparators and seven 8-input gates. A 5-bit circuit requires 31 comparators and nine 16-input gates.

**parallel conversion system** A multichannel conversion system, with one converter for every analog source, in contrast to the conventional analog multiplexed system.

**parallel feed** Refers to a connection using RC or LC coupling.

**parallel input/output card** A circuit board that has the necessary handshake flags for conventional parallel interfacing and contains all the required addressing circuitry.

**parallel operation** The performance of several actions simultaneously using similar or identical devices for each action. Parallel operation can include the processing of all the digits of a word or byte by simultaneously transmitting each digit on a separate channel or bus. Parallel operation can save time over serial operation, but usually requires more equipment.

**parallel-plate package** A method of packaging circuits that uses a stacking arrangement to increase packing density.

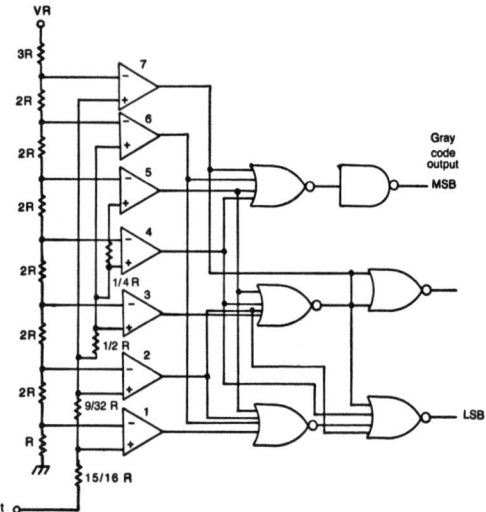

Parallel A/D converter

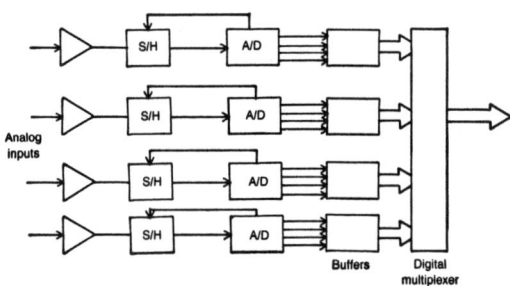

Parallel multichannel conversion system with digital multiplexing

**parallel processing** The processing of more than one program at a time using more than one active processor, in contrast to multiprocessing, where only one processor is active on one program at a time.

**parallel processing system** A microcomputer system (abbreviated *PPS*) that uses a compatible set of LSI chips to achieve the capability of a parallel minicomputer. The system uses a single-chip CPU which receives an instruction word to perform all operations. The large number of instruction words available allows the system to approach the capability of a minicomputer. The large number of available chips in the set allows the implementation of a broad class of data processing products.

**parallel processing system evaluation board** A circuit designed for system development that usually contains a CPU, RAM, input/output ports, and a clock circuit.

**parallel resonance** In a circuit with inductance and capacitance connected in parallel, the steady state condition that exists when the current entering the circuit from the supply line is in phase with the voltage across the circuit.

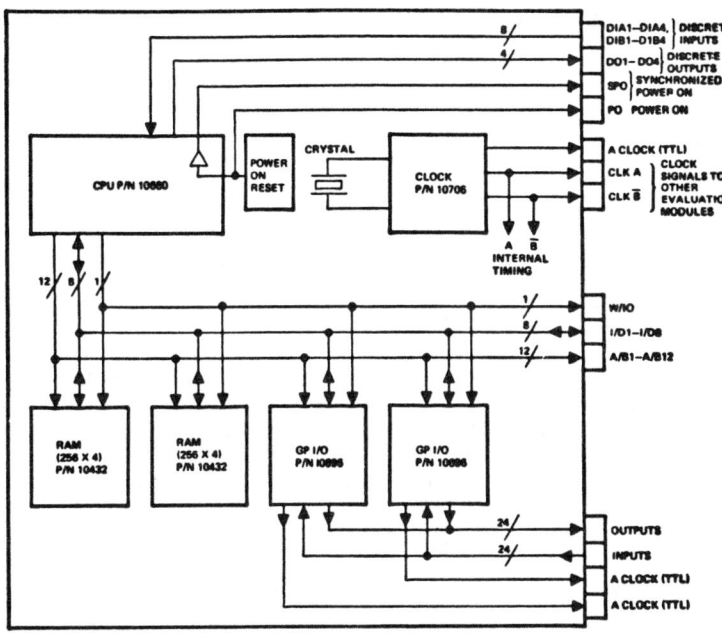

Parallel processing system

**parallel resonant circuit** 1. A resonant circuit in which the applied voltage is connected across a parallel circuit formed by a capacitor and an inductor. 2. An inductor and capacitor connected in parallel to furnish a high impedance at the frequency to which the circuit is resonant.

**parallel search** A memory scanning and sensing operation in which the locations are identified by their contents rather than their addresses. A parallel-search memory allows fast interrogation for retrieving specific data elements.

**parallel search memory** A memory in which the storage locations are identified by their contents rather than their addresses; this enables faster interrogation to retrieve a particular data element.

**parallel-series circuit** A circuit in which several series strings of components are paralleled or in which several paralleled sets of components are series-strung. Also called *series-parallel*.

**parallel storage** Storage in which all characters, words, or bits are equally available. When words are in parallel, the storage is referred to as *parallel by word*. The use of parallel characters or bits implies a storage that is *parallel by character* or *parallel by bit*.

**parallel system** A system that uses two or more processors that may operate on two or more data streams in parallel. The parallel system can also be configured to operate in parallel on a single data stream for high-reliability processing applications.

**parallel transfer** Data transfer in which the characters of an element of information are transferred simultaneously over a set of paths whose number equals the number of bits transferred at one time.

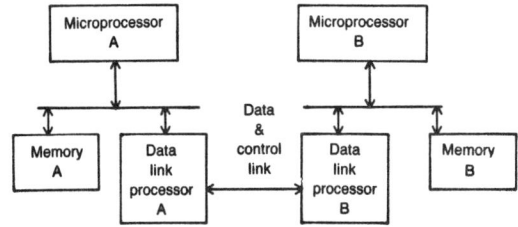

Parallel or linked multimicroprocessor system

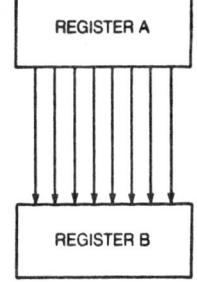

Parallel transfer

**parallel transmission** The simultaneous data transmission of a number of signal elements over separate lines or communication channels.

**parameter** A variable that is usually given a constant value for a specific program or run. In a subroutine, a parameter may have different values when the subroutine is used in different main routines or in different parts of one main routine, but it usually remains unchanged throughout any one such use.

A macro parameter refers to the symbolic or literal elements in the operand part of a macro statement. The macro parameter is usually substituted into specific instructions in the incomplete routine to develop a complete open subroutine.

**parameter and definition lists** These lists explain the function of each parameter and its meaning. The parameters can also be explained in the program.

**parameter, macro** Refers to specific symbolic or literal elements in the operand part of a macro statement that will be substituted into specific instructions in the incomplete routine to develop a complete open subroutine.

**parameter potentiometer** A potentiometer used to represent a parameter such as a coefficient or a scale factor. Also called a *scale factor potentiometer* or *coefficient potentiometer*.

**parametric amplifier** A type of circuit that uses variable reactance elements to transfer energy from pumped power oscillators. There are many circuit arrangements such as negative resistance amplifiers, up converters, and down converters.

**parametric diode** A diode in which the series capacitance can be varied by a biasing voltage.

**parametric oscillator** Refers to a type of oscillator that relies on the fact that certain nonlinear reactors when driven by a pump or other source of frequency, f, may exhibit negative resistance at frequencies of f/2, f/3, ..., f/n where n is determined by the form the nonlinearity takes. If the reactor is an inductor, the device may be referred to as a *parametron*.

**parametric potentiometer** A potentiometer used to represent parameters such as coefficients or scale factors.

**parametric subroutine** A subroutine that involves parameters. The computer is expected to adjust and generate the subroutine according to the parametric values chosen.

**parametron** A device that uses two stable states of oscillation to store binary digits.

**parasitic** An undesirable radiation parameter in an electronic circuit, such as oscillation, which disappears when circuit operation ceases.

**parasitic capacitance** In MOS devices, since most metal-oxide substrate formations are not at channels, parasitic or extraneous capacitance exists. Channel and parasitic capacitances slow down gate switching time because there is a threshold voltage ($V^T$) at which the channel starts to conduct; the time taken to reach this threshold voltage is increased by the presence of capacitance. Parasitic capacitance in MOS devices is caused by a current carrying metal layer, a semiconductor layer, and a thin oxide isolating layer. SOS (silicon-on-sapphire) devices have the current carrying metal separated from a conducting mounting by a thick, isolating sapphire base. The thickness of the sapphire base reduces the parasitic capacitance to negligible proportions.

**parasitic oscillation** Refers to various types of desirable oscillation in an amplifier, or the oscillation of an oscillator at some frequency other than the resonant frequency. It is generally of high frequency, and it may occur during a portion of each cycle of the main oscillation. Also called a spurious oscillation.

**parasitic stopper** A device or component that attenuates or eliminates a parasitic condition.

**parasitic suppressor** A parallel resistance or a parallel combination of inductance and resistance that is used to suppress parasitic oscillations.

**parent population** Refers to a prototype or initial batch of articles or units under study or consideration.

**parity** The anticipated state (odd or even) of a set of binary digits. Parity is achieved by use of a self-checking code employing binary digits in which the total number of ones in each expression is deliberately kept odd or even by the addition of an extra digit whenever necessary. In ASCII, the leftmost digit is used as a parity bit. (See ASCII and associated table.)

**parity bit** In an even-parity system, a bit added to a group of bits whose total of ones would otherwise be odd; in an odd-parity system, an added bit to make an even number of ones total an odd number. The parity bit is error insurance; if odd parity is specified, an error condition will be flagged each time that an even number of bits is counted with a parity bit present. In some systems, the transmission is specified as always odd or even so the parity bit does not change; in others the parity bit is added to make the sum of the bits odd or even when required. In the ASCII table referred to previously, note that the leftmost bit is a parity bit added to character groups whose complement of ones is odd.

**parity check** A check used to determine if the total number of ones or zeros in a word or byte is odd or even. This sum is checked against a previously computed parity digit. Also called *odd-even check*.

**parity check, even** Concerns a technique of detecting when bits are dropped by adding one bit to all odd numbers of bit patterns to signify a character; thus, all characters would be represented by an even number of bits. A failure to have such representation would be called a parity error.

**parity checking** A method of error checking that allows a receiving unit to determine if the message was received correctly. The method involves adding an extra bit, called a parity bit, to each block of data in the message.

**parity, column** A parity system that is applied to all bits in the same bit position in a block or to all bits in the same column. The parity bit is calculated by modulo 2 addition. The combination of row and column parity can detect all 1, 2, and 3 bit errors, all odd number of bit errors, and some even number of bit errors in the block.

**parity error** A condition that occurs when a computed parity check does not agree with the parity bit; that is, when a parity bit exists in a digit group of an even-parity system, a parity error occurs when the total of bits (including the parity bit) is odd.

**parity generator-checker** A hardware unit used to generate and check parity conditions on data words. Available units can be used for either *odd* or *even* parity applications, and cascading allows expansion to any word length.

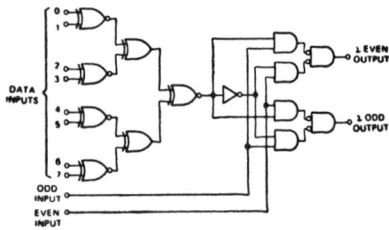

**Parity generator-checker (8 bits)**

**parity interrupt** An interrupt that occurs because of a parity error.

**parity, odd-even** Refers to parity checks using the number of binary ones that is always maintained as an odd or even number. If the ones in the data part of the word or character are even, the parity bit is zero; if they are odd, the parity bit is one.

**parsing** In language theory, the procedures for dividing components into structural forms.

**part** A discrete component in an electronic circuit or system.

**part failure rate** The anticipated or recorded number of occasions in a specified time period when a component will malfunction.

**partial carry** A technique used in parallel addition in which some or all of the carries are stored temporarily, rather than being allowed to propagate.

**particle size** Refers to the average volume of the magnetic particles used in magnetic memories.

**part operation** The part of an instruction that specifies the kind of arithmetic or logic operation to be performed, but not the address of the operands.

**part program** A specific and complete set of data and instructions written in source languages for computer processing or written in machine language for manual programming for the purpose of manufacturing a part of a numerical control machine.

**part programmer** A person who prepares the planned sequence of events for the operation of a numerically controlled machine tool.

**parts family** A set of closely related and compatible IC components, such as a clock and driver, microprocessor, RAM, ROM, and I/O chips. These parts are available as a kit and sold in single quantities by the manufacturer. A ready to assemble kit may have one or more PC cards and a number of ICs and discrete components for assembly on the cards. Once assembled, one has an operative microcomputer. Kits are also available in the form of factory assembled systems. In some kits, the program and data entry uses keyboard switches, and the data output is on a LED display.

**parity line structure** A bus structure in which each device is linked to a single bus through tristate buffers. The bus may be unidirectional, but more often, a bidirectional bus is used so the information can pass among the various sources and acceptors.

**pass** A complete cycle of reading, processing, and writing. Also called *machine run*.

**pass element** An automatic variable resistance device, such as a power transistor, is placed in series with a source of dc power. The pass element is driven by the amplified error signal to increase its resistance when the output needs to be lowered or to decrease its resistance when the output must be raised. This technique is used in regulating power supplies.

**PAT** Abbreviation for *program activity transmissions*. An electronic system for collecting manufacturing and accounting information.

**patch** 1. To insert corrected coding. 2. A section of coding inserted into a routine to correct a mistake or alter the routine. A patch does not have to be inserted into the routine sequence being corrected; it can be placed somewhere else with an exit to the patch and a return to the routine provided. 3. A temporary repair to a malfunctioning system. 4. A wired connection or set of wired connections used in place of switches, usually on a temporary basis.

**pattern** 1. The punching configuration within a card column that represents a single character of a character set; also called *hole pattern*. 2. The waveform produced by a circuit or set of circuits (a pulse train, for example). 3. The configuration of printed circuitry on a board or chip.

**pattern recognition** The identification of shapes, forms, or configurations by automated methods.

**pattern-sensitive fault** A fault that occurs in response to some particular pattern of data.

**PAU** Abbreviation for *position analog unit*. A unit that feeds back to an amplifier, analog information corresponding to the position of a machine slide to be compared with the potential input information.

**PAX** Abbreviation for *private automatic exchange*.

**PBX** Abbreviation for *private branch exchange*. Loosely, this refers to a manual switchboard.

**PBX dictation system** A centralized dictation system using telephone company wiring and dial or touch-tone controls.

**PC** 1. Abbreviation for *program counter*, the index address register. 2. Abbreviation (usually lower case) of *printed circuit*. 3. Abbreviation for *programmable controller, process controller,* and *printer controller*.

**pc board** Abbreviation for *printed-circuit board*, a board prepared from the printing of a chemically resistive ink.

**pc board control point** A contact area on a circuit board to make it easier to reconfigure the circuitry or conduct tests.

**pc board fabricating** There are two major methods for fabricating printed circuit boards, the additive method and the subtractive method. The subtractive method calls for the printing of a chemically resistive ink or paint in a type of stenciling operation on an insulating board with previously applied copper foil. Acid is used to selectively etch away unwanted metal to leave the desired pattern on the board. The additive method also employs a printing process, but the pattern covers only those areas where metal is not desired. Thus selective plating can be performed on the unclad insulating board that has been treated to accept the plating metal.

**pc board package, DIP** Refers to the dual inline package that is becoming the universal form for printed circuit board components. In addition to integrated circuits, DIP packs are used for relays, resistive and capacitive networks, and light emitting diode displays.

**pc board portable testers** These are testers with built-in processors for field service use. These testers have the ability not only to test boards, but also to simulate peripherals. Some can exercise entire instruments and diagnose problems down to the component level.

**pc board power shut-off** A technique that is useful in LSI common bus circuitry on a board. A number of ROMs can be tied to a common bus. One ROM can be isolated from the influence of others by shutting off power to all but that ROM. Power shut off can be controlled by means of a transistor switch or jumper wire. In either case, LSI circuitry or ROMs can be effectively isolated from one another.

**pc board test language** A language used in automatic pc board testing that is specifically designed for the requirements of testing complex boards containing microprocessors and other LSI components. A typical test language is capable of:

1. Loading registers
2. Data transfer between registers
3. Generating repetitive routines
4. Performing limited tests

**pc board test point** An area on a pc board used as a probe contact point during testing.

**pc board tests, wired-OR** Wired-OR circuits present some testing difficulty. The wired-OR circuit often is handled with the addition of another device.

**PCC** Abbreviation for *program controlled computer*.

**p-channel** A p-type semiconductor region that functions as the conducting channel in n-gate FETs.

**p-channel enhancement-mode MOS FET** A metal-oxide field-effect transistor whose conducting channel between source and drain is doped with p-channel impurities.

**p-channel metal gate** The earliest MOS process was the p-channel metal gate. Although there were prior unsuccessful attempts by various manufacturers to develop a process and become established in the MOS business, not until 1967 was it proven that MOS integrated circuits were an economically and technologically viable product. Thus, the p-channel metal gate process became the basis for an entire MOS industry and stimulated the development of a multitude of other processes.

**p-channel MOS** Metal-oxide semiconductor devices that use a p-channel conduction mode. P-channel devices tend to be slower than n-channel units and also exhibit a lower gain.

**p-channel technology** The earliest microprocessors used p-channel technology. This, however, had two disadvantages. Holes have a lower mobility in silicon than electrons; as a result, PMOS transistors are slower than NMOS devices. Also, PMOS circuits provide an active pull up but require a passive pull down of external loads. NMOS amplifiers provide an active pull down, which is more effective for driving the TTL interface circuits common in microprocessors. PMOS is the older technology, which was better understood and thus more economical. It was used successfully in the first microprocessors. It provided good density then (up to 15,000 transistors per chip). It is, however, slower compared to newer technologies, such as NMOS with its many variations. Its main attraction to manufacturers today is that it is a well-understood process, and a complex device can be developed with a high probability of success at a lower cost than newer technologies. But, while p-channel MOS technology provided a low-cost approach to early microprocessor designs, it is not used in designs today.

**PCI** 1. Abbreviation for *peripheral command indicator*. 2. Abbreviation for *program check interruption*.

**PCM** Abbreviation for *pulse-code modulation*, the modulation of a pulse train using a specified code or code system.

**PCP** Abbreviation for *primary control program*.

**pc testing, personality board** The output registers on most personality boards permit the generation of serial and/or parallel test patterns of various lengths; with the appropriate test program control, these boards can also generate pseudo random codes and other types of codes.

**PD** 1. Abbreviation for *pulse driver*. 2. Abbreviation for *pulse duration*.

**PDM** Abbreviation for *pulse-duration modulation*, the modulation of pulse data using varying widths of pulses to convey information.

**PE** Abbreviation for *phase encoding*.

**peak** The maximum instantaneous value of a quantity.

**peak amplitude** Refers to the maximum deviation of a wave from its average position.

**peak clipper** A device that passes signals and cuts off peaks above a predetermined level without otherwise altering the waveform.

**peak data transfer rate** The maximum rate at which data is transmitted through a channel. The peak data transfer rate is usually measured in characters per second, discounting gaps between blocks and words.

**peak distortion** Refers to the worst case displacement of wave components. Also called *jitter*.

**peak follower** A peak follower is composed of a sample hold and a comparator circuit as shown. Balancing the unknown input voltage against some form of internally produced reference, the comparator circuit responds to the polarity of the inequality between input and reference. The sample hold output is biased by a few millivolts of hysteresis signal to avoid ambiguity problems during step inputs and reduce false triggering from noise. When the input is greater than the S/H output, the comparator's positive output forces the S/H to a track mode. When the input becomes less than the S/H output, the comparator causes the S/H to the hold state until the input once again becomes greater than the output. To reset the circuit, the control input is switched into sample, and a low level is applied at the input.

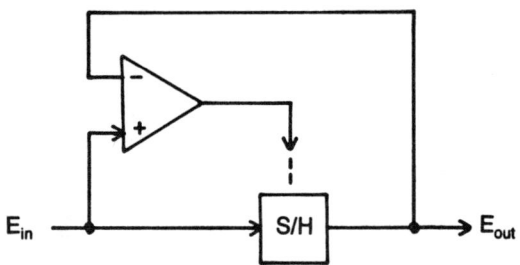

**Peak follower with sample hold**

**peak flux density** Refers to a maximum magnetic condition of magnetic materials.

**peak forward voltage** Refers to the maximum instantaneous voltage in the forward flow direction of anode current as measured between the anode and cathode of a rectifier.

**peaking circuit** A circuit cable of converting an input signal into a peak waveform.

**peaking network** A circuit used to increase the amplification at the upper end of the frequency range for a system.

**peak limiter** A device that passes signals of average amplitude, but that compresses or otherwise restricts signal peaks to some established preset value. Compare *peak clipper*.

**peak load** The maximum instantaneous rate of power consumption for a circuit, load, or system.

**peaks** Refers to momentarily high amplitudes occurring in electronic equipment.

**peak-to-peak amplitude** The amplitude of an alternating quantity, measured from the positive peak to the negative peak.

**peak transfer rate** Peak data transfer rate.

**peak value** The maximum instantaneous value of a varying current, voltage, or power. For a sine wave, it is equal to 1.414 times the effective value of the sine wave. Also called the crest value.

**pecker** A sensing pin used in tape or card reading to determine the presence or absence of a performation at a particular relative location.

**pecker drilling** A canned cycle for deep hole drilling whereby the Z axis feed is reversed at regular intervals for chip relieving in computer-controlled machining.

**peek-a-boo system** An information retrieval system that uses small cards with drilled or punched holes. Also called *batten system* and *cordonnier system*.

**peer network** A configuration that uses mutually cooperating computers in which there is no defined master or slave relationship of one system over the other. The peer network requires that the operating system of each computer be aware of the status of the other computers in the network, and that a scheduling program provide the task distribution. As a job is passed to a computer in the network, the originating computer moves to a new task. A computer that is busy passes the task on to an available computer that executes the task. The time response in peer networks is difficult to predict, since one computer does not know the workload of another and there is no master that can impose tasks.

Peer networks provide access to specialized facilities not available on the originating computer, and the processors share the computing load for a more efficient use of the total facility.

**Peltier effect** A phenomenon where heat is liberated or absorbed at a junction when current passes from one metal to another.

**penetration** A measure of the depth of the skin effect of eddy currents in induction heating or the depth of the magnetic field in superconducting metals.

**pen light** A pen-like device with light and a photosensor on one end for communicating with a computer through a CRT device.

**pentagrid** A frequency converting tube used in heterodyne receivers. The cathode and two grids form an oscillator, and the modulated electron stream is mixed with the incoming signal by the other grids and the anode acting as a pentode.

**PEP** Abbreviation for *program evaluation procedure* (former Air Force designation for PERT).

**PER** Abbreviation for *program event recording*.

**perfect dielectric** A dielectric in which all the energy required to establish an electric field is returned when the field is removed. In practice, only a vacuum conforms to this, and all other dielectrics dissipate heat to varying extents.

**perforated tape** A tape usually made of paper in which data is stored in the form of punched holes. The hole locations are arranged in columns across the width of the tape, and there are usually 5 to 8 positions or channels per column. Also called *paper tape* or *punched tape*.

**performance** Operation with some degree of effectiveness.

**performance characteristic** A characteristic measurable in terms of a useful denominator such as gain, power, or output.

**performance requirements** The set of values, conditions, and operating criteria that define the acceptable operation for a computer system and its subsystems. The computer system must fulfill minimum requirements for online response time, operating time, and record or file size.

**period** 1. The time required for one complete cycle. 2. A specified time duration during which newly installed or modified equipment is evaluated. 3. The reciprocal of frequency.

**periodic** Repeating a cycle regularly in time and form.

**periodic current** An oscillating current, the values of which recur at equal time intervals.

**periodic damping** A damping in which the output of an instrument oscillates about the final position before coming to rest.

**periodic pulse train** A group of pulses that repeat at regular intervals in time sequence.

**periodic quantity** An oscillating quantity in which any value it attains is repeated at equal regular intervals.

**periodic rating** The electrical load that can be handled for alternate periods of load and rest without exceeding the specified heating limits for the equipment, or without significant degradation of circuit or system performance.

**peripheral** An equipment item distinct from the CPU, but which connects to the computing system usually by means of a bus.

**peripheral bus, data direction register** The data direction register (DDR) is used to establish each individual peripheral bus line as either an input or an output. Each of the DDR's 8-bit positions corresponds to a peripheral data line; a zero or a one written into a bit position causes that line to function as an input or output, in some systems.

**peripheral device control, PLA** In order for a central processor unit to communicate with a peripheral device, the CPU must select the device and the mode of communication. During an input/output instruction, the CPU transmits the device address and control information to select a unique device in a specified mode. A PLA (programmed logic array) can be used to monitor the device address and control field bus to issue appropriate control signals to the devices.

**peripheral disk file** A file management system for use with floppy-disk peripherals. The systems can be accessed by macro language programs and include complete sets of utility programs for the updating, copying, purging, or addition of files.

**peripheral equipment** Equipment distinct from the CPU that works in conjunction with it. Peripheral equipment includes all the auxiliary units that may be placed under the control of the computer such as card readers, card punches, magnetic tape units, printers, tape readers, analog-to-digital converters, and typewriters. Peripheral equipment may be used online or offline, depending upon the system job requirements and economic considerations.

**peripheral interface adapter** A device (abbreviated *PIA*) for matching the input/output channels of a microprocessor with peripheral equipment. A PIA is designed to simplify the task of the user by providing the necessary buses for interfacing the peripherals, and the control logic signals for synchronizing the I/O devices with the microprocessor.

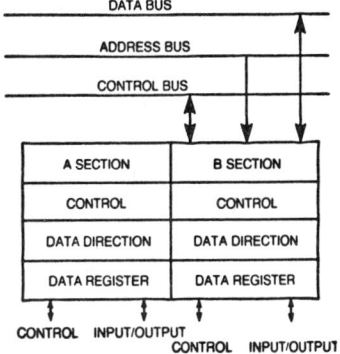

Peripheral interface adapter

A typical PIA uses a data bus line for data flow between the microprocessor and the PIA. The direction of data flow is controlled by the microprocessor using the control bus. When more than one PIA is used, chip select lines allow the selection of the desired PIA. The microprocessor can read or write into the data registers by addressing the unit over the address and control buses. The 8-bit outputs are bidirectional and the control input/output lines can be used for interrupts.

Each half of the two symmetrical sections has a control register, a data direction register, and a data register. The *data direction register* is used to establish the lines to the peripheral units as inputs or outputs. The *data registers* store the data which is on the data bus during a write command; during a read operation, data is transferred directly to the data bus from the peripherals. The *control registers* establish and control the operating modes of control lines to the peripherals.

The functional configuration of the PIA is programmed by the microprocessor during system initialization. Each of the peripheral lines is programmed as an input or an output, and the control lines are also programmed at this time.

**peripheral interface module** The optional interface cards available for selected peripherals. The modules or cards usually plug into a common chassis or card frame.

**peripheral-limited** Descriptive of a system whose processing speed or time is dictated by the limitations of the peripherals.

**peripheral software driver** The programs that allow the user to communicate with and control peripheral devices. A standard approach is to use a microprogrammable microcomputer to emulate a standard minicomputer CPU for which there exists compatible peripheral software.

**peripheral subsystem** A group of one or more peripheral units of the same type that are connected to an available input/output channel. A channel synchronizer-control unit interprets the control signals and instructions issued by the central processor and effects the transfer of data to and from the selected unit and the processor. It also indicates status of the peripheral units and informs the central processor when errors or faults occur.

**peripheral support computer** A computer used for auxiliary operations in support of a large processing complex and compatible with the host computer only to the extent that data interchange is not required for auxiliary conversion. The peripheral support computer is used primarily for card-to-tape, tape-to-card, and tape-to-printer conversions, along with peripheral control operations.

**peripheral transfer** The process of transmitting data between two or more peripheral units.

**permalloy** The group name for a class of high-permeability nickel-iron alloys.

**permanent dynamic storage** A form of dynamic storage in which the maintenance of the data stored does not depend on a flow of energy into the storage medium. Examples include magnetic disks and drums.

**permanent error** An error which is not eliminated by reprocessing.

**permanent fault** Faults are failures in performance in the manner required or specified. Sporadic faults are intermittent, while permanent faults are repetitious, but these may escape attention when they do not result in failure to perform some particular tasks.

**permanent memory** Stored data that remains intact when power is removed.

**permanent storage** Storage that is not altered by computer instructions, such as magnetic core with a lockout feature. Also called *nonerasable storage, fixed storage,* and *read-only storage.*

**permatron** A hot cathode gas discharge diode, gated by an applied magnetic field.

**permeability** The ratio of magnetic field flux density to the magnetizing force.

**permeability constant** Symbol, $\mu_0$. The inductance per unit area in a near-perfect vacuum or in free space. In the International System of Units, the value is $12.566\ 370\ 614 \times 10^{-7}$ henrys per meter.

**permittivity** The ratio of electric displacement to the electric field intensity in a material.

**permittivity constant** Symbol, $\epsilon_0$. The capacitance per unit area in a near-perfect vacuum or in free space. In the International System of Units, the value is $8.854\ 187\ 818 \times 10^{-12}$ farads per meter. $\epsilon_0$ is the reciprocal of the product of free-space permeability and the speed of light squared.

**permutation** Any one of the total number of changes in position or form that are possible in a group.

**permuted cyclic code** A code in which words are represented by a fixed number of bits and arranged in sequence such that the signal distance between consecutive words is always one or unity.

**permuted index** An index developed by producing an entry for each word of interest, including those within the context of meaning. A permuted index is most often used only for title words.

**personality card** A PROM programmer card that contains the specialized instructions for interfacing and programming that are unique for that particular PROM or family of PROMs being programmed. Personality cards may provide the proper timing patterns, voltage levels, and other requirements for the PROM.

**personality module** A module used for PROM interlacing and programming; a personality card.

**PERT** Acronym for *program evaluation and review technique*, a program or project management technique that uses critical path analysis for program and system performance evaluation.

**PES** Abbreviation for *photoelectric scanning.*

**phantom circuit** Refers to a superposed circuit derived from suitably arranged pairs of wires, called side circuits, the two wires of each pair being effectively in parallel.

**phase** The angular relationship between waveforms in AC circuits.

**phase angle** Refers to a measure of the time by which an output lags or leads an input.

**phase-by-phase** Refers to a modular build up or growth of a system according to schedule "milestones."

**phase dictionary** Refers to an abbreviated table of contents that contains the phase name and load addresses of the phases to be loaded for a given programming application.

**phase difference** Refers to the phase angle of the output minus the phase angle of the input using input and output at the same frequency.

**phase discriminator** Refers to a circuit preceding the demodulator in a phase modulation receiver. It converts the carrier to an amplitude modulated form.

**phase frequency distortion** A distortion that occurs when the phase shift is not directly proportionate to the frequency over the range required for transmission. Also referred to as phase distortion.

**phase inverter** Refers to a type of amplifier that supplies a positive and negative half cycle of output for every half cycle of input voltage.

**phase jitter** Refers to a type of undesirable random distortion that results in the intermittent shortening or lengthening of the observed signals.

**phase library** An ordered set of program phases processed and entered by a linkage editor for execution.

**phase-locked loop** A control circuit (abbreviated *PLL*), usually integrated, which locks the phase of the controlled frequency with a reference frequency.

**phase-locked-loop motor control** A motor control system using PLL techniques. With the combination of PLL control and a microprocessor, a single reference or clock can be used to provide high accuracy, and the microprocessor can be programmed to provide flexible counting and to compare functions for tracking.

**phase locked oscillator** A type of parametric oscillator that can be made to oscillate in phases relative to the pumped frequency.

**phase logic** The general instructions that transfer the machine from one operational phase to another, such as *fetch* and *interrupt*. Combinatorial logic can be used to establish the current phase and the next phase. In some systems, a phase may be a microcoded subroutine.

**phase modulation** A modulation system (abbreviated *PM*) in which the carrier angle is varied by an amount proportional to the modulating signal. PM is used in most socalled FM two-way communications systems.

**phase-modulation recording** A recording method in which each cell is divided into two parts and magnetized in opposite senses, with the sequence of the senses indicating if the bit represented is a one or a zero.

**phase shift** The change in the phase of a periodic waveform with respect to a reference point, usually occurring as a direct result of a connection of a component or circuit to the waveform-producing circuit or device.

**phase splitter** Refers to a technique of producing two or more waves that differ in phase from a single input wave.

**phase velocity** The velocity at which a point of constant phase is propagated in a progressive wave.

**phasing** Causing two systems or circuits to operate in phase, or at some established phase difference.

**phasing capacitor** A capacitor used in a crystal filter circuit for neutralizing the capacity of the crystal holder.

**phosphor dots** Refers to the elements in the screen of the CRT that glow in the three primary colors.

**phosphorescence** Refers to the property of emitting light for a period of time after the source of excitation is taken away. Cathode ray tubes (CRT's) use this capability or phenomenon to permit a trace on a screen to remain after a transient signal causing the signal is removed; it is thus a form of temporary storage.

**phosphor trio** Refers to the phosphor dots, arranged in triangular groups accurately deposited in interlaced positions on the phosphor screen of the tricolor CRT. Each trio consists of a green emitting dot, a red emitting dot, and a blue emitting dot.

**photocell** 1. A device that converts light into electricity. 2. A device whose resistance changes with relative linearity according to the amount of light impinging on its surface.

**photocomposition** A form of text production in which each character is exposed photographically on light-sensitive paper, which is then developed to become a reproduction proof.

**photoconductive** Refers to the specific electrical conductivity of some materials dependent upon the intensity and frequency of electromagnetic radiation incident upon the material.

**photoconductivity** A property possessed by certain materials of varying their electrical conductivity under the influence of light.

**photodiode** A junction diode constructed to provide an electrical output under the influence of light. Photodiodes are widely used as optical sensing devices in data processing equipment.

**photoelasticity** A phenomenon in which strain in certain materials results in colored fringes when under the influence of polarized light.

**photoelectric effect** A phenomena resulting from the absorption of photons by electrons, resulting in their ejection with a kinetic energy equal to the difference between the energy of a photon and the surface work function or an atomic binding energy (Einstein photoelectric equation). Among these phenomena are photoconductive, photovoltaic, photoemissive, and photoelectromagnetic effects. The emission of x-rays on the impact of high energy electrons on a surface is an inverse photoelectric effect.

**photoelectric threshold** The limiting frequency for which the quantum energy is just sufficient to produce photoelectric emission. It is given by equating the quantum energy to the surface work function.

**photoelectric yield** The proportion of incident quanta on a photosensitive surface that liberates electrons.

**photoemissive** Refers to the effect in which electrons are emitted from the surfaces of certain specific materials at particular threshold levels of frequency of incident electromagnetic radiation such as visible, infrared, or ultraviolet light.

**photo form** A photo imaging additive printed circuit process. Photoforming needs no resists and provides conductor definition as good or better than that of additive boards using dry film resists. Since a catalytic image is formed photographically, line definition is potentially as good as the quality of the line work used on the photographic negative.

**photographic storage** Storage methods that use photographic processes, such as high-density storage on photographic disks, photographic data shown on CRT screens, or computer-output microfilm and facsimile systems.

**photo-optic memory** A memory or storage system that uses an optical medium such as a light beam to record on photographic film.

**photoresist** A substance that resists the erosion properties of an etchant when exposed to intense light. It is used in fabrication of printed circuits.

**photoresist process** The process used to remove, in a selective manner, portions of a light-exposed surface of a semiconductor chip or a circuit board. The photoresist is usually an organic material that polymerizes on exposure to intense light, which allows it to resist the etchant solution used to eat away nonconductive areas of the board or substrate.

**physical simulation system** An operating computer system designed to represent or simulate physical systems for research and study.

**PI** 1. Abbreviation for *programmed instruction*. 2. Abbreviation for *performance index*.

**PIA** Abbreviation for *peripheral interface adapter*, a hardware unit for matching the input/output channels of a microprocessor with peripheral equipment. A typical PIA provides 8 or 16 bits of external interface and four or more control lines at addressable locations in memory. Each interface bit is individually programmable to act as either an input or an output.

**PIA bus interface** The PIA in many systems is used to provide 8 or 16 bits of external interface as well as control lines at addressable locations in the system memory. The I/O bits may be accessed in two words of 8 bits each, but each I/O bit can be individually programmable to act as either an input or an output system memory. All operating characteristics of the interface can be established by writing from the processor to the data direction and control registers of the PIA. This is required at the time of system reset and permitted at other times in most systems.

**PIAPACS** The psychophysiological information acquisition processing and control system, a system that is conceived as a closed-loop man-machine control system. Its function is to insure that its user is constantly maintained in a state of peak performance capability.

**PIA read-write** A signal generated by the microprocessor unit to control data transfers on the data bus of the PIA.

**pica** 1. The larger of two common typewriter typeface sizes, the smaller being elite. 2. A standard of typewriter spacing, 10 characters to the horizontal inch, also called 10 pitch. 3. A unit of measure, used in printing and the graphic arts, equal to 12 points or about one sixth of an inch.

**pickup** Interference from a nearby circuit or system.

**pickup value** The minimum value that will energize the contacts of a relay, voltage, current, or power.

**pico** Prefix meaning $10^{-12}$.

**picofarad** A capacitance value equal to $10^{-12}$ farad (abbreviated *pF*).

**picoprocessor** A self-contained high-speed miniature digital processor used in intelligent cable systems to provide controller functions for data transfer, control signaling, status monitoring, and interrupt generation. The picoprocessor is usually microprogrammed; because of its small size, it can be attached almost anywhere in the system.

**picosecond** A time period equal to $10^{-12}$ second (abbreviated *ps*).

**picowatt** One ten thousandth of a microwatt.

**PICU** Abbreviation for *priority interrupt control unit*.

**PIE** Abbreviation for *plug-in electronics*.

**piezoelectric** A property of certain crystals that produce a voltage when under mechanical stress, and produce a mechanical vibration at a specific frequency when subjected to a voltage.

**piezoelectric crystal** A crystal transducer that converts mechanical pressure into an electrical signal, or converts an electrical signal into mechanical pressure.

**piezoelectric device** A device that uses the conversion properties of a piezoelectric substance, such as an oscillator crystal used as a frequency reference, or a crystal microphone that produces an electrical analog of the vibrations of a modulated diaphragm.

**piezoelectric effect** Electric polarization arising in some anisotropic (not possessing a center of symmetry) crystals (quartz, Rochelle salt, barium titanate) when subjected to a mechanical strain. Same as *piezoelectricity*.

**piezoelectric flowmeters** Piezoelectric flowmeters were originally developed for aerospace applications in the 1950s. One design uses two transducer pairs to establish an upstream and a downstream sonic path diagonally across the fluid as shown below. The difference in propagation velocity (the doppler effect) between the two paths is then related to the flow rate.

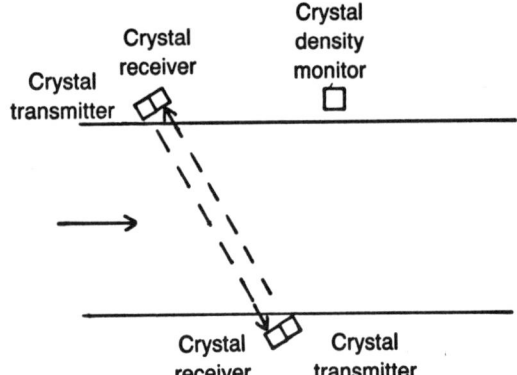

Piezoelectric flowmeter (Doppler type)

**piezoelectric transducer** A transducer that depends upon a material with piezoelectric properties for its operation. Also called ceramic or crystal transducer. See also *piezoelectric crystal* and *piezoelectric device*.

**piezoelectricity** The electrical signal produced by a stressed piezoelectric crystal.

**pilot reference** Refers to a different type of wave from those that transmit the communication signals. It is used in carrier systems to facilitate maintenance and adjustment of the carrier transmission system.

**pilot, synchronizing** Refers to a reference pilot for the purpose of either maintaining the synchronization of oscillators of a carrier system, or comparing the frequencies and/or the phases of the currents generated.

**pilot system** A collection of file records and data obtained from a business over a period of time and used for simulation purposes.

**PINO** Abbreviation for *positive input-negative output*.

**pinboard** A type of control panel that uses pins rather than wires to control the operation of the computer. Some such systems allow the operator to change programs by removing one pinboard and inserting another.

**pinchoff** The cessation of channel (source-to-drain) current in field-effect transistors as a result of increased gate bias. This state is comparable to *cutoff* in bipolar-transistor and vacuum-tube operation.

**pin-connect crystal** A clock crystal that is connected to a microprocessor system with two separate external pins.

**pin connection** Refers to connections made to the base of pins in a connector or socket.

**pin contact** A contact used to mate with a socket or connector.

**pin diode** A semiconductor diode with an intrinsic layer between the p and n junctions. The term "pin" is an acronym for *positive, intrinsic, negative*.

**pin feed** A term applied to typewriter or printer platens having sprocket-like end pieces that help convey continuous forms through the unit.

**PIO** Abbreviation for *processor input/output*.

**pip** A spot of light on a CRT screen for display pointing or calibration, or in radar for target indicating.

**pipeline** An executed serial program using a register at the output of the microprogram memory. Pipelining can produce a faster configuration than a normal series mode of operation. Since only conditional instructions can test the results of previous instructions, the pipelined machine may require more memory. For example, a serial machine may execute as a single microinstruction.

ADD AND BRANCH IF ZERO

The pipeline machine may require two microinstructions for the same operation.

**PLA** Abbreviation for *programmed logic array*, an arrangement of logical AND and OR functions programmed for specific operations. PLAs are used for code conversion, instruction decoding, and command decoding. The output of a PLA is the sum of the products of the input

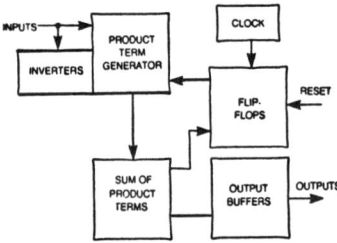

PLA block diagram

addresses programmed by a masking step during manufacture. PLAs offer some advantages over random logic, but generally require more interconnections and board space. Compared to random logic, they are also slow and may cost more than random logic equivalents. PLAs have been used for correct sequencing of instructions in CPUs and to translate codes in microprogramming functions.

**placement algorithm** Refers to an algorithm designed to determine where in internal storage, segments should be placed prior to their use.

**PLA code conversion** A programmable logic array (PLA) can be used efficiently in code conversion applications where all possible combinations of a particular code are not used. The conversion from 12 level Hollerith to 8 level ASCII provides such an example. In the standard solution to this problem, the 12 level Hollerith code is first reduced to 8 levels, with logic before it is presented to a 256×8 ROM. All nonexisting input combinations are decoded as "don't care" output states in the ROM.

**PLA instruction fetch** During an instruction fetch, the instruction to be executed is loaded into the instruction register. A programmable logic array (PLA) can be used for the correct sequencing of the CPU for the appropriate instruction. The state of a priority network decides whether the machine is going to fetch the next instruction in sequence or service one of the request lines.

**planar** Refers to a semiconductor processing technology in which monolithic components extend below the surface of the substrate, but the plane surface remains relatively flat during fabrication.

**planar integrated circuit** An integrated circuit produced using the planar process.

**planar network** A network in which no branches cross when drawn on the same plane.

**planar process** A basic technology of silicon transistors, being a combination of oxidation, selective oxide removal, and heating used to introduce doping materials by diffusion. The introduction of the planar process in 1960 revolutionized the microelectronics field. Silicon, rather than germanium, emerged as the predominant semiconductor material. As applied to semiconductor devices, the term is used to mean that the monolithic components fabricated by this process extend below the surface of the silicon substrate. The plane surface of the semiconductor, however, remains relatively flat and unaltered through the sequence of different fabrication steps. Planar process technology is comprised of five independent processes: epitaxy, surface passivation, photolithography, diffusion, and thin film deposition.

**planar transistor** A transistor constructed by etching a thin slice of semiconductor and characterized by a parallel plane protected by an oxidized surface.

**Planck's constant** A constant that has dimensions of energy × time. The present accepted value is $6.625 \cdot 10^{-27}$ erg. sec. See Planck's Law.

**Planck's Law** The basis of quantum theory, it states that the energy of electromagnetic waves is confined in indivisible packets or quanta, each of which has to be radiated or absorbed as a whole, the magnitude being proportional to frequency. If E is the value of the quantum expressed in energy units, and v is the frequency of the radiation, then $E = hv$, where h is known as Planck's constant.

**plantwide data acquisition configuration** A configuration as shown in which a single computer performs supervisory control and process monitoring. The computer monitors the process by reading analog and digital data from the field via the input/output equipment. It may change an analog controller set point to perform supervisory control by sending either incremental or analog signals to the controller. Analog signals, such as flows or levels are used by both the computer and the analog panel instrumentation. Most peripheral equipment is connected to the I/O channel by interface circuitry. This hardware performs functions related to the operation of both the channel and the peripheral device, such as address detection, decoding, timing, and error detection/correction.

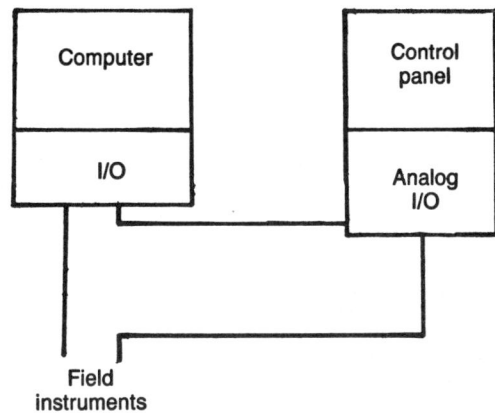

Plantwide data-acquisition configuration

**PLA output latch** A latch available in some microcomputer systems which allows the programmed logic array to be pipelined. The PLA output latch fetches the next control sequence, while the CPU is executing the current sequence.

**plasma** An ionized gaseous discharge within the display units that make use of this effect for segment illumination.

**plasma display** A display panel with supporting electronics that uses the plasma or gas-discharge effect.

**plasma torch** A heating device in which solids, liquids or gasses are forced through an arc within a water cooled tube, with consequent ionization; the deionization on impact results in very high temperatures. It is used for cutting and depositing carbides.

**plasmatron** A discharge tube in which anode current can be regulated by the control of a plasma, either by a grid or through the electron stream originating the plasma.

**plastic deformation** The changes in shape that solids undergo.

**plastic integrated circuits** ICs packaged in plastic. Ordinary plastic ICs may have caused some worries about field failures. To counter this worry and provide reliability plus the economy and ruggedness of plastic, there are gold chip ICs, which have noncorroding gold metalization and leads and contain no aluminum with its potential problems. The chip itself is made hermetic and put in an advanced plastic package with proven reliability in the following areas: temperature/humidity/bias, operating life, thermal fatigue, pressure cooker, thermal shock, and temperature cycle.

**plastic package** An integrated circuit or transistor housed within an inexpensive plastic enclosure. The package is molded directly on the assembled lead frame and semiconductor die. Bonding wire is attached using a thermocompression technique. All materials are thermally matched for expansion.

**plate** 1. The principal electrode to which the electron stream is attracted in an electron tube. Preferably called the anode. 2. One of the conductive electrodes in a capacitor. 3. One of the electrodes in a storage battery.

**plate neutralization** A method of neutralizing an amplifier (preventing its oscillation) by shifting a part of the plate voltage and applying it to the cathode grid circuit with a neutralizing capacitor.

**platinum** A heavy, almost white metal that resists most acids and is capable of high temperatures. It is used in precision resistors.

**platinum contacts** Sparking does not damage platinum as much as it does other metals, and a cleaner contact is assured with minimum attention.

**plantinum resistance thermometers** The International Temperature Scale has been defined by a pure platinum resistance thermometer from the triple point of hydrogen (13.81 K) to the freezing point of antimony (630.74 °C). The R/T relationship of platinum is well known, reproducible, and linear over a wide temperature range. Platinum is chemically inert and not easily contaminated. It does not readily oxidize and can be used up to 1500 °C. It is generally more expensive than other resistance temperature sensors, although some industrial grades are competitive.

**PLA versus ROM** The availability of low-cost ROMs has led to new concepts in digital systems design. The PLA (programmed logic array) offers an alternative to the ROM in some cases and allows regular design concepts to be used in situations where ROMs are impractical. The PLA concept is useful in combinational and sequential digital systems.

**PLL** Abbreviation for *phase-locked loop*.

**PLM** Abbreviation for *pulse length modulation*.

**PL/M** A high-level compiler language developed for microcomputer systems. PL/M is an assembly language replacement that can command the 8080 and other microprocessors to produce object code. It allows the user to concentrate on problems rather than programming. PL/M is derived from PL/1, an extensive high-level language that has some features of FORTRAN and some features of COBOL. Debug and checkout time with PL/M can be less than with an assembly language. Also, the PL/M structure allows the compiler to detect error conditions that could get past an assembler. The PL/M compiler is written in FORTRAN IV and will execute on most large machines without modification.

**PL/M-plus** An extended version of PL/M that can compile programs on microcomputers rather than the larger machines. PL/M-plus allows the user direct access to all bits and fields for manipulation operations. This allows all standard compiler operations on bits, fields, and whole words. Also written *PL/M+*.

**PL/1 programming language** A computer programming language that has some features of FORTRAN and some features of COBOL, among others.

**plotter** A peripheral unit in which a dependent variable is graphed by an automatically controlled pen or pencil as a function of one or more variables. Any position on a two-dimensional area can be referenced, accessed, or written onto by precise control of both vertical and horizontal axes.

**plotting board** An output unit that graphs the curves of one or more variables as a function of its input variables.

**plugboard** 1. A board with removable connections for changing the wiring pattern. 2. A board that can be removed and replaced to change the program or wired connections for a machine.

**plugboard computer** A computer that generally has a punched-card input and output with program instructions on a removable plugboard.

**plugboard, program patching** Refers to a relatively small auxiliary plugboard patched with a specific variation of a portion of a program.

**plugboard unit** A chassis that can be removed or inserted into other equipment by merely plugging in a connecting socket.

**plugging** A system of electric breaking by reversing the motor connections. A series resistance keeps the current at a safe value, and the circuit is opened when the motor stops so that it does not reverse.

**plugging chart** A diagram or chart that indicates where plugs, pins, or wires are to be placed on a plugboard.

**plug-in** Descriptive of devices in which connections are completed using conductors with pins, plugs, sockets, jacks, or other connectors that are readily removed.

**plug-in unit** A self-contained assembly that can be inserted or unplugged easily.

**plug-PROM** A read-only-memory diode array that is programmed by inserting small plugs into edge connectors. After it is connected to the microcomputer system, programming consists of selecting the proper plugs (each representing a 4-bit hexadecimal value) and inserting them into the edge connector of the word being programmed. Changing a program requires only removing and replacing the plugs.

**plug wire** A flexible wire with a metal pin at each end for connecting to the sockets of a plugboard.

**plus zone** Those bit positions in a code that represent the algebraic plus sign.

**PM** Abbreviation for *phase modulation*, a method of modulation in which the amplitude of the carrier remains the same, while the phase is changed as a function of the amplitude of the modulating signal.

**PMD** Abbreviation for *post mortem dump*.

**PMOS** Abbreviation for *p-channel metal-oxide semiconductor*, a field-effect-transistor technology based on use of p-type material for the source-and-drain channel.

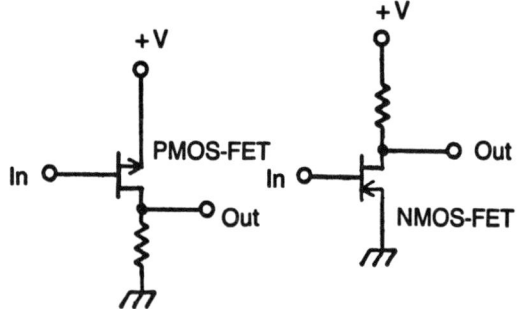

Basic PMOS and NMOS transistor amplifier circuits

**PMOS transistor** A PMOS transistor uses n-type silicon that is doped with p-type impurities in order to create the source and the drain of the transistor. Typical doping agents are boron and phosphorus. The areas to be doped with impurities are defined by a mask, which is made by the photolithographic process or the electron beam process. The impurities are added to the exposed area of the wafer using thermal diffusion.

**pn boundary** The surface where the donor and acceptor concentrations are equal in the transition region between n and p zones in a semiconductor.

**pneumatic interfacing** There are two basic methods of interfacing pneumatic instruments to the computer. One is to use P/I (pneumatic-to-current) and I/P (current-to-pneumatic) converters. In this type of system, the output of the converters are continuous. The other method replaces the P/I converters with a pneumatic multiplexer/converter. This can be accomplished with either a host or remote multiplexing configuration.

**pnip transistor** A transistor with a layer of intrinsic (undoped) material between the base and collector to extend the high-frequency range.

**pn junction** A region of transition between p and n semiconductor materials that has the properties of a diode.

**pn junction, LED** Refers to junctions that use gallium arsenide or phosphide to provide visible or infrared light emitting displays.

**pnp** A transistor consisting of two p-type regions separated by an n-type region and characterized by flow of holes as majority carriers (rather than the more mobile electrons).

**pnpn** Refers to a semiconductor switching device with three junctions.

**pnpn type switch** A semiconductor device made up of three or more junctions, at least one of which is able to switch between reverse and forward voltage polarity.

**pnp transistor** See *pnp*.

**pn type junction** A transition region between p and n (positive and negative) regions in semiconductor materials. The distributions and potential (voltage) gradients permit diode and transistor action.

**point** 1. A printer's measure, equal to .013837 inch or nearly 1/72 inch, used chiefly for specifying type sizes and leadings. 2. In printing, often a synonym for a period or dot.

**point contact** 1. A pressure contact between the semiconductor body and a metallic point. 2. A condition in which current flow to a semiconductor is through a point of metal.

**point contact diode** A diode that obtains its rectifying characteristic from a point contact.

**point contact rectifier** A rectifier made with a metal point pressing on to a crystal of semiconductor.

**point contact transistor** A transistor having a base electrode and two or more point contact electrodes.

**point effect** The phenomenon in which a discharge will occur more readily at sharp points than elsewhere on an object.

**pointer** 1. The indicating needle of an analog meter. 2. The most recently stored word in a stack, which gives the address of another memory location; the word is taken temporarily from a register that is to be used for another purpose or from the program counter during subroutine jumps; it is replaced following the temporary operation or jump.

**point junction transistor** A transistor having a base electrode and both point contact and junction electrodes.

**point of sale central controller** A central controller that polls data entry stations and records the data.

**point-of-sale system** An electronic system for automating the various functions of retail sales operations. Point-of-sale systems include inventory control using electronic cash registers, credit authorization via a reader terminal to a central computer, and electronic funds transfer using card activated systems.

**point of sale terminal equipment** Point of sale recorders or electronic cash register equipment includes: (1) A tag reader for reading merchandise tags, (2) A keyboard with numeric and function keys for operator entry of data, (3) A printer that prints sales slips and an internal audit tape, (4) A display for displaying data entered through the keyboard. Point of sale terminals are used in department stores and other large retail outlets such as supermarkets.

**point-to-point configuration** A network configuration in which all processors have a direct access to every other processor in the point to point network as shown. For n processors, n(n − 1)/2 interconnections are required. With three processors, three communication links are required. For five processors the number of links is ten; for 10 processors the number of links is 45. The number of links quickly becomes excessive. The advantages of this configuration are faster response times, the ability to use lower-grade communications lines, and the ability to use alternate paths to allow messages to continue to be forwarded when some of the links are interrupted.

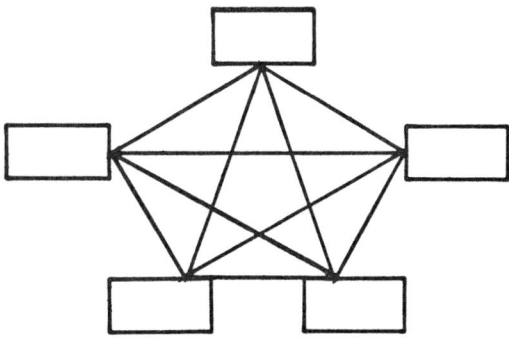

**Point-to-point network configuration**

**POL** Abbreviation for *problem oriented language*.

**polar** 1. A logic technique in which a binary one is represented by current flow in one direction and a zero by current flow in the opposite direction. 2. Having poles (as a magnet). 3. A type of plot showing coordinates over a two-dimensional plane, and used to depict signal distribution from an antenna, the pickup field of a microphone, etc.

**polar axes** The fixed lines from which the angles made by radius vectors are measured in a polar coordinates system.

**polar coordinates** A system of coordinates in which a point is located by its distance and direction (angle) from a fixed point on a reference line called the polar axis.

**polar crystals** Crystals having a lattice composed of alternate positive and negative ions.

**polar diagram** A diagram in which the magnitude of a quantity is shown by polar coordinates.

**polarity** 1. The orientation of any device that has poles or signed electrodes. 2. The value established by the ungrounded electrode of any grounded direct-current electrical system; for example, the polarity of most modern vehicle electrical systems is + 12 volts. 3. Electrical opposition.

**polarized capacitor** An electrolytic capacitor designed for operation only with fixed polarity. The dielectric film is formed only near one electrode, and thus the impedance is not the same for both directions of current flow.

**polarized plug** A plug constructed in such a manner that it can only be inserted into a socket with proper polarity.

**polarizing slot** A cutout in the edge of a circuit board to properly align certain types of connectors or to insure that proper pin polarity is maintained.

**polar mode** 1. Relates to a device that separates or breaks up a quantity, particularly a vector, into constituent parts or elements. 2. A device for resolving a vector into its mutually perpendicular components.

**polar molecule** A molecule with unbalanced electric charges, usually valency electrons, resulting in a dipole moment.

**polaron** An electron in a substance that is trapped in a potential well produced by polarization charges on the surrounding molecules.

**pole** 1. An electrode of an electrical device such as a battery, switch, or relay. 2. Either of two opposite signs (as + or −). 3. One of the regions in a magnetized body where the magnetic flux density is concentrated.

**Polish notation** A system of expressing logical and arithmetic statements without using parentheses. In Polish notation, the expression *A plus B multiplied by C* would be represented by +ABC. Also called *Lukaseiwicz notation, parentheses-free notation,* and *prefix notation.* (Compare reverse-Polish notation.)

**poll** A systematic method for sampling the output of stations on a multipoint system. The computer contacts the stations according to an order specified by the user.

**polled I/O** In the polling or programmed I/O technique, I/O devices are connected to the system bus. They may have to also be connected to some control lines. The principle is to implement a procedure for determining the next input-output device that requires service. The polling technique is a synchronous technique. The microprocessor periodically asks each device connected to the data bus if it requires service. Each device answers with a yes or no. When a no is received, the microprocessor proceeds to the next device and asks it. The microprocessor thus calls each I/O device successively to determine if service is required. In actual practice, a status flag is tested on the device or its interface. If the test is true, action is initiated. This is usually the transfer of a word or block of data to or from the device.

**polling** A technique by which each of the terminals sharing a communications line is periodically sampled to determine if it requires servicing. Polling is also used to determine the source of multiple interrupt requests in multiprocessing systems. If several interrupts occur at the same time, the control program is used to make the decision as to the order of servicing.

**polling characters** The characters that are used to identify a particular terminal during a polling operation. The characters also indicate to the computer whether or not the terminal has a message to send.

**polling interval** The time between polling operations if no data is being transmitted from a polled station.

**polling list** A list containing control information and the order in which terminals are to be polled.

**polling loop** The software used to implement an I/O device-polling algorithm. The process of asking the device and receiving information in return is called *handshaking.* The communications protocol between one device and the next one on a link normally uses some form of handshaking. Before transmitting information to the device, a status bit is checked to test if the device is ready to accept data. Before reading a word from a device, a status bit is checked to test if the word is complete. The basic flowchart of a polling loop is in the next column.

**polling, time sharing** Polling is a technique for controlling the use of lines by an agreed protocol between devices that share a common transmission path. The devices are controlled (so that only one of them sends information along a line at any instant) by an exchange of control signals or messages between them. Sometimes polling is governed by the CPU, which sends a control message to each terminal in turn, inviting it to transmit a message. The terminal replies either with such a message or with a control message indicating it has nothing to report.

**polyesters** A class of thermosetting synthetic resins having good

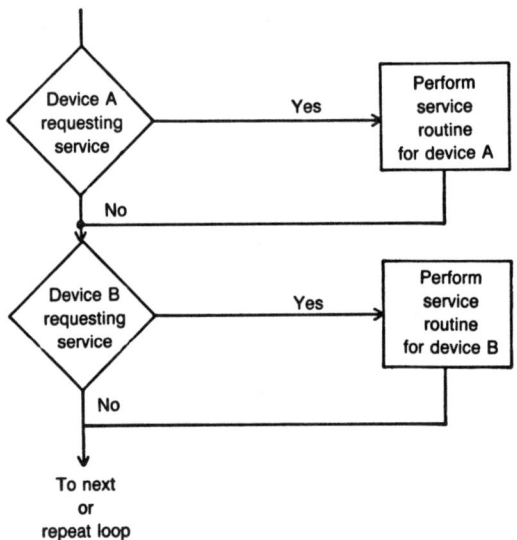

**Basic polling loop**

strength and resistance to moisture and chemicals.

**polymers** Refers to the complex molecular chains that are used to manufacture plastics.

**polymorphic** Capable of existing in several different forms.

**polymorphic system** A system that can take on various forms for the problem at hand by altering its interconnections or functions. A polymorphic system may change its logic construction or operation in order to handle a variety of tasks.

**polyphase** 1. Having or utilizing several phases. A polyphase motor operates from a power line having several phases of alternating current. 2. A set of AC power supply circuits carrying currents of equal frequency with uniformly spaced phase differences, normally employing a common return conductor.

**polyphase synchronous generator** A generator with its AC circuits so arranged so that two or more symmetrical alternating electromotive forces with definite phase relationships to each other are produced at its terminals.

**polystyrene** A clear thermoplastic material with excellent dielectric properties, especially at very high frequencies.

**polystyrene capacitor** A capacitor with a polystyrene dielectric.

**polytheme** Polyethylene, a tough waxy thermoplastic material that is flexible and chemically resistant. It is used as an insulator.

**polyvalence** The property of being interrelated in several ways.

**polyvalent notation** A method of describing characteristics in condensed form in which each character or group of characters represents one of the characteristics.

**population** The total collection of units being considered, sometimes referred to as the universe.

**population inversion** The reversal of the normal ratio of populations of two different energy states, such that fewer and fewer atoms occupy states of successively higher energies. It forms the basis of laser action.

**port** 1. A place of access to a system or circuit. 2. An opening or connection that provides electrical or physical access to a system or circuit. The point at which an input or output is in contact with the CPU can be considered a port, along with any entrance or exit from a network or system. 3. An opening of critical but controllable dimensions in a tuned enclosure (such as a cavity or loudspeaker cabinet).

**portable compiler** A device that edits, enters, and compiles programs in a high-level language and which is capable of being hand-carried from job to job. Portable compilers generate machine-language programs that are loaded into the process controller. They contain a keyboard to enter data and a display or printer for program listings.

**portable data medium** A data medium intended to be easily transportable independently of the mechanism used in its interpretation.

**portable PROM programmer** Refers to a programmer for an MOS or bipolar ROM. Some use a six-digit hexadecimal display that adjusts automatically, along with the formating, to accommodate any PROM type and size. Marginal PROMs are rejected during programming. An operator can program a PROM from the hexadecimal keyboard and automatically duplicate PROMs with or without corrections. The unit may also compare a programmed PROM with a master and display the data stored on a single PROM.

**ports, input-output** Each microprocessor can have a number of I/O ports. Some are associated with external system activity; others are for the information exchange with other system processors. In practice, ports are part of the I/O section of a processor. Low cost microcomputers are particularly adaptable to communications via their I/O ports.

**POS** Abbreviation for *point-of-sale*.

**positional operand** In assembler programming, an operand in a macroinstruction that assigns a value to the corresponding positional parameter, which is declared in the prototype statement of the called macro definition.

**position code** The established positions or sites in recording media in which data may be entered or recorded according to specific conventions adopted to standardize the locations for coding information.

**position readout** A display of absolute slide position as derived from a position feedback device (transducer) normally attached to the lead screw of a machine.

**position sensor** A device for measuring a position and converting this measurement into a form convenient for data transmission.

**position storage** The storage media in a numerical control system containing the coordinate position read from tape.

**positioning/contouring system** A type of numerical control system that has the capability of contouring in two axes, and the ability of positioning in a third axis for such operations as drilling, tapping, and boring.

**positive charge** An electrical charge with fewer electrons than normal.

**positive electricity** 1. A phenomenon in a body associated with a deficiency of electrons, such as when positive electricity appears on glass rubbed with silk. 2. The electricity that predominates in glass or in a glass body after it has been electrified by rubbing it with silk or similar materials.

**positive electrode** The conductor node that serves as the anode terminal of a polarized device such as a battery, an electrolytic capacitor, or a self-contained two-pole circuit.

**positive feedback** A system in which the amplification is increased at the cost of fidelity by returning a part of the output in phase with the input signal. An oscillator, for example, employs positive feedback to sustain self-amplification. Also called *regeneration*.

**positive ion** An atom that has lost one or more electrons and thus has an excess of protons, giving it a positive charge.

**positive ion sheath** Refers to a collection of positive ions that may block normal currents.

**positive logic** A logic convention in which the positive voltage is defined as a 1 and the more negative voltage is defined as a 0.

**positron** A positive electron of the same mass as a normal (negative) electron but with a charge that is of the opposite sign. It is produced in the decay of radioisotopes and in pair production by x-rays of greater than 1 MeV.

**positron quadrapole** A type of ion beam focusing magnet.

**postedit** To edit output data resulting from a previous computation.

**postinstallation evaluation** An evaluation of a computer configuration to determine if it meets the objectives established at the time of acquisition.

**post mortem** 1. The analysis of a condition or malfunction after its completion. 2. Collectively, the routines and listings used to locate a malfunction or an error in the program or system. A post mortem routine can automatically print information on the contents of registers and storage locations at the time the routine is stopped in order to assist in the location of a mistake in coding.

**post mortem routine** A service routine used in analyzing the cause of a malfunction. See *post mortem*, 2.

**postprocessor** A set of instructions used to transform tool centerline data into machine-tool motion in a computer-controlled system. The postprocessor set typically includes rate feed calculations, spindle speed calculations, and function commands for auxiliary operations.

**pot** 1. A potentiometer or variable resistor. 2. To encapsulate a circuit or device into an inaccessible, usually epoxy, package. 3. Abbreviation for potential (as in *hi-pot*, for *high potential*).

**potential** The voltage between two points in a circuit, device, or system; electromotive force; electrical pressure.

**potential difference** The voltage existing between two points in a circuit or system.

**potential gradient** The differences in value of the potential per unit length along the conductor or through a dielectric.

**potentiometer** A usually circular or disk-type resistor with two fixed terminals and a third terminal connected to a variable contact arm.

**potentiometer circuit** A network arranged so that, when two or more potential differences are present in as many branches, the response of a suitable detecting device in any branch can be made zero by adjusting the electrical constants of the network.

**potentiometer function generator** One in which functional values of voltage are applied to points on a potentiometer, which becomes an interpolator.

**potentiometer transducer** A transducer in which a displacement is transmitted to the slider in a potentiometer, thus changing the ratio of output resistance to total resistance.

**potentiometric pressure transducers** The potentiometric pressure transducer was first available in 1914, and is still used today due to low cost and connection simplicity. The potentiometric transducer consists of a resistance element either wirewound or deposited conductive film, and a movable slider or wiper, which is connected to the mechanical sensing element. The motion due to a pressure change results in a resistance change. Depending on the design of the potentiometer, the output can be linear, sine, cosine, logarithmic, or exponential.

These transducers can be used with AC or DC, and no amplification or impedance matching may be required. Other advantages include the low cost to manufacturer and the high output with high input voltages.

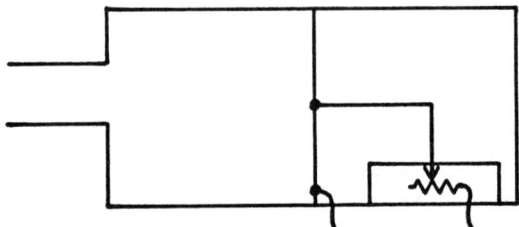

Potentiometric pressure transducer

**powdered iron core** A core consisting of fine particles of magnetic material mixed with a suitable bonding material and pressed into shape.

**power amplifier** 1. An amplifier intended for driving one or more speakers or transducers. 2. A circuit designed to amplify both voltage and current.

**power amplifier with gain** Refers to a unit used to boost the signal handling capability of an operational amplifier. The buffer output allows one to drive up to 50 mA output currents with 20V output swings.

**power derating** The use of computed curves to determine the correct power rating of a device or component that is to be used above its reference ambient temperature.

**power dissipation** The dispersion of the heat generated within a device or component when a current flows through it. This is accomplished by convection to the air, radiation to the surroundings, or conduction.

**powered enclosure** A unit with a recessed frame and power supplies with connectors for specific microcomputers.

**power factor correction** The adding of capacitors to an inductive circuit to increase the power factor by making the total current more nearly in phase with the applied voltage.

**power factor meter** An instrument for measuring power factor with a scale graduated directly in power factor.

**power-fail** A specific interrupt that occurs when a loss of primary power is detected.

**power fail, automatic restart** 1. A facility that provides a processor interrupt when a power low signal is received from the primary power source. Sufficient time is then available to preserve the contents of the working registers in the memory. The automatic restart enables processing to resume at the point of interruption, when power is restored. 2. Refers to a specific power fail interrupt that provides an interrupt when a loss of primary power is detected. Power restart interrupt occurs when the power is applied and is up to normal operating levels.

**power-fail detect module** A unit designed to provide an interrupt or flag at least 500 microseconds before a low-power condition is detected and program execution is halted. Such a device can be used to prevent loss of data in memory for critical applications.

**power fail logic** Refers to logic circuits that protect a system in the event that primary power fails. The circuits automatically store the current operating parameters. When the power is restored, the circuits use this information to continue proper operation.

**power-fail recovery** A system (abbreviated *PFR*) with charging and automatic switching circuitry that provides for computer restart without operator intervention after a power failure. A PFR system can maintain solid-state memory integrity for several hours after a power failure.

**power-fail/restart** An option on some computer systems that monitors power supply voltages and allows an orderly shutdown upon a power failure and an automatic restart when power is restored.

**power-fail/restart diagnostic** A test routine that checks for proper operation of the power-fail/restart option.

**power failure** A usually temporary and inadvertent loss of power to an otherwise functioning machine.

**power frequency** The frequency in hertz at which electric power is generated and distributed.

**power gain** 1. The ratio of output power to input power in an amplifier. 2. The relative level increase of a directional or omnidirectional antenna as compared with (usually) a reference dipole fed with the same signal and measured at a given reference distance from the radiators.

**power ground** A ground that is part of the circuit for the main source of power to or from various units.

**power level** The ratio of power at a point in the system to some arbitrary amount of power chosen as a reference. Power-level differences are usually expressed in decibels.

**power loss** The ratio of the power absorbed by the input circuit to the power delivered to a specified load under specified operating conditions.

**power-on reset** A signal used at power turnon in some systems to initialize the CPU to a known state; it allows the proper sequence of events to occur. The power-on reset signal is generated external to the CPU, which receives the signal and sets the internal logic states and produces a signal which can be used to initialize other circuits.

**power pack** 1. A unit for converting power from AC to DC or DC to AC for electronic devices. 2. A battery of cells for powering electronic equipment.

**power relay** A relay that functions at some predetermined value of power. It may be an overpower relay, an underpower, or a combination of both.

**power response** Refers to the frequency response capabilities of an amplifier running at or near its full rated power.

**power semiconductors** These semiconductors have ratings for a single transistor that are up to 750 volts at several amperes, with turn off times on the order of one microsecond. Slower devices may have turn off times of 2 to 3 microseconds, and ratings can run up to 600 V at 15 amperes.

**power supply** The system and circuitry for converting the ac line power into suitable dc voltages for the electronic equipment in a system.

**power supply circuit** An arrangement of components that convert an ac input voltage into a dc output voltage. A basic power supply includes a transformer, rectifier, and filter. Regulators are often used to supply constant voltages or currents.

**power supply components** A basic power supply has a power transformer that steps up the voltage for high voltage supplies or steps down for a low voltage supply. The voltages at the transformer's secondary then goes through a rectifier system, where it is converted to pulsating dc. The filter system then smoothes out the pulsations to make the dc voltage at the supply's output appear more like the steady state dc characteristic of batteries.

**power switch** 1. A mechanical switch used for high-current control applications or for application of operating voltages to equipment. 2. An electronic circuit that performs a switching action to deliver high-current voltages to equipment.

**power-switch module** A module used to drive solenoids, motor starters, and other such high-current devices.

**power transformer** 1. A transformer used for raising or lowering the supply voltage required by the load. 2. A transformer used to introduce the energizing supply into an instrument or system, distinct from a signal transformer.

**power transistor** A transistor capable of handling relatively heavy current loads.

**power typing** 1. Refers to automatic typing that is essentially repetitive and involves only minimal text editing. 2. A very basic word processing type of application.

**pp junction** A region of transition between two regions having different properties in p-type semiconductor material.

**PPM** Abbreviation for *pulse-position modulation*, a pulse modulation system in which the position of the pulse is a function of the modulating signal.

**pps** Abbreviation for *pulses per second*.

**PPS** Abbreviation for *parallel processing system*, a processor that provides the arithmetic and control section of a general purpose computer. This microprocessor is a small set of circuits that can be used to build equipment requiring digital data processing. This includes calculators, cash registers, credit terminals, electronic scales, billing machines, process controllers and general purpose data processors.

**PRA** Abbreviation for *print alphamerically*.

**preamplifier** A term for a one or two stage amplifier required to strengthen the output of an electrical device so that it can drive a main amplifier.

**preanalysis** An initial review of a computer task, for the purpose of increasing the efficiency of the computer for that task.

**preassembly time** The time used by an assembler to process macro definitions and perform conditional assembly operations.

**precision** The degree of exactness with which a quantity is defined. Precision is related to the number of distinguishable alternatives from which a representation is selected, such as the number of digits or bits in a number or word. Double-length precision pertains to words or operations with twice the normal length of a unit of data in a computing system.

**precision, double length** Pertaining to twice the normal length of a unit of data or a storage device in a given computing system. A double length register would have the capacity to store twice as much data as a single length or normal register; a double length word would have twice the number of characters or digits as a normal or single length word.

**predictive control** A control system that uses a computer for real-time repetitive comparison of pertinent parameters.

**preedit** A checking of application or operational programs before the test run. A preedit run can remove such problems as a disobedience to supervisory or segmentation rules.

**preferred values** A series of resistor and capacitor values adopted by the EIA and military. In this system, the increase between any two steps is the same percentage as between all other steps.

**prefix** An add-on designator for the scheduling and transferring of control between programs.

**prefix multiplier** A scale or conversion factor for increasing a basic unit or quantity.

| PREFIX | FACTOR | SYMBOL |
|--------|--------|--------|
| exa    | $10^{18}$ | E |
| peta   | $10^{15}$ | P |
| tera   | $10^{12}$ | T |
| giga   | $10^{9}$  | G |
| mega   | $10^{6}$  | M |
| kilo   | $10^{3}$  | k |
| hecto  | $10^{2}$  | h |
| deka   | $10^{1}$  | da |
| deci   | $10^{-1}$ | d |
| centi  | $10^{-2}$ | c |
| milli  | $10^{-3}$ | m |
| micro  | $10^{-6}$ | $\mu$ |
| nano   | $10^{-9}$ | n |
| pico   | $10^{-12}$ | p |
| femto  | $10^{-15}$ | f |
| atto   | $10^{-18}$ | a |

**prefix notation** A method of forming mathematical expressions in which each operator precedes its operands. Also called *Polish notation*. (See *reverse-Polish notation*.)

**preliminary review** Refers to an examination or evaluation of matters related to processing procedures of an organization in an attempt to offer guidance in the preparation of plans, proposals, or designs previous to the installation of computer system equipment.

**preparation** In word processing, a task definition that includes paper handling, media loading, and margin, tab, and console adjustments, prior to typing.

**preparatory function** A command for changing the mode of operation of a control system from positioning to contouring, or for calling for a fixed cycle by the machine.

**preprogrammed control ROM** In some microcomputers the definition of the instructions (the microinstructions) are stored in a read-only memory (ROM), which is part of the control chip that makes up a part of the CPU. That chip is a CROM (*control read-only memory*). It can be bought in a preprogrammed form, or the customer can define the contents. Since the microprogram is placed into the CROM by mask programming, the user must have a high volume to warrant the expenses involved in defining the contents.

**preprocessor** A program that converts data from the format of an emulated system to the format accepted by an emulator.

**prerecorded** A term applied to material stored on media for repetitive use, such as programmed instructions or the standard paragraphs of form letters.

**preset** An activity to set the contents of a storage location to an initial value or to establish the initial control value of a loop.

**presettable I/O** A set of switches that allow the programmer to verify microinstructions that perform input/output data transfers before actual peripherals are connected to the system.

**pressure transducer** Almost all electrical output pressure transducers sense pressure with a mechanical sensing element. The elements are generally thin-walled elastic members, such as plates, shells, or tubes, which offer the pressure a surface area to act upon. When the pressure is not balanced by an equal pressure acting on the opposite surface, the element will deflect. The deflection is used to produce an electrical change in the transduction element.

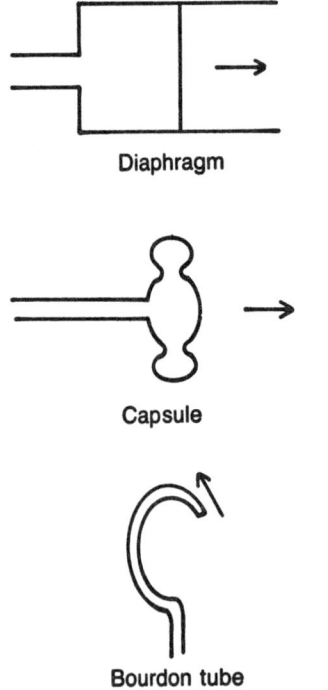

Pressure sensing elements

**presumptive address** The address constant containing the absolute address of a memory location and a relative address; base address.

**pretravel** The distance or angle a plunger or actuator travels from the free position to the operating position.

**preventive maintenance** Precautionary measures designed to forestall system failures.

**prewired external circuitry** Connectors and cable systems that are prewired to extend the input/output system.

**PRD** Abbreviation for *printer dump*.

**PRF** Abbreviation for *pulse repetition frequency*.

**PRR** Abbreviation for *pulse repetition rate*. The measure of the number of electric pulses per unit of time experienced by a unit in a computer; usually a factor of the standard pulse rate.

**PRI** Abbreviation for *primary*.

**primary constants** Refers to the capacitance, inductance, resistance, and leakance of a conductor, usually to earth (coaxial or concentric), or to return per unit length of line for a balanced conductor.

**primary current** The current flowing through the primary winding of a transformer. Changes in this current cause a voltage to be induced in the secondary winding of the transformer.

**primary electrons** 1. Electrons incident on a surface where secondary electrons are released. 2. Electrons released from atoms by internal forces and not by external radiation as with secondary electrons.

**primary emission** Electron emission due to irradiation, including thermal heating, or by the application of a strong electric field to a surface.

**primary flow** The flow of carriers that is determined by the main properties of a device.

**primary ionization** 1. In collision theory, the ionization produced by the primary particles, in contrast to total ionization, which includes secondary ionization. 2. In counter tubes, the total ionization produced by incident radiation without gas amplification.

**primary store** The main storage method in a computer system (not necessarily the fastest).

**primitive** Descriptive of the lowest level of a machine instruction or the lowest unit of language translation.

**printed circuit** A circuit in which interconnecting wires have been replaced by conductive strips bound onto an insulating board.

**printed circuit assembly** 1. A printed circuit board to which separable components have been attached. 2. An assembly of one more printed circuit boards.

**printed circuit board** An insulating board (also called *card*) onto which circuit paths have been printed or etched. Printed circuits boards may be single-sided, double-sided, or multilayer for high-density applications.

**printed circuit breadboard** Refers to a printed circuit board for custom electronic designs in a modular microcomputer system. It is useful in prototyping with pretinned holes, arranged to accommodate standard integrated circuits. ICs may be inserted directly into the board, or sockets may be used.

**printed circuit card** A card, usually of laminate or resinous material of the insulating type, used for the mounting of an electrical circuit.

**printed circuit, ceramic** Refers to a material usually used only for very small printed wiring applications since large ceramic pieces tend to be brittle and are not as flexible as phenolic or glass epoxy. Ceramic material is used when dimensional stability is required at high temperatures.

**printed circuit, double sided** Refers to a printed circuit in which greater complexity is required and both sides of the insulating material contain the printed wiring pattern. The components are mounted only on one side. The connections between conductors of the two opposite sides may be made by the insertion of eyelets, rivets, or wire. For many applications, plated through holes are used. In this process, conductive material is deposited inside the holes connecting the two printed wiring patterns.

**printed circuit epoxy coatings** These coatings offer excellent mechanical and thermal protection, as well as electrical insulation, but do not lend themselves for easy repair. Removal of the epoxy coating to gain access to a solder connection can be difficult.

**printed circuit, glass epoxy laminate** Refers to a widely used PC material, is more translucent than phenolic material and has excellent temperature stability and greater strength than phenolic.

**printed circuit, multilayer** Refers to a printed wiring technique that uses several layers of printed wiring patterns, each mounted on a thin insulating material and carefully aligned and molded together. This technique almost always uses plated through holes to provide the connection of conductors between the conducting layers.

**printed circuit, phenolic** Refers to a brown, board material used in commercial applications where temperature stability, and strength are not critical.

**printed circuit, polyvinyl fluoride** Refers to PC materials that provide excellent insulating capability and withstand extreme environmental conditions, but are more difficult to repair. The polyvinyl fluoride material must usually be scraped away before soldering.

**printed circuit, rhodium plating** A plating material that is used because of its hardness and surface stability for extreme environmental and wear conditions. The fingers on printed circuit boards that mate

**printed circuit, solder plating** Refers to a mixture of tin and lead used on PC boards to improve solderability and prevent corrosion.

**printed circuit switch** A rotary switch that can be soldered in place directly onto a printed circuit board.

**printed component** A type of printed circuit component intended for electrical and/or magnetic functions other than point to point connections or shielding; examples include printed inductors and printed transmission lines.

**printed contact** That portion of a printed circuit that connects the circuit to a plug-in receptacle and performs the function of a plug pin.

**printed element** An element such as a resistor formed on a circuit board by deposition or etching.

**printed wiring** A conductive path formed on the surface of an insulating baseboard by plating or etching.

**printed wiring substrate** Refers to a conductive pattern printed on a substrate.

**printer** A typewriter-like machine that produces human-sensible marks or impressions, usually on paper, and in the form of graphic characters. A typical desktop printer produces up to 100 characters per second and 70 lines per minute.

**printer controller** A device that contains the circuitry necessary to interface a printing unit to a microcomputer. Components are usually mounted on a card that plugs directly into the microcomputer chassis assembly.

**print wheel** A typing element that may be daisy wheel or cylindrical in shape, used on certain typewriters and printer units.

**priority circuits** These circuits of the control unit grant memory access to the various units of the system in a sequence that enables each input/output device and the system's running time to be used most efficiently. The priority circuits receive, store, and grant requests for accesses to memory.

**priority dispatching** Refers to numbers being assigned to tasks and used to determine precedence for the use of the central processing unit in a multitasking situation.

**priority indicators** Code signals that form a queue of data for processing in order of importance.

**priority interrupt controller** A priority interrupt controller provides a mask that allows the programmer to mask selectively any interrupt level. The basic logic is shown. It shows the generation of the level vector but not the address vectoring. These devices typically accept eight interrupt levels, which are shown on the right of the diagram; each one will set a bit in the interrupt register.

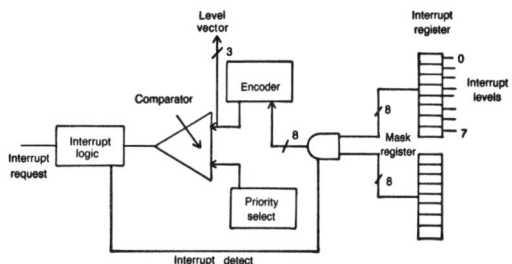

**Interrupt controller**

**priority interrupt control unit** A unit (abbreviated *PICU*) with up to eight levels of priority that is designed to simplify the interrupt system for a microcomputer. A typical unit can accept eight requesting levels, determine the highest priority, compare this priority with the current status register, and issue an interrupt along with vector data to identify the service routine.

**priority interrupt module** A device that acts as the monitor for a number of field contacts and notifies the computer when an external priority request has been made.

**priority interrupt table** A table that lists the priority sequence for handling and testing interrupts in systems without fully automatic interrupt capability.

**priority ordered interrupts** Refers to an interrupt capability that permits a terminal to be attached to more than one interrupt line. If the attached interrupts cover a range of priorities, by selectively arming and disarming the external interrupt lines, the executive program can

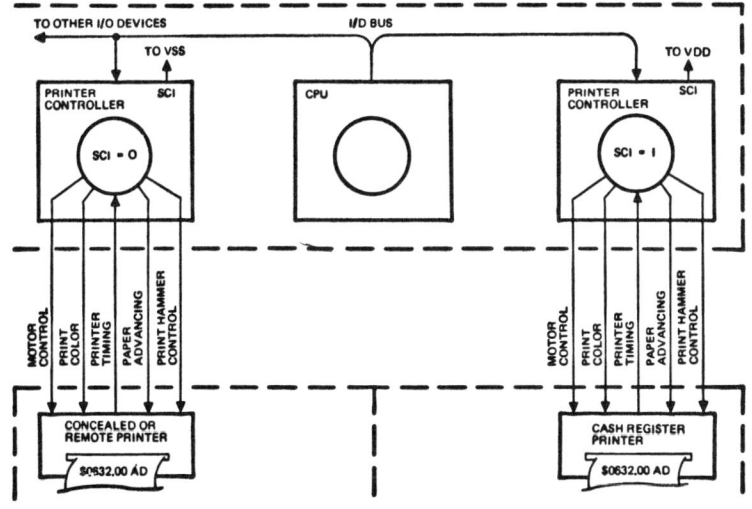

**Printer controllers**

change the relative priority of a terminal's attention requests, allowing different classes of service or response to be given.

**priority scheme** A technique that allows several devices to request service simultaneously. Assume that interrupt 0 is the highest priority, interrupt 1 the next, and so on to the lowest priority device. The microprocessor tests bit 0 of the interrupt register, then bit 1, and so on until it finds a 1. When it finds a 1, the corresponding interrupt line is serviced. Thus the highest level of interrupt is serviced first. After this interrupt is serviced, the microprocessor reads the contents of the interrupt register and services any other waiting interrupts. This is a software implementation of a priority interrupt scheme.

**prise pack** A standard microelectronic functional device proposed by the Navy.

**PRISM** Abbreviation for *program reliability information system* (Navy).

**private automatic branch exchange** A private automatic exchange (abbreviated *PABX*) that provides for the transmission of calls to and from a public telephone network.

**private line** 1. A channel furnished to a subscriber for exclusive use. Also called a *private wire* or *leased line*. 2. Trade name (when capitalized) for a selective calling system in two-way communications characterized by a continuously transmitted low-frequency tone during all station transmissions.

**private wire** The interconnection of a number of points by communication facilities.

**privileged instructions** Specialized restrictions to commands that prevent one subprogram from misusing another subprogram's input/output devices.

**PRN** Abbreviation for *print numerically*.

**probable error** The amount of error that according to the laws of probability, is most likely to occur during a measurement.

**probe** The terminal point at the end of a test equipment's input conductor.

**problem board** A removable panel with an array of terminals which are interconnected by short leads in patterns to simulate specific program problems. The entire problem board can be inserted or removed for different programs.

**problem definition** The act of compiling information in the form of logic diagrams and flowcharts that present a specific problem to the programmer in a clear and concise manner.

**problem description** A statement of a specific problem. The problem description may include the method of solution, the solution, the transformations of data required, and the relationships of procedures, data, and constraints.

**problem determination** The process of identifying a hardware or software failure and determining responsibility and cause.

**problem diagnosis** The analysis used to identify the precise cause of a hardware or software failure.

**problem language** The language used by a programmer in stating the definition of a problem.

**problem-oriented language** A programming language designed for the convenient expression for a given class of problems, usually a source language suited to describe procedural steps. A problem-oriented language is designed for the convenience of program specification in a general problem area, rather than for easy conversion to machine code.

**procedural test** A check of machine control and operation before processing. Procedural test data should cover all or most of the conditions that can occur during the run. A control panel can be used to insert a procedural test program, and results can be compared against predetermined conditions.

**procedure-oriented language** A machine-independent language that describes how the process of solving a problem is to be carried out. The language should be designed for the convenient expression of procedures for problem solution, usually in terms of algorithms. FORTRAN, ALGOL, COBOL, and PL/1 are all examples of procedure-oriented languages. FORTRAN is oriented towards algebraic procedures, while COBOL is oriented towards commercial procedures and applications.

**process chromatograph** An instrument that is used in continuous analysis in process plants. The process chromatograph can be used to measure many components in the same stream. It can also be programmed to measure many streams, each with different concentrations. By the selection of appropriate columns and detectors, the process chromatograph may be used to measure the parts per million concentrations of impurities in gases.

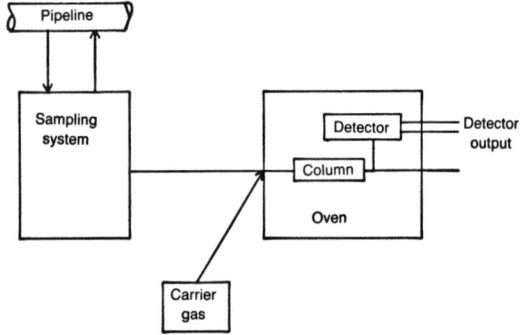

**Process gas chromatograph system**

**process control** The control of industrial processes such as metal production, chemical refining, and other manufacturing operations. Process control usually implies a continuous operation or production.

**process control analog modules** Refers to signal conversion, sample-and-hold, amplifiers, multiplexers, and signal conditioning units designed especially for process control applications.

**process control compiler** A compiler used to program PROMs using a process control language or machine language. The compiler accepts keyboard entry of data, displays the data for verification and editing, compiles the program, and loads it into the PROM chips.

**process control computer** A computer designed for process control applications. It is generally limited in software requirements, instruction capacity, word length, and accuracy.

**process control, industrial** Industrial processing applications for microcomputers are as wide and varied as the degrees of control that the individual processes may require. Some typical process control application areas are precious metals production, cement production, environmental control, chemical processes, and petroleum refining.

**process control language** A language (abbreviated *PCL*) that resembles beginning FORTRAN and is modeled after relay logic for arithmetic and logic commands. PCL allows a control program to be created in English, which is entered using a keyboard and converted into machine language for storage in a PROM. The following features should be a requirement for a powerful process control language:

1. Compatibility with a major language
2. Efficiency of overhead
3. Simplicity for beginners
4. Facility for running multiple tasks
5. All common machine operations
6. Interrupt capability
7. Subroutine and compilation capability

**process control peripheral equipment** Refers to the peripheral equipment available for most control systems including printers, magnetic tape cassettes, floppy disk systems, and CRT displays.

**process controller** A computer that controls the process to which it is connected and executes machine-language programs to accomplish this control.

**process control loop** Refers to a complete process control system in which computers are used for the automatic control and regulation of industrial processes and operations.

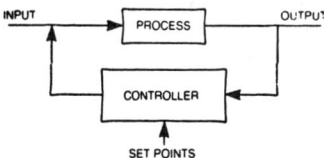

Process control loop

**process control system** A system that uses a computer or digital logic to regulate and control industrial operations such as the production of chemicals. A typical process control system contains:

1. CPU
2. PROM
3. RAM for data storage
4. Input/output modules
5. Communications cables

**processing, interactive** Refers to a type of processing that involves the constant interplay of the operator.

**processing section** The portion of a computer that does the changing of input data into output data. The processing section usually includes the arithmetic and logic sections.

**processing, serial** Pertaining to the sequential or consecutive execution of two or more processes in a single device such as a channel or processing unit.

**process, limited** Refers to the restriction of the speed of the processing unit controls due to the processing time as contrasted with input/output limitations.

**process loop test** A check made to determine the need for loop operations.

**processor** A hardware data processor or a program that performs the functions of compiling, assembling, and translating for a specific language. Processor operations can involve registers, accumulators, program counters and stacks, input/output control, and internal instruction control.

**processor basic instructions** These instructions can be functionally grouped into five categories: register operations, accumulator operations, program counter and stack control operations, input/output operations, and machine operations.

**processor, bit slice** An approach that allows microcomputer organizations of variable word sizes, with processor units separated into two, four, or eight bit slices on a single chip. These devices can be paralleled to yield an 8-, 12-, 16-, 24-, or 32-bit microcomputer when assembled with the other necessary components of the system. Sixteen-bit microprocessors constructed from these components can be assembled into microcomputers that perform in the minicomputer class.

**processor dependent interrupt** A specific example of a processor dependent interrupt condition is the presence bit condition caused by a program being executed on a processor that is executing an operand call that addresses a descriptor with a presence bit of zero.

**processor evaluation module** A circuit card that contains all the necessary components of a microprocessor set. A processor evaluation module contains:

1. CPU
2. RAM
3. Clock generator
4. Input/output circuits
5. Power-on circuits

**processor input/output channel** A channel used to communicate with devices that are generally asynchronous in nature. Each item of data is transferred to or from an addressed device, by executing an input/output instruction for each transfer. Input/output instructions, in addition to transferring data, are also used to test the status of a device and to initiate input or output operations.

**processor interface module** A unit that connects the LSI processor to as many as eight input/output devices. It provides a common interface and standardized software for either serial or parallel operation.

**processor memory, building block** The asynchronous operation of a typical processor provides for the use of various speeds of memories. Memories can be ROM, RAM, or PROM.

**processor module** The circuit card that contains the microprocessor along with the logic and control circuitry necessary to operate as a processing unit. The processor support circuits consist of clock circuits, multiplexer, bus control, input/output control, and interrupt logic.

**processor slices** An approach that allows microcomputer organizations of variable word sizes, with processor units separated into two, four, or eight bit slices on a single chip. These devices can be paralleled to yield an 8-, 12-, 16-, 24-, or 32-bit microcomputer with processing power that is far greater than that presently available from MOS microprocessors.

**processor status word** A word (abbreviated *PSW*) containing information on the current processor status. The PSW may include information on priority conditions of arithmetic or logic results.

**processor transfer time** The time required for data transfer (before the processor acknowledges the data as input or output). Processor transfer time depends on the internal cycle time and channel transfer rate of the processor.

**producer's risk** Associated with an acceptance test, the producer's risk is defined to be the probability of rejecting an item or a lot that is, in fact, satisfactory.

**production automation** The automatic techniques used in such industrial applications as machine tool control, material handling, mixing of materials, inspection systems, and assembly operations.

**production automation microcomputer** A rugged, compact microcomputer system designed for industrial control and automation applications. A typical production automation microcomputer system contains the microprocessor, RAM, input/output channels, DMA channel, interrupt facility, power-fail and automatic restart circuits, and an operating console.

**production automation system components** These system modules include all the basic building blocks to configure a complete working microcomputer system: central processor modules and memories; analog, digital, and power switching modules; clocks, timers and special modules; communication modules; peripheral equipment, programming equipment, test and diagnostic equipment; and power supplies and mounting hardware.

**productive sampling tests** Tests made on a portion of a production run or lot in order to determine the general performance level.

**program** 1. A set of instructions arranged in proper sequence for directing the computer in performing a desired operation, such as the solution of a mathematical problem or the sorting of data. 2. To prepare a set of ordered instructions for automatic computer operation.

A program includes plans for the transcription of data, coding for the computer, and plans for the absorption of results into the system. Programming consists of:

1. Analysis of the problem
2. Preparation of flow diagrams
3. Preparation of subroutines
4. Allocation of storage locations
5. Specification of input/output formats
6. All computer integration tasks

**program address counter** A sequential counter (abbreviated *PAC*) that keeps track of the location of the next instruction to be executed from the program memory. The most significant bits may concern the page, while the other bits contain the word address of the instruction on the page. Also called *program counter* and *index address register*.

**program address register** A register that holds the instruction location to be transmitted to the control ROM.

**program analyzer** A development unit designed for the convenient field service of microcomputer systems. It can be used for software debugging and troubleshooting in the field. The analyzer connects to the CPU and displays the contents of bus lines along with the processor state, including instructions and data.

**program, assembly** Software that translates a symbolic program into a machine-language program. It can also integrate several sections or different programs.

**program, compiling** Refers to a program that translates from one programming language into another programming language. Also called a translator.

**program control unit** A unit or section of the central processor for controlling the execution of computer instructions and their sequence of operation.

**program conversion** Refers to the controlled transition from an old system to a new one. It involves careful planning for the various steps that have to be taken and equally careful supervision of their execution.

**program counter** A counter that contains the address of the next instruction to be fetched from memory. The address is automatically incremented after an instruction fetch except when modified by branch instructions. During interrupts, the program counter saves the address of the instruction.

**program, cross assembler** Refers to the use of another computer to perform assembly. The programs used are called cross assemblers.

**program development system** A development aid that allows users to make, simulate, and debug programs on a system that has a CRT display, keyboard, floppy disk, and printer.

**program, diagnostic trace** Refers to a type of diagnostic program for the performance of checks on other programs or for demonstrating such operations. The output of a trace program may include instructions of the program that is being checked and intermediate results of those instructions arranged in the order in which the instructions are executed.

**program documentation** The hard-copy printout and coding sheets of a program, including program name and function, required hardware and software, interface details between the user and program, and program listing.

**program, editor** A program that allows the user to instruct the CPU to search out and alter certain blocks of data or strings in the program being worked on. The editor is very useful when users desire to make changes that are repeated.

**program error** A mistake made in the program code by the programmer, keypuncher, compiler, or assembler.

**program, executive** 1. Refers to programs that control loading and relocation of routines. 2. A set of coded instructions designed to process and control other sets of coded instructions. 3. A set of coded instructions used in realizing automatic coding. 4. A master set of coded instructions. Effectively, an executive routine is part of the machine itself. Synonymous with *monitor routine, supervisory routine,* and *supervisory program.*

**program forms** These are forms used to describe the routines. The programmer should provide the purpose of the program, the form of the input and output data, the requirements for the memory of the program, and a description of the parameters.

**program generation system** A system (abbreviated *PGS*) that allows the user to output selected areas of memory in object-program format and load programs into memory. It will load programs produced by itself and those produced by the memory load builder or assembler.

**program generator** A program that permits other programs to be written automatically. A character-controlled generator operates like a compiler that takes entries from a library tape. It also examines the control characters and alters the instructions according to directions found in the control characters. A pure generator is a program that writes another program. Most assemblers are also compilers and generators. The generator in an assembler is usually a section of program that is called by the assembler to write one or more entries in another program.

**program instruction** The set of characters that may include one or more addresses that define an operation and cause the computer to operate on the indicated quantities.

**program, internally stored** Refers to a set or sequence of instructions, a program, or a routine that is stored within the computer (internal memory) as contrasted to those programs which might be stored externally on magnetic disk or tape.

**program library** A collection of available computer programs and routines. A microcomputer library might include text editor, loader, assembler, RAM test program, decimal addition, PROM programmer, A/D conversion, logic subroutines, and BCD-to-binary conversion.

**program listing** A step-by-step list of the program operation. The listing may be made up of the machine-language bit patterns or actual instructions.

**programmable** Capable or being set to operate in a specified manner or of accepting remote setpoint or other commands.

**programmable calculating oscilloscope** A programmable instrument for the acquisition and manipulation of electronic data. This instrument combines an oscilloscope and a microprocessor in a single unit with the capability to calculate rise times, integrals, differentials, peak areas, averages, and many other values.

**programmable calculator** A calculating device that is programmed by a keyboard or simple storage devices. High-level programmable calculators may use BASIC keywords and can be used as elements in data communication nets, instrumentation, and peripheral controllers, or to perform remote job-entry functions.

**programmable clock** A system timing device that can be used to synchronize the CPU to external events, measure time intervals between events, and provide interrupts at preset intervals.

**programmable communications interface** A chip designed for data communications and usually referred to as a USART (for *universal synchronous/asynchronous receiver/transmitter*). It is used as a peripheral device and can be programmed by the CPU to operate with any serial data transmission technique. Most USARTs are TTL-compatible, operate from a single 5V power supply, and have a single clock.

**programmable controller** A control unit designed as a direct replacement for a relay panel in industrial control applications. Programmable controllers are usually programmed directly from ladder diagrams or English-like logic statements. In general, programmable controllers sacrifice many of their data-handling capabilities for programming simplicity. Programmable controllers can be configured to handle as few as eight outputs or as many as 256, with or without timing or counting. They can also be used for arithmetic and shift register operations.

**programmable data mover** A custom configured modular data acquisition and transmission device. It can control the signal timing and conditioning for a wide variety of input and output signals. Typical programs can be written in about 20 minutes using a 16-pad keyboard and 32-character display.

**programmable digital logic** Abbreviated *PDL*, logic that can be changed by changing a program in contrast to hardwired logic that must be changed by changing connections. There are a number of economic advantages: (1) the design costs are lower because the systematic approach to logic design is more efficient, and (2) prototype modifications in software are quicker and less costly.

**programmable input/output channel** Refers to the programmed control of information transfer between the central processor and an external device. The programmed input/output channel allows the data to be acted on immediately, thus eliminating the need for a memory reference by either the channel or the program.

**programmable input/output devices** These programmable parallel LSI input/output devices can perform the following functions: address decoding, data input/output buffering, multiplexing, establishing status signals for handshaking, and performing other control functions as shown.

**programmable interval timer** Abbreviated *PIT*, an IC with several independent counters that can operate in input or output modes. In the output mode, one can measure the duration of external pulses. A counter register is loaded with the desired value in micro or milliseconds. A status bit can be set or an interrupt generated when the counter reaches zero; thus, a signal is generated as the desired period of time has elapsed. The 8253 PIT has three 16-bit independent counters counting in binary or BCD with six programmable modes of operation. In some applications, it is necessary to measure the elapsed time for input or output scheduling. Using microprocessor looping techniques is a time consuming task. The availability of a compo-

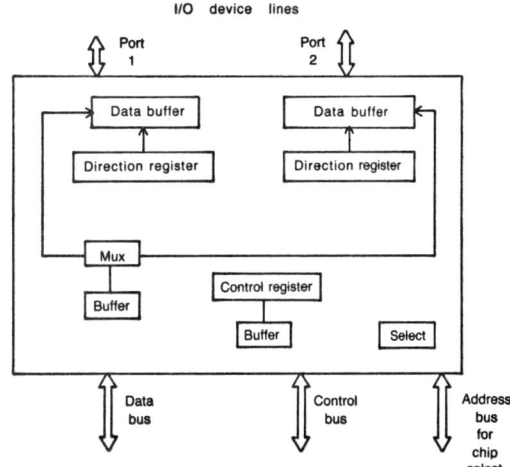

**Programmable I/O device**

nent frees the microprocessor for other tasks.

A PIT is usually required in all real-time operations. In a real-time system using interrupts, software counters cannot provide the accuracy timing. An internal counter could be interrupted by external events, which would result in erroneous time measurements.

An external PIT means adding an extra chip to the system. Some microcomputer chips implement a PIT directly on the chip. It can be predicted that this will be done for more chips in the future: the PIT will be implemented on the same chip as the CPU. To reduce this inconvenience, a PIT is often included on one of the other I/O chips that are used in the system, such as a PIO or a UART.

**programmable logic** Devices and systems that provide logic functions that can be changed by the user. Programmable logic devices include FPLAs, PLAs, ROMs, EAROMs, RAMs, CAMs, and microprocessors. Programmable logic systems include microcomputers, programmable calculators, minicomputers, and large-scale computers.

**programmable logic array** A mask-programmable chip that provides functions from arrays of AND and OR gates.

**programmable LSI** Refers to the LSI chips that have drastically simplified the phases of the design cycle because of the amount of manual engineering work traditionally required. Most phases can now be largely automated by a software design approach that can be implemented with a microcomputer as the development tool. Programmable LSI now allows high performance for most digital systems. Compared to the earliest MOS microprocessors, the new microcomputer systems have 1,000 times the capabilities.

**programmable memory** A memory with locations that are addressable by the program counter. A program within this memory may directly control the operation of the arithmetic and control unit.

**programmable peripheral interface** An input/output device with individually programmable pins. The pins can be programmed either as inputs or outputs.

**programmable point-of-sale terminal** A terminal that has a read-only microprogram memory for retail sales applications.

**programmable read-only memory** 1. A ROM that is user-programmable, generally by electrical methods such as deliberately blowing selected diodes. 2. A circuit board that contains the sockets for PROM along with the necessary address decoding, control, and timing circuits. The sockets allow PROM chips to be added or deleted to satisfy the system requirements.

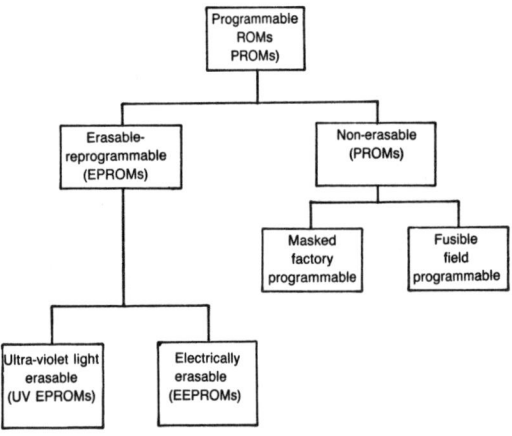

**Types of PROMs**

**programmable read-only memory blaster** A device for changing the protected read-only memory section found in some PROMs. The blaster allows the entire PROM to be changed by the user.

**program maintenance procedures** The checking and testing requirements designed to reduce machine malfunctions or human mistakes in programming.

**programmed acceleration** A controlled velocity increase to the programmed feedrate of a numerical control machine.

**programmed check** A check of machine functions performed by the machine in response to an instruction included in the program. The programmed check may be a sample problem with a known answer.

**programmed data transfer** Programmed data transfer performs data I/O with a minimum of hardware support. The ;maximum rate at which programmed data transfers may take place is limited by the CPU instruction rate. The data rate of the most commonly used peripheral devices, however, is much lower than the maximum rate at which programmed transfers can take place in the CPU. The major drawback associated with programmed data transfer is that the CPU must stay in a waiting loop while the I/O device completes the last transfer and prepares for the next transfer. The technique permits easy hardware implementation and simple, economical interface design. For this reason, many devices rely heavily on programmed data transfer.

**programmed dwell** The capability of commanding delays in program execution for a programmable length of time.

**programmed learning** An instructional method that uses expository material along with questions coupled to branching logic for remedial purposes. Programmed learning has been applied in books called programmed texts, or in computers as computer-assisted instruction (CAI).

**programmed logic** A logic system that is alterable in accordance with a program that controls the equivalent connections of all the gating elements. In programmed logic, the instruction repertoire can be changed to match the machine capability to the problem.

**programmed logic array** See *PLA*.

**programmed search** The automatic finding of various segments of prerecorded material on media for output in some predetermined sequence.

**programmer** 1. A person involved in the writing and testing of programs. 2. A device designed for program generation. An EEROM programmer is a unit that provides a means of programming an electrically erasable ROM from paper tape or from a keyboard and display.

**programmer check** A check procedure designed by the programmer and implemented specifically as a part of the program.

**programmer control panel** A panel that is usually supplied with a microcomputer system to provide access to the CPU registers and memory. It may also include data switches, data and address indicators, and function switches. Through the panel, the operator can address, load, and examine the memory and CPU registers and thus control the operation of the microcomputer.

**programmer's console diagnostic** A routine that tests most of the console logic using an automatic loop-back test. It will also test all lights and switches under control of the operator.

**programmer-defined macro** Refers to specific segments of coding that are used frequently throughout a program and are defined and referenced by a mnemonic code with parameters. This increases the coding efficiency and readability of the program.

**programmer, EEROM** A unit that provides a means of programming electrically erasable ROM (EEROM) from a keyboard and display. EEROMs are electrically erasable and need not be removed from the module or socket to be erased and reprogrammed.

**programmer tools** All hardware and software designed for generating a system's programs. Programmer tools include assemblers, simulators, editors, and assemblers. Some may run on time-sharing systems, while others may be run on the microcomputer system itself.

**program, micro** 1. Refers to a program of analytic instructions that the programmer intends to construct from the basic subcommands of a digital computer. 2. A sequence of pseudocommands that will be translated by hardware into machine subcommands. 3. A means of building various analytic instructions as needed from the subcommand structure of a computer. 4. A plan for obtaining maximum utilization of the abilities of a digital computer by the efficient use of the subcommands of the machine.

**programming** The design, writing, and testing of programs. Programming may consist of:

1. Definition of problem
2. Preparation of flowchart
3. Listing of computer instructions
4. Selecting circuit patterns or control modes

**programming, background** Refers to a type of programming with no specific urgency that may be preempted by a program of greater urgency and priority. Contrast with foreground programming.

**programming control panel** A panel with indicator lights and switches that the programmer can use to enter or change the routines in the program.

**programming flowchart** A flowchart used to represent the sequence of operations in a program.

**programming language** A language used for the preparation of programs.

**programming, machine language** Many microcomputers can be programmed in machine language using an optional keyboard programmer or portable editor, which often consists of a programming unit in a portable case.

**programming module** A discrete identifiable set of instructions that is handled as a unit by an assembler, compiler, linkage editor, or loader.

**programming peripherals** In many systems two distinct functions are relegated to the software: setting the data direction and control register patterns at the time of system initialization and handling interrupts. Setting the data direction and control register patterns establishes the operating characteristics of the I/O device. Handling interrupts in a system is often a problem of software polling. A polling and corresponding program are required.

Such a polling approach is usually the lowest cost alternative for identifying interrupts, but may in some instances be too slow. For such applications, hardware may be added to the system to achieve priority encoding of the various interrupt requests. The encoded value of the interrupt request can then be used as a system address to transfer control to the appropriate response routine. This is referred to as *vectoring*.

**program parameter** An adjustable quantity that can be given different values each time the quantity appears in a different subroutine. The program parameters can be altered by the routine and may vary depending upon the point of entry into the routine.

**program, partial** A program that is incomplete by itself and generally a specification of only a process to be performed on data. It may be used at more than one point in any particular program, or it might be made available for inclusion in other programs; a subroutine, which is often called a *subprogram* or *incomplete program*.

**program redesign** This involves adding new features or meeting new requirements. The redesign should follow the same paths as the previous design stages of software development.

The redesign process may involve making a program meet critical time or memory requirements. When increases of 25 percent or less in speed or reductions of the same order in memory are desired, the program can often be reorganized, but the program structure may have to be sacrificed.

**program reference table** An area of memory (abbreviated *PRT*) for storage of operands or references to arrays, files, or segments of the program. The PRT permits programs to be independent of the actual memory locations occupied by data and parts of the program.

**program register** The computer control register into which the program instruction being executed is stored. The program register controls the computer operation during the cycles required to execute that instruction. Also called *program counter* and *index address register*.

**program run** 1. The actual processing time period of a computer program. 2. Collectively, those steps performed by a computer as it executes all cycles of a program.

**program scheduler** A facility that permits use of the central processing unit among programs based in storage, depending upon priority requirements.

**program segments** The logically discrete units, such as subprograms, that comprise a user's complete program. Program segments consist of sequences of program statements that make up the main program. Control and data can be passed between segments as desired.

**program sensitive error** An error arising from some unforeseen behavior of some circuits, discovered when a comparatively unusual combination of program steps occurred.

**program, service** Refers to the various standard routines that assist in the use of a computing system and in the successful execution of problems, without contributing directly to the control of the system or production.

**program stack** A dedicated memory portion for providing multiple-level nesting capability. The stack nests subroutine addresses and program counter words for orderly return to the main program following subroutine calls. As new values are added to the stack, all previous values are pushed down with the top level being the most recent entry.

**program, stand alone** Refers to programs that operate independently of system control. Generally it is either self loaded or loaded by another stand alone program.

**program statement** A basic unit used to construct programs. A typical assembly language statement begins in character position number one of a source line and is terminated with a carriage return or a semicolon. A semicolon allows multiple statements to be coded on the same physical source line:

LOC 1 ADI 2; (add 2 to accumulator)

**program status word** A word (abbreviated *PSW*) containing information used during processing (such as interrupt status).

**program step** A single operation or phase of one instruction or command in a sequence of instructions.

**program stop** A miscellaneous machining function command to stop the spindle, coolant, and feed after completion of the dimensional move commanded in the block. To continue with the remainder of the program, the operator must initiate a restart.

**program stop instruction** An instruction that is used to automatically stop the machine under certain conditions, such as reaching the end of processing or completing the solution of a problem.

**program storage** The section of internal memory reserved for the storage of programs, routines, and subroutines. Program storage areas are sometimes protected using various schemes to prevent the alteration of the contents.

**program storage unit** An integrated circuit (abbreviated *PSU*) used for the storage of programmed instructions and nonvolatile data constants required for program execution. A PSU may interface directly with the CPU without the need for buffers; the chip may also include a program counter, stack register, plus interrupt control and timing circuits.

**programs, user** A group of programs, subprograms, or subroutines that have been written by the user as contrasted with manufacturer supplied programs.

**program tape** A specific tape that contains the sequence of instructions required for solving a problem.

**program testing time** The time expended for the testing of a machine or system program to ensure that no malfunctions or faults are present. Program testing may include debugging and special diagnostic routines, or circuit and component testing to determine machine status.

**program test system** A checking system in which a sample problem with a known answer is run before running the program to solve the actual problem.

**program, trace** A program that instructs the CPU to display the contents of any combination of registers or memory throughout the execution of the program being developed. Unlike many debug routines that instruct the computer to halt at certain selected breakpoints, trace programs allow users to command the computer to print the contents of any selection of registers in memory and then resume program execution, all automatically.

**project APEQS** A project involving aerial photography of the eclipse of the quiet sun.

**PROM** Abbreviation for *programmable read-only memory*, usually a semiconductor memory that is not programmed during fabrication and requires a physical or electrical operation to program it. A specific PROM consists of a diode array that is programmed by burning out diodes. Other types can be erased by ultraviolet light and reprogrammed electrically. Devices are also available for automatically copying master PROMs quickly and easily.

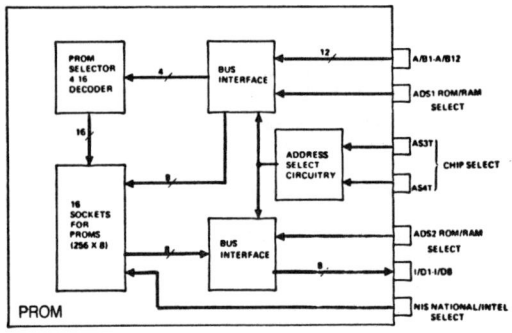

**PROM**

**PROM decoder** Refers to a fixed decoder internal to the device. The internal decoder selects a word by examining the address inputs. For a 512 × 8 PROM, 1 of 512 words are selected by examining 9 address inputs.

**PROM monitor** A program stored in PROM that allows the microcomputer to be programmed using a simple keyboard. Functions of the monitor include:

1. Addressing the memory at any location
2. Reading memory contents
3. Writing data into RAM
4. Executing the user program in RAM

**PROM programmer** Refers to the use of erasable PROMs that plug into a unit for programming. One typical PROM programmer can copy PROMs in less than one minute using a control program.

**PROM programmer card** A card that allows blocks of memory to be automatically programmed into PROM.

**PROM programmer control program** A program used when programming PROMs on a PROM programmer. Data to be programmed is usually read from binary tapes using a teletypewriter or reader, other PROMs, or a keypad.

**PROM programming system** A system for low-cost microcomputer programming that uses PROMs. The system has four basic parts:

1. Prototype board
2. Microprogram control programs
3. Programmer for the PROM
4. Keyboard

**PROM prompting** Refers to a PROM programming system function that helps a user by requesting information such as operands necessary to continue processing.

**PROM simulator** A device that uses RAM for testing and debugging operations prior to PROM programming.

**PROM technology** PROMs are an engineering development aid; they are a special form of semiconductor read only memory. The PROM is similar in size and appearance to a ROM, but while the information in a ROM is written permanently during the process of fabrication, in a PROM, it is programmed after the chip is packaged using one of a number of built in characteristics. Two processing techniques used are fused links or junctions and avalanche induced migration.

Programmable ROM devices fall into two basic categories: (1) those that are erasable and thus reprogrammable and (2) those that are not erasable. The nonerasable PROMs involve some form of fusing process in which a link or junction is fused open or closed. The process involves an action that is basically irreversible, thus making this type of PROM nonerasable. There are three types of fusing technologies in use: (1) metal links, (2) silicon links and (3) shorted junctions. All fusible devices use a relatively short programming time.

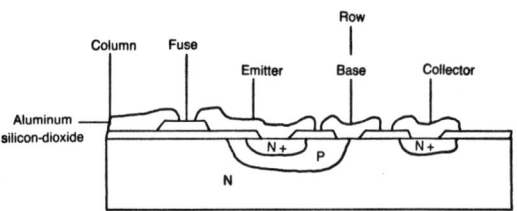

**Fusible link PROM cell structure**

**PROM verifying** Using a PROM programmer, data may be verified while writing a copy or reading a copy. With the verify switch on, data in the master is compared to data in the copy. Any difference in the data will light an error indicator, stop the programmer, and display the data in error.

**proof listing** A report (prepared by the processor) that shows the coding as originally written, with comments and the machine-language instructions.

**propagated error** An error occurring in one operation and affecting data required for subsequent operations, so that the error is spread through much of the processed data.

**propagation** The traveling of waves or pulses through or along a transmission medium.

**propagation constant** A number expressed for the Greek letter Rho to indicate the effect in a transmission line of a wave propagating through it.

**propagation delay** The time required for a signal to travel from one point in a circuit or transmission path to another.

**proportional control** A type of control in which there is a continuous linear relation between the output and the input.

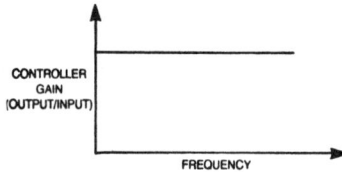

**Proportional control**

**proportional control system** A feedback control system that generates a correction signal that is a linear function of the error.

**proportional gain** The ratio of the change in output due to a change in input in a proportional control system.

**proportional ionization chamber** A chamber in which the initial ionization current is amplified by electron multiplication in a region of high electric field strength, as in a proportional counter, for measuring ionization currents over a period of time.

**proportionality** Refers to that part of a linearity curve when it passes through a zero-error reference point or an origin.

**proportional plus derivative controller** A control action in which the output is proportional to the linear combination of the input and the time integral of the output.

**proportional plus integral controller** A controller that produces proportional plus integral (reset) control action.

**proportional range** A band or set of values of a specific condition being controlled that causes the controller to operate over a linear range.

**proportional spacing** Refers to a technique used for the automatic finding of various segments of prerecorded material on media, for playback in some predetermined sequence.

**proportional speed floating controller** Refers to a unique single action controller that produces integral control action only.

**proprietary program** A program that is controlled by the owner through the legal right of possession and title.

**protected check** A check prepared in such a manner as to prevent alterations.

**protected key** A key on a keyboard that protects a character on the display screen from strikeover.

**protected location** A storage location reserved for special purposes. Data to be stored in these locations is required to undergo a screening procedure. Protected locations may be block locations in main storage or in disk files where data may be read from, but not written into.

**protection key** An indicator in the program status word which is associated with a task and which must match the storage keys of all storage blocks that it is to use.

**protective gap** A spark gap between conductors on an open transmission line or in sets of conductors, to protect the system against excessive high-voltage surges.

**protocol** The set of conventions between communication lines and links on the format and content of messages to be exchanged, especially those conventions that set the precedence among messages. Protocol can be used to define a complex hierarchy for the various level of exchange encountered in information systems. At the lowest level is the synchronous communications protocol used for the exchange of information between switching computers; next, a first level of protocol exists for the exchange of information between a host computer and its interface. The next level of protocol uses these two levels to control the flow of information between host computers. Level-three protocols are used to control the flow of information between processes, where a process may be a program or a terminal. Specific protocols are used to make initial connections in a link, for the transmittal of large files between computers, and for batch communication.

**protocol, database** Refers to database access rules used for information storage and retrieval, in which the host commands what specified data fields will pass between the host and the controller according to set procedures.

**proton** An elementary particle, of positive charge and unit atomic mass; the atom of the lightest isotope of hydrogen without its electron.

**prototype** Refers to an initial design system or package that usually is a model for additional development.

**prototype board** A circuit board used in development systems to evaluate new system concepts.

**prototype development system** A collection of modules and equipment used for software development and PROM programming. A typical system includes the processor, control panel, teletypewriter interface, RAM, PROM programmer, and power supplies. Software includes an assembler, text editor, PROM programmer, plus debug and control programs.

**prototype filter** A filter that has the specified nominal cutoff frequencies, but that must be developed into derived forms to obtain further desirable characteristics, such as the constancy of image impedance with frequency.

**prototype statement** An assembler statement that provides a name to a macro definition for a model or for the macroinstruction that is to call the macro definition.

**prototyping** The initial design and fabrication of a system on a trial basis for "shakedown."

**prototyping components** Refers to hardware that is useful to develop and debug hardware, firmware, and software for the end product. The ingredients of such a prototyping system for microcomputer products includes support software such as assemblers, compilers, loaders, and debug and edit packages. A PROM programmer would be used to provide fast turnaround times when the control programs are modified.

**proving time** The time used in running a test program to check if a particular fault has been corrected.

**proximity effect** The redistribution of current brought about in a conductor by the presence of another current carrying conductor.

**prr** Abbreviation for *pulse repetition rate*, usually expressed in pulses per second.

**PRT** Abbreviation for *program reference table*, a table of the locations reserved for program variables, data descriptions, and other program information. When a program references a word in the PRT, the relative address is used rather than the absolute address. The relative address of any particular location is based upon its position relative to the start of the table.

**ps** Abbreviation for *picosecond* ($10^{-12}$ second).

**psec** Abbreviation for *picosecond* or one trillionth of a second.

**pseudo code** A code that requires translation prior to execution. Pseudo codes are often used to link a subroutine into the main routine, and they usually express programs in terms of source language by referring to locations and operations using symbolic names and addresses.

**pseudo instruction** A group of characters having the same general form as an instruction, but never executed as an actual instruction. Pseudo instructions are used as symbolic representations in compilers, interpreters, and assemblers to designate groups of instructions for performing a particular task. Also called *quasi instruction*.

**pseudo random code** A digital code that has the appearance of a random sequence of finite length. Pseudo random codes repeat themselves and are not truly random, but they are useful for synchronization and sequence control.

**pseudo random-number sequence** A sequence of numbers that is considered random for a given purpose. The sequence may be used to approximate a particular distribution of parameters.

**PSK** Abbreviation for *phase shift keying*.

**PSR** Abbreviation for *processor state register*.

**PSS** Abbreviation for *personal signalling system*.

**PSV** Abbreviation for *program storage unit*.

**PSW** Abbreviation for *program status word*, a word in main storage used to control the order in which instructions are executed and to hold and indicate the status of the computer in relation to a particular program.

**PT** Abbreviation for *paper tape*.

**p-type conductivity** The conductivity in a semiconductor as expressed by the movement of holes.

**p-type crystal rectifier** A crystal rectifier in which forward current flows whenever the semiconductor region is more positive than the metal region.

**p-type semiconductor** A semiconductor in which the hole density exceeds the conduction electron density.

**PU** Abbreviation for *pick-up*.

**PUFF** Abbreviation for *pico farad*.

**pulling by crystal** Refers to the growing of both metal and nonmetal crystals by slowly withdrawing a seed crystal from a molten surface.

**pull operation** An operation in which operands are taken from the top of a pushdown stack in memory and placed in general registers. The operand remains in the stack unchanged; a pointer value is changed to indicate the current top of the stack.

**pulse** A variation in a quantity such as a voltage which is characterized by a rise and decay of finite duration.

**pulse accumulator module** A module with counters for accumulating pulses from several sources for frequency measurements. Input pulses can be accumulated and then held for interrogation by the CPU on the basis of jumpered or preselected intervals ranging from 100 microseconds to ten seconds.

**pulse amplifier** An amplifier with a wide bandwidth that can amplify pulses without excessive distortion.

**pulse amplitude** The level of a pulse or waveform of pulses.

**pulse-amplitude modulation** A form of modulation (abbreviated *PAM*) in which the amplitude of the pulse carrier is varied in accordance with the modulating signal.

**pulse bandwidth** The frequency band occupied by the components of the pulse that have appreciable amplitude and that make an appreciable contribution to the actual pulse shape.

**pulse carrier** 1. A carrier consisting of a series of pulses, usually employed as subcarriers. 2. A carrier wave comprised of a series of equally spaced pulses.

**pulse code** 1. A code in which sets of pulses have been assigned particular meanings, such as in the Morse, Baudot, or binary codes. 2. Pulse code modulation.

**pulse code modulation** A form of pulsed modulation in which the signal is sampled periodically and each sample is quantized and transmitted as a digital binary code.

**pulse counter** A device that gives an indication of or actually records the total number of pulses that has been received during a given time interval.

**pulse counting module** A device to count and store pulse information and transmit this information to a computer upon command.

**pulse decay time** The amount of time required for the trailing edge of a pulse to decay from 90 percent to 10 percent of the peak pulse amplitude.

**pulse delay time** The time interval between the leading edges of the input and output pulses, measured at 10 percent of their maximum amplitude.

**pulse detector** Refers to a circuit designed for use with modulated pulse signals.

**pulse digit** A drive pulse corresponding to a logical 1-digit position in some or all of the words in a storage unit. The pulse digit may be an inhibit pulse or an enable pulse in specific applications.

**pulse discriminator** Refers to a device that responds only to a pulse having some particular characteristic, such as duration, or period. The latter is also called a time discriminator.

**pulse drive** 1. A pulsed magnetomotive force applied to a magnetic core. 2. A particular pulse of current in a winding inductively coupled to one or more magnetic cells, which produces a pulse of magnetomotive force.

**pulse droop** Refers to the exponential decay of amplitude that is often experienced with rectangular pulses of appreciable duration.

**pulse duration** The time interval between the leading and trailing edge of a pulse.

**pulse duration modulation** A type of modulation (abbreviated *PDM*) in which the value of a sample of the modulating wave is used to modulate the duration of a pulse.

**pulse equalizer** A circuit that produces output pulses of uniform size and shape when driven by input pulses that may vary in size and shape.

**pulse flatness deviation** For a rectangular pulse that exhibits pulse droop, the difference between maximum and minimum amplitudes of the top of the pulse, divided by the maximum amplitude.

**pulse frequency modulation** A modulation method (abbreviated *PFM*) in which the pulse repetition rate is varied in accordance with the amplitude and frequency of the modulating signal.

**pulse, gating** A pulse that permits the operation of a particular circuit.

**pulse generator** A device for generating a series of pulses of specific form, duration, and repetition rate.

**pulse interleaving** A process in which pulses from two or more time-division multiplexers are systematically and alternately combined for transmission over a common path.

**pulse jitter** Refers to a slight variation of the pulse spacing in a pulse train. It may be random or systematic, depending on its origin, and it is generally not coherent with any regular pulse modulation characteristics.

**pulse length** The time interval between specified rise and fall points of a pulse.

**pulse length modulation** Pulse duration modulation.

**pulse mode** A coded group of pulses used to select a particular communication channel from a common carrier.

**pulse modulation** The modulation of pulses by a carrier. Pulse modulation includes pulse amplitude modulation (PAM), pulse position modulation (PPM), and pulse duration modulation (PDM).

**pulse noise** Refers to spurious signals of short duration that occur during reproduction of a tape and are of a magnitude considerably in excess of the average peak value of the ordinary system noise.

**pulse origin time** Refers to the start of a pulse. It is defined as the time at which it first reaches some given fraction, such as 10 percent of full amplitude; this time is called the *time origin*.

**pulse position modulation** A form of modulation in which the positions in time of pulses are varied without modifying their duration.

**pulse ratio** The ratio of the length of a pulse to its total period.

**pulse repeater** A device that receives pulses from one circuit and transmits corresponding pulses at another frequency or wavelength into another circuit. Also called a *transponder*.

**pulse repetition frequency** The rate at which pulses occur in a given unit of time. More correctly termed *pulse repetition rate*, since pulses are digital in character and "frequency" is generally applied to analog (AC) signals.

**pulse repetition rate** The number of pulses per unit time experienced at a point in a device, circuit, or system, usually expressed in terms of pulses per second (pps).

**pulse resolution** The minimum time separation, usually in microseconds or milliseconds, between input pulses that allows proper circuit or component response.

**pulse shaping** Intentionally changing the shape of a pulse.

**pulse string** A sequential group of pulses; a pulse train.

**pulse, strobe** Refers to a pulse used to gate the output of a memory sense amplifier or similar circuit.

**pulse, sync** Refers to a pulse transmitted to a circuit by a master unit in order to operate the slave in synchronism with the master.

**pulse time modulation** Modulation in which the modulating wave is used to vary a time characteristic of the pulse carrier, such as in pulse duration modulation and pulse position modulation.

**pulse train** A group or sequence of pulses with similar characteristics.

**pulse train generator** A circuit or device that produces a fixed number of usually equally spaced pulses.

**pulse transformer** Refers to a transformer designed for pulses using square hysteresis loop material for the core or other techniques to maintain the output currents or voltages at the proper pulse levels.

**pulse, unidirectional** Refers to single polarity pulses that all rise in the same direction.

**pulse-width modulation** Pulse duration modulation.

**pulse-width recording** A method of recording in which each storage cell is made up of two regions magnetized in opposite senses with unmagnetized regions on each side. A zero bit is represented by a cell containing a negative region followed by a positive region.

**pulse, write** Refers to a drive pulse or the sum of several simultaneous drive pulses that under suitable conditions can write into a memory cell or set a circuit, usually to a one condition.

**pumping** The use of electromagnetic radiation to raise the energy levels of electrons in devices such as lasers.

**punch** 1. A perforation in a punched card or tape. 2. To make a paper-tape or card perforation. 3. The machine or device used to make coded paper perforations.

**punch, automatic feed** Refers to a card punch having a hopper, a card track, and a stacker. The movement of cards through the punch is automatic.

**punch card** A card suitable for punched patterns of holes that are used to represent data.

**punch-card check** A bank check that has perforations either in the body of the draft or along a portion of its border.

**punched card** A precisely sized heavy paper material on which information can be coded in the form of holes. The holes can be of many shapes and may be punched either by machine or by hand.

**punched card reader** A device that senses hole patterns in punched cards and performs some operation as a result of the content, such as translating them into machine language.

**punched-card verifier** A machine that ensures that data punched into cards is the same as the data on original documents from which it was punched. The process of punching from the initial documents is repeated, and the machine detects any differences between the holes and the key depressions.

**punched paper tape** Paper tape on which information is or may be stored in the form of punched holes. Each character of information is punched in an established code across the width of the tape. There are usually 5 to 8 punch positions which represent channels or levels along the length of the tape. Also called *paper tape* and *punched tape*.

**punched tape** Punched paper tape.

**punch, hand** A keyboard punch into which punched cards can be fed manually one at a time. The card is moved as a result of the punching and at the end of the punching the card is manually removed.

**punch position** A defined location on a card or tape where a hole may be punched.

**punch station** An area in a given facility where a punching unit is located for the coded perforation of punched cards or tape.

**PUP** Abbreviation for *peripheral unit processor*.

**pure generator** A routine that is capable of writing another routine. The pure generator may be a section of a program in an assembler on a library tape. It can then be called by the assembler to perform.

**purity** Refers to complete color saturation; freedom from white in CRTs.

**pushdown list** A list that uses the last-in-first-out system. The item to be retrieved is the most recently stored item in the list, and the last item entered becomes the first item retrieved from the list.

**pushdown queue** A last-in-first-out method of ordering data in which the last item attached to the queue is the first to be withdrawn.

**pushdown stack** A segment of memory used to receive information from the program counter and store address locations of the instructions which have been pushed down during an interrupt. The pushdown stack can be used for subroutining; its size determines the level of subroutine nesting. When instructions are returned, they are "popped back" on a last-in-first-out basis. The stack tends to minimize register transfers, facilitate counting and sorting, and limit transfers to and from main memory.

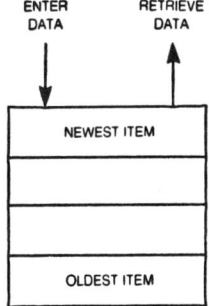

Pushdown stack

**push operation** The operation in which operands from a general register are stored in the top location of a pushdown stack in memory.

**push-pull** 1. Refers to a system in which one leg of a balanced circuit is driven by a periodic waveform, while the other leg is driven by the same waveform with the phase reversed. 2. A term applied to sound tracks that carry sound recordings in antiphase. They are class A when each carries the whole waveform and class B when each carriers half the waveform; both halves are united optically using a push-pull photocell.

**push-pull circuit** A circuit containing two like elements that operate in 180 degree phase relationship to produce additive output components of the desired wave and the cancellation of certain unwanted products. Push-pull amplifiers and oscillators use such a circuit.

**push-push amplifier** An amplifier that uses two similar devices or transistors with their control electrodes in phase-opposition but with their output electrodes parallel connected to a common load. By this means the even order harmonics are emphasized.

**pushup list**  A list that uses a first-in-first-out order. The next item to be retrieved and removed is the oldest item on the list. Each item is entered at the end of the list, and the previous items maintain their same relative position in the list.

**pushup storage**  A method of storage in which the next item of data to be retrieved is the oldest and has been in the queue the longest.

**PVR**  Abbreviation for *precision voltage reference*.

**PW**  Abbreviation for *pulse width*.

**PWC**  See PWM.

**PWE**  Abbreviation for *pulse width encoder*.

**PWM**  Abbreviation for *pulse-width modulation*, a pulse modulation technique in which the modulating wave is used to vary the width of a pulse proportionally.

**pyroelectricity**  Polarization developed in some hemihedral crystals by an inequality of temperature.

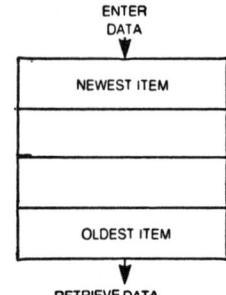

**Pushup list**

# Q

**Q** 1. Symbol for *figure of merit* for a resonant circuit or device. 2. Symbol for *electric charge*. 3. Schematic designation of active solid-state devices (usually followed by a numeral). 4. Abbreviation for *accumulator extension*.

**QCW** A 3.58 mHz continuous wave signal having Q phase. Generally restricted to reference the receiver local oscillator (3.85 mHz) and associated circuits in color TV.

**QF** Abbreviation for *quality factor*.

**QIL** Abbreviation for *quad-inline*, a dual-inline package (DIP) with four similar functional units or circuits.

**QISAM** Abbreviation for *queued indexed sequential access method*.

**Q output** The reference output of a flip-flop. The Q output corresponds to a one condition, and the Q output is the Q output inverted or a zero in the normal state.

**Q phase** A color television signal carrier phase separated by 147° from the color subcarrier, also referred to as the *quadrature carrier*.

**QPL** Abbreviation for *qualified products list*.

**QR** Abbreviation for *quick reaction*.

**QT** Abbreviation for *queuing theory*.

**QTAM** Abbreviation for *queued teleprocessing access method*.

**quad** 1. A packaged integrated circuit containing four identical stages. 2. Four-channel stereophonic sound. 3. Containing four identical or nearly identical electrodes, terminals, or leads (as outputs).

**quad clock driver** A driver circuit with four separate outputs. It is useful for driving the address, control, and supplementary timing circuits for various logic systems.

**quad MOS clock driver** An IC used for supplying the voltage and current drive requirements for address, control, and timing inputs for MOS devices. This device is usually configured as a quad NAND driver with two common enable inputs per gate pair. It will operate on a wide variety of supply voltages.

Positive logic: Y = $\overline{AB}$

**Quad NAND gate**

**quadrant** Any of the four parts into which a plane is divided by the rectangular coordinant axes lying in that plane.

**quadratic programming** A type of nonlinear programming used in operations research in which the function to be maximized or minimized is a quadratic function and the constraints are linear functions.

**quadrature** Displaced 90 degrees in phase angle.

**quadrature component** Refers to a reactive component of a current or voltage due to the inductive or capacitive reactance in a circuit or device.

**quad tabulation** A function that provides for the automatic alignment of a character or group of characters within a column.

**qualification** 1. Testing of a program, equipment, or system prior to its delivery from the manufacturer to the user. 2. In COBOL, a technique used to make a name or situation unique by adding IN or OF.

**qualification testing** The testing of programs, equipment, or systems prior to delivery to the user.

**qualified name** A data name accompanied by the class to which it belongs in a given classification system.

**qualifier tester** A benchtop system for testing DTL, TTL, and CMOS devices. This tester uses a microcomputer to control all internal test functions, and it can be used with RS-232C terminals.

**quality assurance** The systematic methods that are used to provide suitable confidence that an item will perform satisfactory.

**quality control** The process of monitoring, in an organized and formal manner, workmanship, processes, and materials to produce a consistent, uniform product. Quality control may involve the keeping of batch logs, error summary reports, and evaluation records.

**quality diagnostic** Software that verifies the proper operation of the CPU, memories, and input/output functions. Quality diagnostics include routines to check instructions, memory, real-time clock, printer and associated keyboard, power-fail/restart, automatic loader, etc.

**quality engineering** An engineering program used to establish quality tests and acceptance criteria along with interpreting quality data.

**quantity** Any positive or negative number used to specify a value; it may be a whole number, a fraction, or a combination of both.

**quantization** The subdivision of an element or parameter into a finite number of distinct values such as occurs in analog-to-digital conversion and some forms of multiplexing.

**quantization distortion** A comunications process in which the range of values of a wave is divided into a finite number of smaller subranges, each of which is represented by an assigned or quantized value within the subrange. *Quantized* is used as an adjective modifying various forms of modulation such as quantized pulse amplitude modulation.

**quantization uncertainty** Refers to a measure of the uncertainty, which may cause irretrievable information loss, that occurs as a result of the quantization of a function in an interval in which it is continuous.

**quantize** To subdivide an element or parameter into a number of distinct values.

**quantum** 1. A unit of processing time in a time-sharing system that may be allocated for operating a program during its turn in the computer. 2. A subrange in a quantization operation. 3. The smallest indivisible element of a quantized signal. 4. An indeterminate quantity; an amount. 5. The smallest increment into which an energy form can be described.

**quantum clock** The timing of an interval of processing time according to developed priorities in a time-sharing system.

**quantum efficiency** 1. The number of electrons released in a photocell per unit of incident radiation. 2. The ratio of energy output to input in an energy conversion system.

**quantum electronics** Refers to a branch of science concerned with the amplification or generation of microwave power in solid crystals, governed by quantum mechanical laws.

**quantum number** One number of a set describing the possible states of a magnitude when quantized.

**quantum statistics** The statistics dealing with the distribution of particles of a given type among the various possible energy values.

**quantum theory** Refers to those theories that were developed from Planck's Law. There is a quantum theory for most branches of classical physics.

**quantum yield** Refers to the ratio of the number of photon-induced reactions occurring to the total number of incident photons.

**quark** A proposed measure of the fractional charges in strongly interacting particles.

**quartz** A piezoelectric material used in the manufacture of crystals for oscillators. It may be natural or man made. Quartz exhibits a variety of predictable characteristics that vary according to the axis from which it is cut.

**quartz crystal** A frequency-determining crystal cut to oscillate at some precise fixed frequency over a specified temperature range. It exhibits the properties of a resonant RLC circuit and is used in close-tolerance oscillators as a source for clock signals.

**quartz delay line** A delay line that uses quartz as the medium.

**quartz oscillator** An oscillator that uses a quartz crystal for frequency control.

**quartz plate** Refers to a quartz crystal finished for a generalized frequency range but not trimmed to a specific frequency within that range. Also called a *blank*.

**quartz pressure transducers** Some capacitive pressure transducers utilize materials such as quartz. The sensor consists of two thin quartz disks, each having a platinum electrode on its inner surface. The disks are fused at their periphery to form a capsule, with the electrodes separated by a 0.002 inch gap. When a vacuum is drawn inside the gap, absolute pressures of up to 30 psi are measured. Gage pressures of up to 30 psi can also be measured with one port vented to the atmosphere.

**quartz thermometer** A transducer that determines temperature from the frequency difference between a temperature-dependent quartz oscillator and a temperature-independent one.

**quench** Refers to resistor or resistor-capacitor shunting used to reduce the high frequency sparking when a current is broken in an inductive circuit.

**quenched spark gap** A spark gap in which the discharge takes place between cooled or rapidly moving electrodes.

**quenching circuit** A circuit that inhibits multiple discharges from an ionizing event by suppressing or reversing the voltage.

**query station** A terminal or station that introduces requests for data or information while the system is computing or communicating.

**queue** 1. To form a waiting line for service. 2. The waiting line for items to be serviced. Queues may be last-in-first-out (LIFO) or first-in-first-out (FIFO).

**queue, automatic** Refers to a specific series of events or registers that are designed to implement either a LIFO (last-in-first-out) series or a FIFO (first-in-first-out) series without program manipulation. For a FIFO queue, new entries to the queue are placed in the last position and automatically jump forward to the last unoccupied position, while removal of the front entry results in all entries automatically moving forward one position. Also called *push-down storage* and *push-up storage*.

**queued content addressed memory** Refers to an automatic memory structure that contains a series of parallel automatic queues. The front member of each queue is content-addressable.

**queue control block** A control block used for regulating the sequential use of a set of competing tasks.

**queued access** An access method that synchronizes the transfer of data between the program and input/output devices with minimal delays.

**queue discipline** Refers to the method used to determine the order of service in a queued system.

**queued sequential access** A method of sequential access in which queues are formed of input data blocks that are awaiting processing, and output data blocks that have been processed and are awaiting storage or transfer to an output device.

**queued telecommunications access method** A method (abbreviated *QTAM*) used to transfer data between main storage and remote terminals. A macroinstruction is used to request the transfer, which is performed by a message control program that synchronizes the transfer with minimum delays.

**queues, direct access** A group of queues or message-segment chains of queues residing on a direct access storage device. The group may include destination and process queues.

**queues, ready** Refers to a condition such that when a user task is in a ready status, it can be executed or resumed. Generally a separate queue of ready tasks is maintained by the executive. When a processor is available, the executive activates the task at the head of the ready queue and changes its status to running.

**queuing** The patterns and methods used in studying delays and waiting lines for servicing devices or items.

**queuing list** A list used for scheduling actions in real time on a time priority basis.

**queuing theory** A form of probability theory used in the study of delays or lines at servicing points. Queuing theory is concerned with minimizing the delays due to waiting lines at servicing areas or junctions.

**queuing theory problems** Refers to conditions when a row of objects or data is bottle necked at a particular servicing point; losses accumulate in the form of lost information, idle equipment, and unused labor. Minimizing such costs involved in waiting lines, or queues, is the object to queuing theory.

**queuing (waiting line) theory** A branch of study that provides techniques to determine such conditions as the average queuing (waiting line) length or average waiting time.

**quick break** A characteristic of a switch or circuit breaker when it has a fast contact opening speed that is independent of the operator.

**quickcharting** A flowcharting technique that does not require knowledge of standard flowchart symbols.

**quick-disconnect** A type of connector that allows quick locking and unlocking of all contacts.

**quiescence** 1. At rest, waiting for an input signal or command. 2. In a class A amplifier, the condition in which the input electrode is biased to the midpoint of the linear range (between cutoff and saturation), but no input signal is applied.

**quiescent** 1. At rest; the condition of a circuit when no input signal is applied to it. 2. A term for a system waiting to be operated.

**quiescent current** The current in an amplifier or control device in the absence of a command or control signal.

**quiescent push-pull amplifier** An amplifier in which one side passes current for one phase and then the other side passes current for the other phase.

**quiescing** The process of bringing a device or system, including a multiprogrammed system, to a halt by the rejection of new jobs or new requests for work.

**quinary** Sometimes used as a shortened form of *biquinary*.

**Quincke's method** Refers to a technique for determining the magnetic susceptibility of a substance in solution by measuring the force acting on it in terms of the change of height of the free surface of the solution when placed in a suitable magnetic field.

**qume** The trade name for a typing mechanism that uses a high speed, interchangeable printwheel.

**quoted string** A character string used in assembler programming in which the string is enclosed by apostrophes to represent a value that can include blanks in a microinstruction operand.

**qwerty keyboard** The standard typewriter keyboard, named for the arrangement of the first six letters.

**R** Rise time factor in transistors.

**race** In any multisignal logic system, a condition in which the timing between two coincident signals is unpredictable even though the system operation requires a specific timed sequence for proper operation.

**rack** A free-standing metal frame or cabinet into which panels of equipment may be installed.

**rack-mounting** Descriptive of a piece of equipment whose front panel is designed to fasten to a standard, usually 19-inch, rack (cabinet) in such a way that the equipment is contained within the rack, but the controls are accessible from the front.

**RAD** Abbreviation for *rapid access disk*.

**RADA** Abbreviation for *random-access discrete address*.

**RADC** Abbreviation for *Rome Air Development Center*, USAF.

**RADCM** Abbreviation for *radar countermeasures and deception*.

**radiation** The propagation of energy through space or a medium.

**radiation error** The variance between the true gas temperature indicated due to the transfer of heat by radiation between a junction and surrounding areas.

**radio circuit** A communication system consisting of a radio link with a transmitter and antenna, the radio transmission path, and a receiving antenna and receiver.

**radio-frequency interference** The unwanted interference (abbreviated *rfi*) in a circuit or device caused by electromagnetic radiation from another circuit or device.

**RADIST** Abbreviation for *radar distance indicator*.

**radix** The quantity of characters for use in each of the digital positions of a numbering system. Also called *base*.

| SYSTEM | CHARACTERS | RADIX |
|---|---|---|
| binary | 0, 1 | 2 |
| octal | 0, 1, 2, 3, 4, 5, 6, 7 | 8 |
| decimal | 0, 1, 2, 3, 4, 5, 6, 7, 8, 9 | 10 |

**radix complement** A complement obtained by subtracting each digit from one less than its radix, adding one to the least significant digit, and executing all carries required. Examples include the tens' complement in decimal notation or the twos' complement in binary notation. Also called *true complement*.

**radix-minus-one complement** A complement obtained by subtracting each digit from one less than the radix. Examples include the nines' complement in decimal notation and the ones' complement in binary notation. Also called *diminished-radix complement*.

**radix notation** A positional representation in which the significance of any two adjacent positions has an integral ratio which is the radix of the least significant of the two positions. The permissible values of the digit in any position range from zero to one less than the radix of that position.

**radix point** The real or implied character that separates the digits associated with the integral part of a numeral from those associated with the fractional part.

**RALU** Abbreviation for *register and arithmetic logic unit*, a collection of logic elements such as accumulators, stack, and arithmetic logic unit, which provide data storage and processing functions. A typical RALU is designed so that up to 8 units can be combined in parallel to allow the implementation of processors from 4 to 32 bits wide. All elements in the unit are tied together by a set of buses, and data flow can be defined using microprogramming (usually with a CROM chip).

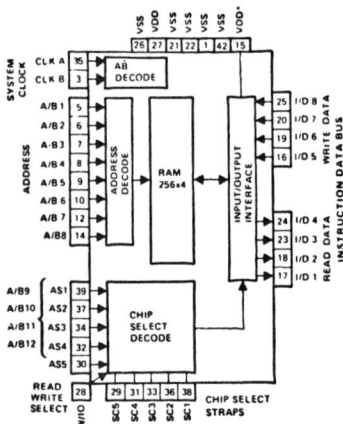

RALU

**RAM** Abbreviation for *random-access memory*, a mass store that provides fast access to any storage location point by means of vertical and horizontal coordinates. Information is written in or read out using the same procedure. A RAM system can be divided into three main sections:

1. Address buffers, read-write logic, and chip-select logic.
2. Data bus buffers and memory array.
3. Refresh and control logic.

During a cycle, a 1 on a write input/output line will be interpreted by the RAM as a write enable command, and data on the bus will be written in. Available RAMs have access times from two nanoseconds to three microseconds and range in size from 4 to 4096 bits per chip. RAMs provide the means for designers to program the logic of all programmable logic systems in use. They are also used as ROM and PROM emulators in many systems.

RAM

**RAM address register** A register that contains the address location to be accessed in RAM.

**RAM alarm** An alarm triggered when the data on a given channel in the memory system does not agree with alarm setpoint values. The microprocessor then prints out a complete data scan from memory, regardless of which channel is in alarm.

**RAM alarm option** A low cost option in some systems that allows the user a great deal of alarm flexibility. The flexibility. The flexibility is built into the underlying architecture of the microprocessor, memory, and alarm programming on a channel by channel basis. Signal input channels and alarm setpoints are interchangeable.

**RAMARK** Abbreviation for *radar marker system*.

**RAM card system** Refers to a complete RAM with control logic on a single circuit board or card.

**RAM CCD cell** Refers to a RAM array of two electrode CCD cells. Negative potentials produce a depletion region potential well in the n-type layer beneath the electrodes. To write a logic 1 in the cell, the p-type channel is pulsed positive, thus allowing holes into the well. To write a logic 0, both electrodes are grounded, letting any holes recombine.

**RAM circuit** The circuit for a four-by-three RAM is shown. It has four words of three bits each for a total of 12 storage cells. Each cell contains the circuit of a binary cell. The address lines use a two-by-four decoder with a memory enable input.

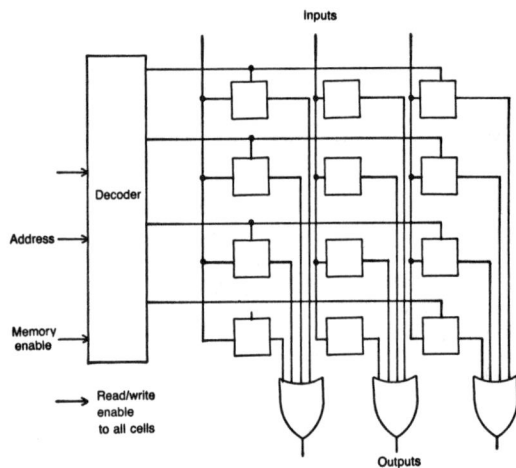

12-word RAM

When the memory enable is 0, all the outputs of the decoder are false and none of the words is selected. When the memory enable input is true, one of the four words is selected, depending on the bit combination of the two address lines. With the read/write at 1, (read) the bits of the selected word go through the OR gates to the output. The nonselected cells produce 0s at the inputs of the OR gate, and thus have no effect on the outputs. When the read/write control is 0, the data at the input lines is transferred into the flip-flops of the selected word. The nonselected cells in the other words are disabled by their address selection line so their previous values remain unchanged. When the memory enable is 1, the read/write line initiates the required read and write operations. An inhibited operation is obtained when the memory enable is 0. This condition leaves the contents of all words in memory as they were, regardless of the read/write control input. RAMs sometimes use cells with outputs that can be tied to form a wired-OR or a wired-AND function. Other RAMs may provide tristate outputs. These outputs are useful when a high impedance path is desired for isolation from the other integrated circuits in the microcomputer system.

**RAM control memory** Many systems use RAMs in their control memories. When RAM is used in the control memory, it is often referred to as *WCS* (writable control store).

**RAM enable** A RAM control line that allows new data to be written into the address field.

**RAMP** Abbreviation for *Raytheon airborne microwave platform* (sky station).

**ramp** A signal that increases in level linearly with time. Usually the ramp is repetitive, operating at a predetermined rate.

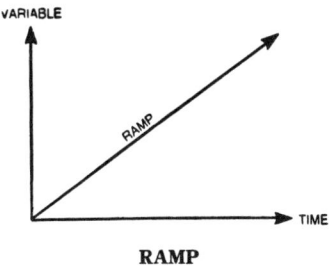

**RAMP**

**RAM print-on-alarm** An operation mode in which continuous scanning takes place but data is read out only when an alarm is interpreted by the CPU.

**RAMPS** Abbreviation for *resources allocation and multiproject scheduling*.

**RAM refresh** The periodic signals that must be applied to dynamic MOS RAMs to insure that stored data is retained. The refresh operation consists of a specified number of write cycles and sometimes read cycle as well, on the least significant address bits within a given period of time. The number of cycles may vary from 16 to 64 within a 2 ms period. The refresh requirement tends to increase system costs and reduce the overall memory system performance due to the additional required timing logic circuitry.

**RAM refresh clock** The source of the timing signals required for refreshing dynamic RAMs. A typical system uses a ripple counter to generate the sequential states and a multiplexer for gating these states with the CPU.

**RAM refresh cycle** The period required for dynamic RAM refresh.

**RAM register simulator** A program that functionally simulates execution of microcomputer programs. Such simulators are interpretive and provide bit-for-bit duplication of instruction execution timing, register contents, and other functions.

**RAM/ROM pattern processor** A test system that can be used to check RAM and ROM patterns.

**RAM save** An option that prevents data in ROMs from being lost due to power outages. One type of system uses a custom initialization ROM that restores the full program to the ROMs, restarts the clock, and begins data scanning. Other types use battery banks or other units to provide power for five minutes, or until external power is returned.

**RAM storage functions** RAM consists of a number of random access memory devices that are used to store the user program under execution. Its size varies with the user requirements and is limited by the addressing capability of the microcomputer.

**RAM terminals** Terminals offer an attractive area for the use of RAM. A large number of terminals are multifunction devices and used in different applications. By using RAM, local control can be put in the terminal to tailor its characteristic to the application. One of the key problems in terminal system design is to diagnose failures precisely and to separate machine failures from operator errors. The use of RAM can facilitate the diagnosis of failures. Diagnostic routines can then develop information about the system malfunction.

**RAM test program** A program that uses a PROM that plugs into prototyping boards for complete checkout.

**RAM text editor** Refers to a RAM resident character oriented text editor with search, substitute, insert, and delete commands that facilitate alternation.

**RAN** Abbreviation for *read around number*.

**random-access** 1. The process of obtaining information from or placing information into a storage system in which the time required for access is independent of the location of the information most recently obtained or placed in storage. 2. An access mode in COBOL in which specific logical records are obtained from or placed into a mass storage file in a nonsequential manner.

**random access, buffer memory system** Refers to a static memory system designed to meet the reliability and cost requirements of random access buffer storage applications. The compact size of these systems makes them ideal for use as buffer storage for various computer peripheral applications. The memory systems can be easily modified to interface with most microprocessors.

**random-access device** A unit in which access time is independent of data location and system history.

**random-access memory** A memory (abbreviated *RAM*) in which information elements are organized into discrete sections with each location uniquely identified by an address. Data may be obtained from such a memory by specifying the data addresses.

A random-access memory may be implemented in many ways, such as core, drum, disk, or cards; however, popular usage of the abbreviation RAM usually refers to semiconductor types. A typical semiconductor RAM has bidirectional input/output lines that are directly compatible with the microprocessor data bus. A particular RAM in a system is selected by applying the correct signals to the chip-select lines via the address bus. Locations in a particular RAM are addressed by applying the correct code to the address inputs. The

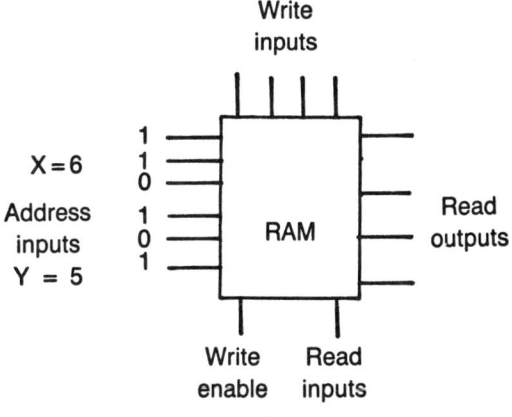

**Semiconductor RAM**

read or write function is programmed by the correct signal on the read-write line.

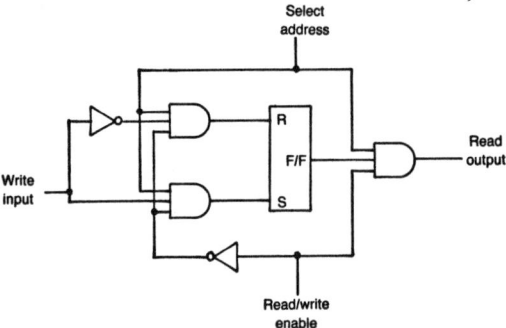

**Typical RAM cell**

**random access memory system, bipolar** Refers to a bipolar unit designed to meet the needs of control memory, disk controllers, scratch pad, and signal processing applications. The unit provides fast access and cycle times in a TTL compatible memory system. Utilizing bipolar technology and solid state integrated circuitry, the memory provides high reliability and performance. They can be expanded to any word or bit length through the use of additional memory cards. Each system includes all address and data registers.

**random access memory technology** RAMs are used in microcomputer systems for storing new results or new data for use in current processing operations. The memory cycle time is the same for any location addressed because there is no waiting or sorting time required as there is when data items are stored sequentially.

**random access programming** Programming without regard to the time for access to the information in the registers called for in the program.

**random access, removable** Refers to storage devices like magnetic disk packs that can be physically removed (not permanently attached).

**random-access storage** Storage in which the time required to obtain information is independent of the location of the information.

**random-access time** The average time period between the end of readout of a word from storage at a randomly chosen address, and the end of readout of another word from any other randomly chosen address. The readout operations are performed as fast as the microcomputer can carry them out, so no waiting period for the arithmetic and logic unit is included in this time period. Minimum random access time is used to define the time period between the end of readout of a word at any given address and the end of readout of the word in the most favorable other address in the storage unit.

**random assembly** A word processing feature that eases the production of documents by automatically putting together parts from separately recorded material. Also called *programmed search*.

**random failure** A failure whose occurrence at a particular time is unpredictable. Also called *chance failure*.

**random logic** Logic circuits and collections of circuits that use discrete integrated circuits for individual functions. Random logic uses hardware gates to implement the logic equations. Design aids include Karnaugh maps, state diagrams, computer simulation, and breadboarding.

**random logic devices** The SSI and MSI integrated circuits used to design random logic systems.

**randomness** A condition of equal chance for the occurrence of any of the possible outcomes.

**random, pseudo** Refers to a sequence of numbers, determined by some defined arithmetic process that is satisfactorily random for a given purpose, such as satisfying one or more of the standard statistical tests for randomness. Such a sequence may approximate any one of several statistical distributions, such as a uniform distribution or a normal (Gaussian) distribution.

**random pulsing** Varying the repetition rate of pulses by noise modulation or continuous frequency change.

**random noise** Refers to a large number of different overlapping transient disturbances. Also called fluctuation noise and white noise.

**random number** A number in a series of numbers that is obtained completely by chance. Random numbers are considered to be free from bias and thus they are used for statistical testing.

**random-number generator** A routine or device designed to produce a random number or a series of random numbers according to specified limitations.

**random variable** A variable that may assume any one of a number of values, each having the same probability of occurrence. Also called a *variate*.

**random walk** A method used in problem analysis in which experiments with probabilistic variables are traced to determine if the results are significant.

**range** 1. The set of values between two limits that a quantity may assume. 2. The usable operating sphere of a communications system.

**range conversion** A signal conditioning technique that uses a dc offset to bias odd ranges, such as 2.5 to 7 volts, to levels more compatible with standard converters as shown.

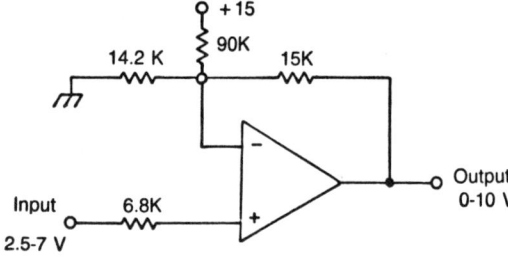

**Range conversion**

**range, dead band** The range through which an input can be varied without initiating response; a dead band is usually expressed in percent of span. Resolution sensitivity can be defined as one-half dead band. When the output is at the center of the dead band, it denotes the minimum change in the measured quantity required to initiate a response.

**range, error** 1. Refers to the range of all possible values of the error of a particular quantity. 2. The difference between the highest and the lowest of these values.

**RAP** Abbreviation for *random-access program*.

**RAPCON** Abbreviation for *radar approach control center*.

**rapid-access loop** A section of storage that has a much faster access than the remainder of storage. Such loops are found in some disk, drum, and tape units. Sometimes called *revolver*.

**RAPTAP** Abbreviation for *rapid access parallel tape*, Dept. of Commerce.

**RAR** Abbreviation for *ROM address register*.

**raser** Abbreviation for *radio amplification by stimulated emission of radiation*.

**raster** An illuminated gray cathode-ray screen without an image-forming video input.

**raster count** The number of coordinate positions addressable on a cathode-ray screen.

**raster count, horizontal** Refers to the number of coordinate positions addressable across the width of a cathode-ray tube.

**raster count, vertical** The number of coordinate positions addressable across the height of a cathode-ray tube.

**RAT** Abbreviation for *rocket assisted torpedo*.

**RATAN** Abbreviation for *radar and television aid to navigation*.

**RATCC** Abbreviation for *radar air traffic control center*.

**rated capacity** A term for the output of equipment, which can continue indefinitely, in conformity with some criterion, such as heating, or distortion of signals or of waveform.

**rated output** The output power, voltage, or current at which a device is designed to operate under normal conditions.

**rated power output** The normal power-output capability (peak or average) of a device under optimum adjustment and operational conditions.

**rated voltage** The voltage at which a device or component is designed to operate under normal conditions.

**rate gain** Refers to the ratio of maximum gain resulting from proportional plus derivate control action to the gain due to proportional action alone.

**rate-grown transistor** A variation of the double doped transistor, in which N- and P-type impurities are added to the melt. Also called a graded-junction transistor.

**rate test** A test in which problems are run with known solution times to determine if a computer is operating correctly.

**rating** A value that determines the limiting capacity or limiting conditions for a device. Ratings are determined for specified values of environment and operation.

**rating system** The set of principles upon which ratings are established and interpreted.

**ratio, amplitude** Refers to the ratio of peak height of an output signal to the peak height of a related input signal.

**ratio, noise signal** Refers to the ratio of the number of signals conveying information to the number of signals not conveying information.

**RATO** Abbreviation for *rocket assisted takeoff*.

**RATT** Abbreviation for *radio teletype*.

**RAYSISTOR** Abbreviation for *Raytheon resistor*, a photoelectric control device.

**RB** Abbreviation for *read buffer*.

**RBDE** Abbreviation for *radar bright display equipment*.

**RC** 1. Abbreviation for *resistance-capacitance*. 2. Abbreviation for *radio-controlled*. 3. Abbreviation for *resistance-coupled*. 4. Abbreviation for *remote control*.

**RC amplifier** An amplifier that uses resistance-capacitance coupling.

**RC circuit** A circuit that uses resistors and capacitors to form a time constant.

**RCA 1800 family** The RCA 1800 series of microprocessors is based on CMOS (complementary metal-oxide semiconductor) technology. The 1802 is an 8-bit silicon gate CMOS device that has an on-chip single-phase clock. The CMOS unit requires a minimal power supply. It may be operated with unregulated supplies over a wide voltage range. Noise immunity is high, and there is compatibility with other logic families such as TTL and NMOS. The power requirements can be lowered at slower operating speeds to allow the use of small batteries in remote or isolated applications.

The 1802 architecture is shown below. The register file uses sixteen 16-bit scratch pad registers. Registers in the array are designated and selected using a 14-bit code from one of the 4-bit designator/registers, P, X, or N.

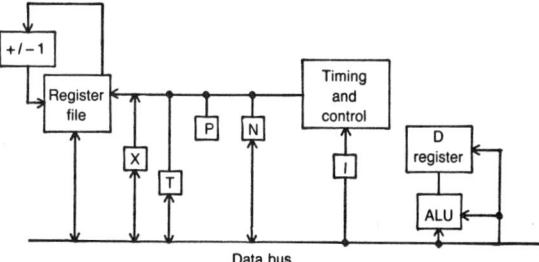

1802 architecture

The registers in the file can be used as program counters, data pointers, or as scratch pad locations for holding data. When a register is used as the main program counter, its register number must be stored in the P register. Other registers in the array can then be used as subroutine program counters. When a call is required, the contents of the P register are changed by an instruction that allows the call to be made.

**RCA 1800 system** A basic 1800 system with ROM, RAM, and input/output is configured as shown below.

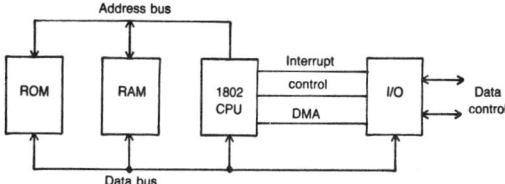

Basic 1820 architecture

**RC network** A circuit using resistors and capacitors to perform a particular function, such as filtering, timing, differentiation, integration, etc.

**RC oscillator** An oscillator circuit in which the frequency of oscillation is determined by resistor and capacitor elements.

**RCTL** Abbreviation for *resistor-capacitor-transistor logic*, a logic family that uses discrete transistors with RC coupling.

**RD** Abbreviation for *research and development*.

**RD CHK** Abbreviation for *read check*.

**RDR** Abbreviation for *receive data register*.

**RDT** Abbreviation for *remote data transmitter*.

**RE** 1. Abbreviation for *real number*. 2. Abbreviation for *reset*.

**reactance chart** A chart of logarithmic scales so arranged that it is possible to read directly the reactance of a given inductor or capacitance at any frequency.

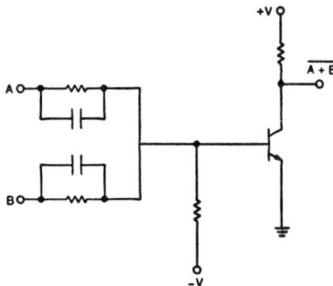

RCTL NOR gate

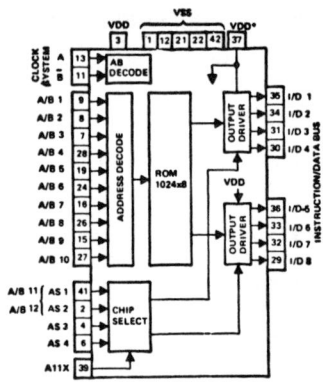

ROM block diagram

**reactance modulator** In FM communications, a circuit that modulates the capacitive reactance of a stage in accordance with the applied signal amplitude.

**reactive document** A routine document that is rarely revised and infrequently proofread.

**reactive mode** A condition of communications between remote terminals and a computer in which each entry causes an action of the computer, sometimes without an immediate reply.

**read** 1. To sense information contained in some storage medium. 2. To acquire and interpret information from a storage device.

**read-after-write verify** A check for determining information currently being written is correct as compared to the information source.

**read-around ratio** The number of times a location in a storage medium may be consulted before deterioration results in the loss of data.

**read-back check** A check in which the information that was transmitted to an output device is returned to the source and compared with the original information to insure accuracy.

**reader** A device for sensing information stored in memory and for generating signals that represent such sensed data.

**reader-interpreter** A service routine that reads an input stream, stores programs and data for later processing, identifies control information in the data stream, and stores this information in the proper control list.

**read in** 1. Refers to the act of placing data in storage at a specified address. 2. To sense information contained in some source and transmit this information to an internal storage.

**reading, computer** 1. To copy, usually from one form of storage to another. 2. To sense the meaning of an arrangement of hardware representing information. 3. To extract information.

**reading rate** The number of characters, words, or items that can be sensed by an input unit in a given time.

**read-only memory** A memory (abbreviated *ROM*) whose contents are not intended to be alterable by instructions. A typical semiconductor read-only memory is programmed by a mask pattern as part of the final manufacturing stage. ROMs are usually permanent, although some can be erased electrically or with the aid of ultraviolet radiation. ROMs are used to store microprograms or fixed programs in microcomputer systems.

The size of a ROM varies with system requirements, and the maximum size is usually dictated by the addressing capability of the microprocessor. A ROM does not need any store control circuitry; instructions can be fetched from a ROM in half the time it would take with a RAM. But programs must be correct, since ROM gives no flexibility for changing the instruction sequence.

**read-only memory, blastable** Refers to fusible read-only memory, which provides a nondestructive memory in applications in which the contents of memory do not change.

**read-only memory programmer** A ROM programmer for providing a capability for writing programs in chips used on a programmable read-only memory (PROM) module. Operating as an on-line peripheral device to a microcomputer system, the unit can be a fully self-contained subsystem that will load and verify user-generated routines in individual PROM chips. Source data for loading PROMs is binary code, previously generated by an assembler or the debugging programs.

**read-only storage** Read-only memory.

**readout** An array of addressable display characters that collectively form numbers or words that are the result of a machine operation; thus, a display of alphabetical, numerical, or alphanumeric characters.

**readout device** The collective addressable characters that indicate a computer or calculator output or result; thus, a display.

**read pulse** A pulse applied to one or more binary storage cells to determine if a bit of information is stored there.

**read punch** A unit of input/output equipment that punches coded holes (representing results) into cards, reads input data into the system, and segregates output cards. The read punch usually contains a card feed, a read station, and a punch station.

**read wire** The wire used to couple read pulses into magnetic storage cells.

**read-write counter** A device used to store the starting and current addresses being transferred by a read-write channel between the main memory and peripheral devices.

**read-write head** The electromagnetic device that is used for recording or erasing information on magnetic tapes, drums, or disks.

**read-write memory** A memory (abbreviated *RWM*) that can be altered at will. Read-write memories are used where it is desired to change the system application by the operator.

**read-write memory module** A circuit board that contains a random-access memory along with all necessary timing, control, and decoding logic.

**ready** The status or condition of being prepared to run. A program or device that is in a ready condition needs only a start signal to begin operation.

**ready condition** Refers to a specification or circumstance of a job or task when all of its requirements for execution other than control of the central processor have been satisfied.

**ready line** A line on some processors designed to interface the processor to a slow memory or to a slow input/output device.

**ready status word** A status word used to indicate that the remote computing system is waiting for entry from the terminal.

**real-time** The actual time during which a physical process occurs. In a real-time system the results of the computation can be used in guiding the physical process.

**real time BASIC satellites** Refers to a technique used in some systems that combines the speed and ease of conversational real time BASIC language programming with the operation of a number of time and event-scheduled tasks.

**real-time clock** 1. A device that provides interrupts at twice the line frequency and allows for the maintenance of an accurate time-of-day clock. 2. A timed device that produces output signals that correspond exactly with actual time—usually in hours, minutes, seconds, and tenths of seconds—and which may be used to indicate cumulative elapsed time, elapsed time, or time of day.

**real-time clock diagnostic** A routine that tests for the proper functioning of a real-time clock.

**real-time clock interrupt operation** The real-time clock interrupt occurs when a present clock count in a unique memory location is incremented to zero. The clock count location is automatically advanced at each clock time. The real time clock interrupt is enabled and disabled under program control.

**real-time clock module** A circuit board or unit that provides programmable time bases for real-time clocking.

**real-time debug routine** A program that allows the user to test, examine, and modify a program task while the real-time application program is running.

**real-time executive** A multitasking program system that can handle all aspects of priority scheduling, interrupt servicing, input/output control, intertask communications, and all queuing functions. Executives are designed for operation with specific microcomputer systems. Tasks operating under executive supervision provide the mechanism to real-time events. The occurrence of an event typically results in the scheduling of a response task. This scheduling is performed using a priority structure which associates each task with a distinct priority level. A given task may be interrupted while in the process of execution and temporarily suspended while a higher priority task is executed.

**real-time executive system** A multiprogramming foreground-background system with priority handling, interrupt capability, and program load-and-go capabilities.

**real-time guard** A mode that results in an interrupt to an address in central store when any attempt is made to perform a restricted operation. The guard mode is terminated by the occurrence of an interrupt.

**real-time information system** A system that provides information fast enough for the process to be controlled by the operator using this information.

**real-time input** An input that goes to the computer as the activity occurs.

**real-tine input/output** Refers to signals that are accepted by the system as they occur, or output signals that are generated to control external devices in real time such as required in industrial process control.

**real-time interface** An interface used for such tasks as controlling relays, solenoids, limit counters, and controllers.

**real-time mode** A mode of operation in which data necessary for the control or execution of a transaction are affected by the results of the processing. Real-time modes eliminate slow information-gathering procedures along with lax reporting techniques and slow communications. It insures that facts within the system are as timely as the prevailing situation. The real-time mode provides answers when answers are needed and delivers data when the need for that data occurs.

**real-time monitor** An operating and programming system designed to monitor the construction and execution of programs. An effective monitor will tend to optimize the utilization of hardware and to minimize programmer effort and operator intervention. The system is usually of a modular construction, tailored for a specific microcomputer and application.

**real-time operating system** A comprehensive software operating system designed to support the microcomputer in dedicated real-time applications. The system usually includes a system generation program, input/output routines, and analog-to-digital conversion routines.

**real-time operation** Data processing that allows the machine to use information as it becomes available. Real-time operation is opposed to *batch operation*, which processes information at a time unrelated to the time when the information was generated.

**real-time option board** A circuit board that contains most of the interface circuits and other options that users need for real-time operation. A typical option board includes:

1. Real-time clock
2. Programmer console
3. Input/output interface
4. Time-share control
5. Power-fail/restart circuits

**real-time remote inquiry** Online inquiry stations that allow users to interrogate computer files and receive immediate answers.

**real-time system** A system in which information is processed and responses are generated in a time interval directly related to the operational requirements of the system. Many real-time systems may also perform batch processing while concurrently processing inquiries. A typical microprocessor real-time system uses a compact memory-resident executive requiring in its simplest form less than 700 words of memory. It can be used in cost-sensitive applications such as controllers, which previously could not operate with the high overhead of real-time software. Some systems control 60 to 70 tasks on a fixed-priority basis.

**real time system, microprocessor** Refers to a multitask, real-time microprocessor-based system that is capable of handling concurrent priority-structured tasks in a multiprogramming environment.

**real-time trignometric-function generation** An approach to synchro-to-digital conversion that uses a real-time triognometric-function generator.

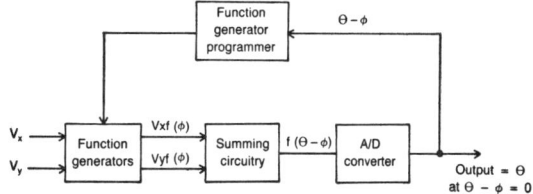

**Real time trignometric function generator S/D converter**

**reasonableness check** A test made on information in a computer system to insure that the data is within a desired range of values.

**receive-data register** In some communications systems data is automatically transferred to a receive-data register from a receiver deserializer register when it receives a complete character. This causes the receive-data register full bit in the status buffer to go high. Data may then be read through the bus by addressing the ACIA and selecting the receive-data register when the ACIA is enabled. When the receive-data register is full, the automatic transfer of data from the receiver shift register to the data register is inhibited.

**receiver** A device equipped for reception of incoming signals that are then transformed into a desired format.

**receiver card** A circuit board that accepts incoming data and translates it into some other usable form. A typical receiver card accepts ASCII data and translates it into parallel digital data.

**receiver gating** Refers to the application of gating voltages to one or more stages of a receiver, during the time when reception is desired.

**receiver holding register** A register that holds and then presents assembled receiver characters to the bus lines when requested by a read operation.

**receiver isolation** Refers to the attenuation between any two receivers in a system.

**receiver register** A register used to input received data into the system at a clock rate determined by the control register.

**receiver throughput, processor** The receiver throughput is dependent on the number of characters identified in the control bytes as being special (interrupt generating) and the size of the message buffers for received characters. As a receiver interrupt is generated, the received characters may be accumulated in a first-in/first-out FIFO storage buffer until the interrupt is handled.

**receiver/transmitter communication controller** An asynchronous controller that can interface data sets to a microcomputer. The controller consists of timing and control interface circuits, a receiver, and a transmitter.

**receiving perforator** A tape punch that converts coded electrical signals into perforations in tape.

**recirculating loop memory** A section of magnetic memory in which stored information recirculates continuously to provide rapid access.

**REC MARK** Abbreviation for *record mark*.

**record** 1. A collection of related items of data which can be treated as a unit. One line of an invoice may form a record, and a complete set of records may form a file. 2. A set or collection of related fields.

**record blocking** The grouping of records into data blocks that can be read or written using magnetic tape in one operation. Record blocking allows for more efficient tape operation and reduces the time to read or write files.

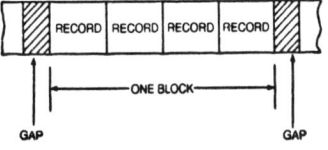

Record blocking

**record format** The design and organization of a record, usually a part of the program specification.

**record gap** An area on a data medium which indicates the end of a block or record. Also called *interrecord gap*.

**recording density** The number of bits in a single linear track measured per unit length of the recording medium.

**recording head** A transducer that accepts electrical variations and produces a corresponding field that selectively magnetizes a storage medium.

**record interface, audio cassette** Refers to a low cost storage device that allows off-line memory storage for data or software. It operates by the modulation of audio frequencies in the record mode and demodulates the recorded data in the playback mode.

**record layout** The arrangement and structure of a data record, including the sequence and size of components. Also called *record format*.

**record length** A measure of the size of a record, usually specified in characters or words.

**record separator** The information separator used to identify a logical boundary between the sets of items called records. Abbreviated *RS*.

**records, overflow** Refers to those records that cannot be accommodated in assigned areas of a direct access file and that must be stored in another area where they can be retrieved by means of a reference that is stored in the original assigned area.

**recoverable error** An error condition that allows the continued execution of a program.

**recoverable synchronization** An operational feature that allows synchronization to be recovered or reestablished when upset by disturbances.

**recovery factor** For a thermocouple sensor, this is a measure of its ability to indicate total temperature.

**recovery from fallback** Refers to the restoration of a system to full operation from a fallback mode of operation after the causes of the fallback has been removed.

**recovery procedures error** Refers to procedures designed to help isolate, and where possible, to recover from errors in equipment. The procedures are often used in conjunction with programs that record the statistics of machine malfunctions.

**recovery program** A program that allows a computer system to continue functioning when certain equipment fails.

**recovery time** Specifies the time required for the output voltage of a power supply to return to a value within the regulation specification after a step load or line change. Recovery time, as opposed to response time, is a more meaningful way of specifying power supply performance since it relates to regulation specifications.

**rectangular loop** Refers to a magnetic hysterisis loop that is not an S-shaped curve but tends to be square or rectangular in shape.

**rectifier** A device for converting alternating current into direct current by permitting the passage of signals in one direction only.

**rectifier crystal** Refers to diodes that are manufactured with a junction of crystalline elements, such as, silicon or germanium.

**rectifier diode** A device intended for power rectification applications (as opposed to signal detection applications).

**rectifier instrument** Refers to an instrument that uses a rectifying device so alternating currents or voltages can be measured.

**rectifying nonlinearity, Schottky diode** Refers to the rectifying nonlinearity of a Schottky diode, which results from the presence of a potential barrier at the metal semiconductor interface. The carriers must surmount this barrier by thermionic emission before they can flow through the junction. The barrier potential can be reduced by a forward bias to increase the carrier flow from the semiconductor into the metal. Under reverse bias, the Schottky diode behaves similarly to a pn-junction diode; the reverse current is small and almost voltage independent unless the breakdown voltage is exceeded.

**recursion** The continued repeating of the same operation or group of operations.

**recursive digital filter** This filter uses a feedback path to provide input signals from the previously calculated outputs.

**recycling programs** Refers to an organized arrangement for recycling programs through a computer where alternations have been made in one program that may change or have an effect on other programs.

**red-tape operation** An operation that is necessary to process data, but does not contribute to the final answer.

**redundancy** 1. That part of the information content that can be eliminated without loss of essential data. 2. The employment of several devices to perform the same function in order to improve the reliability of a particular portion of a system.

**redundancy check** The systematic insertion of bits or characters in a message for error detection. The added bits are redundant, since they can be eliminated without the loss of message information. Parity checking is one form of redundancy checking.

**redundancy-check character** A character used for checking the parity on a tape track. It is usually the last character recorded in each block.

**redundancy check, longitudinal** An error control device or system based on the arrangement of data in blocks according to some preset rule, the correctness of each character within the block being determined on the basis of the specific rule or set.

**redundancy check, vertical** Refers to an odd parity check performed on each character of a transmitted block of coded data as the block is received. Abbreviated RCV. See also *redundancy check, longitudinal*.

**redundant character** A character added to a group of characters to insure conformity with certain rules designed to detect errors.

**redundant code** A self-checking code that uses an added check bit. Examples of redundant codes include the biquinary code and the two-out-of-five code.

**reed switch** Refers to a switching device that consists of magnetic contactors that are sealed in a glass tube. The contactors are actuated by the magnetic field of an external solenoid, electromagnet or a permanent magnet.

**reenterable** A routine that can be shared by several tasks concurrently by calling itself or a program that then calls it.

**reenterable load module** A loading module that can be used repeatedly or concurrently by two or more jobs or tasks.

**reference address** The common address or address portion for a group of relative addresses.

**reference block** A block within a numerical control program identified by an "O" or "H" in place of the word address and containing sufficient data to enable resumption of the program following an interruption. This block should be located at a convenient point in the program that enables the operator to reset and resume operation.

**reference current** A current to which a varying current can be referred, especially when the current gains are expressed in decibels.

**reference-input signal** Refers to a signal that is external to a control loop; it serves as the standard of comparison for the directly controlled variable.

**reference listing** A list printed by a compiler to indicate instructions as they appear in the final routine; the listing usually includes details of storage allocation.

**reference noise** The magnitude of electrical noise that will produce a reading equal to that produced by 10 watts of electric power at 1 kHz.

**reference point** A terminal that is common to both the input and the output circuits.

**reference pressure** Pressure sensing can be designed to measure differential, gage, or absolute pressure depending on the reference pressure maintained in the reference side of the sensing element. These configurations are shown. The reference side of an absolute-pressure transducer is evacuated and sealed. Gage pressure is measured when ambient pressure is allowed on the reference side.

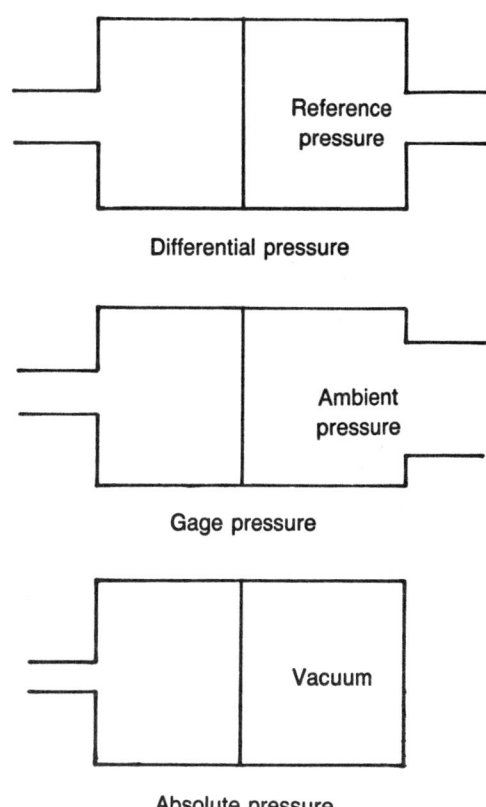

**Pressure reference configurations**

**reference program table** A section of storage that is used as an index for operations, variables, and subroutines.

**reference record** A compiler output that lists the operations and their positions in the routine, along with information on the segmentation and storage allocation of the routine.

**references, D/A converters** The most common D/A (digital-to-analog) reference is the temperature-compensated zener diode. It is often used with operational amplifiers for operating-point stabilization or transducing to current. Some typical reference circuits are shown on the next page.

**reference time** In a computer, an instant chosen near the beginning of switching as an origin for time measurements. It is taken as the first instant at which either the instantaneous value of the clock pulse reaches a specified fraction of its peak pulse amplitude.

# reference voltage

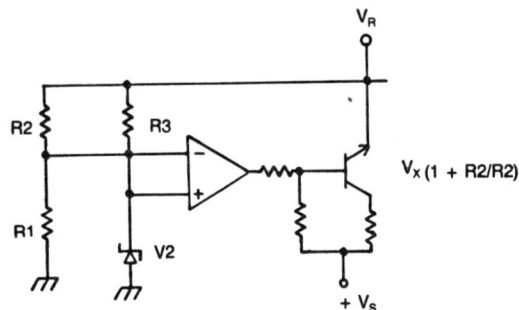

**A** Operating point stabilization

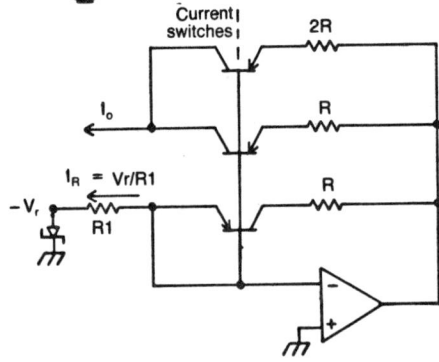

**B** Voltage-to-current conversion

**D/A converter reference circuits**

**reference voltage** A voltage used as a comparison standard for various circuit operations.

**reflected binary unit distance code** A binary code in which sequential numbers are represented by expressions that are the same except in one place, and in that place, differ by one unit; thus in moving from one decimal digit to the next sequential digit, only one binary digit changes its value.

**reflected impedance** The impedance at the input terminals of a transducer, device, or circuit as a result of the impedance characteristics at the output terminals.

**reflection** 1. A phenomenon that occurs when a wave meets a surface of discontinuity between two media, and part of it has its direction changed so as not to cross this surface, in accordance with the reflection laws. 2. A reduction of power from the maximum possible, because a load is not matched to the source, and only a part of the energy is transmitted. The loss of power is usually measured in decibels below the maximum possible.

**reflection gain** Refers to the gain received in a load from a source due to the introduction of a matching network, such as a transformer; usually measured in dBs.

**reflection loss** The loss in power from a source as a result of an impedance mismatch between source and load.

**reflectometer** An instrument for measuring the ratio of energy of a reflected wave to that of an incident wave.

# register arrangement

**reformatting** The changing in the representation of data from one format to another. Reformatting may include the translation of data values from one character set to another, such as from ASCII to EBCDIC.

**refresh** To restore signals or data states in a volatile storage system such as a dynamic MOS RAM.

**REG** Abbreviation for *register*.

**regenerate** 1. To restore information that is electrostatically stored, such as on a cathode-ray tube screen. 2. To produce a new pulse of proper shape when keyed by a degraded pulse.

**regeneration** 1. The process of restoring information or signals to specified requirements in amplitude or timing. 2. Positive feedback in usually a single amplifier stage.

**regeneration, pulse** Refers to the process of restoring a series of pulses to their original timing, form, and magnitude.

**regeneration signal** Refers to a restoration of signals that comply with specified requirements for amplitude, shape, and timing. Such signals are often generated from another signal, and the requirements are often conventions or rules of specific computers or systems.

**regenerative feedback** A positive feedback of part of the output in a circuit or system to the input such that it causes an increase in the output. See *regeneration*.

**regenerative memory** A memory or storage system that requires refreshing of the data to avoid loss of the contents.

**regenerative read** A read operation that automatically refreshes or rewrites the data back to the positions from which it was extracted.

**regenerative storage** Storage that requires periodic refreshing.

**register** A set of flip-flops used as a storage device for usually one or two words. It is used for temporary storage of subsets of data to facilitate arithmetic, logical, and transfer operations. Typical registers in microcomputers include the accumulator, index address register, instruction counter, stack pointer, and others. These registers should have good accessibility to the CPU.

**register, accumulator** Refers to that part of an arithmetic unit in which the results of an operation remains, and into which numbers are brought to and from storage.

**register address** An address where the operand lies in one of the general registers. In the 8080 system, an instruction such as:

$$\text{ADDC} \;;(A = A + C)$$

will add the contents of C to the accumulator and then place the results in the accumulator.

**register address field** The part of a computer instruction that contains a register address.

**register addressing, microprocessor** Register addressing is used when the CPU has several possible registers that may be used for reference. Since the number of registers is usually small, only a few bits are necessary to select a register.

**register and arithmetic logic unit** See *RALU*.

**register, arithmetic** Refers to the particular register in a computer that holds operands for certain operations, such as the multiplier for multiplication.

**register arrangement** This is a part of the microcomputer architecture, along with the addressing modes. Registers not dedicated to any specific function can be used as determined by the instruction that is decoded. They can contain the address of an operand or serve as pointers to the address of an operand. They can be used for autoincrement or autodecrement features or they can be used as index registers for data and program access.

**LOGIC DIAGRAM**

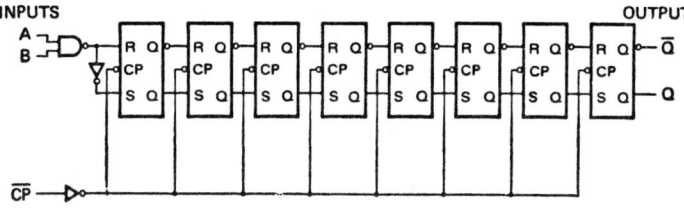

Register

**TRUTH TABLE**

| $t_n$ | | $t_{n+8}$ |
|---|---|---|
| A | B | Q |
| L | L | L |
| L | H | L |
| H | L | L |
| H | H | H |

NOTES:
$t_n$ = Bit time before clock pulse.
$t_{n+8}$ = Bit time after 8 clock pulses.

**register, base** Refers to a register whose contents are used to modify a computer instruction prior to its execution.

**register, buffer memory** 1. A register in which a word is stored as it comes from memory (reading) or just prior to its entering memory (writing). 2. The memory buffer serves as a buffer register for all information passing between the processor and the main memory, and serves as a buffer between the main memory and peripheral equipment.

**register, designation** Refers to a register into which data is to be placed.

**register, double-word** Refers to a register used to hold a double word.

**register, external** Registers that can be referenced by the program and are located in control storage as specific addresses.

**register, input/output** Refers to registers that are used to temporarily hold input and output data.

**register, memory-address (MAR)** The location in memory that is selected for data storage or retrieval is determined by this register. It can be used to directly address all words of the standard main memory or in any preselected field of an extended main memory.

**register, multiplier-quotient** The register used to contain a multiplier in multiplication and the quotient in division.

**register, sequence control** A register that is used to control the location of the next instruction to be processed.

**register, shift** A register capable of shifting data as directed.

**register, standby** Refers to a register containing information that may need to be available in case of an error or malfunction.

**register transfer module** A functional register unit (abbreviated *RTM*) designed for the construction of register logic systems.

**registration** The accuracy of the positioning of punched holes in a card.

**rejection, common mode** Refers to the ability of a circuit to discriminate against common mode voltage; usually expressed as a ratio or in decibels.

**rejection, normal-mode** Refers to the capability of a circuit to discriminate against normal-mode voltage, most often expressed as a ratio or in decibels.

**relating coding** To form or use a relative code.

**relation** The comparison of two expressions in assembler programming to determine if the value of one is greater than, equal to, or less than the other.

**relational operator** An operator used in assembler programming to indicate when a comparison is to be performed between different terms.

**relative address** An address that is to be altered to an absolute address at the time the program is being run.

**relative address label** A label used to identify the location of data by reference to its position with respect to some other location in the program.

**relative addressing** A type of addressing that shortens the address part of an instruction by allowing a reference within some range relative to a register. In the 6800 system, a relative addressing instruction is formed by adding the second byte of the instruction to the op code plus two. Because the addition is in twos' complement arithmetic, the result is plus 127 or minus 128 of the original value, and the relative address lies between plus 129 and minus 126 of the current instruction. As an example:

BBC 12 ;(branch if carry clear)

transfers control to the current location plus 14 if the carry bit is cleared.

**relative addressing mode** An addressing mode that specifies a memory location in the program counter or another register for reference. The relative addressing mode can be used for branch instructions, in which case an op code is added to the relative address to complete the instruction.

**relative code** A code in which all addresses are specified or written with respect to an arbitrary position or represented symbolically in a computable form.

**relative frequency** Refers to a measure or calculation of the ratio of numbers of observations in a class or subset to the total number of observations or elements constituting a population, such as a universal subset.

**relative magnitude** Refers to the magnitude relationship or comparison of one quantity to another, most often related to a base magnitude and expressed as a difference from or a percentage of the base or reference.

**relative time clock**  A clock system (abbreviated *RTC*) used to allow the executive to keep track of time and service interrupts. At every relative time-clock interrupt, the program control is returned to the executive, which determines the priority of action.

**relaxation oscillator**  An oscillator that operates by being driven to a regenerative state rapidly and repetitively. Upon reaching the saturated regenerative state, the device "relaxes" to return to its original state and is immediately driven again to saturation.

**relay**  1. An electromechanical switching device usually composed of a solenoid, a movable armature containing at least one contact point, and a set of fixed contact points. Applying a voltage to the solenoid sets up a magnetic field that attracts the armature, thus causing it to make or break a circuit completed by the touching contact points. 2. A radio repeater system, usually automatically operated and controlled.

**relay contacts**  Refers to the contacts that are closed or opened by the movement of a relay armature.

**relay driver**  A circuit that produces an output powerful enough to drive relay solenoids when a low-current logic signal is applied.

**relay, electromagnetic**  Refers to an electromagnetic switching device having multiple electrical contacts that are operated by an electrical current through a coil.

**relay input module**  Refers to a unit that connects relay coils to the computer. The contacts of the relays are presented to the processor's I/O bus.

**relay output module**  Refers to a unit that provides a set of relay contacts that may be used to drive devices such as lamps.

**relay, reed**  A switching device that consists of magnetic contactors that are sealed into a glass tube. The contactors are actuated by the magnetic field of an external solenoid, an electromagnet, or a permanent magnet.

**relay tree**  A group of relays whose contacts are interconnected, but whose solenoids are independently driven; so called because each relay in the array has twice the contacts of the prior relay. Relay trees perform binary-to-decimal conversion (for driving 7-segment displays) and permit selection of a number of power-driving functions with only a few input signals.

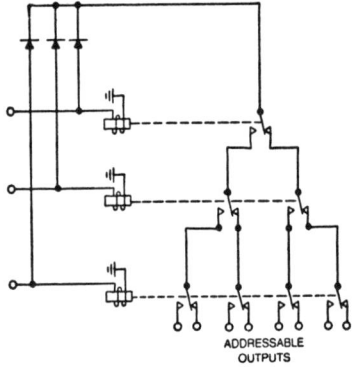

Relay tree

**release-guard signal**  A signal sent in response to a clear-forward signal that indicates that the circuit is free at the incoming end.

**reliability**  The probability that a device will perform without failure for a specified time period under specified operating conditions.

**reliability control**  Refers to the coordination and direction of reliability activities.

**reliability index**  The figures of merit that are used to denote relative reliability.

**reliability testing**  Tests that are designed to determine the anticipated failure-free performance, or life expectancy of a product or system under specified conditions.

**relocatability**  The ability to situate a program or data in an area of memory at different times without modification to the program.

**relocate**  To move a routine from one part of storage to another and make the necessary adjustments to allow the routine to be executed.

**relocatable assembler**  An assembler that generates an object program with memory addresses entered as displacements from a relative program origin or as external references.

**relocatable expression**  An assembly expression whose value is affected by program relocation. A relocatable expression may represent a relocatable address.

**relocatable program**  A program designed so that it may be located and executed from many areas in memory.

**relocatable program loader**  Refers to a program that assigns absolute origins to relocatable subroutines, object programs, and data. It assigns absolute locations to each of the instructions or data, and modifies the reference to these instructions or data.

**relocatable term**  A term in assembler programming whose value is affected by program relocation.

**relocating object loader**  A program used to load and link object programs produced by assemblers. It satisfies external references between separate program segments, generates linkages as required, and loads only those segments required to satisfy external references.

**relocation dictionary**  RLD. Refers to a part of a program that contains the information necessary to change addresses when it is relocated.

**reluctance**  The opposition in a magnetic circuit to flux.

**reluctive transducers**  Transducers that use the ratio of the reluctance of two coils. They are less sensitive to temperature effects than one coil devices. Reluctive transducers use a small motion of 0.003″ to yield an ac output voltage of about 100 mV.

**REMAD**  Abbreviation for *remote magnetic anomaly detection*.

**remanence**  Refers to a unit of measure for determining the magnetic flux density after removal of an applied magnetic force.

**remote access**  The capability for communication with a processing facility by one or more stations that are distant from that facility.

**remote batch processing**  Batch processing where an input device is located at some distance from the main installation and has access through the communications system to the computer.

**remote console**  A terminal located some distance from the processor.

**remote control**  Operation of a system from a distant location.

**remote control signals**  Refers to signal lines that allow the microcomputer to be operated from a remote control panel. Remote control signals include REMOTE HALT, REMOTE LOAD, and REMOTE POWER-ON.

**remote data concentration**  Refers to communications processors that are used for the multiplexing of data from low-speed lines or terminals or low-activity lines or terminals onto one or more higher-speed lines.

**remote debugging**  The use of remote terminals for the testing of programs.

**remote inquiry**  The interrogation of the contents of a data processing storage unit from a device displaced from the storage unit site. Remote inquiry stations allow the computer to be interrogated from various locations for immediate answers to inquiries.

**remote job entry** The processing of stacked jobs over communication lines via terminals that are usually equipped with line printers. Small computers are also used to operate as RJE stations. A typical RJE station operates at 4800 baud for tasks such as data transmission, report transmission, file updating, and program compilation in FORTRAN or COBOL.

**remote monitoring and control, microcomputer systems** The microcomputer can be used as a programmable remote station to be addressed from a central computer. It can be given operating setpoints strategies or can send data from a number of sensors and then implement decisions based on complex combinations of conditions. In addition, distributed digital processing allows the central controller to receive refined status reports rather than raw data from remote stations. Since information is then exchanged only when established limits are exceeded or when remote units are specifically interrogated, communication burdens are reduced. This can save money by reducing the complexity of the central computer programming and decrease the wiring or line cost by having each remote unit do more. Data can also be stored, timed, and dated at a remote site by using a data storage peripheral unit such as magnetic tape cassettes. By relieving the central computer from routine data manipulation and control tasks, the machine can do more computations and better optimize the control of the total system.

**remote multiplexing system** Remote multiplexing uses a configuration like that shown below. The remote multiplexers are located throughout the plant. Analog and digital signals are sent to the nearest remote multiplexer.

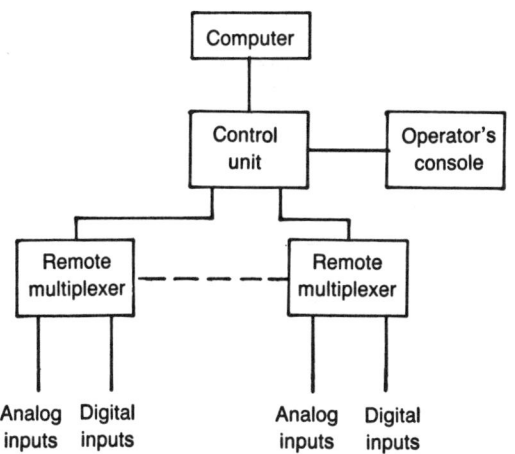

Remote multiplexing configuration

**remote real-time terminal** These terminals can include controllers and buffers for microcomputer computer I/O equipment, a real time clock, a sensor, instrument and control interfaces with discrete I/O lines, a/d converters, d/a converters, analog multiplexers, and communications modems.

**remote station** Terminal equipment for communicating with a processing system from a distant location.

**remote terminal** An input or output terminal that can be located at some distance from the processor.

**repeatability** The closeness of agreement among a number of consecutive measurements of a constant signal approached from the same direction. Repeatability is expressed as maximum nonrepeatability in percent of span or counts of error.

**repeat counter** A counter used to control repeated operations, such as block transfer and search commands.

**repeated addition multiplication** There are several possible circuits for multiplication by repeated addition or by the shifting technique. Multiplication by repeated addition requires a counter. The figure shows the technique used for repeated-addition multiplication. The value of the multiplicand is loaded into its register, and the value of the multiplier is loaded into the multiplier counter.

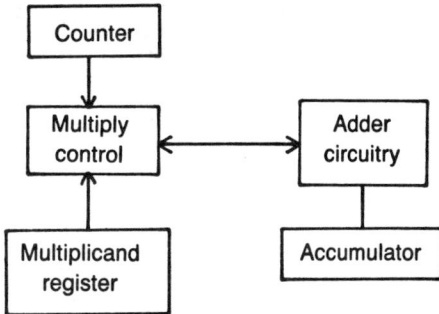

Multiplication using repeated addition

**repeated subtraction division** Refers to a method of division in which the number of subtractions that take place is loaded into the counter. The counter then holds the answer. The repeated subtraction technique of division is shown.

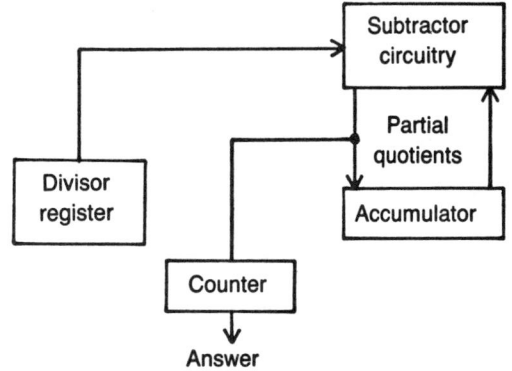

Division using repeated subtraction

At the start, the dividend is loaded into the accumulator, and the divisor into the divisor register. As each subtraction takes place, the value in the accumulator becomes smaller and smaller, finally reaching zero (or some remainder); the value in the counter becomes larger and larger, finally yielding the correct quotient. The divider circuit does not stop when the accumulator reaches zero (or a remainder). The subtracter will try to continue subtracting beyond the point of zero remainder; when it does, the value in the accumulator becomes a negative quantity. The negative sign can be recognized with a "sign comparator." This stops the divide process, and the machine adds-back the subtrahend and produces the correct positive remainder.

Often in dealing with large binary numbers, many of the arithmetic processes drop a few of the least significant bits in the answers. The final result may be in error, but it is usually more accurate than required.

**repeater** 1. A device that reconstitutes signals into standard or desired requirements. 2. A communications system that automatically retransmits received signals on a different fixed frequency within the same band.

**repertoire** The set of instructions that a processor is capable of performing or a coding system is capable of assembling.

**repertoire, instruction** 1. Refers to the set of instructions that a computing or data processing system is capable of performing. 2. The set of instructions that an automatic coding system assembles.

**report** A presentation of data or information in tabular, graphic, narrative, or any other form.

**report generation** The automatic creation of reports according to user specifications of the desired content and arrangement.

**report generator** A routine designed to produce an object routine that can then be run to produce a desired report. To use the report generator, the programmer prepares a set of parameters defining control fields and report lines. These parameters are used to produce a symbolic program. The assembled version of this program accepts the raw data as input, edits it, and generates the desired reports.

**report program generator** 1. A program (abbreviated *RPG*) used to generate object programs that produce reports from existing data. 2. The RPG language.

**report program generator language** A problem-oriented language for commercial programming. Especially useful in smaller applications, RPG is like COBOL in having powerful and simple file manipulation capabilities, but it lacks algorithmic facility.

**representative calculating operation** A method of evaluating the speed performance of a computer. One method is to use one tenth of the time required to perform nine complete additions and one complete multiplication. A complete addition or a complete multiplication time includes the time required to procure two operands from high speed storage.

**reproducibility** The closeness of agreement among repeated measurements of the output for the same value of input made under the same operating conditions over a period of time, approaching from either direction.

**reprogrammable associative ROM** A term sometimes used for a programmable logic array.

**reprogrammable read-only memory** Refers to a ROM that is erasable. A transparent lid allows the user to expose the chip to ultraviolet light to erase the bit pattern. A new pattern can then be written into the device.

**request for repetition, automatic** Refers to a system employing an error-detecting code and arranged such that a signal detecting as being in error automatically initiates a request for retransmission. Abbreviated *ARQ*.

**request to send** One of the basic data set interchange leads defined in the EIA Standard RS-232.

**required hyphen** A program instruction entered to insure that the hyphen is not omitted. Also known as *embedded hyphen*.

**rerun point** One of a set of preselected points in a program that is used as a restarting point in the event of error detection.

**rerun routine** A routine that uses rerun points for restarting.

**rescue dump** A dump on magnetic tape of the entire memory, along with a starting point to allow the rerun from this point. Rescue dumps can prevent the rerunning of an entire program when the run is interrupted by an error or power shutdown.

**reset** To return a device such as a register to zero or to an initial or selected condition.

**reset key** A key or switch on the computer console used to reset the error-detection system and to restart the program after an error has been discovered.

**reset pulse** A pulse used to set a flip-flop or a magnetic cell to its original state.

**reset switch** A switch used for either an error reset or a master reset. For a master reset, all registers are set to zero, the interrupt system is disabled, the input/output interface is initialized, and the program counter is set.

**resident compiler** A compiler that uses the computer itself to produce programs. A resident compiler may require several passes in a microcomputer system to reduce a source program to machine language.

**resident module** A module that keeps track of program execution status.

**resident program** A program that is permanently located in storage.

**residual charge** The charge remaining on the plates of a capacitor after a discharge.

**residual current** The vector sum of the currents in an electric circuit after the source of power is removed.

**residual resistance** The resistance persisting at temperatures near zero on the absolute scale, arising from crystal irregularities and impurities.

**residue** The residue of a number is calculated by dividing it by the modulus, resulting in an integer and a remainder. The remainder is the residue. Residue codes can be used to detect or even correct errors from an arithmetic unit or faults produced by data transfers or memory operations.

For control functions it may be necessary to employ fixed-weight or m-out-of-n codes. Here the weight of the code word is the number of nonzero components in the code word.

**residue check** A check in which each operand is accompanied by the remainder obtained by dividing this number by *n*, the remainder then being used as a check digit or digits. Also called a *modulo n* check.

**resillator** A miniaturized frequency standard combining a resonator and oscillator in a single package.

**resist** The material used in printed circuit board manufacture to protect desired portions of the conductive material during additional processing steps. Also called *photoresist*.

**resistance** A property of conducting materials that determines the current produced by a given voltage. The unit of resistance is the ohm. The value of resistance of a given circuit component is equal to its voltage divided by its current.

**resistance box** 1. An assembly of resistors and the necessary switching or other means for changing the resistance connected across its output terminals by known, fixed amounts. 2. A device containing carefully constructed and adjusted resistors, which can be introduced into

**resistance drop** The voltage drop occurring across two points on a conductor when current flows through the resistance between those points. Multiplying the resistance in ohms by the current in amperes gives the voltage drop in volts.

**resistance ladders** A network that uses a limited number of repeated values, with attenuation. One approach, as shown, uses a binary resistance quad, consisting of the four values 2R, 4R, 8R, 16R for each group of 4 bits, with an attenuation of 16:1 for the second quad and 256:1 for the third quad. The proper quad weights for BCD conversion can be achieved with an attenuation between quads of 10:1.

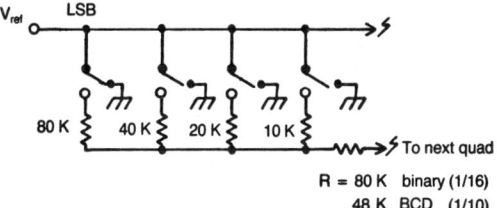

Quad resistance ladder

**resistance lamp** Refers to a lamp used to limit the current in a circuit.

**resistance material** A material used for the construction of resistance elements. Typical materials are nichrome wire and carbon.

**resistance temperature detectors** Abbreviated *RTDs*, these sensors operate on the principle that the resistance of a material to electric current flow is temperature dependent. The resistance of metals used as sensing elements increases with increasing temperature, as shown, while most semiconductor materials decrease in resistance. One component of the total resistivity is due to impurities and is known as residual resistivity. It is lowest for the pure metals. The residual resistivity can change if the RTD is used at too high a temperature or if the wire is contaminated by the environment or materials in contact with the wire.

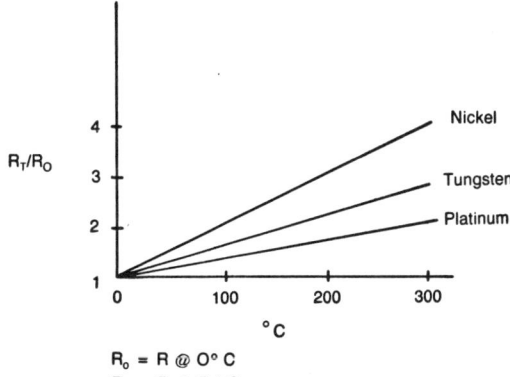

Temperature dependence of common RTD materials

**resist-etchant** A material deposited onto a copper-clad base material to prevent the conductive area underneath from being etched away.

**resistive component** Refers to those parts of the impedance of an electrical system that lead to the absorption and dissipation of energy in the form of heat.

**resistive coupling** The use of resistors to connect or link two circuits or gates.

**resistor** A component with a specified resistance value designed to restrict the flow of current.

**resistor-transistor logic** A logic family (abbreviated *RTL*) that uses resistors with discrete transistors.

**resolution** 1. The smallest incremental step in separating a value into constituent parts. 2. The smallest inseparable constituent part of a value.

**resolver** 1. A device that breaks up a quantity, such as a vector, into components or elements. 2. A small section of storage that has much faster access than the rest of the storage.

**resolver differential** A device used to obtain zero shift or offset in control systems that use resolver feedback. It is connected between the reference and the feedback to furnish a signal to the position feedback unit.

**resolving potentiometer, flat card** Refers to a type of potentiometer that uses an element that is a square slab or card wound with resistance wire.

**resonance** Refers to the sympathetic electrical vibration of a circuit or device to a signal.

**resonant-gate transistor** A type of field-effect transistor with a mechanically tuned input.

**resonator** A device exhibiting a sharply defined electric, mechanical, or acoustic resonance effect such as a piezoelectric crystal.

**resource allocation mapping** Refers to the use of visual aids or maps to allow register, memory, or I/O space assignments as they are required.

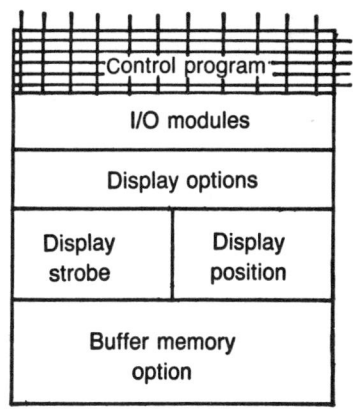

Resource allocation map

**response time** The time elapsed between generation of an inquiry at a terminal and receipt of a response at that same terminal.

**restart** To reestablish the execution of a routine by using a checkpoint.

**restart procedure** A procedure that allows processing to continue from the last checkpoint, rather than the beginning of the run. Restart procedures are used in machines with heavy scheduling, since complete reruns due to errors or interruptions cannot be tolerated.

**restoration** Returning the dc component to an ac signal after passing the signal through a capacitive circuit.

**restore** 1. To return an index, address, word, or character to its initial state, sometimes by periodic recharge or regeneration. 2. To superimpose a dc level on an ac signal after loss of the original dc in a stage.

**restorer generator** A device that generates the signals required to restore specific conditions in a system.

**restorer pulse generator** Refers to a circuit designed to generate pulses for special timing or gating purposes. These pulses are used as inputs to gates to aid in pulse-shaping and timing.

**retentivity** The degree or expression of the ability of a material to retain magnetic flux.

**retransmit error checking** Communications channel may be sensitive to intermittent noise and signal failures, thus it is necessary to determine if the transmitted message is received without errors. One technique requires that the receiving station to retransmit the message received back to the transmitting device. The message must then be transmitted twice. This can be done for most applications.

**retrofit** Work done to an existing machine tool from simply adding special jigs or fixtures to the complete re-engineering and manufacturing, often involving the addition of a numerical control system.

**return address** Refers to that part of a subprogram that connects it with the main program or routine. A return address can be used to unite two or more separately written, compiled, or assembled programs or routines into a single operational unit.

**return from zero time** The elapsed time between the end of a pulse at full strength and the start of the absent electrical flow or some lower level of electrical flow.

**return to bias** A mode of recording (abbreviated *RB*) in which the state of the medium changes from a bias state to another state and then returns to record a binary one or zero.

**reverse bias** A voltage applied to a P-N crystal such that the positive terminal of the voltage is applied to the N section and the negative to the P section.

**reverse-blocking PNPN switch** A PNPN-type switch that exhibits a reverse-blocking state when its anode-to-cathode voltage is negative and does not switch in the normal manner of a PNPN-type switch.

**reverse direction** The direction of greater resistance to current flow through a diode or rectifier; that is, from the positive to the negative electrode. Also called inverse direction.

**reverse gate current** The direct current into the gate terminal of a MOS device with a reverse gate-source voltage applied.

**reverse-Polish notation** A system for expressing mathematical statements wherein the operators follow the numbers, and the answer appears without an equal (=) sign. See *Polish notation*.

**reverse printer** Another term for a bidirectional printer.

**reverse recovery time** In a semiconductor diode, the time required for the current or voltage to reach a specified state after being switched instantaneously from a specified forward current condition to a specified reversed bias condition.

**reverse scan** An editing operation used to suppress zeros by replacing them with blanks.

**reverse search** The searching in a nonplay direction for reference points on a magnetic tape.

**reversible capacitance** For a capacitor, the limit, as the amplitude of the applied sinusoidal voltage approaches zero, of the ratio of the amplitude of the inphase, fundamental frequency component of

transferred charge to the amplitude of the applied voltage, with a specified constant-bias voltage superimposed on the sinusoidal voltage.

**reversible process** Refers to a mechanism of flux change within a magnetic material where the flux returns to its initial state when the magnetic field is removed.

**revision cycle** The path of a document through a series of corrections after its initial release.

**revision work** Refers to the typing of corrections and editing changes after the original release of a document.

**REW** Abbreviation for *rewind*.

**rewrite** The restoring of information in storage by repeated writing. Also called *regeneration*.

**rf** Abbreviation for *radio frequency*.

**rf amplifier** An amplifier capable of operation at radio frequencies.

**RFI** Abbreviation for *radio frequency interference*.

**rheostat** Refers to an electric component in which the resistance introduced into a circuit is variable by a knob or handle or by a mechanical means, such as an electric motor.

**RHI** Abbreviation for *range height indicator*.

**rhythm generator** A circuit designed for electronic organs and other musical electronic instruments. One type contains an internal oscillator, a counter, and a ROM that drives the rhythm instruments and a seven segment sequence count display. The oscillator frequency is determined by an external network.

**RI** Abbreviation for *reliability index*.

**right-justify** To adjust the printing positions on a page such that the right margin is flush.

**right shift** An operation in which digits of a word are displaced to the right. A right shift has the effect of division if the word represents a binary number.

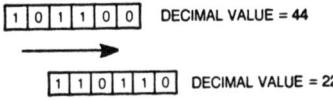

**Right shift**

**ring counter** A loop of connected bistable elements in which one and only one is in a specified state at any one time; as input signals are counted, the position of this state moves in an ordered sequence around the loop.

**ring oscillator** 1. An oscillator in which a number of devices feed each other in a circle or circuit. 2. An oscillator in which the frequency is determined by a ring cut from a quartz crystal suspended at its nodes to minimize damping.

**ring system** An array of processors distributed along one or more rings or loops. Data is transferred around the ring or loop and used by a particular processor according to a predetermined address or tag.

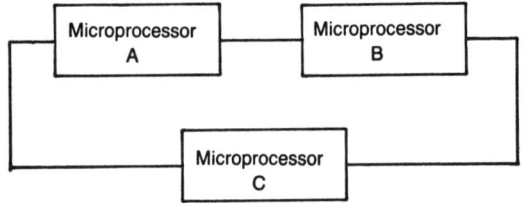

**Ring multimicroprocessor system**

**ripple** 1. The ac component arising from sources within a dc power supply. Ripple is the ratio, expressed in percent, of the root-mean-square value of the ripple voltage to the absolute values of the total voltage. 2. The excursions above and below the average peak amplitude.

**ripple counter** A counting circuit in which flip-flops are connected in series, with one flip-flop affecting the next in sequence until the last flip-flop is triggered.

**ripple factor** The amount of ac voltage in the output of a rectifier after rectification. It is measured, in percent, by the ratio of the rms value of the ac component to the algebraic average of the total voltage across the load.

**ripple filter** A filter designed to reduce the ripple or ac variation produced by a rectifier circuit.

**ripple generator** A thermoelectric generator powered by heat from a radioactive source and suitable for long periods of maintenance-free operation on remote sites; it is used for lighting marine navigational buoys and other radioisotope powered pulsed light equipment.

**RIPS** Abbreviation for *range instrumentation planning study*.

**RISE** Abbreviation for *research in supersonic environment*.

**rise time** The time required for the leading edge of a pulse to rise from 10 to 90 percent of its final value. It is proportionate to the time constant and is a measure of the slope of the wavefront.

**rise time, overshoot** Refers to the measured time necessary for the output of a system (other than first order) to make the change from a small specified percentage (often 5 or 10) of the steady-state increment to a large specified percentage (often 90 or 95) either before overshoot or in the absence of overshoot.

**RJE** Abbreviation for *remote job entry*.

**rms pulse amplitude** Root-mean-square pulse amplitude, the square root of the average of the squares of the instantaneous amplitudes taken over the duration of the pulse.

**ROAMA** Abbreviation for *Rome air materiel area*.

**robot** 1. A device or system that can detect input signals or environmental conditions and perform calculations for resultant actions of a control mechanism. Robots are being used for visual inspection and identity-and-attitude analysis. They have been used to determine the two-dimensional outline of an object, locate corners, find holes and grip points, separate multiple objects, and identify objects based on characteristics. 2. A mechanical simulation of a human and a human's movements; an automaton.

**robot capability** Properly programmed, a robot can solve problems in the two general areas of visual inspection and identity and attitude analysis. Available routines have the capability to extract the two-dimensional outline of the image of an object, locate corners, find holes, separate multiple objects, identify an object on the basis of its distinguishing features, specify the grip points, and acquire and orient a workpiece. Some systems identify different foundry castings and determine their position and orientation so that the system manipulator can pick them up off a conveyor belt.

**robotics** An area of artificial intelligence that deals with the development and use of robots.

**Rockwell 6500/1** A microcomputer chip that combines the 6502 microprocessor with 2048 bytes of ROM, 64 bytes of RAM, 32 bidirectional I/O lines, four interrupts and a 16-bit programmable counter/timer. The 6500/1 single chip microcomputer has a separate pin for RAM power, which may be used to maintain data in the RAM on 10 percent of the total power for the chip. The programmable 16-bit counter/timer can operate as either an interval timer, pulse generator, or event counter.

**ROI** Abbreviation for *return on investment*.

**rollback** A programmed return to a prior checkpoint.

**rollback snapshot** A recording of data taken at periodic intervals in a program to allow the program to restart at the last recording after a system failure.

**roll-in** To restore to main storage the data that had previously been transferred from main storage to auxiliary storage.

**rollout** To record the contents of main storage in auxiliary storage.

**ROM** Abbreviation for *read-only memory*, a memory whose contents are not alterable by computer instructions. A semiconductor ROM is programmed by a mask pattern as a part of the final manufacturing process. The organization of the storage cells determines the number of input and output lines required for a given ROM. The address pins are the means by which a specific word is accessed or selected. If the ROM is organized as 32 words of 8 bits, then each word can be addressed using 5 input lines, since $32 = 2^5$ and:

$$\text{WORD ONE ADDRESS} = 00000$$
$$\text{WORD TWO ADDRESS} = 00001$$

The number of output lines is determined by the number of bits in the word. ROMs can be used to store microprograms or fixed programs, depending upon the application. A ROM can be used to implement in one package the functions that previously took up to 50 TTL packages.

**ROM address lines** Refers to the lines or pins that are used to select a specific word in ROM.

**ROM assimilator** A self-contained microcomputer system with assembly and utility programs that can develop, debug, and simulate proposed ROM programs. The system includes a debug console and terminal interface for input and output. Proposed ROM programs are stored in RAM and modified directly from the terminal.

**ROM bootstrap** Refers to a ROM program that is used as a bootstrap loader. The bootstrap loader is a minimum program that, if everything in memory is wiped out, will allow the programmer to recreate a main memory load.

**ROM, chip enable** Most types of ROMs have a pin labeled CE for *chip enable*. This permits the output to be isolated from the rest of the circuitry inside the IC. Thus, if a 1 is placed at CE (while the address is being changed), the outputs will be at logic-1 level.

**ROM loader** A loader program that is implemented in ROM. A typical ROM loader is contained on a printed-circuit card for plugging into the microcomputer system.

**ROMON** Abbreviation for *receive only monitor*.

**ROM-oriented architecture** A system in which the microprocessor instruction set can be executed completely from ROM without the need for external RAM. This system requires an internal stack for subroutines and internal registers for indirect addressing operations. The instruction set needs logical instructions for bit manipulation.

**ROM/RAM** A circuit containing a mask programmable MOS ROM as well as a RAM. The ROM/RAM is designed for applications requiring only a small amount of ROM and RAM. One specific unit has a ROM section of 704 words of 8 bits and a RAM of 76 words of 4 bits.

**ROM/RAM/CPU** A chip for low cost applications that contains a processor along with RAM and ROM memories.

**ROM self-test** To check the contents of a ROM, the microprocessor reads out every word in the ROM and performs a cumulative parity check, an exclusive-OR operation on each bit. At the end, the result should be a 1 in every bit position of the accumulating register. If the specific microprocessor's instruction set doesn't include an exclusive-

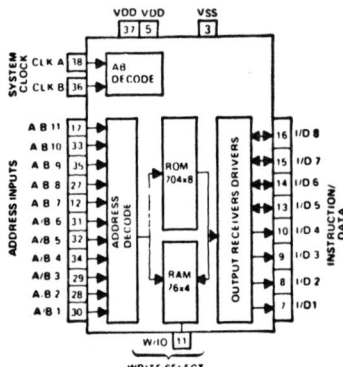

ROM/RAM

OR instruction, it can execute the equivalent operation in a subroutine. This self-test always detects single errors, whole-word errors, data output lines stuck at 1 or 0, and address input lines stuck at 1 or 0. It sometimes detects address lines short-circuited to each other, output lines short-circuited to each other, and multiple random errors.

**ROM simulator** An instrument designed to replace ROM or PROM during program development and debugging. The instrument can be used to simulate PROM or ROM configurations and provides an inexpensive means of altering microprograms. The memory modules are loaded and verified through the ROM simulator or front-panel address and data switches. Simulation is achieved by extending control of the read-only function to the user's equipment using simulation cables.

**ROM terminal** A terminal that uses a ROM for storing instructions.

**root segment** The master or controlling segment of an overlay structure which resides in the main memory. The root segment is usually the first segment within the program, and it is always the first to be loaded at program initiation time.

**rope lay** Refers to the bunch and concentric stranding to build wire diameter to the required size and flexibility.

**ROS** Abbreviation for *read-only storage*.

**rotate** The process of moving each bit in a register in a circular manner, either to the right or the left. Each bit that leaves one end of the register enters the other end. Also called *circular shift*.

**round** The deletion of the least significant digits with or without modifications to reduce bias. Also called *round off*.

**rounding error** An error due to roundoff.

**roundoff** Deletion of the least significant digit or digits and adjustment of the part retained to reduce bias.

**round robin** The cyclical multiplexing of a resource among jobs with fixed time slices.

**routine** An ordered set of instructions used to direct the computer to perform one or more specific tasks or operations. A closed routine is one that is not entered as a block of instructions within the main routine, but entered by a linkage from the main routine. A routine may be considered as a subdivision of a program with two or more instructions that are functionally related.

**routine, closed** Refers to a routine that is not inserted as a block of instructions within a main routine but is entered by basic linkage from the main routine.

**routine, correction** Concerns a particular routine that is designed to be used in or after a computer failure, malfunction, or program or operator error.

**routine, floating point** A set of subroutines that allows a computer to execute floating point arithmetic. These routines may be used to simulate floating point operations on a computer with no built in floating point hardware.

**routine, input** A routine, sometimes stored permanently in a computer, to allow reading of programs and data into the machine. Also known as a bootstrap.

**routine, minimum-latency** Refers to a program that operates in such a way that minimum waiting time is required to obtain information out of storage.

**row binary** A method of representing binary numbers on a card where bits are represented by punches in a row as opposed to a series of columns. Row binary is useful in systems with words of 40 bits or less where the card can be used to store 12 words on each half of the card.

**row pitch** The distance measured along paper tape between the centers of adjacent holes.

**RPG** Abbreviation for *report program generator*.

**RS** Abbreviation for *remote station*.

**R-S flip-flop** A flip-flop consisting of two cross-coupled NAND gates and having two inputs, a *set* and a *reset*.

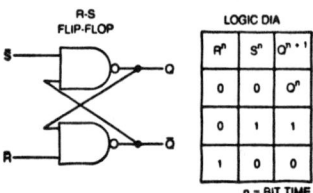

R-S Flip-flop

**R-S-T flip-flop** A flip-flop that operates like an R-S flip-flop with an additional input (the trigger), which is used to cause the flip-flop to change states.

**RS-232** An interface standard designated by EIA and spelled out in *Standard RS-232*.

**RS-232 compatible controller** A module designed to interface a microcomputer system to most asynchronous modems. Baud rates include 110, 300, 1200, 2400, 4800 and 9600, with selectable words lengths from 5 to 8 bits and either odd or even parity.

**RS-232 interface** An interface used to connect a modem with associated data terminal equipment that is standardized by EIA Standard RS-232.

**RS-449** This bus standard accommodates data rates as high as two megabits a second. It differs from RS-232 in other ways as well. It introduces a few more signals and uses two connectors: a 37-pin unit for the most frequently used signals and a 9-pin unit for a secondary channel. A single 37-pin connector is used in most applications. RS-449 is intended to replace RS-232C. In the meantime, new equipment conforming to the RS-449 standard will require an adapter to mate to RS-232 devices. Some applications may require cables with 36-, 9-, and 25-pin connectors to interconnect newer and older equipment. The RS-449 standard adapter requires resistors for the logic conversion.

**RT** Abbreviation for *research and technology*.

**RTC** Abbreviation for *relative time clock*.

**RTCM** Abbreviation for *radio technical commission for Marine services*.

**RTE** Abbreviation for *real-time executive*, a program that provides a multiprogramming foreground-background system with priority scheduling, interrupt handling, and load-and-go capabilities.

**RTF** Abbreviation for *radio telephone*.

**RTL** Abbreviation for *resistor-transistor logic*, a logic family that uses discrete transistors with resistive coupling.

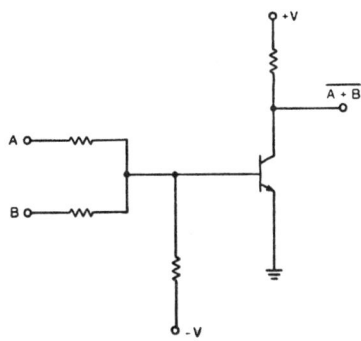

**RTL NOR Gate**

**RTOS** Abbreviation for *real time operating system*.

**ruby laser** Refers to an optically-pumped ruby crystal producing a very intense and narrow beam of coherent red light. It is used in light-beam communication and for localized heating.

**ruly English** A language based on English in which every word has one and only one meaning, and each concept has one and only one word to describe it.

**run** The performance of one computer program or several routines linked together so that they form an operating unit. Usually during a run, manual operations are minimal; a typical run may involve loading, reading, processing, and writing.

**runaway** Refers to a condition that arises when one of the parameters of a physical system undergoes a large, sudden, undesirable, and often destructive increase.

**run book** The material needed to document a computer application, including problem statement, flow charts, and coding and operating instructions.

**run indicator** An indicator used to indicate that the processor is in a run mode.

**run switch** A switch that allows the processor to begin instruction execution, beginning at the address contained in the program counter.

**run time** The time required to complete a single, continuous execution of an object program.

**RUSDIC** Abbreviation for *Russian dictionary*.

**R-2R ladder** A ladder network that allows an inexpensive range of resistance values. The R-2R ladder is a convenient form. The illustration shows its use with an inverting operational amplifier. If all bits but the MSB are off and therefore grounded, the output is $(-R/2R)V_{REF}$. If all bits except bit 2 are off, it can be seen that the output voltage will be $1/2(-R/2R)V_{REF} = 1/4V_{REF}$. The lumped resistance of the LSB circuit to the left of bit 2 is 2R. The equivalent circuit looking back from the MSB toward bit 2 is $V_{REF}/2$, and the series resistance is 2R. The grounded MSB series resistance, 2R, has no influence since the amplifier is at ground. The output voltage is therefore $-V_{REF}/4$. The same reasoning can be used to show that the nth bit produces an output increment equal to $2^{-n}VREF$.

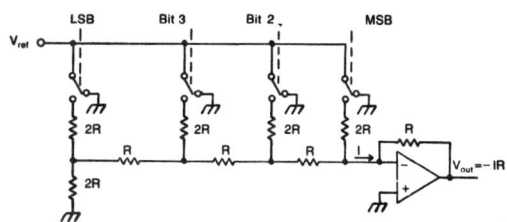

**R-2R resistance ladder**

**RWI** Abbreviation for *read or write initialize*.

**R/W RAM refresh** Dynamic R/W RAMs require refreshing. The refresh process can create problems in I/O-to-memory and CPU-to-memory interaction. The balancing of the CPU, asynchronous-memory refresh, and real-time semiasynchronous I/O memory bandwidth demands must be solved in the system design.

**R/W RAM volatility** Refers to the volatility of the data in R/W semiconductor RAMs. While the problem can be overcome with a battery backup power subsystem, the cost, complexity, and inconvenience of such a subsystem can prohibit its use.

**RX** Abbreviation for *receiver*.

**RY** Abbreviation for *relay*.

**RZ** Abbreviation for *return to zero*.

# S

**S** 1. Abbreviation for *store*. 2. Abbreviation for *spool*.
**SABRE** Abbreviation for *secure airborne radar equipment*.
**SAC** Abbreviation for *store and clear*.
**safeguard timer** A system for fault detection. Here a hardware timer is run continuously; it is periodically reset if nothing delays the main program within its appointed window of time. If an error causes the main program to be delayed, the timer is not reset, and an error is detected.
**SAM** Abbreviation for *surface to air missile*.
**sample and hold** A circuit used to increase the interval during which a sampled signal is available by maintaining an output equal to the most recent input sample.
**sample hold acquisition time** The time in a sample and hold from when the sample command is given to the point when the output enters and remains within a specified band around the input value. At the end of the acquisition time, the output is tracking the input.
**sample hold amplifier** The use of a sample hold amplifier can increase the system data acquisition throughput rate and increase the highest frequency signal that can be encoded within the converter resolution.

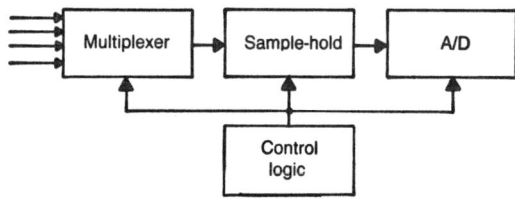

**Data acquisition system with sample hold**

System throughput rate, without the sample hold, is determined mainly by the multiplexer's settling time and the a/d conversion time.
**sample hold aperture time** The time between the hold command and the point at which the sampling switch is completely open. Also called turn off time.
**sample hold aperture uncertainity time** The variation in the aperture time. The difference between the maximum and minimum aperture times.
**sample hold applications** In data acquisition systems, sample holds are used either to hold fast signals during conversion or to store multiplexer outputs while the signal is being converted and the multiplexer is seeking the next channel. In analog data-reduction, they are used to determine peaks or valleys, establish amplitudes, and allow computations involving signals obtained at different times.
**sample hold characteristics** An ideal sample and hold, or *zero order hold* as it is also called, takes a sample in zero time and then holds the value of the sample indefinitely with perfect accuracy. In practical devices, a sample is taken in a time period that is short compared to the holding time. During the holding time there is some change in the output that may effect the system accuracy. The effect on a continuous analog input signal can be determined by finding the transfer function of the sample hold. By use of the impulse response of the device and the Laplace transform method, the transfer function is found for the ideal sample hold:

$$G(jw) = \frac{2\pi}{w_s} \frac{\sin \pi w/w_s}{\pi w/w_s} e^{-j\pi(w/w_s)}$$

where T is the sampling period and $w_s$ is the sampling frequency. The

269

magnitude and phase of this function are shown below. This shows that the sample hold acts like a low-pass filter with a cutoff frequency of approximately $f_s/2$ and a phase delay of $T/2$, or on half the sampling period.

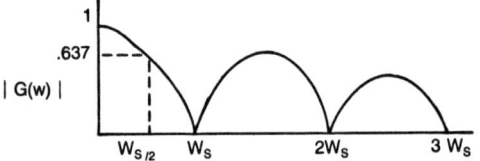

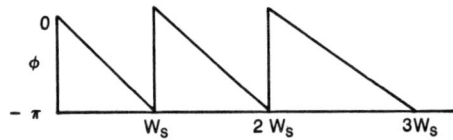

Sample-hold transfer function

**sample hold decay rate** The change in output voltage with time in the hold mode.

**sample hold devices** The sample hold is a device with a signal input, an output, and a control input. It has two operating modes: the hold mode and the sample, or track mode, in which it acquires the input signal and tracks it until commanded to hold, at which time it retains the value of the input signal at the time the control mode changed. Sample holds are also known as *track holds* if a large portion of time has been spent in the sample mode tracking the input. Sample holds normally have unity gain and are noninverting. The control inputs are usually TTL-compatible. Logic 1 is usually the sample command, and logic 0 the hold command.

A sample and hold in its basic form consists of a switch and a capacitor. When the switch is closed, the unit is in the sampling or tracking mode and will follow the changing input signal. When the switch is opened, the unit is in the hold mode and retains a voltage on the capacitor for a period of time, depending on capacitor size and leakage resistance. Practical sample hold circuits may also use input and output buffer amplifiers along with sophisticated switching techniques. The output buffer amplifier should be a low input current FET amplifier in order to have a small effect on leakage of the capacitor. The electronic switch used should also have a low leakage.

**sample hold feedthrough** The amount of input signal appearing at the output when the unit is in the hold mode. Feedthrough varies with signal frequency and is sometimes expressed as an attentuation in dBs.

**sample hold settling time** The time from the command transition until the output has settled within a specified error band around the final value.

**sampled data** Data in which the information content can be, or is, ascertained only at discrete intervals of time.

**sampling** 1. Obtaining the values of a usually analog function by making automatic measurements of the function at periodic intervals. Each sample thus obtained becomes a digital value and is processed with digital circuitry. 2. A representative value of a population of values.

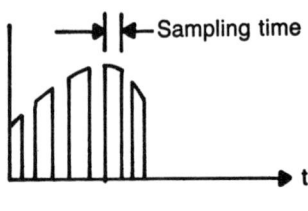

Sampled date

**sampling gate** A device activated by a selector pulse usually to extract instantaneous-value information for a system.

**sampling oscilloscope** An oscilloscope in which the input waveform is sampled at successive points along the waveform instead of being monitored continuously.

**sampling period** The time between observations in a periodic sampling system.

**sampling thermocouple** This has the means for collecting samples of the gas stream at two or more locations and mixing the samples at the thermocouple junction so that an average temperature will be indicated.

**sapphire** A material used as a substrate for some types of integrated-circuit chips.

**sapphire substrate** The substrate used in silicon-on-sapphire (SOS) MOS chips. Silicon-on-sapphire chips have reduced parasitics and permit tighter geometries for high-speed applications.

**satellite** 1. A computer used to relieve a larger computer of simple but time-consuming tasks, such as editing and compiling. 2. An earth-orbiting usually electronic system for scientific, defense, or communications operations, observations, or measurements.

**satellite computer** 1. A computer connected to a larger computer and performing simple tasks or time-consuming operations. A satellite computer is usually subordinate to the central processor and sometimes independent. 2. An earth-orbiting system consisting principally of a usually dedicated computer or processor.

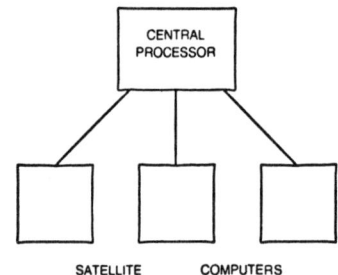

Satellite computer system, 1

**satellite, synchronous** Refers to satellites with an orbital period equal to the time of rotation of the earth on its axis and launched so that they remain directly above the same geographical point on the earth's surface. This facilitates the control of the antenna assemblies of ground stations operating in conjunction with the satellite.

**SATIN** Abbreviation for *SAGE air traffic integration*.

**SATIRE** An automated information retrieval system. It can be tailored to the needs of the individual user and can also be utilized from remote locations by means of computers.

**saturated molecule** One in which each bond of every atom in the backbone of the molecule holds another atom.

**saturating integrator** Refers to a digital integrator modified so that the output increment is maximum negative, zero, or maximum positive, according to whether the value of the input is negative, zero, or positive. Same as an incremental integrator.

**saturation** 1. In an amplifier, a condition in which an increase in the input signal no longer produces a significant change in the output. 2. The condition of maximum signal-carrying ability in any medium.

**saturation current** The current that flows between the base and collector of a transistor when an increase in the emitter-to-base voltage causes no further increase in the collector current.

**saturation limiting** Limiting the maximum output of an active device by operating the device in the region of saturation. When the input signal increases, saturation occurs immediately and the output is held at approximately the value of saturation.

**saturation noise** 1. Extra bits or words that can be removed or ignored before the data is used without affecting the data represented. 2. Errors introduced into a system due to disturbances occurring when the signal-carrying medium is at saturation.

**saturation point** The point (in an amplifier) beyond which an increase in input signal magnitude produces no further increases in output signal magnitude. This is in contrast to the *cutoff point*, where usually negative-going signal inputs in excess of the cutoff-point value cause the amplifier to shut off momentarily. Linear amplifiers are operated in the relatively linear region between the two extremes.

**sawtooth** A triangular waveform consisting of a fairly linear voltage or current ramp of ascending value that returns abruptly to the original value.

**sawtooth generator** An oscillator-type circuit used to produce a sawtooth waveform, usually at some specific frequency or within a specific frequency range.

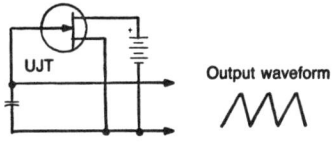

Sawtooth generator

**sawtooth wave** A signal composed entirely of a recurring sawtooth. Also called *sawtooth waveform*.

**sawtooth waveform** A sawtooth wave such as the type used to establish the timebase in a cathode-ray oscilloscope.

**SBT** Abbreviation for *surface barrier transistor*.

**SC** Abbreviation for *shift control*.

**scalar** Having a value that may be plotted on a graduated scale.

**scalar product** The product of two quantities that itself has magnitude but no direction. In the example:

FORCE × DISTANCE = WORK

two vector quantities produce the scalar product, work.

**scalar quantity** A quantity that has magnitude without direction, such as a real number.

**scale** 1. A range of values usually dictated by the computer word length or the routine being processed. 2. To change the units of a variable so that the quantity may be measured by a system whose limits are in a different range. Scaling can bring the values of a variable within the bounds required by register size or other factors. 3. Any value range that permits identification of any incremental value within that range, as a *temperature scale*.

**scale factor** A value used to convert the magnitude of a variable to a usable value in another range or to convert from one notation to another. Scale factors are often used to adjust the radix point so that the significant digits occupy specified positions in a word or register.

**scaler** 1. A unit that produces an output equal to the input multiplied by a constant. 2. A converter used at the input of a device (such as a frequency meter) to bring the quantity being measured to within the range of measurement of the instrument (a *frequency scaler*, for example).

**scale span** The algebraic difference between the values of the actuating electrical quantity that corresponds to the two ends of the scale of an instrument.

**scaling** 1. The changing of a quantity from one notation to another, or from one value range to another, using scale factors. 2. Refers to the uniform reduction of dimensions in integrated circuit fabrication.

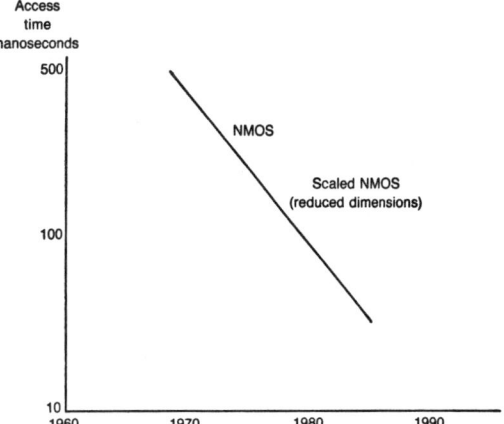

The effect of scaling on dynamic MOS RAM speed

**scamp** Loose acronym for a small cost-effective microprocessor. Addresses are generated by four 16-bit pointer registers with processor timing generated on the chip.

**scan** 1. To examine sequentially using a part-by-part technique. 2. The successive trace-and-flyback operation required to produce a raster or image on a TV screen.

**scanner** A device that samples or interrogates the state of a process or processes, including files and physical conditions. It then may initiate action or cause another device to initiate action based upon the information obtained. A typical scanner might connect a specified sensor to measuring or monitoring equipment for transmission to the processor.

**scanner, analog point** Refers to a device that will, upon command, connect a specified sensor to measuring equipment and cause the generation of a digit count value that can be read by the computer.

**scanning rate** The speed per unit time at which a scanner operates. Also called *scan rate*.

**scan rate** The rate or speed at which a scanner operates.

**scan, sensor** Refers to a type of sequential interrogation of lists of information or devices under process control. This develops a collection of data from process sensors by a computer for use in calculations, usually through a multiplexer.

**SCAR** Abbreviation for *submarine celestial altitude*.

**scattering** A phenomenon in which waves or particles are reflected or dispersed irregularly, such as in acoustic waves in an enclosure leading to a diffuse reverberant sound.

**scattering loss** The loss of energy from a beam of radiation as a result of various scattering processes arising either at a surface of discontinuity or in the medium traversed.

**scatter load** A method of loading a program into main memory such that each section occupies a single connected memory area without the sections being adjacent to one another. The sections are usually a page, and the system is usually implemented with a virtual memory structure.

**scatter loading** The process of loading a program into main memory using pages which are not adjacent.

**scatter read** The ability to distribute data into several memory areas as it is being entered into the system from magnetic tape.

**SCE** Abbreviation for *single cycle execute*.

**scheduled maintenance** Maintenance that is carried out in accordance with an established plan.

**schematic** A diagram that uses symbols to show components and their interconnections for a system or circuit.

**schematic diagram** A diagram that shows the scheme of a circuit or system using graphic symbols. A schematic diagram permits tracing of circuit and flow paths for continuity; a *schematic*.

**Schmitt limiter** A bistable pulse generator that gives a constant amplitude output pulse provided that the input voltage is greater than a predetermined value.

**Schmitt trigger** A monostable circuit that has a sensitive, accurate, and stable trigger level.

**Schmitt trigger circuit** A circuit that acts as a one-shot multivibrator with an accurate and stable trigger level. It is often used to restore pulses and pulse information.

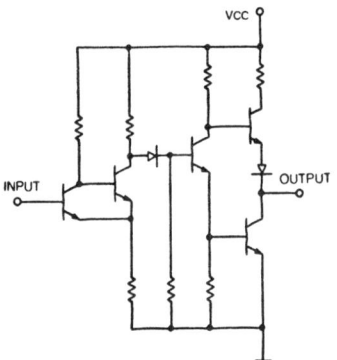

**Schmitt trigger circuit**

**Schmoo plot** A graphical representation of the relative output parameter failure condition resulting from varying two input parameters at the same time. This graph facilitates the establishment of an operating envelope within which input parameters may be varied without resulting in circuit or system failure due to parameter interdependence.

**Schottky** Rectifying metal semiconductor contacts were discovered and investigated by Ferdinand Braun in 1874. Despite many attempts to understand their current flow mechanism, the correct physical model was not discovered until half a century later by Walter Schottky. Researchers at Bell Labs in the late forties were investigating metal semiconductor interfaces when they accidentally discovered the transistor. From then on, most efforts in the semiconductor industry have been directed toward pn-junction devices. Only in the recent past have manufacturers gained the understanding of surface phenomena and developed the metallization techniques required to produce reliable Schottky barrier diodes.

**Schottky barrier** 1. In a hot-carrier diode, the metal-semiconductor junction. 2. Hot-carrier diode junctions incorporated into some TTL devices to increase switching speed (transit times) and reduce system noise.

**Schottky bipolar** TTL devices that use a Schottky clamping diode to prevent transistor saturation and improve switching speeds. With the use of integrated Schottky diodes, the saturation delay normally encountered is avoided. The process is simple and does not have a significant effect upon manufacturing costs.

**Schottky bipolar latch** A latch circuit designed with the Schottky TTL process. It is used where high speed is important.

**Schottky bipolar look-ahead carry** A high-speed circuit capable of anticipating a carry across the central processing array. In systems with multiple arrays, the carry circuit can provide high-speed look-ahead capability for any word length.

**Schottky bipolar memory** A memory that uses Schottky barrier diodes to obtain fast switching speeds. Their high speed makes them ideal for scratchpad applications.

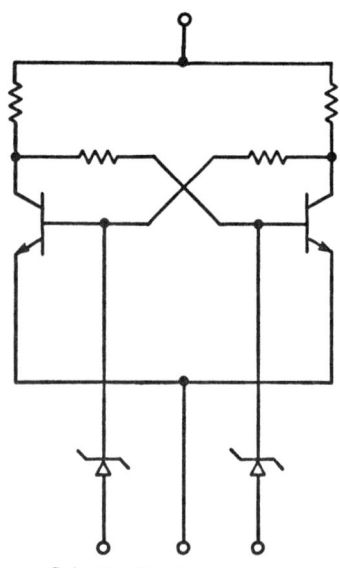

**Schottky bipolar memory**

**Schottky bipolar microcomputer** A set of bipolar chips designed with the Schottky bipolar process for high speed. A typical microcomputer set of this variety includes:

1. Central processing elements
2. Bipolar PROM
3. Microprogram control units

Schottky bipolar microcomputer chips can be much faster than available MOS chips. The chips allow a design that is fast, but smaller and less expensive than equivalent designs using SSI or MSI integration.

**Schottky bipolar read-only memory** A ROM that is manufactured using Schottky barrier diode clamped transistors, which allows higher switching speeds than those devices made with a conventional gold diffusion process.

**Schottky-clamped transistor** A bipolar transistor that is limited by a Schottky diode to prevent saturation and improve switching speeds.

**Schottky diode** A hot-carrier diode that has a short recovery time and a low forward-voltage drop. It is formed by the metal-to-semiconductor contact at the surface of the crystal.

**Schottky effect** Refers to the increase of saturation with an increasing potential gradient near the cathode.

**Schottky process** The manufacturing process used to produce Schottky diodes in bipolar circuits. The process is simple and does not have significant effects upon manufacturing costs.

**Schottky TTL** TTL devices that use Schottky diodes for improved speed performance.

**Schottky TTL memory** A memory made with Schottky diodes used to isolate the transistor bases.

**Schottky II** A TTL process that uses ion-implanted techniques and minimum geometry to extend the performance of Schottky devices into the 1 ns range. A Schottky II microprocessor chip set with a cycle time of 50 ns is available.

**SC/MP** Abbreviation for *simple cost-effective microprocessor*, a microprocessor developed by National Semiconductor.

**SC/MP applications** A simple SC/MP system can be constructed with three integrated circuit packages as shown below. The timing capacitor is connected to the CPU for clock timing and a ROM, and RAM completes the system along with the power source. This system has three serial data input ports and four serial data output ports, for applications like games, traffic controls, simple industrial controllers, appliances, and vending machines.

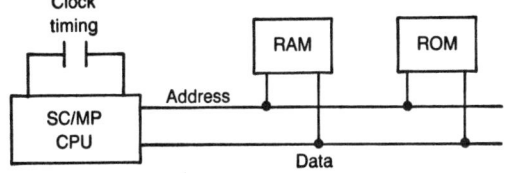

**Basic SC/MP microcomputer system**

**SC/MP expansion** The input/output capability of the SC/MP unit may be increased by adding the three CMOS devices shown below. To increase the number of serial data input and output ports, the following has been added: a hex D flip-flop, an 8-channel digital multiplexer, and a 1-to-8 demultiplexer.

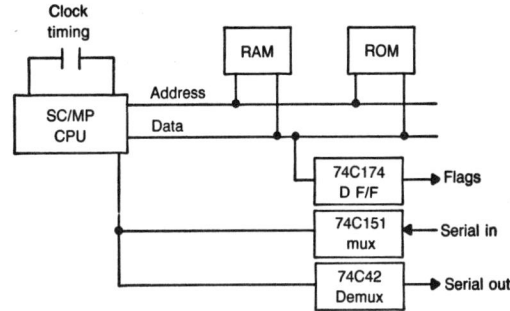

**Expanded SC/MP microcomputer system**

This system has four latched control flags and can address 4K bytes of memory. It can be used to implement industrial controls with up to eight loops or complex traffic controllers.

**SC/MP multiprocessing** The SC/MP chip has two control lines that allow implementation of a multiprocessor system. The CPUs are tied together through two enable control lines. When a CPU requires the bus, it requests access to the bus and then waits for a bus enable signal. Until the CPU receives this signal, it waits with its address and data busses in the high impedance state. This provides the user with the flexibility of adding extra processors to achieve additional throughput without changing the processor or software.

**SC/MP programmed delay** The SC/MP has a feature in its delay instruction that is useful in control interfaces. The delay instruction can be used to program delays for control input/output timing for an interface as shown below. For this serial interface, SIN is the receive data line and SOUT the send data line. A single control word communication contains a start bit, data bits, and a stop bit. The delay instruction may be used to cause a delay of time according to the formula:

$$\text{delay} = 13 + 2^* \text{ accumulator} + 514^* \text{ displacement}$$

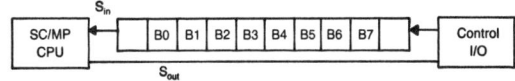

**SC/MP programmed timing delay**

**SC/MP II** The SC/MP II or INS8060 microprocessor is an NMOS version of the original SC/MP PMOS microprocessor.

**SCORE** Abbreviation for *signal communications by orbiting relay equipment*.

**SCR** Abbreviation for *silicon controlled rectifier*.

**scratchpad** A memory used to hold temporary results in a computer system. It is usually the fastest memory in the system.

**screen** 1. The face of a TV tube (video monitor) on which graphic or other visual material is displayed. 2. To sift or cull a collection of data or data elements for the purpose of extracting only those of use in a subsequent process or operation. 3. In a vacuum tube, a shielding grid positioned adjacent to the control grid (between control grid and anode) to reduce interelectrode capacitance.

**screen current** The electron current existing in the screen circuit of a vacuum tube.

**screen grid** See *screen, 3*.

**screen voltage** The voltage applied to the screen of a vacuum tube; it is usually of lower value than, but obtained from, the anode supply.

**SCT** Abbreviation for *subroutine call table*.

**SD** Abbreviation for *sample delay*.

**S/D converter** Abbreviation for *synchro-to-digital converter*.

**SDLC** Abbreviation for *synchronous data link control;* a standard protocol.

**SDO** Abbreviation for *source data operation*.

**SEA** Abbreviation for *Subterranean Exploration Agency*.

**sealed circuits** Refers to circuits that use components that are sealed in place.

**search** A function in word processing in which specific material is located in memory.

**search algorithm** An algorithm developed for minimizing the number of accesses needed to find an item in a random access memory. The time required to find an item in memory can be reduced if the stored data can be identified by the content of the data rather than the address.

**search procedure** The strategy for choosing a sequence of addresses, reading the content of memory at each address, and comparing the data read with the item being searched for until a match occurs.

**second** The international unit of time and equal to the duration of 9,192,631,770 periods of the radiation corresponding to the transition between the two hyperfine levels of the ground state of the cesium-133 atom.

**secondary** 1. Any output winding of any transformer that contains multiple windings. 2. Relating to the second order in a string of ordinally identified functions or values.

**secondary constants** Those constants for a transmission line that are derived from the primary constants. They are the characteristic impedance of the line and the propagation constants (attenuation and phase).

**secondary electrons** Refers to electrons that are emitted from a surface by electronic bombardment, as distinct from the primary bombarding electrons or photoelectrons.

**secondary emission** The phenomenon in which electrons bombarding the anode of a vacuum tube cause electrons to be dislogged from that electrode; the dislodged electrons comprise secondary emission.

**secondary grid emission** The electrons released by bombarding electrons; dependent on the surface of the grid material.

**secondary-level address** That portion of an instruction that indicates a location where the address of the referenced operand is to be found. Multiple levels of addressing can be terminated by control or by a termination symbol.

**secondary memory** A memory used to transfer large blocks of data into main storage; it usually has a large capacity, but a long access time.

**secondary winding** See *secondary*.

**second generation** 1. In the numerical control industry, the period of technology associated with transistors (solid state). 2. The period of technology in computer design utilizing solid state circuits, off-line storage and a significant development in software, the assembler.

**second-level addressing** A type of addressing in which instructions use a referenced location for the address of the operand.

**second-source** To manufacture a product designed, developed, and also produced by another manufacturer. Second-sourcing results from the reluctance of the government to purchase devices available from only one maker, and it had its birth when government specifications for devices and systems were written after prototype development.

**sector** The smallest addressable space on a disk's media. A sector is the evenly divided subsections on a track that hold the stored data or programs.

**seek** 1. The process of locating specific data in a random-access store. A seek refers to each memory location searched and the number of seeks determines the total search time. 2. To search a memory array.

**seek time** The time required to locate data in a direct-access storage device, including the time needed to position the access mechanism.

**see-trac** Doppler navigation for helicopters.

**segment** 1. To divide a routine into parts with each one capable of being completely stored in internal storage and containing the necessary instructions to jump to other segments. 2. A part of a routine short enough to be sorted entirely in the internal storage of a computer, yet containing the coding necessary to call in and jump to other segments. A segment can be placed anywhere in memory and addressed relative to a common origin. 3. One of the components of a single-character numeric or alphanumeric display. (See also *seven-segment display*.)

**segmentation overlays** A segment of a program is that portion of memory that is defined by a single reference to the loader. Usually a segment overlays some other segment and may have within itself other portions, called subsegments, that in turn overlay one another. That part of a segment that is actually brought into memory when the loader is referenced is called the fixed part of a segment. Segments are built up from separate relocatable elements, common blocks, or other segments.

**seising signal** Refers to a signal that is often translated at the start of a message to initiate a circuit operation at the receiving end of a circuit.

**selection check** A check that verifies the choice of devices in the execution of an instruction.

**selective dump** A dump of one or more desired storage locations. A selective dump is usually a library subroutine that is called when other programs are running and a dump is desired.

**selective fading** 1. Fading that unequally affects different frequencies within a specified band. 2. Fluctuation in which the components of a signal fade or decrease disproportionately, such as the rise and fall of only the high or low frequency components.

**selectivity** The degree of "narrowness" of a circuit's frequency response bandwidth. High selectivity implies high Q, narrow bandwidth, and single-frequency sensitivity. Low selectivity implies low Q, broadband response, and relatively uniform sensitivity over the response frequency range.

**selector** 1. A switching operation based on previous processing which allows a logical choice to be made in the program or system. 2. A mechanical multiposition switch. 3. Cursor.

**selector circuit** Refers to a circuit that selects a specified output, magnitude, waveform, amplitude, phase or frequency.

**selectric** An IBM trademark applied both to the company's interchangeable ball typing elements and to the entire mechanical assembly that activates the typing elements.

**selenium (Se)** Atomic number 34, atomic weight 78.96, specific gravity 4.81, melts at 217°C, boils at 685°C. A nonmetallic element that is a semiconductor and exists in a number of allotropic forms. One form becomes electrically conducting when irradiated with light.

**selenium rectifier** A rectifier that uses a barrier layer of crystalline selenium on an iron base.

**self-adapting** The ability of a system to change its performance characteristics in response to environmental changes.

**self-defining** Refers to terms in assembler programming with a value that is absolute and implicit in the specification of the term itself.

**self discharge** 1. The loss of capacity of a primary cell as a result of internal leakage. 2. The loss of charge from a capacitor due to finite insulation resistance between the plates.

**self induction** The property of an electric circuit or component by which it resists any change in the current flowing; Lenz's law.

**self-instructed carry** A carry process in which information is allowed to propagate to succeeding places as soon as it is generated, without requiring an external signal.

**self-organizing machine** A machine (abbreviated *SOM*) in which the internal organization is conducted by the machine itself, without external intervention.

**self-oscillation** Usually unwanted oscillation that is generated in a circuit as a result of inadvertent positive feedback, as through the interelectrode capacitance of an active device.

**self-powered** Containing an independent power source, as a special voltaic cell or group of cells.

**self-pulse modulation** A modulation that uses an internally generated pulse.

**self-relocating program** A program that can be loaded into any area of main storage that uses an initialization routine to adjust its address constants so that it can be executed at that location.

**self-resetting loop** A loop that contains instructions for restoring all locations affecting the operation of the loop to their initial condition upon entry of the loop.

**self-test techniques** These utilize the microcomputer in the system to test the system functions. Self-test employs time outs, start up routines, or other programs stored in a self-test ROM. Many simple products can easily be tested upon each reset or powerup. The self-test program can usually detect major faults in the system or its boards.

**semantic error** An error results from an ambiguous meaning in a program statement. Semantic errors are the responsibility of the programmer and can be removed by debugging prior to use of the program.

**semantics** The relationship between symbols and their intended meanings.

**semicompiled** Descriptive of a program converted from source language to object language but not called by the source program.

**semiconducting material** Intrinsic or extrinsic material, such as germanium and silicon, used in the manufacture of active solid-state devices.

**semiconductor** 1. A material with a conductivity between a metal and an insulator. 2. Any member of the class of devices constructed from a semiconductor. Semiconductors include diodes, transistors, and the complex integrated circuits that are fabricated from wafers of semiconducting material.

**semiconductor contact** Refers to the section of a semiconductor device where the interconnects for the leads are made.

**semiconductor device** See *semiconductor, 2.*

**semiconductor diode** A two-terminal semiconductor device with a pn junction possessing a nonlinear voltage-current characteristic.

**semiconductor doping** Refers to the adding of impurities to semiconductor materials to produce desired conducting characteristics.

**semiconductor functional blocks** Refers to the functional blocks that are used in microcomputer design. Not only are conventional parts of the CPU being integrated on LSI chips, but many specialized functions previously performed by software are being converted to hardware. Multiply operations, for example, can be done using LSI multiplier chips. These chips can multiply two 16-bit numbers in less than a microsecond.

**semiconductor integrated circuits** Complex single-package circuits fabricated from semiconductor wafers.

**semiconductor, intrinsic** Refers to a pure crystal of germanium or silicon that conducts electric currents due to the presence of mobile holes and electrons, but is not as efficient a conductor as is copper, silver, gold, and aluminum, in which the carrier density is much greater. Since the property is that of a pure crystal, it is called intrinsic.

**semiconductor junction** The region between $p$ and $n$ areas in a semiconducting material.

**semiconductor memory** A memory that uses semiconductors for data storage. A typical semiconductor memory is contained on a single circuit card and contains all refresh, control, and interface logic required to operate as a memory unit.

**semiconductor, n-type** Refers to a semiconductor crystal material that has been doped with small amounts of an impurity that will produce donor-type centers of electrons in the crystal lattice structure. Because electrons are negative particles, the material is called n-type, and conduction is primarily by electrons as the majority carriers.

**semiconductor, p-type** A semiconducting crystal material that has been doped with small amounts of an impurity that will produce acceptor-type centers in the crystal lattice structure. Since the main current carriers are positive particles, the material is called p-type. These carriers are called *holes* in the p-type semiconductors.

**semiconductor radiation detector** Under reverse voltage conditions semiconductor diodes are sensitive to ionization in the junction depletion layer and can be used as radiation counters or monitors.

**semiconductor RAMs** A semiconductor memory is a collection of storage registers, together with the circuits necessary for transferring information in and out of the registers. When the memory can be accessed for information as required, it is a random-access memory, or RAM. Sometimes these use a single line for the read/write control. One binary state specifies the read operation and the other state specifies the write operation. Enable lines are included in the IC to provide a means for accessing a single chip in a group of devices.

**semiconductor strain gage elements** Semiconductor strain gage elements are usually bonded or deposited so that the semiconductor foil and diaphragm appear as a single part. Semiconductor types feature larger output than wire types, but tend to be more temperature sensitive.

**semiconductor trap** Refers to the lattice defects in a semiconductor crystal that produce potential wells in which electrons or holes can be captured.

**semimetals** Material such as bismuth, antimony, and arsenic having characteristics between semiconductors and metals.

**semistor** A semiconductor resistor that uses the resistance of silicon.

**sense** The action required to examine or determine the arrangement of coded items, as in reading the holes in punched cards or tape; read.

**sense wire** A wire that carries the output signal in a magnetic core unit.

**sensing** The process of determining the state or condition of an item.

**sensing element** Refers to the specific portion of a device that is directly responsive to the value of the measured quantity.

**sensitive relay** A relay requiring only a small current, such as those used in photoelectric circuits.

**sensitivity** The relative response of a device to an incoming signal or stimulus. The sensitivity of a receiver is the minimum input signal required to produce a specified output signal.

**sensitivity analysis** A test or trial of a range of values at the input to determine the response and interdependence of the output values. Sensitivity analysis can be conducted using parametric programming in which parameters are allowed to vary in order to determine the solution of a problem.

**sensitivity ratio** The measured ratio of the change in output to the change in input that causes it.

**sensor** A transducer or other device that can be used to provide a quantity whose value is a measure of some physical phenomenon.

**sensor-based** Refers to systems whose primary function is to monitor physical processes using transducers or sensors.

**sensor-based computer** A computer designed to be used to receive real-time data from transducers or sensors that monitor a physical process. In a typical application, the computer might receive data from a pressure transducer or a flow meter, compare the data to required conditions, and then produce a signal to operate a control device.

**sensor-based system** A system whose primary source of data is from sensors and whose output can be used to control a physical process.

**sentinel** A character or indicator used to mark some condition, such as the beginning or end of a word.

**separator** A specific character used for the demarcation of the logical boundary between items that can be considered as separate and distinct units.

**sequence** An orderly progression of items and the act of putting items into such a progression.

**sequence checking** A routine that checks every instruction executed and prints desired data. The printout may include coded instructions, the contents of registers, or transferred data.

**sequence counter** A hardware register used by the computer to remember the location of the next instruction to be processed.

**sequence number** A number identifying the relative location of blocks or groups of blocks on a magnetic tape.

**sequencer** A device or circuit used to trigger a predetermined series of events as a result of a specific action. The circuit selects the order of occurrence in accordance with the action to which it responds.

**sequence readout** A display of the number of the block of tape being read by the tape reader.

**sequencer register** A counter that is reset following the execution of an instruction to form a new memory address for locating the next instruction.

**sequence timer** A succession of time delay circuits arranged so that completion of the delay in one circuit initiates a delay in the following circuit.

**sequential access** A type of access in which items of information are available in an ordered progression regardless of the amount of information required.

**sequential-access storage** A form of storage in which the items of stored information are available in sequence regardless of the information desired.

**sequential alarm** A device that monitors a group of alarm contacts and signals a priority interrupt to the computer when an alarm condition occurs. The computer can then establish an alarm sequence based on current and previous information.

**sequential computer** A computer with built-in logic that executes instructions in a fixed sequence which can usually be overridden or changed by another instruction.

**sequential control** A control mode in which instructions are set up in an ordered progression and fed into the machine consecutively during the solution of the problem.

**sequential logic** A logic methodology in which the output state is determined by the previous state of the input.

**sequential sampling** A type of sampling inspection in which the decision to accept, reject, or inspect another unit is made following the sampling of each unit.

**serial** The time-sequential handling of individual items, such as the processing of a sequence of instructions one at a time. Serial transmission uses a time sequence for words with the same facilities required for successive parts.

**serial access** The sequential or consecutive transmission of data to or from storage.

**serial-access system** A computer system in which the access time is dependent upon the location of the data most recently obtained or placed into storage.

**serial adder** A device that adds two binary words one bit-pair at a time. The least significant digit is performed first, and the more significant digits are added in succession with carries until the sum is formed. Serial adders require less hardware but are slower than parallel units.

**serial computer** A computer that manipulates all bits of a word serially. It usually has a single arithmetic and logic unit.

**serial data controller** A typical serial data controller unit will provide a flexible interface for full duplex, synchronous or asynchronous serial communications. Both transmitter and receiver may be double buffered; the device is capable of data rates up to 250Kbps (synchronous) or 16Kbps (asyncrhonous). Data formatting, (bits per character, character framing, odd/even parity) is usually programmable under CPU control. Interrupt and/or direct memory access modes may also be selected.

**serial I/O port** This consists of two single-bit serial data buses linked to the serial input and serial output lines of a shift register, which is usually 16 bits long. The shift register is loaded or read via parallel input and output lines and shifted one bit at a time under software control. The serial I/O port is often used as a simple asynchronous serial data communications interface. The shift register performs parallel to serial and serial to parallel code conversions under programs control.

**serially reusable** Descriptive of a reusable program that is not necessarily reenterable. The same copy of the routine or program can be used by another task after the current use has been concluded in main memory.

**serial memory** A memory in which items are stored and obtained sequentially, one at a time. Serial memories are used in large-volume applications that require low cost and high reliability, such as CRT storage. A typical serial memory contains 20,000 words of ten bits each on a memory card. The system is expandable in capacity and word length by stacking memory cards.

**serial memory system** Refers to systems designed to meet the high-reliability and low-cost requirements of large volume storage and CRT refresh applications. These systems are available as self-contained memory units or as units that can be expanded to virtually any size in either word or bit length through the use of additional memory cards. They are designed for the replacement of small fixed head disk systems and for CRT refresh applications.

**serial operation** 1. Computer operation in which numbers are processed one character at a time. 2. The flow of information in time sequence.

**serial-parallel** The property of being partially serial and partially parallel, such as serial by character and parallel by bits that make up the character.

**serial-parallel converter** A unit designed for changing data in serial

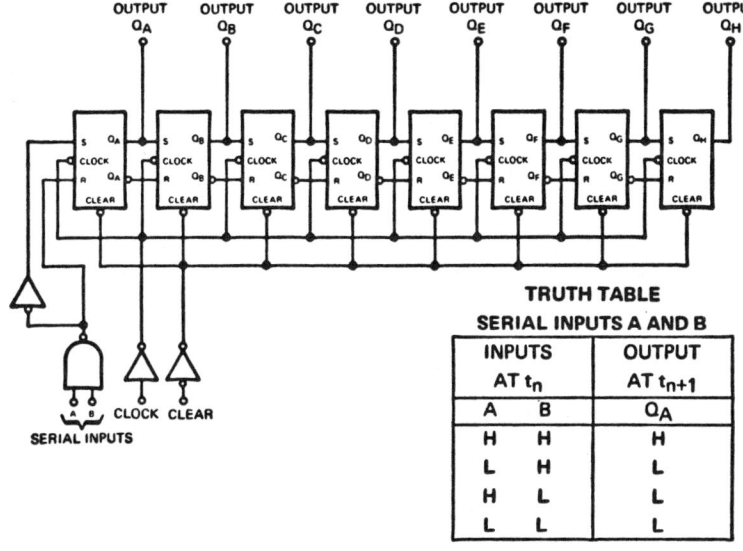

Serial-parallel register

format to parallel format. A typical unit allows full-duplex operation between a CPU and a remote location. The modules are used in pairs, with one at the central processor and the other at the remote location.

**serial-parallel register** A shift register that can be used to perform serial-to-parallel data conversion.

**serial programming** Programming in such a way that only one arithmetic or logical operation can be executed at one time.

**serial storage** Storage in which one of the storage parameters is in time sequence. Storage in which words appear one after another is *serial-by-word*. Bits that must appear in time sequence are found in serial-by-bit systems. Devices such as magnetic drums may be part serial and part parallel.

**serial transfer** Data transfer in which the characters of information flow in sequence over a single path.

**serial transmission** A sequential transmission of characters or items of data over a single path.

**serial work flow** A system of operations in which each operation is performed singly, and not at the same time when other tasks are being operated on. The work moves along a single line or path where each operation is performed at a station, with none being performed at the same time.

**series** 1. The condition of being wired so that a single current flows through several devices. 2. A set of related terms in a mathematical expression. 3. A group. 4. Appearing in a string of individual but related items or values.

**series circuit** A circuit in which a single current value flows through all elements sequentially.

**series interface board** A circuit board designed to allow custom interfaces to be used with different types of series memory systems.

**series-parallel circuit** A circuit that contains branches that are connected in both series and parallel configurations.

**series-parallel network** 1. A network in which successive branches are connected in series and/or in parallel. 2. One in which the electrical components are composed of branches that are successively connected in series and/or parallel.

**series resistor** Refers to a resistor used for adapting an instrument or device so that it will operate on some designated voltage or voltages. It forms an essential part of the voltage circuit and may be either internal or external to the device.

**service organization** A company that offers contract maintenance and operation of computers.

**service routine** A routine in general support of the operation of a computer. Service routines are designed to assist in the maintenance and operation of the computer as well as for the preparation of programs. Service routines include monitoring and supervisory routines and are generally standardized to meet the needs at a particular installation for a wide variety of programs.

**servo** A system in which electrical signals are used to produce mechanical movement in a remote device, wherein the rate and direction of motion are represented by specific signal characteristics.

**servo link** Refers to a mechanical power amplifier that permits low strength signals to operate control mechanisms that require larger power.

**servomechanism** A feedback control system in which at least one of the system signals represents a mechanical motion.

**servomechanism, rate** A servomechanism in which the mechanical shaft is translated or rotated at a rate proportional to an input signal.

**servomotor** A motor in a servo system that is controlled by a corrective electric signal.

**servomotor controller** A microcomputer-based unit capable of running multiaxis dc servomotor-controlled machines. It is usually controlled by a tape reader that accepts commands in ASCII format. The microcomputer reads an encoder on the motor and calculates motor speeds and positions, allowing precise control with programmable variables.

**servo multiplier** An analog device capable of multiplying several different variables by a single variable or constant.

**servo system** An automatic control system that compares an actual mechanical position with a desired position and generates an error signal to adjust the control element in accordance with this difference.

**set** To place a storage device into a desired state. 2. A collection of values or items, such as all even numbers or positive integers. 3. An equipment system.

**set breakpoint** A command that causes a breakpoint to be set in a specified location.

**set point** Refers to the value of a variable to which specific control actions, such as alarms or process changes, are desired.

**set-point control** A control system that operates from commands or information from variable set points in the system or process.

**set symbol** A variable symbol used in assembler programming to communicate values during conditional assembly processing.

**set theory** The mathematical study of groups, sets, and elements.

**settling time** The time required for a signal to attain a final value within a specified fraction of full scale.

**seven-segment display** A single-character readout with seven individually addressable segments that are illuminated selectively to form numerals and other symbols.

**sexadecimal digit** A digit that is a member of the following group when used as a radix-16 system:

0, 1, 2, 3, 4, 5, 6, 7, 8, 9, A, B, C, D, E, F

Also called *hexadecimal digit*.

**sexadecimal notation** A notation using the base of sixteen. Also called *hexadecimal notation*.

**SF** 1. Abbreviation for *shift forward*. 2. Abbreviation for *signal frequency*. 3. Abbreviation for *skip flag*.

**SFM** Abbreviation for *semiconductor functional module*.

**SG** Abbreviation for *symbol generator*.

**shaft encoder** A simultaneous data converter in which all bits appear at once and can be read in parallel at any one time. There is an equivalent form of simultaneous a/d converter having a Gray code output. It uses a chain of biased comparators and the outputs provide a quantized indication of the analog input level. All comparators above are 0 and all comparators below are 1. Logic gates are used to obtain the parallel Gray code output. Such converters are fast, being capable of 10 million conversions per second. But they require a number of comparisons that is a geometric function of the required resolution, as well as large numbers of logic gates.

**Shannon equation** An expression in information theory that gives a theoretical limit to the rate of transmission of binary digits with a given bandwidth and signal/noise ratio.

**shaped card potentiometer** Refers to a function generator for functions of one variable, in which the input variable sets the angular position of a potentiometer shaft.

**shared logic** Term applied to a system in which several terminals simultaneously use the memory and processing powers of a single CPU.

**shared storage** The ability to share main storage between two processors. In shared storage, either machine can insert information into storage, and either machine can access the data and use it.

**sharing** 1. The use of a device for two or more purposes during the same time interval. 2. The apportionment of time intervals for different tasks by interlacing or interleaving.

**sheath** 1. An excess of positive or negative ions in a plasma, giving a shielding or space charge effect. 2. The covering on a cable. 3. The can protecting a nuclear fuel element.

**Sheffer stroke operation** Same as *NOT-BOTH operation, stroke operation, nonconjunction, NAND operation,* and *NOT-AND operation*.

**shell** 1. A shell-like magnet in which the magnetization is always normal to the surface and inversely proportional to the thickness. The strength of the shell is the product of magnetization and thickness of shell. 2. The theoretical concept of a double layer of poles; multitudinous magnetic dipoles that in general do not form a plane. 3. A pattern of orbital electrons surrounding the nucleus of an atom and characterized by quantum numbers.

**SHF** Abbreviation for *Superhigh Frequency:* 3,000-30,000 megahertz.

**shield** A screen or other housing of conducting material placed around devices to limit magnetic fields or noise from them. Also called shielding.

**SHIELD** Abbreviation for *Sylvania high intelligence electronic defense*. A system for aircraft protection against radar guided weapons that can lock-on to targets and destroy them.

**shielded-conductor cable** A cable in which the insulated conductor or conductors are enclosed in a conducting envelope or envelopes, with almost every point on the surface at ground potential or at some predetermined potential with respect to ground.

**shielded line** A transmission line that is enclosed in a conducting material to protect it from inadvertent signal pickup from stray radiation, or to protect adjacent circuits from radiation of the line.

**shielded pair** Refers to a balanced pair of transmission lines within a screen used to mitigate interference from outside.

**shielded transmission line** An unbalanced line used for the transmission of information. It possesses a known characteristic impedance and exhibits predictable properties of inductance, capacitance, and resistance.

**shielding** 1. The protection of circuits, components, and conductors from radiated interference by enclosing them with conducting material. 2. The physical barriers placed within the confines of a chassis to minimize interaction between separated stages or circuits.

**shift** To move digits or characters in a register to the right or left, either transferring the information or performing an arithmetical operation. If a register holds 8 digits:

23456789

a shift to the right produces

12345678

**shift, end around carry** A carry sent directly from the high-order position to the least-significant position in a machine operation.

**shift-in character** A code extension character (abbreviated *SI*) used to return a register to its prior state before shifting operations.

**shifting register** A register that is designed or adapted to perform shifts.

**shift instruction** A computer instruction that causes the contents of an accumulator register to shift to the right or the left. A right shift instruction is equivalent to dividing by two; a left shift instruction is equivalent to multiplying by two, or adding the contents of the register to itself.

**shift out** To move information within a register towards one end so as to clear the register.

**shift-out character** A code extension character (abbreviated *SO*) that can be used to replace one set of characters in a register with another set, or the null set.

**shift pulse** A pulse that initiates the shifting of characters in a register.

**shift register** A register for the short or long-term storage of serial or parallel data in which data may be shifted to the right or left, shifted out, and shifted in. A typical shift register operates at speeds of 5 MHz

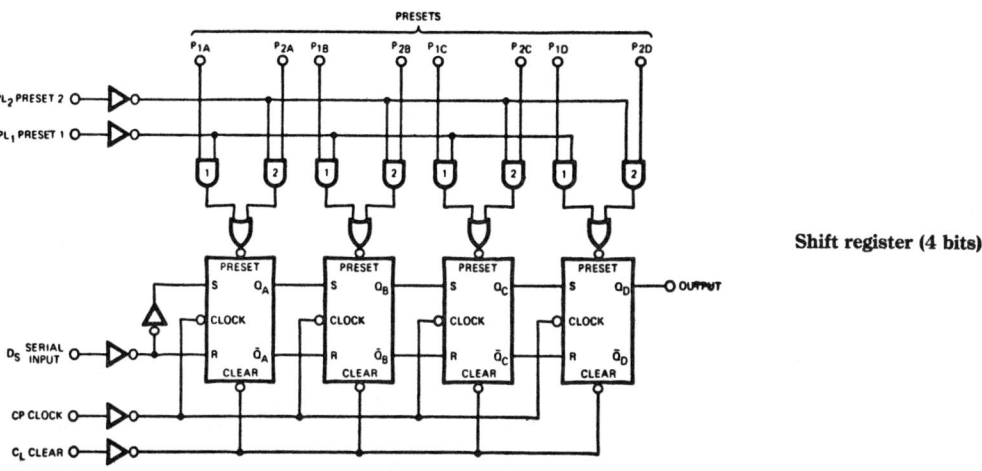

Shift register (4 bits)

from standard TTL voltage levels. It is composed of a series of flip-flops connected in tandem. Registers may be connected together to form larger memory units.

**shift register, flip-flop** Shift registers are made up of a number of flip-flops joined together in tandem or chain fashion. Each flip-flop is triggered at the same time by the same clock pulse, and this shifts the 0 and 1 states from one flip-flop to the next. In addition to shifting, individual flip-flops can be set. Their outputs are individually available. This means that data can be entered serially (shifted) or in parallel, and data can be taken from the shift register in either serial or parallel form.

**Shillelagh** Abbreviation for *surface to surface guided missile for antitank capability against heavy armor.*

**SHORAN** Abbreviation for *short range aid to navigation.*

**short circuit** 1. A direct resistance-free connection between two points in a circuit or system that normally are not connected or are not intended to be connected. 2. To cause a short circuit.

**short-circuit impedance** The input impedance of a device when the output or voltage source is shortcircuited.

**short circuit parameters** In an equivalent circuit of a device, the resultant parameter when independent device terminals are shorted.

**short code** A system of instructions that causes an automaton to behave as if it were another, specified automaton.

**shorted junction devices** This technology consists of two semiconductor junctions that appear as a high-impedance circuit of back to back diodes as shown.

Generally an npn double diffused transistor structure is used with only the emitter and collector contacts metallized. As shown below, the base is left open, forming the back to back diodes, $D_1$ and $D_2$. This structure is the result of an irreversible process that occurs on the migration of aluminum through silicon to the diffused junction. $D_2$ is reverse biased, and the large flow of electrons in the reverse direction causes aluminum atoms from the emitter contact to migrate through the emitter to the base, causing an emitter-to-base short. The avalanche technique requires a higher voltage and current than the fuse technique. The remaining junction is thus usable as a forward-based diode and represents a programmed data bit. Shorted junction devices are also referred to as the *AIM (Avalanche-Induced Migration)* technology.

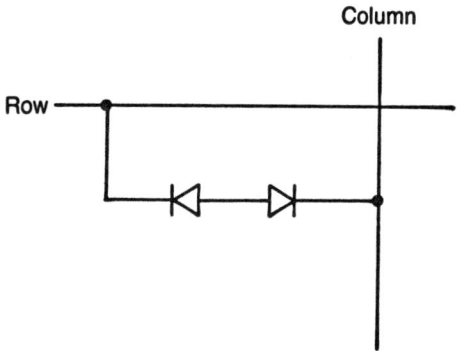

Shorted junction or AIM PROM cell

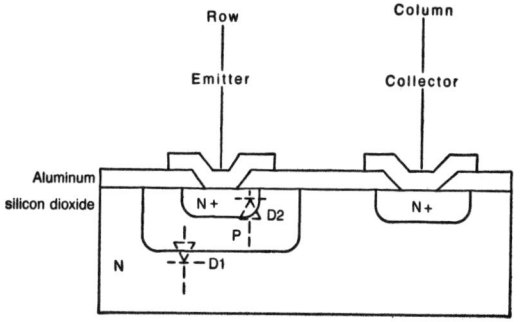

Shorted junction or AIM PROM cell structure

**shorted out** Made inactive by connecting a wire or other low resistance path around a device or portion of a circuit.

**short instruction** The standard one-word instruction format, as opposed to a multiple-word instruction.

**short stack** A stack of only a few bytes that is used to allow the monitor

**shot noise** program to store flags temporarily when interrupts occur. The short stack improves the interrupt handling capability of the microprocessor at minimal cost.

**shot noise** Noise that is generated as a result of the random passage of discrete carriers across a barrier or discontinuity such as a semiconductor junction.

**shunt** A precision low-value resistor placed across the terminals of a device to increase its range. 2. Any part connected in parallel with some other part; also the act of connecting such a part. 3. In an electric circuit, a branch the winding of which is in parallel with the external or line circuit. 4. The addition of a component to divert current in a known way. 5. The diversion of flux from the gap in a magnetic circuit by a magnetic slide or screw in a moving coil instrument.

**shunt leads** The leads that connect the circuit of an instrument to an external shunt. The resistance of these leads must be taken into account when the instrument is adjusted.

**SI** 1. The shift-in character. 2. Abbreviation for *International System of Units*.

**sidebands** The frequency bands on both sides of the carrier frequency. The frequencies of the wave produced by modulation fall within these bands. During amplitude modulation with a sine-wave carrier, the upper sideband includes the sum (carrier plus modulating) frequencies, and the lower sideband includes the difference (carrier minus modulating) frequencies.

**side circuit** Refers to a circuit arrangement for deriving a phantom circuit. In four-wire circuits, the two wires associated with the on-channel form one side circuit and those associated with the return-channel form another.

**side circuit repeating coil** Refers to a repeating coil which is designed to function as a transformer at a side circuit terminal. Often used as a means for superimposing one side of a phantom channel on that circuit.

**sides** The number of floppy disk sides that are used to record information on. The abbreviations used are *SS* for single-sided and *DS* for double-sided recordings.

**SIE** Abbreviation for *single instruction execute*.

**sign** 1. A symbol that distinguishes negative from positive quantities. 2. Flag.

**signal** The intelligence, message, or effect to be conveyed over a transferral system; it may be electrical, visual, or audible, and it is the event or phenomenon for conveying the data from one point to another.

**signal converter** A transducer that converts from one type of transmission signal to another.

**signal distance** The number of digit positions in which the corresponding digits of two words are different. Also called *Hamming distance*.

**signal element** The part of a signal that occupies the shortest interval of the signaling code.

**signal frequency noise** Refers to noise that lasts for a significant time period and is highly localized in frequency about some common reference.

**signal generator** An oscillator used to provide a test voltage over a wide range of frequencies.

**signal level** The magnitude of a waveforms or pulse trains voltage amplitude, either absolute or with respect to a reference value. Often expressed in decibels.

**signal power** An expression of the absolute signal strength at a specific point in a circuit.

**signal processor** A device that performs complex processing of waveforms for analysis and transmission. A typical signal processor is used with a host computer to provide the functions of a fast Fourier transform processor, array processor, display processor, and voice processor.

**signal pulse-repetition** The basic frequency or pulse repetition rate of a signal has no intrinsic intelligence until it is modulated by another signal that does have intelligence. A signal may be amplitude, phase, or frequency modulated; for example, an 8-MHz sound wave carrier can be amplitude or pulse modulated by a 1-MHz pulse code signal; the presence or absence of a pulse determines whether a one or a zero is present in the binary number being represented.

**signal strength** The strength of the signal produced by a transmitter or other device at a particular location. Usually it is expressed in millivolts per meter.

**signal-to-noise ratio** The ratio of the magnitude of the signal to the magnitude of the noise at the same point when the signal is removed, and usually expressed in decibels.

**signal tracing** The methodological following of a signal path in hardware or on diagrams in order to locate faults.

**signal transducer** Refers to a transducer designed to convert one standard transmission signal to another.

**signature analysis** A testing technique that uses a test mode or pattern to exercise a digital system. Four hex digits can be used to represent a pattern for 16 bits. A test sequence will use these signatures within a certain window of time at a desired clock rate to detect timing related faults.

There are several basic methods that can be used for isolating faults using digital signatures. The signal can be traced from the point of application to the output. As the test point moves, the signature will change at a particular point. The faulty component is then one of the devices connected to the point at which the signature change appears.

**sign bit** A binary digit occupying the sign position in a word to give the value direction.

**sign control flip-flop** Refers to a specific flip-flop that is used to store the algebraic sign of numbers.

**sign digit** A character used to designate the algebraic sign of a number.

**Signetics 2650** A single chip 8-bit microprocessor that uses the ion implanted n-channel silicon gate process. It has 576 bits of ROM and about 250 bits of registers.

The 2650 architecture is shown. Instructions are read in the CPU from the data bus and loaded into the instruction holding and data bus registers. The instructions are decoded using ROM along with decode logic.

The ALU can be used for Boolean and combinatorial shifts as well as arithmetic operations. It operates in a parallel mode on eight-bit words using a carry look ahead system. The address adder is used for incrementing the instruction address register and calculating the operand addresses for the indexed and relative addressing modes. A general purpose stack and subroutine stack for return addresses are mechanized with RAM. The general purpose stack may hold up to eight 15-bit addresses for eight-level nesting operations. Separate 15-bit registers for instruction and operand addressing are used.

**Signetics 2650 instructions** About 40 percent of the 2650's 75 instructions apply to arithmetic, another 30 percent apply to branch operations, and the remaining instructions are used for input/output operations and status. Automatic incrementing and decrementing of index registers is allowed using the arithmetic indexed instructions. All branch instructions except those for indexed branching are condi-

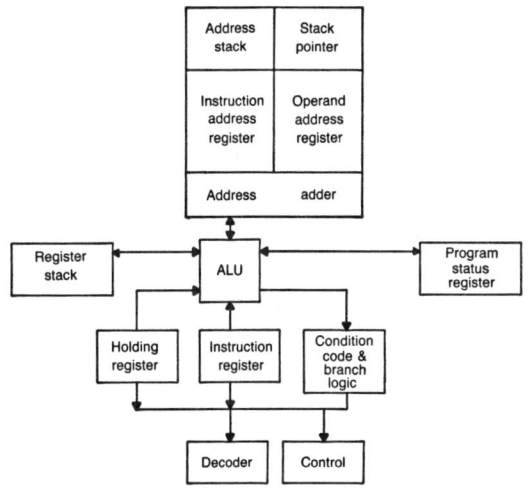

**2650 architecture**

tional. The register-to-register instructions are one byte long, and register-to-memory instructions are two or three bytes long. The register to memory instructions may use either immediate or relative addressing modes.

**significance** The weighting factor in positional representations which is dependent on the digit place and by which a digit is multiplied to obtain its additive contribution in the representation of a number.

**sign magnitude bipolar d/a conversion** A type of digital-to-analog conversion in which the converter's current output can be inverted, and circuitry controlled by the MSB determines if the output amplifier's input is direct or through the current inverter. One technique is shown.

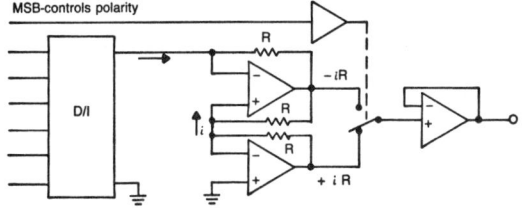

**Sign magnitude bipolar D/A converter**

**sign position** In an array of binary digits, the position that contains an indication of the algebraic sign of a number.

**SIL** Abbreviation for *speech interference level*.

**silica gel** A moisture absorbent chemical used for dehydrating wave guides, coaxial lines, pressurized components, shipping containers, and other equipment.

**silicon** A nonmetallic element having semiconducting properties; it is widely used in the manufacture of active electronic devices.

**silicon controlled rectifier** A three-junction rectifying device (abbreviated *SCR*) that is triggered by means of a voltage applied to a gate terminal. The SCR is a member of the *thyristor* family of devices, which includes diacs, triacs, and a variety of 4-layer diodes.

**silicon diode** A rectifying device that uses silicon as the semiconducting material.

**silicon dioxide** In MOS device manufacturing, the layer used to insulate the metal gate from the $p$ or $n$ regions.

**silicon-gate CMOS** A complementary MOS technology that allows high packing density with good speed performance and noise immunity along with low power dissipation. The internal logic structure for a microprocessor using this technology is fully static, which allows the clock to be stopped between instructions, cycles, and minor cycles. It requires only a single supply, and all signals are TTL compatible.

**silicon link PROMs** Silicon link PROMs use notched strips of polycrystalline silicon material. Programming of these polysilicon fuses involves melting the links using a mechanism similar to that in metal fuses. During programming, a current of 20-30 mA is used to blow the fuse link. This current generates heat estimated at 1400 °C. At this temperature, the silicon oxidizes, forming an insulating material around the open link. The use of silicon results in the absence of contact problems or difficulties caused by the use of a dissimilar material. Additionally, the use of silicon eliminates the existence of conductive materials in the open gap between the formerly linked polysilicon fuse ends. Thus, growback is greatly reduced, although not completely eliminated.

**silicon nitride passivation** A semiconductor manufacturing process that involves use of a layer of silicon nitride to protect the surface of devices from ionic contamination. The silicon nitride layer is covered with a layer of phosphorous silicon dioxide. The double layer prevents both mechanical and ionic damage and enhances device reliability.

**silicon-on-sapphire** A semiconductor technology (abbreviated *SOS*) in which a thin layer is grown on a sapphire substrate; sections of it are then removed, leaving small silicon pads or islands that are made into MOS transistors. All standard MOS techniques can be used with SOS; and because the sapphire substrate is a nearly ideal insulator, parasitic capacitance and leakage are greatly reduced.

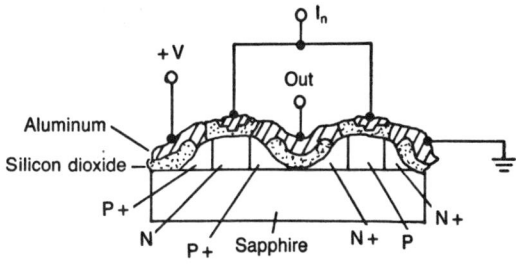

**SOS structure**

**silicon processing** Refers to the basic techniques of forming a dielectric layer on a semiconductor surface by thermally oxidizing a silicon surface. The low diffusion coefficients of most dopants in the resulting silicon dioxide and the task of etching without attacking the silicon itself are key factors in silicon processing. The silicon dioxide is not often a sufficient final passivation. Silicon nitride is often used because of its properties.

**silicon PROM fuse** In PROM programming, a fuse made of polycrystalline silicon, which is deposited in a thick layer during the manufacturing process. The fuse is used to selectively blow gating elements of the device to program it for a specific application.

**silicon rectifier** Refers to one or more silicon rectifying cells or cell assemblies.

**silicon resistor** A resistor of silicon material that has an almost constant positive temperature coefficient, making it suitable as a temperature sensing element.

**silicon solar cell** A photovoltaic cell that consists of a thin wafer of specially processed silicon designed to convert light energy into electrical energy.

**silicon steel** Steel containing three to five percent silicon, its magnetic qualities make it desirable for use in the iron cores of transformers and other ac devices.

**silicon transistor** A transistor formed from a silicon crystal, as opposed to a germanium transistor.

**silver mica capacitor** A high stability, low power factor fixed capacitor prepared by the vacuum deposition of silver on thin mica sheets.

**SIM** Abbreviation for *simulated*.

**simplex** A communications system or channel that is not capable of simultaneous transmission and reception.

**simplex circuit** A communications circuit derived from an existing two wire circuit by the use of a center-tapped repeating coil. This additional circuit must use another conductor or ground return to complete its path.

**SIMULA** Abbreviation for *simulation language*.

**simulate** To employ one system to duplicate the principal operational characteristics of another, using software to effect the simulation so that the imitating system accepts the same data, executes the same instructions, and performs the same operations.

**simulation** 1. The representation of physical systems by computers and models. 2. The technique of setting up a routine or program in one computer to make it simulate as nearly as possible the operational characteristics of another computer.

**simulation language** A language designed for the simulation of systems using computers. Simulation languages include *Simscript* and *GPSS* (general-purpose simulation system). They tend to have more comprehensive diagnostics than general-purpose languages such as FORTRAN or PL/1. Both Simscript and GPSS have an event monitor that tracks events and can be used for clocking.

**simulator** A program that can be used to emulate or imitate the operation of a given microprocessor. They are designed to execute object programs generated by a cross assembler on a machine other than the one being worked on. A simulator offers a powerful and flexible design support system which can reduce development time and allow products to get to market sooner.

A hardware simulator is a program which is usually stored in RAM which is used to simulate the execution of a test program, tracing its progress and detecting errors. It allows the user to interact with and modify the program in order to simplify the debugging process. A typical hardware simulator for a microprocessor comes complete with all timing details, breakpoints, and debug commands. Direct user control over RAM and register contents, interrupts, and input/output data is usually provided.

**simulator/debug utility** Refers to a program or routine that allows microcomputer programs to be simulated and debugged on other computers or prototype systems.

**simulator programs** These are special programs to emulate the execution of microprocessor programs. Most simulators are interpretive and provide bit-for-bit duplication of microprocessor instruction executing timing and register contents. Direct user control over the execution conditions is normally provided.

**simultaneity** The facility of a machine to allow input/output operations on peripherals to continue in parallel with operations in the central processor.

**simultaneous access** 1. Immediate access. 2. Parallel access.

**simultaneous computer** A computer that contains a separate unit to perform each portion of the computation concurrently. The units can be interconnected in a manner determined by the run.

**simultaneous I/O bus interface** I/O bus interfaces generally consist of drivers and receivers of the I/O bus. In many systems the I/O command register can simultaneously contain the I/O commands to control devices and buffer memories.

**simultaneous multichannel system** A data acquisition system in which a shared a/d converter with a multiplexer is used for switching among the outputs of a number of sample holds. As shown in the configuration, this is used in situations in which the sample holds must be updated rapidly or even simultaneously, and then read out in some sequence. It is usually a high-speed system, in which items of data indicating the state of the system must do so as at the same approximate time. Multiplexing may be sequential or may be done by some random addressing method. The sample holds must be relatively free from droop to avoid accumulating excessive errors while awaiting readout, which may be longer than in the case of a converter-per-channel circuit. Increased throughput can be obtained by using additional converters if desired. Typical applications that use this approach include wind tunnel measurements, seismographic experiments, and the testing of radar or fire control systems. Usually the event is a one

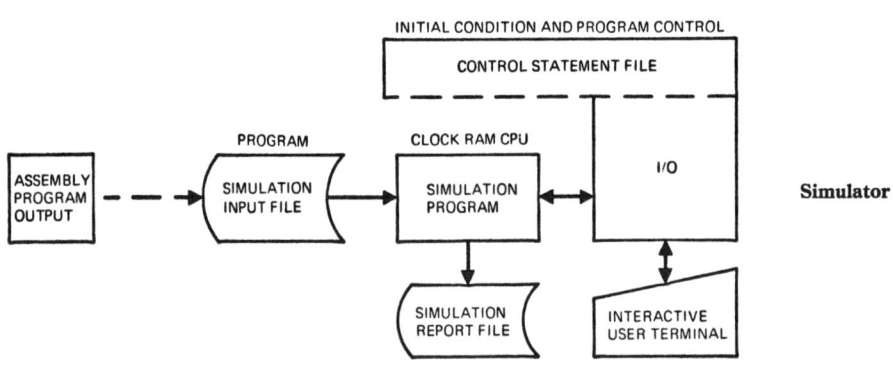

Simulator

time phenomenon, and the information is required at a critical time during the event, for example, when a ground shock or air blast hits the test specimen.

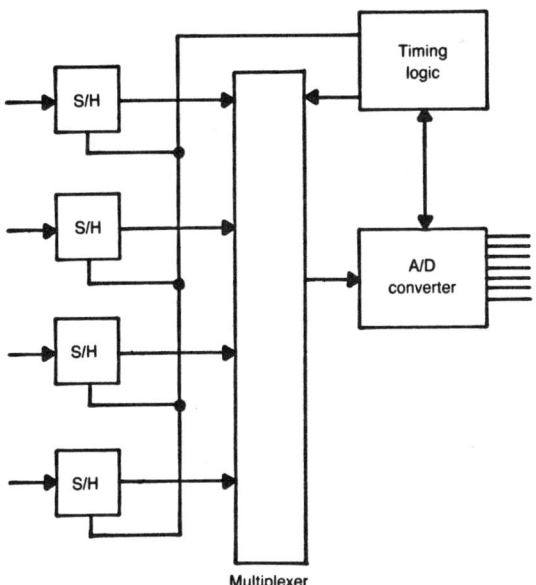

**Simultaneous multichannel system**

**simultaneous multiplication** If speed is essential, then one can perform multiplication in one step. A simultaneous type multiplier for multiplying four bits in approximately one bit time would use seven full adders and six half adders.

**simultaneous sample hold s/d converter** A circuit in which each input has its own pair of sample holds, and all samples are taken at the carrier peak as shown in the configuration.

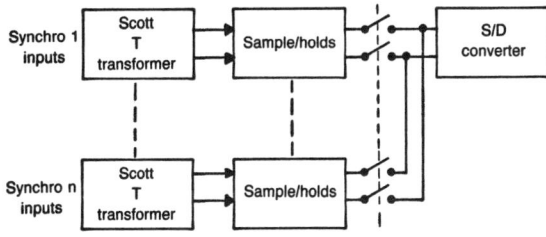

**Simultaneous sample-hold S/D converter system**

**sine** The sine of an angle of a right triangle is equal to the side opposite that angle divided by the hypotenuse (the long side opposite the right angle).

**sine injunction gate** Same as *gate, A AND NOT B* and *gate, B AND NOT A.*

**sine law** The law that states that the intensity of radiation in any direction from a linear source varies in proportion to the sine of the angle between a given direction and the axis of the source.

**sine potentiometer** A dc voltage divider (potentiometer), the output of which is proportionate to the sine of the shaft angle position.

**sine wave** A wave that is the sine of a linear function of time or space; a sinusoidal waveform.

**single and multiple passes** A single pass program generates the desired end result in one computer run. A multiple pass program generates intermediate outputs that require additional processing or loops to obtain the end result.

**single-bus operation** A microcomputer system that uses a single path or bus for all data transfers. Any device transmitting data can become bus master, while any device receiving data becomes a bus slave. Any master can transmit data to any slave without CPU intervention.

**single card connector** Usually refers to a 144 pin, two-piece connector, mounted in a sheet metal plate to simplify chassis mounting and to provide mechanical rigidity. The connector includes plastic alignment ears that simplify card insertion and provide some support for a circuit board.

**single card IEEE 488 bus interfaces** These boards link directly to the microcomputer bus. This relieves the microcomputer of some of the detailed transactions required to transfer blocks of data using this bus standard.

**single channel system** The simplest data acquisition system is a single A/D converter that performs repetitive conversions at a free running rate. It has an analog signal input, and its outputs are a digital coded word with an over range indication, polarity information if necessary, and status output to indicate when the output is valid. A well-known example of this system is a digital panel meter, which consists of an A/D converter and a numeric display. In many applications, the purpose of digitizing is to obtain the numerical display, and use the DPM as a meter, rather than as a system component. Some DPM's allow connection to the A/D output for transmission or digital processing.

Since most converters designed for system applications are single-ended in reference to signal ground and have normalized analog in-

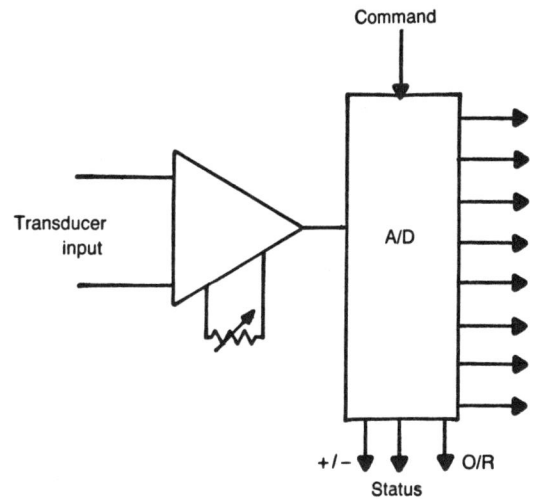

**Single channel system with scaling**

put ranges of the order of 5 or 10 volts (single-ended or bipolar), one should scale signal inputs up or down to the converter input level to allow the fullest possible use of the converter's resolution.

When the signals are of a reasonable magnitude (perhaps already preamplified) or they are the outputs of an analog power device, the scaling might be accomplished with operational amplifiers in a single-ended or differential configuration. If the signals are small or have a large common-mode component a differential instrumentation amplifier might be used. The amplifier characteristics will depend on the gain required, signal levels, and possible cost tradeoffs. If the input signals must be galvanically isolated from the system, a light or transformer-coupled isolation amplifier can be used to break the conductive signal paths. This isolation is essential in many medical instrument applications. It is also used when large common-mode spikes are possible for applications requiring intrinsic safety and for applications in which the source is at a high potential.

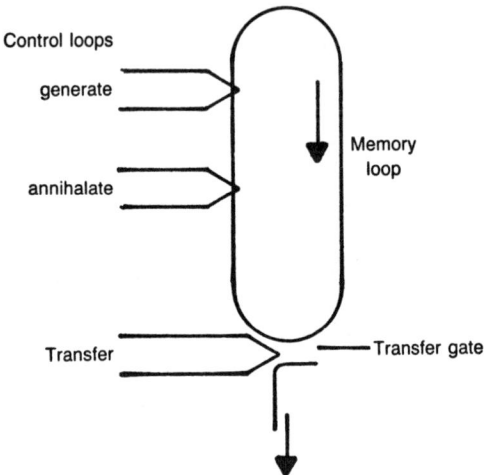

**Single-loop bubble memory architecture**

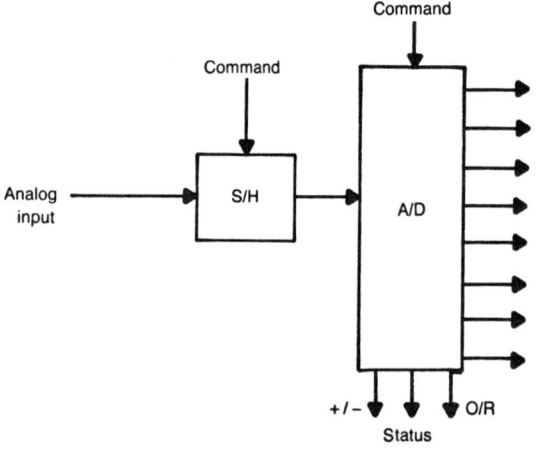

**Single channel system with sample hold**

**single element** A term applied to a typing mechanism in which all print characters are contained on a single unit, such as a printwheel or typing ball.

**single ended** A unit or system designed for use with unbalanced signals, having one input and one output terminal permanently earthed.

**single loop memory** An architecture used for magnetic bubble memories. Single loop memories (see the figure) are simple to operate, since they require the minimum number of current loop functions and have a higher data access time. A single defective location in the loop makes the entire memory inoperative.

**single pass** Refers to a program that generates the desired end result in one computer run.

**single pole** Refers to a switch or relay in which connections to only one circuit can be made. A single-pole single-throw switch is a basic on-off switch.

**single ramp A/D converter** This A/D converter uses a reference voltage of opposite polarity to the signal, which is integrated while the counter tracks clock pulses until the integrator output is equal to the signal input. At this time, called $\Delta t$, the output of the integrator is $V_R \Delta t / RC$. The number of counts is proportional to the ratio of the input to the reference. This circuit has the disadvantage that its accuracy depends on the capacitor and the clock frequency. The multiple ramp types provide increased compensation.

**single-RC phase shift S/D converter** The single-RC phase shift synchro-to-digital converter shown operates by comparing the zero crossing times of the reference wave and the phase shifted sine to cosine (resolver-format) wave. It may be shown that, if WRC = 1 (where W = $\pi$2 times the reference carrier frequency), then the phase shift between the voltage from A to ground and the reference wave is equal to $(\theta - \alpha)$. If $\alpha$ (the time phase error caused by rotor to stator phase lead) is small compared to $\theta$, the time interval between the zero crossings of $V_A$ and $V_r$ is a measure of $\theta$. A counter totals the number of digital clock pulses during the time interval, and the clock frequency is scaled to make the count read directly in a digital coded angle.

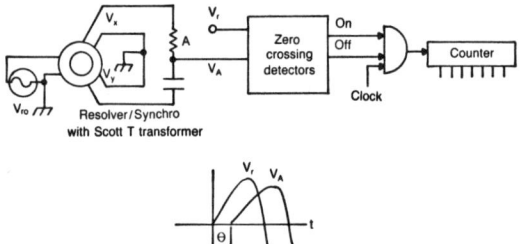

**Single RC phase-shift synchro-to-digital converter**

**single-sideband** A method of amplitude-modulated communications in which either the lower or upper sideband-frequency signals produced as a result of modulation are retained and transmitted, and the carrier itself is suppressed. The signals are detected at the receiver by heterodyning them with an oscillator whose output is a modulated beat-frequency tone.

**single-step** A method of operating a computer in which each step is performed under manual control.

**single-step debug** A debugging method that uses short routines to set up system states for checking the response of the microprocessor.

**single-step operation** A method of operating a computer manually in which a single instruction or part of an instruction is performed in response to a single operation of the manual control. Single-step operation is usually initiated to detect mistakes in programming.

**single throw circuit breaker** A circuit breaker in which only one set of contacts need to be moved to open or close the circuit.

**single tuned circuit** A circuit that may be represented by a single inductance and capacitance, together with their resistances.

**single-word instruction** An instruction format that requires only one memory location. A single-word instruction format is typical of microcomputer systems.

**sink** 1. A device that drains off power or energy from a system. 2. A place where power or energy from several sources is collected or drained away.

**SINS** Abbreviation for *shipboard inertial navigation system*.

**sintering** Refers to the formation of a solid from powders.

**sinusoidal field** A field in which the magnitude of the quantity at any point varies as the sine or cosine of an independent variable such as time, displacement, or temperature.

**sinusoidal wave** A wave in which the displacement varies as the sine (or cosine) of an angle that is proportional to time and/or distance.

**SI** Abbreviation for *super impose:* refers to the process that moves data from one location to another, superimposing bits or characters on the contents of specified locations.

**SIP** Abbreviation for *single inline package*.

**SISS** Abbreviation for *submarine integrated sonar system*.

**SI units** The modern Scientific International system of units, identical to the electric MKSA system, but more general, using six fundamental units.

**skeleton table** A macro assembly program table that contains all the prototypes of the macro definitions in a program.

**skew** The presentational differences between the input and output signals of a propagation system when the response of the processing circuits is not linear over the full signal range.

**skewness** A statistical measure of the asymmetry in a distribution.

**skin effect** An effect that occurs when metallic conductors are used to carry high frequency currents, which are limited to a surface layer equal in thickness to the skin depth; it produces a large value for the high frequency resistance of the conductor.

**skip** An instruction that directs the program to proceed to the next instruction. Also called a *blank* instruction or a NO OP.

**skip bus** Refers to a central processor bus, that is shared by I/O interfaces and utilized to test devices associated with each interface and provide conditional branching of the program as a result of the testing.

**skip flag** A flag produced by a 1-bit register to represent the true or false condition with respect to the instruction being executed by the processor.

**skip test** A microinstruction designed for conditional operations based on the state of readiness of devices or conditions in a register.

**sky noise** Refers to noise produced by radio energy from stars.

**slab** A relatively thick crystal from which blanks are cut.

**SLAM** Abbreviation for *supersonic low altitude missile*.

**SLAM package** The single layer metallization package, a dual-inline package that offers a lower cost alternative to three layer ceramic packages. The package uses the same basic materials as ceramic, but in a simpler and thereby more reliable manner. It uses a 96 percent alumina base, one basic refractory metallization layer, an alumina passivation layer, and brazed-on Kovar leads. The leads are suitable for either socket insertion or soldering. A glazed ceramic lid is attached with a low temperature controlled devitrified glass frit sealant. A gold silicon eutectic solder is used for Kovar lids. It is available in 14 to 40 pin configurations.

**slave** A unit or device which is under the control of another unit or device. At any point in time, there is one device that has control of the communication bus—the *bus master*. The bus master may in turn communicate with any other device, which is called the *slave*.

**slaved tracking** A system of interconnecting two or more regulated power supplies in which one (the master) operates to control the others (the slaves). The output voltages of the slave units may be equal or proportional to the output voltage of the master unit. The slaved output voltages track the master output in a constant ratio.

**slave mode** Refers to a mode of computer system operation in which most of the basic controls affecting the state of the computer system are protected from outside interference.

**slave tube** Refers to a cathode ray tube that is connected to a master tube; both tubes are identical. The slave tube follows the master, most often to change the storage contents of an electrostatic storage tube.

**slewing rate** 1. The rate at which a device can be driven from limit to limit over the dynamic output range. 2. The maximum rate at which a circuit, device, or system can be cycled through its operational states.

**slew rate, amplifier** This term is comparable to rise or fall time in a digital circuit. It is a measure of how fast the output can change. If an amplifier output could go from 0 volts to 10 volts in 2 microseconds, it would have a slew rate of 5 volts/sec.

**slice** Refers to the type of microcomputer architecture that permits the cascading or stacking of devices to increase word length.

**slice architecture** A microcomputer architecture that uses a section of the register file and ALU in one package. Each end of each 2- or 4-bit register is accessible through the chip's edge to allow registers (slices) to be cascaded together to form larger word lengths.

**slice latch/mask** The latch/mask controls data to one input port of an arithmetic slice unit. A holding latch is used to provide temporary storage for data entering through the output bus port. The latch clock input controls the latch operation. When not latched, data ripples through the latch and need not be clocked. By using mask select lines, it is possible to mask data on the output bus.

**slice look-ahead** A circuit that allows high-speed look-ahead arithmetic operations in bit-slice systems.

**slice memory** An interface device that connects the slice packages to a main memory system. The chip contains the data and address storage and logic along with the logic for the more complex addressing methods required for the slice configuration.

**slice system** A computing system that can handle large amounts of data at high speed by using the slice concept. Typical applications for slice systems include minicomputers, high-speed instrumentation, communications processors, real-time analysis, scientific computers, and time-sharing systems.

**slope** The essentially linear portion of the characteristic curve of a vacuum tube or solid state amplifying device. This is where the operating point is chosen for linear amplification.

**slot** Refers to the cells under a set of heads at one time in a magnetic memory.

**slow death** A term used to describe the gradual deterioration of semiconductor devices, usually due to contamination of surfaces.

**SLR** Abbreviation for *storage limits register.*

**SLT** Abbreviation for *solid logic technology.*

**slug** 1. A heavy metal ring or short circuit winding used on a relay core to delay operation of the relay. 2. A metallic core that can be moved along the axis of a coil for tuning purposes. 3. A thick copper band, on a relay, that, through induced eddy currents, retards the operation and fall off of the relay.

**SM** Abbreviation for *strategic missile.*

**SMAC** Abbreviation for *Submicron Airosol Collector.*

**small signal current gain** The output current of a transistor with the output circuit shorted divided by the input current. The current components are understood to be small enough that linear relationships hold.

**small signal drain source on-state resistance** The small signal resistance between the drain and source terminals of a FET device with a specified gate source voltage applied to bias the device to the on state.

**small signal, open circuit forward transfer impedance** The ratio of the ac output voltage to the ac input current when the ac output current is zero in a transistor or similar device.

**small signal, open circuit input impedance** The ratio of the ac input voltage to the ac input current when the ac output current is zero in a transistor or similar device.

**small signal, open circuit output admittance** In a transistor or similar device, the ratio of the ac output current to the ac voltage applied to the output terminals when the ac input current is zero.

**small signal power gain** The ratio of signal power delivered to the load, to the signal power delivered to the input. Usually expressed in dB.

**small signal short circuit forward transfer admittance, common source** The ratio of rms drain current to rms gate source voltage in a FET device with the drain terminal short circuited to the source terminal for alternating currents.

**small signal short circuit input admittance, common source** The ratio of rms gate current to rms gate-source voltage in a FET device with the drain terminal short-circuited to the source terminal for ac signals.

**small signal short circuit output admittance, common source** The ratio of rms drain current to rms drain source voltage for a FET device with the gate terminal short-circuited to the source terminal for ac signals.

**small signal short circuit reverse transfer admittance, common source** The ratio of rms gate current to rms drain source voltage with the gate terminal short circuited to the source terminal for ac signals.

**smart terminal** A terminal in which part of the processing is done using a microcomputer in the terminal itself. Sometimes called an intelligent terminal, the unit allows the user to program the terminal for his application. A typical smart terminal contains a CRT, keyboard, serial input/output device, and microcomputer. The microcomputer controls editing, formatting, and the protocol of communication with the central computer. Editing may include character, line, field, and page deleting and inserting as well as line, page, and memory clearing.

**SMI** Abbreviation for *static memory interface.*

**smooth contact** Refers to a socket or pin contact that has a significantly smooth profile with a flush surface.

**smoother** Refers to a combination of capacitors and inductors for removing the ripple from a rectifier supply.

**SMP** Abbreviation for *sampler.*

**SNA** Abbreviation for *Systems Network Architecture.* Refers to IBM's standard protocol between its virtual telecommunication access method (VTAM) and the network control program (NCP/VS).

**SNAP** 1. Abbreviation for *system for nuclear auxiliary power.* 2. Abbreviation for *simplified numerical automatic programmer,* a two axis, point-to-point technique or program for NC or CAD systems.

**snaper effect** The automization of a solid, fluid, or gas when an ultrasonic impingement of sufficient force to disrupt the molecular cohesion of the material is instituted. Named after Dr. Alvin Snaper.

**snapshot** A dump performed by a snapshot system.

**snapshot debugging** Refers to a type of diagnostics and debugging technique in which the programmer specifies the start and end of program segments for which he wants to examine the contents of various registers and accumulators. The snapshot tracing may indicate the contents not only of the various accumulators and registers but also of specified memory locations.

**snapshot dump** A dynamic partial printout during computing at breakpoints and checkpoints, or selected areas of storage.

**snapshot system** A system that will (1) plant unconditional transfer orders to the system at arbitrary points in another program, (2) execute dumps of specified registers and storage locations at these points during the running of the program, and (3) return to the program at these points in such a manner that the running of the program is unaffected by the snapshot system.

**SNR** Abbreviation for *signal to noise ratio.*

**SO** Abbreviation for the *shift-out* character.

**SOA** Abbreviation for *state of the art.*

**SOFAR** Abbreviation for *sound fixing and ranging.*

**soft drop** A phenomenon in RAM memory where a memory location(s) is altered due to background radiation or other electrical interference. The soft drop rate in most RAM memory is once in every several trillion memory accesses. Most soft drops occur in unused memory locations and are not noticed.

**soft limited** Refers to a limiting action with an appreciable tolerance in the limiting value.

**software** The programs, routines, languages, and procedures used in a computer system. Software items include assemblers, generators, subroutines, compilers, and operating systems.

**software cross assembler** A software system for translating a symbolic representation of instructions and data into a form which can be loaded and executed by the microcomputer. The cross assembler acts like an assembler executing on a machine other than the one to be used, which generates the code for the desired unit.

**software development process** Refers to the cycle or systematic method used to develop the software for a system. A typical development process includes:

1. Problem statement
2. Design of algorithms
3. Flowchart construction
4. Program coding
5. Preparation of source code
6. Translation to object code
7. Loading of object code
8. Checkout and debugging
9. Documentation

**software development system** Hardware to be used for the rapid development of software. A typical system includes an editing CRT, a hard-copy device, mass storage (such as magnetic tape or disk), and a paper-tape unit.

The CRT terminal is used to construct and edit source programs. A hard-copy device such as a printer is required to create the hard-copy listings for debugging and documentation. A cassette or floppy disk unit is used to obtain rapid access to assemblers, editors, and debug programs, and a high-speed paper-tape unit is needed to handle the programs that come with many microcomputer development system packages.

**software documentation** The total documentation for a program can include general flowcharts, detailed programmer's flowcharts, a description of the test plan, a written description of the program, a listing for each program module, a list of the parameters and definitions, memory maps, and I/O maps. Documentation is best generated during the design, coding, debugging, and testing stages of software development.

**software documents** Written or printed material associated with the microcomputer, including manuals, diagrams, and listings.

**software evaluation and development modules** Refers to a software system of modules that allow a means of building up and testing a proposed microcomputer system before committing the design to hardware. First the functional specifications and programs are established, then the ROM program is assembled and simulated on a time-shared system, using the software modules.

**software house** A company that offers software support services to users. This support usually includes consulting services along with programming support.

**software interrupt** An interrupt instruction that can be used for debugging purposes. The instruction usually saves the current value of the program counter and then branches to a specified memory location. This memory location may be used as the starting point for a debugging program that then lists or displays selected status information.

**software interrupt instruction** Some microprocessors like the 6800 have a software interrupt instruction (SWI) that can be used to decrease memory requirements. This instruction uses the subroutine address that is stored in memory locations FFFC and FFFD. It is quite similar to a restart except that its address is not fixed since it comes from the memory.

SWI can be used to simulate hardware interrupts, in order to allow debugging without special hardware.

**software kit** A collection of programming aids for a microprocessor system. A typical software kit includes:

1. Language editor for source programs
2. An assembler for source programs
3. PROM programmer
4. Debug program

**software library** The collection of programs used by an operating system. A microcomputer software library may include a machine-language assembler, Teletype operating system, tape editor, simulator, cross assembler, map generator, and utility and diagnostic programs.

**software modularity** Refers to the flexibility in the programming and operating aids furnished with systems. Most types of programs in the software library are offered in several versions to run in system configurations of different sizes and compositions. Most software versions written for large systems are designed to take advantage of the increased internal and input/output processing capacities of these systems.

**software network components** The software components available through a time-sharing service. These include cross assemblers, interactive simulators, and other software packages to aid software development.

**software package** The programs or sets of programs used in a particular application or function. Many software packages include diagnostic programs for verifying processor and memory operation along with cross assemblers.

**software priority interrupts** Here the interrupt priorities are defined and controlled by the microprocessor. After an interrupt request occurs, it is transmitted to the microprocessor and the address is compared with a multibit interrupt enabling mask. If the address is equal or less than the mask, the request is recognized. The mask is forced to one less than the address and servicing begins. If the address is greater than the mask, the request is queued. In this scheme only interrupts from a device with an address lower than that of the device being serviced are recognized. So the lower the address, the higher the priority as shown below. The interrupts are nested for rapid service of high priority interrupts even when they occur when a low priority interrupt is being serviced.

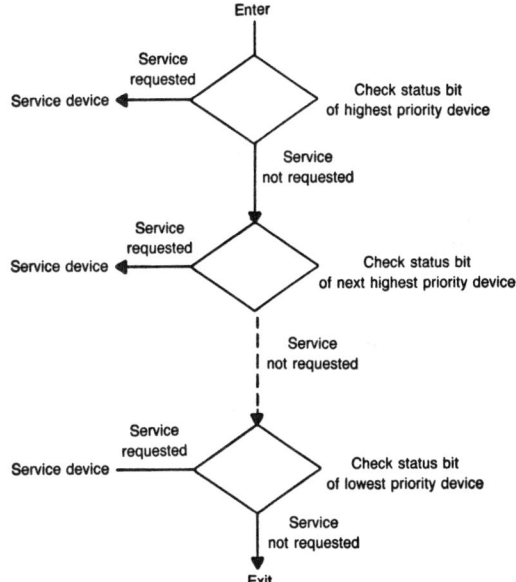

Software priority interrupt system

**software simulator** Major aids to programing of a microcomputer system are software assemblers and simulators. Software simulators are useful to check out central processor coding, and they sometimes prove to be successful in checking out peripherals or input/output equipment. A programming problem can be related to the timing and quality of the signal on a computer input or output or can be related to an external device fault, which can be difficult to isolate with only a simulator.

**software stack register** A status register that sometimes provide latched flag outputs and accepts sense inputs. It can be tested under program control. The status register may contain the interrupt enable flag as well as arithmetic carry and overflow flags. The carry flag can also be used as a link for multiple byte shift and rotate instructions. The provision of the interrupt input means that the processor does not have to use valuable computing time looping through a scan or polling sequence.

**software system** The entire set of program and software development aids used in a microcomputer system.

**software test set** A set of programs used to support the development of custom programs and to verify the design under actual operating conditions prior to release of the ROM pattern to manufacturing. The software set usually consists of a cross assembler, simulator, and test-program generator.

**software tools** Programs that assist the programmer during the development cycle. Software tools include editors, assemblers, compilers, loaders, linkage editors, debuggers, and simulators.

**SOH** The *start-of-heading* character; in ASCII it is designated as a seven-bit binary 1.

**SOL** Abbreviation for *simulation oriented language*.

**solder** A tin-lead alloy used for making electrical connections. In use, molten solder is applied to conductor joints. When the solder cools, it solidifies to hold the conductors permanently in place.

**solder covered wire** Copper wire coated with solder instead of tin, used to facilitate connections between components in electrical and electronic equipment.

**solderless breadboard** A circuit breadboard that contains sockets and socket pins to allow temporary solder-free connections during test or debugging operations.

**solderless connector** A device for clamping two wires together without the use of solder.

**solderless wrap** A method of connection in which a solid wire is wrapped around a metal terminal using a special hand or power tool. Also called *wire wrap*.

**solder short** A circuit or component defect that occurs when solder forms a short circuit path between two or more conductors.

**solenoid** A current-carrying iron-core coil of wire typically used as a controllable magnet for opening or closing mechanical contacts or valves.

**solid** Matter which has the definite shape and volume of a crystal structure, as opposed to a liquid or a gas.

**solid conductor** A wire or conductor composed of a single strand.

**solid-state** Descriptive of circuits or systems constructed with active devices other than vacuum tubes; or the active devices themselves.

**solid-state component** A component that depends upon the control of electrical or electromagnetic phenomena in a solid material; thus, a transistor, diode, or integrated circuit.

**solid state element** Refers to electronic components whose operation does not require current to pass through a space or a vacuum. As a direct result, the power needed by the element is greatly reduced, and the need for special cooling is reduced because there is less heat.

**solid state integrated circuit** The class of integrated circuit components in which only solid state materials are used.

**solid-state memory** A memory constructed entirely of circuits employing semiconductor devices.

**solid-state physics** The branch of physics that deals with the properties of solid materials, especially conduction in semiconductors and metals.

**SOM** 1. Abbreviation for *self-organizing machine*. 2. Abbreviation for *start of message*.

**SONAR** Abbreviation for *sound navigation and ranging*.

**sonic delay line** A device for simulating the acoustical delay of a long transmission line and used to emulate the effect of reverberation, or for providing phase changes to input signals under controlled conditions.

**sonic flowmeters** Sonic and ultrasonic flowmeters are used with liquid or sonically conductive slurries through pipes or open channels. They are used in water and waste sewage plants, industrial process plants, and power stations.

**sonic thermocouple** A thermocouple designed for a gas velocity at the junction of Mach 1 or greater, resulting in maximum heat transfer to the junction.

**SONOAN** Abbreviation for *sonic noise analyzer*.

**SOP** Abbreviation for *standard operating procedure*.

**sophisticated vocabulary** Refers to an advanced and elaborate set of instructions.

**sort** To rearrange or segregate usually listed items into groups according to a specified order. For example, a list of subjects in a book can be entered into a computer in order of page number, and a sort operation can cause the list to be printed out in alphabetical order.

**sorter** A device or routine used as the basis for determining the sequential order of the items in a set and for producing the list in that order.

**sort key** A key used as the basis for determining the sequential arrangement of items in a set.

**SOS** Abreviation for *silicon-on-sapphire*, a semiconductor process that uses a sapphire base to "grow" silicon for the production of MOS transistors. SOS devices achieve bipolar speeds, provide radiation protection for military applications, and are well suited for CMOS designs. SOS technology can be applied in memories, microprocessors, high-speed counters, and multiplexers.

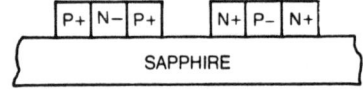

SOS structure

**SOS CMOS** Abbreviation for *silicon-on sapphire complementary metal-oxide semiconductor*, a low-power, high-speed MOS device.

**SOS RAM** Abbreviation for a type of RAM that uses the silicon-on-sapphire technology. A typical unit uses the SOS MOS technology for a 1024-bit memory that operates with +4.5 to 6V and consumes only 4 mW of power. The unit is static with no requirement for refreshing, clocking, or pulsing circuitry.

**SOS transistor** Abbreviation for *silicon-on-sapphire* transistor, an active device on a sapphire substrate that is electrically isolated from all others on the substrate.

**SOTIM** Abbreviation for *sonic observation of the trajectory and impact on missiles*.

**source** 1. A circuit or device which serves as a distributor (of voltage, data, timing pulses, etc.) to other devices. 2. An element in a circuit which serves as the starting point for an energy pulse of a given polarity (as a charged capacitor, for example). 3. Originator.

**source code** Program statements, arguments, and codes generated by keyboard inputs to a system.

**source-code instruction** An instruction used as a pointer in microprogrammed systems to emulate a particular instruction set being executed.

**source data** Data generated in the course of research, design, and development.

**source data automation** The recording of information in coded form on punch cards, paper tape, tags, and other media which may be used again and again without rewriting to produce other records of the data. Abbreviated *SDA*.

**source deck** A stack of coded cards that contain a source program.

**source editor** A program that allows the entry and modification of source code into the system for later translation or storage. Without a source editor, a program would have to be built up on a medium such as punched cards or paper tape.

**source file editor** A line-oriented editor that operates on programs in a sequence determined by their assembler-produced statement line numbers. The editor produces an updated file while preserving the original master file.

**source impedance** The impedance presented to the input of a device by the source.

**source language** 1. The language from which a statement is translated. 2. The original form in which a program is prepared prior to processing by the machine.

**source language translation** The translation of a program to a target program, as from FORTRAN to machine language.

**source library** A collection of programs (compiler or assembler) for a specific machine.

**source module** A set of statements in a source language recorded in machine-readable form and suitable for input to an assembler or compiler.

**source program** A program that can be translated automatically into machine language to become an object program. Source programs are usually written in a language designed for ease of expression. A generator, assembler, translator, or compiler routine is used for translation into the object program in machine code.

**source statement** A statement written in other than machine language. Source statements are written in symbolic terms for translation to machine code.

**source tape** Refers to the tape that contains the source program.

**source tape preparation** A program used to prepare and edit symbolic source tapes. The program allows the tape to be edited by typing commands on the keyboard to perform corrections and produce a new source tape.

**source utility** A program that aids in the preparation and modification of symbolic assembly-language tapes.

**space** 1. A site intended for the storage of data, such as a specific position on a page in memory. 2. A unit of area for a single character on a line. 3. To advance a reading or display position in order to create a desired format.

**space character** 1. A nonprinting character used to separate words. 2. A format effector which controls the printing or display position in a system. Abbreviated *SP*.

**space charge** 1. The electrical charge caused in space by the presence of electrons or ions. 2. The electron cloud around the hot cathode of a vacuum tube.

**space lattice** The three-dimensional regular arrangement of atoms, characteristic of a particular crystal structure. The 14 such simple symmetrical arrangements are known as Bravais lattices.

**SPADATS** Abbreviation for *space detection and tracking system*.

**SPANDAR** Abbreviation for *space range radar*.

**spandex** A manufactured fiber in which the synthetic substance is a long chain synthetic polymer composed of at least 85 percent polyurethane.

**spark** The result of the breakdown of insulation between two conductors when the potential is sufficient to cause ionization and rapid discharge.

**spark absorber** A resistance and/or capacitor placed across a break in an electrical circuit to damp any possible oscillatory circuit that would tend to maintain an arc or spark when the current is interrupted.

**spark spectra** An important way of exciting spectra is by means of an electric spark. The high temperature reached will generate the spectrum lines of multiple-ionized atoms as well as of uncharged and singly ionized ones, as distinct from the arc spectrum. The evaporation of metal from the electrodes leads to additional lines not associated with the gas through which the discharge takes place.

**spark timing system** A microprocessor spark timing system is shown. Sensors supply the microprocessor with the required information. Inputs include the engine vacuum, crankshaft position, reference timing, and coolant temperature. The main output is the timing signal to the distributor. The other two outputs of the system are status information. A special purpose microprocessor was designed for this application. The system functions in a table-driven mode. There is no algorithm that determines the proper timing for the spark as a function of the input conditions. Every engine type is extensively tested. The manufacturer then establishes tables that determine the desired timing as a function of the external parameters. The system implements an automated version of the table look up mechanism. A subset of the tables is stored in memory. For each set of external conditions measured by the system, the closest match in the tables are found. Interpolation techniques are used to compute the intermediate values. Instructions exist in the custom microprocessor to do this. This microprocessor has input/output lines, as well as analog-to-digital facilities.

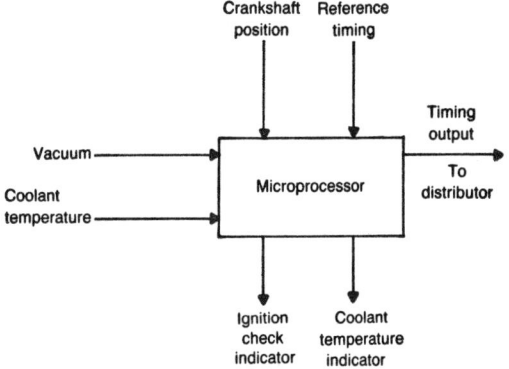

**Microprocessor spark timing system**

**SPASUR** Abbreviation for *space surveillance*.

**SPC** Abbreviation for *silver plated copper*.

**SPEC** Abbreviation for *stored program educational computer*.

**special character** A graphic symbol that is neither a letter, a numeral, nor a space character.

**special function keys** Refers to functional keys on a keyboard that add functional capability to provide ease of operation. On some systems special function keys are offered for data retrieval functions and display formats.

**special purpose bus interface** A bus system that may use one or more integrated circuits to link the microprocessor to a particular I/O device. In addition to the basic bus interface circuits, the interface may contain circuits for specific functions peculiar to the I/O device. A keyboard interface would require matrix encoding and perhaps parity generating functions. A line printer interface would require message formatting, character storage, and print heat control and timing functions. A communications interface could require serial-to-parallel/parallel-to-serial conversion, parity generation, message formatting, and modem control.

**special-purpose computer** A computer designed to handle a restricted class of problems.

**specific address** Absolute address.

**specific code** Absolute code.

**specific conductivity** The conducting ability of a material in mhos per cubic centimeter. It is the reciprocal of resistivity.

**specific dielectric strength** The dielectric strength per millimeter of thickness of an insulating material.

**specific gravity** The weight of a substance compared with the weight of the same volume of water at the same temperature.

**specific magnetic moment** Refers to the value of the saturation moment per unit weight of a magnetic material, expressed in emu/gm. The specific magnetic moment is a convenient quantity in which to express the saturation magnetization of fine particle materials. The specific magnetic moment of pure gamma ferric oxide is approximately 75 emu/gm at room temperature.

**specific resistance** The resistance of a conductor. It is expressed in ohms per unit length per unit area.

**specific routine** A routine used to solve a particular arithmetic, logic, or data-handling problem in which each address refers to explicitly stated registers and locations.

**spectral luminosity profile** Refers to a high luminosity phenomena observed when a vehicle reenters the earth's atmosphere.

**spectrometer** 1. A test instrument that determines the frequency distribution of the energy generated by a source and displays all components simultaneously. 2. An instrument used for the measurement of wave length or energy distribution in a heterogeneous beam of radiation.

**spectrum** 1. Refers to the arrangement of components of a complex color or sound in order of frequency of energy, thereby showing the distribution of energy or stimulus among the components. A mass spectrum is one showing the distribution in mass or in mass to charge ratio of ionized atoms or molecules. 2. The range of electromagnetic waves to the shortest cosmic rays. Light, the visible portion of the spectrum, lies about midway between the two extremes. 3. A graphical representation of the distribution of the amplitude (and sometimes phase) of the components of a wave as a function of frequency. A spectrum may be continuous or contain only points corresponding to certain discrete values.

**spectrum, frequency** A portion of the range of frequencies of electromagnetic radiation waves.

**split keyboarding** A production technique in which material is keyboarded and edited on one word processing unit and played out on another.

**spin out** An effect that occurs when a relay is subjected to high inrush currents of relatively long duration.

**spooling** A procedure of temporarily storing data on disk or tape files until the CPU is ready for additional processing of the information.

**sporadic** Intermittent.

**sporadic fault** Faults are failures to perform in the manner required under specified conditions; sporadic faults are intermittent faults.

**spreadsheet program** A "super calculator" program, that provides you with a giant electronic grid that functions analogously to the traditional spreadsheet. When you change the values of numbers in the grid, the program automatically calculates what effect, if any, there is on all the other numbers. The spreadsheet can provide answers within seconds to all sorts of financial "What ifs."

**spring finger action** Refers to operations of electrical contacts that permit a stress-free spring action to develop contact pressure. They are used in sockets of printed circuits and in many types of connectors.

**SPS** 1. Abbreviation for *series-parallel-series*. 2. Abbreviation for *solar power satellite*.

**spurious pulse** A pulse not purposely generated or directly due to circuit or system operation.

**spurious pulse mode** An unwanted pulse mode that may be formed by the chance combination of two or more pulse modes. It may be indistinguishable from a normal pulse mode or reply.

**sputtering** Refers to the removal of atoms from a cathode by positive bombardment, as in a cold evaporation. These atoms deposit on any surface and can be used to coat dielectrics with thin films of various metals.

**square loop** Refers to a hysteresis loop that is not like an S-shaped curve but is square or rectangular in shape.

**square wave** A pulse with very rapid (theoretically infinite) rise and fall times, and a pulse duration equal to half period of repetition.

**squareness ratio** The ratio, for a magnetic material in a symmetrically cyclically magnetized condition, of the residual magnetic flux density, or the flux density at zero magnetizing force, to the maximum flux or density.

**SR** 1. Abbreviation for *study requirement*. 2. Abbreviation for *shift register*. 3. Abbreviation for *send-receive*.

**SRBM** Abbreviation for *short range ballistic missile*.

**SS** 1. Abbreviation for *single-sided* (for using one side of the floppy disk for recording information.) 2. Abbreviation for *Solid State*. 3. Abbreviation for *Single Side-band*.

**SSB** Abbreviation for *single side-band*.

**SSD** Abbreviation for *space systems division*.

**SSI** Abbreviation for *small scale integration*.

**SSM** Abbreviation for *surface to surface missile*.

**stability** The freedom from undesirable deviation, used as a measure of process controllability.

**stable** 1. A system not exhibiting sudden changes, such as those with atoms that are not radioactive. 2. A term used to indicate the incapability of following a stated mode of spontaneous change. 3. The state of an amplification or control system when it satisfies a stability test such as the Nyquist criterion, either conditionally or unconditionally.

**stable oscillation** A condition in which amplitude and/or frequency will remain constant indefinitely. A statically stable system may be dynamically unstable and follow a divergent oscillation when subjected to a disturbance. Dynamically stable means that an induced oscillation will be convergent, with a decreasing amplitude.

**stable state** In a digital circuit, a phase that will continue each time the circuit is restarted, until the circuit is switched to the opposite state or phase by another input signal.

**stable trigger** A circuit with two binary states, each state requiring a trigger signal for transition from one state to another. Also known as *binary pair, trigger pair* and *R-S-T flip-flop*.

**stack** A block of successive memory locations that are accessible from one end and coordinated with a stack pointer that keeps track of storage and retrieval of each word in the stack. A *pushdown* stack operates as a last-in-first-out (LIFO) buffer; as data is added, the stack moves down with the last item occupying the top position. The stack hardware is a collection of registers with a counter that indicates the most recently loaded register. The registers are unloaded in the reverse order in which they were loaded.

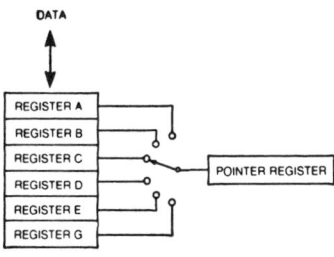

**Stack**

**stack architecture** Descritptive of a microcomputer that uses a stack for part of its internal memory. Stack architecture reduces the number of registers required for temporary storage and can decrease the number of steps required in a program. Multiplelevel interrupts can easily be handled with a stacked system, since system status can be saved when an interrupt occurs and restored after the interrupt.

**stack control** Refers to the ability to process stacked service requests and status words. The type of stack control used is important in conversing processor time.

**stacked job processing** Refers to a procedure of automatic job-to-job transitions with little or no operator intervention.

**stack manipulation** Refers to a system that has instruction addressing modes that allow temporary data storage structures for the convenient handling of data which is frequently processed. The register used to keep track of stack manipulation is called the *stack pointer*. Stack manipulation is often used in microcomputers to offset the shortcomings of their smaller instruction sets.

**stack pointer** The register used to keep track of the most recent register data stored in a stack.

**stack push-down** Refers to a procedure that develops a reserved area of memory into which operands are pushed and from which operands are pulled on a last-in-first-out basis.

**stack register** A register that receives the contents of the program counter and aids in developing a multilevel program function.

**STALO** Abbreviation for *stable local oscillator*.

**stand alone** A term applied to a system that is self-contained and not connected to other systems or system components.

**standard** An established unit of measurement, or a reference instrument of component, suitable for use in the calibration of other instruments. Basic standards are those possessed or set by national or international laboratories or institutes.

**standard component** A component that is regularly produced by one or more manufacturers and arrived by one or more distributors.

**standard deviation** The square root of the mean of the squares of a set of numbers representing statistical variations from an average value.

**standard interface** An interface which allows several units or systems to be easily interconnected.

**standard subroutine** A subroutine that is applicable to a specific class or set of problems.

**standby** 1. A nonoperating-but-ready condition of equipment which allows resumption of operation when permitted. 2. A duplicate set of equipment which is used when the primary equipment malfunctions.

**standby application** An application where two or more machines are tied together as a part of the system design and stand ready for activation and processing of system inquiries.

**standby register** A register in which information is stored for a rerun in the event of a mistake in the program or a malfunction in the machine.

**standby time** The time between inquiries in a system, or the time two or more computers are connected for a standby application.

**standing-on-nines carry** A high-speed carry in which a carry input to a given digit place is bypassed to the next digit place if the current sum in the given digit place is nine.

**star configuration** A network configuration in which the host processor is the center of the system and each processor communicates with the host. Communication between satellite processors is through the host. This is also known as a radial or centralized configuration. This configuration lends itself to control by the host. More than one satellite can talk to the host at the same time, and the host may be burdened with supervising data flow between satellites.

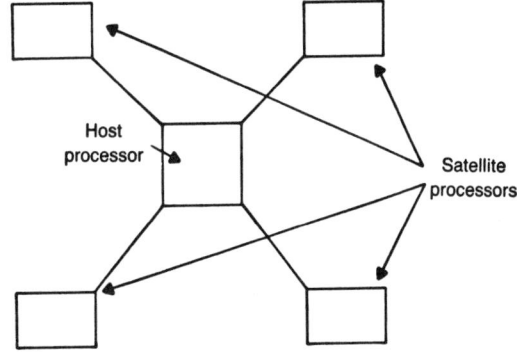

**Star network configuration**

**starter voltage drop** In a glow-discharge, cold cathode tube. The voltage drop across the starter gap after conduction is established there.

**start-of-heading character** A communications control character (abbreviated *SOH*) used as the first character of a heading in a message.

**start-of-text character** A control character (abbreviated *STX*) which indicates the beginning of text and the end of the heading.

**start-stop multivibrator** Refers to a type of multivibrator that has one stable state and one unstable state and goes through a complete change cycle. The circuit provides a single signal of the proper form and time from a varying shaped, randomly timed signal. Upon receipt of a trigger signal, it assumes another state for a specified length of time, at the end of which it returns of its own accord to its original state.

**statement** A meaningful expression or generalized instruction in a program.

**static** 1. Nonmovable or nonrotating; a transformer or rectifier is a static converter. 2. Electrostatic. 3. Refers to electrical disturbances that arise through electrostatic induction, particularly from lightning flashes.

**static behavior** Refers to the behavior of a control system or a unit under fixed conditions; as contrasted to dynamic behavior, which occurs under changing conditions.

**static charge** Refers to the accumulated electric charge on an object.

**static CMOS memory** A memory of memory cells that use a flip-flop arrangement in which the transistors function as the loads are combined into a complementary circuit. The static CMOS memory allows low-power dissipation with less density than standard MOS. It is also compatible with TTL logic for easy interfacing.

**static drain-source on-state resistance** The dc resistance between the drain and source terminals with a specified gate source voltage applied to bias the device to the on state.

**static dump** A dump that is performed at a specific time in a machine run, usually at the end of the run.

**static error** An error that is independent of time.

**static forward-current transfer ratio** The ratio, under specified test conditions, of the dc output current to the dc input current in a transistor.

**static gain** Refers to the gain of a device under steady-state conditions.

**static input resistance** The ratio of the dc input voltage to the input current in a transistor.

**staticizer** A storage device for converting serial or time-sequential information into parallel static data.

**static magnetic cell** A storage cell in which the two values are represented by different patterns of magnetization.

**static magnetic storage** Storage of information bits on a medium that holds the data in place so that it is available at any time, such as in a core cell.

**static memory** A semiconductor (usually) memory that holds data indefinitely as long as power is applied.

**static memory card** A circuit board that contains a semiconductor memory.

**static MOS** MOS memory circuits that are cross-coupled bistable units for storing information in one of two stable states.

**static MOS RAM** A read-write memory that stores data in integrated flip-flops.

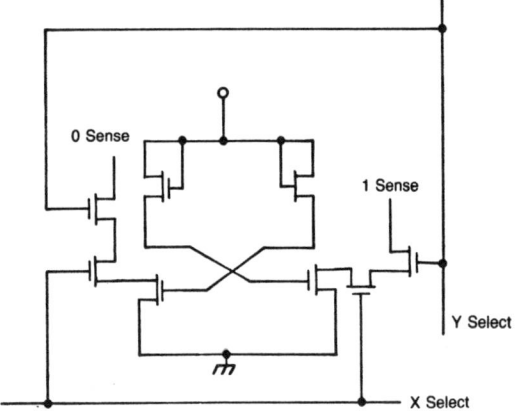

**Basic static MOS RAM cell**

**static MOS ROM** A static read-only memory based on MOS technology. Static MOS ROMs offer low-cost, simple interfacing and high performance for applications requiring large capacity. Applications include microprogramming, table lookup, code conversion, and character generation. Inputs and outputs are usually TTL compatible.

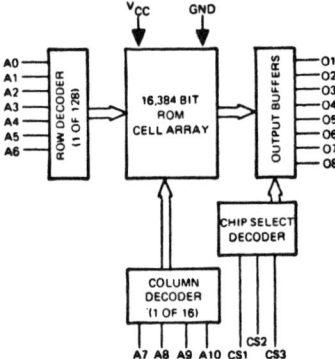

**Static MOS ROM**

**static read/write memory** Refers to a memory in which clocks or refreshing are not needed. A typical static N-channel MOS memory is designed and organized to be compatible with the various microprocessors. Its data, address, and control line organization and functions match those of the microprocessor and all signal levels are TTL compatible.

**static storage** A memory that requires no refresh logic since data does not degenerate or leak away as long as power is applied to the memory elements. Compare *dynamic storage*.

**static subroutine** A subroutine involving no parameters other than the addresses of the operands.

**stationary gap** A device used in conjunction with a pulse forming line to form short period high voltage pulses for modulating microwave oscillators.

**statistical error** Refers to the error arising in measurements of random events, as a result of statistical fluctuations in the data.

**statistical universe** A complete set of items that are similar or related in certain respects.

**stat typing** Refers to priority typing.

**status bit** A bit used in many systems to designate interrupt conditions. The status bit is tested by the program to check for the presence of an internal interrupt condition. The status bit can be used to check for console interrupts, DMA termination, clock interrupt, power-fail/restart interrupt, and others. Microprograms can be shortened with the use of status bits. Branches can be made after the status bits are set to eliminate premature branching and reduce the number of microinstructions required.

**status register** A register used to hold information on communication errors, data register status, and communication device status. Some systems use several status registers and exchange data between the registers to allow limited nesting capability.

**status word** 1. A word used to resume processing after the servicing of an interrupt. 2. A word used to indicate the status of an internal or external device. The status word may provide information on the sign of a number, overflow conditions, carry bits, accumulator conditions, and interrupts.

**status word, device** Refers to a computer word containing bits whose conditions indicate the status of devices. Abbreviated *DSW*.

**status word register** Refers to a group of binary numbers that inform the user of the present condition of the microprocessor. In some systems the status register may provide the following information: plus or minus sign, overflow indication, carry bit, all zeros in the accumulator, and interrupt bit status.

**STDM** Abbreviation for *synchronous time-division multiplexing*.

**STE** 1. Abbreviation for *special test equipment*. 2. Abbreviation for *segment table entry*.

**steady-state** A condition in which all values remain essentially constant or recurring in a cyclic manner.

**steady-state deviation** The difference between the final value assumed by a specified variable after the expiration of transients and its ideal value.

**steady-state oscillation** Oscillation in which the motion at each point is a fixed periodic quantity.

**step-by-step switch** A stepper switch.

**step counter** A counter used in the arithmetic unit to count the steps in a process such as multiplication, division or shift operations.

**step-down amplifier** Refers to an amplifier that is used to reduce an input signal.

**step-down transformer** An electrical transformer that provides the transfer of energy from a high to a low voltage.

**step function** A function that is zero preceding time zero, and then has a constant value after time zero.

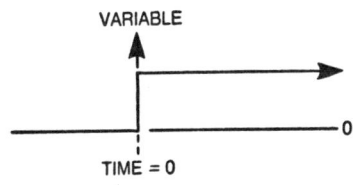

Step function

**stepper** A stepper switch.

**stepper motor** A motor in which rotation occurs in a series of discrete steps that can be controlled by pulses.

**stepper switch** An electromechanical relay with a number of contact positions. The wiper arms are rotated from contact to contact by applications of driving pulses to the relay coil.

**stepping motor** A motor that can be stepped to rotate in a series of partial rotations using pulses.

**stepping-motor controller** A module used to provide an interface between the microcomputer and the stepping-motor power amplifier. In a typical system the CPU uses a 16-bit word, with 12 bits for the number of pulses and 4 bits for direction and channel control.

**stepping switch** A type of relay that advances its position each time it receives a pulse; a stepper switch.

**step response** The response of a device to an instantaneous change in the input.

**step up transformer** An electrical transformer with more secondary than primary turns. It thus transforms low to high voltages and matches low to high impedances.

**STIL** Abbreviation for *statistical interpretive language*.

**sticking relay** A relay that makes (closes) when dc current passes through the operating coil and continues to operate on the cessation of current, thereby saving current. It may be released with a reversed current.

**STL** Abbreviation for *synchronous transistor logic*.

**stochastic** An operation in which the element of chance cannot be avoided or excluded from consideration.

**stochastic noise** Refers to noise that maintains a statistically random distribution.

**stochastic process** Refers to a process characterized by a family of random variables.

**stochastic simulation** Refers to a simulation of the random variables and the properties of the system, rather than the system itself.

**STOP** Abbreviation for *stable ocean platform*.

**stop bit** The last element of a character in start-stop asynchronous serial transmission. The stop bit is used to insure recognition of the next start element. Also called *stop element*.

**stop element** The last element or bit of a character in asynchronous serial transmission. Also called *stop bit*.

**stopper** 1. A resistance used to reduce high-frequency potentials and the consequent build up of parasitic oscillations. 2. A resistor-capacitor combination for decoupling supply circuits, in order to prevent oscillation or motorboating in amplifiers.

**storage** A device or medium on or into which data can be entered, held, and retrieved later; a memory. Storage may use electrostatic, magnetic, acoustic, optical, electronic, or mechanical methods.

**storage allocation** 1. A specific cell or group of cells in memory. 2. The assignment of sections of data to specified sections of storage.

**storage area** The section or space in memory used for specific data.

**storage capacity** The amount of information that can be retained in a storage device, usually expressed in bits or words. Also called *memory capacity*.

**storage, cathode ray tube** Refers to the (usually) electrostatic storage characteristic of cathode ray tubes in which the electron beam is used to sense the data.

**storage cell** The elemental unit of storage in a storage system.

**storage cycle** The sequence of events required when information is transferred to or from the storage device of a computer. The storage cycle may include storing, sensing, and regeneration.

**storage cycle time** The time required for a complete storage cycle.

**storage device** The medium or device in which data can be inserted, retained, and retrieved. Mass-storage devices are used to collect, organize, and retrieve large volumes of data.

**storage, disk cartridge** Refers to a removable type of magnetic disk system used for economical mass storage. Disk cartridge systems can provide millions of words of high density memory per disk drive. Drives have a typical access time of 50 milliseconds (average random move) and can transfer a 16-bit word in about 12 microseconds.

**storage element** A unit of memory capable of storing a single bit of information.

**storage fragmentation** The sectionalizing of memory required as a result of the inability to assign actual storage locations to virtual addresses when the available spaces are smaller than the page size.

**storage key** A special set of bits associated with every word or character in some block of storage; it allows tasks with matching sets of key bits to use that block of storage.

**storage, magnetic core** Refers to a storage device in which binary data are represented by the direction of magnetization in each unit of an array of magnetic material, usually in the shape of toroidal rings, but also in other forms such as wraps on bobbins.

**storage module** A usually add-on circuit card or package that functions as an auxiliary memory for the storage and retrieval of data. A typical module uses a 4096-word RAM with two stack pointers. The processor accesses the memory using transfer instructions which reference the addresses assigned to the stack pointers.

**storage oscilloscope** An oscilloscope in which the displayed trace of an extremely short-duration phenomenon is retained as long as desired. It is used for observation of nonrecurring pulses, a periodic repetitive pulses, and transients.

**storage, primary** Refers to the fastest storage device of a computer and the one from which instructions are executed as contrasted with auxiliary or off-line storage.

**storage protection** An arrangement for preventing access to storage for reading, writing, or both. Storage protection usually operates with a programmed protection key that prevents one program from destroying or covering another by protecting a specific area of storage.

**storage, static** Refers to the storage of information that is fixed and cannot be changed easily.

**storage switch** A switch provided on the console to allow the operator to read the contents of selected registers.

**storage tube** A CRT-type tube capable of retaining a trace resulting from a nonrecurring phenomenon.

**storage, virtual** Refers to a conceptual system of main storage that does not really exist, but is made to appear as if it does through the use of hardware and programming.

**storage volatility** The inability of a storage device to retain data when power is removed.

**store** 1. Memory. 2. To enter or retain information in a storage device for later retrieval.

**store and forward** Refers to communication systems in which messages are received at intermediate routing points and recorded (stored). They are then retransmitted to a further routing point or to the ultimate recipient. Also known as the packet concept.

**stored input/output method** A diagnostic technique in which a truth table with the input/output responses is stored in memory and executes the system. Most automatic functional test systems use some variation of this method. The principal differences are in the mechanization of the hardware or software. A major disadvantage in many systems is cost because thousands of digital states must be generated to provide the stimulus.

**stored program** A set of instructions in a computer memory that specify the operations to be performed and the location of the data on which the operations are to be performed.

**stored-program computer** A computer controlled by internally stored instructions that are used to synthesize, store, or alter data or other instructions.

**STR** Abbreviation for *synchronous transmit/receive*, a transmission mode used in communications.

**STRAC** Abbreviation for *Strategic Army Corps*.

**straight cut system** An N/C system that has feedrate control only along the axes and can control cutting action only along a path parallel to the linear (or circular) machine ways.

**straight-line code** To code using repetitions of sequences of instructions by explicitly writing the instructions for each repetition, with or without address modifications.

**straight-line coding** Coding in which loops are avoided by explicitly writing the instructions for repetition of parts of the coding when required. Straight-line coding can require less execution time and more space than loop coding. A generator is usually required if the number of repetitions is large, since the coding is limited by the variable number of instructions required as well as the space available.

**strain** The dimensional change in a medium when subjected to a stress.

**strain gauge** A transducer that detects changes in pressure of mechanical stress and delivers a corresponding electrical analog of that pressure.

**strain gauge pressure transducers** Strain gage transducers convert a pressure change into a change in resistance due to a mechanical strain. Usually four or sometimes two arms of a Wheatstone bridge are used for temperature compensation.

The pressure sensing element can be a flat or corrugated diaphragm or a straight tube, because the deflection required is small. The strain gages can be mounted right on the tube, which is sealed at one end.

A pressure differential causes a slight expansion or contraction of the tube diameter. Other designs use a secondary sensing element or auxiliary member as the deforming member.

**stray radiation** Refers to direct and secondary radiation from irradiated objects that is not serving a useful purpose.

**stray resonance** Resonance due to unwanted inductance and capacitance, such as that found in leads between conductors, in leads inside canned capacitors, or between turns of inductors.

**STRESS** Acronym for *structural engineering system solver*, a language used in civil engineering for solving structural analysis problems.

**string** A linear sequence of items which are grouped in series according to certain rules. A string may be a set of records grouped in ascending or descending sequence according to a key contained in the records.

**string manipulation** The process of creating strings for the control of groups of items.

**stripe recording** A magnetic recording in which a stripe of magnetic material is deposited on a document or card.

**strobe** 1. A term for the detailed examination of a designated phase or epoch of a recurring waveform or phenomenon. 2. The enlargement or intensification of a part of a waveform. 3. The process of viewing vibrations with a stroboscope; colloquially the stroboscope itself. 4. The selection of a desired point or position in a recurring event or phenomenon, such as a wave, or the device or circuit used to make the selection or identification of the selected point.

**strobed I/O** Refers to input/output ports that use a strobed enable signal. As shown in the illustration, these ports can be built from SSI devices and other components; they are also available in lower-cost higher-integration packages.

**strobe pulse** A pulse used to gate the output of a circuit or device.

**stroboscope** An aperature producing device that gives the appearance of slow or zero motion when a vibrating or rotating object is intermittently illuminated by short flashes from a xenon or neon gas discharge tube or other source, at a suitable integral or aliquot frequent.

**stroke** A straight line or arc used as a segment of a graphic character in character recognition.

**stroke centerline** A line midway between the two stroke edges.

**stroke edge** The line of discontinuity between the side of a stroke and the background, obtained by averaging the irregularities between the printing and detecting processes.

**stroke width** The distance between the two stroke edges.

**structured design** Structured design utilizes measures, analysis techniques, and guidelines in order to control the flow of data through the system, which in turn is used to formulate the program design. The data flow is traced by charting each data transformation, each transforming process, and the order of occurrence. A system specification is

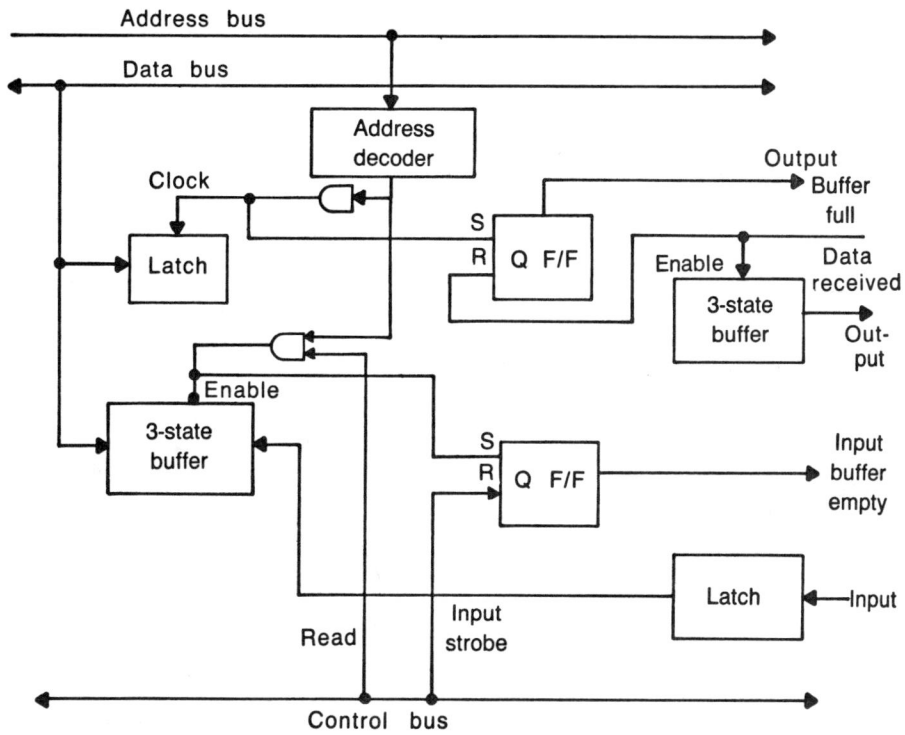

**Typical strobed I/O bidirectional port**

then used to produce a data flow diagram, and the diagram is used to develop a structure chart. The structure chart is then used to develop the data structure, and these results are used to reinterpret the system specification. The process is iterative, but the order of iteration is not rigid.

**structured programming** Structured programming tends to use only simple logic structures, including sequential structures, conditional structures, and looping structures. When sequential structures are used, the instructions or routines are executed in the order written. Conditional structures can be of the IF-THEN-ELSE type: IF A THEN $R_1$ ELSE $R_2$, where A is a logical expression and $R_1$ and $R_2$ are routines consisting of the permitted structures. If A if true, the processor executes $R_1$; if A is false, the computer executes program $R_2$. $R_2$ is not necessary if the computer is to do nothing if A is false. Here is an example of the structure for THEN AND ELSE: IF X $\neq$ 0, THEN Y = 1/X, ELSE Y = 0. This structure ensures that the processor will never try to divide by zero, and it defines Y in the case in which X is zero. An example of the structure for THEN only follows: IF CENTS > 50 THEN DOLLARS = DOLLARS + 1. This structure rounds DOLLARS to the nearest dollar. No action occurs if CENTS < 50.

Loop structures can be of the DO-WHILE TYPE, as in DO WHILE X, where X is a logical expression and R is a routine with the permitted structures. The processor checks X and executes R if X is true; then it returns to check X again. The processor execute R for as long as X is true. A example of the structure for DO-WHILE is shown below:

INDEX = 1
DO WHILE INDEX $\leq$ MAX
    BLKA (INDEX) = BLKB (INDEX)
    INDEX = INDEX + 1
END

This structure moves the number of elements specified by MAX from memory locations in one array (BLKA) to the memory locations in another array (BLKB).

**structured programming languages** Languages that contain the actual structures of structured programming include the high-level languages based on PL/I such as Intel's PL/M and Motorola's MPL. Structured programming could be used in the design stage and then the structured program translated to assembly language.

**structured programs** Structured programs are usually slower and require more memory than unstructured programs. In large programs, however, execution time and memory usage are not as critical as the time required for program development.

Structured programs can make the debugging, testing, and maintenance stages of software development much simpler. Two major difficulties with FORTRAN are the GO TO and IF statements. These can complicate the program structure, since the programmer may not know how the program reached a particular point. Many users of structured programming do not use GO TO statements, which cause unconditional transfer of program control. The simpler flow of control produces clearer, more reliable, and more easily traced programs. The

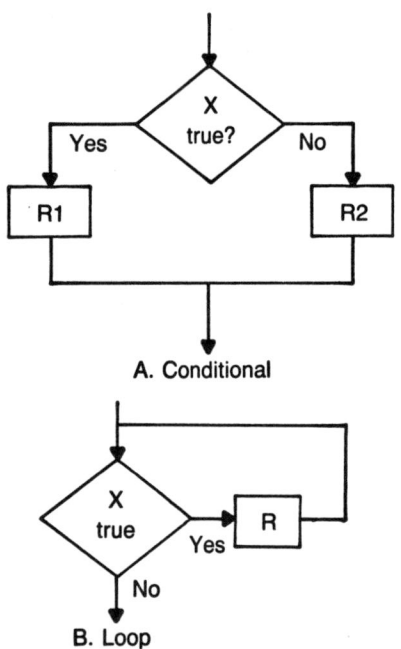

**Logic structures used in structured programming**

results of structured programming in various applications has been rewarding, especially in large programming projects.

**STRUDL** Acronym for *structural design language*, an extension of the STRESS language for the analysis and design of structures.

**stunt box** A term for the unit that controls the nonprinting functions of a printing terminal or the response of stations to selective calling signals in a communications terminal.

**STX** The *start-of-text* character; in ASCII it is designated as a seven-bit binary 2.

**SUB** 1. Abbreviation for *subtract*. 2. Abbreviation for the *substitution character*.

**subaddress** An order code that allows access to an input/output device. In a disk system, the subaddress might be the module number.

**subcommand** Refers to a portion of an input/output device that is ac-

cessible through an order code. For disk storage units, the module number is the subaddress.

**SUBIC** Abbreviation for *submarine integrated control system*.

**submicron** A particle whose diameter is less than a micron.

**subminiaturization** The technique of packaging miniaturized parts using increased methods to obtain increased densities.

**submodulator** Refers to a low-frequency amplifier that immediately precedes the modulator in a transmitter.

**subprogram** A segment of a program that can perform a specific function. Subprograms can reduce programming time when a specific function is required at more than one point in a program. If the required function is handled as a subprogram, the statements for that function can be coded once and executed at the different points in the program. Subroutines, functions, and macroinstructions may be used to provide subprograms, and they may be linked in one of two ways:

1. The subprogram reference is replaced by a jump to the desired procedure.
2. The subprogram reference is replaced with the actual statements for the desired procedure.

**subroutine** A routine that can be part of another routine. A subroutine can be a portion of another routine which allows the computer to carry out a defined mathematical or logical operation. A subroutine may be used to perform a specific task for many other routines and may be distinguished from a main routine in that it requires a location specifying where to return to the main program after its function has been accomplished.

A *closed* subroutine may obtain control from a master routine and then return control to the master routine upon concluding its function by branching or jumping.

**subroutine address stack** A stack register used to save the program return address for subroutines.

**subroutine call instruction** Some microprocessors use a subroutine call instruction for restarts (RST). This instruction is the same as CALL i, where i = restart number, O – N. The difference between a restart call and its equivalent subroutine call is that the subroutine call can use three bytes of memory, while the restart call (RST) may use only one byte.

**subroutine library** A set of standard, proven subroutines that are kept on file for use at any time in various programs. A subroutine library for floating-point operations might include decimal-to-floating-point conversion, addition, subtraction, multiplication, division, fixed-point-

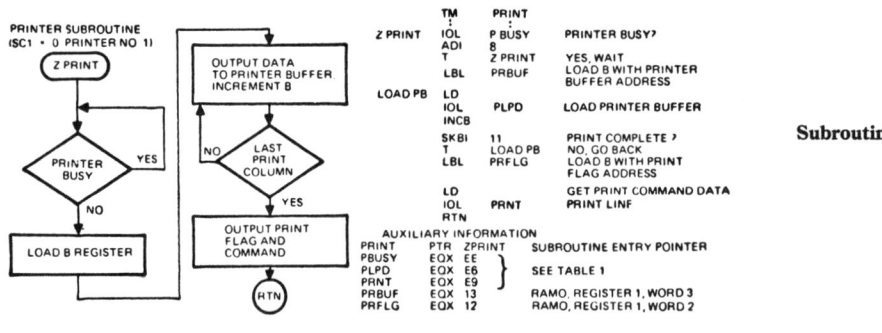

**Subroutine**

**subscript** 1. Refers to integer numerals or symbols attached to a quantity to indicate its location in an array such as a matrix. They are often used below a set name to identify a particular element or elements of that set. 2. An indexing notation for elements of a set. 3. An indexing notation for elements in an equation or other expression.

**subsequent counter** An instruction counter designed to step through or count micro operations or parts of larger programs.

**substitute character** An accuracy control character (*SUB*) used to replace a character that has been determined to be invalid or in error.

**substrate** The base material upon which or in which a transistor or integrated circuit is fabricated.

**subsystem** A secondary or subordinate system, which may be a self-contained portion of a major system. A subsystem may be used to provide one of the major system functions, with only minimal interaction with other portions of the system.

**subtract** To find the difference between two quantities.

**subtracter** A device used to perform the subtraction operation. Subtracters may use parallel or serial configurations.

**subtracter-adder** An element designed to act as adder or subtracter, depending on the control signal or command issued to it.

**subtracter instrumentation amplifiers** Subtracter instrumentation amplifiers require high-precision feedback networks. Their drift, linearity and noise-rejection capability make them useful for extracting and amplifying low-level signals in the presence of high common-mode-noise voltages. They are used as transducer amplifiers for thermocouples, strain-gauge bridges, and biological probes. As preamplifiers, they can be used for extracting small differential signals superimposed on large common-mode voltages.

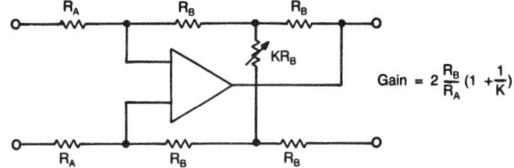

**Subtractor instrumentation amplifier**

The figure above shows a simple subtracter that uses one operational amplifier. It has a problem with source unbalance characteristics, with its low input impedance since CMRR depends on resistance matching. When a FET-input amplifier is used with very large values of resistance, noise and bandwidth problems can also occur.

**subtraction** The process of finding the difference between two quantities.

**subtrahend** The number or quantity subtracted from another number (the minuend).

**successive-approximation A/D converter** This technique consists of comparing an unknown input against a precisely-generated internal voltage at the output of a D/A converter. The input of the D/A converter is the digital output number of the A/D converter. The conversion process is similar to a weighing process with a set of n binary weights.

When the conversion command is applied, the converter has been cleared, and the D/A converter's MSB output (1/2 full scale) is compared with the input. If the input is greater than the MSB, it remains ON and the next bit is tested. If the input is less than the MSB, it is turned OFF, and the next bit is tested. If the second bit doesn't have enough weight to exceed the input, it is left ON, and the third bit is tested. If the second bit exceeds the input, it is turned OFF, and the third bit is tested. The process continues until the last bit has been tested. When the process is completed, the status line changes to indicate a valid conversion. The output register now holds the digital code corresponding to the input signal.

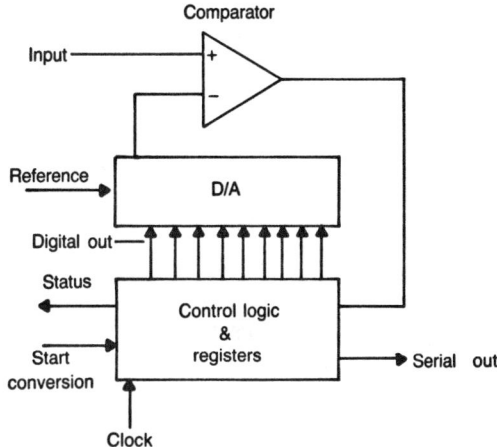

**Successive-approximation A/D converter**

**successive-approximation conversion interface** In the successive-approximation converter, each bit is compared with the analog input voltage, and the bit is left on by the register if less than this voltage or turned off if greater than the input. If the register is part of the microprocessor, this converter can be implemented with only a comparator and digital-to-analog converter as shown on the next page. The comparison operation is repeated for each bit-related position in the register until a close approximation of the input voltage is completed. The successive approximation method is fast, and it does not require a large amount of hardware. This method tends to be sensitive to temperature and voltage drifts. It is normally used only when high-speed conversions are required.

**successive-approximation sampling S/D converter** A successive-approximation sampling synchro-to-digital converter is shown. This is one type of sampling S/D converters. Part of the circuit is similar to the quadrant-selector and sine/cosine multiplier section of a tracking S/D converter. The main differences are (1) the signals from the sampler are sampled sine and cosine dc levels, rather than continuous modulated carriers; (2) the circuit that stores the digital angle output is a sequentially addressed register, instead of an up-down counter; (3) the error processor performs a simpler function. The error processor has two elements: a comparator to sense the polarity of the input signal, sin ($\theta - \phi$), and a clock-pulse generator.

**successive-approximation system** Refers to a successive approximations type of converter that uses a sample hold device at its input. Between conversions, the sample hold acquires the input signal. Just before conversion takes place, it is in hold, where it remains throughout

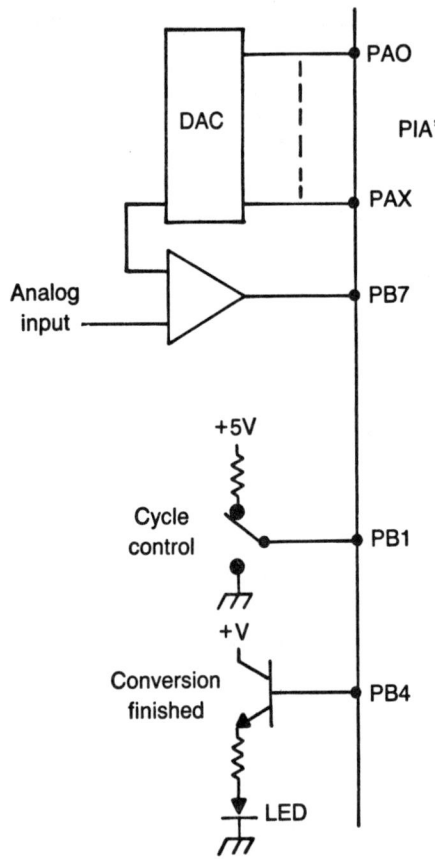

**Successive approximation conversion interface**

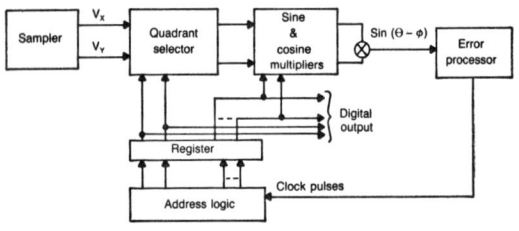

**Successive-approximation S/D converter**

the conversion. If the S/H responds quickly and accurately enough, the converter will convert the changes from the preceding sample accurately, at a speed up to the conversion rate.

**sudden death** A term used to define an abrupt failure of a working device or system.

**SUM** Abbreviation for *surface to underwater missile*.

**sum check** A check developed when groups of digits are summed. The check is usually made without regard to overflow, and this sum is compared with a previously computed sum to verify that no digits have changed since the last summation.

**summation check** Sum check.

**summing junction** A junction used in computing amplifiers and operational amplifiers to sum voltages and currents for computation.

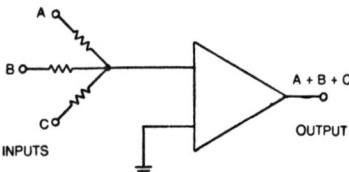

**Summing junction**

**summing point** A point in a circuit or system at which signals are added algebraically.

**super band** The frequency band from 216 to 600 MHz, used for fixed and mobile radios and additional television channels on a cable system.

**superconductivity** 1. The decrease in resistance of certain materials such as lead, tin, and thallium as their temperature is reduced to nearly absolute zero. When the critical (transition) temperature is reached, the resistance will be almost zero. 2. The physical characteristic displayed by certain materials whose resistance to the flow of electric current becomes zero below a specified temperature.

**superheterodyne** Refers to a receiver in which carrier frequencies at the forward end are reduced through heterodyning.

**superposed circuit** Refers to an additional channel obtained from one or more circuits normally provided in such a manner that all channels can be used simultaneously, without interference.

**supervising system** A set of coded instructions designed to process and control other sets of instructions. Supervising systems provide a master set of instructions to control the loading and relocation of routines and may also be used for automatic coding. Also called *supervisory routine*, *supervisory program* and *monitor routine*.

**supervisor** A monitor or executive routine that controls the proper sequencing and positioning of segments of the program during execution.

**supervisor mode** A mode of operation in which certain operations, such as memory protection instructions and input/output operations, are permitted.

**supervisor overlay** A routine that controls fetching of overlay segments using information recorded in the overlay module by the linkage editor.

**supervisory console** A system console that contains the operator control panel and operator input/output devices for system control.

**supervisory control action** A mode in which control loops operate independently, subject to intermittent corrective action.

**supervisory program** A program used to organize and control the flow of work in an automatic data processing system. An *executive program*.

**supervisory routine** A routine that controls the execution of other routines; an *executive routine*.

**super-voltage** A voltage, of over one million volts, used in X-ray tubes or accelerators.

**supply voltage** 1. The steady-state dc potential required to operate an electronic system. 2. The ac line voltage required to power the circuits which produce system operating potentials.

**support** Support includes both hardware and software facilities. Support also refers to the availability of persons familiar with the components who are accessible to the user. These persons should be engineers or experienced individuals that can support the effort. This often means the difference between the success or failure of a project.

**support system** A collection of programs, hardware, and skills used to develop, operate, and maintain a data processing system.

**suppression** 1. The elimination of any component of an emission, such as a particular frequency or group of frequencies. 2. The reduction or elimination of noise generated by a motor or generator.

**suppressor** 1. A resistor used in a circuit to reduce or prevent oscillation or the generation of unwanted signals. 2. A resistor in the high-tension lead of an ignition system. 3. A component, usually a resistance, which is used to reduce the conditions that promote parasitic oscillations. 4. A component, such as a capacitor or resistor, that damps high-frequency oscillations.

**surface barrier** The potential barrier across the surface of a semiconductor junction due to the diffusion of charge carriers.

**surface leakage** The leakage along the surface of a nonconducting material or device. It can vary widely with contamination and humidity.

**surface lifetime** The lifetime of current carriers in the surface layer of a semiconductor where recombination takes place.

**surface resistivity** The resistance between opposite sides of a unit square inscribed on the surface of a material. Its reciprocal is the surface conductivity.

**surge** A sudden current or voltage change in a circuit.

**surge voltage (or current)** A large, sudden change of voltage (or current), usually caused by the collapse of a magnetic field or by a shorted or open circuit element.

**swamping resistor** A resistor used to minimize the effects of undesirable variations in a circuit or device parameter.

**swap** To write the main storage image of a job to auxiliary storage and read the image of another job into main storage.

**swapping** A type of memory multiplexing in which jobs are transferred between auxiliary and main storage. Swapping is usually found in time-sharing applications.

**sweep circuit** A circuit used to guide the movement of the electron beam in a cathode-ray tube.

**SWIFT** Abbreviation for *society for worldwide interbank telecommunications*.

**swish noise** The noise produced by convection currents in a gas surrounding certain control or sensing elements.

**swiss cheese** A technique of circuit fabrication using a thin board containing a lattice of holes into which dot type circuit elements are dropped. Also referred to as *imitation 2-D*.

**switch** 1. To make or break a connection between two stations or points. 2. The mechanical or electronic device that makes or breaks the circuit between two points. 3. A multivibrator (bistable, astable, or monostable).

**switchboard loop panel** A patch panel with rows of jacks for access to local loops.

**switch bounce routine** In applications in which switches are used to control the inputs to the microprocessor, it may be desirable to have a delay in the program to allow for switch bounce. A mechanical switch can cause on and off transients for as long as 40 milliseconds. A sequence like the following can be used to ensure that the processor does not sample this input until the transients have settled.

```
        LDX     #5000       ; load index
                              register, 3
                              cycles
LOOP    DEX                 ; decrement index
                              register, 4 cycles
        BNE     LOOP        ; branch to LOOP,
                              4 cycles
```

**switched message network** A communications service that allows customers to communicate among themselves. Switched message networks include TELEX and TWX systems.

**switched system** 1. An array of processors connected by crossbar switches that directly couple any one processor to any other processor. 2. A telephone switching system.

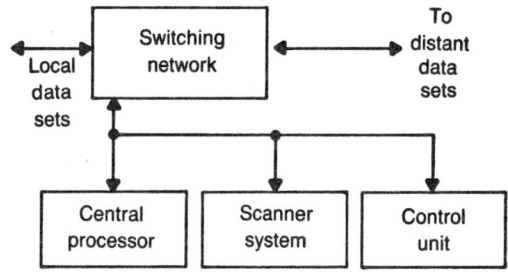

**Switched system**

**switched telephone networks** A telephone switching system provides communication links between lines in response to subscriber requests. Systems range in size from small private automated branch exchanges (PABX) with under 100 lines, to central office or tandem systems with tens of thousands of lines. A block diagram of a central office switching system is shown. The diagram shows the main elements of the system—the switching network and the processor. The switching network allows for selectively interconnecting the two wire paths by internal junction circuits. The interconnections allow a path between a subscriber station and a trunk that connects to other central offices.

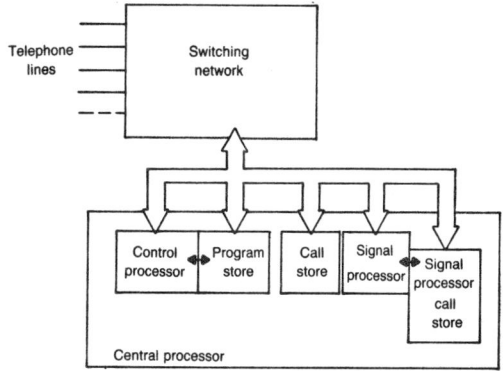

**Central telephone switching system**

**switch, function** Refers to a circuit having a fixed number of inputs and outputs designed such that the output information is a function of the input information, each expressed in a certain code, signal configuration, or pattern.

**switching** Refers to the making and breaking of connections in a circuit or network. In message switching applications, the computer can be used to accept messages from terminals and route the messages over trunk lines to remote switching devices, while providing an audit trail along with the error control.

**switching circuit** A circuit that can be used to perform a switching function, such as the connection of two or more inputs. Switching circuits include gates and the logic devices made from them.

**switching device** A device or mechanism that can be electrically placed in a desired state or condition.

**switching diode** A diode designed for high-speed switching applications.

**switching module** A module used to provide isolated output voltages for driving solenoids and other high-power devices.

**switching time** The time required for switching action to be completed from reference level to a final level, usually a fraction or percentage of the peak value.

**switch matrix** An array of circuit elements interconnected to perform a specific function. The array elements may be transistors, diodes, or gates for functions, such as encoding, decoding, transformation, code conversion, or word translation.

**switch register** An array of data entry switches that can be used to manually alter the contents of the accumulator, program counter, or memory data register. The switch register can also be read under program control.

**switch, stepping** Refers to a device or relay that has a particular number of discrete conditions and advances from one condition to the next each time it receives an input pulse.

**switch-type function generator** A function generator that uses multitap switch rotated in accordance with the input and has its taps connected to suitable voltage sources.

**SWR** Abbreviation for *standing wave ratio*.

**symbol** A graphic representation of a concept or item, such as a letter representing a quantity in a formula. Although a symbol usually consists of a single character, in some computer systems a symbol may consist of up to eight letters. Symbols may be used as statement labels or equality symbols in these systems. The value of the symbol, when defined as a label, is the value of the location counter at the time the symbol is encountered. When used as an equality, the symbol is defined by the value of the expression.

**symbol cross reference table** A table of all identifiers or entry points used in the program modules. The identifiers can be listed in alphabetical order followed by the name of the module in which they are defined as well as the modules referencing them.

Combined with the assembler cross reference listings, this table can provide good traceability of the identifiers and their references as shown below:

| IDENTIFIER | ADDRESS | DEFINED | REFERENCED |
|---|---|---|---|
| ADD | 016B | ARITH | MAIN |
| DIVIDE | 01A6 | ARITH | MAIN |
| MULTIPLY | 028B | ARITH | MAIN |
| SUBTRACT | 0270 | ARITH | MAIN |

**symbolic address** An address expressed in symbols convenient to the programmer. Also called a *floating address*, the symbolic address is used as a label to identify a particular word, function, or other item which is independent of the location of the information within the routine. If the programmer can refer to memory locations by symbolic name rather than numeric addresses, the assembler can translate these as well as the instructions. The assembler requires less time than manual translation, so fewer coding errors result.

| LABEL | MNEMONIC | OPERAND |
|---|---|---|
| XO | PTR | LXO |
| CLRX | LB | XO |

Symbolic Addresses

**symbolic assembler** A programming system that translates mnemonic instructions into binary machine-readable form.

**symbolic assembly system** The use of an assembler to translate mnemonic instruction into machine format. A symbolic assembly system provides the means of entering linkages, mapping common data, and using address modifiers.

**symbolic code** A code used to express programs in source language. The symbolic code allows the programmer to refer to storage locations and machine operations by symbolic names and addresses which are independent of their hardware-determined labels and addresses.

**symbolic coding** A coding system that uses symbols rather than actual machine addresses and instructions.

**symbolic concordance** A program used to produce a cross-referenced list of all the symbolic names in a program. Symbolic concordance programs are used for debugging and modification of larger programs.

**symbolic language** A language that expresses addresses and codes in terms convenient to humans (rather than in machine form). A program prepared in any coding other than a machine language uses a symbolic language which requires assembly or compiling.

**symbolic logic** The study and discipline of formal logic using expressions that seek to avoid the ambiguity and inadequacy of ordinary language and expressions.

**symbolic name** A label used in programs written in source language to reference data elements, peripherals, or instructions.

**symbolic parameter** A variable symbol used in assembler programming to call a macro definition. The symbolic parameter is usually assigned a value from the corresponding operand in the macroinstruction that calls the definition.

**symbolic programming** The use of symbols to represent addresses in order to facilitate programming. An assembly program is used to translate the symbolic program and assign instruction locations.

**symbolic unit** A designation used to refer to an external storage area or input/output device during coding. The actual location or device to be used is determined at a later time.

**symbol string** A string of characters consisting entirely of symbols.

**symbol variable** A symbol used in macro assembly processing that can assume any of a given set of values.

**symmetrical** Refers to circuits, networks, or transducers for which the impedance level (image impedance or iterative impedance) is the same in both directions.

**symmetrical transistor** A transistor in which the collector and emitter are identical, so either can be used interchangeably.

**symmetry** The measure of a device's ability to provide corresponding outputs on each side of zero when the polarity of the applied energy is reversed.

**symmetry-breaking effects** Refers to effects that violate the invariance of a given symmetry.

**sync** 1. Synchronous operation. 2. To synchronize.

**sync character** A character used to establish character synchronization in communications systems. When the receiving station recognizes the sync character, the station is in synchronization with the transmitting station and communication can begin.

**synchro** A rotary position indicator consisting of an induction machine with a stator and a rotor.

**synchro differential generator** Refers to a shafted device with rotor and stator coils that normally produce a three-terminal output signal equal to the sum or difference of an input signal and an input shaft rotation.

**synchronization** The matching or coordinating of two systems, devices, or functions.

**synchronization of oscillators** A phenomenon that occurs when two oscillators having nearly equal frequencies are coupled together. When the degree of coupling reaches a certain point, the two suddenly pull into step and appear to be synchronized.

**synchronization pulse** 1. Refers to pulses introduced to keep all components operating in order or step. 2. Timing pulses sent to a master clock to keep all logic gates operating in synchronous order.

**synchronize** To lock the elements of a system into step with one another, such as synchronizing the operations of a computer to clock pulses.

**synchronizer** A device or unit used to maintain synchronism between two devices or systems. Synchronizers include buffers or storage devices that are used to compensate for differences in the rate of flow of data or occurrence of events between devices or systems.

**synchronous** Refers to a constant time interval between bits, characters, and events in a circuit or system.

**synchronous capacitor** A rotating machine running without mechanical load and designed so that its field excitation can be varied in order to draw a leading current (like a capacitor) and thereby modify the power factor of the ac system or influence the load voltage through such a change in the power factor.

**synchronous clock** A system in which events are controlled by signals from a clock generator at a desired rate or frequency.

**synchronous communications interface** An interface for providing two-way communications between devices in a synchronous mode. A specific interface for data-set applications operates at up to 9600 baud in half- or full-duplex modes. Programmable functions include parity checking, special character recognition, and synchronization modes.

**synchronous computer** A computer in which each event is constrained by signals from a clock.

**synchronous data** Synchronous data usually contain a specified bit pattern for synchronization. The pattern is defined by the protocol.

**synchronous data line control** A type of protocol (abbreviated *SDLC*) used in data transmission.

**synchronous data transmission** A system in which timing is derived by synchronizing characters at the beginning of each message.

**synchronous gate** A gate that is controlled by time pulses and that in turn may be used to synchronize other operations in the computer system.

**synchronous idle character** A communication control character (abbreviated *SYN*) used in synchronous transmission to provide a signal so that synchronism can be achieved between devices.

**synchronous input** An input that allows data to be entered only when a clock pulse is present.

**synchronous machine** A machine that has an average speed exactly proportionate to the frequency of the system to which it is connected.

**synchronous mode comparator** A comparator that is used in the synchronous mode to compare the assembled contents of registers. The comparator output allows character synchronization following successive matches of data.

**synchronous operation** A mode of operation in which each event is timed by a signal generated by a clock.

**synchronous preprocessor** A device used for interfacing synchronous lines to computers. It is designed to reduce the overhead for the computer by handling most of the interrupt processing and character manipulation.

**synchronous receiver** A receiver that assembles characters from serial communications lines and asserts a flag as each character is received.

**synchronous serial data adapter** A device that converts parallel data to serial or serial data to parallel in a synchronous system. The adapter usually provides error detection and correction during transmission and reception.

**synchronous speed** A speed value related to the frequency of an ac power line and the number of poles in the rotating equipment. Synchronous speed in revolutions-per-minute is equal to the frequency in hertz divided by the number of poles, with the result multiplied by 120.

**synchronous time division multiplexer** A multiplexer (abbreviated *STDM*) which shares a synchronous data line by scanning and interleaving bits into frames of the incoming data stream.

**synchronous transmission** A mode of transmission that uses a timed stream of bits or characters.

**sync pulse** A pulse used by all system elements as a reference point for operational timing.

**syndetic** 1. Refers to connections or interconnections. 2. Pertaining to a document or catalog with cross references.

**synergetic** Refers to a combination of every unit in a system that when combined develop a total larger than their arithmetic sum. Also called synergistic.

**SYN register** A register used in some systems to hold the synchronous character code used for receiver character synchronization.

**syntactic error** An error due to incorrect structure or symbols. Syntactic errors include typographic errors, incorrect punctuation, mixed-mode expressions, illegal statements, illegal transfers, references to nonexistent statement numbers, etc.

**syntax** The relationship among characters and groups of characters and their structure in a language.

**syntax checker** A program that tests source statements in a programming language for violations of syntax.

**syntax error** Syntactic error.

**syntax error list** A linked list of syntactic errors provided so the program can be scanned to locate the errors.

**syntax transducer** Refers to a subroutine designed to recognize the phase class in an artificial language, normally expressed in Backus normal form.

**synthesis** 1. The act of combining parts to form a desired result based on the performance requirements, such as the formation of an analog signal by a rapid series of digital pulses. 2. The process of generating any one of a variety of fixed-frequency signals using special electronic techniques and devices.

**synthetic language** A pseudo code or symbolic language; a fabricated language.

**SYSIN** Abbreviation for *system input*.

**SYSLIB** Abbreviation for *system library*.

**system** A collection of methods, devices, programs, equipment, or other items which are united by some form of regulated interaction to create an organized whole. A system could be a collection of routines for providing sequencing control or debugging operations, or it could be an overall relationship between hardware, programs, procedures, and management at a particular computer installation. An operating computer, for example, is a system.

**system check** A performance check based on external program tests rather than built-in hardware circuits.

**system check module** A device which monitors a system for power failure or deviations from desired performance, and when necessary, initiates emergency actions.

**system command executive** An executive program which accepts and interprets commands by a user. Typical commands include:

1. LOG IN, LOG OUT
2. SAVE OR RESTORE PROGRAM
3. COMPILE, EXECUTE
4. INTERRUPT, TERMINATE
5. EDIT, LIST
6. REQUEST STATUS

**system controller and bus driver** A single-chip unit that generates all signals required to interface RAM, ROM, and input/output devices to the microcomputer system.

**system data bus** A bus designed for communications between all external units and the CPU. A typical bus transfers information between any two devices connected to the bus by granting access through a priority network for bus control.

**system design** The specification of the working relationship between all parts of the system in terms of their characteristic actions.

**system design aids** Hardware and software support items used in design of the various types of equipment encountered in microcomputer applications. Systems design aids include:

1. Evaluation modules and support hardware
2. Development and test equipment
3. System design documentation and manual
4. Support software

**system diagnostic** A program used to detect overall system malfunctions rather than isolate errors or faults.

**system engineering** An engineering approach in which all aspects of the system are considered in arriving at a solution.

**system firmware** Many systems include system firmware building blocks. They can be used in various systems and often assure that only application software peculiar to the application need be written by the user. The following are typical of these firmware/software system building blocks: multiprogramming executive, macro assembly language interpreter, input/output control, and disk file management.

**system handbook** A document that provides a concise reference of all the major characteristics of the microcomputer system. The system handbook will contain operation codes, addressing modes, device status details, interfaces, timing diagrams, and data flow.

**system interface** Any device that connects support hardware to the microprocessor.

**system interface module** A circuit board or card that provides the interface for external devices to the system. Modules are available for power switching, analog transducers, and communications in parallel or serial modes.

**system loader** A supervisory routine used to retrieve program phases from an image library and load them into main storage.

**system log** A set of records containing all job-related information, such as descriptions of unusual occurrences, and all commands and messages from or to the operator.

**system monitor** A program that allows the user to load and execute programs stored on paper tape or other external devices. The system monitor usually has four sections which may be associated with a physical device or unit, and which controls the console, reader, punch, and list devices. The user controls the assignment of each physical device through a system command.

**system multiplex** To interleave sequentially and transmit two or more messages on a single data channel.

**system noise** 1. The extra bits or words that must be removed from the data before it is used. 2. Any disturbance tending to interfere with the normal operation of the system by creating signals that can be read as pulses.

**system-oriented** Descriptive of applications that use a common bus system for all data and communications within the microcomputer system itself.

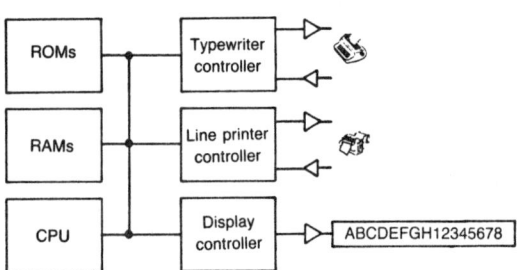

**System-oriented application**

**system reliability** The probability that a system will perform its specified tasks under specific environmental conditions.

**systems analysis** The examination and study of an activity, method, technique, procedure, or business operation to determine what operations must be accomplished and how they should be accomplished. The examination is usually aimed at achieving the maximum result at minimum cost and may include feasibility studies, identification of areas for study and correction, identification of requirements for information, assessment of costs and benefits, and definition of purpose and objectives.

**systems analyst** Refers to one who defines the applications problem, determines system specifications, recommends equipment changes, designs procedures, and devises data verification methods. She or he also prepares block diagrams and record layouts from which programmers prepare flowcharts and may assist in or supervise the preparation of flowcharts.

**systems and support software** Refers to the wide variety of software that includes assemblers, compilers, subroutine libraries, operating systems, and application programs.

**systems approach** The examination of an overall situation or problem with the aim of devising a total solution, as opposed to dealing with the separate functions that constitute the whole.

**system support** Generally refers to the support furnished by the manufacturer to simplify the application of the microprocessor and the design and development of the microcomputer system. System support may include manuals, literature, field and factory engineering specialists, prototyping hardware, and development software.

**system-support program** A program that contributes directly to the use and control of the system and the production of end results. System support programs include linkage editors, job control processors, and utility packages.

**system test** A running or simulation of the total connected set of components of a system to obtain test data and check the adequacy of the design.

**system tester** A test device used to check modules in modular industrial control systems. Some system testers use thumbwheel switches to select the test program desired.

**system timing, microprocessor** A typical processor instruction cycle might consist of five states, two states in which an address is sent to memory, one state for the instruction or data fetch, and two states for the execution of the instruction. If the processor is used with slow memories, a READY line may synchronize the processor with the memories. When the memories are not available for either sending or receiving data, the processor may go into a WAIT state. Instructions for some systems require one, two, or three machine cycles or states for complete execution. The first cycle is usually an instruction fetch cycle. The second and third cycles are often data reading, data writing, or I/O operations. The processor controls the use of the data bus and determines whether it will be sending or receiving data. State signals inform the peripheral circuitry of the state of the processor. Many of the multicycle instructions do not require the two execution states. As a result, these states are omitted when they are not needed, and the system operates asynchronously with respect to the cycle length.

**tab** 1. A nonprinting spacing action on a typewriter or other preparation device whose code is used to separate words or groups of characters in a sequential format. 2. A tabulate switch.

**table** A graphically arranged collection of data in which each item is uniquely identified by a label or position relative to other items. The items are usually laid out in rows and columns for reference or stored in memory as an array.

A *decision* table contains all contingencies that are to be considered in the solution of a problem, including all the actions to be taken. Decision tables can be used in place of flow charts for problem description.

A *lookup* table can be used to obtain a derived value of a variable which corresponds to an argument or table address.

**table addressing** Refers to multilevel indirect addressing methods that allow user constructions for effective table addressing.

**table, decision** Refers to a table of all contingencies that are to be considered in the description of a problem, together with the actions to be taken. Decision tables are sometimes used in place of flowcharts for problem description and documentation.

**table lookup** The procedure used to obtain the value of a function from a table of function values using the proper argument or address. Table lookup methods are used primarily to obtain a value for one variable when given another, where the relationship cannot be stated easily with a formula or algorithm (such as converting from one code to another).

**table lookup instruction** An instruction that allows a reference to stored data arranged in tabular form. The instruction usually directs the computer to search for a named argument and to locate and retrieve a desired value. This operation is performed in place of a calculation.

**tab sequential format** A means of identifying a word by the number of tab characters preceding the word in a block. The first character of each word is usually a tab character.

**tabsol** Refers to software for the structuring of table solutions to problems involving multiple sequential decisions such as those in manufacturing planning, engineering design, and inventory control.

**tabulate** 1. To form data into an array or table format. 2. To print out the totals of a section of storage.

**tabulator** Mechanical calculating machine driven electrically or manually.

**TACAN** Abbreviation for *tactical air navigation*.

**tachometer** A speed measuring instrument generally used to determine revolutions per minute. In N/C it is used for velocity feedback.

**Tac-Nav** Abbreviation for *tactical navigational display system* (Temco Display System unit of Ling-Temco-Vought, Inc.)

**TACS** Abbreviation for *tactical air control system*.

**tactile keyboard** A pressure-sensitive keyboard with conductive sheets.

**taffeta weave** A plain, fairly tight weave, in which the warp and filling yarns cross each other at each row in both directions; used in semiconductor clean rooms.

**tag** One or more characters attached to an item for the purpose of identification, and sometimes used in place of a *flag*.

**tandem transistor** Refers to two transistors in one package that are internally connected together.

**tape** 1. Generally, paper or magnetic tape used as a medium for storage of data. 2. To record on tape.

**tape cable** A type of cable that contains flat ribbon conductors imbedded side by side with an insulating material separating them.

**tape cartridge** A self-contained continuous loop of magnetic tape in a plug-in package. A typical tape cartridge can store over two million 8-bit bytes.

**tape cassette** A self-contained supply of magnetic tape and the reels (one for supply and one for takeup) for containing it. The cassette is a small plug-in package.

**tape conversion program** A program (abbreviated *TCP*) for duplicating paper tapes and converting from one tape format to another. The program can be used to convert from hexadecimal to binary format, or binary to hexadecimal format. The conversion requires a minimum of 2000 bits of RAM.

**tape deck** A device that contains a tape drive unit along with reading and writing heads and associated control circuitry. Also called *tape unit*.

**tape drive** The mechanism used to move tape past read and write heads allowing tape rewinding.

**tape-drive controller** A unit designed to interface one or more tape drive units to a microcomputer. The controller usually provides error checking and may provide buffering.

**tape leader** The front or lead portion of a tape.

**tape load point** The position on a magnetic tape where reading or writing can begin.

**tape, magnetic** Refers to a storage device consisting of metallic or plastic tape coated with magnetic material. Binary data are stored as small, magnetized spots arranged in column form across the width of the tape. A read-write head is usually associated with each row of magnetized spots so that one column can be read or written at a time as the tape is moved relative to the head.

**tape operating system** A software package (abbreviated *TOS*) designed for computers having at least 16,000 words of memory with no random-access storage, and at least four magnetic tape systems. It is used for smaller systems without disk drives.

**tape perforator** A unit for creating paper tapes. Tape perforators are used for recording data in environments that demand rugged equipment. The cost is lower than magnetic tape and extreme cleanliness is not required. Recording density is lower, making it suitable for applications with smaller data requirements. Also called *tape punch*.

**tape perforator interface** A circuit that provides the buffering and matching required to drive a tape perforator. It can be specified for connection to a desired microcomputer system.

**tape preparation** The act of translating command information into punched or magnetic tapes.

**tape reader-punch** A device designed to read and create paper tapes. Read operations are asynchronous at 300 characters per second. Punching is also asynchronous at 75 characters per second.

**tape reader-punch controller** A device designed to interface paper tape equipment to a microprocessor system. The controller may also include tape handlers for folding and reel-to-reel operations.

**tape recorder** A device containing a magnetic tape drive with read and write heads and associated controls. Magnetic tape recorders offer high recording speed and high density storage. Disadvantages include vulnerability to dust, temperature, and humidity.

**tape recorder interface** A device designed for incremental recording of one multibit character. Each magnetic tape character describes a single printer character such as a letter, space, or punctuation mark.

**tape trailer** The trailing end portion of a tape.

**tape transport** The mechanism that moves the magnetic tape past the sensing and recording heads. Also called *tape drive*.

**tape unit** A device containing a tape transport with read and write heads and associated controls. Also called *tape recorder*.

**tapped line** Refers to a delay line having more than two terminal pairs associated with a single delay channel.

**tapped potentiometer function generator** A technique used for generating functions of one variable in which the input variable sets the angular position of a potentiometer shaft. A number of taps along the potentiometer are positioned to represent the table of values for the function.

**target language** The language into which a program is to be translated.

**target phase** The time when a number of target statements comprising a target program are run, usually during compiling operations.

**target program** A fully compiled or assembled program that is to be loaded into the computer. Also called an *object program*.

**TASC** Abbreviation for *terminal area sequence and control*.

**TASI** Abbreviation for *time assignment speech interpolation*, a communications technique used to increase the capacity of telephone cables.

**task** Refers to an assigned piece of work.

**task data sheet** A record of jobs by time period, usually for a day or week.

**tasking** A capability in a system that allows the handling of several tasks during the same time interval using task scheduling commands.

**task management** A set of functions in the control program for allocating the hardware and software resources of the system by tasks.

**task queue** A waiting line or list of all the task control blocks that are in the system at any one time.

**TASR** Abbreviation for *terminal area surveillance radar*.

**TATSA** Abbreviation for *transportation aircraft test and support activity* (Army).

**TC** 1. Abbreviation for *tinned copper*. 2. Abbreviation for *Time to Computation*. 3. Abbreviation for *Transmission Controller*. 4. Abbreviation for *thermocouple*.

**TCAM** Abbreviation for *telecommunications access method*.

**TCP** Abbreviation for *tape conversion program*.

**TCS** Abbreviation for *terminal control system*.

**TDR** 1. Abbreviation for *time-domain reflectometry*. 2. Abbreviation for *transmit data register*.

**TELCO** Abbreviation for *telephone company*.

**telecommunications** The communication of information in written or coded verbal or pictorial form by electrical means using wire or radio waves.

**telecommunications access method** A communication subsystem (abbreviated *TCAM*) designed to exchange information between a communications network and a set of message queues. The exchange is carried out according to information contained in the control blocks and headers. The control program is coded for each particular installation using a set of system macroinstructions.

**teleconference** A conference between persons linked together by a telecommunications system.

**telemeter** To transmit or cause the transmission of analog or digital data such as measurement results from a remote fixed or moving station to a control or recording station using radio waves.

**telemeter service** A metered telegraph service between paired telegraph instruments over a time-shared circuit.

**telemetry** The remote sensing of systems using transmitted electrical signals which are coded using a suitable modulation method.

**telephone dialer** A circuit that converts pushbutton closures or stored information into dial pulses compatible with standard telephone systems. The circuit may store the last number dialed for automatic redialing.

**teleprinter** A communications terminal that includes a printing device.

**teleprinter interface** A serial interface that makes the computer system compatible with a teleprinter. In typical use, data is fed to the teletypewriter punch and stored for later transmission or fed to the computer and printed out at the same time. Standard output for the interface is a two-wire 20 mA current loop, with simplex operation at 110 baud, or 10 characters per second.

**teleprocessing** A term for describing systems that transmit data from one point to another during the course of processing the information.

**Teletype** Trade name for a terminal with a typewriter-printer that is used to send or receive messages by wire or radio.

**Teletype controller** A device that contains parallel-to-serial and serial-to-parallel conversion circuitry to interface a Teletype terminal to a computer for asynchronous operation.

**Teletype/CRT utility** A package of programs for performing the most common input/output functions for a Teletype or CRT terminal.

**Teletype diagnostic** A diagnostic program for testing the keyboard, printer, and tape reader and punch, along with the motor operation. The program uses a lookback diagnostic mode.

**Teletype exchange** The exchange services such as TELEX or TWX, which provide direct-dial point-to-point connections using Teletype equipment. Facilities are also available to allow computers to interface through these services.

**Teletype microcomputer system** A system that includes a microcomputer with Teletype interface.

**Teletype modification kit** A kit that contains the circuitry for converting TTL signals to 20 mA loop currents for Teletype units. It also contains incremental control circuits for the tape reader.

**Teletype network** A system of points connected together by private telegraphic channels. Typically up to 20 channels time-share a single circuit.

**Teletype utility** A software package for programming input/output functions through a Teletype.

**teletypewriter** A teleprinter that is part of a communications terminal.

**teletypewriter controller** A controller that allows the CPU to control the interface for full-duplex communication with a teletypewriter.

**teletypewriter exchange service** A teletypewriter service (abbreviated *TWX*) for direct point-to-point communications for subscribers.

**teletypewriter KSR** A keyboard send-receive unit that receives and prints incoming data. It also has a keyboard for manually sending out signals, but contains no paper tape.

**teletypewriter KTR** A keyboard typing reperforator that receives, punches, and types on paper tape. It can punch and send simultaneously.

**teletypewriter pulse spacing** A spacing pulse or space is the signal pulse that corresponds to an open circuit or no current condition.

**TELEX** The international network of teleprinter subscribers.

**Telpak** A leasing service of wideband channels for communications.

**TEMP** Abbreviation for *temporary register*.

**temperature coefficient of delay** Refers to the variation of delay with temperature measured in parts per million per degree centigrade. It may be nonlinear, in which case, the average coefficient over some interval is used.

**temperature coefficient of voltage drop** Refers to the ratio of the change in voltage drop across a glow discharge tube to the change in operating temperature.

**temperature influence** The change in an indication due solely to a change in ambient temperature from a specified reference temperature.

**temperature rating** 1. The maximum temperature at which insulating material may be used continuously without breaking down. 2. The maximum temperature at which a device or unit may be operated without overheating.

**temporary register** A register used as a latch to avoid race conditions. It can also be used as an internal register for microprogram control.

**temporary storage** Storage that is reserved for intermediate results. Also called *working storage*.

**temporary storage area** An area of memory reserved for data in process or in an intermediate state of computation. Also called *scratchpad memory*.

**ten-pitch** A term applied to typewriter spacing of 10 characters per horizontal inch. Also known as *pica spacing*.

**tera** Prefix for the numerical quantity of $10^{12}$ as in, for example, tera ohm.

**terminal** A point in a system or communications network at which data can be entered or retrieved. Some terminals have hard-copy and display capabilities. In systems where computers must communicate with each other, asynchronous and synchronous interfaces are used with modems for communications. A complete terminal facility may include a keyboard, display, microprocessor, memory, printer, modem, and adapters.

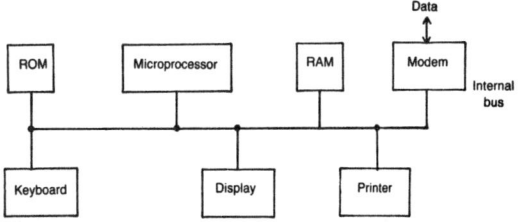

**Terminal block diagram**

**terminal area** In a printed circuit, the portion of the conductive pattern to which electrical connections are made.

**terminal, badge reader** Refers to a self-contained, remote data-entry terminal that offers a reliable method of identifying and controlling access to an area. The alphanumeric display can permit complete interaction between the computer and the operator, and therefore it can be tailored to the specific application. Options that allow a combination of controls over an audible signal, function lights, badge ejector, and keyboard lockout are available. This versatility permits the user to configure the terminal to offer a specific response to a badge input.

**terminal components** Refers to the components needed to perform most functions required of terminals including keyboard, display, microprocessor, memory, storage, printer, modem, and adapters.

**terminal controller** A unit that contains the circuitry to interface a teletypewriter or data terminal to a microcomputer. It contains a receiver which converts incoming serial data in parallel format with parity, framing, and overrun detection. The internal transmitter converts outgoing parallel data into serial format with start and stop bits.

**terminal control system** A control program (abbreviated *TCS*) designed to handle multiterminal operations in a computer system. The program schedules the use of hardware and all input/output processing.

**terminal cursors** Most terminals have a cursor of some sort. On the smarter terminals, the cursor can be moved around freely, but usually the movements are more restricted. Typical cursors include a line under the character at hand, a nondestructive blinking white block, and a white block on which an existing character on the screen is reversed. Typical cursor keyboard commands are up, down, left, right, home, and return left to next line on new line command. With the up, down, left and right keys, there is usually a repeating feature for rapid

**terminal display mode** long distance cursor movement. When cursor control keys are not enough, other interactive control devices are sometimes available as options. These include joysticks, light pens, trackballs, and a set of thumbwheel controls. These techniques are more useful on graphical terminals.

**terminal display mode** The manner in which points are to be displayed on the CRT screen. Terminal display modes include vector, increment, characters, point, or vector continue.

**terminal equipment** The equipment at the end of a communications channel used for the reception and transmission of messages. Terminal equipment may include telephone and teletypewriter switchboards in which communications circuits are terminated.

**terminal fanout** The number of circuits designed to be supplied with input signals from an output terminal.

**terminal forward-gate current** The direct current into the gate terminal with a forward gate-source voltage applied.

**terminal gate current, dc** The direct current into the gate terminal.

**terminal human factors** The key elements of human factors for terminals include the size of the screen; the number, shape and size of the characters on the screen; the color and appearance of the screen; the arrangement of the keyboard; and the sound of the keyboard.

**terminal interface** The connections, voltage levels, and impedance matching circuitry between data processing equipment and data communication equipment.

**terminal keyboard** The keyboard that is part of a communications terminal and is normally used for manual input of data or control signals.

**terminal reliability** Many terminals have features that make them easy to diagnose and service. These include self-testing and diagnostic circuitry and modular construction.

**terminals, daisy-chaining** Daisy-chaining is generally similar to multidropping, except that no modems are used; however, the terminals share the same data link. The data link comes from the computer, goes to the first terminal, comes out of the first terminal, and goes on to the second terminal. All terminals share the same data link and the same computer port.

**terminals, interactive** Refers to terminals that are generally equipped with a display and a keyboard. Such terminals support interactive, conversational, demand, inquiry, and transaction-oriented applications.

**terminated line** Refers to a transmission line with a resistance/impedance attached across its far end equal to the characteristic impedance of the line, so that there is no reflection and no standing waves when an input signal is placed at the near end.

**termination** 1. The connection or load at the end of a propagating medium. 2. The end of a program or program run.

**ternary** 1. The characteristic involving a selection or choice in which there are three possibilities. 2. A number system with a base of three.

**ternary incremental representation** An incremental representation in which the value of the increment is rounded to one of three values.

**tertiary** A separate output winding on a multiwinding transformer, but not the principal output for which the transformer is designed.

**test bench** Refers to equipment designed specifically for making overall bench tests on equipment using a particular test set-up under controlled conditions.

**test, bias** Refers to a form of test, usually as part of preventive maintenance or as a fault-finding or correcting operation, that is used to test against safety margins for faults.

**test card** A card that can be used to test all input/output functions and simulate regular and DMA controllers. The card includes special-purpose test logic for a complete test of every input/output bus signal. Connections typically are provided to check the power-failure restart system and to test automatic loaders.

**test data** The data developed to check the adequacy of the run or computer system; including data from previous runs and data created from simulated runs for test purposes.

**tester, bench-top** Refers to a small self-contained unit such as a tester for semiconductor memories, RAM's, ROM's, and shift registers. These may use a standard library of personality cards for the popular memory chips.

**tester devices and adapters** Refers to the various devices that allow one to test the various types of chips used in systems. A functional test is usually performed on each chip. Some testers provide fast, thorough, automatic testing of devices in a dynamic mode.

**testing nominative** A standard of performance established for quantitative and qualitative testing.

**testing, printed circuit board** It is common for a printed-circuit board assembly to go through engineering changes after it has been put into production. Some of the changes will be temporary fixes. The manner in which these changes are incorporated will affect the tests. If a bed-of-nails fixture is to be used, consideration must be given to accessibility.

**testing to destruction** The intentional operation of equipment or a portion thereof to ultimate failure.

**test macro** An ordered set of software and hardware designed for the testing of LSI devices. The total system includes a conditioning module, a memory, and a programmable clock generator with the associated software package.

**test program package** A collection of test and diagnostic programs for microcomputers and peripheral devices. A typical package might consist of:

1. Processor exerciser
2. Interface test
3. Interrupt test
4. RAM

**test program system** A checking system used before a program containing a sample problem of the same type with a known solution is run.

**test to failure** The process of submitting an item to stress levels within design limits until failure occurs. Accelerated tests to failure require that an item is subjected to stress levels beyond design limits to induce early failure.

**tetrad** A group of four pulses used to express a digit.

**tetrode** A four-electrode active device, especially a vacuum tube, which contains cathode, control grid, screen grid, and anode.

**tetrode field-effect transistor** A field effect transistor having two independent gates, a source, and a drain. An active substrate terminated externally and independently of other elements is considered to be a gate.

**tetrode transistor** A transistor with four electrodes.

**Texas Instruments 9900** The Texas Instruments 9900 microprocessor is a single-chip 16-bit CPU that is available in a NMOS silicon gate version or an $I^2L$ equivalent. The 9900 design has a 16-bit capability on both address and data buses. The buses use a parallel configuration that allows access to 16 bit words in one cycle. The basic architecture of the 9900 is similar to some minicomputers. There are no general purpose registers in the CPU itself; instead the general registers are found in memory. All data goes directly from memory to the ALU or to special purpose registers for interrupts or data status and then back to memory again. Since all data resides in external memory, register capacity is not limited by on-chip register capacity. This system can save time during interrupts since register data does not have to be saved, but it can also slow processing speed for arithmetic calculations.

The heart of the chip is the ALU as shown below. Three internal registers are accessible to the user. PC (the program counter) contains the address of the next instruction. This address is referenced by the processor for fetching the next instruction from memory; it is then incremented. The status register is used to contain the previous state of the processor including the interrupt mask level and information pertaining to the instruction operation.

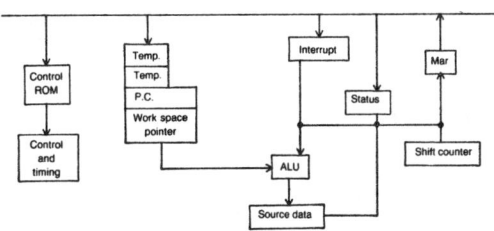

**9900 architecture**

The workspace pointer register is a 16-bit register that holds the address of the first general register in memory. A workspace-register file uses 16 memory words of the general memory. Each workspace register can hold data or addresses and function as an accumulator, an address register, an operand register or an index register. During the execution, the processor addresses a register in the workspace by adding the register number to the contents of the workspace pointer register and then initiating a memory for the word.

The workspace system may be useful when there is a change from one program environment to another due to an interrupt or a subroutine. With a conventional register arrangement, at least part of the file must be stored and reloaded. A memory cycle is used to store or fetch each word. The 9900 goes through a program environment change by exchanging the program counter, the status register, and the workspace pointer register in three stores and three fetch cycles. After the exchange, the workspace pointer holds the starting address of a new 16-word workspace for the new routine. Time can also be saved when returning back to the original program environment.

The instruction set of 69 16-bit words provides 26 arithmetic, logic, and data manipulation instructions; 14 internal register to memory operations; 5 data transfer commands; and 24 control functions. Instructions include binary multiply and divide as well as programmed DMA I/O capability.

The instruction set is more powerful than any 8 bit microprocessor, but since it is word-oriented, memory requirements must be larger and the 64 pin package also tends to increase costs.

Memory access is organized so that any 16-bit memory address can specify the location of one byte of data. The memory space for a 9900 system is 65,536 bytes which is organized as 32,768 16-bit words. Access to memory is via 15 bits on the memory bus for all 32,768 words. The 16th bit is maintained in a register to specify the byte that the processor must use during instruction execution. During byte operations, the unused byte is held, and at the end of an instruction, the two bytes are merged and returned to memory.

The 9900 does not use a stack like other microprocessors for subroutine return addresses. The programmer normally saves each return address in a general register like R11 if only a few subroutine calls are required. For applications with many subroutine levels, storage in RAM may be used.

**Texas Instruments 9900 microprocessor system** A small 9900 microprocessor system is shown. The memory contains a 16-bit by 1,024 word ROM system and a 256 by 16 RAM system.

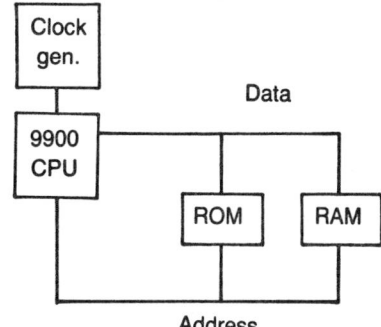

**Minimum 9900 system**

**Texas Instruments 9940** The 9940 single-chip microcomputer was designed to be compatible with the 9900 family of microprocessors. It copies the memory oriented architecture of this family.

This compatibility may be an advantage to those who are familiar with the 9900 series. But it may be a disadvantage to those not familiar or prepared to handle it.

Program memory is a 1K by 16 ROM, which is not expandable. An erasable reprogrammable version is also available.

Data memory is a 64 by 16 RAM divided into four workspace areas. The workspace concept is useful in a multiprocessing environment where a portion of memory can be used for each task. The processor can change tasks by switching to a new workspace area in memory.

The 9940 provides an extensive I/O structure for a single-chip device. It has 32 general purpose I/O lines. It has provisions for expansion to 256 additional lines. The 9940 has a serial I/O system designed for multiple processor applications. This feature can be useful for distributed processing applications. The 9940 has an internal 14-bit binary counter, which may be used as a timer or event counter.

**Texas Instruments 99000** The TI 99000 microprocessor uses n-channel, silicon-gate scaled MOS (SMOS) circuitry and runs on a 6-MHz microinstruction cycle. These microinstructions, or machine states, carry out the instructions. Using code-compression, the control ROM decodes the assembly-language instructions into a 162-bit control word.

**Texas Instruments SBP 0400** The Texas Instruments SBP 0400 is a 4-bit slice microprocessor that uses nonisolated $I^2L$ technology. SBP stands for Semiconductor Bipolar Processor. It is microprogrammable with up to 512 microinstructions and uses a single phase clock. The 4-pin package draws 200 ma at 0.85 volts, and the current drain can be adjusted to be as low as 1 $\mu$a.

This processor contains about 1,450 logic gates, which would be equivalent to 30 or 40 standard TTL packages. It contains the functions required for 4-bit parallel processing except for sequence controls. The architecture of the 0400 is organized as shown below. The ALU has 16 functions with full carry-look-ahead logic. It receives inputs from a multiplexed A port and a multiplexed B port. The eight general purpose registers have access to the A port, while the data-in bus has access to the A or B ports or the working registers. The output from the ALU is multiplexed and transferred out or along the data bus to the general registers or the working register and its extension. The eight word general register file includes a program counter and incrementor; the working register and extension can handle either single or double length operations.

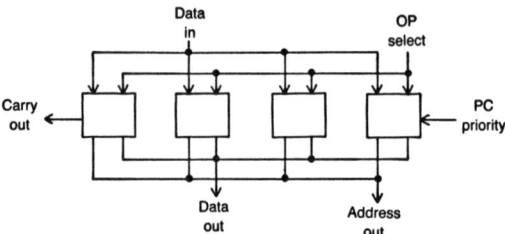

**16-bit SBP 0400 circuit**

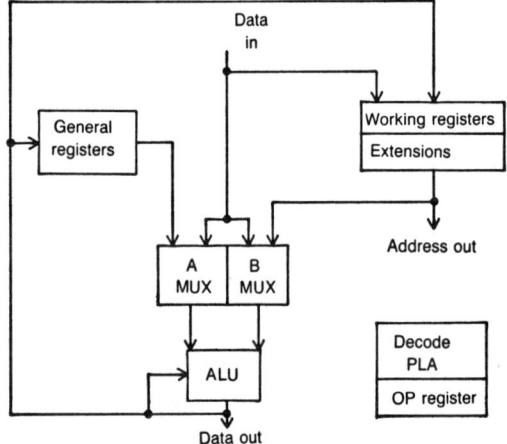

**SBP 0400 architecture**

A programmable logic array (PLA) is used to define the instruction set desired by the user. Up to 512 operations can be programmed into this on-chip array compared to 50 to 100 instructions for the typical fixed instruction set microprocessor. The user can define an instruction set that is unique to a particular application. Each instruction is represented as a 9-bit operational select word as an input to the PLA, which is operated under the clock to decode this input into a specific operation for the 20-bit operation register. The control word in the operation register then provides commands to the ALU, the general and working registers, and the bus lines for executing the machine operation. The PLA concept can allow a greater system security and integrity. The PLA is programmed at the factory and it would be difficult to copy the software instruction set; thus the developed software remains proprietary with the developers. The PLA technique also allows emulation of larger systems.

The chip architecture is expandable in 4-bit multiples. A 16-bit machine can be made up with four chips as shown below. A multichip system like this uses parallel access to control, data, and address functions along with carry-look-ahead capability. A 16-bit system as shown can be used to emulate low-level minicomputers.

**Texas Instruments TMS 1000 Family** The Texas Instruments TMS 1000 series is a family of four-bit devices that uses PMOS technology and include the ALU, ROM, and RAM on a single semiconductor chip. The user's application determines the ROM pattern, which is produced during manufacture. The 1000 and 1200 units use 1K-bit instruction ROMs. The 1070 and 1270 units are designed to interface with high voltage displays; otherwise they are identical to the 1000 and 1200 devices. The 1100 and 1300 units provide twice the ROM and RAM capacity of the 1000 and 1200.

The architecture for the 1000 series is shown. The ROM holds the program that is used to control data input, processing, storage, and output. All data processing is done by the ALU with temporary storage in the 4-bit accumulator. Data storage in the 256 bit RAM is organized as 64 four bit words. The words are grouped into four 16-bit files, which are addressed by a two bit register. Decode logic is a programmable logic array (PLA) that is changed by mask tooling. Thirty programmable-input NAND gates are used to decode the 8 bits of each instruction word. Each gate output selects a combination of 16 microinstructions, and these are used to control the ALU, and the status and write inputs to the RAM.

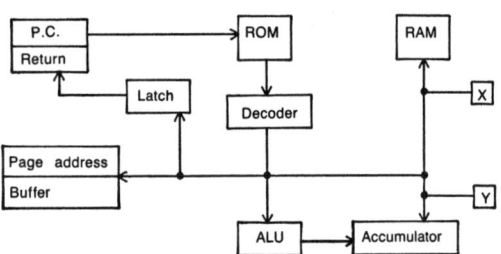

**1000 microcomputer architecture**

Device operation is determined by the sequence of the 1,024 eight-bit instructions. There are 16 pages of instructions with 64 instructions per page.

**text** A sequence of usually a great many characters treated as an entity.

**text editing** An editing facility designed into the program to allow the keyboard entry of text or copy without regard to the final format. After the copy has been placed in storage, it can be edited and justified by specifying the desired format.

**text editing typewriter** A word processing typewriter; one that records or captures keystrokes on a medium and that has the ability to make additions, deletions, corrections, and format changes in the recorded text prior to the printing of finished documents. Text-editing typewriters may be part of a larger system or may stand alone.

**text editor** The software that provides the user with a source text generation system. The text editor permits the stored text statements to be altered at any time. The user can insert, delete, or replace lines in the text buffer. Some systems also allow editing on a word or character basis.

**text processing** A term generally synonymous with word processing, though often applied specifically to applications dealing with lengthy documents, such as articles or books for publication, which may go through several editing cycles.

**text string search** A machine function that allows a user to access a point or points within a document by keying in a set of unique characters identifying the locations.

**T flip-flop** A flip-flop that has only one input electrode that causes the device to be triggered (to change from one state to another). T flip-flops are used in ripple counter applications.

**TFM** Abbreviation for *thin film module*.

**TFT** Abbreviation for *thin film transistor*.

**TFX** Abbreviation for *tactical fighter experimental*.

**thermal** A general term used for all forms of thermoelectric thermometers, including a series of couples, thermopiles, and single thermocouples.

**thermal agitation** 1. Refers to the movement of the free electrons in a material. In a conductor they produce minute pulses of current. When these pulses occur at the input of a high-gain amplifier in the conductors of a resonant circuit, the fluctuations are amplified together with the signal currents and heard as noise. 2. The minute voltages arising from random electron motion, which is a function of absolute temperature expressed in degrees Kelvin. Also called *thermal effect*.

**thermal converter** The combination of a thermoelectric device, such as a thermocouple, and an electrical heater; this device can convert an electrical quantity into heat and into a voltage. They are used in telemetering systems. Also called a *thermo-element*.

**thermal light** Refers to a display signal that is visible to a computer operator when the temperature in a piece of equipment is higher than normal.

**thermal noise** The electromagnetic noise due to thermal agitation in a material. Also called *Johnson noise*.

**thermal printer** A hard copy output device that uses chemically treated paper that darkens when exposed to heat. The pins on the print head are heated which creates the character's dots on the paper. Thermal printers produce approximately 30 cps and are used principally in low cost applications where print quality is not critical.

**thermal pyrometers** When temperatures are too high to allow a thermocouple or other temperature sensing element to be used, pyrometers can be used. All hot bodies emit radiant energy with an intensity that bears a relation to the absolute temperature of the emitting surface. Radiation pyrometry measures the radiant heat emitted or reflected by a hot object. Practical radiation pyrometers are sensitive to a limited wavelength band of radiant energy. The operation of thermal radiation pyrometers is based on blackbody radiation concepts and has made possible the measurement and automatic control of temperature under conditions not feasible with other temperature sensing elements.

**thermal runaway** A condition in semiconductor devices where an increased temperature results in increased power dissipation, which accordingly increases the temperature until ultimate destruction occurs.

**thermal shock** An abrupt temperature change.

**thermal traverse** Refers to a plot of measurements made to determine the time necessary for components of greatest thermal inertia to stabilize at a new temperature under controlled heat transfer conditions.

**thermionic conduction** Refers to the conduction that arises through electrons being liberated from hot bodies.

**thermionic relay** Refers to three (or more) electrode valves in which the on-off potential applied to one electrode controls the current flowing to another, usually without any loss of energy at the control electrode.

**thermistor** A temperature-sensitive device whose resistance varies with temperature. Its temperature coefficient of resistance is usually high, typically nonlinear, and either positive or negative.

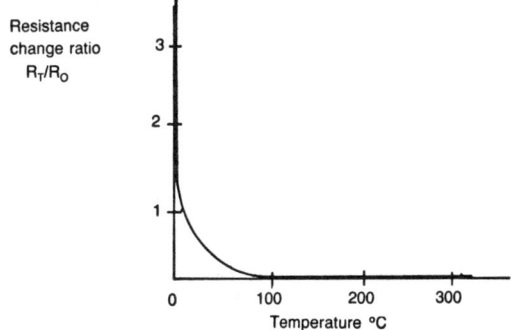

**Thermistor temperature characteristics**

**thermocouple** A junction of two dissimilar metals, which produces a voltage by virtue of the difference in the response of the atoms in the two metals to applied heat. The emf developed is typically very small and must be amplified or conditioned before use.

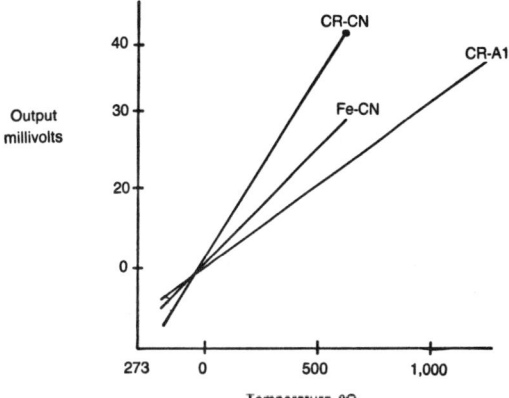

**Typical thermocouple temperature characteristics**

**thermocouple linearization** A technique for correcting errors in a thermocouple measurement system and compensating for the known nonlinearity. Linearization can be accomplished using ROMs with a specific ROM for each calibrated thermocouple.

**thermoelectric effect** The phenomenon whereby a small emf is produced by the difference in temperature between two junctions of dissimilar metals in a circuit.

**thermographic printer** A nonimpact printer that creates images through heat impressions.

**thick-film circuit** A usually integrated circuit in which layers of appropriate conducting paths and components are deposited on an insulating substrate.

**thin-film capacitor** Refers to a capacitor formed by the evaporation of two conducting layers and an intermediary dielectric film, such as silicon monoxide, on an insulating substrate.

**thin-film circuit** An integrated microelectronic circuit formed by means of a thin film, usually equal to the molecular thickness, deposited in a vacuum on a substrate.

**thin-film integrated circuits** Microminiature circuits produced on a passive substrate. Terminals, interconnections, resistors, and capacitors are formed by depositing a thin film of various materials on the substrate. Microsize active components are then inserted separately to complete the circuit. Also called two-dimensional circuitry.

**thin-film magnetic module** A storage cell that uses thin films of magnetic alloys for switching action. The thin film cells allow fast switching speeds and miniaturization of magnetic storage units.

**thin-film memory** A memory made up of plates or disks of thin film magnetic layers deposited on a nonmagnetic base.

**thin-film microelectronics** Circuits that use thin-film technology to achieve miniaturization.

**thin-film platinum temperature sensors** Thin-film platinum temperature sensors are made by depositing a thin film of platinum on an insulating substrate. This construction technique yields high resistances and small sensing elements with fast response times. The construction techniques used are similar to those used to manufacture ICs. Platinum wire RTD elements generally are delicate, and thermal cycling can cause aging. Thin-film platinum deposition and laser trimming results in small, rugged thermal sensors at a lower cost. Problems in applying the high purity films, however, can cause the R/T relationship to behave differently from pure, annealed, strain-free platinum. The temperature coefficient at room temperature is typically in the range of 30 to 80 percent of pure platinum.

**thin-film processing** Thin-film processes involve conducting layers that are a few hundred angstroms thick and are important in the reliability of integrated circuits. There are a number of important limitations in the techniques used. For example, electromigration in aluminum conductors can cause problems that result in a reduction in aluminum thickness at the oxide steps.

**thin-film resistor** A high-stability resistor that is formed by a conducting layer a few hundred angstroms thick on an insulating substrate.

**third generation** 1. In the N/C industry, the period of technology associated with integrated circuits. 2. The period of technology in computer design utilizing integrated circuits, advanced programming concepts and time sharing.

**third-generation computer** A computer utilizing solid-state electronic logic blocks in the form of integrated circuits.

**third party lease** An arrangement whereby a vendor sells equipment to a buyer, often a leasing company, who in turn leases it to a user.

**THOR** Abbreviation for *tape handling option routine*.

**three-address** An instruction format that contains three address parts.

**three-card connector cage** Refers to a cage that consists of a U-shape bracket with edge connectors mounted along the bottom and card-guide ridges formed in the sides. The connector spacing is made to allow the mounting of three wire-wrapped circuit boards.

**three-D process** Refers to a triple-diffusion process for complementary integrated-circuit structures.

**three-plus-one address** An instruction that contains three operand addresses and one control address.

**three-tier hierarchical system** An example is shown below. This configuration might be a computer control system for two plants. The top tier is a large data processing computer. Two supervisory minicomputers, one in each plant, are shown in the middle tier. The bottom tier uses microcomputers for direct control operations.

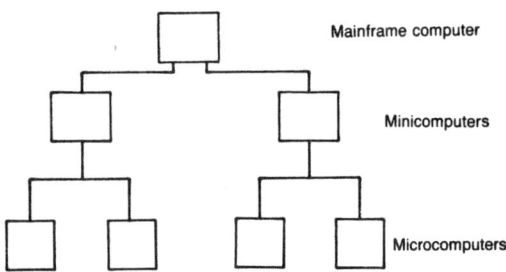

**Three-tier hierarchical network configuration**

**three-wire system** A system of electrical supply using three conductors; one of these (the neutral wire) is maintained at a potential midway between that of the other two, which are called the outer conductors.

**threshold** 1. The point at which an effect is first observed or measured. 2. A logic operator having the property: if P, Q, and R are statements, then the threshold of P, Q, R is true if at least *n* statements are true; it is false if less than *n* statements are true. In this context, *n* is a nonnegative integer called the *threshold condition*.

**threshold element** A device that performs the logic threshold operation in which the truth of each input statement contributes to the output determination.

**threshold energy** The minimum energy for a particle that can just initiate a given endoergic or exoergic reaction.

**throughput** The rate at which work can be handled by a system. Throughput is a measure of system efficiency, and it relates to the speed at which problems, programs, or routines are performed. Throughput can be measured as the total information processed in a specified time period, and includes input time, processing time, and output time.

**thru-put** Thru-put (or through-put) is a measure of processing information per unit time, and speed is a measure of how rapidly that is accomplished. Thus, a thru-put is the measurement of productivity. Speed can increase the thru-put, but greater processing volume is also attained by increasing information paths.

**thumbwheel control** An operator at a central control terminal can select various status conditions to be displayed or change alarm limits through a set of BCD thumbwheels. The microcomputer terminal controller works primarily with character data for the supporting peripherals, and it can process data from the thumbwheels or the monitor controller. Either binary or BCD data from the thumbwheels can be processed directly.

**thyratron extinction** The termination of the flow of current through a thyratron by the reduction or interruption of the anode supply.

**thyristor** A thyratron-like semiconductor device for bistable switching. There are various pnpn types, using silicon, that provide a phase-controlled rectifier, similar to a thyratron tube. Voltage ratings of up to 600 V are common, while current handling capability can be on the order of 50 A.

**tilt** Input-to-output waveform differences when the processing circuits are not fully linear; skew.

**time constant** In an RC circuit, the product of $R$ (ohms) and $C$ (farads) expressed in seconds, which is the time required for an uncharged capacitor to charge to 63.2% of the applied voltage. After five such periods, the capacitor is considered to be fully charged (except in pulse circuits, where seven periods are considered necessary to completely charge the circuit).

When voltage is removed from an RC circuit, the time constant describes the complementary arrangement: the amount of time required for the capacitor to lose 63.2% of its charge (drop to the 36.8% voltage level). In an RL circuit, the time constant in seconds is equal to L/R (in henrys and ohms) and follows the same charge and discharge curves. See *time constant chart*.

**time-constant chart** A chart showing universal charge and discharge curves for RC and RL circuits, where voltage or current is shown as a decimal fraction of 1.

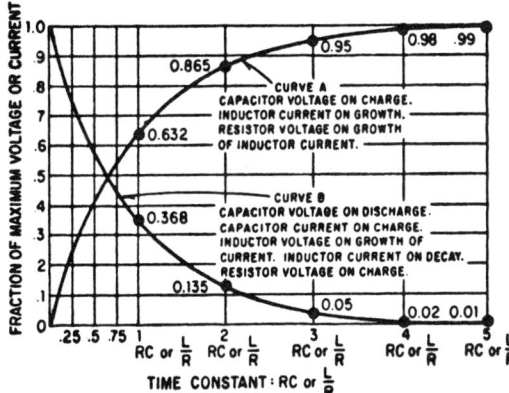

Time constant chart

**time, cycle** 1. Refers to the minimum nonoverlapping time interval between successive accesses to one storage location. 2. Refers to the time required to process an instruction. Cycle time is one parameter that allows a comparison of speeds. Because other factors, such as the instruction set and cycles/instruction, affect computer speed, benchmark programs similar to the required application program should be used to compare speeds.

**time-delay circuit** A circuit or device that provides (1) electrical contact after a specified time, (2) the breaking of electrical contact after a specified time, or (3) the delayed transmission of input signals.

**time discriminator** Refers to a type of circuit with an output proportional to the time difference between two pulses, its polarity reversing if the pulses are interchanged.

**time-division multiplex** A multiplexing method (abbreviated *TDM*) that transmits two or more coincident signals over a common path using a sampling technique for sensing each signal alternately.

**time domain measurements** These are frequency measurements on clocks and timed devices and circuits that are taken and compared over a period of time.

**time-domain reflectometry** The study or measurement of phenomena associated with signal propagation along wires or other related media.

**time origin** Refers to a start of a pulse defined as the time at which it first reaches some given fraction, such as 10 percent of its full amplitude.

**time pulse distributor** A device or circuit that allocates timing or clock pulses to one or more conducting paths in a specified sequence.

**timer, internal** An electronic timer that facilitates the monitoring or logging events at predetermined intervals.

**time schedule controller** A controller whose actions adhere automatically to a predetermined time schedule.

**time series** Refers to a discrete or continuous sequence of quantitative data assigned to specific moments in time, usually studied with respect to their distribution in time.

**time-share** To use a device or system for two or more interleaved purposes.

**time-shared BASIC** An enhancement of BASIC that is used as a conversational language to provide access to a computer system for a maximum number of users.

**time-shared computer** A computer system that allows usage by a large number of subscribers, usually through data communication subsystems. Certain data and programs may be shared by all users, while other data and programs may only be provided and used by certain subscribers. Documentation for general programming on the system is available with the time-sharing service which provides system-dependent operating instructions. The programmer may be assigned a work area in the system for storing programs that can be edited using the system editor.

**time-sharing** A computer technique in which a device or facility is shared by several other devices or users by allocation of separate time slots. Time-sharing programs are available for several microprocessors, and time-sharing services are available from a number of service organizations. Time-sharing allows a microcomputer system to be developed on a pay-as-you-go basis, since there is not normally a fixed overhead charge.

**time-sharing, conversational** The simultaneous utilization of a computer system by multiple users at remote locations, each being equipped with a remote terminal. The user and the computer usually communicate by way of a keyboard and CRT display.

**time slice** A designated interval of time during which a job or task uses a resource without being preempted.

**time-slicing** 1. The allocation of time slots to terminal jobs in time-sharing systems. 2. A feature in some systems which prevents a task from monopolizing CPU time in a system and delaying other jobs or tasks.

**timing clock** The source of timing signals or clock pulses required for sequencing computer operation. This source usually consists of a clock generator and a cycling unit to derive the sets of pulses required at specific intervals. Sometimes called *timing master*.

**timing master** The primary source of timing signals in a computer system; *timing clock*.

**timing, processor** Microprocessor timing and clock generation methods affect the system, because instruction times are based on maximum clock frequencies and cycle times.

**timing signals** The electrical pulses that are required at specific intervals to ensure synchronization in processors. The synchronous logic used in most machines is based on a clock signal to trigger operations on pulses of a fixed period. Instruction times are based on the maximum clock frequency of the microprocessor, and other lower-frequency signals may be desired to optimize other functions, such as memory access time.

**timing specifications, real-time clock**  In some systems a crystal controlled, 100 day clock is used; the maximum readout is 99 days, 23 hours, 59 minutes, and 59 seconds. The time is outputed or printed at the beginning of each data scan. The accuracy is 0.025 percent.

**TIMM**  Abbreviation for *thermionic integrated micro-module*.

**tinkertoy**  Refers to one of the early attempts at modularization in which wafers, with one more component parts printed or mounted on them, were stacked vertically with interconnecting wiring stiff enough to provide support running through holes around the periphery of the wafer. The multiplatform-like appearance of the stacked wafers and support wiring inspired the name of the technique, which with modifications, is still employed for some high density packaging.

**TIPS**  Abbreviation for *terminal interface processors*.

**TIPSEY DOG**  A ground-based radar.

**TL**  Abbreviation for *transmission line*.

**TMS 5501**  This chip has a PIO with an 8-bit input port, an 8-bit output port, plus an asynchronous serial line, two interrupts, and five programmable interval timers. It interfaces directly to the 8080 without the 8228. This component is a combination of a PIO, UART, and PIT (programmable interval timer).

**TNF**  Abbreviation for *transfer on no overflow*.

**TNZ**  Abbreviation for *transfer on non zero*.

**toggle**  A bistable trigger circuit such as a flip-flop which switches between two stable states.

**toggle switch**  A circuit or switch that holds one of two states until changed.

**token**  A distinguishable unit in a sequence of characters.

**tolerance**  A permissible deviation from a specified value. A frequency tolerance is expressed in cycles or as a percentage of the nominal frequency, and a temperature tolerance, in degrees centigrade.

**tool function**  A tape command identifying a tool and calling for its selection.

**tool length compensation**  A manual input technique that eliminates the need for preset tooling and allows the programmer to program all tools as if they are of equal length.

**tool offset**  1. A correction for tool position parallel to a controlled axis. 2. The ability to reset tool position manually to compensate for tool wear, finish cuts, and tool usage.

**TO package**  A semiconductor package, usually metal, used to house discrete transistors.

**top-down design**  The top-down design technique is based on the philosophy that the problem can be broken down into smaller tasks or sections that can become modules. In top-down design the testing and integration can occur along the way rather than at the end; thus some problems may be discovered early. Testing can be done closer to the actual system environment instead of using driver programs. The top-down design technique tends to combine the design, coding, debugging, and testing stages.

An example of top down design for A/D conversions follows:

1. The flowchart is written as shown. The program initially calls the A/D input routine, which is a program stub, and then calls the other routines or program stubs if the input data is not zero; it then returns to reading the A/D input.
2. The routine that reads the A/D input is expanded, the input from the converter consists of three BCD digits that the CPU fetches one at a time. The expansion results in the following tasks:

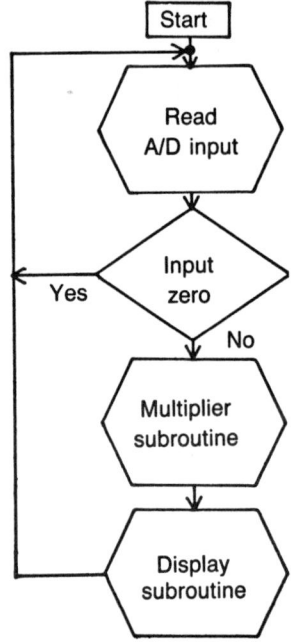

**A/D general flowchart for top-down design**

a. Send a START CONVERSION signal to the A/D converter.
b. Check the CONVERSION COMPLETE line. Wait if the conversion is not complete.
c. Fetch a digit.
d. Check the digit for zero.
e. Repeat (c) and (d) three times.
f. If all the digits are zero, repeat starting with step (a).
g. Check if the converter has reached the final value by waiting and then repeating (a) through (f).
h. If the inputs are not equal, repeat step (g) until equal within the converter accuracy requirement.
i. Save the final input value.

**top octive synthesizer**  Refers to a frequency synthesizer designed to generate the highest frequencies used in electronic organs. They are applicable to any electronic musical instrument based on the equal tempered scale. These products facilitate the design of instruments that never require tuning and offer automatic transposition. The outputs contain both odd and even harmonics and do not jitter or produce undesirable subtones.

**Torr**  1 mm of mercury.

**TOS**  Abbreviation for *tape operating system*.

**total capacitance**  The capacitance between a given conductor and all other conductors in a system.

**totalizing**  Registering a precise total count from a mechanical, electromagnetic, or electronic device.

**total multiplexing**  A system that allows both analog and digital signals to flow either to or from a central control and the remote multiplexers.

**total temperature**  A temperature that represents the total energy of the gas stream and is the sum of the static temperatures that would result if the kinetic energy of the stream were entirely converted into heat.

**total transition time** The time interval between the point of 10 percent input change and the point of 90 percent output change. It is equal to the sum of the delay time and rise or fall time.

**touch control** A device that adjusts the pressure required to operate a keyboard.

**townsend avalanche** A multiplication process in which a single charged particle that is accelerated by a strong field causes a large increase in ionized particles through collisions.

**townsend criterion** A relationship expressing the minimum requirement for breakdown in terms of the ionization coefficients.

**TPM** Abbreviation for *tape preventive maintenance.*

**TPI** Abbreviation for *tracks per inch,* a measure of disk recording capacity. The higher the TPI, the more information the media can record.

**TPR** Abbreviation for *teleprinter.*

**TRACALS** Abbreviation for *traffic control, approach and landing system.*

**TRACE** Abbreviation for *taxiing and routing of aircraft coordinating equipment.*

**trace** 1. An interpretive diagnostic method which provides an analysis of each executed instruction and writes it on an output device as each instruction is executed. A selective trace may be used to trace instructions which satisfy certain specific criteria such as instruction type or data location. 2. The graphic representation of a waveform on a CRT screen. 3. To troubleshoot a circuit or system by monitoring signals at various points along the signal route.

**trace program** A diagnostic program used to perform a check on another program. The trace program may include instructions as its output.

**trace routine** A routine used to provide a time history of machine registers and controls during the execution of the object routine. A complete tracing routine can provide the status of all registers and locations affected by each instruction each time the instruction is executed.

**track** 1. The path along which information is recorded on a storage medium such as a drum or tape. 2. To properly follow a master control signal or control element.

**tracking converters** A tracking synchro converter is shown. Three-wire synchro-angle data are sent to a Scott-T transformer, isolated from ground and translated into two signals, the amplitude of one being proportional to the sine of $\theta$ and the other proportional to the cosine of $\theta$. These amplitudes are the carrier amplitudes at the reference frequency. The cosine wave is $\cos \theta \cos wt$; the carrier term, $\cos wt$, is removed in the demodulator. The quadrant selector circuit selects the quadrant in which $\theta$ lies and also sets the polarities of the sine $\theta$ and $\cos \theta$ signals for computations. The outputs of the quadrant selector are then sent to the sine and cosine multipliers.

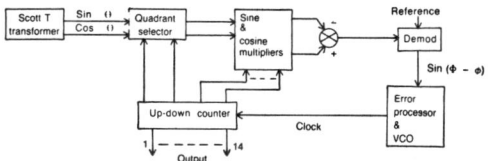

**Tracking S/D converter**

The multipliers are digital programmed resistive networks. The transfer functions of these networks are determined by a digital input that switches in resistors in such a manner that the instantaneous value of the output is the product of the instantaneous values of the analog input and the sine or cosine of the digital encoded angle $\phi$. When the instantaneous value of the analog input to the sine multiplier is $\cos \theta$ and the digital encoded word sent to the sine multiplier is $\phi$, then the output is $\cos \theta \sin \phi$. Thus the outputs from the multipliers are:

Sine multiplier: $\cos \theta \sin \phi$.
Cosine multiplier: $\sin \theta \cos \phi$.

These outputs are sent to a subtractor, thus the input to the demodulator is:

$$\sin \theta \cos \phi - \cos \theta \sin \phi = \sin (\theta - \phi)$$

This identity indicates that the output represents a carrier frequency sine wave with an amplitude proportional to sine of the difference between $\theta$ and $\phi$. The demodulator has access to the reference

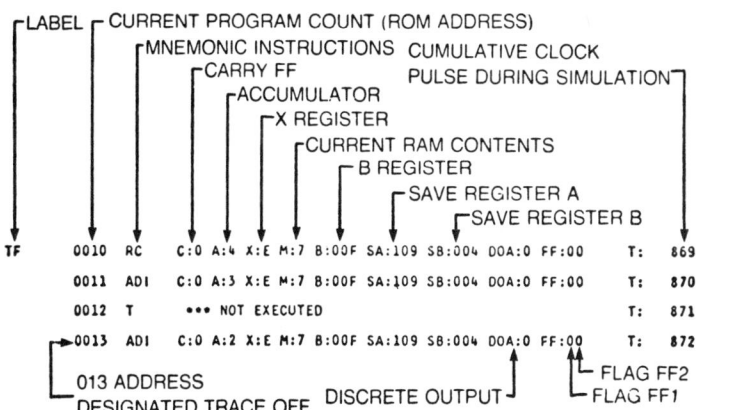

Trace, 1

voltage, which has been isolated from the reference source and scaled by the reference isolation transformer. The output of the demodulator is an analog DC level proportional to sin $(\theta - \phi)$. This is the sine of the error between the angular position of the synchro and the digital encoded angle, $\phi$, which is the output of the counter. For small errors, sin (error) $\cong$ (error). This analog error signal is then fed to the error processor and VCO block.

This circuit block consists of an analog integrator output (the time-integral of the error) that controls the frequency of a voltage controlled oscillator (VCO). The VCO produces clock pulses that are counted by an up-down counter. The sense of the error ($\phi$ too high or $\phi$ too low) is determined from the polarity of $(\theta - \phi)$. This is used to generate the counter control signal, which determines if the counter is up or down. It is normal practice to add a small amount of hysteresis into the reaction of the error processor.

The two most significant bits of the angle $\phi$, which are stored in the up-down counter, control the quadrant selection, and the remaining 12 bits are fed in parallel to the inputs of both multipliers. The up-down counter acts as an incremental integrator. Therefore the tracking converter acts as a closed loop servomechanism (continuously attempting to null the error to zero) with two lags, since there are two integrators in series. This is then a Type 11 servo loop, which has advantages over Type 1 or Type 0.

**track, primary** On a direct access device, the original track on which data are stored.

**traffic control, microcomputer** A microcomputer at each intersection allows a large central master traffic control system to know the traffic flow at each intersection. The intersection microcomputer can implement light changes operating (1) on its own information, (2) in conjunction with a group of intersections, or (3) under central master control. This multimode control is now practical with microcomputers and has become low in cost.

**trailer card** A card that contains information related to the data on preceding cards.

**transaction telephone** A credit validation system that uses either a dedicated line to the central computer or an acoustical coupler with an ordinary telephone. The transaction telephone was developed by Bell Telephone Laboratories and uses the Rockwell PPS-4 microprocessor with other Western Electric components. The Rockwell PPS-4 (4-bit Parallel Processing System) is a 4-bit CPU. It is packaged in a 42 pin flat pack.

The transaction telephone user inserts a credit card into the card reader of the telephone system. The card reader senses the data on the magnetic stripe of the card and converts this data into digital signals. The microprocessor checks that the card has been read correctly by performing a parity check of the read information. If the card has been read correctly, the microprocessor interprets the data to control the touch-tone oscillators of the telephone set, sending the data over the telephone network to a computer. After the computer performs a credit check from the serial number on the card, a signal is sent back to the transaction telephone indicating if credit should be authorized. The microprocessor receives this signal and actuates the appropriate light on the telephone system to indicate to the user if the transaction is authorized. Although the transaction telephone was designed for retail establishments for credit validation purposes, other uses of the product have been utilized. Bank customers can automatically check their account balances by inserting their bank credit card into a transaction telephone system equipped with a numeric display. Electronic funds transfer may occur through a transaction telephone.

**transceiver** A terminal device that can be used to transmit and receive signals. A typical asynchronous transceiver provides a data communications interface for operation in full- or half-duplex modes. The unit accepts parallel data words from a computer or terminal and converts the data into asynchronous serial format. Received information is converted into parallel data for transmission to the computer or terminal. Baud rates, bits per character, parity mode, and number of stop and start bits are typically selectable by control signals or jumper leads.

**transcribe** To copy, with or without translating, between storage media or between computers and storage media.

**transcriber** The equipment used for translating data recorded in one format to another format, and recording this data for later use elsewhere.

**transducer** A device that converts one form of energy into another form. The energy may be electrical, mechanical, acoustical, thermal, etc.

**transducer-coupling system efficiency** The power outputs at the point of application divided by the electrical power input into the transducer.

**transducer, expandor** Refers to a transducer, designed for a given amplitude range of input voltages, that produces a larger range of output voltages. One type of expandor uses the information from the envelope of speech signals to expand their volume range.

**transducer, feedback** Refers to a transducer that generates a signal depending on the quantity to be controlled. A potentiometer, synchro, or tachometer might be used, giving proportional, derivative, or integral signals respectively.

**transducer loss** A ratio of the power from the source to the power that the transducer delivers to the load under specified operating conditions.

**transducer pulse delay** The interval of time between a specified point on the input pulse and on its related output pulse.

**transducer translating device** Refers to a device for converting the error of the controlled member of a servomechanism into an electrical signal that can be used for correcting the error.

**transfer** 1. To jump or cause to jump. 2. To transmit or copy information from one device to another.

**transfer admittance** The ratio of the current at a pair of terminals of an electrical device to the voltage applied between another pair, with all terminals being terminated in a specified manner.

**transfer check** 1. A check to determine if a transfer or jump operation was successfully completed. 2. A verification of data by temporarily storing, retransmitting, and comparing. The transfer check can be implemented by comparing each character with a copy of the same character transferred at a different time or by another route.

**transfer circuit** A circuit which connects two or more communications networks to transfer the traffic between the networks.

**transfer command** An instruction which changes control from one part of the program to another by indicating a remote instruction.

**transfer current** The current in a gas tube control electrode required for ionization and gas discharge.

**transfer function** The expression relating the output of a control system to its input.

**transfer impedance** The ratio of the potential difference between a pair of terminals of a network to the resultant current at another pair of terminals with all terminals being terminated in a specified manner.

**transfer rate** The rate at which information is transferred between various units in a system. It is limited by the transfer capabilities of the memory itself and of the memory bus. The transfer rate is sometimes called the memory bandwidth and measured in words or bits per second.

**transfer ratio** Refers to the ratio of transfer of a parameter such as power or current in a circuit or transducer at a specified frequency.

**transfer table** A table that contains a list of all transfer instructions of programs in main memory. The transfer table allows the transfer of control between programs.

**transfer time** The time required to complete a transfer operation in a computer.

**transform** To change the form of data according to specific procedure, usually leaving some feature of the data invariant. The structure or composition may be changed, but the meaning or value is not significantly altered.

**transformer** An inductive electrical device which uses electromagnetic energy to transform voltage and current levels in a circuit.

**transformer coupled isolation amplifier** Isolation amplifiers, employing transformer coupling, offer total galvanic isolation, a low capacitance of < 10 pF between input and output ground circuits, a CMR of 115 dB at 60 Hz, and common-mode voltage ratings to 5 kV. Capable of transmitting millivolt signals with unity or adjustable gain, these devices are used for medical applications where an ECG waveform is the input to isolate patients from ground-fault currents.

Like the instrumentation amplifiers, these amplifiers use committed gain circuits with internal feedback networks and can operate from dc to 2 kHz. They are designed in two parts: an isolated amplifier section and an output section.

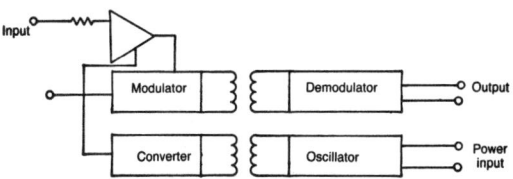

**Transformer coupled isolation amplifier**

The amplifier section includes a fixed-gain op amp, a modulator, and a dc-regulator enclosed in a floating guard-shield. The output section contains the demodulator, filter, and power supply oscillator circuit, operating from a single supply. Operating power is transformer-coupled into the shielded input circuits and capacitively or magnetically coupled to the output demodulator circuit. A typical ECG application in a medical electronics data acquisition system is shown.

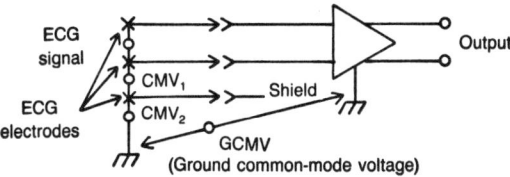

**ECG amplifier**

**transformer step-down** Refers to a transformer in which the output voltage is less than the input voltage.

**transformer step-up** Refers to a transformer in which the output voltage is greater than the input voltage.

**transient** A sudden pulse in a signal; it is usually of extremely short duration and may be difficult to detect, but it often causes problems because it may be read by the system as a signal element. High-voltage transients can be destructive to unprotected components in a system.

**transient analyzer** A device used for the study and observation of transient electrical phenomena in circuits and systems.

**transient distortion** A distortion due to the inability of a system to reproduce transients linearly.

**transient motion** Any motion that has not reached or has ceased to be a steady state.

**transient oscillation** A momentary oscillation that may occur in a circuit during switching.

**transient response** The fidelity with which a circuit responds to step voltages, pulses, or waveforms with extremely fast rise times.

**transient wave** A wave-pulse that results from changes in the current amplitude and/or frequency. The effects decay rapidly but are propagated along transmission lines.

**transistor** A usually three-terminal active solid-state device that can be used for amplification and switching. Some two-terminal transistors have no input lead and are controlled by incident light.

**transistor action** Refers to the physical mechanism of amplification in a transistor.

**transistor amplifier** An amplifier that uses one or more transistors.

**transistor and diode automatic test system** A computer-operated system for the testing of transistors and other semiconductor devices, including diodes, SCRs, and FETs.

**transistor, binary counter** A combination of flip-flops and gates in which a pulse train or clock changes a flip-flop according to the "0" or "1" condition of the inputs. When a set of these flip-flops is connected, a binary counter is obtained. As successive pulses enter into the first trigger or "clock" input, the "0" or "1" condition of the flip-flops change.

**transistor current gain** The slope of the output current against input current characteristics for a constant output voltage. In a common-base circuit it is somewhat less than unity, but in a common-emitter circuit it may be relatively large.

**transistor, depletion-type field-effect** A field-effect transistor having an appreciable channel conductivity for zero gate-source voltage. The channel conductivity can be increased or decreased according to the polarity of the applied gate-source voltage.

**transistor, drain cutoff current** The direct current that goes into the drain terminal of a depletion transistor with a specified reverse gate-source voltage applied to bias the device to the off state.

**transistor, dual-gate field-effect** An alternate term for a tetrode field-effect transistor.

**transistor flip-flop** A flip-flop consisting of two cross-connected transistors.

**transistor, insulated-gate field-effect** A field-effect transistor having one or more gate electrodes that are electrically insulated from the channel.

**transistorized** Fabricated using transistors for active signal processing functions.

**transistor logic** Circuits that use transistors with other components for performing logic functions.

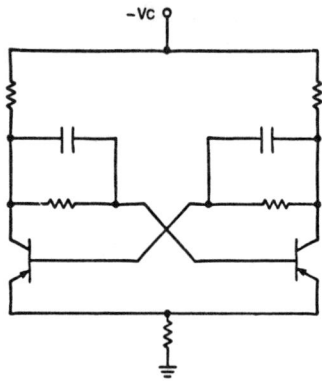

**Transistor flip-flop**

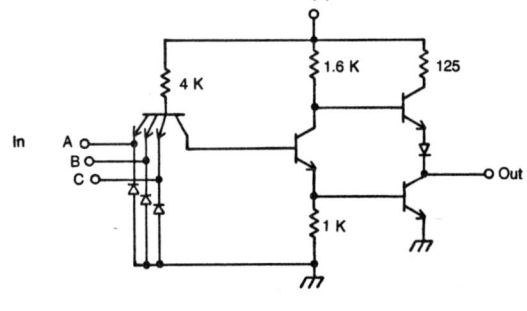

**TTL NAND gate**

**transistor, metal-oxide semiconductor** An insulated gated field-effect transistor in which the insulating layer between each gate electrode and the channel is an oxide material or an oxide and nitride material.

**transistor NAND circuit** In diode logic circuits, the input and output signals are of the same polarity, but if transistors are used instead of diodes, it is possible to invert the polarity and perform the logic function in a single stage. It is therefore simple to change the AND circuit into a circuit in which there is a "1" output only when both inputs are not "1." Since this circuit has an output only in the NOT AND condition, it is called the NAND circuit.

**transistor, n-channel field-effect** A field-effect transistor that has an n-type conduction channel.

**transistor oscillator** An oscillator that uses at least one transistor to produce its output signal.

**transistor, p-channel field-effect** A field-effect transistor that has a p-type conduction channel.

**transistor, pentode** A transistor designed for mixing, modulating, or switching, and containing four electrodes.

**transistor power-pack** Refers to a power supply unit that uses transistor inverters or converters.

**transistor seconds** Transistors in a production run that do not meet the primary manufacturing specifications, but that are functioning units suitable for less rigorous applications than specified.

**transistor tetrode** A transistor designed to operate at high frequencies, having an emitter, collector, and two base connections.

**transistor-transistor logic (TTL)** The circuit for a TTL NAND gate is shown. This circuit uses four transistors and four resistors.

TTL is a saturated form of logic; during turn-on both the emitter-base and collector-base junctions are forward biased, which causes an accumulation of charged carriers in the base region. As the device is turned off, this charge must be discharged through the collector. The time required for this discharge results in a delay in turning the transistor off. All saturated logic experiences this storage time delay. There are other versions of the TTL gate. Five versions are listed below, together with propagation delay, power dissipation, and the product of these two parameters which serves as a figure of merit.

The standard TTL gate was the original version of the TTL family. Improvements were made as TTL technology matured. In the low-power version, the propagation delay was sacrificed to reduce power dissipation. In the high-speed version, power dissipation is increased to reduce the propagation delay. Schottky TTL increases the speed of operation without an excessive increase in dissipated power. The low-power Schottky version sacrifices some speed for reduced power dissipation. It compares with the standard TTL in speed but requires less power. The fan-out of TTL gates is 10 when the standard loads of the same circuit version are used. The noise margin is greater than 0.4 volt with a typical value of about 1 volt.

**transistor width to ratio length** An important dimension-related design parameter of the transistor channel, this ratio determines the total resistance of the channel and is one determinant of speed. It also relates to the overall size of the transistor and thus affects the final chip size.

**transit angle** The product of delay or transit time and the angular frequency of operation. In a velocity-modulated tube, the transient time corresponds to the time taken for an electron to pass through a drift space.

**transition card** A card used to signal the computer that the reading

| TTL Version | Abbreviation | Propagation Delay (ns) | Power Dissipation (mW) | Speed Power Product | Input Pull-Up Resistor |
|---|---|---|---|---|---|
| Standard | TTL | 10 | 10 | 100 | 4K |
| Low-power | LTTL | 33 | 1 | 33 | 40K |
| High-speed | HTTL | 6 | 22 | 132 | 2.8K |
| Schottky | STTL | 3 | 19 | 57 | 2.8K |
| Low-power Schottky | LSTTL | 9.5 | 2 | 19 | 25K |

of a program has ended and the execution of a program has begun.

**transit time** 1. The time taken by an electron to go from cathode to anode of a tube. 2. The time necessary for injected charge carriers to diffuse across the barrier region in a semiconductor device. 3. The time taken for a charge carrier to cross a given path. 4. The average time a minority carrier takes to diffuse from emitter to collector in a junction transistor.

**translate** To change information from one form of representation to another without significantly affecting the meaning of the data. A translation may convert a source language program in FORTRAN or COBOL to a target program in machine language.

**translating program** A program designed to convert programs or data from one form to another.

**translator** 1. A device or program which converts programs or data from one form to another. Translators include code converters, assemblers, compilers, and interpreters. Translators allow the user to express data or write programs using codes or languages that are convenient to humans. 2. An automatic radio relay station (repeater) that receives an entire frequency band and retransmits it in another frequency range.

**transliterate** To convert the characters of one alphabet to the corresponding characters of another alphabet.

**transmission** 1. The sending or conveying of electrical energy or data along a path between locations of recipients. Transmission methods and systems include telemetering, telephony, broadcasting, facsimile, and television. 2. A message conveyed by wire or radio.

**transmission preprocessor** A unit designed to remove a part of the processing overhead from the central processor in a system. A typical preprocessor handles protocol modes and performs block checks for redundancy.

**transmission system** The collection of elements that are capable of functioning together for the transmission of signals and information.

**transmission technology** This is concerned with the means for transmitting signals. In telephone communications, there is the grade of the line—low-speed, voice, or broadband—and the type of line—private, switched or WATS. There are also a number of alternatives to telephone communications, including microwave and satellite transmission.

**transmit** To send signals or data from one location to another.

**transmit data register** A register (abbreviated *TDR*) used in ACIA transmission systems to hold data ready to be transmitted out.

**transmitter** The equipment used to generate and amplify carrier signals for the transmission of information.

**transmitter card** A card that converts parallel digital data into asynchronous serial data in ASCII format. It contains a transmitter module, a clock module, and conditioning circuitry.

**transmitter-distributor** A device used in a teletypewriter terminal to make and break the transmission line in timed sequence.

**transmitter holding register** A register used to hold parallel transmitted data transferred from the data access lines by a write operation.

**transmitter-receiver serial/parallel module** A unit used to convert (1) parallel data for serial transmission and (2) received serial data into a parallel format.

**transmitter register** A register used to serialize data for the transmitted data output section. It may accept data from a holding register or the SYN register.

**transponder** A type of transmitter-receiver which transmits signals automatically when it detects correct interrogation code.

**transponder efficiency** For a given deployed transponder, the ratio of the number of replies to the number of interrogations.

**transponder suppressed time delay** Refers to the overall fixed delay between the reception of an interrogation and the transmission of a reply.

**transposition** An interchange of the positions of the conductors of a circuit, the characters in a printed word, or the data in a stream or block.

**trap** 1. A form of a conditional break-point activated by hardware or operating conditions. Traps are usually set by unexpected or unpredictable occurrences which cause an automatic transfer of control or jump to a known location. In some systems the program can only set or clear a trap bit by popping a new program status word off the stack. When set, a processor trap will occur through a specific location at the completion of the current instruction execution, and a new processor status word will be loaded from another specific location. This is useful in debugging programs because it is an efficient method of installing breakpoints. 2. A device to selectively filter a single frequency or a small frequency band.

**trapped flux** The magnetic flux linked with a closed superconducting loop in a material in the superconducting state.

**trapped instruction** An instruction that is executed by a software routine when the hardware is unavailable.

**trapping** A feature in which an unscheduled jump is made to a predetermined location in response to a machine condition. Trapping is used by monitor routines to provide automatic checking.

**trapping mode** A method used for program diagnostic procedures. If the trapping mode flip-flop is set and the program includes a certain instruction of a set, the instruction is not performed, but the next instruction is taken from a specified location.

**trap setting** Establishment of conditions to control interrupt signals when using trapping methods.

**TREAT** Abbreviation for *transient reactor test facility*.

**tree structure** A pyramid system such as a file or data addressing structure that selects an element by fan-in cascading, or all the members of a set by fan out cascading.

**triac** A thyristor equivalent to a solid-state three-terminal ac relay; it is the structural equivalent to reverse-parallel connected SCRs, and can be gated by signals of either polarity.

**triad** A group of three bits or three pulses, usually in sequence on one wire or simultaneously on three wires.

**trigger** 1. To start a circuit action. 2. The pulse used to start a circuit action. 3. The electrode on which a start pulse is applied. 4. The circuit which initiates an action as a result of a signal change, as a Schmitt trigger.

**trigger action** Refers to the instantaneous initiation of current flow by a smaller controlling impulse in a circuit or device.

**trigger, bistable** Refers to circuits that have two stable states requiring excitation triggers to cause switching from one state to the other. Also called binary pair, trigger pair, bistable circuit and flip-flop.

**triggering** The starting of a circuit action that usually continues for a predetermined time under circuit control.

**triggering circuits** The circuits used for triggering flip-flops or registers in a system.

**trigger level** 1. The minimum input required to cause an output. 2. The minimum receiver input capable of causing the transmitter to emit a reply in a transponder.

**trigger pair** A circuit that has two stable states and requires a trigger to cause a transition from one state to the other.

**trigistor** A bistable pnpn semiconductor that acts as an R-S-T flip-flop, or bistable multivibrator.

**trigonometric conversion** A synchro-to-digital conversion technique in which the synchro signals are applied to trigonometric function generators (either tangent bridges or sine/cosine nonlinear multipliers). By manipulating the generator outputs in accordance with trigonometric identities, an analog voltage proportional to the difference between $\theta$ and the function-generator setting $\theta_r$ is developed. The integral of this voltage is digitized, and this digital value is fed back, as $\phi$ to drive $(\theta - \phi)$ to null; then $\phi$ equals the shaft angle $\theta$.

**trimmer capacitor** A small variable capacitor usually associated with another capacitor and used for fine adjustment of the total capacitance of the combination. Also called a trimmer.

**trinistor** A three-terminal semiconductor device that operates like a thyratron for controlling large amounts of power.

**triode** A three-electrode electronic device that is active, such as a vacuum tube or transistor, and can be used as an amplifier.

**triode field-effect transistor** A field effect transistor having a gate, a source, and a drain. Also called a field-effect triode.

**triode pnpn-type switch** A pnpn type switch having an anode, a cathode, and a gate terminal.

**triple diffusion** A semiconductor process in which three impurity depositions are prepared on the substrate.

**tripler** A circuit or device that multiplies an input frequency or voltage by three.

**triple-state gates** The bus buffers that control the direction of information flow are shown. The control input of each triple-state buffer controls its output. When the control input is enabled, the output of the gate is equal to its input value. When the control input is disabled, the output of the buffer may be disabled regardless of the input condition. By controlling the selection lines, the data bus lines are placed in an input or output status. The selection lines can also be used to inform external modules of the status condition in which the data bus is at a particular time.

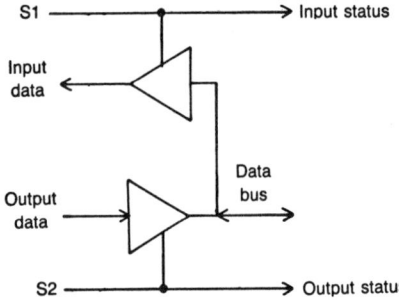

| S1 | S2 | |
|----|----|---|
| 0 | 0 | Bus disabled |
| 0 | 1 | Input status |
| 1 | 0 | Output status |
| 1 | 1 | Not allowed |

**Using triple-state gates for the bidirectional data bus**

**TRL** Abbreviation for *transistor-resistor logic*.

**TROLL** A language for the implementation and testing of models using systems of linear and nonlinear equations. Capabilities include:

1. Continuous simulation
2. Regression methods
3. Statistical analysis
4. Vector transformations

**trouble-location problem** A test problem which supplies information on the location of a fault. It is usually applied after a check problem has been used to show that a fault exists.

**troubleshoot** To search for the cause of a failure for the purpose of isolating the responsible stage or device and correcting the problem.

**truncate** 1. To terminate a computational process in accordance with some procedure or rule. 2. To intentionally drop digits of a word or series. For example, 3.141 592 653 may be truncated to 3.1415, but 3.1416 would be the rounded-off value.

**truncation** 1. The ending of a computational procedure according to a specified rule. 2. The rejection of the final digits in a number, reducing precision.

**truncation error** The error resulting from a truncation operation.

**trunk** 1. A single message circuit between two points, both of which are switching centers and/or individual message distribution points. 2. A communications channel between two different offices or between groups of equipment within the same office.

**truth table** A table that describes a logic device or function by listing all possible logic-state combinations with the appropriate output values.

**truth table generator** A technique that uses a microprocessor to develop the truth table from a diagnostic written in the microprocessor machine code or assembly language.

**TSMT** Abbreviation for *transmit*.

**TSO** Abbreviation for *time-sharing option*.

**TSO command language** The set of commands, subcommands, and operands recognized under the time-sharing option for a machine.

**TSS** Abbreviation for *time-sharing system*.

**T-test** A comparison test of two units of quantitative data for the determination of which is greater.

**TTL** Abbreviation for *transistor-transistor-logic*, a bipolar integrated-circuit logic that uses transistors with multiple emitters. The multiemitter transistors are easy to fabricate, requiring only a single isolated collector region upon which a single base region and then the several emitter regions are diffused. Operation is simple, but complex configurations require a lot of components or chip area with high power dissipation in comparison to other logic types. Noise immunity can also be a problem in some applications.

**TTL character generator** A device that furnishes the correct drive to character displays from a coded set of inputs.

**TTL compatibility** The capability of being directly interfaced with TTL circuits.

**TTL dual digital-to-analog converter** A digital-to-analog converter subsystem that incorporates the circuitry necessary to interface two analog output channels to the microcomputer. It consists of a dual-channel D/A converter with intensity control for point-plotting applications, a digital input group, and a buffered digital output group. The subsystem accepts digital data from the processor and produces analog output signals having full-scale ranges of 0 to +10 V +5 V or +10 V.

**TTL input/out** Refers to standard modules that provide an interface with TTL compatible processor peripheral devices. A typical unit contains 16 bits of digital input and 16 bits of digital output with flag and interrupt capabilities. Data outputs are fully buffered, allowing output data to be stored on the module.

**TTL-level clock** Many CPUs operate directly from a high-frequency crystal with a single-phase, TTL-level clock.

**TTL logic** TTL logic uses two dc flips-flops with one single-phase clock pulse to control the logic steps in a classic master-slave relationship. Standard TTL is relatively fast and is unsurpassed for a variety of functions. It has at least four disadvantages: high power dissipation, limited noise immunity, inadequate speed for some applications, and limited complexity. TTL is simple to operate, but it requires a lot of components and consequently a lot of chip area for LSI.

**TTL parallel data controller** A unit (abbreviated *PDC*) which provides a flexible programmable interface between peripherals and the microcomputer. A typical PDC includes full handshaking under CPU control, and a direct memory-access function for data rates to 256,000 bps, along with four interrupt inputs.

**TTL, Schottky** Schottky TTL speed is twice to three times that of conventional TTL units. It is available at a component cost of about twice that of conventional TTL. Schottky ICs can be used for upgrading TTL systems by using them in critical paths and high speed areas. See *Schottky TTL*.

**TTS** Abbreviation for *teletypesetter*.

**TTTL** A modified TTL configuration in which a third transistor is added to the output of the TTL gate to increase drive and improve noise immunity.

**TTY** Abbreviation for *teletypewriter*.

**TTY controller** A unit that provides the 20 mA loop transfer currents, and the control between low- and medium-speed serial devices such as teletypewriters, CRT terminals, and microcomputers. Typical transmit and receive speeds range from 110 to 2400 baud.

**TU** 1. Abbreviation for *tape unit*. 2. Abbreviation for *timing unit*. 3. Abbreviation for *transmission unit*.

**tuned circuit** A circuit consisting of inductance and capacitance that can be adjusted for resonance at the desired frequency.

**tuning** Refers to the adjustment of coefficients governing the various modes of control of a circuit.

**tuning capacitor** A variable capacitor for adjusting the natural frequency of an oscillatory or resonant circuit.

**tunnel diode** A pn diode to which a large amount of impurity material has been added. Its operation is based on the tunnel effect of quantum mechanics. As the voltage across this diode increases, the current first increases, then decreases, and finally increases again. The region where the current falls as the voltage rises is called the negative-resistance region. This negative resistance is useful in microwave amplifier oscillators and converters. Also called an *Esaki diode*.

**tunnel effect** The probability that a particle of given potential energy can penetrate a finite barrier of higher potential.

**turbine flowmeters** The turbine flowmeter uses the moving fluid to turn a turbine wheel. The speed of the rotor varies with the flow rate. Turbine flowmeters supply the flow information as a precise number of pulses for the volume of fluid displaced between the rotor blades. The relationship is linear within limits for flow rate and viscosity.

The transducer case must be made of a nonmagnetic metal. The amplitude of the output voltage from the coil is dependent on the gap between the pole piece and turbine blade tips. Most turbine flowmeters use an electromagnetic coil of the permanent-magnet type. The turbine blades are then made of a ferroelectric material.

**Turing machine** A mathematical model of a machine that changes its internal state and reads from, writes on, and moves an infinite tape, providing a computer-like model. The behavior of the machine is specified by listing an alphabet of symbols for the control of tape motion and read-write operations.

**turnaround time** The total time between the submission of a job to a data processing facility and the return of the results.

**turning center** A lathe-type numerically controlled machine tool capable of automatically boring, turning outer and inner diameters, threading, and facing multiple diameters and faces of a part. It is often equipped with a system for automatically changing or indexing cutting tools.

**turnkey front panel** A "turnkey" front panel eliminates all controls except the one that restarts the processor. It is used in a number of applications in which it is desirable to eliminate the possibility of having an operator affect the contents of the memory or the computing cycle. An example might be a sophisticated intruder-detection system in which the only control provided for the operator is essentially on/off.

**turnkey system** A dedicated computer system whose hardware and software have been fully debugged before installation. The user's responsibility is then reduced to the task of learning the essential operational instructions only.

**turn-off delay time** The time interval from a point 90 percent of the maximum amplitude on the trailing edge of the input pulse to a point 90 percent of the maximum amplitude on the trailing edge of the output pulse. This corresponds to the storage time for a bipolar transistor.

**turn-on delay time** The time interval from a point 10 percent of the maximum amplitude on the leading edge of the input pulse to a point 10 percent of the maximum amplitude on the leading edge of the output pulse. This corresponds to delay time for a bipolar transistor.

**TUT** Abbreviation for *tube under test*.

**tutorial light** An indicator that is used on a terminal to show the transaction history or provide indications of keyboard action.

**twelve-pitch** A term applied to typewriter spacing of 12 characters per horizontal inch. Also known as *elite spacing*.

**twelve-punch** A punch in the top row of a Hollerith punched card. Also called a *Y-punch*.

**twin check** A continuous computer check that uses a duplication of hardware and a comparison of results.

**twill weave** A weave in which the filling yarns are interlaced with the warp yarns in such a way as to form diagonal ridges across the fabric, which is used in clean rooms.

**twin crystal** Refers to the imperfect growth of crystals, whereby two lattices have a common face, leading to a double resonance and unsuitability for oscillator use.

**twinning** 1. The intergrowth of crystals of near symmetry such that, for quartz, the piezo-electric effect is not sufficiently determinate. See twin crystal. 2. One of two defects that occur in quartz crystals. Either defect results from structural misgrowth of otherwise perfect crystals, yet it cannot be seen in ordinary light. *Optical twinning* is the presence of both right and left hand quartz in the same crystal. *Electrical twinning* is the presence of adjacent regions of quart having electrical axes of opposite poles.

**two-address** An instruction format that includes an operation and specifies the location of two registers, one for the operand and the other for the result of the operation.

**two-chip microprocessor** A microprocessor whose complete architecture is developed using only two integrated-circuit chips.

**two-level subroutine** A subroutine that contains another subroutine within its own structure.

**two-out-of-five code** A positional notation in which decimal digits are

**two-plus-one address** An instruction that contains two operand addresses and one control address.

**two's complement** The radix complement in binary notation. All positive numbers are the same as in standard binary, while negative numbers are the reverse of the negative standard binary number plus one.

**two's complement code** This consists of a binary code for positive magnitude with a 0 sign bit and the two's complement of each positive number to represent its negative equivalent. The two's complement is formed by complementing the number and adding one LSB. The two's complement of 3/8 (binary 0011 ) is the complement plus the LSB: 1100 + 0001 − 1101. Two's complement is easy to work with since it may be thought of as a set of negative numbers. Thus, addition can be used instead of subtraction. To subtract 3/8 from 8/8, one adds 4/8 to −3/8, or 0100 to 1101. The result is 0001, or 1/8, neglecting the extra carry.

**two-valued variable** A variable that assumes values in a set of two elements, usually symbolized as one or zero. Alco called *binary variable* or *two-state variable*.

(Note: preceding entry continues from previous page: represented by five binary digits of which two are one kind (zeros or ones) and the others are another kind.)

**two wire circuit** Refers to a circuit formed by a pair of metallic conductors that are insulated one from the other and that, in turn, feed a load in one direction at a time.

**TWX** Abbreviation for *teletypewriter exchange service*, a subscriber service for teletypewriter interconnections with communication rates of up to 100 words per minute.

**typebar** 1. A term applied to typewriters having a conventional basket typing mechanism, with one capital and lowercase character-pair per key-bar. 2. An individual typing element in the basketed set.

**typeface** A synonym for font, though it is often used to designate the specific hardware component, such as a typing element or printing chain, that produces text in a given font.

**typing element** The unit that produces a character or characters of typing. Individual typebars, printwheels, and typeballs are all typing elements.

**typing mechanism** Refers to the subassembly within a typewriter that includes both the typing element (or elements) and the linkages that position and power them.

**typing station** Refers to an individual workstation at which documents are typed.

**TYPOUT** Abbreviation for *typewriter output*.

# U

**U** Abbreviation for *temporary accumulator*.

**UADS** Abbreviation for *user attribute data set*.

**UART** Acronym for *universal asynchronous transmitter-receiver*, a device used to interface a parallel controller or data terminal to a bit-serial communications network. An asynchronous terminal can be connected to a UART, which converts the parallel data inputs into a serial stream for communications, or converts received serial data input into parallel format. A typical UART is a single-chip MOS LSI device. It will transmit or receive words of 5, 6, 7 or 8 bits.

Options allow the generation and checking of odd or even parity, which is automatically added to the word for transmission. UARTs use double buffering, which allows one character to be read from a buffer as a shift register receives another. The UART has separate clock input pins for the receiver and transmitter sections so that receiving rates can be different from transmitting rates. This allows different rates to be used between terminals than from terminals to a microcomputer. The receiver in the UART has priority on simultaneous interrupts.

**UART controller** In an asynchronous terminal, data input and data output lines are connected to a universal asynchronous receiver transmitter (UART) circuit, which converts a serial bit stream to 8 bits of parallel data. An 8 bit character is transferred off the data input lines to a buffer memory area for processing. Error conditions are tested to ensure the character integrity and finally a receive flag is cleared, indicating that the previous character has been transferred.

**UART double buffering** A UART receiver may use double buffering, so that one character can be read from a buffer as a shift register operates on another.

**UART functions** Standard UART's have three sections: a receiver, a transmitter, and a control section, as shown below. The receiver takes

**UART**

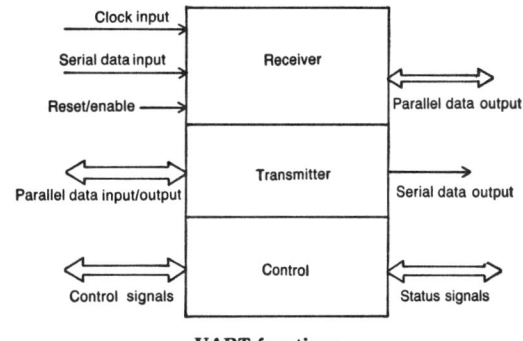

**UART functions**

the serial input and a clock, and supplies a parallel 8-bit output. The transmitter section receives an 8-bit parallel input along with a clock and supplies a serial output. The control section receives the control signals from the microprocessor and implements the required operations. It also supplies the status and control outputs to the microprocessor.

**UART simulator** A program that simulates UART operation in the microcomputer system. The UART has a complexity comparable to a 4-bit microprocessor and its functions can be transformed for execution into an 8-bit microcomputer. The program passes characters to the UART simulator as if it were a hardware device.

**UBC** Abbreviation for *universal buffer controller.*

**UC** Abbreviation for *uppercase.*

**U-contact** A type of contact and connector system that pierces the insulation of the conductors and compresses them in a firm connector grip.

**U-contact flexible cable/connector** A connector system technique that accurately spaces conductors for termination in a U-contact connector, which assures a firm contact between flexible cables and the connectors on printed circuit boards.

**U-contacts, cable** A system for the transition from flexible cables to rigid printed-circuit boards. It simplifies the harness assembly. Flat-ribbon cable/connectors are used in many areas such as peripherals, readout devices, machine tool controls, and other applications. The system uses a method of termination that involves the use of U contacts in the connector. These contacts pierce the insulation without cutting the conductors.

**UCS** Abbreviation for *universal character set.*

**UHF** Abbreviation for *ultrahigh frequency,* the range of frequencies from 300 to 3000 MHz.

**ultrafiche** A sheet of film containing images or frames that have been reduced more than 100 times by photographic means.

**ultrastrip** A film, usually 1.5 inches by 7 inches, containing images or frames which have been reduced 150 times by photographic methods.

**ultraviolet** Electromagnetic radiation with frequencies higher than visible light and with wavelengths from about 200 to 4000 angstroms.

**ultraviolet erasable PROM** A type of PROM that can be erased by concentrated ultraviolet light. The device package has a quartz top that is transparent to ultraviolet light. Unwanted bit patterns are erased by directing an ultraviolet source through the quartz window.

**ultraviolet erasing lamp** A lamp designed for erasable PROMs. One model can be mounted for a constant height from the work surface, or moved over the PROMs as a portable hand unit. Typical erasing time ranges from 5 to 10 minutes.

**ultraviolet radiation** Electromagnetic radiation in the frequency range between X-rays and visible light rays.

**ultraviolet rays** Radiation in the ultraviolet region.

**ultraviolet safety goggles** Short wave ultraviolet light can cause sunburning of the eyes and skin. Operators should never look directly into the lighted lamp. Long-sleeved clothing and gloves should be worn. Due to the high intensity of the lamps, UV safety goggles are essential in protecting the eyes from short wave exposure and avoiding eyestrain.

**umbilical cord** A cable for interconnecting an equipment with a "mother" system which contains vital functions for system operation; because of this, it may be given special requirements or precautions.

**UNACOM** Abbreviation for *universal army communication system.*

**unallowable digit** A character or digit combination that is not accepted as a valid representation by the program or computer.

**unary operation** An operation on one operand, such as negation.

**unary operator** An arithmetic operator having only one term, such as the negation operator.

**unbalanced** 1. Lacking the conditions for balance. 2. A circuit having one side grounded. 3. Refers to a line, circuit, or network in which the impedances measured from corresponding points on opposite sides are unequal.

**unbalanced circuit** A circuit with two sides that are electrically unlike.

**unbalanced instrumentation amplifier system** An unbalanced system does not use symmetry in the configuration. As shown below, a major application of instrumentation amplifiers is in eliminating the effects of ground-potential differences in these single-ended systems.

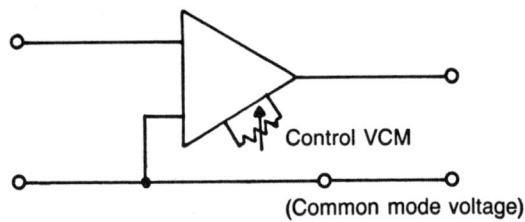

**Unbalanced system**

**unbalanced line** A transmission line, such as a coaxial line, in which the voltages on the two conductors are not equal with respect to ground.

**unbalanced wire circuit** A circuit with two sides that are electrically unlike.

**unbonded strain-gage elements** Unbonded wire elements are stretched and unsupported between a fixed and a moving end. The wire is usually looped one or more times over supporting posts. They tend to have high sensitivity, but are unusually sensitive to vibration.

**unbranched chain molecule** A large molecule whose components are lined up in a single row.

**unbundling** The separate pricing of software items from total equipment costs.

**uncommitted storage list** A list of blocks of storage that are not allocated for any particular use.

**unconditional branch** An instruction that switches the sequence of control to a specified location. Also called *unconditional jump* and *unconditional transfer of control.*

**unconditional control transfer** An instruction which always causes a jump.

**unconditional jump** An instruction that interrupts the normal process of obtaining instructions in ordered sequence and specifies the address from which the next instruction is taken.

**unconditional transfer of control** An instruction that causes the instruction following it to be taken from an address that becomes the first one of a new sequence. Also called *unconditional branch* and *unconditional jump.*

**uncorrectable error** An error in which the intent of the programmer cannot be determined. The CPU usually rejects the statement and continues processing.

**undercut** In a printed circuit board, the reduction of the cross section of a metal-foil conductor due to the removal of metal from beneath the edge of the resist by the etchant.

**underdamped** Descriptive of a circuit in which the value of resistance is lower than the *critical resistance* and the response is oscillatory or the output level momentarily exceeds the input level.

**underflow** A condition which occurs when a machine computation yields a result that is smaller than the smallest possible quantity capable of being stored.

**undermodulation** In an AM system, a modulation percentage substantially below 100%. In an FM system, modulation insufficient to permit full carrier deviation to channel limits on amplitude peaks.

**underscoring** In word processing, the automatic underscoring of designated words and phrases.

**undershoot** 1. The tendency of a numerical-control machine to round off corners of a programmed path as a result of servo lag. 2. A mechanical or electrical system lag due to the inability of the system to react at the same speed as the input or driver.

**unichassis** A memory chassis designed for mounting memory and control cards in a rack panel.

**UNICOM** Abbreviation for *universal integrated communication system*.

**unidirectional** Characterized by operation in one principal polarity or direction.

**unidirectional bus** A bus over which signals are permitted to pass in one direction only.

**unidirectional current** A direct current that is always positive or always negative and never alternating.

**unidirectional pulses** Single polarity pulses that always rise in the same direction.

**unidirectional transducer** A transducer that can only be actuated by signals at its input; there is no response at the input if the signal is applied to the output terminals. Also called a unilateral transducer.

**unijunction transistor** A three-terminal semiconductor that exhibits stable negative-resistance characteristics. It is used in relaxation oscillators and trigger circuits.

**unilateralization** Refers to the neutralization of feedback so that a transducer or circuit has a unilateral response (it responds only in one direction). Many vacuum tube circuits are inherently unilateral, but most equivalent transistor circuits require external neutralization.

**uninterruptable power supply** A power supply designed to provide power in the event of commercial power failure. Abbreviated *UPS*.

**union** A logical operator having the property: if P and Q are statements, then the union of P and Q is true if either P or Q is true; it is false if both P and Q are false.

**unipolar** Refers to devices and signals having only one pole.

**unipolar devices** Refers to devices that use charge carriers of only one polarity, such as field-effect transistors made with MOS technology. The transistors are created on the surface of a small piece of silicon, called the substrate.

To make a MOS circuit, a single crystal of silicon must be grown. This crystal is then cut into thin circular slices called wafers. The crystal must be cut in a specific direction of the crystal lattice. Several hundred chips can be made from a wafer. These chips may be used for microprocessors, memory, or other functions.

**unipolar field-effect transistor** A transistor structure containing a semiconductor current path the resistance of which is modulated by applying a transverse electric field.

**unipolar transistor** A transistor in which the charge carriers are of only one polarity.

**unit** 1. A portion or subassembly of a system, usually one piece, which provides the means of accomplishing a specific operation or function. 2. The standard qualitative element by which a quantity is measured;

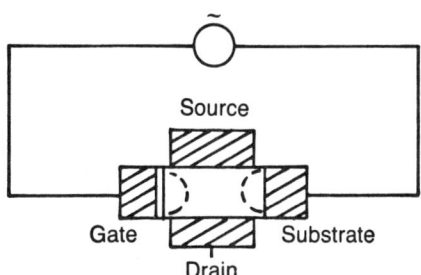

Unipolar field-effect transistor

for example, the ohm is the internationally accepted unit for measuring resistance, impedance, and reactance. 3. A whole, as *one*. 4. A digit in the least significant position of a whole number.

**unit approach** A control technique in which a separate control system is used for each unit in a plant with a microcomputer assigned to each unit. For example, a microcomputer might be assigned to the control of a milling machine.

**uniterm** A word, symbol, or number used as a descriptor for the retrieval of information from a collection, especially from one using a coordinate indexing system.

**uniterm indexing** An indexing system that uses uniterm descriptors.

**uniterming** The selecting of words or parts of words that are considered descriptive of the contents of an item. The selected words or phrases are then included in a uniterm index.

**uniterm system** A data recording system that is based on classifying keywords in a coordinate indexing array.

**unit record** A card containing a complete record.

**unit record equipment** Typically, punched-card equipment such as collators and tabulating machines.

**units, absolute** Those units derived directly from the fundamental units of a system and not based on arbitrary numerical definitions, such as the internationally adopted fundamental units of the meter and second.

**unit separator** The information separator (abbreviated *US*) intended to identify a boundary between units of information.

**unit string** A string with only one entity.

**unitunnel diode** A diode similar to a tunnel diode, but characterized by peak reverse currents in the microampere region while it is providing high forward conductance at low voltage levels.

**unity** Contained as one.

**unity-gain** Exhibiting a voltage amplification of 1 or less, as applied to follower circuits.

**universal asynchronous receiver-transmitter** See *UART*.

**Universal Product Code** Abbreviated *UPC*, a symbol of the supermarket industry. The UPC symbol provides an automated reading of product information in point-of-sale systems. The UPC symbol contains 10 digits of information divided into two 5-digit fields. The data in the fields is also represented as numerals below the symbol. In a specific representation the left-hand 5-digit field contains the characters 12345, and the right-hand 5 digit field contains the characters 67890. In the grocery industry, the left hand five digits will identify the manufacturer of the product, while the right hand five digits will identify the product. The representation of a specific digit in the UPC symbol is shown below. Each character position consists of a region of seven bar positions. A dark bar represents a 1, while a light bar represents a 0. Thus the code represented by the character shown has bits 1000100 which indicates the decimal value 7.

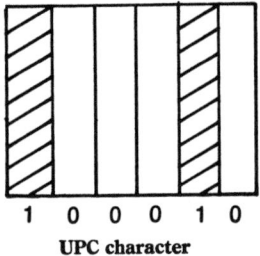

UPC character

**universal PROM programmer**  A device that allows users to program and verify PROMs using commands from the system console. The PROMs are programmed by plugging personality cards into the programmer card sockets.

**universal synchronous-asynchronous transmitter-receiver**  A chip (abbreviated *USART*) designed as a peripheral device for data communications. It is programmed by the PCU to operate in a desired serial data mode. The chip accepts data from the CPU in parallel and converts the data into a continuous serial stream for transmission. It also converts received serial data into parallel format for the PCU. The USART signals the CPU when it can accept new characters for transmission, or when it has new data for the CPU. The CPU can check the status of the USART at any time period. The USART may operate in the synchronous or asynchronous mode.

**universal synchronous receiver-transmitter**  A single-chip LSI device (abbreviated *USRT*) that provides serial-to-parallel and parallel-to-serial conversion to interface a parallel controller or terminal with a serial synchronous communication network. The device consists of separate receiver and transmitter sections with independent clocks, status, and data lines. The transmitter and receiver have common word lengths and parity modes. Data is transmitted and received at a rate equal to the clock frequency. Data messages are transmitted in a data stream which is bit-synchronous with the clock and character-synchronous with respect to framing or sync characters which start and stop each message. The receiver compares the contents of the sync register with the incoming data, and when a match is made, the receiver becomes character-synchronous using a 5-, 6-, 7-, or 8-bit character.

**universal terminator board**  Refers to a single height, standard length module. It is an etched and drilled module that can be used for mounting user-selected and user-supplied discrete components to provide a variety of termination or voltage source circuits. Each signal pin can have two components connected to ground and one component connected to a common tie point.

**universal transistor**  Refers to a common transistor for specific applications categories. Such a transistor would not break down under any practical reverse voltage. It would also have a high beta and a high frequency response. It would be free from internal noise and immune to external noise, with little or no internal capacitances, and could operate at several amperes of current. No universal transistor exists because the design criteria to maximize certain transistor characteristics are diametrically opposite to the optimization of others. Thus, it takes a variety of transistor designs to meet the wide spectrum of performance requirements.

**universal Turing machine**  A Turing machine that can simulate any other Turing machine.

**unmodulated**  Refers to a signal with no modulation.

**unpack**  To separate or decompose combined items or packed information into a sequence of items, words, or elements.

**unwind**  To code in full all the operations of a cycle in order to eliminate red-tape operations in the final coding. Unwinding is performed during assembly, generation, or compilation of programs.

**UOC**  Abbreviation for *ultimate operating capability*.

**update**  1. To put into a master file changes required by current transactions. 2. To modify an instruction so that the address numbers it contains are increased by a desired amount each time the instruction is performed.

**up-down counter**  A binary counting unit that can change its counting mode from up to down or vice versa without disturbing the count stored up to that time.

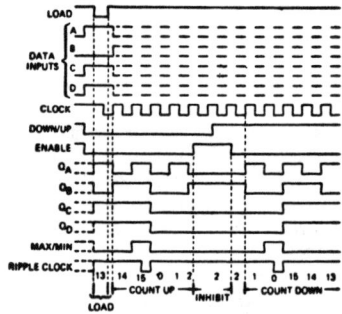

**Up-down counter timing**

**up-down counter module**  A module used to provide event counting for the microcomputer system. The module is capable of detecting count overflows and setting up flags for this condition. Count parameters are fully programmable along with reset conditions.

**uppercase**  1. The capital letters of type, in contrast to small letters or lower case. 2. Typing done all in capital letters.

**UPS**  Abbreviation for *uninterruptable power supply*, a power supply that is designed to provide power in the event of commercial power failure.

**up time**  1. The time during which equipment is either operating or available for operation as opposed to down time when no productive work can be accomplished. 2. The time a computer is operating free of component failure and the computer is capable of such operation.

**upward reference**  A reference made in an overlay system from one segment to another segment higher in the same path and closer to the root segment.

**US**  Abbreviation for *unit separator*.

**USART**  Abbreviation for *universal synchronous-asynchronous transmitter-receiver*.

**USART application**  A typical application of the 8251 USART in asynchronous mode is shown. In this system, the UART reads serial information from a keyboard and sends display information to a CRT. A baud rate generator is used to supply the clock pulses. The slowest mode of operation is normally 110 baud, where a baud is a bit per second. Most CRT controllers use a baud-rate generator, where the rate may be selected from 110 baud to 9,600 baud. The main applications for the UART mode are for communications with devices such as a printer or a modem connected to a telephone line.

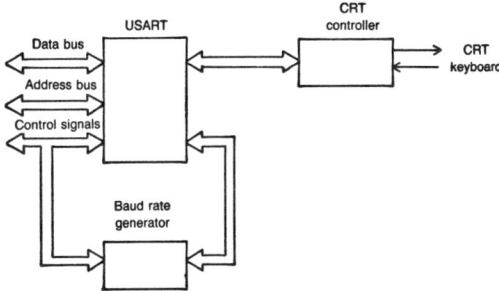

**USART CRT control**

**USART chips** The Intel 8251 is a UART as well as a USRT (Universal Synchronous Receiver Transmitter). It can be used either in asynchronous or synchronous mode. In most designs, the system will be either synchronous or asynchronous. The organization of the 8251 device appears below. The functional blocks shown are the transmitter section, the receiver section, and the control section. The data bus buffer communicates with the other sections. The connections to the microprocessor are on the left side. The connections to the peripherals are on the right side. There are two signals per I/O function: a data line and clock signal. There is also a synchronization line for the synchronous mode.

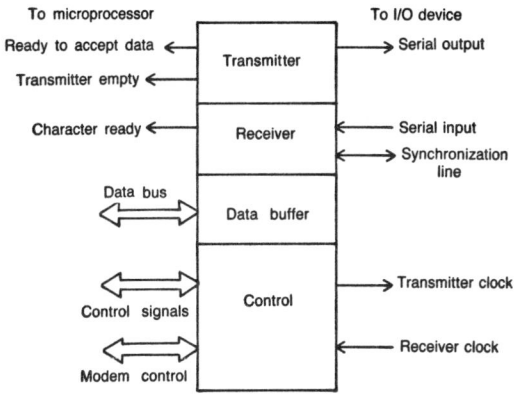

**8251 USART**

**USASCII** See *ASCII*.
**USASI** Abbreviation for *United States of America Standards Institute*, a former name of the American National Standard Institute (ANSI).
**use, joint** Refers to the simultaneous use of a communications or computer system by more than one user.
**user** Anyone who requires the use of services or products from a computing system or facility.

**user-microprogrammed processors** Refers to microprogrammable processors having a variety of microinstruction sequencing capabilities. A primary use of microprograms is as an alternative to hardwired control sequencers in the implementation of the control function in computers with conventional instruction sets. These microprograms are used to implement tasks that have a relatively simple logical structure. Microprograms can also be used to support special purpose architectures with instruction sets chosen to simplify the programming of certain classes of algorithms. These microprograms may be used to implement tasks that have a relatively complex logical structure.
**users group** 1. A group that is both a means of communication among users and a method of building a comprehensive library of programs. Specific system purchasers are often entitled to membership in such a group. Members of the users group are encouraged to submit programs they have created. User groups often have newsletters that contain updates on hardware and software developments, programming tips, and other useful information. 2. Refers to organizations made up of users of computing systems who share knowledge, exchange programs, and jointly influence vendor software and hardware support policy.
**user's manual** 1. A book of instructions outlining procedures for proper operational use of equipment. 2. A guide for programming and data processing procedures that sets forth the other documents, the style, and the standards used in the organization or system.
**USNUSL** Abbreviation for *U.S. Navy Underwater Sound Lab*.
**USRT** Abbreviation for *universal synchronous receiver-transmitter*.
**utility** A utility routine or program.
**utility debug** A design-aid program for the testing and debugging of utility functions. The utility debug may allow memory and register changing, punching and loading of paper tapes, selecting breakpoints, and searching memory.
**utility program** A program designed for such functions as changing or extending indexing structures or similar operations.
**utility routine** A routine used to assist in the operation of the computer. Utility routines may include conversions, sorting, printout operations, tracing, mathematical functions, read and write for all peripherals, and text generation for Teletypes, CRTs, or other terminal devices. The utility routines may involve a large package for a variety of operations, but only those required for the application need to be loaded into memory.
**utility typing** Refers to short, out of the ordinary typing tasks that are handled more or less informally.
**U.V. EPROM technology** The ultraviolet (U.V.) light erasable PROM uses a floating silicon gate that is erasable by ultraviolet light and reprogrammable after each erasure. The floating gate is located in the silicon dioxide layer, and it effectively isolates the source from the drain under normal operating conditions. During programming, a high negative voltage is applied; this action forces the junction of the desired cell into a breakdown condition. This results in the injection of electrons into the floating gate area. After the voltage is removed, the gate retains this negative charge because it is electrically isolated by the silicon dioxide layer. The negative charge on the gate results in the formation of a conductive inversion region in the substrate, which provides a channel between the source and the drain. It is the presence or absence of this conductive channel that determines if a one or zero is stored in the memory cell.

A lid is provided in the sealed package of the chip in order to allow erasure by illuminating the chip surface with ultraviolet light. The lids may be opaque or transparent in appearance, but they allow U.V. light

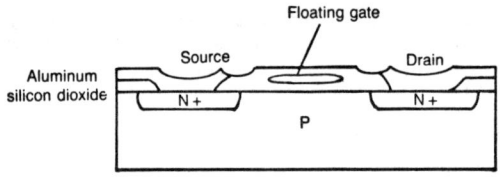

**UV EPROM structure**

to pass through for the erasing process. The technique for erasing U.V. EPROMs is to illuminate the window with an ultraviolet lamp that has a wavelength of 2537 A. The U.V. source is placed at a distance of 2-3 cm from the lid, and the radiation is allowed to fall on the element for 10-45 minutes, depending on the type of device and source. The U.V. radiation raises the conductivity of the silicon dioxide and allows the floating gate charge to leak away. The erasing process is not selective and results in the resetting of all cells in the device. Also, it may be necessary to check the U.V. source periodically since it may age with time, and its intensity may diminish.

# V

**VA** 1. Abbreviation for *value analysis*. 2. Abbreviation for *video amplifier*.

**VAB** Abbreviation for *voice answer-back*, an audio response unit that can link a computer system to a telephone network and provide voice responses to inquiries made from telephone terminals. The audio response is composed from a vocabulary prerecorded on a disk storage device.

**valid** Legitimate; permissible; operationally acceptable.

**validity** Correctness; especially the degree of closeness by which iterated results approach the correct result.

**validity check** A check based on limits related to a specific problem; for example, in a validity check, a computed time of day would be rejected if greater than 24 hours.

**validity checking** A screening procedure in which data records are checked for range, valid coding, illogical bit combinations or storage addresses, and similar factors.

**valid memory address** An output line that indicates to peripheral devices that there is a valid address on the address bus.

**varactor diode** Refers to pn junction reverse-biased diode types that are used in voltage controlled parametric amplifiers and multipliers.

**variable** A quantity that can assume any of the numbers of some set of numbers, or a condition, transaction, or event which changes or may be changed as a result of processing data.

**variable address** An address that is to be modified by an index register or similar device. Also called *indexed address*.

**variable area meters** These are flowmeters that use a float in a tapered section of tubing (called a *rotameter*), a spring-restrained plug, or a spring-restrained vane. The displacement of these elements causes the area of flow passage to vary while the differential pressure or head remains constant. The displacement is measured to provide an output proportional to the flowrate.

**variable block format** A format that allows the number of words in successive blocks to vary.

**variable capacitance diode** A semiconductor diode in which the junction capacitance has been accentuated. An appreciable change in the thickness of the junction-depletion layer and a corresponding change in the capacitance occur when the dc voltage applied to the diode is changed. Abbreviated *VDC*.

**variable capacitor** A capacitor that changes its capacitance by varying the useful area of its plates, as in a rotary capacitor, or by altering the distance between them, as in some trimmer capacitors.

**variable connector** 1. The collective instructions that cause a logical chain to take one of several paths. 2. The device inserting such instructions. 3. A flowchart symbol representing a connection that is not fixed, but which can be varied by the program or procedure.

**variable-cycle operation** Computer action in which any cycle or operation may be of a different time length. Variable-cycle operation is characteristic of asynchronous machines.

**variable field** A field in which the vectors at any point can change during the time under consideration.

**variable field length** A data field that can have a varying number of characters from record to record.

**variable function generator** Refers to a function generator that operates using a set of values of the function that are preset within the device with or without interpolation between these values.

**variable length record** A file that contains records that are not uniform in length.

**variable master clock** A clock that provides frequencies from 100 kHz to 1 MHz for evaluation of microcomputer system components.

**variable-point representation** A positional notation in which the position of the radix point is indicated by a character at that position.

**variable reluctance pressure transducer** In the diaphragm-type of variable-reluctance pressure transducer a diaphragm of magnetic material is supported between two symmetrical inductance assemblies. The diaphragm deflects when there is a difference in pressure between the two input ports. This tends to increase the gap in the magnetic flux path of one core and decreases the gap in the other. The reluctance varies with the gap. The overall effect is a change in inductance of the two coils. The inductance ratio is usually measured in a bridge circuit to produce a voltage proportional to the pressure difference.

Most manufacturers of reluctive transducers offer dc to ac to dc conversion circuitry in separate or integral packaging. Reluctive transducers with dc excitations of 28 and 5 V are available for absolute, gage, and differential pressure measurements. Typical range is 1 inch of water to 12,000 psi.

The performance of reluctive transducers, with or without dc to dc converters, is comparable in most respects to the best available versions of other transducer types. Static-error is typically ± 0.5 percent with nonlinearity producing the major portion. Errors due to hysteresis and nonrepeatability can be below 0.2 percent. Proof pressure ratings of greater than six times range are available. Errors can be introduced by stray magnet and electric fields.

Most ac transducers operate at a carrier frequency in the range of 60 Hz to 30 kHz. When dc conversion is used, the internally-generated carrier frequency may be much higher, permitting smaller coils and capacitors in a smaller package.

Temperature effects are minimized by similar sensing element and coil materials. Temperature errors are typically 1 or 2 percent to 100 °F. Pressure transducers without dc conversion operate over a wide temperature range with an upper limit of 350 °F. The solid-state components of dc converters may limit the operating temperature of this transducer to less than the ac version. Frequency response is flat from 50 to 1000 Hz but depends on the particular design.

**variable resistance pickup** A transducer whose operation depends upon the variation of resistance, such as a thermistor or strain-gauge element.

**variable-resistance transducer** A transducer that produces an electrical analog of the resistance value of its input device.

**variable resistor** A wirewound or composition resistor, the resistance of which may be changed. (See *potentiometer*.)

**variable symbol** 1. A symbol used in assembly programming that does not have to be declared since it is assigned a read-only value. 2. A symbol used to denote a variable quantity.

**variable word length** Descriptive of a computer in which the number of characters addressed is not a fixed number but is varied by the data or instruction.

**varistor** A silicon, carbon, or selenium device used for surge suppression or contact protection. Its resistance is a function of the applied voltage.

**VAX** A popular and quite powerful minicomputer produced by Digital Equipment Corporation.

**VDS** Abbreviation for *variable depth sonar*.

**VDT** Abbreviation for *visual display terminal*.

**vector** 1. A symbol for a directed quantity. 2. A quantity that has direction, magnitude, and sense and which can be expressed graphically as a line segment referred to other coordinate line segments.

**vector algebra** The manipulation of symbols representing vector quantities according to the laws of addition, subtraction, multiplication, and division

**vector diagram** An arrangement of vectors showing the relationships between the representative quantities.

**vectored interrupt system** An interrupt system in which the microprocessor recognizes the interrupting device since each I/O device is assigned a unique interrupt address. This address is then used to generate an interrupt trap address for the device. The trap addresses are usually located sequentially in program memory to form the interrupt vector. Each location contains the starting address of a device-service program. The contents of the interrupt vector are loaded into the program counter and program control is transferred to the correct device-service program.

Some vectored systems, instead of transmitting an address, use an I/O device to transmit a single byte instruction to the microprocessor after the request has been acknowledged. The interrupt control logic loads the instruction code into the instruction register. Normal operation continues after this instruction is executed. Vectoring is achieved by a single byte jump instruction that derives the jump address from a part of the instruction code. A unique jump address is defined for each I/O device in the system.

**vectored priority interrupt** An interrupt that automatically determines priority.

**vector feedrate** A programmed motion at a specified rate over a given distance in a given direction.

**vector field** In a given region of space, the total value of some vector quantity that has a definite value at each point of the region, such as the distribution of magnetic intensity in a region surrounding a current carrying conductor.

**vector function** A function that has both magnitude and direction such as the magnetic intensity at a point near an electric circuit.

**vector impedance** The ratio of the complex harmonic potential difference to the corresponding complex current.

**vector instruction** An instruction that can accept an interrupt and branch to the correct routine or device.

**vector potential** A vector quantity in an electromagnetic field, whose component along any axis at any point is equal to the sum or i. dl/r, where i. dl is a current element parallel to the axis at a distance r from a point, the summation extending throughout all space.

**vector power** A vector quantity equal to the square root of the sum of the squares of the active and reactive powers. The unit is the vector-ampere.

**vector quantity** A quantity with magnitude, sense, and direction.

**vector ratio** A ratio between two complex quantities in which both the amplitudes and phases are expressed as vectors.

**vector transfer table** A transfer table used to communicate between two or more programs. The transfer vector provides the communication linkage between the programs.

**Veitch diagram** A graphical technique used for the solution of problems arising in digital circuit design.

**velocity** 1. A vector quantity that includes both magnitude (speed) and direction in relation to a given frame of reference. 2. The rate of motion in a given direction. 3. In a wave, the distance travelled by a given phase of a wave divided by time taken. It is a vector quantity such that it has a magnitude and a direction expressed relative to some frame of reference.

**velocity of propagation** Refers to the speed of a wave within a media such as a cable. This speed is usually compared with the same wave in free space.

**Venn diagram** A diagram in which each region represents an individual parameter. Sets are represented by the overlapping of regions. Basic

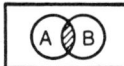
C = A AND B

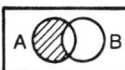
C = A AND NOT B

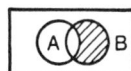
C = NOT A AND B

**Venn diagrams**

logic relations, operations, and propositions are illustrated and defined by the inclusion, exclusion, and intersection of the regions.

**VER** Abbreviation for *vision electronic recording*.

**verbs, processor** Refers to verbs that specify to the processor the procedures by which a source program is to be translated into an object program.

**verification** The process of checking the results of one data transcription against those of another.

**verification mode** A mode of operation in time-sharing systems in which all edit subcommands are acknowledged and text changes are displayed as they are made.

**verifier** A device on which a record or data can be compared or tested for identity, character by character, with a retranscription of copy as it is being prepared.

**verify** To make a certain determination that a computer operation has been accomplished accurately.

**vernier capacitor** A variable capacitor placed in parallel with a larger tuning capacitor and used to provide a fine adjustment.

**vertical parity check** A check in which the binary digits of a character column are added and the sum is checked against a previously computed parity digit to test whether the number of ones is odd or even.

**vertical polarization** Refers to the state of an electromagnetic wave when the electric component lies in the vertical plane and the magnetic component in the horizontal plane.

**vertical redundancy checking** A type of error checking that adds a parity bit to each block of data.

**vertical tabulation character** A format effector (abbreviated *VT*) that causes the printing or display position to be moved up or down a predetermined number of lines.

**very high frequencies** Those frequencies between 30 and 300 MHz.

**very low frequencies** Those frequencies between 20 and 30 kHz.

**vestigial sideband** The incomplete suppression of one sideband in an AM system to reduce the total signal bandwidth without degradation of information content.

**vestigial-sideband transmission** Refers to a method of communication in which frequencies of one sideband, the carrier, and only a portion of the other sideband are transmitted.

**vf band** Abbreviation for *voice-frequency* band, that frequency range between 600 and 3000 Hz that is adequate for transmission of speech with good intelligibility.

**VFO** Abbreviation for *variable frequency oscillator*.

**V format** A data record format with records of variable length. Each record begins with a record length indicator.

**VFT** Abbreviation for *voice frequency terminal*.

**VGA** Abbreviation for *variable gain amplifier*.

**VHD** Abbreviation for *video high density*. A video disk system in competition with Philips's laser reading (VLP) system and RCA's grooved capacitance (CED) video.

**VHF** Abbreviation for *very high frequency*. The range of frequencies from 30 to 300 MHz.

**VHP** Abbreviation for *very high performance*.

**vibrator** Multivibrator.

**VIDAT** Abbreviation for *visual data acquisition*.

**videodisc** The video counterpart of the phonograph record; it stores visual and audio matter that can be displayed on the television set through a special turntable. It is being developed in three different, incompatible formats: LV (Lasvision—MCA/Phillips' reflective laser optical system), CED (RCA's capacitance electronic disc), and VHD (the Japanese video high density system).

**video signal** Refers to that part of a TV signal that conveys all the information (intensity, color, and synchronization) required for establishing the visual image on a monochrone or color TV.

**VIG** Abbreviation for *video interface group*.

**VIPS** Abbreviation for *voice interruption priority system*.

**virtual** Conceptual rather than actual, but possessing the essential characteristics of a real function.

**virtual address** A symbol or word that can be used as a valid address part, but does not necessarily refer to an actual memory location.

**virtual address space** In a virtual storage system, the storage area assigned to a job, user, or task.

**virtual circuit** A circuit or function that is established in a computer operation.

**virtual earth** Refers to a terminal of a device such as an amplifier that remains approximately at earth potential although not connected to earth.

**virtual image** The apparent spatial position of a reflection in a mirror.

**virtual machine** A system that uses multiple copies of another computer's hardware and software to create a machine environment that can be used to test software and hardware designs. The virtual machine allows a large memory capacity through the use of virtual memory, and provides simplified software and improved development reliability. The technique maps the memory plus the instructions; when instructions are executed, the machine traps and implements them directly.

**virtual memory** A memory technique that transfers information one page at a time between primary and secondary memory, and adds only the page-swapping time to the operating time. The technique allows the programmer to address storage without regard to whether primary or secondary storage is being addressed. The technique has been used in large system development programs where an executive system allows the programmer to write programs as if memory capacity were unlimited. The executive keeps the programs on disks and out of use until required. Each disk is loaded into the system when called for by the program.

**virtual memory pointer** A pointer used to keep track of the parts of programs and data that is scattered between main memory and auxiliary storage in a virtual memory system. The pointer system is usually transparen. the user.

**virtual memory technique** A memory system (abbreviated *VMT*) which operates as if all instructions and data were on main memory when they may be actually segmented between main memory and secondary storage. The virtual memory technique locates the instruction and operands, and if not in main storage, transfers them from secondary storage sites which act as the virtual memory sites. The system permits a program to be larger than main memory, and with the use of a pointer arrangement, software can be much less that other types of segmentation systems.

**virtual memory, user-coded** Refers to a virtual memory that can be provided by a user-determined form of code segmentation. This approach permits a program to be larger than the main memory and avoids problems that may result when segmentation is totally machine determined.

**virtual radiator** In an antenna system consisting of a quarter-wave vertical radiator over a ground plane, the label applied to the virtual image of the vertical element as "reflected" by the ground plane in the analysis of the antenna's propagation or radiation characteristics.

**virtual storage system** See *virtual memory*.

**virtual terminal network** A network that allows the user to select the type of terminal to be used at each location independently. A user computer supporting the network has the capability to handle a wide range of terminal types without additional software.

**virtual unbundling** A marketing concept in which manufacturers sell as much or as little computer system hardware as the applications require. The user needs may call for a complete computer system, subsystem, boards, kit parts, or components, which are all furnished by one manufacturer.

**VIS** Abbreviation for *visual instrumentation system*.

**visual display** A unit that can display characters of information, such as tables, graphs, charts, or the lines and curves of drawings as a series of connected points. Computer console displays may indicate the next instruction, parity, the contents of any memory location, or the status of interrupts in the system.

**visual display interface** The circuitry required to connect the results of a measurement or computation to a display device for observing and recording.

**visual display station** An input/output unit that allows the interrogation of a CPU using a CRT or similar display.

**visual display terminal** A device (abbreviated *VDT*) that permits inputs to a computer system through a keyboard or other manual input device such as a light pen, and whose primary output is visual through a CRT unit or other type of display. The terminals allow keyboarding, verification, editing, correction, and reformatting of material. They may be user programmable using parameter designations or data entry languages.

**visual inquiry station** Refers to an input/output unit that permits the interrogation of the data processing system by the immediate processing of data from a terminal.

**visual terminal** A unit that allows the interrogation of a processor along with the input of data using a visual display technology. Visual terminals use cathode-ray tubes, magneto-optics, light-emitting diodes, and gas-discharge displays.

**VLF** Abbreviation for *very low frequency*.

**VLR** Abbreviation for *very long range*.

**VMOS** A MOS transistor technology in which devices are formed using a vertical structure, which permits high power dissipation capability.

**VMT** Abbreviation for *virtual memory technique*.

**VOC** Abbreviation for *voice operated circuit*.

**vocoder** Voice encoder.

**voice answer-back** See *VAB*.

**voice channel** A circuit of sufficient bandwidth to allow a data transfer of 2400 bits per second.

**voice grade** A classification for a communication line used in normal telephone service that is capable of handling speech data without significant degradation of signal regardless of path length.

**voice-operated device** A device that allows the presence of an audio signal to actuate a desired operation or function. Also called *VOX box*.

**volatile** Refers to memory units that lose stored information with time or when the power is turned off. IC memories are volatile because their cells require power to maintain the stored information. A nonvolatile memory unit such as a magnetic disk retains its stored information after power is removed. This is because the stored information is determined by the direction of magnetization, which is retained when power is off. Microcomputers with volatile memories may use backup batteries or power supplies that continue to provide power for some time after a power interruption occurs.

**volatile dynamic storage** A type of dynamic storage that depends upon the supply of power along with refresh circuitry to maintain stored information. Without such circuitry, stored data would be lost with the removal of power.

**volatile storage** A storage medium in which stored data is lost when power is removed.

**volt** The international unit of electromotive force (abbreviated *V*), equal to the product of current and resistance.

**voltage comparator** A device that can compare two voltages and issues an output that is a function of the comparison.

**voltage doubler** A power supply circuit in which both half cycles of an ac supply are rectified, and the resulting dc voltages are added in series.

**voltage, drain gate** The dc voltage between the drain and gate terminals.

**voltage, drain gate breakdown** The dc breakdown voltage between the drain and gate terminals with the source terminal open.

**voltage, drain source on-state** The dc voltage between the drain and source terminals with a specified forward gate source applied to bias the device to the on state.

**voltage, drain-substrate** The dc voltage between the drain and substrate terminals.

**voltage drop** The reduction of voltage along a conductor or through a device as a result of the conductor's (or device's) resistance.

**voltage, forward gate-source** The dc voltage between the gate and source terminals of such polarity that an increase in its magnitude causes the channel resistance to decrease.

**voltage gain** The ratio of the output to input voltage in a circuit or device.

**voltage, gate-source** The dc voltage between the gate and source terminals.

**voltage, gate-source threshold** The forward gate source voltage at which the magnitude of the drain current of a field-effect transistor has been increased to a specified low value.

**voltage jump** Refers to an abrupt discontinuity in voltage drop across a device, normally associated with a marked change in the device characteristic.

**voltage level** The value of the voltage at any point in a network expressed relative to a specified reference level.

**voltage multiplier** A circuit for obtaining a high dc potential from a low voltage ac supply. A ladder of half-wave rectifiers charges successive capacitors connected in series on alternate half-cycles. It is effective only when the load current is small, such as for the anode supply to a CRT.

**voltage regulation** A measure of the degree in which a power source maintains a stable output under varying load conditions, usually expressed as a percentage.

**voltage regulation/load** Refers to the change in output voltage of a power source for a specified change in the load. This is often expressed as the percentage ratio of the voltage change.

**voltage regulator** A circuit or device used in conjunction with a power supply to maintain a stable voltage under different load and environmental conditions.

**voltage regulator diode** A diode that is used as a stable reference source in a voltage regulator application.

**voltage, reverse gate-source** The dc voltage between the gate and source terminals of such polarity that an increase in its magnitude causes the channel resistance to increase.

**voltage, source-substrate** The dc voltage between the source and substrate terminals.

**voltage stabilizer** Refers to the use of a zener or stabilizer diode to reduce the voltage across a device.

**voltage standard** An accurately known voltage source, such as a standard cell, that is used for comparison with or for the calibration of other voltages.

**voltage supply drain** Refers to the current drain, shown in the specifications for a module, that is consumed by the circuit in its worse-case state. This is usually the maximum specified current from all voltage sources simultaneously.

**voltage-to-frequency converter** A device for changing an input voltage into a proportional frequency that can then be counted by a digital device or processor.

**voltaic cell** A device with an *electrolyte* (ionized chemical compound in water) and two differing electrodes that are used to establish a difference of potential.

**voltaic couple** Refers to a contact with two dissimilar metals, resulting in a contact potential difference.

**voltaic pile** A voltage source consisting of alternate pairs of dissimilar metal discs separated by moistened pads, which form a number of elementary primary cells in series.

**volt-ammeter** An instrument designed to read both voltage and current.

**volt ampere** 1. The product of actual voltage (in volts) and actual current (in amperes) in a circuit. Abbreviated VA. 2. A unit of apparent power in an ac circuit containing reactance. It is equal to the potential in volts multiplied by the current in amperes, without considering phase.

**volt-ampere hour** The MKSA unit of apparent power, equivalent to the watt-hour.

**volt-ampere meter** An instrument for measuring the apparent power in an alternating current circuit. Its scale is graduated in volt-amperes or kilovolt-amperes.

**Volta's law** When two dissimilar conductors are placed in contact, the same contact potential is developed between them, whether the contact is direct or through one or more intermediate conductors.

**voltmeter** An instrument for measuring voltage (potential difference), usually in any of a number of voltage ranges.

**voltohmmeter** A portable instrument for measuring voltage and resistance. Abbreviated *VOM*.

**voltohmmilliammeter** A generally portable instrument for measuring voltage, subampere current levels, and resistance.

**voluntary interrupt** An interrupt caused by an object program's deliberate use of a function known to cause an interrupt.

**VOM** Abbreviation for *voltohmmeter* (or *voltohmmilliammeter*).

**VOR** Abbreviation for *VHF omnidirectional range*.

**VOX** Abbreviation for *voice-operated device*.

**VOX box** A modular voice-operated device for interconnection to a tape recorder, radio transmitter, etc.

**VR** Abbreviation for *voltage regulator*.

**VRR** Abbreviation for *visual radio range*.

**VS** Abbreviation for *virtual storage*.

**VSB** Abbreviation for *vestigial sideband*.

**VSW** Abbreviation for *very short waves*.

**VSWR** Abbreviation for *voltage standing wave ratio*.

**VT** The vertical tabulation character.

**VTAM** Abbreviation for *vortex telecommunications access method*, a software package designed to simplify the data communications programming required to serve remote user stations with a host computer.

# W

**W** Symbol for *watt*.

**WAC** Abbreviation for *write address counter*.

**wafer package** Refers to a wafer package of transistor or IC chips. The wafer is supplied unscribed, and except for the aluminum bonding pads, the chips are completely covered with silicon dioxide to minimize damage due to handling. They are 100 percent tested to electrical specifications. When the wafers are ordered, dice that fail the electrical test are inked out. Extra dice may be included to cover possible breakage and/or rejects.

**waiting list** A queue of unprocessed data or operational programs.

**waiting state** The state of an interrupt level that is armed and has received an interrupt signal, but has not yet been allowed to become active.

**wait time** The time interval during which a processing unit is waiting for information. This time interval may occur while information is being retrieved from a serial access file or located by a search.

**wall energy** Refers to the energy per unit area stored in the domain wall bounding two oppositely magnetized regions of a ferromagnetic material.

**wall-less ionization chamber** A chamber in which, due to the use of a guard ring, the collecting volume is defined by the applied field.

**warmup time** The time required for a device to reach a stable state after application of power.

**waste instruction** An instruction which specifically instructs the processor to do nothing but process the next instruction in sequence. Also called a *blank, skip,* or NO-OP.

**watchdog timer** In utilizing duplexed processors one must consider when the backup processor should be activated to take over. The primary processor can set a watchdog timer in the backup unit on a periodic basis. Failure to set the timer causes the backup to assume control and disable the primary unit.

**WATS** Acronym for *wide-area telephone service*, a telephone-subscriber service that permits a customer to make calls to other telephones in distant zones on a flat-fee rather than a toll-call basis.

**watt** The international unit of electric power (abbreviated *W*), equal to the product of voltage and current in dc circuits.

**wattage rating** The maximum power that a device can safely handle.

**watt-hour** The MKSA unit of electrical energy, being the work done by one watt acting for one hour, and equal to 3600 Joules.

**wave** 1. A single cycle of a periodic propagated disturbance such as a radio wave, a sound wave, or a carrier wave for transmitting data signals. 2. A graphic representation of a recurring cyclic signal; a waveform.

**wave amplitude** The maximum change from zero characteristic of a wave.

**wave analyzer** An instrument used to measure the amplitude and frequencies of the components of an electrical wave.

**wave angle** The angle at which a wave is propagated from one point to another.

**wave band** The band of frequencies assigned to a particular function or application.

**wave carrier** Refers to the basic frequency or pulse repetition rate of a signal bearing no intrinsic intelligence until it is modulated by another signal that does bear intelligence. A carrier may be amplitude, phase, or frequency modulated. In a pulse coded signal, the presence or absence of a pulse determines whether a one or a zero is present in the binary number being represented.

**waveform** The graphic representation of the shape of a wave, showing the variations in amplitude with time.

**waveform analyzer** An instrument that measures or displays the components in an electrical waveform, usually with a variable-timebase capability.

**waveform generator** A circuit used to produce a desired waveform in a system.

**waveform influence** The change in indication, caused solely by a change in waveform from a specified waveform, of the applied current and/or voltage.

**wave function** In a wave equation, a point function that specifies the amplitude of a wave.

**wave guide** 1. A system of material boundaries capable of guiding electromagnetic waves. 2. A transmission line comprising a hollow conducting tube within which electromagnetic waves are propagated on a solid dielectric or dielectric-filled conductor. 3. A hollow metal conductor within which very high frequency energy can be transmitted efficiently in one of a number of modes of electro-magnetic oscillation. Dielectric guides, consisting of rods or slabs of dielectric, can also be used, but these normally have higher losses.

**wave interference** A phenomenon that results when waves of the same or nearly the same type and frequency are superimposed. It is characterized by variations in the wave amplitude that differ from that of the individual superimposed waves.

**wavelength** 1. The distance between two similar and successive points on a periodic wave. 2. The approximate length in meters (abbreviated $\Lambda$) of any signal wave within a given band, used to express the approximate range of frequencies represented. The 6-meter band, for example, refers to frequencies between 50 and 54 MHz.

The formula for wavelength is $\Lambda = c/f$ where c is the propagation speed of the wave (300 million meters per second) and $f$ is the frequency of the wave in hertz.

**waveshape** The graphic representation of one cycle of a wave, usually referenced against time. Principal waveshapes are sine, triangle, and square.

**wave theory** Refers to the explanation of diffraction, interference, and optical phenomena, as in electromagnetic waves, predicted by Maxwell and verified by Hertz for radio frequency waves.

**WC** Abbreviation for *write and compute*.

**WCS** Abbreviation for *writeable control store*.

**wearout failure** A failure that is due to normal deterioration or mechanical wear, the probability of which increases with use.

**weber** The MKSA unit of magnetic flux. An emf. of one volt is induced in a circuit through which the flux is changing at a rate of one weber/second. The weber is also used as the MKSA unit of magnetic pole strength.

**WEDISC** A family of digital computers that are built around the nucleus of a magnetic disk storage unit.

**weighted average** An average adjusted to give a different significance to each item according to its importance to the problem being studied.

**weighting technique** A technique that can be used in selecting equipment such as a microcomputer for a particular application. One can analyze a number of issues, both technical and nontechnical, and rate the microprocessor accordingly. The various factors can then be given a weight for the application being considered, and the optimum choice can be computed.

**weights** The set of numbers associated with digits in positional notation, such as the holes punched in paper tape or cards.

**WF** Abbreviation for *write forward*.

**Wheatstone bridge** A basic circuit for measuring electrical resistance by the null method, comprising two parallel resistance branches, each branch consisting of two resistances in series. It is the basic prototype of other bridge circuits that can be used for measuring other electrical parameters.

**Whirlwind I** A very early large computer which used ferromagnetic cores in its main memory. It was built at M.I.T.

**whisker resistance** Refers to the resistance of a catwhisker element in a semiconductor device.

**white noise** Noise that has equal energy at all frequencies, as opposed to *pink noise*, which has equal energies within a specified band and very little energy elsewhere.

**Wicking** Refers to the flow of solder up under the insulation on a covered wire.

**wicking** The act of drawing liquid through a fabric or thread, such as in the action of a wick in an oil lamp as it draws oil up. Cotton thread and some synthetic threads will "wick" perspiration through a seam.

**width, pulse modulation** The duration of a pulse in the time interval between the points of the leading and trailing edges at which the instantaneous value bears a specified relation to the pulse amplitude.

**Williams tube** A cathode-ray tube designed by F. C. Williams of the University of Manchester, England, for the electrostatic storage of information.

**winchester disk** A fixed, rigid magnetic disk that is in a sealed unit. This concept allows the read/write heads to move over the surface of the disk at a distance less than the width of a human hair and allows more compact storage of data. Winchester disks for microcomputers may store between 5 and 90 megabytes (million bytes). Winchester disks are more expensive than floppies but offer a more rapid access type of mass storage.

**winding drive** A pulse of current in a winding, such as a drive wire or drive winding, that is inductively coupled to one or more magnetic cells; also the pulse of magneto motive force produced.

**wire** A solid or stranded group of solid cylindrical conductors having a low resistance to current flow, together with any associated insulation.

**wire printer** A high-speed printer that uses a character-like configuration of wire fingers from a matrix of wire ends, rather than from a selection of type faces.

**wired-AND** The stringing together of a number of circuits or functions such that when all circuits are at a logic 1, a desired connection point is a logic 1.

**wired-OR** The connecting of separate circuits or functions such that the combination represents an OR function or operation. The point at

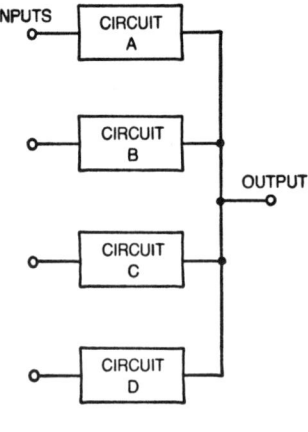

**Wired OR**

which the separate circuits are wired together will be a 1 if any of the wired-together circuits are a 1.

**wired-program computer** A computer in which a majority of the instructions are determined by the placement of interconnecting patchcords or pins using a device such as a plug or patchboard. If the wires are permanently soldered, the computer is a *fixed-program machine*.

**wire harnesses, U contact** Refers to the handling that allows mass termination of individual wires in connectors originally designed for flat cable. During assembly, the conductors of multiple conductor cable harnesses must be aligned with the U contacts in the connector. The conductors in flat cable are accurately spaced during cable manufacture, but those in a twisted pair woven cable must be separated and accurately spaced before they can be terminated in a U-contact type of connector.

**wire-in** Refers to components that are too small to be plugged safely into a connector or holder.

**wirewrap** An alternative to soldering connections in which a number of turns of a stripped solid conductor are wrapped around a metal post by special tools. With the proper technique, a good metal-to-metal contact results with enough corrosion resistance, mechanical stability, and conductivity to be used in military equipment. Wirewrap offers ease of design, freedom of layout, ease of design change, and good densities for logic designs.

**wirewrap board** A board that allows users to adapt portions of a microcomputer system for special applications or changes during the development process.

**wirewrap module** A module designed to fit into a microcomputer system that has wirewrap pins along with IC sockets for easy circuit modifications.

**wirewrapped panel** A panel designed to accommodate a random-access memory system along with the read-only memory and microprocessor required for a microcomputer system. A typical panel has 200 to 300 input or output pins for wirewrap connections.

**wirewrapped socket board** A board containing sockets and wirewrap pins for maximum flexibility of design of the microcomputer system. The sockets will accept components with 14 to 40 pins.

**wirewrapping** The process in which a solid conductor is wrapped, using a special tool, around a metal post.

**wirewrap tool** The hand or power tool used to accomplish prototype or production wirewrapping. Tools are available with electrical ac power, battery power, or air power.

**wiring diagram** A circuit diagram that indicates the physical layout of equipment and the point-to-point distribution and interconnection of conductors.

**wiring pencil** A prototype aid which contains a replaceable spool or wire and a pencil-like tip to guide and cut the wire. The wire is wrapped around the terminal and cut. Heat from a soldering iron melts the insulation and completes the connection as the solder bond is made.

**WO** Abbreviation for *write out*.

**word** 1. An ordered set of characters which occupies one storage location and is treated as a unit. Usually a word is treated by the control unit as an instruction, and by the arithmetic unit as a quantity. Words lengths may be fixed or variable, depending on the system configuration. 2. A byte containing as many bits as the word-length capacity of the machine permits.

**word address format** The order of appearance of the character information within a word.

**word and byte addressing** Some systems provide both word and byte addressing for most memory reference instructions. This means that users can deal directly with either bytes or full words, as the application requires, without the complications required in microcomputers without both types of addressing.

**word comparator time** Refers to circuitry that compares a word-time counter with the specified word time at the moment of the coincident pulse. This is done in order to verify that the correct word is being read.

**word count** The number of words in a record or other data item.

**word counter** A register that holds the transfer word count during block transfer operations. See also *word count register*.

**word count register** A register used to keep track of input/output transfers. In a typical application, the word count register is loaded at the start of an operation with the number of data words to be transferred and then decremented after each transfer. When the register reaches zero, it signals the completion of the operation by generating an interrupt.

**word generator** A circuit or device for providing words and sequences for testing and checkout. Many units are interactive and respond to

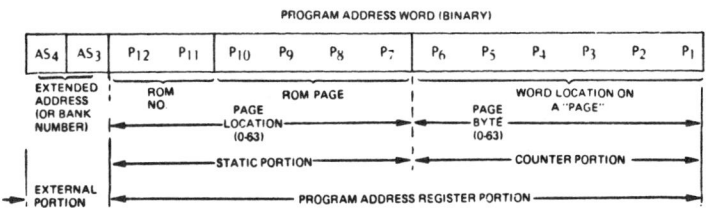

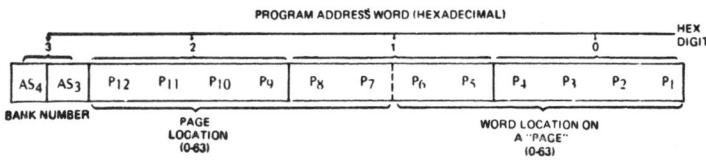

**Word address format**

levels or pulses from the device under test. Some word generators can perform program loops, generate serial or parallel data, generate data from selected locations in memory, and generate data continuously or in single words.

A word generator can be used to test logic states in a system. With the generator supplying the desired signals, operation of the circuit or system is checked using an oscilloscope or logic state analyzer. It may also be used to test serial devices such as shift registers, disk memories, and terminal hardware.

**word index**  An index based on the selection of words as used in a document, without consideration to synonyms or generic concepts related to the term selected.

**word length**  A measure of the size of a word specified in characters or bits. Longer word lengths in a microcomputer system increase efficiency and accuracy but add to the system complexity and cost. For greater precision and memory access, multiple-word operands and instructions are used, although they increase execution time and complexity. In a fixed-point arithmetic system, a double-length word is stored in two registers.

**word-length, double**  Many arithmetic instructions produce two-word results. With fixed-point multiplication, a double length product is stored in two registers of control storage for integer and fractional operations. Integer and fractional division can be performed upon a double length dividend; the remainder and the quotient will be retained in the registers.

**word-length, I/O compatibility**  The efficient handling of 8-bit words is important in communications processing, in which 8-bit ASCII characters are typical; 8- or 16-bit machines with good byte handling capabilities are required in such applications. Incompatible I/O word lengths increase the difficulties encountered in interfacing computers with communication lines and peripherals.

**word mark**  An indicator used to signal the beginning or end of a word.

**word-organized storage**  A type of magnetic storage in which each word of storage has a winding common to all the magnetic cells of the word.

**word originator**  1. A person who dictates copy for transcription into final documents. 2. An individual who originates documents.

**word pattern**  The smallest meaningful language unit recognized by a machine. It is usually composed of a group of syllables and/or words.

**word processing**  The preparation of printed material for publication using automatic data processing equipment.

**word processing center**  1. An area of equipment and personnel for the production of typed documents. 2. A centralized location in which word processing operations take place.

**word processing system**  Refers to equipment and personnel dedicated to the production of typed documents in a cost-effective manner.

**word processing terminal**  Refers to the equipment or the area used for the preparation and dissemination of letters, memoranda, reports, and articles produced using typewriters and word processing systems.

**word processing typewriter**  See *WP typewriter*.

**word-select, memory section**  Refers to the word-select steering technique that is used for memory addressing. An important consideration for dynamic memories is nondestructive readout with positive, automatic restoration that prevents an accidental loss of memory information.

**word size**  See *word length*.

**word time**  The amount of time required to transport a word past a given point, or from one storage device to another.

**word, trap**  Refers to the storage location used to store the instruction counter and trap identification data.

**work area**  A section of storage where data items may be processed or temporarily stored. The work area is used to retain intermediate results of a calculation, especially those results which do not appear as output in the program.

**work distribution center**  A consolidation of tasks and activities that a particular department does, with each station in the center fitting into the department's overall activities.

**working register**  A register reserved for data on which operations are being performed. Working registers can be specified using fewer bits than working-storage memory locations, and execution time can be faster.

**working storage**  A portion of storage reserved for data upon which operations are being performed. Working storage can be used in a microcomputer as buffer storage or for storage of intermediate program data.

**work output queue**  A list of data which is output, but is stored temporarily in an auxiliary medium until a printer or other output device is available.

**WOROM**  Abbreviation for *write-only read-only memory*.

**worst-case**  Refers to an analysis or design that considers the worst possible combination of possible parameter variations.

**worst-case circuit analysis**  A type of circuit analysis in which the worst possible effects are determined due to all possible combinations of circuit parameters.

**worst-case design**  A conservative design approach in which the circuit is designed to function assuming the worst possible combination of operating characteristics.

**worst case noise pattern**  The noise appearing in a magnetic storage system when half of the selected cores are in a logic 1 state and the other half in a logic 0 state.

**WP**  Abbreviation for *word processing*.

**wpm**  Abbreviation for *words per minute*, a measure of user speed in various signal processing and operator keypunch rating systems.

**WP typewriter**  A text-editing typewriter that records or captures keystrokes on a medium and has the ability to make additions, deletions, corrections, and format changes in the recorded text prior to the automatic printing of the finished documents. These units may be either interactive or stand-alone.

**wraparound**  The continuation of an operation such as:

1. A change in the storage location from the maximum addressable location to the first addressable location.
2. The shift of a register address from the highest address to the lowest.
3. A shift in a read or cursor movement from the last character position to the first position.

**WR CHK**  Abbreviation for *write check*.

**write**  To transfer, record, or copy, usually from one storage device to another. The information may be recorded in a register or any other storage location or medium.

**writeable control storage**  A read-write memory used in the control portion of a system. The read-write memory, or RAM, replaces a ROM and gives the designer additional capability to change the characteristics of the microcomputer system.

**writeable control store**  The control portion of a read-write memory that allows the user to microcode a specialized instruction set for the system application. This technique is especially suited for some communications and signal processing applications where a few well-designed algorithms are required.

**write addressing**  To direct or control a write operation in a device, such as with a binary counter, in which the first location address contains all zeros, and each successive address is incremented by one bit, such as:

| | |
|---|---|
| FIRST WRITE ADDRESS | 00000000 |
| SECOND WRITE ADDRESS | 00000001 |
| THIRD WRITE ADDRESS | 00000010 |

**write-head**  Magnetic-tape recording head.

**write operation, cache memory**  Typically, a logical address is sent from the CPU to the memory-cache subsystem. A page address is presented to a CAM memory for a presence check. If the page is present in the cache, a match occurs and a signal is sent to the control logic, indicating that the page is in the cache; the memory access is then made from the cache. If the operation is a WRITE, the field changes to indicate a WRITE has taken place on that page. If the page is not present, the control logic transfers the desired page from main memory to the cache, completing the memory request in the process.

**write-read**  1. An operation in which a block of data is read in while simultaneously processing the previous block and writing out the results of that block. 2. Possessing the capability of both read and write operations.

**write-read process**  To read in one block of data while simultaneously processing the previous block and writing out the results of the preceding processing block.

**writing head**  Refers to the magnetic head that is designed to write as contrasted with the read head. The two are often combined.

**writing rate**  The maximum speed at which the spot on a cathode ray tube can move and still produce a satisfactory image.

**writing speed**  The rate of registering signals on a storage device.

**WRU**  The who-are-you character.

**WS**  Abbreviation for *working storage*, an area of storage designed to hold dynamic or working data. The working storage area provides a user area for semipermanent data storage.

**W-shaped plugboard**  A plugboard with a W cut that allows easier insertion than conventional plugboards.

**WTS**  Abbreviation for *word terminal synchronous*.

**Wullenweber**  A type of directional antenna array. A large Wullenweber is operated by the University of Illinois. It consists of 960 reflecting wires arranged in a 995 foot circle. The receivers are in the 5 to 15 MHz range, and it is used for studies of signals reflected from the ionosphere.

**X** The horizontal deflection on a CRT.

**xasers** A family of giant pulse lasers.

**x-axis** 1. The horizontal axis, as on a CRT screen, graph, printer, or plotter. 2. The reference axis of a quartz crystal.

**xerographic printer** A device for printing an optical image on paper in which light and dark areas are represented by electrostatically charged areas on the paper. A powdered ink is dusted on the paper. The ink adheres to the charged areas and is melted into the paper by heat.

**xerography** A dry copying process in which light is used to discharge an electrostatically charged plate, which is then dusted with a dielectric powder to make the image visible. Fixing is usually done by heat directly after the dusting.

**Xerox** Trade name for a particular line of xerographic equipment.

**XIO** Abbreviation for *execute input/output*.

**XMT** Abbreviation for *transmit*.

**XMTR** Abbreviation for *transmitter*.

**X-punch** A punch in the X or 11 row of an 80-column card. The X-punch is used to control, select, or indicate a negative number. Also called an 11-punch.

**XTAL** Abbreviation for *crystal*.

**x-y plotter** A device used to plot coordinate points in the form of a graph.

**x-y recorder** A recorder that traces the relationship between two variables on a chart or graph. The chart or graph may move such that one of the variables becomes time-dependent.

**x-y switch** A type of switch in which the wipers are moved first in one direction and then in the other.

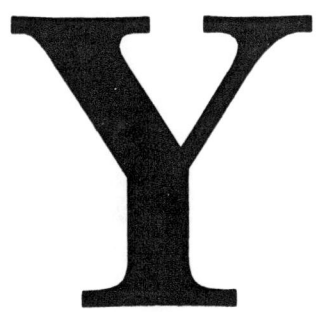

**Y** The vertical deflection on a CRT.

**y-axis** The vertical axis, as on a CRT screen, graph, printer, or plotter.

**Y-circuit** A star connected three-phase power circuit, so called because of its resemblance to the letter Y. Also called *wye circuit* and *delta circuit*.

**yig** Acronym for *yttrium-iron-garnet*, a crystal used in tuning devices in microwave circuits.

**yig device** A device using a yig crystal with a magnetic field for functional applications in wideband circuits. Yig devices include filters, discriminators, and multiplexers.

**yig filter** A filter that uses a yig crystal in a magnetic field provided by an electromagnetic coil.

**yig oscillator** A microwave oscillator that uses a yig filter in a tunnel-diode oscillator circuit.

**yoke** 1. A piece of ferromagnetic material that connects two cores or heads for reading or writing operations. 2. A coil assembly used to provide electromagnetic deflection in a CRT.

**Y-punch** A punch in the Y or 12 row of an 80-column card. A Y-punch is used to indicate a positive number. Also called a *12-punch*.

**Y signal** In color TV, a luminance primary transmission signal.

# Z

**Z** Abbreviation for *impedance*.
**ZA** Abbreviation for *zero and add*.
**z-axis** The longitudinal or optical axis of a quartz crystal slab; it is perpendicular to both the x and y axes.
**zener** A semiconductor diode with a high ratio of reverse to forward resistance until breakdown occurs. The voltage drop after breakdown remains essentially constant and the current is limited mainly by the circuit in which the device is connected. The zener is commonly used as a voltage regulator, reference, and ac clipper.
**zener breakdown** The avalanche of a semiconductor device due to field emission of charge carriers in the depletion layer.
**zener current** The current produced in an insulator by electrons that have been raised in energy from the valence bond to the conduction bond through the use of a strong electric field.
**zener diode** A diode that exhibits a sharp increase of reverse current at a certain negative potential, which is called the zener or breakdown voltage.
**zener diode coupling** A method of coupling circuits using zener diodes to provide a high degree of noise rejection.
**zener diode regulator** A power or voltage regulator that uses one or more zener diodes as the basic regulating element.

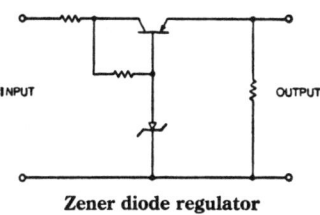

**Zener diode regulator**

**zener effect** A reverse-current breakdown due to the presence of a high electric field at the junction of a semiconductor or insulator.
**zener voltage** The negative breakdown voltage of a zener diode, which remains essentially constant over a wide range of current values.
**zero** 1. A numeral denoting lack of magnitude. Some machines may have distinct representations for plus zero or minus zero. 2. The bit or state representing *false* or *off* in a two-state logic system.
**zero access storage** A storage in which waiting time is negligible and information is immediately available.
**zero address instruction** An instruction consisting of an operation that does not require an address in the usual sense. For example:

SHIFT LEFT 0002

has in its address portion the amount of shift desired.
**zero adjust** A control for setting the reading of a device to the zero mark in the absence of any signal.
**zero-based conformity** Refers to a specific condition or value that is determined after various translations and/or rotations of the actual data curves are made to make it coincide with zero on the specified curve that minimizes the maximum deviation.
**zero beat** The condition in which two signals, combined in a nonlinear element, are brought to the same frequency by nulling the element's output as a result of shifting the frequency of one of the two signals.
**zero bit** A bit used in the program counter to indicate that the accumulator has been cleared.
**zero compression** A method of data compression in which all non-significant leading zeros are eliminated.
**zero-cut crystal** Refers to a crystal cut at such an angle to the axes as to have a zero frequency/temperature coefficient. Such a crystal can be used for a frequency standard.

**zero error** 1. The error on any instrument when indicating zero. 2. The residual time delay that has to be compensated for in determining readings of range.

**zero-error reference** Refers to a constant ratio of incremental cause and effect. Proportionality is a special case of linearity in which the straight line passes through the origin. Zero-error reference of a linear transducer is a selected straight-line function of the input from which output errors are measured. Zero-based linearity is transducer linearity defined in terms of a zero-error reference where zero input coincides with zero output.

**zero fill** To fill in characters with the representation of zeros without changing the meaning or content.

**zero gate voltage drain current** The direct current into the drain terminal when the gate source voltage is zero. This is an on-state current in a depletion type device and an off-state current in an enhancement-type device.

**zero gate voltage source current** The direct current into the source terminal when the gate-drain voltage is zero. This is an on-state current in a depletion-type device and an off-state current in an enhancement type device.

**zero gradient synchrotron** An atomic accelerator capable of accelerating protons with 12.5 billion electron volts of energy.

**zero level** 1. The usually abitrary reference point for measuring signal levels in decibels. 2. In audio and telephone work, a reference level established by a power of 1 mW across a 600Ω line; the decibel value is abbreviated *dBm* to specify the reference point.

**zero level address** An instruction address in which the address part of the instruction is the operand. Also called *immediate address*.

**zero offset** A characteristic of a numerical machine tool control permitting the zero point on an axis to be shifted readily over a specified range. The control and machine, in this case, do not have a permanently located zero.

**zero page addressing** A page-addressing method that uses only the second byte of an instruction and assumes a zero address byte. The technique is used in some systems with an index register in which the second byte is added to the contents of the register to produce an effective address.

**zero potential** Refers to the potential of a point at infinite distance, such as used for defining capacitance.

**zero power level** An arbitrary power level for referring other power levels, either in decibels or nepers. Zero power level in the U.S., is now defined as 1 mW, for a standard 600 ohm impedance.

**zero shift** A characteristic of a numerical machine tool control permitting the zero point on an axis to be shifted readily over a specified range. The control and machine do not have a permanently located zero.

**zero stability** Refers to the drift in the no-signal output level of an amplifier or device, either with time or with the operating conditions.

**zero suppression** The elimination of nonsignificant zeros, usually before printing or display.

**ZGS** One of the largest atomic accelerators. A beam of protons with an energy of 12.7 billion electron volts can be obtained from it.

**Zilog Z8** The Z8 single-chip microcomputer provides an on-chip ROM of 2048 bytes, a RAM of 124 bytes, 32 I/O lines, two counter/timers, and a programmable UART. I/O is software configurable on some ports and dedicated on others. One port is set up as four input and four output lines; another has eight lines that are bit programmable as inputs or outputs; another port programmable in four bit sections; the fourth port is byte programmable. Up to 64 kilobytes of external memory may be addressed by the processor, which also contains a 64 byte ROM test memory.

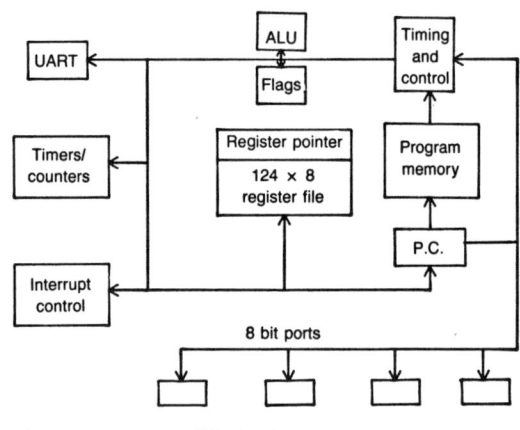

**Z8 structure**

**Zilog Z80** The first Z80 appeared in April 1976. By using a depletion mode load and n-channel MOS fabrication, only a single +5 – V power supply is required for this microprocessor. The Z80 does not multiplex status information on the data bus, as is done with the 8080. It is contained in the same 40 pin DIP that is used for the 8080.

The Z80 architecture is shown. An accumulator register is used to store data from the accumulator. This additional register tends to improve response time during interrupts. The temporary registers W and Z have been replaced with a set of temporary registers that serve as the general registers B, C, D, E, H, and L. This set of temporary registers also improves the interrupt response time. The Z80 microprocessor has four 16-bit registers; a program counter that provides the same functions as in the 8080, a stack pointer like one in the 8080 to hold the address of the next available location in the last-in-first-out (LIFO) stack stored in RAM, and two index registers X and Y.

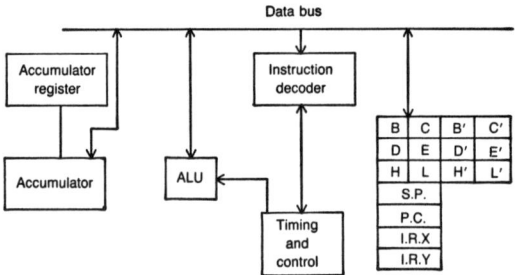

**Z80 architecture**

A clock generator is on the CPU chip, along with circuitry for dynamic RAM refresh capability. There is also a special register for controlling interrupts. This allows the microprocessor to operate in a mode in which an indirect call to memory may occur from an interrupt. The added special purpose register can be used to hold the upper 8 bits of the indirect address while the lower 8 bits is furnished by the interrupting device.

**Zilog Z8000** The Z8000 is a 16-bit microprocessor with an instruction set based on an expanded Z80 instruction set. Z80 users must use a translator to convert programs to the Z8000. Although the Z8000 uses a different architecture, both processors are register-oriented, and the addressing modes of the Z80 are a subset of the Z8000 modes. The Z8000 has a greater addressing space, and a larger number of instructions, which are more powerful than those found in the Z80 instruction set. To make full use of the Z8000 the user should record Z80 programs for the Z8000 rather than translating for most applications.

The Z8000 is a random-logic-based CPU; its structure is shown. An internal 16-bit data bus is used for internal addressing and data communication. Instructions are fetched over the bus interface and executed by the instruction control unit. Throughput is enhanced by lookahead pipelining, which allows prefetching of the next single-word instruction or the first word of the next multiword instruction.

The Z8000 is available either in a 40-pin package or a 48-pin package. The 40-pin Z8000 is able to address 64K of memory, while the 48-pin device will address 8 megabytes of memory. In the Z8000 units, addresses are expressed in bytes. Single bytes are read and written using the byte/word output line. The eight megabytes of directly addressable memory is split up into 128 segments, each of 64K bytes. The CPU generates information that enables the address range to be increased by separating code, data, and stack spaces. External logic is used for this extension.

**zone** 1. A portion of storage allocated for a particular purpose or function. 2. The top row of 12, 11, and 0 on certain punched cards. A second punch used with positions 1 to 9 can be used to represent alphabetic characters.

**zone bit** 1. A bit in a group of positions used to indicate a specific class of items. 2. A bit used as a key to a code.

**zone digit** A digit used as a key to a section of code. Zone digits can be used independently of other markings for control significance in a system.

**zone punch** A punch in the 11, 12, or 0 row of a punched card. Also called an *overpunch* when the card column already contains holes.

**zoo event** Refers to a radio signal from space that has no known source or cause. A flash may be called a *zoo event*, a signal of unknown origin,

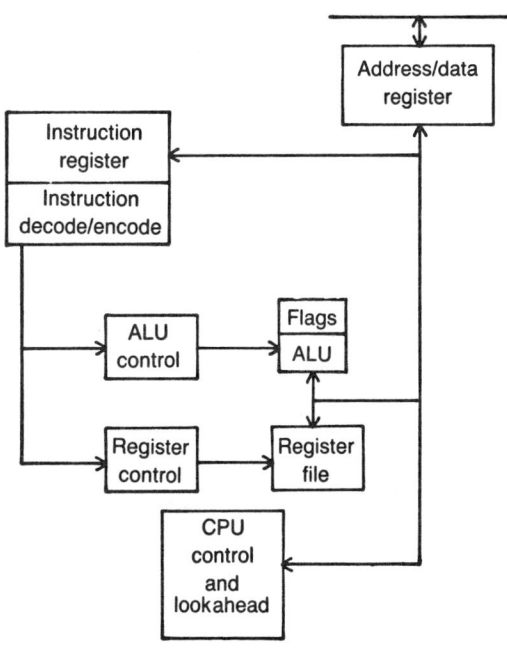

**Z8000 structure**

which possibly was caused by the impact of a small meteoroid on the satellite, if no supporting evidence, such as radioactive debris, can be found to confirm a nuclear explosion. So called because the enormous variety and number of possible sources of the signal are comparable to the number and variety of animals in a zoo.

**zoom** Refers to the capability of a graphics system to switch to a close-up rendering of the subject or image.

**z-parameters** The open circuit impedance parameters of a transistor.

**ZPR** Abbreviation for *zero power reactor*.

**zwitterion** A dipolar ion, such as an electrically neutral molecule that has a dipole moment. Many aminoacids form such dipolar ions.

# Appendix

# Symbols and Programming Information

## SCHEMATIC SYMBOLS

| | |
|---|---|
| AMMETER | |
| AND GATE | |
| ANTENNA, BALANCED | |
| ANTENNA, GENERAL | |
| ANTENNA, LOOP, SHIELDED | |
| ANTENNA, LOOP, UNSHIELDED | |
| ANTENNA, UNBALANCED | |
| ATTENUATOR, FIXED | |
| ATTENUATOR, VARIABLE | |
| BATTERY | |
| CAPACITOR, FEEDTHROUGH | |
| CAPACITOR, FIXED, NONPOLARIZED | |
| CAPACITOR, FIXED, POLARIZED | |
| CAPACITOR, GANGED, VARIABLE | |
| CAPACITOR, VARIABLE, SINGLE | |
| CAPACITOR, VARIABLE, SPLIT-STATOR | |
| CATHODE, DIRECTLY HEATED | |
| CATHODE, INDIRECTLY HEATED | |
| CATHODE, COLD | |
| CAVITY RESONATOR | |
| CELL | |
| CIRCUIT BREAKER | |
| COAXIAL CABLE | |
| CRYSTAL, PIEZOELECTRIC | |
| DELAY LINE | |
| DIODE, GENERAL | |
| DIODE, GUNN | |
| DIODE, LIGHT-EMITTING | |
| DIODE, PHOTOSENSITIVE | 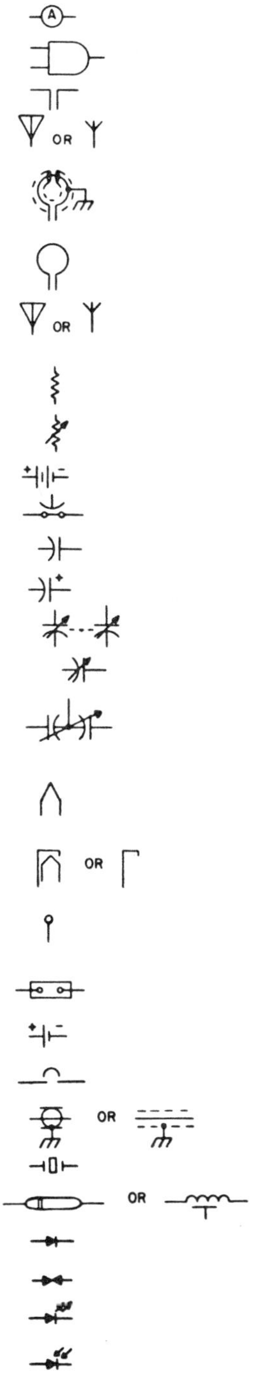 |
| DIODE, PHOTOVOLTAIC | |
| DIODE, PIN | |
| DIODE, VARACTOR | |
| DIODE, ZENER | |
| DIRECTIONAL COUPLER OR WATTMETER | |
| EXCLUSIVE-OR GATE | |
| FEMALE CONTACT, GENERAL | |
| FERRITE BEAD | |
| FUSE | |
| GALVANOMETER | |
| GROUND, CHASSIS | |
| GROUND, EARTH | |
| HANDSET | |
| HEADPHONE, DOUBLE | |
| HEADPHONE, SINGLE | |
| INDUCTOR, AIR-CORE | |
| INDUCTOR, BIFILAR | |
| INDUCTOR, IRON-CORE | |
| INDUCTOR, TAPPED | |
| INDUCTOR, VARIABLE | |
| INTEGRATED CIRCUIT | |
| INVERTER OR INVERTING AMPLIFIER | |
| JACK, COAXIAL | |
| JACK, PHONE, 2-CONDUCTOR | |
| JACK, PHONE, 2-CONDUCTOR INTERRUPTING | |
| JACK, PHONE, 3-CONDUCTOR | |
| JACK, PHONO | |
| KEY, TELEGRAPH | |
| LAMP, INCANDESCENT | |
| LAMP, NEON | |

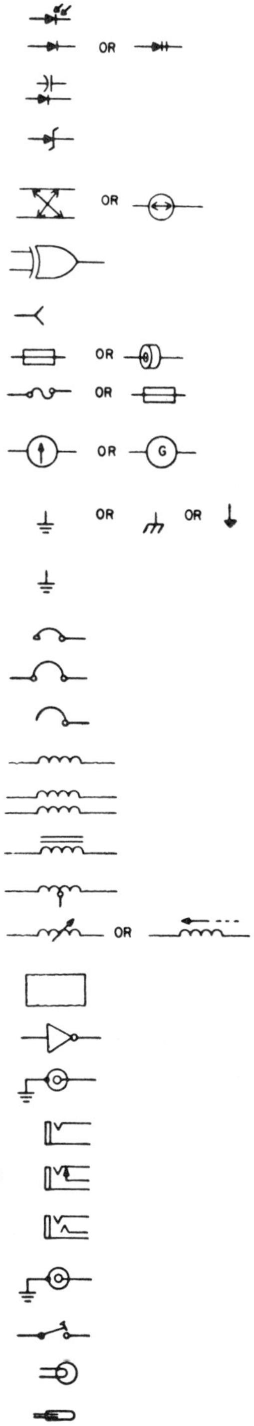

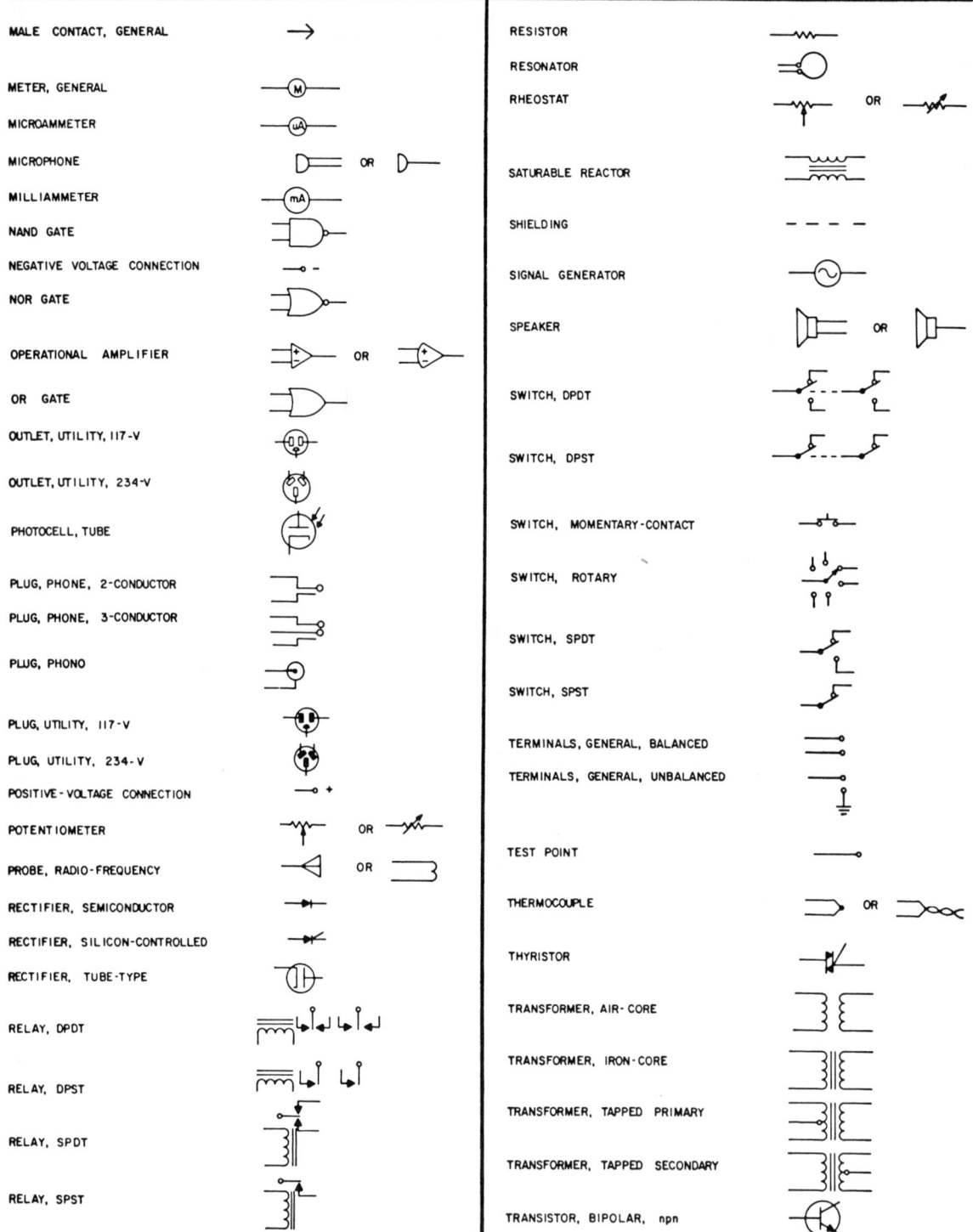

| | |
|---|---|
| TRANSISTOR, BIPOLAR, pnp | |
| TRANSISTOR, FIELD-EFFECT, N-CHANNEL | |
| TRANSISTOR, FIELD-EFFECT, P-CHANNEL | |
| TRANSISTOR, METAL-OXIDE, DUAL-GATE | OR |
| TRANSISTOR, METAL-OXIDE, SINGLE-GATE | OR |
| TRANSISTOR, PHOTOSENSITIVE | OR |
| TRANSISTOR, UNIJUNCTION | OR |
| TUBE, DIODE | |
| TUBE, PENTODE | |
| TUBE, PHOTOMULTIPLIER | |
| TUBE, TETRODE | |
| TUBE, TRIODE | |
| UNSPECIFIED UNIT OR COMPONENT | |
| VOLTMETER | |
| WATTMETER | OR |
| WIRES, CROSSING, CONNECTED | OR |
| WIRES, CROSSING, NOT CONNECTED | OR |
| WIRES, CONNECTED (3-WAY) | |

## Typical BASIC Reserved Words Used on Microcomputers

| | | | | |
|---|---|---|---|---|
| ABS | AND | ASC | AT | ATN |
| AUTO | BEEP | BLOAD | BSAVE | CALL |
| CDBL | CHAIN | CHR$ | CINT | CLEAR |
| CLOSE | CLR | CLS | CMD | COLOR |
| COM | COMMON | CONT | COS | CSNG |
| CSRLIN | CVD | CVI | CVS | DATA |
| DATE$ | DEF | DEFDBL | DEFINT | DEFSNG |
| DEFSTR | DELETE | DIM | DRAW | EDIT |
| ELSE | END | EOF | EQV | ERASE |
| ERL | ERR | ERROR | EXP | EXT |
| FIELD | FILES | FIX | FLASH | FN |
| FOR | FRE | GET | GET# | GOSUB |
| GOTO | GR | HCOLOR | HEX$ | HGR |
| HIMEM | HLIN | HOME | HPLOT | HTAB |
| IF | IMP | IN# | INKEY$ | INP |
| INPUT | INPUT# | INPUT$ | INSTR | INT |
| INVERSE | KEY | KILL | LEFT$ | LEN |
| LET | LINE | LIST | LLIST | LOAD |
| LOC | LOCATE | LOF | LOG | LOMEM |
| LPOS | LPRINT | LSET | MERGE | MID$ |
| MKD$ | MKI$ | MKS$ | MOD | MOTOR |
| NAME | NEW | NEXT | NORMAL | NOT |
| NOTRACE | OCT$ | OFF | ON | ONERR |
| OPEN | OPTION | OR | OUT | PAINT |
| PDL | PEEK | PEN | PLAY | PLOT |
| POINT | POKE | POP | POS | PRINT |
| PRINT# | PR# | PSET | PUT | RANDOMIZE |
| READ | RECALL | REM | RENUM | RESET |
| RESTORE | RESUME | RETURN | RIGHT$ | RND |
| RSET | RUN | SAVE | SCREEN | SCRN |
| SGN | SIN | SOUND | SPACE$ | SPC( |
| SPEED | SQR | STATUS | STEP | STICK |
| STOP | STORE | STR$ | STRIG | STRING$ |
| SWAP | SYS | SYSTEM | TAB( | TAN |
| TEXT | THEN | TIME | TIME$ | TO |
| TRACE | TROFF | TRON | USING | USR |
| VAL | VARPTR | VARPTR$ | VERIFY | VLIN |
| VTAB | WAIT | WEND | WHILE | WIDTH |
| WRITE | WRITE# | XOR | | |